LAW AND MIND

Are the cognitive sciences relevant for law? How do they influence legal theory and practice? Should lawyers become part-time cognitive scientists? The recent advances in the cognitive sciences have reshaped our conceptions of human decision making and behavior. Many claim, for instance, that we can no longer view ourselves as purely rational agents equipped with free will. This change is vitally important for lawyers, who are forced to rethink the foundations of their theories and the framework of legal practice. Featuring multidisciplinary scholars from around the world, this book offers a comprehensive overview of the emerging field of law and the cognitive sciences. It develops new theories and provides often-provocative insights into the relationship between the cognitive sciences and various dimensions of the law, including legal philosophy and methodology, doctrinal issues, and evidence.

Bartosz Brożek is Professor at the Faculty of Law and Administration and the director of the Copernicus Center for Interdisciplinary Studies at the Jagiellonian University in Kraków. He holds PhDs in law and philosophy, and specializes in legal philosophy, epistemology, and theories of argumentation, as well as moral and mathematical cognition. He is the author of twenty book monographs and more than 100 research papers, and the editor of twenty-four volumes. Brożek has received numerous scholarships and awards, including the Humboldt Fellowship.

Jaap Hage holds the chair for Jurisprudence at Maastricht University. His research has focused on the ontology and logic of law, basic legal concepts, the methods of legal science, and – most recently – law and the cognitive sciences. His scientific publications include *Reasoning with Rules*, *Studies in Legal Logic*, and *Foundations and Building Blocks of Law*.

Nicole A Vincent is Senior Lecturer, Faculty of Transdisciplinary Innovation at the University of Technology Sydney. An analytic philosopher, she focuses on the social, legal, policy, and ethical implications, applications, challenges, and opportunities of advances in science and emerging technologies. Her publications have been cited in the Supreme Court of the United States and by the Presidential Commission for the Study of Bioethical Issues. She also spearheaded the development of the Australian Neurolaw Database. Her edited volumes, *Neuroscience and Criminal Responsibility* (2013) and *Neurointerventions and the Law: Regulating Human Mental Capacity* (2020) are core neurolaw reference texts.

LAW AND THE COGNITIVE SCIENCES

Law and the Cognitive Sciences publishes book monographs exploring connections between law and the cognitive sciences. The books will be of interest to academics, students, and practitioners, and in particular to the scholars in the fields of legal theory, philosophy of law, psychology of law, the theory of law and artificial intelligence, general theory of private and criminal law, and evidence.

General Editors
Bartosz Brożek, *Jagiellonian University*
Jaap Hage, *University of Maastricht*
Francis X. Shen, *University of Minnesota Law School*
Nicole A Vincent, *University of Technology Sydney*

Law and Mind

A SURVEY OF LAW AND THE COGNITIVE SCIENCES

Edited by

BARTOSZ BROŻEK
Jagiellonian University

JAAP HAGE
Maastricht University Faculty of Law

NICOLE A VINCENT
University of Technology, Sydney

CAMBRIDGE
UNIVERSITY PRESS

Shaftesbury Road, Cambridge CB2 8EA, United Kingdom

One Liberty Plaza, 20th Floor, New York, NY 10006, USA

477 Williamstown Road, Port Melbourne, VIC 3207, Australia

314–321, 3rd Floor, Plot 3, Splendor Forum, Jasola District Centre, New Delhi – 110025, India

103 Penang Road, #05–06/07, Visioncrest Commercial, Singapore 238467

Cambridge University Press is part of Cambridge University Press & Assessment, a department of the University of Cambridge.

We share the University's mission to contribute to society through the pursuit of education, learning and research at the highest international levels of excellence.

www.cambridge.org
Information on this title: www.cambridge.org/9781108736923

DOI: 10.1017/9781108623056

© Cambridge University Press & Assessment 2021

This publication is in copyright. Subject to statutory exception and to the provisions of relevant collective licensing agreements, no reproduction of any part may take place without the written permission of Cambridge University Press & Assessment.

First published 2021
First paperback edition 2024

A catalogue record for this publication is available from the British Library

Library of Congress Cataloging-in-Publication data
NAMES: Brożek, Bartosz, editor. | Hage, J. C. (Jacob Cornelis), editor. | Vincent, Nicole A., editor.
TITLE: Law and mind : a survey of law and the cognitive sciences / edited by Bartosz Brożek, Jagiellonian University (Poland) Department of Philosophy and Law; Jaap Hage, Maastricht University Faculty of Law; Nicole A Vincent, University of Technology, Sydney.
DESCRIPTION: Cambridge, United Kingdom ; New York, NY : Cambridge University Press, 2021. | Series: Law and the cognitive sciences | Includes bibliographical references and index.
IDENTIFIERS: LCCN 2020046962 (print) | LCCN 2020046963 (ebook) | ISBN 9781108486002 (hardback) | ISBN 9781108623056 (ebook)
SUBJECTS: LCSH: Law – Psychological aspects. | Cognitive science.
CLASSIFICATION: LCC K346 .L375 2021 (print) | LCC K346 (ebook) | DDC 340/.19–dc23
LC record available at https://lccn.loc.gov/2020046962
LC ebook record available at https://lccn.loc.gov/2020046963

ISBN   978-1-108-48600-2   Hardback
ISBN   978-1-108-73692-3   Paperback

Cambridge University Press & Assessment has no responsibility for the persistence or accuracy of URLs for external or third-party internet websites referred to in this publication and does not guarantee that any content on such websites is, or will remain, accurate or appropriate.

Contents

List of Figures		*page* viii
List of Contributors		ix
Acknowledgements		xiv

1. Introduction: Between Law and the Cognitive Sciences – A Manifesto   1
   Bartosz Brożek and Jaap Hage

   I   METATHEORY AND METHODOLOGY

2. Are the Cognitive Sciences Relevant for Law?   17
   Jaap Hage

3. Social and Normative Facts   50
   Carsten Heidemann

4. Law, Folk Psychology and Cognitive Science   55
   Łukasz Kurek

5. Law and the Cognitive Science of Ordinary Concepts   86
   Kevin Tobia

   II   ONTOLOGY AND EPISTEMOLOGY

6. Cognitive Science and the Nature of Law   99
   Corrado Roversi

7. The Architecture of the Legal Mind   138
   Bartosz Brożek

8. The Psychology of the Trial Judge   165
   Morris B. Hoffman

9	Institutional Design and the Psychology of the Trial Judge Adi Leibovitch	193
10	Bias at the Surface or the Core? A Comment on the Psychology of the Trial Judge Eyal Aharoni	207

III LEGAL DOCTRINE AND COGNITIVE SCIENCES

11	Private Law and Cognitive Science Przemysław Pałka	217
12	Private Law and Cognitive Science: A Methodological Commentary Bartosz Brożek and Marek Jakubiec	249
13	Responsibility, Liability, and Retribution Jaap Hage and Antonia Waltermann	255
14	Guilt in Criminal Law: Guilt in Us or in the Stars? Mikołaj Małecki and Marek Sławiński	289
15	The Insanity Defense Gerben Meynen	317
16	Thoughts on the Insanity Defence Lisa Claydon and Paul Catley	342

IV EVIDENCE

17	Implications of Neurotechnology: Brain Recording and Intervention Pim Haselager	353
18	Neuroimaging Evidence in US Courts Jane Campbell Moriarty	370
19	Neuroscientific Evidence in Context Deborah W. Denno	412
20	Some Issues in Interpreting Neuroscientific Evidence Bartłomiej Kucharzyk	421
21	Explanation-Based Approaches to Reasoning about Evidence and Proof in Criminal Trials Anne Ruth Mackor, Hylke Jellema and Peter J. van Koppen	431

V DISSENTING OPINIONS

22 A Non-Naturalist Account of Law's Place in Reality 473
George Pavlakos

23 The Law and Cognitive Sciences Enterprise: A Few Analytic Notes 490
Pierluigi Chiassoni

24 The Cognitive Approach in Legal Science and Practice:
A History of Four Revolutions 507
Jerzy Stelmach

Figures

6.1a	Sociality	page 126
6.1b	Legality	127
13.1	Determinism	261
13.2	Fatalism	264
13.3	Libet's experiment	267
13.4	Identity of mind (M) and brain (B)	268
13.5	Epiphenomenalism	269

Contributors

Eyal Aharoni is an associate professor of Psychology, Philosophy and Neuroscience at Georgia State University, USA. His research investigates risk factors for anti-social behaviour and the impact of cognitive bias on legal decision-making. He has a specific interest in the formation of punishment attitudes as a result of conflicts between moralistic and consequentialist reasoning processes.

Bartosz Brożek is a full professor at the Faculty of Law and Administration and the director of the Copernicus Center for Interdisciplinary Studies at the Jagiellonian University in Kraków. He holds PhDs in law and philosophy. He specializes in legal philosophy, epistemology and theories of argumentation, as well as moral and mathematical cognition. He is the author of numerous monographs and research papers and editor of many volumes. He has received numerous scholarships and awards, including a Humboldt Fellowship. He is the co-creator of the Copernicus Festival in Kraków as well as the MOOC platform Copernicus College.

Paul Catley is Head of the Open University Law School. With over 9,000 undergraduate students studying law modules, the Open University is the largest law school in the United Kingdom. Paul's research focuses on the use and potential use by legal systems of developments in the cognitive sciences.

Pierluigi Chiassoni is Professor of Jurisprudence at Genoa University. His research has focused on the law and economics movement (from a juristic perspective), legal interpretation and argumentation, judicial precedent, legal positivism and the history of analytical jurisprudence. His most recent publications include the monographs *El discreto placer del positivismo jurídico* (The Subtle Pleasure of Legal Positivism), *Da Bentham a Kelsen. Sei capitoli per una storia della filosofia analitica del diritto* (From Bentham to Kelsen. Six Chapters for a History of Analytical Jurisprudence), and *Interpretation without Truth: A Realistic Enquiry*.

Lisa Claydon is Senior Lecturer in Law and Head of the Centre for Life, Law and the Brain Sciences at The Open University Law School. Her research interests lie in the relationship between the cognitive sciences and the criminal law.

Deborah Denno is the Arthur A. McGivney Professor of Law and Founding Director of the Neuroscience and Law Center at Fordham University School of Law.

Jaap Hage holds the chair for Jurisprudence at Maastricht University. His research has focused on the ontology and logic of law, basic legal concepts, the methods of legal science and – most recently – law and the cognitive sciences. His scientific publications include the monographs *Reasoning with Rules*, *Studies in Legal Logic* and *Foundations and Building Blocks of Law*.

Pim Haselager is an associate professor at the Radboud University and a Principal Investigator at the Donders Institute for Brain, Cognition and Behaviour, in Nijmegen. He focuses on the ethical and societal implications of cognitive neuroscience and AI. He publishes in journals such as *Nature: Biotechnology*, *Science and Engineering Ethics*, the *American Journal of Bioethics*, *Neuroethics*, the *Journal of Cognitive Neuroscience* and the *Journal of Social Robotics*.

Carsten Heidemann wrote his thesis on Hans Kelsen's concept of norm. Since it was published in 1997, he has written diverse papers on topics including the Pure Theory of Law, law's claim to correctness, discourse theory and John Searle's conception of social reality. He is working as a practising lawyer.

Morris B. Hoffman is a District Judge, Second Judicial District, State of Colorado; Member of the John D. and Catherine T. MacArthur Foundation's Research Network on Law and Neuroscience; Research Fellow, Gruter Institute for Law and Behavioral Research; and Adjunct Professor of Law, University of Denver.

Marek Jakubiec holds a PhD in legal philosophy and currently works as an assistant professor at the Department of Philosophy of Law and Legal Ethics at the Jagiellonian University in Kraków. His research interests include law and the cognitive sciences, legal concepts, philosophy of mind and embodied cognition.

Hylke Jellema is a PhD candidate at the University of Groningen, Faculty of Law. His main research topic is the connection between inference to the best explanation and Bayesianism in criminal law. Recent publications include Jellema, 'Case Comment: Responding to the Implausible, Incredible and Highly Improbable Stories Defendants Tell: a Bayesian Interpretation of the Venray Murder Ruling' (in *Law, Probability and Risk* 18(2–3), 2019), and Jellema, 'The Reasonable Doubt Standard as Inference to the Best Explanation' (in *Synthese*, 2020).

Bartłomiej Kucharzyk holds a PhD in law and an MA in psychology. His research interests include empirical legal studies, law of evidence and psychology.

Łukasz Kurek is an assistant professor in the Department of Philosophy of Law and Legal Ethics at the Jagiellonian University. His research has focused on issues at the intersection of legal philosophy and philosophy of mind such as moral and legal responsibility, the role of folk psychology within law and the issue of naturalism in legal philosophy.

Adi Leibovitch is an assistant professor at the Hebrew University of Jerusalem, Faculty of Law. Her research focuses on the economic analysis of law, behavioural theory and empirical methods, as applied to the study of the institutional design of courts, litigation and legal decision making, with a particular interest in the criminal justice system. She received her JSD and LLM from the University of Chicago Law School, her LLB and MBA, both *magna cum laude*, from the Hebrew University of Jerusalem, and her MA, *summa cum laude*, in public policy, mediation and conflict resolution from Tel Aviv University.

Anne Ruth Mackor is Professor of Professional Ethics, in particular of legal professions, at the University of Groningen. She has published on topics including the nature of legal science, criminal responsibility and free will, and models of rational proof in criminal law, amongst others. A recent publication is van Koppen and Mackor, 'A Scenario Approach to the Simonshaven Case', in Prakken, Bex and Mackor (eds.), *Models of Rational Proof in Criminal Law*, special issue of *TopiCS*, 2020.

Mikołaj Małecki has a PhD in law and is an assistant professor at the Department of Criminal Law at the Jagiellonian University. He is also the President of Krakowski Instytut Prawa Karnego Fundacja (Kraków Institute of Criminal Law Foundation). He is the author of books on preparation as a stage of perpetration of a crime, and on the attribution of guilt in criminal law. His main areas of interest include the principles of criminal liability, theoretical foundations of criminal law and interdisciplinary issues concerning law and philosophy.

Gerben Meynen is Professor of Forensic Psychiatry, Willem Pompe Institute for Criminal Law and Criminology (Utrecht Centre for Accountability and Liability Law, UCALL), Utrecht University, and Professor of Ethics and Psychiatry, Department of Philosophy, Humanities, Vrije Universiteit Amsterdam. His research interests include legal insanity and the implications of neuroscience for criminal law and forensic psychiatry.

Jane Campbell Moriarty is a professor and the Carol Los Mansmann Chair in Faculty Scholarship at Duquesne University School of Law in Pittsburgh, Pennsylvania. Her research focuses on scientific evidence, neuroscience and law, and legal ethics. Her publications include several law review articles, interdisciplinary chapters, a textbook on scientific and expert evidence and a two-volume treatise on scientific evidence. She is also the co-editor of a book series and is currently working on a book for NYU Press, entitled *Are You Lying Now? Neurotechnology and Law* (forthcoming 2020–2021).

Przemysław Pałka is a Research Scholar at the Jagiellonian University in Cracow (Future Law Lab, the Faculty of Law and Administration), Associate Research Scholar at Yale Law School and a Visiting Fellow at the Information Society Project at Yale. His research interests encompass the intersection of law, science and new technologies, especially property law, contract law, consumer law, personal data protection law, cognitive science, machine learning, data analytics and automation of legal tasks.

George Pavlakos is Professor of Law and Philosophy at the School of Law, University of Glasgow. He has held visiting posts at the Universities of Antwerp, Kiel, Luzern, the European University Institute, the UCLA Law School, the Cornell Law School and the Beihang Law School in Beijing. In recent years his work has focused on understanding the existence of legal obligations outwith the context of state institutions or other particular institutional arrangements. His published work includes the monograph *Our Knowledge of the Law* (Hart Publishing) and two co-edited volumes on moral and legal responsibility published by Cambridge University Press, as well as papers in legal philosophy in journals such as *Legal Theory*, *Ratio Juris* and *The Canadian Journal of Law and Jurisprudence*. He is the general editor of the book series Law and Practical Reason at Hart Publishing and joint general editor of the academic journal *Jurisprudence*, published by Routledge.

Corrado Roversi is Associate Professor at the University of Bologna, where he teaches Philosophy of Law. His research is focused on legal ontology and the phenomenology of institutional concepts. Amongst his publications are 'On the Artifactual – and Natural – Character of Legal Institutions', in *Law as an Artefact* (Oxford University Press, 2018), 'Conceptualizing Institutions' (*Phenomenology and the Cognitive Sciences* 13, 2013), and 'A Marriage is an Artefact and Not a Walk that We Take Together: An Experimental Study on the Categorization of Artefacts' (with L. Tummolini and A. Borghi, *Review of Philosophy and Psychology* 4(3), 2013).

Marek Sławiński has an MA in Law and a BA in Philosophy. He is currently preparing a PhD thesis in which he adopts Roman Ingarden's conception of responsibility as a framework to explain the notion of criminal liability. He collaborates with the Department of Criminal Law at the Jagiellonian University, and the Krakowski Instytut Prawa Karnego Fundacja (Kraków Institute of Criminal Law Foundation). His main areas of interest include constitutional principles of criminal law, theory of criminal law, contemporary notions of responsibility and the notion of moral agency in ancient Greek philosophy.

Jerzy Stelmach is the Head of the Department of Philosophy of Law and Legal Ethics at the Jagiellonian University. His research interests include interpretation within law, legal argumentation, legal negotiations and the methodology of law. He is the author of numerous highly acclaimed books, articles and contributed chapters which have appeared in leading publishing houses and scholarly journals. He holds honorary degrees awarded by Heidelberg University and the University of Augsburg.

Kevin Tobia is an assistant professor of law at Georgetown University. His research focuses on legal interpretation and the cognitive science of legal concepts.

Peter J. van Koppen is a psychologist and emeritus professor of legal psychology at the Faculty of Law at VU University Amsterdam, and Professor of Legal Psychology at Maastricht University. His research encompasses issues concerning evidence in legal cases, especially witness and suspect statements, behaviour of police officers and judges and miscarriages of justice. Van Koppen has served as an expert witness in many cases, advises police teams and has published some 35 books, 125 articles and 100 chapters in edited volumes on various subjects in legal psychology. In 2014 he was awarded the Tom Williamson Award for lifetime achievement by the International Investigative Interviewing Research Group (iIIRG) and in 2016 received the Lifetime Achievement Award of the European Association of Psychology and Law (EAPL).

Antonia Waltermann is Assistant Professor of Legal Theory and Philosophy at Maastricht University. Her research focuses on explicating foundational concepts of (public) law and, more recently, on non-human agency. For the latter research in particular, she draws also from the cognitive sciences. Her scientific publications include the monograph *Reconstructing Sovereignty* and the edited volume *Law, Science, Rationality*.

Acknowledgements

We would like to thank all of the contributors to this handbook for their willingness to take part in its creation, as well as for their thoughtful and inspiring contributions. We would also like to thank Aeddan Shaw for proofreading the texts. Finally, we would like to extend our sincere thanks to Matt Galloway from Cambridge University Press for his encouragement and patience.

This volume was supported by research grant no 2017/27/B/HS5/01407, funded by the Polish National Science Center.

1

Introduction

Between Law and the Cognitive Sciences – A Manifesto

Bartosz Brożek and Jaap Hage

1.1 A SCIENTIFIC REVOLUTION

Recent decades have brought about a genuine scientific revolution. It did not take place overnight, but the cumulative efforts of psychologists, neuroscientists, specialists in AI and philosophers have given us a picture of human cognitive processes and behaviour that is radically new. The revolution has led us to recognize and account for the important role played by unconscious decision making, the central role that emotions play in the human psyche and the intricate relationship between mind and body. In doing so, it has significantly reshaped the way in which we understand our mental lives and the sources of our actions.

Of course, it is debatable whether the theoretical and methodological shifts brought about by the cognitive sciences deserve the label of a 'revolution'. One may argue that it is better to speak of a gradual evolution, one which errs more often than it finds a grain of truth. However, such terminological disputes are ultimately useless. Whether we have a revolution on our hands or 'merely' a slow evolution, the fact is that – when compared to the science of the first half of the twentieth century – the contemporary cognitive sciences provide us with a fresh, often intriguing and surprising view of human thinking and agency.

All of this poses a challenge to legal scholars and practitioners. The law is preoccupied with guiding human behaviour by means of rules. Thus, it would seem that lawyers should take careful notice of the advances in the cognitive sciences. After all, if one wishes to influence the behaviour of people, one should understand what drives this behaviour in the first place. Nevertheless, for various reasons, lawyers have paid relatively little attention to developments in psychology and other cognitive sciences over the last century. Arguably, they have often adopted the strategy of splendid isolation, where law is considered an island far removed from the mainland of the empirical sciences. Of course, not everybody has been an isolationist, and hence the employment of the terms 'relatively', 'arguably' and 'often'. However, it is difficult to escape the conclusion that the prevalent attitude of legal scholars and practitioners has been to safeguard their sceptred isle from the intrusions of economists, sociologists and psychologists.

Perhaps there are good reasons for this isolation. A century ago, Hans Kelsen forcefully spelled out what he believed to be such reasons. According to Kelsen, the law remains the law only when it is considered as a sphere of Ought, based upon, but not part of, social reality. In this way, legal decision making could remain free from external considerations. Yet does this argument, based on the alleged nature of law, provide us with a sufficient justification for remaining aloof from the sciences? Arguably (again!) not. At the very least, lawyers should seriously consider whether the cognitive sciences have any significant bearing on the law. Of course, there are numerous obstacles to doing so successfully. Let us comment here on a few of them.

1.2 (DO NOT) MIND THE GAP!

Cognitive sciences are about human behaviour and so is the law. Therefore, each must be highly relevant for the other. Superficially this is how it may seem, but if one takes a closer look, it transpires that the cognitive sciences investigate the way we actually act, uncovering the mechanisms behind human behavioural patterns, while the law tells us what our behaviour should be. For many centuries, philosophers have been telling us that this difference in modalities is crucial: there is an unbridgeable gap between Is (as investigated by the natural sciences) and Ought (as considered in law or ethics). Because of the gap – and not an ordinary, but an unbridgeable one! – lawyers, preoccupied with what *ought* to be the case, are engaged with something *completely different* than the cognitive scientists, who are interested in what *is* the case. This means that there is no theoretical or methodological bridge to be built between Is and Ought and, consequently, that no dialogue between the law and the cognitive sciences is possible! Lawyers who are not interested in the findings of the cognitive sciences are not unreasonable. To the contrary: they act fully reasonably by trying to avoid violating the fundamental methodological precepts that define their discipline.

Some people are indeed happy to accept the analysis outlined above and tend to adopt a dualist approach in relation to norms (moral or legal) and empirical facts: the methods of the normative sciences differ fundamentally from those of the empirical sciences. However, others are quick to point out that, in the real world at least, the law is significantly limited by various factual constraints, from the purely physical to the economic. For example, one cannot impose an obligation which is impossible or extremely hard to fulfil. Such observations force one to adopt a position which is the polar opposite, one which denies the existence of the sphere of Ought altogether. Legal norms become descriptions in disguise: to say that one ought not to steal is nothing other than saying, for example, that if one does steal something, one will (with such and such a degree of probability) be punished by the court.

These two extreme stances, dualism and reductionism, are both philosophically defensible, but they are far from being the only available options. Their persistence is but a reflection of the human propensity to think in terms of crude oppositions. It is certainly easier this way: when the choice is limited to well-defined and highly contrasted options, one lives in a theoretically simple universe. The problem is that such a universe is not only simple, but also simplistic. Things get much more interesting when one moves beyond the celebrated opposition. There, one finds an abundance of possibilities for depicting the relationship between Is and Ought and it is by accepting this complexity that one may achieve deeper insight into the functioning of the law.

There are at least two strategies which may be employed to help overcome the simplistic dualism of Is and Ought. The first is to realize that sentences expressing norms may stand in a special relation to sentences expressing empirical facts. In this context, one interesting route – albeit obviously not an uncontested one – is to take advantage of the concept of supervenience. On this account, no change at the level of legal norms (obligations), that is, the supervenient level, would be possible without a change at the level of empirical facts (that is, the subvenient level). Another intriguing route is to utilize the concept of presupposition: some empirical facts would be necessary for some statements expressing legal obligations to be meaningful. For example, the sentence 'Crimes may be committed only intentionally' presupposes that human beings are capable of acting intentionally; if humans lack this capability, the requirement that crimes be committed intentionally is meaningless.

The second strategy for blunting the Is–Ought distinction is to downplay its importance. That is not as difficult as some imagine. The claim that there is an 'unbridgeable gap' between what is and what ought to be seems to assume a very poor and highly polarized view of language. In addition to descriptive and imperative sentences, language offers a broad spectrum of other kinds of expressions. Perhaps the most powerful picture of the richness of language has been sketched in Ludwig Wittgenstein's *Philosophical Investigations*, where he writes:

> But how many kinds of sentence are there? Say assertion, question, and command? – There are countless kinds: countless different kinds of use of what we call 'symbols', 'words', 'sentences'. And this multiplicity is not something fixed, given once for all; but new types of language ... come into existence, and others become obsolete and get forgotten. ... Review the multiplicity of language-games in the following examples, and in others: Giving orders, and obeying them – Describing the appearance of an object, or giving its measurements – Constructing an object from a description (a drawing) – Reporting an event – Speculating about an event – Forming and testing a hypothesis – Presenting the results of an experiment in tables and diagrams – Making up a story; and reading it – Play-acting – Singing catches – Guessing riddles – Making a joke; telling it – Solving a problem in

practical arithmetic – Translating from one language into another – Asking, thanking, cursing, greeting, praying.[1]

The opposition between Is and Ought only becomes so strict if we focus exclusively on two kinds of speech acts, those expressing norms and those expressing facts. However, once we broaden our perspective and realize that there are also questions (which come in many varieties), value judgements, mathematical truths, logical tautologies, evocative metaphors, *onomatopoeias*, dirty and abstract jokes, crossword puzzles and so on and so forth, we will plainly see that there is something artificial in concentrating on the Is–Ought gap. Given the abundance of ways in which we use language, the gap is but one of many.

Moreover, it may be argued that even the category of Is-sentences is not as uniform as it seems. Let us consider the following four sentences: 'Dobrochna entered the room', 'The total entropy of an isolated system can never decrease over time', 'Every positive integer can be written as the sum of at most four squares' and 'If Manuel is happy then Manuel is happy'. Arguably, all of these sentences are Is-sentences, but it is quite clear that the facts they express and the manner in which they do so is completely different. 'Dobrochna entered the room' is a description of a concrete situation, and it is true if and only if Dobrochna has indeed entered the room. The second law of thermodynamics is a general law and as such it is a hypothesis pertaining to the structure of the universe. Of course, it has turned out to be a very good hypothesis – one which has not been falsified so far (and may never be falsified) – but one cannot say with absolute certainty that it is true. Lagrange's four-square theorem expresses a mathematical truth: it is not an empirical truth, but rather a necessary one. Finally, 'If Manuel is happy then Manuel is happy' is a tautology; it is also necessarily true, but – in contraposition to Lagrange's theorem – it has no discernible content. Its truth hangs together exclusively with its form.

We encounter a similar diversity in normative expressions. 'One ought not to steal' is substantially different from 'One ought to use the word "bald" by referring to bald people only', which is still different from 'If one wants to kill bacteria, viruses and protozoa in the water, one ought to heat it to 100 degrees Celsius'. It is easy to see that the 'oughts' involved in these three sentences are quite different. The first is considered by many to be a 'full-blooded' ought: the norm that it contains expresses a moral (and legal) obligation. The second is used to set (or describe?) a criterion of linguistic correctness. The third, in turn, is an instrumental recommendation, rooted in some facts discovered by the natural sciences.

We do not want to suggest that the distinction between Is and Ought is completely irrelevant. However, the above considerations clearly show that the issue is much more complex and not as clear-cut as may transpire from some philosophical discussions. Even if there is a gap between Is and Ought, there exist many other

---

[1] L. Wittgenstein, *Philosophical Investigations*, translated by G. E. M. Anscombe, §23 (Oxford: Basil Blackwell, 1953).

gaps of various kinds: between descriptive and evaluative statements, descriptions of concrete facts and general laws, mathematical truths and empirical truths, moral obligations and linguistic standards, legal norms and instrumental recommendations, and so on. Therefore, the conclusion is that the Is–Ought distinction cannot be considered as fundamental; to the contrary: a small shift of focus leads to highlighting different conceptual distinctions. Moreover, it transpires that intriguing theoretical and practical problems emerge in the space delineated by the extreme views of dualism and reductionism. The way is quite open to explore this territory, and hence to engage in reflections which combine the perspectives of both lawyers and cognitive scientists. At the same time, it is obvious that this is no easy task. In particular, it requires a lot of methodological awareness as well as the use – and perhaps also the development – of new conceptual tools.

1.3 SCOPE AND DEPTH

It would be unfair to claim that the cognitive sciences have had no influence in (and on) the law. There has been substantial effort to organize and discuss the research in the field, especially within the *neurolaw* movement. Hundreds if not thousands of papers have been published, and dozens of international conferences dedicated to this topic have been organized. Even if this constitutes but a tiny fraction of the publications and events devoted to legal scholarship, one cannot pretend that nothing has been done.

However, a closer inspection of the ongoing debates reveals that they are somewhat narrow in scope. Usually, the research and discussions in question revolve around three main issues: legal reasoning (in particular, unconscious decision making and the pitfalls of relying on heuristics in the law); evidence (in particular, the use of neuroscientific evidence in the courtroom); and the existence of free will in the context of legal agency (although this topic is usually considered within a broader, ethical perspective). These are all extremely important issues, and the research targeting them often leads to interesting, if not groundbreaking ideas. The problem is, however, that the insights they bring are rather fragmentary. Let us consider the research in law and psychology pertaining to legal reasoning. It is almost exclusively devoted to the decision-making processes which take place at the unconscious level. Many important contributions have shown that professional lawyers are prone to commit errors while tackling legal problems due to their (unconscious) use of heuristics. At the same time, little if any attention is given to other aspects of legal thinking: conceptual structures, theory construction, argumentation or imagination. This may generate the false impression that the cognitive sciences are only useful to the extent that they help us to uncover the unconscious processes that interfere with 'correct' legal thinking, while they have nothing to say about our conscious efforts to solve legal problems. It is true that the cognitive sciences have done much to reaffirm the power of the unconscious mind – but it is not all they have done. To sketch a full and methodologically sound picture of legal thinking, one must also take the theories developed by cognitive sciences into consideration that pertain to language processing or the mechanisms underlying mental imagery.

The same argument applies to other law-related issues that are addressed from the perspective of the cognitive sciences. There is a substantial amount of research directed at particular problems, but a more comprehensive picture is missing. We believe that the cognitive sciences may shed new light on virtually any problem to be found in legal scholarship, from the philosophy of law (legal ontology and epistemology), through legal doctrine (criminal and private law), to the law of evidence. All these areas may be – to a lesser or greater extent – informed by the cognitive sciences.

Of course, some of them are a more natural fit for such an approach than others. For example, it is quite easy to understand how insights from the cognitive sciences may alter our picture of legal decision making, while it is much more difficult to see this happening in relation to legal ontology. Moreover, it must be observed that at least in some of the areas of legal science there are powerful inertial forces at work, which make it difficult to embrace the insights coming from outside, in particular from the natural sciences. A case in point is contemporary legal philosophy, largely dominated by the analytical tradition, a paradigm which is often tinged with conservatism and isolationism. The basic tenet of analytical jurisprudence is that the goal of legal philosophy is to uncover the conceptual scheme of the law and map the interconnection between various legal concepts as they are actually used. Questions pertaining to the origin of the said concepts, their evolution or function, are relegated to the (often ignored) background of this kind of philosophy.

A similar isolationist attitude may be discerned in legal doctrine. A typical criminal or international lawyer is interested in the interpretation and application of legal provisions or in putting together a coherent 'narrative' linking past precedents with current and future cases. They are also engaged with questions pertaining to the practical use of science, and especially scientific evidence, in legal procedures. However, more fundamental problems which potentially lead to the questioning of the dominant paradigm are rarely raised or addressed. As a consequence, there is little need to open up legal doctrine to impulses coming from the outside.

Thus, our suggestion is not only that the theories and insights from the cognitive sciences should be used in a much wider way in legal science; we believe that such an endeavour should penetrate the fabric of law much more deeply. Much of the existing research on the subject may be described as 'scratching the surface'. The cognitive sciences are not taken seriously as a point of reference in discussing the foundations of law, or the key legal concepts. Instead, relatively smaller issues are addressed and investigated.

Our plea to adopt a wider involvement of the cognitive sciences in the science and practice of the law is a plea for more coherence. Fragmentary and shallow attempts to illuminate legal problems from the perspective of this or that conception developed by neuroscientists or experimental psychologists may be fashionable, provocative and may arouse a considerable degree of controversy. However, from the methodological standpoint, they are essentially flawed. Only a kind of reflection which aims at the development of a more embracing picture of the relationship between law and the cognitive sciences may lead to real insights and progress.

This is closely connected to yet another issue: our understanding of the cognitive sciences. In the existing legal literature, the cognitive sciences are often equated with neuroscience or experimental psychology – the 'real' natural sciences. In this way, they are opposed to less well-defined and less highly regarded fields of inquiry. In truth, however, the cognitive sciences are a more complex beast. They also embrace other branches of psychology, as well as evolutionary theory, research in artificial intelligence, logic, and philosophy of mind and of action. Moreover, the complexity of the cognitive sciences is tied up with the nature of the theories developed therein. Most of the work done in neuroscience and experimental psychology pertains to well-defined, but comparatively small problems investigated in the controlled environment of a laboratory with the use of somewhat artificial cognitive tasks.

At the same time, there exist attempts to synthesize this mosaic of data and small-scope theories into a larger narrative of how the human mind functions. Naturally, these attempts exhibit less methodological rigour than a well-designed experiment: they are largely based on philosophical argument more than anything else. They also generate considerably more doubt and criticism than the more focused research. The point is, however, that without such synthetic approaches the enterprise of law and the cognitive sciences (as well as literature and the cognitive sciences, economics and the cognitive sciences, political science and the cognitive sciences, etc.) would remain shallow and fragmented. Any fruitful exchange between these different fields of reflection can only take place at an appropriate level of generality: one where the image of mankind depicted by the contemporary cognitive sciences may be meaningfully confronted with the image of mankind presupposed by the law.

1.4 THE PROMISE AND THE OBSTACLE

The above considerations are underpinned by what may be called 'the promise of law and the cognitive sciences'. This promise may be understood in two distinct ways: either moderate or revolutionary. The moderate promise is that the cognitive sciences may and will constitute an important point of reference for the law. This will happen regardless of what the lawyers do now. The continuous advances in neuroscience, experimental psychology, artificial intelligence and related disciplines, which lead to a better understanding of the functioning of the human mind and the mechanisms behind human behaviour, will – in one way or another – force legal science into rethinking the law in light of the findings of the cognitive sciences. If so, it is only reasonable to develop conceptual tools which would facilitate this process. In particular, much needs to be done in connection to legal method as well as in relation to opening up the legal sciences to the dialogue with other disciplines. In other words, the moderate promise will be fulfilled to a higher degree and in a smooth and coherent manner if lawyers are ready – and know how to – respond to the challenges posed in the future by the cognitive sciences.

The revolutionary promise goes much further: it is a claim that the law of the future will be substantially different from what the lawyers are accustomed to. Key legal concepts such as crime, contract, personhood or ownership will be abandoned, completely reinterpreted or at least given new theoretical foundations. Similar changes will transpire in legal practice, where the methods of the cognitive sciences and neuroscientific technologies will be used more commonly. Legal scholars will be part-time psychologists and will devote as much time to reading the Damasios and Blooms of their time as to the more traditional reading list. Law students, in turn, will be required to complete an intensive course in cognitive science. Thanks to these revolutionary changes, the law of the future, created, interpreted and applied with constant support from the relevant natural sciences, will become more efficient and fair (or, at least, commonly considered as fair).

The revolutionary promise is, of course, much stronger and it is unlikely that the law will change to such a degree. There is a very powerful argument to this effect, one that constitutes, in our opinion, the greatest obstacle to applying the findings of the cognitive sciences in the sphere of law. The law is based on a particular conceptual scheme, one which is deeply rooted in what psychologists call 'folk psychology'. This is a set of concepts that people use (also unconsciously) to understand and predict the behaviour of others. Folk psychology uses concepts such as 'belief', 'intent', 'voluntary', 'reason', 'guilt' and so on. Their legal counterparts are not so very different; rather, they constitute a more detailed specification of these common notions. Because of this shared set of concepts, people are generally able to understand the law. Even if, on occasion, the law involves a high degree of abstraction, it remains connected to the well-known folk-psychological way of thinking about human behaviour.

Meanwhile, the explanation of human behaviour offered by the cognitive sciences is, more often than not, at odds with folk psychology. When our common understanding is that we make decisions in a conscious and informed way, forming intent and acting on the basis of well-established beliefs, the cognitive sciences suggest a picture in which most of our decisions are unconscious. When folk psychology ignores or, at best, downplays the role of emotions in the human mental life, the cognitive sciences place emotions centre stage in the theatre of the human mind. While we tend to think that we are free in our decision making, the cognitive sciences raise serious doubts as to the common understanding of the will.

The relationship between these three conceptual schemes – the legal, the folk-psychological and the scientific – is fascinating. The legal conceptual apparatus is a refinement of the folk-psychological one, making the law understandable to its addressees. The scientific perspective uncovers the real mechanisms behind human behaviour: it provides an explanation of why we act and think in the given way. (As such, it also explains the emergence and role of folk psychology.) It transpires that the law is based on an essentially flawed picture of the architecture of the human mind. It misinterprets the real motivational factors at play in our behaviour and, in turn, this leads to serious doubts regarding the efficacy of the law. At the same time, a legal system based exclusively on the view of the human decision making provided by the cognitive sciences would most probably be difficult to understand, and a rudimentary understanding of what is required of us seems to be a prerequisite of following legal rules. Therefore, legal regulations based on a picture of the human mind which is alien to the common folk-psychological understanding of what it means to think and act would also be inefficient. This leaves us with a puzzle or, better yet, a certain tension.

We believe that this is an unavoidable, but creative dialectic. It shows that what we should be looking for is neither the moderate nor the revolutionary approach; what matters lies in-between. It will be intriguing to see where this creative tension leads us and what it generates in the future. The present volume is but one attempt to decipher this future.

1.5 THE CONTENTS

In line with the above considerations, this handbook aims to encompass a wide scope of subjects at the intersection of law and the cognitive sciences. It may be divided into five parts. The first is devoted to metatheoretical and methodological issues, in particular the Is–Ought problem and the relationship between the legal and folk-psychological conceptual frameworks and the cognitive sciences. The second part tackles some of the key topics in legal philosophy: ontology of law, legal epistemology and the rationality of legal decision making. In the third part, important doctrinal issues in both private and criminal law are addressed. The fourth part is devoted to some of the more prominent themes in evidence law. The fifth and final part consists of three 'dissenting opinions', where substantial doubts and questions are raised in relation to 'law and the cognitive sciences'.

Most of the chapters are accompanied by shorter commentaries. The role of these is not to criticize merely for the sake of criticizing, but rather to add a new perspective, or highlight an aspect of the problem which has perhaps not been fully explored in the main chapter. It is our hope that a more comprehensive picture of the use of the cognitive sciences in the law may be formed in this way.

1.5.1 *Part I*

Here is a short outline of the contents of the handbook. The first part, on the metatheoretical and methodological issues, opens with a chapter by Jaap Hage, where he argues that the cognitive sciences are important for the law for three different reasons: because facts that can be established by the cognitive sciences are important for application of the law, because the content of the law is (partially) determined by such facts and – most importantly – because the law assumes a descriptive view of mankind which is challenged by the cognitive sciences. Hage underscores the fact that, while the first reason is quite straightforward, the remaining two are subject to argument.

Carsten Heidemann disagrees with Hage's account of the relationship between Is and Ought and defends this distinction, pointing out the internal tensions in the second part of Hage's argument, as well as some additional external reasons.

Łukasz Kurek, in turn, considers the relationship between the law and folk psychology, that is, a conceptual scheme we use to understand the intentions and actions of ourselves and others. He analyses in some detail three different stances with regard to this relationship: autonomy and revision of law with regard to the role of folk-psychological concepts and integration of the conceptual frameworks of folk psychology and the cognitive sciences in the law.

This problem is also taken up by Kevin Tobia, who advances 'the folk law thesis' in his commentary, that is, the view that ordinary (folk-psychological) concepts are at the heart of key legal concepts.

1.5.2 *Part II*

In the second part of the volume, which is devoted to legal ontology and epistemology, Corrado Roversi's chapter starts from two theses pertaining to legal metaphysics: that legal facts are a subset of social facts and that they are the outcome of rules that organize sanctions and authority in a formal way. Building on these assumptions, he develops the view that complexity in human society is based on the kind of intentional states involved, and the way in which these states are interrelated. In particular, Roversi distinguishes four levels of sociality. Level 0 is the baseline of sociality, that is, acting together; level 1 is a fundamental element, the acceptance of norms; level 2 is a specific thing we can do together, namely, attribute a status; and, finally, level 3 combines levels 1 and 2 in the attribution of a status through social norms. In the passage from level 0 to level 3 the creation of social facts, and therefore also legal facts, is made possible.

In his chapter, Bartosz Brożek provides an overview of the architecture of the legal mind. He posits that legal thinking is possible through the simultaneous utilization of three different but interlocking mental mechanisms: intuition, imagination (or mental simulation) and linguistic constructs.

Morris Hoffman addresses the issues connected to the psychology of trial judges. He considers the question of whether general insights from psychology are applicable to trial judges, and also discusses the use of heuristics in judicial decision making. The chapter closes with some general reflections on the challenges psychology poses to judicial reasoning.

Adi Leibovitch, in her commentary on the work of Hoffman, underscores three more specific issues connected to judicial decision making: how context dependence can change substantive outcomes reached by the courts, the tension between the tendency to retributivism and the rehabilitative goals of the law, and the difficulty of disregarding irrelevant or inadmissible evidence.

In turn, Eyal Aharoni – adopting a broad evolutionary perspective – considers the fundamental question pertaining to the psychology of judging, that is, of the relationship between the emotional and the rational aspects thereof, and – more in particular – the desire to use criminal law for retribution.

1.5.3 Part III

The third part of the handbook is devoted to the relationship between the cognitive sciences and legal doctrine. Przemysław Pałka's chapter addresses the intersection of private law and the cognitive sciences. In particular, he draws the reader's attention to the image of *homo legalis privatus*, the man of the private law, that is, a set of presuppositions regarding the functioning of the human mind and the sources of human behaviour as presupposed by contract law and related branches of the legal system. He observes that the image is not fully compatible with the findings of the cognitive sciences and shows how this fact can illuminate the tasks of a private lawyer.

Bartosz Brożek and Marek Jakubiec, in their commentary on Pałka's chapter, discuss the concept of a presupposition which is needed to account for the descriptive level of the legal rules. They also consider in some detail what it means to say that the legal image of the human decision-making processes is incompatible with the scientific one.

The next chapter, by Jaap Hage and Antonia Waltermann, revolves around the concepts of responsibility and liability in criminal law. They describe and analyse three central positions in the ongoing debates on the subject: libertarianism, hard incompatibilism and compatibilism. They also suggest that the emphasis in these debates should gravitate towards the question of whether the reductionist perspective on the world and on agency is compatible with the folk-psychological perspective.

Mikołaj Małecki and Marek Sławiński's chapter is also embedded in the framework of the criminal law. They present and analyse the most popular conceptions of guilt in continental criminal law: psychological, complex normative, pure normative and functional. They observe that these conceptions are troubling from the perspective of the cognitive sciences: they either assume an explanation of the human mental machinery which is incompatible with the current state of knowledge, or become incomprehensible to an average addressee of the law. Małecki and Sławiński consider whether – and how – this weakness may be turned into an opportunity for the further development of the theories of guilt.

Gerben Meynen's chapter is devoted to the insanity defence. He considers various aspects of this multidimensional phenomenon, from the justification of its inclusion in the legal system, through the criterion for legal insanity and the problem of the burden of proof, to the question of whether the advances in the cognitive sciences, and neuroscience in particular, may lead to a more useful and fair construction of the insanity defence.

In their commentary to Meynen's chapter, Lisa Claydon and Paul Catley point out that, on the one hand, neuroscience can never become the sole basis for establishing insanity, while, on the other, it is imprudent to think that neuroscience is of no value in this context.

1.5.4 Part IV

Meynen's chapter and Claydon and Catley's commentary constitute a natural transition to the fourth part of the volume. Pim Haselager addresses some questions of neurotechnologies, which enable the recording or stimulation of brain processes. In particular, his focus is on neurotechnology that measures brain activity to drive applications in order to perform actions, stimulates brains in order to change, restore or improve aspects of cognition, or combines recording and stimulation to enable informational loops within or between brains. In this context, the questions of agency, identity and responsibility become more prominent and may be seen in a new light.

In her chapter, Jane Campbell Moriarty provides a detailed consideration of neuroscience and neuroimaging evidence in federal and state courts of the United States. The issues addressed include the admissibility of evidence and some problematic aspects of neuroscience evidence, as well as the potential ways in which neuroscience has affected legal policy and evidentiary decisions.

In turn, Deborah Denno tries to provide an additional context to Moriarty's discussion in her commentary. She examines the scientific environment in which neuroscientific evidence has taken hold, as well as the complexities that can arise when attempting to decipher the influence of such evidence in the much broader framework of a criminal case that involves hundreds of factors, with neuroimaging tests simply being one component.

In a similar vein, the commentary by Bartłomiej Kucharzyk underscores the fact that neuroscientific evidence is often beset by a number of traps and weaknesses. They are closely connected to the methods used in neuroscience: a lawyer must be aware of them in order to fairly assess the strength of the arguments based on neuroscientific evidence.

In their chapter, Anne Ruth Mackor, Hylke Jellema and Peter van Koppen consider the way in which people reason about evidence. They discuss in detail the explanation-based theories of reasoning which are deeply rooted in the cognitive psychology of decision making. They conclude that this approach remains close to how people reason in everyday life and that – in reasoning about evidence and proof in criminal cases – it may help to avoid certain fallacies and biases.

1.5.5 *Part V*

The fifth and final part of the volume consists of three dissenting opinions, which raise some doubts regarding the relevance of the cognitive sciences for the law.

George Pavlakos offers a broad non-naturalistic account of legal phenomena. Along the way, by demonstrating the failure of naturalistic facts to meet the requirements of explanation, he calls into question the relevance of cognitive science to law.

In turn, Pierluigi Chiassoni – adopting a broadly analytic perspective – critically considers four issues: the relevance of the cognitive sciences for law, the need for a 'renewed' metaphysics of law informed by the cognitive sciences, Hume's law, and the limits of the psychological account of legal reasoning and interpretation.

Finally, Jerzy Stelmach outlines the history of four revolutions, emphasizing that law and the cognitive sciences is not the first attempt to approach the law from a naturalistic perspective. Against this background, he attempts to answer the question of what contemporary cognitive science can offer legal science and practice. He responds by identifying a number of consequences which any serious consideration of the theories and data from the cognitive sciences may bring to the theory and practice of law.

I

Metatheory and Methodology

2

Are the Cognitive Sciences Relevant for Law?

Jaap Hage[*]

2.1 INTRODUCTION

'Are the cognitive sciences relevant for law?' At first glance this question seems superfluous. Of course the cognitive sciences are relevant for law, just like many other sciences! On second thoughts, the question turns out to make some sense. Sciences aim to provide us with information about the world, about its facts and about the laws that govern these facts. Law aims to guide human behaviour; it does not aim to provide information at all. To state it by means of slogans: sciences deal with what IS the case, while law deals with what OUGHT to be done. From this perspective, law and sciences seem to be worlds apart, and the question of the use of the cognitive sciences for law does make sense.

Before starting our discussion, it will be useful to delineate the topic further. By law I mean a set of rules, rights and principles, compliance with which is by and large enforced by collective means such as the power of the state.[1] By the cognitive sciences, in a broad sense that transcends pure cognition, we will mean all those sciences that study the functioning of mind and its physical substrate. They include relevant parts of psychology, biology, cognitive neurosciences, sociology, economy, philosophy and artificial intelligence.

The first part of the discussion will deal with the question of why there may be an issue at all regarding the relevance of the cognitive sciences for law. Sections 2.2 and 2.3 address this question and provide some historical and jurisprudential information which explains the doubts that some may have. These doubts are in the last instance based on a strict distinction, if not division, between IS and OUGHT.

Section 2.4 argues that, even if this distinction is taken as strictly as some do, there is still room for the cognitive sciences in law.

---

[*] The author thanks Antonia Waltermann for valuable comments on an earlier version of this text.
[1] This definition limits law to positive law and defines positive law as law that is enforced by state organs. Moreover, it ignores the institutional side of law, the organizations which make law, adjudicate or enforce, and only focuses on the 'rule-aspect' of law. Other definitions are certainly possible, but for a sharp opposition between law and the sciences, the given definition, which focuses on the content of law, is attractive.

There are good reasons not to make the distinction between IS and OUGHT too strictly. Section 2.5 presents these reasons. This section differs from the rest of the chapter because the argument presented there, which introduces different categories of facts, including the category of 'constructivist facts', is philosophical, and addresses the cognitive sciences only superficially. Section 2.5 closes with a discussion of what the implications are for the role of the cognitive sciences in law, if the distinction between IS and OUGHT is downplayed.

The argument up to this point will be focused on the relevance of the cognitive sciences for law as it is presently conceived. In Section 2.6, the angle is reversed, and the question becomes how law should be conceived from the perspective of the cognitive sciences. This section focuses on the image of humankind that underlies law as it presently is, and addresses the question of whether this image is disrupted by the recent insights from the cognitive sciences. It also raises the question of whether the foundations of law can remain the same in light of those findings. For example, does it still make sense to guide human behaviour by imposing duties or by threatening with sanctions, and should we still treat people as responsible beings?

2.2 LEGAL SCIENCE AS A NORMATIVE SCIENCE

The tendency to see the relation between empirical sciences and legal science as problematic was promoted in the early twentieth century by the writings of Hans Kelsen (1934). Kelsen propagated a 'pure theory of law', by which he meant a non-empirical, non-moral science of law. In his early work, Kelsen was strongly influenced by the philosophy of Immanuel Kant. Kant was, in turn, influenced by David Hume, if only by opposing Hume's views (Brożek, 2013, pp. 115–28). To get a proper understanding of Kelsen's view of law and legal science proper, we will first pay some attention to these two major influences.

2.2.1 *Hume on Reason and Passion in the Motivation of Human Behaviour*

Hume's work on moral philosophy is famous for, amongst others, his view on the relation between reason and passion in the motivation of human behaviour and his suggestion that it is impossible to derive ought-conclusions from is-premises only.[2] According to Hume, there are two components in the motivation (the will) that a person has to do something. One component is passion, the other reason. Traditionally these two were, according to Hume, seen as competing sources of motivation, but wrongly so, as the one needs the other as complement:

---

[2] As with any important work, Hume's *Treatise on Human Nature* is the object of interpretational discussions. This is not the place to enter into these discussions. The views that are ascribed to Hume here have certainly been inspired by Hume, but there is no claim that they represent the, or even a, correct Hume interpretation. Cf. the introduction of Railton (2006).

> Nothing is more usual in philosophy, and even in common life, than to talk of the combat of passion and reason, to give the preference to reason, ... In order to shew the fallacy of all this philosophy, I shall endeavour to prove *first*, that reason alone can never be a motive to any action of the will; and *secondly*, that it can never oppose passion in the direction of the will. (Hume, 1978, p. 413; Book II, Section III. Italics in the original)

Hume continues to claim that reason by itself – conceived as empirical knowledge, mathematical knowledge and knowledge about causal relations – cannot motivate. In the last instance, the passions drive people, and reason can only steer this driving force of the passions. For example, if a person P is thirsty, they desire to drink. This desire would, in the Humean classification, belong to the area of passion. In itself the desire does not motivate P to take a glass of water. However, P also believes that there is water in the tap, that this water can be collected in a glass and that having a glass with water allows them to drink. These beliefs in themselves do not motivate any action either, but in combination with the desire to drink, they motivate P to fill a glass with water from the tap and to drink it. Here we have in a nutshell Hume's belief/desire theory of motivation. Passions, expressed in desires, are the force that drive people to act, and reason, in the form of means/end beliefs, transforms these abstract desires into the motivation to perform particular actions.

A crucial aspect of this belief/desire model is that beliefs and desires – reason and passion – are, *in the last instance*, distinct entities. Some desires may be derived, such as the desire to take a glass of water, which is derived from the desire to drink and the belief that taking a glass of water is a means of drinking. The ultimate desires, however, are not the outcome of any reasoning process, but just happen to a person. Being thirsty and the closely related desire to drink are states of a person that happen to exist, and they are not the result of belief-based reasoning. Analogously, beliefs depend on sensory information and on reasoning, but not on passions or desires. Because beliefs and desires are distinct types of entity, the one type cannot be reduced to the other. They exist in the last instance independently of each other, and they are both necessary for a proper understanding of motivation.

There seems to be a natural transition from this belief/desire model of motivation to the (onto)logical distinction, or even the gap, between IS and OUGHT:

> Beliefs concern what *is* the case according to the agent; their satisfaction conditions are met when the agent gets the facts right. ... Desires and values, by contrast, concern what *is to be* or *ought to be* the case according to the agent; they 'aim the agent toward an end', namely, the desired object of valued state. They have action-guiding force on behalf of what they represent, not simply credence in it. They therefore lack straightforward truth conditions, and one cannot straightforwardly apply the same notions of objectivity, or norms of logic and evidence, to desire and to reasoning that concludes in action, *practical reason*. (cf. Railton, 2006)

There is much in this brief argument that can be questioned, but the main message seems convincing: on the one hand we have beliefs that describe an independently existing reality, and on the other hand desires which express how an agent wants reality to be. These are – according to the message – different things (the ontological distinction). Moreover, because they are different things, it is logically impossible to derive one from the other. The logical gap between IS and OUGHT reflects the ontological gap between beliefs and desires.

If these gaps between reason and passion and between IS and OUGHT really exist, and if law belongs to the realm of OUGHT, the gaps explain why the role of the cognitive sciences in law, which deal with what IS the case, can at best be limited.

2.2.2 Kant's Distinction Between Theoretical and Practical Reason

Where Hume's major distinction was between, on the one hand, passion and desires and, on the other, reason and beliefs, Kant's major distinction was between theoretical and practical reason. Theoretical reason deals with matters of fact and our explanation or prediction of them. Practical reason, by contrast, deals with the question of what one ought to do, or what would be the best thing to do (Wallace, 2020).

Both theoretical and practical reason are manifestations of reason. This means that Kant does not have a role for the Humean passions in the determination of what ought to be done. There is not necessarily a conflict with Hume here, as Hume's theory is a theory of motivation, of what actually moves human behaviour, while Kant's theory is a theory of what an agent ought to do. A theory of motivation would, in Kantian terminology, belong to the domain of theoretical, not of practical reason. It is important to notice, however, that the consistency between the views of Hume and Kant is then rescued by emphasizing the distinction between IS (motivation) and OUGHT (justification). By assuming that Hume and Kant tried to answer different questions, one presupposes the distinction between what the facts are and what ought to be done.

According to Kant, the OUGHT-question should be answered by means of practical reason and there is no role for the Humean passions in this connection. Passions are the passions of concrete persons, while reason is connected to humanity as such and not to individual persons. The ultimate moral command is, according to Kant, the categorical imperative. In one of its formulations, this categorical imperative reads that one should only act according to that maxim whereby one can at the same time will that it should become a universal law. This imperative 'is categorical because it commands and constrains us … without regard to our personal preferences or any empirically contingent ends' (Wilson & Denis, 2018).

Although Kant's views differ considerably from those of Hume, they have the same implications for the role of the cognitive sciences in relation to law considered as a normative enterprise. Kant might have stated it as follows: as law deals with the question what ought to be done, it belongs to the sphere of practical reason. The cognitive sciences, which aim at explanation and prediction, belong to the sphere of theoretical reason. Because the cognitive sciences and law belong to these two different spheres, the former cannot be relevant for the latter (Mackor, 2013).

2.2.3 *Kelsen's* Reine Rechtslehre

Kelsen's *Reine Rechtslehre*, the Pure Theory of Law (Kelsen, 1960, 1992), was perhaps the most influential reflection of the Kantian style of thinking in legal theory. In the very first section of the first edition of the *Reine Rechtslehre*, Kelsen sets out his programme. The Pure Theory of Law strives for cognition of its object, the law.[3] It aims to answer the questions of what the law is and how law is made, and not what the law ought to be, or how law ought to be made. The purity of the Pure Theory of Law consists in the fact that this theory aims to free legal science from all foreign elements. These foreign elements would include – on the factual side – psychology and biology, and – on the normative side – ethics and theology.

Kelsen strongly emphasizes that law is not a branch of morality. He distinguishes between the moral and the legal ought, and assumes that law deals with what legally ought to be done or ought to be the case. In this respect, he differs from Kant, who sees both morality and law as aspects of one single practical reason.

According to Kelsen, legal norms exist because they have been created, for example by a legislator or a judge. Kelsen denotes the mode of existence of norms as the 'validity' of norms. This validity is the result of the meaning that is attached to some norm-creating event by another valid norm. For instance, a decision taken by the municipality council to prohibit cars that produce pollution from entering the city centre creates a valid legal norm, because there is a 'higher' norm which empowers the municipality council to create norms like this. This higher norm gives the decision of the council the meaning of valid law. The result is a chain of valid norms, alternating with norm-creating events. Lower norms are created by legislation, where the competence to legislate is conferred by higher norms.

A plurality of norms forms a system or order, if all the validity chains can be traced to a single norm as the basis of their validity. All other norms in the system can then be said to derive their validity from this basic norm, which Kelsen calls the *Grundnorm* of the system. Since the validity of a norm can only be based on the validity of another norm, the validity of all norms in a legal system is traced back to the validity of this *Grundnorm*. There is one exception, and that is the *Grundnorm* itself. By definition, its validity cannot be traced back to some other norm.

This creates the theoretical problem from where the validity of the *Grundnorm* stems. It seems that there is an infinite regress of norms that can only be valid on the

---

[3] The text of this section uses fragments of Hage (2018, chapter 1).

basis of another valid norm.[4] Kelsen solves this problem by positing the *Grundnorm* as a presupposition of a factually existing legal system:

> The Pure Theory of Law works with the basic norm as a hypothetical foundation. Given the presupposition that the basic norm is valid, the legal system resting on it is also valid. ... Rooted in the basic norm, ultimately, is the normative import of all the material facts constituting the legal system. The empirical data given to legal interpretation can be interpreted as law, that is, as a system of legal norms, only if the basic norm is presupposed. ... The basic norm is simply the expression of the necessary presupposition of every positivistic understanding of legal data. It is valid not as a positive legal norm – since it is not created in a legal process, not issued or set – but as a presupposed condition of all law-making, indeed, of every process of positive law. (Kelsen, 1992, p. 58)

A presupposed basic norm must explain the validity of all ordinary norms that constitute a legal system. When should such a presupposition be assumed? It only makes sense to speak of a legal system, and therefore also to interpret a set of norms as valid, if the norms are actually used, if the system is by and large efficacious. Therefore, the validity of a legal system depends *in a certain way* on the efficacy of the system. The clause 'in a certain way' is meant to emphasize the gap between IS and OUGHT; the efficacy of the legal system cannot make its own basic norm valid. And yet, in a certain way, the validity of the basic norm seems to depend on the efficacy of the system.

Kelsen is caught on the horns of a dilemma: the existence of law is a matter of fact, and at the same time it cannot be a matter of fact as law belongs to the realm of OUGHT. What does this mean for the role of the cognitive sciences in law? To answer this question, it is necessary to delve into the theory of legal reasoning.

2.3 LEGAL REASONING

Legal reasoning, and in particular legal decision making, depends on theories about what counts as law. These theories are often implicit and are therefore seldom discussed in legal practice. Still, they are present in the background and influence legal thinking, including our thinking on the relevance of the cognitive sciences for law.

There are many forms of legal reasoning, including reasoning about what the law should be, what the law was in the past, how the law should be explained, and how the law will develop. However, most legal reasoning is devoted to the question of what legal consequences the law attaches to a particular (kind of) case. This is the kind of reasoning that must be performed by legal decision makers such as courts and arbiters, but also by practising lawyers and legal scientists. It aims at the

---

[4] This problem will return, and will be solved in a non-Kelsenian way, in Section 2.5.4.

justification of judgements about the correct outcome of legal cases. Here we will focus on this kind of reasoning, which aims at legal justification.[5]

For analytical purposes, legal justification is sometimes divided into two 'stages'. These 'stages' are logical constructs and do not necessarily succeed each other in time. One stage consists in applying a legal 'rule' to the facts of a case; the other stage is the establishment of the rule that is to be applied. The distinction has been labelled as the distinction between first- and second-order justification (MacCormick, 1978, p. 100–1; Wróblewski, 1992, pp. 198–203), or as the distinction between internal and external justification (Alexy, 1978, chapter C II). It is closely related to the distinction between questions of fact and questions of law. The outcome of a legal case depends both on the facts of the case and on the content of the law. The facts are assumed to exist objectively, although there may be disagreement on what they are. For instance, did the suspect really kill the victim? If there is uncertainty about the facts, evidential reasoning plays an important role, but this is not reasoning about the law proper.[6] Sometimes there is disagreement about the content of the law, and then it is necessary to use arguments to justify the rule that is applied to the facts. This justification would be the second-order or external justification, while the application of the rule to the facts would be the first-order or internal justification.

The distinction between evidential reasoning and external justification (to use Alexy's terminology) is complex. The worn-out example of vehicles in the park (Hart, 2012, pp. 128–9) can illustrate why this is so. Suppose that there is a by-law prohibiting vehicles from being brought into the park. War veterans bring an old tank that is out of use into the park to serve as a war memorial. Is this forbidden under the law? We will not attempt to answer that question here, but raise the question of whether the legal rule that must be used reads that it is forbidden to bring vehicles into the park, or that it is forbidden to bring out-of-use tanks into the park as war memorials?

In the former case, the formulation of the legal rule can remain close to the formulation of the by-law by means of which the rule was created. However, if the rule is to be applicable, the facts of the case must then be classified as bringing a vehicle into the park.

In the latter case, the description of the facts can be much more concrete: the war veterans brought an out-of-use tank into the park to be used as a war memorial. However, the formulation of the rule is much less obvious now, as there is no direct connection anymore between the formulation of the by-law and the rule. Clearly,

---

[5] The relevance of the cognitive sciences for the process of legal reasoning itself is shown in Brożek (Chapter 7 in the present volume).
[6] Actually, things are a bit more complicated. Evidential reasoning is governed by legal rules (e.g. what kinds of evidence are allowed; what is the probative force of a statement of the suspect) and there may be disagreement about these rules. If that is the case, reasoning about the content of the law plays a role in evidential reasoning. Here, we will ignore this complication.

somewhere in the decision-making process, it is necessary to answer the question of whether the introduction of the tank into the park falls under the prohibition of the by-law, but it is less obvious whether this decision is a decision about the facts of the case or rather the content of the rule. Because the final decision cannot be based on the by-law alone, additional justification is unavoidable, and it is important to determine what kinds of arguments are allowed in this justification. For those who assume that the argument is an argument about the law, theories about the nature of law become practically relevant, as they inform us what are good arguments in the external justification of a concrete legal judgement.

Let us consider a different example to illustrate the relevance of this discussion for law and the cognitive sciences. In the case *Roper* v. *Simmons* (543 US 551, 2005), the Supreme Court of the United States held that it is unconstitutional to impose capital punishment for crimes committed while under the age of eighteen. According to Morse (2013), the rational capacities of the defendant are at stake. Those with diminished or undeveloped rationality are, according to Morse, less responsible than people with normal or fully developed rational capacities. Let us assume that it is unconstitutional in the USA to impose capital punishment on persons who were insufficiently responsible at the time they committed their crime.

Morse correctly emphasizes that neuroscience can provide us with information about the less developed brains of juveniles, but that it cannot tell us whether a defendant was sufficiently responsible when they committed a crime. There is a logical step from the stage of brain development to the legal classification of (in)sufficient responsibility.[7] The issue at stake is whether this logical step is based on law. If it is a matter of establishing the applicable legal rule, as Morse implicitly assumes, the logical step is a legal matter. In that case, the relevant expertise is legal and the decision should arguably not be decided by neuroscientists or psychiatrists, but by lawyers. However, if it is a matter of classifying the case facts – was the crime committed by an insufficiently responsible person? – lawyers would not have any privileged knowledge and neuroscientist or psychiatrists would be at least equally competent to answer the question. The relevance of neuroscience and the cognitive sciences in general would then be greater.

The division of questions between law and non-law is a legal matter. As Kelsen pointed out (Kelsen, 1960, p. 282), law resembles the legendary King Midas. Everything that King Midas touched turned into gold. Similarly, everything that law deals with becomes a legal matter. Therefore, the law determines who counts as responsible. Moreover, if the law wants to, it can also determine who counts as – legally speaking – rational. If legal reasoning is divided into legal and non-legal questions, the law draws the borderline. This means that if the role of the cognitive sciences is limited to non-legal issues, this role is determined by the law.

---

[7] See also the discussion of the insanity defence and the role of experts in Meynen (Chapter 15 in the present volume).

2.4 THE ROLE OF THE COGNITIVE SCIENCES IN A TRADITIONAL VIEW OF LAW

Traditionally, law draws its own borders broadly. Many questions that are legally relevant are considered to be legal questions. Moreover, if law and the sciences are opposed for the reason that law deals with what OUGHT to be done while the sciences deal with what IS the case, a broad interpretation of law entails a narrow interpretation of the role of the sciences in the context of answering legal questions, including the cognitive sciences. In this section we will, for the sake of argument, adopt this traditional view of law and its relation to the sciences, and try to delineate the room that is left to the cognitive sciences in relation to law. Even in this traditional view, according to which cognitive sciences cannot be relevant for the content of the law, there is still a role for the cognitive sciences in at least the following three areas:

1. proof of case facts (evidential reasoning);
2. classification of case facts; and
3. reasoning about good law.

2.4.1 Evidential Reasoning

Evidential reasoning deals with the question of what are the facts of a case. The same holds for classificatory reasoning, and it is not always easy to keep the two apart. Although the next subsection, which deals with classification, will illustrate the distinction by means of some examples, it is useful to first define it here. Classification deals with the question of which facts also *count as* other facts. For instance, does pain count as damage, or does the absence of a particular brain function count as a lack of rationality? Evidence addresses the question whether the presence (or absence) of some facts makes it *rational to believe or accept the presence (or absence) of some other facts*. For instance, should we believe or accept in law that the defendant committed the crime, if a polygraph suggested that they were lying when they denied their involvement?

It is quite obvious that the cognitive sciences are relevant for evidential reasoning. In her introduction to a chapter on brain imaging techniques, Roskies (2013) mentions a role for these techniques in the determinations of competency (to comply with the law) and lie detection. She might as well have mentioned a role of the same techniques in the establishment of damage or other legally relevant facts with an important neurological element, such as the presence of pain (Goodenough & Tucker, 2010), or the lack of working capacity.[8] It is well known that neuroimaging evidence plays a role in judicial decision making (Moriarty, Chapter 18 in this volume).

---

[8] The reason that Roskies did not mention these may well have been that she was writing for a primer on *criminal* law and neuroscience.

A very different branch of the cognitive sciences, the logic and computational theory of evidential reasoning, is also highly relevant for law. In this connection, logic should be taken in a broad sense, to include not only formal logic, but also logically precise forms of epistemology. It includes, for example, the theory of defeasible reasoning applied to legal evidence (Prakken, 2001; Bex, 2009; Di Bello & Verheij, 2018),[9] the legal application of Bayesian statistics (Fenton, Neil & Berger, 2016), the theory of scenarios (Wagenaar, Van Koppen & Crombag, 1993; Bex, 2009; Mackor, Jellema and Van Koppen, Chapter 21 in the present volume) and coherentist theories of evidence (Hage, 2005; Amaya, 2015, 2018).

2.4.2 Classification

Classification occurs when some facts are also considered to be facts of some other kind. We then say that the former facts count as the latter facts (Grossi, Meyer & Dignum, 2008). Because such a step from one kind of facts to another kind is always rule-based, we can say that the relation between the one kind of facts and the other kind is based on counts-as rules.[10] For instance, the step from the fact that somebody negligently damaged goods that belong to somebody else to the fact that the former person committed a tort is based on the counts-as rule that negligently damaging somebody else's goods counts as a tort. Other examples would be that the President of the United States counts as the Commander in Chief of the US army, or that skateboards count as vehicles for the purposes of the Traffic Act (Hage, 2018, pp. 102–15).

The cognitive sciences can provide support for the counts-as rules that underlie legal classification. For example, if somebody has a particular kind of brain damage, they may not be able to follow rules any longer and therefore lack the responsibility that is required for criminal liability. The classificatory step from suffering from a particular kind of brain damage to the inability to comply with rules can be supported by neurological findings to the effect that persons with that kind of brain damage tend not to follow rules.

This example also illustrates that the role of the cognitive sciences in legal classification lies in the support for classificatory or counts-as rules. These sciences cannot directly support a classification for two reasons. One reason is that classificatory judgements are universalizable: if facts of one kind in a particular case also count as facts of some other kind, facts of the former will in similar circumstances generally count as facts of the latter kind. This is the same point as that which states that classification is always rule-based. If the cognitive sciences support a particular

---

[9] Also see Floris Bex, 'Evidence for a Good Story' (PhD thesis, University of Groningen, 2009).
[10] Classification is a traditional topic in the theory of legal argumentation. See, for example, MacCormick (2005, p. 41).
Counts-as rules were made popular by Searle in his work on social ontology (Searle, 1995, pp. 43–8). The issue at stake in both fields is essentially the same, however.

concrete classification, they do so by supporting the counts-as rule that underlies this classification.

The second reason is that classification of facts comes on top of establishing the facts that are classified. Classification of brain damage as the inability to comply with rules comes on top of establishing brain damage. Sciences, including the cognitive sciences, can only establish the facts at the bottom of a chain of classification, not the classificatory additions to these 'bottom facts'. However, the cognitive sciences can support the classificatory rule that leads from the presence of brain damage to the inability to follow rules.

This argument implies that the role of the cognitive sciences in legal classification always consists in support for classificatory, or counts-as rules. This is not an independent role but falls under the third role of the cognitive sciences in the ordinary view of law: reasoning about good law.

2.4.3 Reasoning About Good Law

Legal rules have a purpose, and their quality – are they good or bad rules? – depends on the quality of the purpose and on the efficacy of the rules in achieving their purpose without having undesirable side effects. For example, rules that promote health in people are *pro tanto* good rules, while rules that discriminate against some part of the population are *pro tanto* bad ones. A rule that is efficacious in promoting public health is *pro tanto* better than a rule that is less successful in promoting this goal. A rule with many undesirable side effects is *pro tanto* worse than a rule with fewer of these side effects.

The quality of a rule may also depend on whether it implements another rule and on the quality of this latter rule. Consider for example a rule that defines insanity for the purposes of a law on the insanity defence in criminal law. If the rule defines insanity in such a way that it promotes the purposes of the insanity defence, it is *pro tanto* better than a rule that defines insanity in a manner that conflicts with the point of this defence. Of course, this presupposes that the insanity defence has a good point.

These examples all illustrate that the causal effects of rules are crucial for the quality of these rules. Other examples can easily be given. It is important to know whether a projected rule will succeed in motivating people to comply (Epstein, 2006), as it is important to know how rules will affect the mental states – happiness or unhappiness – of the persons who will have to apply them or against whom they will be applied. The cognitive sciences, in particular the relevant parts of game theory (Bowles & Gintis, 2011; Zaluski, 2013), (moral) psychology and cognitive neuroscience (Sinnott-Armstrong, 2008a and b; Doris & the Moral Psychology Research Group, 2010) and other areas of biology (Zaluski, 2009; Sapolsky, 2017), are highly relevant for producing this causal information. This means that there is an important role for the cognitive sciences in the legislative process and in judicial decision making that leads to precedents. Court procedures should, for instance, be designed in such a way that they give as little leeway to judicial biases as possible, and cognitive sciences can inform us under which circumstances such biases occur (Kahneman & Tversky, 1982; Rachlinski, Guthrie & Wistrich, 2007; Kahneman, 2012; Rachlinski et al., 2009; Hoffman, Chapter 8 in the present volume; Leibovitch, Chapter 9 in the present volume; Aharoni, Chapter 10 in the present volume) and what procedures may mitigate their effects (Gigerenzer, 2006; Haidt & Bjorklund, 2008).

Also, when courts and administrations exercise discretionary powers, the cognitive sciences can play an important role in determining how these powers are best exercised. An example would be the choice of a particular form or amount of punishment, where cognitive sciences can inform the decision maker what kind of punishment would be most efficacious in achieving the intended purpose of the punishment (Roskies, 2013).

2.4.4 *Summary on the Traditional View*

If law is approached from the traditional perspective, it is seen as normative – belonging to the realm of OUGHT. If it is also assumed that descriptive sciences belong to the realm of IS, and that there is a logical gap between IS and OUGHT, then the cognitive sciences cannot inform us about the content of the law. However, even from this perspective it turns out that there is an important role for the cognitive sciences in law, in particular in evidential reasoning and in reasoning about what would be good law. The sceptical question with which we started this chapter can therefore be given a reassuring answer: for sure, there is an important role for the cognitive sciences in law, even if law is approached from a traditional perspective.

As we will see in the next section, this role for the cognitive sciences becomes even more important if we are prepared to question the traditional perspective and do not separate the OUGHT-law from the IS sciences.

2.5 CHALLENGING THE IS–OUGHT DISTINCTION

Hardly anyone would question the existence of *some* role for the cognitive sciences in law, and in the previous section we have seen why. The principled scepticism about the role for the cognitive sciences does not concern the 'ordinary' use of insights of cognitive sciences in the application of law or in thinking about what good law would be, but the pretension that law can be 'naturalized' and that, amongst others, the cognitive sciences would be able to answer the question of what the law is. This is a recurring theme, one which has already played a role in Kelsen's Pure Theory of Law and the reactions to it from, amongst others, Alf Ross (1946, chapter 3) and Herbert Hart (2012, chapter 4). In the present volume, this theme is revisited in the contributions by Pavlakos (Chapter 22), Stelmach (Chapter 24) and Heidemann (Chapter 3).

2.5.1 Ross: Validity as Projection

Kelsen distinguished two elements in law, a factual and a normative one, neither of which can be reduced to the other. According to the Danish legal philosopher (and pupil of Kelsen) Alf Ross, there lies a problem in the dual nature of law, according to which the normative aspect depends on the factual aspect, and the other way around. Both aspects depend on each other and this seems to lead to an infinite chain with alternating elements of normativity and factuality without an element that can exist independently. The way in which the factuality and normativity of law depend on each other is destructive for the legal phenomena.

> The sting of the problem lies in the very fact that the two points of view cannot be distinguished and isolated; the thesis is bound to lead to the antithesis and vice versa. The interpretation by means of reality cannot be carried through without recourse to the category of validity, and the reverse. The two points of view reflect each other like mirrors with an endless perspective. This is the really awkward dilemma of the concept of law. (Ross, 1946, pp. 76–7)

In Ross' view, neither the factual nor the normative aspect of law can exist independently from the other, and this seems to make the existence of law impossible because of a lack of foundation. And yet, law exists, so there must be something wrong; the mutual dependence must be shown not to exist.

Ross aims to prove this by showing that the normative aspect of law can be reduced to hard facts. In doing so, he takes an approach which later became known as projectivism. Projectivism was mainly developed in ethical theory as the view that moral value judgements express valuations which are not part of reality proper, but are in a sense 'projected' upon the world (Blackburn, 1984, pp. 181–2; Joyce, 2016). Analogously, Ross held the view that the validity of legal rules is not a characteristic of rules which actually exist 'out there', but rather something that legal subjects project upon legal phenomena. In particular, he held the view

> that every extant theory of law is in its foundation characterized more or less by three elements, viz. 1) the element of reality, more precisely defined as an actual element of compulsion; 2) the element of validity; and 3) a logical interdependency of these elements. (Ross, 1946, p. 78)

The basic idea is that the validity of legal norms is nothing more than a projection upon legal reality of the fear of compulsion that legal subjects experience. Analogously, the experience of validity would be a causal factor contributing to the exercise of compulsory measures. Basically, what Ross does is replace normative notions like 'validity' and 'competence' with psychological ones and explain the existence of these notions as a projection of mental experiences on the legal phenomena. It will be clear that Ross's approach to the validity of law would make the cognitive sciences directly relevant for the determination of what the law is. However, against this approach it may be objected that Ross completely disposes of normativity, in order to avoid what he thought to be a mistaken view of what normativity is.

2.5.2 Hart and the Internal Aspect of Rules

In his book *The Concept of Law*, the English legal philosopher Hart tried to give an account of law's normativity that holds the middle ground between Kelsen's view that normativity is a realm of its own, and Ross's reduction of normativity to a feeling of compulsion. Hart's view is based on the distinction between being obliged and having an obligation (Hart, 2012, pp. 5–6 and 82–3). The story attached to this distinction is familiar amongst legal philosophers. A gunman orders somebody to hand over their money and threatens to shoot their victim if they do not obey. The victim is obliged to hand the money to the gunman, but – and this is the crucial point – there is no obligation to do so. Being obliged and having an obligation are quite different things. The victim was obliged to hand over the money because they believed that otherwise they would be shot, and because they did not want to be shot. In a sense, handing over the money was the only option available.

The threat of a sanction may also be attached to an obligation, but it does not constitute the obligation. An obligation is imposed by a rule, and it can also exist if there is no sanction attached. As a matter of fact, an obligation could even exist if the person having it were not aware of it, and (therefore) felt no desire to comply with it. In other words, obligations presuppose some form of normativity, while being obliged does not have any such presupposition. This is where Hart differs from Ross.

Hart tried to explain his notion of normativity through a discussion of social rules and how they differ from habits. The members of a group have a habit if their behaviour converges. For example, members of the group tend to attend dance parties when there is one in their city. Convergence of behaviour suffices for the existence of a mere habit, but not for the existence of a rule:

> where there is such a rule, deviations are generally regarded as lapses or faults open to criticism, and threatened deviations meet with pressure for conformity . . . .
>
> Secondly, where there are such rules, not only is such criticism in fact made, but deviation from the standard is generally accepted as a *good reason* for making it. Criticism for deviation is regarded as legitimate or justified in this sense, as are demands for compliance with the standard when deviation is threatened. (Hart, 2012, pp. 55–6; italics in the original)

The criticism which arises when a social rule is violated, the demands for conformity and the facts that these criticisms and demands are considered to be justified by the rule are all manifestations of the internal aspect of rules. What, then, does this internal aspect of rules involve? Not merely a feeling of being bound, as was claimed by Ross:

> The internal aspect of rules is often misrepresented as a mere matter of 'feelings' in contrast to externally observable physical behavior. . . . But such feelings are neither necessary nor sufficient for the existence of 'binding' rules. . . . What is necessary is that there should be a critical reflective attitude to certain patterns of behavior as a common standard, and that this should display itself in criticism (including self-criticism), [and] demands for conformity, ... all of which find their characteristic expression in the normative terminology of 'ought', 'must', and 'should', 'right' and 'wrong'. (Hart, 2012, p. 57)

Social rules share a convergence in behaviour patterns with mere habits, but are distinguished by the fact that people following a social rule have a critical reflective attitude towards the behaviour of themselves and of others to whom the rules apply. This critical reflective attitude is called the 'internal aspect' of rules. It is not a mere feeling, but neither is it a separate sphere of normativity, as Kelsen would have it.

Hart locates the internal aspect of rules, the counterpart of Kelsen's normativity, in an actually existing social practice. With this theory of normativity as the 'internal aspect' of rules, Hart seems to have found a middle ground between the extremes of Kelsen and Ross. However, this 'middle ground' seems to be closer to the psychological approach of Ross than to the Kantian approach of Kelsen, as it locates the internal aspect of rules in social reality and the sphere of IS. This means that it leaves more room for a role for the cognitive sciences than Kelsen would have permitted when it comes to establishing the validity of legal rules.

2.5.3 Brute Social Facts

Elsewhere (Hage, 2018, pp. 192–4), I have argued that compliance with rules is better construed as compliance with duties or obligations that are often, but not always, imposed by rules. The internal aspect of rules that Hart tried to characterize is on this view nothing other than the internal aspect of duties or obligations. A person who recognizes that they have a duty to do something will normally *ipso facto* be motivated to act accordingly (Rosati, 2016). On Ross's view, this internal aspect would be the essence of the duty: the OUGHT of the duty is a feeling of obligatoriness, comparable to being obliged in Hart's sense. Duties are in this view psychological entities. Hart amended Ross's view by elevating duties to the social level: the existence of a duty is a complex phenomenon in social reality with accompanying psychological aspects. Arguably, both accounts miss something in their analysis of normativity, something that might be referred to as that aspect of normativity that Kelsen had in mind when he claimed that the OUGHT cannot be reduced to an IS

(Kelsen, 1960, p. 5). The challenge is to identify this aspect without claiming, as Kelsen did, that there is a separate and rather mystical realm of OUGHT.

Constructivism might be a solution to the puzzle of how law can be a matter of fact, while at the same time transcending mere psychological and sociological phenomena.[11] Constructivism in the sense used here is a refinement of the acceptance theory of social reality.

Before continuing the argument, it may be useful to give a brief overview of kinds of facts. First, there are objective facts, which are assumed to exist independent of (human) minds. If such facts exist, typical examples would be that there is water in the oceans on Earth, or that John is taller than Jean. Then there are purely subjective 'facts', such as the 'fact' that chocolate tastes better than cauliflower. Because these are purely subjective, depending on taste or subjective judgement, some would prefer not to call them 'facts' at all. And then there is an intermediate category of facts, which are mind-dependent, but which do not depend entirely on personal taste or subjective judgement, but in the last instance on social acceptance. These facts are called 'social facts'. Some of them are rule-based, such as the fact that Anton has the obligation to pay his landlord Violet €700 on the first of every month. The gist of the present argument is that some social facts are so-called 'constructivist facts', which depend not only on acceptance, but also on arguments, and that ought-facts belong to this category.

According to the acceptance theory of social reality, a fact exists in social reality if sufficiently many[12] members of a social group:

a. accept that this fact exists,
b. believe that sufficiently many members of the group accept that this fact exists and
c. believe that the fact belongs to a kind of fact that exists in social reality (as opposed to objective reality).

Let us study the following example: Jean is the leader of a cycling club. The members of the club are for our present purposes the relevant social group. Most likely these members do not believe that leadership is a fact of nature, which exists independent of social practices. Leadership depends, in their opinion, on acceptance. This means that condition c is satisfied.

Almost all members of the club consider Jean to be the leader. They not only believe that Jean is the leader, but they also act accordingly, by complying with Jean's decisions, and giving (self-)criticism if a member of the group does not

[11] The following argument is rather technical and dense. Some readers may want to skip it. The argument pleads for the conclusion that an ought is a kind of fact, and that the cognitive sciences can be relevant for establishing the existence of ought-facts. Therefore, if law deals with what ought to be done, the cognitive sciences may also in this way be relevant for law.

[12] Because of a division of cognitive labour, the purely numerical definition of what exists in social reality may have to be replaced by a definition that assigns an important role to 'experts'. This complication will be ignored here.

comply. (That would be Hart's internal aspect.) This means that condition a is satisfied.

Finally, almost all members of the club believe that almost all members consider Jean to be the leader. This means that the group members know of each other that they recognize Jean's leadership. This means that condition b is also satisfied.

The acceptance theory of social reality holds that facts exist in social reality by being accepted in the manner described above. Let us call the facts that exist in this way *brute social facts*. Because in the case of the cycling club and its leader, all three conditions are satisfied, Jean is the leader of this cycling club as a matter of brute social fact.

2.5.4 *Constructivism*

Many social facts are brute: they exist because and to the extent that they are accepted as existing. However, some social facts are different. It does not merely suffice that they are accepted; there is also a normative aspect involved.[13] I will call such facts *constructivist facts*.[14] A constructivist fact exists if and only if:

- it exists as a brute social fact, and it is not the case that it ought not to exist; or
- it ought to exist.

In this connection it is crucial that ought-facts, including the fact that some other fact ought not exist, are a kind of constructivist fact themselves, and that this definition invokes the presence or absence of constructivist facts as conditions for the existence of a constructivist fact. Technically speaking, this means that the definition of constructivist facts is recursive: it invokes itself.[15] Recursive definitions run the risk of leading to an infinite regress. A good example is Kelsen's definition of the legal validity of norms, which invokes the validity of other norms. This definition threatens to lead to an infinite regress, and Kelsen only avoided the regress by positing the validity of the basic norm *ex hypothesi*. The present definition of constructivist facts avoids this regress by including acceptance – the mode of existence of brute social facts – as a foundation on which the recursive definition can 'bottom out'.

As a first approximation, constructivist facts may be seen as facts that exist if they ought to exist. For these facts, the alleged gap between OUGHT and IS does not exist: they are by definition what they ought to be. However, this approach leads to

---

[13] In order to avoid complicating the discussion even further, the fact that many social facts are rule-based is ignored here.
[14] The name 'constructivist facts' derives from the connection between these facts and the term 'constructivism' as it is used in ethical theory (Bagnoli, 2017). The details of the connection are beyond the scope of this contribution.
[15] The notion of recursion is most often used in computer science, and a readable introduction can be found in the *Wikipedia* encyclopaedia as the lemma <Recursion (computer science)>. A useful discussion of recursion in a legal setting can be found in (Ruiter, 1993, pp. 20–6).

an infinite regress, as we saw in the discussion of Kelsen's *Reine Rechtslehre*, which – without using the present terminology – defined the legal ought and legal validity as constructivist facts.

A simple example can elucidate this further. Take fact F and assume that it is a constructivist fact. We adopt for the sake of argument that a constructivist fact exists, if and only if it ought to exist. Let us, finally, formalize that F ought to exist as O(F). The theory then boils down to the following formula that holds by definition for all constructivist facts: $F \equiv O(F)$. Since O(F) is a constructivist fact itself, it then also holds that $O(F) \equiv O(O(F))$. O(O(F)) is, in turn, equivalent to O(O(O(F))), and so on. As this example illustrates, the adoption of a too-simple recursive definition of constructivist fact brings about that a constructivist fact can only exist if an unending series of ought-facts exists.

It is necessary to find a way to escape from this regress which is better than Kelsen's 'solution', which is to assume a foundational ought as the presupposition of legal systems. This solution is to use a three-valued logic: for every constructivist fact holds that it ought to exist, or that it ought not to exist, or that neither of these is true (the third possibility). A constructivist fact exists if it ought to exist, and does not exist if it ought not to exist. In the third case – if neither it ought to exist nor ought not to exist – and only then, it exists if it exists as a brute social fact.

If a query for the existence of a constructivist fact ends in an infinite regress of oughts, as illustrated by the example above, the fact does not exist. So, in our example, the constructivist fact F would not have existed, as the condition for its existence leads to an infinite regress.

The same holds if there is an infinite regress in establishing that a fact ought not to exist. Suppose again that F is a constructivist fact. If it were a mere brute social fact, it would have existed, because we will assume for the sake of argument that the conditions a–c, mentioned in the previous section, are all satisfied. However, as F is constructivist, a fourth condition must be met: it should not be the case that F ought not to exist. This means that if an attempt to prove that F ought not to exist ends in an infinite regress, we can take it that it is not the case that F ought not to exist. Because F would have existed if it had been a brute social fact, F exists as a constructivist fact.

The upshot of the given definition of constructivist facts is that these facts can also exist if they are merely accepted, and thus, in this respect, they are like brute social facts. However, there is a crucial difference at play here. A real brute social fact exists if it is accepted, even if it ought not exist. For example, if everybody accepts Jean as the leader of the cycling club, she is the leader, even if she ought not to be. Being the leader of a social group is a brute social fact, and acceptance is all that is needed for the existence of such a fact. It does not make sense to say that Jean is not the leader, because she is – for instance – unsuitable as a leader.

This is different for the constructivist fact that Jean ought to buy all the members of the club a drink. Even if everybody accepts this, it is still not a fact if it should not be a fact. If there are good reasons why Jean should not buy everybody a drink – for example, unknown to the club members, the drinks have been poisoned – Jean ought not buy the drinks. Moreover, Jean ought to buy all members of the club a drink if this ought to be a fact, even if it is not broadly accepted as a social fact.

Constructivist facts differ from brute social facts because there is always the possibility of raising the question of whether they should really exist, a possibility that does not exist for brute social facts. However, the conclusion that a fact ought or ought not to exist must *in the end* be based on acceptance. This means that ultimately all ought-facts exist in the form of acceptance, either of the ought-fact itself, or of some other ought-fact on which it is based. This acceptance is itself a matter of non-social fact.

2.5.5 Application to Law

This discussion about constructivist facts is very abstract. Let us therefore see what this means for law. Suppose that Anton rented his home from Violet for €700 a month, to be paid on the first day of the month. It is the first of March, and the question that needs to be answered is whether Anton ought to pay Violet €700.

As a matter of brute social fact, the legal rule exists that contracts lead to the legal consequences they were intended to establish.[16] Anton and Violet have a contract that creates an obligation for Anton towards Violet to pay her a monthly rent of €700. Given this obligation, which exists as a matter of rule-based fact, Anton ought to pay Violet the money. This obligation is the result of the acceptance of its underlying social rule in the legal community in which Anton and Violet participate. This social rule is also a legal rule at the same time, because the consequence of this rule is that Anton has a legal obligation towards Violet, an obligation that the state apparatus will normally enforce.

Normally, if somebody has a legal obligation to do something, this person legally ought to do it (the step from obligation to ought). If there is no reason why Anton ought not to pay the money to Violet, Anton ought to pay her the money. However, if there is such a reason, it has to be balanced against the obligation as a reason why Anton ought to pay. Suppose, for example, that Anton needs the money to feed his hungry children. As a matter of social fact, parents have the duty to feed their children. So, at least *pro tanto*, Anton ought to feed his children, and since the only way to do so (we assume) is to spend his money on food instead of paying the rent, Anton ought not pay the rent.

If these facts are all that is relevant, there are two reasons: one for why Anton ought to pay Violet €700 and one for why he ought not to do that. The first reason is rule-based, where the existence of the rule is a matter of social fact. The second reason is

---

[16] Interestingly, the rule that contracts lead to their intended consequences is not codified everywhere in the civil law world. Apparently, this rule is assumed to exist even without a statutory foundation.

a duty which exists directly as a matter of social fact. Both social facts can be established by sciences, including social sciences.

If there are both reasons for and against an ought-conclusion, the proper outcome depends on the relative weight of these reasons. Which reason 'outweighs' the other reason is a matter of social fact again, at least if there are no reasons dealing with this issue. (Such a reason might be based on an earlier judicial decision.)

The argument as described up to this point is *in the end* completely based on social facts, which depend *in the end* completely on what people believe and accept. However, this is not the full story. There may be other reasons why Anton ought, or ought not, to pay his monthly rent to Violet. Whether these reasons exist depends, again *in the end*, on social facts, and can in principle be established by means of sciences which describe what IS the case. Every step in the relevant chains of argument is open to discussion, but *in the end* all arguments in this discussion must be based on premises that are true because of objective or social facts.

2.5.6 *A New Perspective on Law and the Cognitive Sciences*

Let us assume that ought-facts are constructivist facts which differ from brute social facts, but nevertheless depend on a social practice of acceptance for their existence. Then, there is no fundamental difference between the OUGHT and the IS. As the expression 'ought-facts' suggests, an ought is a fact. This means that sciences, including the cognitive sciences, which give us information about the facts, can also give us information about what ought to be done. The Kelsenian argument is that IS and OUGHT are different realms, that the sciences can give us information about the realm of IS, but that law belongs to the realm of OUGHT, for which the sciences are not relevant. This argument turns out to be based on an incorrect view of what the OUGHT is. Speaking of 'realms' is not very illuminating, but if we nevertheless do so, we should conclude that the realm of OUGHT belongs to the realm of IS. The next conclusion is, then, that sciences that deal with what is the case can also deal with what ought to be done. And the conclusion that then follows is that the cognitive sciences may be relevant for law by answering the question of what ought to be done. They would be relevant, for instance, by specifying the circumstances under which people accept legal ought-facts. This a topic that has not received much attention yet, but which may be highly relevant for a proper understanding of law.

2.6 DISRUPTIVE COGNITIVE SCIENCES

In the previous section it was argued that when the recursion bottoms out, the question of what ought to be done is ultimately a matter of social fact. If the law deals with the question of what ought to be done, as many believe it does, it can still be the object of science and in particular also the cognitive sciences. The objection to the use of the cognitive sciences to establish the content of the law is based on a false ontological presupposition. As soon as this presupposition is abandoned, the relevance of the cognitive sciences for establishing the content of law becomes apparent.

2.6.1 *Law's Image of Humankind*

The cognitive sciences are also relevant in a different way, since underlying law there is an image of humankind. A long philosophical tradition has cast doubts on this image, and these doubts have been confirmed by the modern cognitive sciences. If it turns out that law is based upon a fundamentally false image of humankind, there is reason to redesign law completely, assuming that there will still be a role left for law at all. The role of the cognitive sciences in this connection may be labelled as a contribution to reasoning about good law (see Section 2.4.3). However, the impact of a substantially changing image of humankind on law is so big that the role of the cognitive sciences in this connection deserves a separate discussion.[17]

The image of humankind that underlies Western[18] law is that human legal subjects are mostly rational creatures, who are – to use a word that has become fashionable – reasons-responsive. This reasons-responsiveness is closely connected to the notions of free will and rationality. The following fragment provides a good illustration:

> consider again the case of Allison and her decision to walk her dog. A reasons-responsive view of the will says that Allison's volition to walk her dog is free if, had she had certain reasons for not walking her dog, she would not have decided to walk her dog. Imagine what would have happened had Allison turned on the television after waking from her nap and learned of the blizzard before deciding to walk her dog. Had she known of the blizzard, she would have had a good reason for deciding not to walk her dog. Even if such reasons never occur to her (that is, if she doesn't learn of the blizzard before her decision), her disposition to have such reasons influence her volitions shows that she is responsive to reasons. Thus, reasons-responsive views of the will are essentially dispositional in nature.
>
> Coercion and manipulation undermine free will, on this view, in virtue of making agents not reasons-responsive. If Allison has been brainwashed to walk the dog at a certain time, then even if she were to turn on the news and sees [sic] that it is snowing, she would attempt to walk the dog despite having good reasons not to.

---

[17] One illustration of how cognitive sciences may change the image of humankind that underlies law is the discrepancy between the concepts used in modern psychological theorizing, and the concepts used by law to categorize human behaviour. See Kurek (Chapter 4 in the present volume).
[18] It is hazardous to assume that all law is based on the same image of humankind. However, it seems more likely that the main Western legal traditions, the Roman law tradition and the Common Law tradition, by and large share the same image which is described here.

Thus, manipulated agents are not reasons-responsive, and in virtue of this lack free will. (Timpe, n.d.)

The notion of reasons-responsiveness is used in this fragment to illustrate a particular view of free will. However, the disposition to act rationally – on the basis of reasons – also defines reasons-responsiveness.

The next step taken in Western legal systems is to use reasons-responsiveness as a precondition for responsibility. Only persons who are reasons-responsible are responsible for their own actions and can be fault-liable in tort law,[19] or liable to be punished in criminal law.

Law assumes that adult people who do not suffer from exceptional mental conditions are reasons-responsive and in this sense rational. This assumption justifies that legal subjects can undertake contractual obligations (freedom of contract) and can – more in general – perform juridical acts by means of which they modify the legal positions of themselves and sometimes also of other persons.[20] It also justifies that persons who have committed crimes can be punished by way of retribution (Golding, 1975; Claessen, 2019). And, finally, it justifies that political decisions are, directly or indirectly, made by taking votes (democratic elections).

A noteworthy side effect of this assumption of rationality is that (justificatory) theories of rational action can be used to explain and predict human behaviour. This happens in the discipline of law and economics, where economic theories of rational action are used to explain and justify legal rules.[21]

2.6.2 Knowing Why

It is far from obvious that people are rational or reasons-responsive in the way that law presupposes.[22] One ground for doubting this rationality lies in the limited capabilities that people have to recognize the determinants of their own actions. If people are to be held responsible for their actions, they should at least know why they did what they did. One of the findings of cognitive science is that this is often not the case. Several studies suggest that people confabulate to explain their own behaviour.

One study dealt with post-hypnotic suggestion. Under hypnosis, people were prompted to do weird things after their hypnosis has ended, such as wearing a lampshade, and the victims sometimes really did what had been suggested to them. Because the behaviour was weird, it is highly unlikely that it had any other cause than a suggestion made under hypnosis, a suggestion which they did not

---

[19] Obviously, tort law recognizes a broad spectrum of situations in which a person is liable for the damage of somebody else. Different versions of fault liability exist, as well a different versions of strict liability. For a summary overview, see Hage (2017).
[20] See Hage (2018, chapter 10).
[21] See, for instance, Friedman (2000, p. 8).
[22] The title of this subsection and the examples discussed in it were inspired by the similarly titled chapter in Wilson (2002).

remember. When asked why they behaved in such a strange way, the victims came up with explanations which sounded somewhat plausible, but which were patently false (Estabrooks, 1943).

Another study dealt with split-brain patients. To 'cure' them from severe epileptic attacks, these patients had their *corpus callosum*, the bundle of nerve fibres that connects the left and the right hemispheres of the brain, cut through. As a result, information stored in one hemisphere could not be used to steer the hand controlled by the other hemisphere. Moreover, this information could not be used to explain the movement of this hand, and the patient would confabulate an explanation when asked for one (Gazzaniga & LeDoux, 1978).

Both the post-hypnotic and the split-brain cases concern extraordinary situations. However, confabulation of reasons for action also takes place in more ordinary situations, as shown in a study about nylon tights. Customers in a shop were asked to evaluate tights that were stored in a row from left to right. It was known from earlier studies that people had a relative preference for objects on the right-hand side of such a row. This case study confirmed this preference. However, when the customers were asked to justify their preferences, they did not mention the position of the preferred tights in the row, but other characteristics such as superior knit, sheerness or elasticity. The tights were identical, however, and the explanations of the preferences were confabulated (Nisbett & Wilson, 1977).

A number of case studies does not suffice to show that people always confabulate the reasons that moved them to act in certain ways, but these cases strongly suggest that people quite frequently do not know what has moved them. Moreover, all mentioned cases deal with causes, unknown to the agents, which were not very rational. Apparently, people are often motivated to act by irrational causes of which they are not aware.[23] Publicity agents are no doubt aware of this, and in developing commercials they use this knowledge to the advantage of their clients.[24] Law should use this knowledge too.

2.6.3 *Dual-System Decision Making*

In a series of path-breaking articles, Daniel Kahneman and Amos Tversky (1982) developed a theory of human decision making that explains cognitive biases. This theory was developed into a model of human decision making in which two systems play a role (Kahneman, 2012, Part I). The systems, called System 1 and System 2, were defined functionally – in terms of what they do – but were also cautiously associated with different parts of the brain, the limbic system and the cortex respectively (Taleb, 2008, pp. 82–3). System 1 performs unconscious decision making, based on intuition and heuristics. It works quickly and smoothly, but may lead to mistaken, biased

---

[23] This is the central theme of Ariely (2009). See also the contribution of Leibovitch to the present volume (Chapter 9).
[24] See Pałka's contribution to this volume (Chapter 11).

judgements. System 2 is the system that 'thinks'. Its operation is often conscious, and takes effort. It makes fewer mistakes than System 1, and mistakes are made consciously and are therefore more easily corrected.

The precise relation between systems 1 and 2 is still the object of discussion. Some see System 2 as a correction mechanism for System 1, which comes into play when the decision maker has time to think about the decision. Others, including Haidt (Haidt & Bjorklund, 2008 and Haidt, 2012), see it primarily as a tool to rationalize the spontaneous decisions of System 1. In the latter function it might perform the role of confabulator that we encountered in the previous subsection.

Whatever the details, if decisions need to be taken swiftly, only System 1 can be involved and the decision-making procedure is based on heuristics and is not always rational.[25] Because of this important role of System 1, the presupposition that human beings are reasons-responsive and act on the basis of balanced reasons is not always correct.

2.6.4 Who Is Acting?

Actions are by definition performed by agents, and the stereotypical agent is an adult human being. So if a particular decision to act was taken by System 1 or by System 2 in the brain of a particular person, we ascribe this decision to the person, not to the relevant part of the brain. The temptation to ascribe actions to parts of the brain, no matter whether they are defined functionally or physically, is therefore called the 'mereological fallacy' (Bennett & Hacker, 2003; Pardo & Patterson, 2013).

Notice that the mereological fallacy is a fallacy only if we follow common parlance, in which actions are ascribed to agents and in particular to human beings, and not to their brains. The 'temptation' to ascribe decisions and the actions based upon them to parts of the brain might well be interpreted as a proposal that we change our terminology. Such a change may be justified by the growing insight into what happens when decisions are being made. If this proposal is adopted, the ascription of actions to parts of the body, more specifically to the brain, would be permissible.

The distinction between systems 1 and 2 indicates that it is not obvious to map one person to one brain. There may be more 'systems' in the brain, and it is not immediately clear whether a person should be correlated to one full set of brains, or to a particular subsystem of the brain, whether physically or functionally defined, or to something else again. The possibility that one body 'embodies' multiple personalities or selves also suggests that there is no simple match between, on the one hand, a body or a brain, and on the other hand, a self, person or agent (Radden, 2011). Even if we ignore psychopathology, there are reasons to assume that a person's

---

[25] Because heuristics may have been developed during evolution and have then been selected on survival value, their products need not be irrational. Heuristics may be 'fast and frugal' (Gigerenzer, 2008).

mind has no single top-level decision maker (Dennett, 1991, chapter 5). Also, the unity of a person in time has been disputed, for instance in the work of philosophers such as Thomas Nagel (1970), Derek Parfit (1984) or Galen Strawson (2011).

The opposite also occurs: some agents apparently consist of two or more entities which, from a different perspective, are seen as separate agents themselves. A well-known example from the world of non-human animals, popularized in Hofstadter, (1980, pp. 310–36), is the ant colony. The individual ants can be seen as separate agents, but the combined behaviour of these agents constitutes an agent at a higher aggregation level: the ant colony. In law, an analogous phenomenon exists in the form of organizations with a recognized legal personality. These organizations include businesses, but also state agencies and full states (Hage et al., 2017, pp. 37–8).

In short, recent results from the cognitive sciences cast doubt on the very concepts that underlie the legal approach to actions, responsibility and liability. Human agents often do not act rationally, do not always know what drove them and are only loosely associated with bodies or parts thereof. If we take a closer look at the perennial discussion about free will and determinism, these doubts are confirmed.

2.6.5 *Free Will and Determinism*

Law typically presupposes that humans are reasons-responsive and have (in that sense) a free will. However, there is a long-standing philosophical tradition, starting from the doctrine of determinism, that questions the existence of a free will. Determinism is the view that all events are uniquely determined by what went before, and that given a particular state of the universe at some point in time, only one particular development of the universe after that point in time is possible.[26] If determinism is true and applicable to human actions, there is at every moment in time only one possible action for every agent. In other words, the agent has no alternative possibilities next to the action that they will actually perform. Therefore, the argument continues, the agent has nothing to choose and cannot respond to the reasons for action that exist. The agent is not reasons-responsive and has no free will.[27]

It is debatable whether determinism is generally true, and whether it holds for the domain of human action.[28] One thing is certain: determinism is not a scientific theory that can be falsified or verified. It is better characterized as a paradigm in the Kuhnian sense (Kuhn, 2012), or as the hard core of a Lakatosian research programme (Lakatos, 1970). Causal determinism would be a presupposition of a particular way

---

[26] A more specific circumscription, which emphasizes the role of causal laws in determinism, can be found in Hoefer (2019).

[27] It is not necessary to include reasons-responsiveness in this argument; an alternative would be to make the existence of alternative possibilities a direct condition for free will. The result remains the same: determinism means no alternative possibilities, which in turn means no free will.

[28] See the contributions by O'Connor and Kane in Kane (2002).

of doing scientific research: assume that every event has a cause and that cause and effect are connected by laws that have no lawless exceptions.[29]

As a paradigm or as the core of a research programme, determinism has proven fruitful in many scientific domains. In the humanities, the fruitfulness of determinism has not been so obvious. However, one important consequence of the recent developments in the cognitive sciences is that it has become clear that the determinist paradigm is more fruitful for the explanation and prediction of human behaviour than would have been expected on the basis of earlier experiences.

Determinism may or may not be true and applicable to human behaviour, but the question of whether it is so may be less important for the existence of free will than some believe. If determinism is true and applicable to human behaviour, there is seemingly no free will because of a lack of alternative possibilities. If determinism is false, or not applicable, human behaviour seems to be arbitrary, to such an extent that perhaps we should not even speak of behaviour anymore. Suppose, for instance, that my arm rises, without this being the result of a decision of mine. Can we then say that I raised my arm?[30] The issue at stake here is the authorship of actions. The falsity or non-applicability of determinism suggests that 'actions' lack a proper author. Seemingly, there is nobody who performed them, and it becomes questionable whether they can still count as actions at all. To turn it into a slogan: No action without an agent, and no agent without authorship.

The attractiveness of determinism is based on the success of the physical sciences, which have proven to be able to predict future events with a large degree of detail and reliability. If it turns out to be possible to explain mental phenomena in terms of 'underlying' physical regularities, there is hope that the success of the physical sciences can be translated to psychology and perhaps also sociology.

2.6.6 Compatibilism, a True but Irrelevant Side Track

The discussion of determinism and its relation to free will is important, not because the determinism issue is itself important, but because it draws our attention to the question of how bodily events are related to mental events. To what extent should we pay attention to bodily states when we answer questions about responsibility and liability? This question directly relates to the relevance of the cognitive sciences for law, as the sciences tend to focus on bodily states, while law deals with mental states or events.

Compatibilism is, in one of its meanings, a theory about the relation between determinism and free will. It holds that the existence of free will is compatible with

---

[29] The word 'lawless' was included here to account for the possibility that there are exceptions to physical laws, but that these exceptions are themselves governed by laws. If that is the case, physical laws may be subject to exceptions, but these exceptions do not subtract from the determinism brought about by the physical laws collectively.

[30] See Schlosser (2015) on the role of intention in defining actions and agency.

the truth of determinism and its applicability to mental phenomena. There are several variants of compatibilism, but they have in common that determinism plays no role in establishing the free will that is required for the attribution of responsibility and liability. Free will is tightly connected to responsibility and liability in the sense that a person's will is taken to be free in the relevant sense if we hold this person responsible or liable. If the truth and applicability of determinism play no role in establishing responsibility or liability, determinism is not relevant for free will either (Haji, 2002). A follow-up question would then be what the precise grounds are for holding a person responsible or liable and, consequently, for holding this person's will to be free. For the relation between free will and determinism this is not relevant, however. The issues of free will and determinism have been detached from each other and therefore free will and determinism have become compatible.

A similar argument can be used to argue why the findings of the cognitive sciences are not relevant for the attribution of free will, responsibility or liability. As a matter of fact, our practice of attributing responsibility, liability and free will assigns only a small role to the findings of the cognitive sciences and therefore these findings are not very relevant for our practice.

The argument for compatibilism as applied to the relevance of the cognitive sciences for legal practice was deliberately presented very succinctly in the previous paragraph. In this way the serious defect in the argument becomes obvious: it is claimed that the cognitive sciences are only minimally relevant, because we have a social (legal) practice that attaches little relevance to these sciences. This argument is either circular, or it is based on an illegitimate move from IS to OUGHT. It is circular if interpreted as: the cognitive sciences are not relevant because they are not relevant. It makes an illegitimate move from IS to OUGHT if it is interpreted as: our practice does not assign much importance to the cognitive sciences and therefore our practice should not assign much importance to them.

The proper line of argumentation with regard to free will and determinism – or rather: responsibility and the cognitive sciences – must turn the tables. First, we must establish whether the cognitive sciences have something to say that is relevant for the attribution of responsibility and liability, and if that turns out to be the case, we should determine what consequences to attach to the findings of the cognitive sciences. In this connection, relevance cannot be determined at the hand of the existing social practice, because that would repeat the mistake that was pointed out above. Compatibilism, as the theory that our actual practice does not pay much attention to determinism and related issues, and that determinism is therefore compatible with free will and responsibility as they function in our actual practice, may very well be true. However, for our theoretical investigations it is irrelevant, as we are not interested in what our actual social practice is, but in what it should be. For this latter question, determinism and – for similar reasons – the cognitive sciences, are highly relevant.

2.6.7 Back on Track: Integrating the Physical Approach to Human Action

Determinism poses a dilemma. Either human action is determined, and then human agents lack alternative possibilities for their behaviour, cannot respond to available reasons, have no free will and should not be held responsible for 'their' actions. Or human action is not determined, and then:

- it is arbitrary what happens with human bodies,
- the events in question cannot properly be called actions any more,
- human agents lack alternative possibilities for their behaviour,
- these agents cannot respond to available reasons and so on.

The dilemma turns out to be constructive: there are two possibilities which complement each other in the sense that either one of them must be realized. Both possibilities lead to the same conclusions, and therefore these conclusions hold irrespective of whether determinism is true and applies to human action.

How is it possible that merely raising the issue of determinism means that human agents should not be held responsible for their actions, even without taking a stance on the truth or applicability of determinism? This is possible because raising the issue of determinism frames the discussion about free will and responsibility in physical terminology. Events are either determined or random, and in both cases there is no room for free will and responsibility. Law does not frame its questions in this terminology, and therefore typical legal discussions about the circumstances under which agents can be held responsible for their actions seem to make sense.

This discrepancy between the physical and the legal approach to bodily events, including human actions, is not identical to the discrepancy between the psychological approach to decision making, with theories about dual systems and disappearing selves, and the legal conceptualization of the 'same' issues in terms of agents, intentions and actions. However, it is related to this discrepancy. The cognitive sciences, with their associated conceptualization of 'agency' in terms of neural processes and decision-making systems, disrupt the legal approach. There seems to be a conflict between the different conceptualizations of what goes on, and it is not obvious how this conflict is to be solved.

The easy way out is to assume that there are two 'languages' that describe the same phenomenon, that neither one of these languages is better than the other and that we can happily continue to use the two conceptualizations in parallel. This is the solution adopted by compatibilists, and it has the advantage of an intellectual holiday: there is nothing to worry about and therefore we should not worry. However, if we consider our actual practice of attributing responsibility and liability, we find that sometimes the findings of the cognitive sciences are already considered relevant (see also Section 2.4). For example, if somebody was involuntarily drugged and committed a crime under the influence of those drugs, we would excuse this behaviour and not punish the agent. The influence of drugs on human behaviour falls under the scope of the cognitive sciences, broadly conceived. Apparently, these sciences are sometimes treated as relevant. Consistency demands that if the findings of the cognitive sciences are sometimes treated as legally relevant, then they should be considered relevant in general, unless an explanation if offered for the differences in relevance. At present, such an explanation is lacking, unless it is the circular explanation that this is our social and legal practice (see Section 2.6.6).

If the results of the cognitive sciences are legally relevant, it is necessary to reconcile the vocabularies of the two approaches to bodily events, including human actions. That would mean that the cognitive sciences are relevant for law, if only in that they demand a reconsideration of the way in which law conceptualizes its domain.

2.6.8 Consequences

If the image of humankind that underlies law should be changed under the influence of the cognitive sciences, to reflect that humans are often not rational, not reasons-responsive and do not know what motivates them, what would be the consequences for law? Clearly this is a question that goes beyond the scope of this chapter, but it is possible to provide the beginnings of an answer nevertheless.

The influence of a change in the image of humankind from rational to (often) irrational should be greatest in those areas of law that are strongly based on the assumption of rationality. Private law is the obvious candidate here, as it assigns an important role to the autonomy of legal subjects. This assignment can only be beneficial if the autonomy is used wisely or rationally. If, and to the extent that, it is to be expected that legal subjects will not exercise their autonomy in a rational fashion, measures should be taken to protect their interests, and these measures will include a limitation on the possibility for a legal subject to arrange their own affairs. For examples of what this may entail, we can look at the protective measures that are in place for juveniles and for mentally impaired persons. It is unlikely that similar measures will be desirable for persons that we consider mentally healthy adults, but the protective measures for juveniles and for mentally impaired persons at least provide a glimpse of what direction the new law may go in.

In the sphere of constitutional law, a rationality assumption is in place as one of the grounds for allowing people to vote about the course of their governments and about future legislation. If we cannot rely on people voting for what is in their own proper interests or those of society at large, at least one ground for democratic decision making seems to be lost. Perhaps a counterweight can be – and has already been – found in the safeguards of human rights, the rule of law and lengthy bureaucratic decision-making procedures. Measures like these provide another glimpse of the direction in which new law might go.

Perhaps criminal law is the field where the impact of a modified image of humankind will be most strongly felt. It has already often been pointed out that a lack of reasons-responsiveness takes away criminal responsibility and that this makes retributive criminal law impossible (Pereboom, 2001, chapter 6). If a role for criminal law is to remain, it must be confined to measures that promote a better future. In other words, criminal law must become completely consequentialist. This is, by the way, not the same as saying that criminal law should aim at the prevention of crimes. Prevention of crimes may be a way to create a better society, but it is not the only way.[31]

2.7 CONCLUSION

This chapter addressed the question of whether the cognitive sciences are relevant for law. The answer to this question turned out to be a threefold 'yes'. First, if law is traditionally conceived as a set of rules that prescribe what ought to be done, there is a role for the cognitive sciences in determining the facts of the cases to which the law is to be applied (evidential reasoning). Moreover, the results of the cognitive sciences may also be important for the evaluation of law and determining what would be good law. This includes the evaluation of potential counts-as rules that can be used for legal classification (Section 2.4).

Second, there is reason to assume that there is no hard difference between IS and OUGHT and that even if law belongs to the realm of OUGHT, cognitive sciences may still be relevant for determining the content of the law. In this connection it turned out to be important that ought-facts are constructivist facts that depend in the last instance (when the ought-recursion bottoms out) on acceptance by the members of some group (Section 2.5).

Finally, the cognitive sciences may disrupt the image of humankind that underlies law. It turns out that people are less rational than they may seem at first sight, that they often do not know what motivates them, that it is not obvious what actions and agents are and that it is unclear what the best level of explanation is for human actions or bodily movements. A change in the image of humankind that underlies law to reflect the recent insights of the cognitive sciences, but also of ancient philosophical debates, may have important consequences for the contents of law (Section 2.6).

Summarizing, we can confidently claim that the cognitive sciences are highly relevant for law.

REFERENCES

Alexy, R. (1978). *Theorie der juristischen Argumentation*. Frankfurt am Main: Suhrkamp.
Amaya, Amalia. (2015). *The Tapestry of Reason*. Oxford: Hart.

---

[31] Bentham (1970) is an example of how utilitarianism can wrongly be narrowed down to a theory of crime prevention.

Amaya, Amalia. (2018). Coherence and Systematization in Law. In G. Bongiovanni, G. Postema, A. Rotolo, G. Sartor, C. Valentini & D. Walton (eds.) (2018), *Handbook of Legal Reasoning and Argumentation*. Dordrecht: Springer, pp. 637–72.

Ariely, Dan. (2009). *Predictably Irrational: The Hidden Forces that Shape Our Decisions*. New York: Harper.

Bagnoli, Carla. (2017). Constructivism in Metaethics. In Edward N. Zalta (ed.), *The Stanford Encyclopedia of Philosophy* (Winter 2017 edition). https://plato.stanford.edu/archives/win2017/entries/constructivism-metaethics/

Bennett, M. R., & Hacker, P. M. S. (2003). *Philosophical Foundations of Neuroscience*. Oxford: Blackwell.

Bentham, Jeremy. (1970). *An Introduction to the Principles of Morals and Legislation*, ed. J. H. Burns & H. L. A. Hart. London: Methuen.

Blackburn, Simon. (1984). *Spreading the Word: Groundings in the Philosophy of Language*. Oxford: Clarendon Press.

Bowles, Samuel, & Gintis, Herbert. (2011). *A Cooperative Species: Human Reciprocity and Its Evolution*. Princeton and Oxford: Princeton University Press.

Brożek, Bartosz. (2013). *Rule-Following*. Kraków: Copernicus Press.

Claessen, Jacques. (2019). Theories of Punishment. In Johannes Keiler & David Roef (eds.), *Comparative Concepts of Criminal Law*, 3rd ed. Cambridge: Intersentia, pp. 11–34.

Dennett, Daniel C. (1991). *Consciousness Explained*. London: Penguin Books.

Di Bello, M., & Verheij, B. (2018). Evidential Reasoning. In G. Bongiovanni, G. Postema, A. Rotolo, G. Sartor, C. Valentini, & D. Walton (eds.) (2018), *Handbook of Legal Reasoning and Argumentation*. Dordrecht: Springer, pp. 447–93.

Doris, John M., & the Moral Psychology Research Group. (2010). *The Moral Psychology Handbook*. Oxford: Oxford University Press.

Epstein, Richard A. (2006). The Optimal Complexity of Legal Rules. In G. Gigerenzer & C. Engel (eds.), *Heuristics and the Law*. Cambridge: MIT Press, pp. 141–57.

Estabrooks, G. H. (1943). *Hypnotism*. New York: E. P. Dutton.

Fenton, Norman, Neil, Martin, & Berger, Daniel. (2016). Bayes and the Law. *Annual Review of Statistics and its Application* 3, 51–77.

Friedman, David D. (2000). *Law's Order*. Princeton: Princeton University Press.

Gallagher, Shaun (ed.) (2011). *The Oxford Handbook of the Self*. Oxford: Oxford University Press.

Gazzaniga, M. S., & LeDoux, J. E. (1978). *The Integrated Mind*. New York: Plenum.

Gigerenzer, G. (2006). Heuristics. In G. Gigerenzer & C. Engel (eds.), *Heuristics and the Law*. Cambridge: MIT Press, p. 17–44.

Gigerenzer, G. (2008). Moral Intuition = Fast and Frugal Heuristics? In Sinnott-Armstrong, 2008a, pp. 1–26.

Golding, Martin P. (1975). *Philosophy of Law*. Englewood Cliffs, NJ: Prentice Hall.

Goodenough, Oliver R., & Tucker, Micaela. (2010). Law and Cognitive Neuroscience. In *Annual Review of Law and Social Science* 6, 61–92.

Grossi, Davide, Meyer, John-Jules, & Dignum, Frank. (2008). The Many Faces of Counts-As: A Formal Analysis of Constitutive Rules. *Journal of Applied Logic* 6, 192–217. https://doi.org/10.1016/j.jal.2007.06.008

Hage, Jaap. (2005). Law and Coherence. In *Studies in Legal Logic*. Dordrecht: Springer, pp. 33–68.

Hage, Jaap. (2017). Tort Law. In Jaap Hage, Antonia Waltermann, & Bram Akkermans (eds.), *Introduction to Law*, 2nd ed. Cham: Springer, pp. 109–28.

Hage, Jaap. (2018). *Foundations and Building Blocks of Law*. The Hague: Eleven.

Hage, Jaap, Waltermann, Antonia, & Akkermans, Bram (eds.) (2017). *Introduction to Law*, 2nd ed. Cham: Springer.
Haidt, Jonathan. (2012). *The Righteous Mind: Why Good People Are Divided by Politics and Religion*. London: Penguin.
Haidt, Jonathan, & Bjorklund, Fredrik. (2008). Social Intuitionists Answer Six Questions about Moral Psychology. In Sinnott-Armstrong 2008a, pp. 181–218.
Haji, Ishtiyaque. (2002). Compatibilist Views of Freedom and Responsibility. In Kane, 2002, pp. 202–28.
Hart, Herbert L. A. (2012). *The Concept of Law*, 3rd ed. Oxford: Oxford University Press (1st ed. 1961).
Hoefer, Carl. (2019). Causal Determinism. In Edward N. Zalta (ed.), *The Stanford Encyclopedia of Philosophy* (Spring 2016 edition). https://plato.stanford.edu/archives/spr2016/entries/determinism-causal/
Hofstadter, Douglas R. (1980). *Gödel, Escher, Bach: An Eternal Golden Braid*. New York: Basic Books.
Hume, David. (1978). *A Treatise of Human Nature*, ed. L. A. Selby-Bigge & P. H. Nidditch. Oxford: Oxford University Press (1st ed. 1738–40).
Joyce, Richard. (2016). Moral Anti-Realism. In Edward N. Zalta (ed.), *The Stanford Encyclopedia of Philosophy* (Winter 2016 edition). https://plato.stanford.edu/archives/win2016/entries/moral-anti-realism/
Kahneman, Daniel. (2012). *Thinking, Fast and Slow*. London: Penguin.
Kahneman, D., & Tversky, A. (1982). *Judgment under Uncertainty: Heuristics and Biases*. Cambridge: Cambridge University Press.
Kane, Robert (ed.). (2002). *The Oxford Handbook of Free Will*, 1st ed. Oxford: Oxford University Press.
Kelsen, Hans. (1934). *Reine Rechtslehre*, 1st ed. Leipzig: Franz Deuticke.
Kelsen, Hans. (1960). *Reine Rechtslehre*, 2nd ed. Vienna: Franz Deuticke.
Kelsen, Hans. (1992). *Introduction to the Problems of Legal Theory*. Translation of the first (1934) edition of the *Reine Rechtslehre* by Bonnie Litschewsky Paulson and Stanley Paulson. Oxford: Clarendon Press.
Kuhn, Thomas S. (2012). *The Structure of Scientific Revolutions*. Chicago: The University of Chicago Press (1st ed. 1962).
Lakatos, Imre. (1970). Falsification and the Methodology of Scientific Research Programs. In I. Lakatos, & A. Musgrave (eds.) (1970). *Criticism and the Growth of Knowledge*. Cambridge: Cambridge University Press, pp. 91–196.
MacCormick, Neil. (1978). *Legal Reasoning and Legal Theory*. Oxford: Clarendon Press.
MacCormick, Neil. (2005). *Rhetoric and the Rule of Law*. Oxford: Oxford University Press.
Mackor, Anne Ruth. (2013). What Can Neurosciences Say About Responsibility? Taking the Distinction Between Theoretical and Practical Reason Seriously. In Nicole A. Vincent (ed.), *Neuroscience and Legal Responsibility*. Oxford: Oxford University Press, pp. 53–84.
Morse, Stephen J. (2013). Introduction. In Stephen J. Morse & Adina L. Roskies (eds.), *A Primer on Criminal Law and Neuroscience*. Oxford: Oxford University Press, pp. xv–xxiii.
Nagel, Thomas. (1970). *The Possibility of Altruism*. Princeton: Princeton University Press.
Nisbett, R. E., & Wilson, T. D. (1977). Telling More Than We Can Know: Verbal reports on mental processes. *Psychological Review* 84, 231–59.
Pardo, Michael S., & Patterson, Dennis. (2013) *Minds. Brains and Law*. Oxford: Oxford University Press.
Parfit, Derek. (1984). *Reasons and Persons*. Oxford: Clarendon Press.

Pereboom, Derk. (2001). *Living Without Free Will*. Cambridge: Cambridge University Press.
Prakken, H. (2001). Modelling Reasoning About Evidence in Legal Procedure. In *Proceedings of the Eighth International Conference on Artificial Intelligence and Law*. New York: ACM Press, pp. 119–28.
Rachlinski, J. J., Guthrie, C., & Wistrich, A. J. (2007). Heuristics and Biases in Bankruptcy Judges. *Journal of Institutional and Theoretical Economics*, 163, 167–86.
Rachlinski, J. J., Johnson, S., Wistrich, A., & Guthrie, C. (2009). Does Unconscious Racial Bias Affect Trial Judges? *Notre Dame Law Review*, 84, 1195–1246.
Radden, Jennifer. (2011). Multiple Selves. In Gallagher, 2011, pp. 547–70.
Railton, Peter. (2006). Humean Theory of Practical Rationality. In David Copp (ed.), *The Oxford Handbook of Ethical Theory*. Oxford: Oxford University Press, pp. 265–81.
Rosati, Connie S. (2016). Moral Motivation. In Edward N. Zalta (ed.), *The Stanford Encyclopedia of Philosophy* (Winter 2016 Edition). https://plato.stanford.edu/archives/win2016/entries/moral-motivation/
Roskies, Adina L. (2013). Brain Imaging Techniques. In Stephen J. Morse & Adina L. Roskies (eds.), *A Primer on Criminal Law and Neuroscience*. Oxford: Oxford University Press, pp. 37–74.
Ross, Alf. (1946). *Towards a Realistic Jurisprudence*. Copenhagen: Einar Munksgaard.
Ruiter, Dick W. P. (1993). *Institutional Legal Facts*. Dordrecht: Kluwer Academic Publishers.
Sapolsky, Robert M. (2017). *Behave: The Biology of Humans at Our Best and Worst*. London: Bodley Head.
Schlosser, Markus. (2015). Agency. In Edward N. Zalta (ed.), *The Stanford Encyclopedia of Philosophy* (Fall 2015 Edition). https://plato.stanford.edu/archives/fall2015/entries/agency/
Searle, John R. (1995). *The Construction of Social Reality*. New York: The Free Press.
Sinnott-Armstrong, Walter (ed.) (2008a). *Moral Psychology*, vol. 2, *The Cognitive Science of Morality: Intuition and Diversity*. Cambridge, MA: MIT Press.
Sinnott-Armstrong, Walter (ed.) (2008b). *Moral Psychology*, vol. 3, *The Neuroscience of Morality: Emotion, Brain Disorders, and Development*. Cambridge, MA: MIT Press.
Strawson, Galen. (2011). The Minimal Subject. In Gallagher, 2011, pp. 253–78.
Taleb, Nassim Nicholas. (2008). *The Black Swan: The Impact of the Highly Improbable*. London: Penguin.
Timpe, Kevin. (n.d.) Free Will. https://iep.utm.edu/freewill/#SH2c
Wagenaar, Willem A., Van Koppen, Peter J., & Crombag, Hans F. M. (1993). *Anchored Narratives: The Psychology of Criminal Evidence*. Englewood Cliffs, NJ: Prentice Hall.
Wallace, R. Jay. (2020). Practical Reason. In Edward N. Zalta (ed.), *The Stanford Encyclopedia of Philosophy* (Spring 2020 Edition). https://plato.stanford.edu/archives/spr2020/entries/practical-reason/
Wilson, Eric Entrican, & Denis, Lara. (2018). Kant and Hume on Morality. In Edward N. Zalta (ed.), *The Stanford Encyclopedia of Philosophy* (Summer 2018 Edition). https://plato.stanford.edu/archives/sum2018/entries/kant-hume-morality/
Wilson, Timothy D. (2002). *Strangers to Ourselves: Discovering the Adaptive Unconsciousness*. Cambridge, MA: The Belknap Press.
Wróblewski, Jerzy. (1992). *The Judicial Application of Law*, eds. Zenon Bankowski and Neil MacCormick. Dordrecht: Kluwer Academic Publishers.
Zaluski, Wojciech. (2009). *Evolutionary Theory and Legal Philosophy*. Cheltenham: Edward Elgar.
Zaluski, Wojciech. (2013). *Game Theory in Jurisprudence*. Kraków: Copernicus Center Press.

3

Social and Normative Facts

Carsten Heidemann

Perhaps the most remarkable feature of Hage's text, in the present volume, on the relevance of the cognitive sciences for law is his dismissal of the 'classical' separation of Ought from Is (Chapter 2, Section 2.5). It is central for his enterprise to show that cognitive sciences can give an answer to the normative question of what ought to be done. To achieve this aim, Hage relies on a subtle conception of 'constructivist facts'. The core passage of his text runs as follows:

> Ought-facts are constructivist facts which differ from brute social facts, but nevertheless depend on a social practice of acceptance for their existence. Then, there is no fundamental difference between the Ought and the Is. As the expression 'ought-facts' suggests, an Ought is a fact. This means that sciences, including the cognitive sciences, which give us information about the facts, can also give us information about what ought to be done. (Chapter 2, Section 2.5.6)

Thus, Hage maintains that an Ought always takes the form of an 'ought-fact', and he defines ought-facts as constructivist social facts. Constructivist social facts stand in a complicated relation to 'brute' social facts. For a 'brute' social fact to exist, three conditions have to be fulfilled: First, a sufficient number of members accept that this fact exists; second, they believe that enough members of the group accept that this fact exists; third, they believe, and take the other members to believe, that this fact belongs to social reality (not to objective reality) (Section 2.5.3). According to Hage, a constructivist fact exists if it ought to exist, and does not exist if it ought not to exist. In the third case, if neither it ought to exist or ought not to exist, and only then, it exists if it exists as a brute social fact (Section 2.5.4). So there are seemingly two alternatives for a constructivist fact to exist: To take up Hage's example, 'that Jean is the leader of the club' denotes a constructivist fact, either if Jean is accepted as the leader of the club, while at the same time it is not the case that she ought not be the leader of the club, or if she ought to be the leader of the club, while it is not a brute social fact that she is the leader of the club.

Hage takes this definition to be recursive, because the Ought, and thus a constructivist fact, is part of the definition of a constructivist fact again: A constructivist fact exists, if it ought to exist; that it ought to exist is in turn a constructivist fact, if it ought to be the case that this fact ought to exist, and so on (at least that's how I read the text; Hage draws a parallel to Kelsen's chain of validity but does not give an example). But if there were an infinite regress, the chain could not establish the existence of a constructivist fact. Therefore – at this point the second part of the definition of a constructivist fact comes in – the chain must 'bottom out' on a brute social fact where it is not the case that it ought not to exist: Hage holds that, in the end, every ought-fact depends on its social acceptance (Section 2.5.4). Hence, any chain of constructivist facts, be they ought-facts or not, will always end with a brute social fact which counts as a constructivist fact if it is not the case that it ought not to exist.

Hage's notion of a constructivist fact needs three special features to do its work. First, the clause 'it is not the case that fact x ought not to exist' does not denote an ought-fact itself – that's why not all constructivist social facts are ought-facts. Second, if because of an infinite regress it cannot be established whether a fact x ought not to exist, the proposition 'it is not the case that fact x ought not to exist' is true. Third, the proposition 'fact x ought to exist' does not presuppose that fact x exists (else the second part of the definition would be superfluous).

It is by basing them on social acceptance that constructivist facts are, says Hage, like all facts in general accessible by sciences. Hence, cognitive sciences, conceived as empirical sciences, may also give an answer to the question of what ought to be done, for example by specifying the circumstances under which people accept legal ought-facts (Section 2.5.6): To determine what ought to be done can be accomplished by pointing to is-facts.

If it were really that easy to dismiss the dualism of Is and Ought, Hage would have solved a centuries-old problem. And the conception he employs to reach this goal is ingenious. But there are several difficulties.

The most important one stems from the dual nature of constructivist facts. Ought-facts belong to just one category of constructivist facts (facts that ought to be the case), the other category is made up, according to Hage, of non-normative facts (brute facts where it is not the case that they ought not to exist). Although it is plausible to say that constructivist facts of the latter category bottom out on social acceptance, does this really count in the same way for ought-facts? If a chain of ought-facts ends with an ought-fact which cannot be derived from any other ought-fact, why and how could it possibly be derived from a non-normative fact? To say, for example, 'that nobody should hurt any other human being wilfully' cannot be derived from another ought-fact, but it can be derived from the brute social fact of its acceptance, simply begs the question. It is a pure stipulation which is not in accordance with the general use of ought-language. If, in a totalitarian society, it is generally accepted that dissenters ought to be snubbed, does it really follow that dissenters ought to be snubbed? It certainly does not for anybody who is not part of this society. But does it follow for the members of this society? If I am part of this society, but do not believe that dissenters should be snubbed, why should I accept that they ought to be snubbed? Simply because the majority of the members of the society think so? Is it, for a member of this society, meaningless to ask: 'The majority of my society accept that dissenters ought to be snubbed, but should dissenters (in my society) really be snubbed?'[1] This does not seem to be the case. The question would be absurd only if the general normative rule is presupposed that for any participant in a social practice those things ought to be done which are accepted inside the social practice, by the majority of its participants, as things that ought to be done. But this 'ultimate rule' would, first, be part of the Ought-domain; second, it would, again, only be valid by stipulation.

To assess this problem correctly, it is useful to have a look at the line of thought which Hage refers to for his conception: metaethical constructivism. Metaethical constructivism is

> the view that insofar as there are normative truths, they are not fixed by normative facts that are independent of what rational agents would agree to under some specified conditions of choice.[2]

Examples are the theory of justice of John Rawls, or discourse theory as proposed by Jürgen Habermas. Now, there is one decisive difference between their view and Hage's view. Hage's concept of normativity defines the Ought, in the end, by social acceptance. For him, a normative fact exists if it is accepted as such inside a social practice (the restriction that it must not be 'forbidden', i.e. ought not to exist, is not of much avail, as I'll try to show in a moment). It is exactly this move which enables Hage to regard the Ought as part of the domain of Is. But metaethical constructivism neither defines the Ought in a reductive way, nor does it point to factual acceptance as its criterion; instead, it envisages a hypothetical *ideal* situation in which certain norms would be agreed upon. This ideal situation functions as a standard for accepting a norm as valid. Metaethical constructivism is, unlike Hage's conception, a normative theory of validity, and not a sociological theory.

And there are some other problems with Hage's notion of an ought-fact: That part of the definition of a constructivist fact, 'that it is not the case that it ought not to exist', expresses, according to Hage, a non-normative fact. But does it really? In a footnote, Hage explains that, while the formula $O(\sim p)$ expresses an ought-fact, the formula $\sim O(p)$ does not. This, however, is doubtful. To say that p is not obligatory is a way of partially describing the normative domain just as much as saying that p is obligatory. To illustrate this point it is helpful to draw a parallel to the domain of empirical objects and is-facts: To be sure, a non-existing object is not an object. But a negative fact is still a fact. The sentence 'It is not the case that it is raining' expresses an is-fact just as much as the sentence 'It is raining'. For both sentences describe the domain of Is, and their truth-value depends on this domain. Why should this be different in the case of ought-facts?

---

[1] This is, of course, a variant of G. E. Moore's famous 'open question-argument' (see Moore, 1903, p. 15).
[2] This is the definition in the *Stanford Encyclopedia of Philosophy*, which Hage refers to.

Besides, how could we possibly establish whether a constructivist fact *x* that is generally accepted ought not to exist? For the chain of ought-facts founding the conclusion that fact *x* ought *not* to exist would also bottom out on general acceptance; and it is scarcely conceivable that both a constructivist fact *x*, and another ought-fact *y* saying that constructivist fact *x* ought not to exist, could be accepted by a majority in the same social group at the same time. It would follow that the demand that for a fact to be a constructivist fact 'it must not be the case that it ought not to exist' is superfluous.

And then the question arises of whether Hage's concept of Ought is reductive or not. If every ought-fact is a constructivist fact, and if a constructivist fact is *defined* by pointing to a finite chain of constructivist facts, then the Ought is ultimately reduced to an Is by definition, because the chain, according to Hage, necessarily bottoms out on purely factual general acceptance: That something is an ought-fact *means* that some other ought-fact says so, and so on; if there is an ought-fact where no other ought-fact says that it ought to be, then social acceptance suffices to secure its status. If social acceptance is taken account of in this way, as a matter of the definition of Ought, then the Ought *is* 'reduced' to social acceptance: That Jean ought to be the leader of the club – to take up Hage's example – means, in the end, nothing else but that it is accepted that she is the leader of the club; quite in accordance with Alexander Pope's 'Whatever is, is right', as it were.

This might only be different if recurring to another Ought, and finally to social acceptance, were not a matter of a recursive *definition* of a constructivist fact, but (simply) a matter of the *criteria* for something being a constructivist fact. In this case one might say that the fact that Jean ought to be the leader of the club depends for its validity on social acceptance, but social acceptance does not define it. But there is no hint in this direction in Hage's text, apart from his short allusion to Kelsen's chain of validity.[3] Besides, that kind of solution would afford the existence of a rule defining the empirical criteria for something to be an ought-fact (like Kelsen's basic norm).

Finally, the dualism of Is and Ought is traditionally conceived, for example by Kelsen and the neo-Kantians, to be comprehensive; that is, the Ought covers all manifestations of normativity there might be: moral and legal norms, norms guiding cognition, logical rules, rules of meaning and so on. It is difficult to regard some of these more abstract, implicit or necessary forms of normativity as being embodied in constructivist facts. It is not a matter of social acceptance that I ought not to think p and ~p, or that I ought to add 3 and 4 up to 7. Neither is any kind of social acceptance presupposed if I follow the rule that connects little black dots in the score with movements of the fingers on the keyboard of the piano.

To conclude, my main objection would be that the gap between Is and Ought has not been successfully challenged by Hage's conception, due to several problems in

---

[3] For Kelsen does not take the derivability from a higher norm to be defining validity; rather, for him, validity is the *existence* of the norm, which is given if one 'really' ought to act in the way described by the norm. Derivability from a higher norm is just a criterion of validity.

the definition of 'constructivist' fact, so that the transition from the factuality of general acceptance to an Ought remains implausible. While the usefulness of cognitive science as an ancillary discipline for legal science cannot be doubted, its ability to directly answer the question of what ought to be done must remain doubtful.

*

Hage's conception is problematic for internal reasons. But there are also external reasons which favour the notion that normativity is irreducible in the sense that an Ought cannot simply be established by answering an empirical question. It is an old objection to naturalism that, as far as it is deemed to be all-encompassing, it is self-refuting, simply because, as a theoretical position, it can only be advocated with a claim to correctness or truth; and correctness and truth are notions for which there is no room in a naturalist world. An alternative metaphysical view would be the (neo-)Kantian one. The starting point of Kantian philosophy was the insight that it is impossible to compare a cognitive act about an object with the object itself, because the only way to get at the object is by means of cognitive acts (Kant, 1992, 557–8). It follows that ascertaining the truth of a cognitive judgement can only be conceived of as a process of determining whether the rules guiding cognition have been met. The central part of Kant's metaphysics is, accordingly, a theory of the normative presuppositions of judging correctly, which replaces classical ontology. This was elaborated especially by the neo-Kantians of the Baden school, for whom some kind of value or normativity is the most basic metaphysical notion (cf. Rickert, 1921). In more recent philosophy, a similar conception is contained in Hilary Putnam's internal realism, where 'facts' dissolve into bundles of obligations to think in a certain way.[4] On this philosophical basis, one might just as well turn the tables and maintain that the dualism between Is and Ought is a relative one, because any Is might be reduced to an Ought – and not the other way round.

REFERENCES

Kant, I. (1923). Logik. In *Kants gesammelte Schriften*, ed. B. Jäsche, vol. 9. Berlin: Königlich Preußische Akademie der Wissenschaften.
Kant, I. (1992). The Jäsche Logic. In *Lectures on Logic*, trans. and ed. J. M. Young. Cambridge: Cambridge University Press.
Moore, G. E. (1903). *Principia Ethica*. London: Cambridge University Press.
Putnam, H. (1990). Why Is a Philosopher? In H. Putnam, *Realism with a Human Face*. Cambridge, MA and London: Harvard University Press.
Rickert, H. (1921). *Der Gegenstand der Erkenntnis*, 4th and 5th ed. Tübingen: J. C. B. Mohr.

---

[4] 'If I dared to be a metaphysician, I think I would create a system in which there were nothing but obligations. What would be metaphysically ultimate in the picture I would create, would be what we ought to do (ought to say, ought to think). In my fantasy of myself as a metaphysical super-hero, all "facts" would dissolve into "values". That there is a chair in this room would be analyzed . . . into a set of obligations: the obligation to think that there is a chair in this room if epistemic conditions are (were) "good" enough, for example' (Putnam, 1990, p. 115).

4

Law, Folk Psychology and Cognitive Science

Łukasz Kurek

4.1 INTRODUCTION

Folk psychology (henceforth FP) is the common-sense understanding of the human mind.[1] The main idea behind this chapter is that the legal understanding of the human mind – that is, how the human mind is conceptualized within criminal law, tort law, contract law or jurisprudence – has its roots in FP. A provisional justification of the claim that law's outlook on the mind is folk psychological is as follows. Law aims at influencing action. On many accounts, one of the principles which is somehow inherent in our concept of law is that legal rules should be possible to obey. To know when legal rules are possible to obey, at least some basic account of how the mind works is required. When the possibility of obeying legal rules is in question, one's legal responsibility for infringing them is diminished or even ruled out. There are factors pertaining to how the mind works – or, to be precise, how the mind malfunctions – which are recognized by virtually all legal systems as making it difficult or even impossible to follow legal rules. These factors – such as being underage or acting under duress – undermine an agent's control or knowledge about their actions to such an extent that they diminish or even rule out legal responsibility. What is of note for our purposes is that it seems to be a part of our common-sensical knowledge about the human mind that such factors undermine responsibility for the aforementioned reasons. These factors are recognized as limiting moral responsibility as well.

That law draws from FP is perhaps not a very surprising claim. Law is an artefact, and if there is any information about human beings within law, this information should be aligned with how humans view themselves. As for the relationship between cognitive science and FP, the former has had the latter in its sights for several decades. Various claims – both of an empirical and philosophical nature – have been made as to what the features of FP are. Despite this long-lasting interest in FP, considerable disagreement remains in connection to even its most basic

---

[1] This paper has been prepared within the project 2017/26/D/HS5/00688 funded by the National Science Centre, Poland.

features. An example of such a feature, and one which will often resurface in this chapter, is whether FP makes any commitments as to how the mind really works. If FP makes such claims and they turn out to be false, this could be used as an argument against the usefulness of FP. In a way, it would be surprising if the empirical commitments of FP – if there are any – would not, at least to some extent, turn out to be false. Science has already revealed how our common sense gets things wrong in the context of our everyday understanding of the physical world. Some think, however, that FP should not be viewed as making empirical commitments. They will not regard as serious the threat which cognitive science is supposed to pose for how we understand ourselves.

FP is viewed as the source of our knowledge not only about ourselves, but also about other people. Because knowledge of this kind is of interest to philosophers, numerous contemporary thinkers have become interested in this phenomenon and their interest in FP has only increased since cognitive scientists began to investigate it. Therefore, much of this chapter will pertain to various philosophical arguments and positions which have emerged at the intersection between FP and cognitive science. It does not mean that there are no problems connected with FP which are specific to law. After all, law aims at directly influencing real-world situations and, in contrast to philosophy, its aims are mainly practical. The practical nature of law influences the debate about FP, law and cognitive science to a considerable extent. For example, those dubious as to the usefulness of FP for legal purposes should propose how FP could be replaced. For if our legal practices are rooted in FP, these legal practices would be crippled without it and completely replacing FP would not be an easy task. Some would even argue that the elimination of FP would be 'the greatest intellectual catastrophe in the history of our species' (Fodor, 1987, p. xii). As we can see, the topic raises some emotions.

In the first part of the chapter I will present the philosophical and scientific issues pertaining to FP. In particular, I will focus on the issue of the nature of our FP conceptual network and what the features of the cognitive architecture underpinning it are. Then I will attempt to reconstruct the folk-psychological conceptual framework present within law. In the last part of the chapter, I will discuss three viewpoints on the law–FP–cognitive science relationship: autonomy, revision and integration.

4.2 WHAT IS FOLK PSYCHOLOGY?

The term 'folk psychology' has at least two meanings. According to the first meaning, the term refers to the prescientific, conceptual framework used by ordinary people. We use this conceptual framework to predict, explain and manipulate the behaviour of our fellow human beings as well as to explain and understand our own behaviour. The conceptual framework in question includes, but is not limited to, concepts such as belief, desire, pleasure, memory, knowledge, intention, love, hate, joy and anger.

It is the core of our understanding of what a human being is as a person, that is, as a thinking, feeling and acting creature. In its second meaning, the term 'FP' refers to the aforementioned practices of predicting, explaining and manipulating behaviour. Investigations into mind reading underscore the fact that it consists of a lot more than just explaining, predicting or manipulating behaviour (Malle, 2004, pp. 64–72). The conceptual apparatus of FP enables practices such as, *inter alia*, greeting, promising, congratulating, threatening, joking and advising (Wilkes, 1984, p. 347). These practices are crucial to virtually all social phenomena, including language, morality and law (Humphrey, 1976, p. 308; Malle & Nelson, 2003, pp. 563–4; Tomasello, 2003, *passim*; Knobe, 2005, p. 357).

It is notoriously difficult to state precisely what the scope of our folk-psychological conceptual framework is, and how it enables the aforementioned practices. This is primarily because we are skilled at describing behaviour in terms of various influencing factors. Character features are one prominent type of such factors: although my sister often has her head in the clouds, I know I can count on her when it really matters. Also, some of my academic colleagues take criticism really badly and they become easily frustrated when someone disagrees with them. When we turn to social psychology – the field within cognitive science which is especially interested in FP – we are provided with information that when people explain others' behaviour, they use concepts pertaining not only to what they understand to be the immediate causes of behaviour, such as thoughts or emotions, but also concepts pertaining to traits or moods such as cheerful, gloomy, sincere, intolerant, critical or imaginative (Malle, 2004, p. 47).

We should keep in mind that there are many factors here – such as beliefs, desires, emotions, traits or moods – which we readily include in our common-sense descriptions of others and ourselves. However, within philosophy and cognitive science, special attention has been accorded to mental states, especially beliefs and desires (Nichols & Stich, 2003, pp. 14–15). Beliefs are mental states which provide the agent with information about how things are. Desires are mental states which contain information about what the agent wants. What beliefs and desires have in common is intentionality: they have representational content, in the sense that they are about something. Beliefs are about how the world is and desires are about how one wants the world to be. The understanding of ourselves and others in terms of intentional states is the core of what is usually described as 'FP'. Despite its limitations, this is also the understanding of FP which is adopted in this chapter. It is this understanding of FP which is usually at stake when the relationship between FP, law and cognitive science is investigated.

4.2.1 *The Emergence of Folk Psychology*

That there is a practical side to FP – that people actually explain or predict behaviour with the aid of intentional states – is perhaps its least controversial aspect.

It is hard to dispute the fact that we frequently mind-read others in this way and talk about what they think, want or feel. Thus, when I explain why John became a lawyer by saying that 'He wanted to help others' it reveals, *inter alia*, that I think that John believed that by becoming a lawyer he would be able to help other people.

What is more problematic than indicating when we mind-read is to explain how mind reading is possible. Here the investigations pertain to the nature and scope of our psychological knowledge which underpins the aforementioned practices. For instance, many would agree that certain linguistic practices reveal people's knowledge about the relationship between various intentional states and between intentional states and behaviour (Gopnik, Meltzoff & Kuhl, 1999 p. 101; Malle, 2004, p. 147). For instance, if I say 'They said it because they were angry' this reveals that I know something about how anger influences verbal behaviour. The psychological knowledge in question is a body of information a person finds plausible whenever they tap into their conceptual framework pertaining to how intentional states are interrelated and how they are interrelated with behaviour.

The conceptual framework linking intentional states with other intentional states and intentional states with behaviour is a hypothesized structure, the existence of which is supposed to explain observable behaviour. For example, if my friend has come to the meeting we earlier agreed upon, I may explain their behaviour by referring to their beliefs about the time and place of the meeting and to their desire to meet me. The conceptual framework of FP is often understood to be of a theoretical nature (Sellars, 1956, pp. 317–18). It means that this framework postulates the existence of unobservable objects of a mental nature, such as beliefs and desires.

Its attitude towards intentional states is what differentiates the folk-psychological mode of behaviour explanation from its behavioural counterpart. Behaviourists object to FP because they allow explanations based only on observational criteria (e.g. 'They are violent because they have a history of violent behaviour'). Behavioural explanations have some attractions, especially for theorists with a more pragmatic outlook. Their major advantages are that they are more parsimonious in comparison to FP explanations, as they avoid postulating suspicious and elusive inner episodes which are only indirectly accessible to the observer.

One might question, therefore, the existence of FP. The reason why FP exists is that the deficiencies of the behavioural account far exceed its advantages of simplicity. For instance, the behavioural account is too coarse-grained to give us a glimpse into the intricacies of how feelings, desires and thoughts interplay and influence behaviour. Therefore, folk-psychological explanations allow us to better understand the meaning of actions – for example, to determine whether a particular comment was a snide remark or a good-natured jest.

The behaviourist theory has other difficulties. Imagine Jane, who always drives to work. Then, one day, Jane's car breaks down. Will she take a bus or ride a bike? That depends on many things, such as the extent to which she cares about her physical condition or concerns for the environmental impact of mass-transit systems. So the explanation of her taking a bus by her being disposed to do so involves her beliefs and desires and other folk-psychological phenomena. Furthermore, it would be peculiar if we were to reduce our self-knowledge to the knowledge of our behavioural dispositions. We have a lot of introspective evidence that we actually think about what to do and that our actions are often in line with our practical deliberations. This suggests that our thoughts play an important role in producing behaviour.

Further drawbacks of behaviourism include accounting for the behaviour which consists in following legal rules. Imagine you see a person who is not smoking in a non-smoking area. Are they not smoking because they are following the rule or because they just had a smoke and do not feel like smoking? To differentiate between rule-following behaviour and merely acting in accordance with rules, one needs to postulate what the target person was thinking.

Perhaps the clearest edge which folk psychologists have over their behavioural counterparts is of a practical nature: the former are better equipped to manipulate others. They are better able to manipulate others because they realize that people's knowledge of the world is mediated through their thoughts about the world. In consequence, they are able to recognize that others may not know what they themselves know. The daily struggles of living in a society tempt us to exploit this ignorance.

4.2.2 The Ontological Status of Folk-Psychological Entities

A thorny issue pertaining to FP is whether it makes any empirical commitments, that is, whether it at least aims to correspond with reality. This issue has been a bone of contention between realists, eliminativists and pragmatists. Realists claim that our concepts of intentional states refer to real phenomena and that these phenomena exist. Eliminativists claim that our concepts of intentional states refer to real phenomena, but that these phenomena do not exist. Pragmatists argue that FP is not committed to the existence of intentional states. This philosophical debate has consequences for legal FP. If there is no correspondence between FP and reality – that is, if FP can be accounted for without the assumption of such correspondence – then cognitive science poses no major threat to law. For one of the goals of cognitive science is to make empirical commitments, and to compare it with FP would be fallacious. On the other hand, if FP actually postulates the existence of things like beliefs and desires and cognitive science would give us reasons to doubt their existence, this could mean that we should reconsider the role of FP within law.

4.2.2.1 Realism

That FP should be interpreted in realist terms is perhaps the most natural position to take. After all, when I explain someone else's behaviour by referring to their belief that by becoming a lawyer they will be able to help people, it appears that I assume that the target person had this particular belief when they were deciding on what to do in their life and that this particular belief influenced their decision.

Despite the initial plausibility of realism, immediate difficulties follow for its proponents. For instance, we now have scientific knowledge at our disposal about how the mind actually works. Some of this knowledge pertains to biology, especially how the brain works. But FP does not include any claims as to the neurobiological nature of our mentality. Some even argue that there is a mind–body dualism present within FP, that is, that according to FP we are composed of two different things: the physical body and the ethereal mind, which resembles what in some religions is described as a 'soul' (Knobe, 2014, p. 71). So if there are claims within FP as to the relationship between the mind and the brain, and if, to makes matters worse, FP postulates entities resembling souls, then one may wonder if FP is not only a superficial way of thinking about the mind which should be superseded by a more scientific outlook.

The standard realist view on intentional states is well equipped to deal with such objections. First of all, virtually all realists agree that we should not think about FP as making any commitments as to the constituent nature of intentional states – such as claims pertaining to the neural architecture of the human brain. Instead, many realists think that the folk knowledge about the mind makes 'functional' claims, that is, it characterizes intentional states in terms of how they are produced by external and internal stimuli and by their effects on other intentional states and behaviour (Putnam 1975, pp. 435–9). For instance, we can provide the following functional analysis of pain without knowing anything about its neurological underpinnings: (1) people who suffer bodily harm generally feel pain; (2) people who feel pain will generally have a characteristic look on their face; (3) people who feel pain will generally try to alleviate it, for example by taking painkillers. This list accounts for different functions which pain plays within our lives. The idea behind functionalism is that sometimes the knowledge stored in our concepts of things pertains to what these things do, and not to what they are.

According to functionalism, our everyday knowledge about the mind is at just the right level of behaviour explanation to provide us with the tools necessary to coordinate social interactions. Some compare it to classical physics, which is highly useful when aimed at the level of large-enough objects, but incapable of explaining events at the quantum level (Malle, 2004, p. 33). What is interesting about functionalism is that adopting this position leaves open the issue of the constituent nature of intentional states. It may be that their constituent nature is physical, but at the same time this viewpoint is consistent with there being ephemeral mental stuff, the different functions of which we can observe. Despite this non-commitment of functionalism, the contemporary consensus of opinion is that, in order to explain the mind, we have to find what its place in the natural world is, that is, in the world which is the target of explanation for empirical sciences. This excludes from the picture otherworldly, soul-like objects. So functionalism is almost always paired with a claim of some kind which grounds the mind in what is physical.

Perhaps the driving idea behind realism pertaining to intentional states is that it cannot be a coincidence that our everyday psychological knowledge actually works (Fodor, 1987, p. 3). The extent to which it works remains – as we will see – a moot point, but that it sometimes aids us in the prediction of behaviour is a plausible claim. Just to give an example: it is my everyday psychological knowledge which leads me to the conclusion that people whose beliefs about some aspect of reality differ from mine might act differently than me. When I realize that my friend's belief about the place we agreed to meet tomorrow evening differs from mine, I will come to the conclusion that, if I do not intervene, tomorrow evening they will not be at the place I have in mind, but somewhere else. And it is not only the fact that predictions grounded in FP are sometimes correct which supports the claim about the correspondence between FP and reality. This claim is also supported by the introspective evidence that I have beliefs, desires and other intentional states and that they influence my behaviour in a particular way. When this introspective evidence is paired with the observation that others behave similarly to me, it seems plausible to reason analogically and infer that they also have intentional states which influence their behaviour. Thus, functionalism can be easily paired with the claim that, at least for our practical needs, there is a sufficient correspondence between our everyday understanding of the mind and how the mind actually works.

4.2.2.2 Eliminativism

Yet there is another very different understanding of FP. This viewpoint is usually described as 'eliminativism' and consists of four core claims: (1) that our conceptual framework pertaining to intentional states takes the form of a theory of mind, (2) that the folk theory of mind commits itself to the existence of intentional states it postulates, (3) that the folk theory of mind is false because the intentional states it postulates do not exist and (4) that the folk theory of mind should be eliminated (Churchland, 1981). Claims (1) and (2) have already been discussed. However, claims (3) and (4) are certainly a novelty and, because of their revolutionary character, need some explication.

For eliminativists, the crucial claim is (3), since claim (4) is merely the consequence of (3). Despite the uncompromising nature of (3) we should notice that it remains at least a logical possibility if we understand the folk-psychological conceptual framework as an empirical theory of mind, that is, a theory which aims at explaining what the mind is and how it works. That is, if the theory makes a commitment about the existence of X, and it turns out that X does not exist, the theory is false.

Eliminativists have much more up their sleeves than merely pointing to the logical possibility of FP being a false theory of mind. The philosopher Paul

Churchland, one of the proponents of this view, points to at least three empirical failures of this theory (Churchland, 1981). Firstly, FP is unable to explain various psychological phenomena of central importance, such as mental illness, intelligence, sleep, creativity or memory – and this is just the tip of the iceberg. In the case of memory, for example, we know that it is divided into various subsystems such as working memory, procedural memory or semantic memory. The conceptual apparatus provided by the folk theory of mind is insufficient to arrive at this fragmentation of memory – it is the result of scientific experimentation. Secondly, FP is a stagnant theory as it has not evolved in any significant manner since at least the Ancient Greeks. When we read Aristotle's *Nicomachean Ethics*, for example, we notice that the conditions of responsibility ascription pertaining to beliefs and intentions of the perpetrator are in many ways the same as those of today. According to Aristotle, the two main factors which undermine responsibility pertain to the lack of control over one's action and the lack of knowledge about it (Aristotle, 2000, p. 37). Lastly, there is no evidence that the core of FP, the intentional states it postulates, can be integrated with cognitive science. Because the folk theory of mind is false, eliminativists conclude that it should be superseded by a mature, scientific theory of mind of a neurobiological character.

As we will see, many of the eliminativist doubts pertaining to the truth of folk psychology are referred to by those who argue that findings within cognitive science will revolutionize law. Yet if the eliminativists are right, and FP should be disposed of, then we can suspect that it is not only law that will change as a result. After all, according to the eliminativists, no one believes or desires anything. If this is true, then to understand ourselves we would need to develop a completely novel conceptual framework and a vocabulary to accompany it.

4.2.2.3 Pragmatism

The last influential view on the nature of intentional states – pragmatism – is opposed to both realism and eliminativism. Although pragmatists do not deny that there is a folk-psychological conceptual framework which underpins such everyday abilities as explaining, predicting and manipulating behaviour, they reject the claim that there is any strong correspondence between what we think about the mind and what it actually is or how it works (Dennett, 1991, p. 30). Pragmatists aim at explaining how we attribute intentional attitudes, and consider the issue of the nature of mental states as being of secondary importance. In a nutshell, these theorists claim that to attribute mental states to a target person is to rationalize them, that is, ascribe to them beliefs and desires that make them emerge as a rational agent.

Pragmatists often claim that there is a profound difference between the folk-psychological and scientific explanations of behaviour. Proponents of this view typically think of intentional states as causally influencing thought and behaviour, but at the same time they deny that this causal influence can be described by a linguistic structure resembling a scientific theory. This is because the process of mind reading is somehow normative that is, that various rules of rationality plays an important role in the folk-psychological understanding of behaviour (Davidson, 1984, p. 169). An example of such a rule of rationality is the following: if a person believes that p and q, then they should believe that p and they should believe that q. This, in fact, should be the case because the conjunction is true if and only if all of its conjuncts are true. But many pragmatists argue for a stronger claim: if a person believes that p and q, then they *will* generally believe that p and believe that q. Of course, it would be unrealistic to suppose that people actually use the formal principles of logic or another normative system such as probability theory – on this view, it is usually not clear which rules of rationality people follow when they folk-psychologize – to guide them in their attributions of intentional states (Dennett, 1978a, pp. 10–11). This is unrealistic mainly because it would often require carrying out mental activities of intractable complexity. Rather, the capacities to use the rules of rationality should be understood in dispositional terms, that is, as tendencies which people demonstrate when they mind-read. So the rules of rationality should not be understood as laws describing the transitions between intentional states of the mind reader – that is, their beliefs about intentional states of the target person – but as approximations or idealizations of what actually happens in their mind. Pragmatists claim that such a mind-reading procedure is very different from scientific explanation, which uses general – and often statistical – laws correlating events to be explained and their causes.

The important role of rationality in folk-psychologizing may be illustrated when we imagine how difficult mind reading would be without it. Even the simplest mind-reading tasks allow for numerous solutions without there being some rules which simplify them. For instance, imagine I attempt to predict where Jane will look for her umbrella. I know that she left it in the closet, but I also know that her daughter took it and put it in the bathroom. It seems obvious to me that – despite the fact that the umbrella changed location – Jane will look for it in the closet. But why is it obvious? After all, Jane may know that her daughter always moves the umbrella to the bathroom. Or perhaps, for some reason, Jane told her daughter to move the umbrella? One might even posit, due to a quirk of some kind, that Jane always looks for her umbrella in the bathroom. All of these possibilities can be discarded if I assume that Jane is rational – that is, that she looks for things in the places where she has left them. In the more complex cases, when there are several competing folk-psychological explanations of behaviour – all of which could be convincing to reasonable interpreters – pragmatists claim there are just no facts of the matter which could determine which explanation is correct. This is because all of these explanations are merely approximations of the actual sequence of events which lead to the particular decision.

To sum up the pragmatist proposal, the possibility of an inquiry into the nature of intentional states in this view is denied because folk-psychological explanations are understood to be at best idealizations of what actually happens when we act. What is more, these idealizations are of a different kind than the ones which we usually encounter in science. This is because folk-psychological idealizations require people to be interpreted as rational, that is, as following the appropriate rules in their practical deliberations. From the scientific standpoint, it is not only far from obvious that people have such capacities, but, given the prevailing outlook on this matter, it may seem entirely dubious. It is almost a truism these days to point to the fact that human rationality is limited (Kahneman, 2011, *passim*). But pragmatists such as Dennett tend to hold to such idealizations because they find them useful.

4.3 FOLK PSYCHOLOGY AND COGNITIVE SCIENCE

The claim that people possess a folk-psychological conceptual framework which takes the form of a theory has proven to be stimulating for philosophers and cognitive scientists alike. Within philosophy, this conceptual framework was understood as providing us with an understanding of ourselves and others. For cognitive scientists, the claim that people possess a theory of mind was a hypothesis which could be tested empirically.

4.3.1 *Theories of Mind*

The empirical research pertaining to FP was initiated by two primatologists, David Premack and Guy Woodruff, who coined the term 'theory of mind' in their 1978 paper (Premack & Woodruff, 1978, p. 515). Building on the results of their experiments involving chimpanzees, they hypothesized that chimpanzees also possess a theory of mind. To be specific, they claimed that a chimpanzee is able to recognize that others behave in a certain way because they want something. But is difficult to ascribe intentional states solely on the basis of the observed behaviour, since behaviours usually yield many explanations, some of which do not require intentional state ascription (e.g. does chimpanzee X recognize that chimpanzee Y wants a banana or did X merely learn that whenever there is a banana near Y, Y will try to get it?).

The philosopher Daniel Dennett, who wrote an influential commentary on the paper by Premack and Woodruff, proposed that the evidence which would suggest that an animal has a theory of mind should consist in that animal behaving as if it understood that others may have *false* beliefs (Dennett, 1978b, p. 569). It is more difficult to explain behaviour influenced by false beliefs purely in behavioural terms because it requires taking into account that an animal responds to what is not in its environment – the false information is stored in the mind of the animal. Dennett's idea has been used by the developmental psychologists Heinz Wimmer and Josef

Perner to determine at what age children begin to recognize that others may have false beliefs (Wimmer & Perner, 1983). To examine this, they presented the children with a short scenario. Maxi puts a chocolate in location A and then he goes out to play. During his absence, Maxi's mother moves the chocolate to location B. After the mother leaves, Maxi returns. The children participating in the experiment were asked the question 'Where will Maxi look for his chocolate?' While four- and five-year-old children tended to give the correct answer – that Maxi will look in place A – there was no three-year-old child who gave this answer. Wimmer and Perner came to the conclusion that when children are four years old they begin to realize that others may have false beliefs. Wimmer and Perner's study has been replicated in various formats and the term 'false-belief task' is commonly used to refer to these experiments.

There is a point which the empirical research on FP raises and which is worth highlighting as it touches upon one of the thorniest issues concerning FP. This is whether the conceptual framework of FP is an empirical theory in any interesting way. Not everyone agrees that FP should be associated with having a folk-psychological theory of mind. Some argue, for instance, that FP is more like a set of platitudes pertaining to how the mind works (Lewis, 1972, p. 256). These platitudes are unsystematic and shallow and one should not attach much importance to their content. On this view, there could never be any serious conflict or even tension between FP and cognitive science, since it is only the latter which makes any genuine claims pertaining to what the mind is and how it works.

4.3.2 *Theory or Simulation?*

For some time, the scientific dispute pertaining to FP was dominated by proponents of the so-called theory-theory and simulation theory. Proponents of the theory-theory claim that FP is an information-rich process, that is, people possess and use a considerable amount of information about the mind in their folk-psychological practices. At least some of this information pertains to the common-sense psychological laws which link stimuli with thoughts, thoughts with each other and thoughts with behaviour (e.g. 'People who suffer bodily harm generally feel pain', 'People who are angry generally talk louder' or 'People who desire P, believe that Q-ing is the best means to achieve P, and do not have any desires conflicting with P, generally attempt to Q'). Proponents of the simulation theory argue that FP is an information-poor process. Simulationists claim that when people mind-read they generalize from their own situation, that is, they use their own decision-making mechanism to get at the sought-after explanation or prediction of behaviour, even though in such cases their decision-making mechanism works in an offline manner (Goldman, 2006, pp. 27–9). The story goes as follows: to predict or explain the behaviour of another person, we input a set of 'simulated' or 'pretend' intentional states into our decision-making mechanism that we think the target person has and see what decision it generates. We do not act in accordance with this decision – hence the caveat that the mechanism works offline – but we ascribe the decision to the target person. In comparison to the theory of mind, simulation requires less information about the person who is simulated to arrive at the prediction or explanation. This is because simulation supplants this information with the information about the person who simulates.

Despite the fact that for some time the dispute between the so-called 'theory-theorists' (proponents of the theory that people possess a theory of mind) and simulationists had been viewed as a 'winner takes it all' situation, this dichotomy is now understood by many as a false one – and rightly so. For although simulationists reasonably highlighted the fact that mind reading does not seem to require an elaborate theory of mind, their account also rests on the assumption that people possess some psychological knowledge about intentional states. For it is difficult to explain how the person who simulates is able to determine which intentional states to ascribe to the target person if one precludes appeals to such psychological knowledge. What is more, generalizations from one's own case may often be too weak to sustain the full range of mind reading. After all, we sometimes make corrections to our common-sense explanations of behaviour which take into account the difference between us and the person whose behaviour we are attempting to explain. Such corrections also require some degree of psychological knowledge.

Because the simulation account and the theory-theory account are not mutually exclusive, and they both seem to contribute to our understanding of what underpins FP, various hybrid accounts of FP have been proposed. Particularly interesting developments pertaining to FP are connected with the so-called 'model' approach (Maibom, 2003; Godfrey-Smith, 2005). According to this view, mind reading consists of utilizing a model of mind. Model building involves the construction of a hypothetical and relatively simple structure for the purpose of understanding a more complex and real-world phenomenon. As we will see, this is a promising development if we want to account for the relationship between FP and law.

The important feature of the model approach to FP is that it is more nuanced than the theory-theory and simulation approaches. On the model approach, different construals of the model of mind are available, and the choice of a particular construal depends on the context. In some cases, particularly when fast prediction of behaviour is required, the psychological model of the target person will be generic. This might happen when I go to a restaurant and order a meal. The simple action of ordering a meal would not be possible without the appropriate interpretation of the behaviour of the person who is approaching my table with a menu in his hand. But to interpret this person as a waiter who will take my order, it seems that I do not need to ascribe to this person beliefs or desires and, using these mental states as premises, reason who they are and what they will do. It is likely that I will interpret the person in question with the use of a default behavioural rule such as 'people approaching my table in a restaurant who carry a menu are waiters'. My model of the mind of the person approaching my table is, in this case, generic. Things become more complicated if the waiter asks me whether I would like to order the same as usual when I have never been in this restaurant before. To understand that they probably took me for someone else, I need to add this mistaken belief to my model of their mind.

Sometimes, however, the interpretation of behaviour will require a much more detailed model of mind. This is the case when one attempts to explain the behaviour of a friend who has acted out of character. In such a situation, when we are especially motivated to get at the bottom of things, the explanation will often be the result of a more careful investigation into the thought which most probably preceded the action. The model of the mind used here is more complex and it includes, *inter alia*, beliefs and desires which we ascribe to others, on the basis of our knowledge of them. What is important for our purposes is that there are few areas where we are more motivated to arbitrate what was going on in the mind of a particular person than in the area of law. This can be illustrated with an example of the criminal trial, which – in order to justify holding the perpetrator legally responsible for his actions – requires us to justify that the perpetrator had a guilty mind. It appears, therefore, that the model of the mind required for the purposes of law is more complex than in some other situations in which we use FP.

4.4 FOLK PSYCHOLOGY AND LAW

Now that the basic philosophical and scientific issues pertaining to FP have been outlined, let us inquire into the relationship between FP and law. I will attempt to assess this relationship by focusing on the legal variant of one of the central concerns pertaining to FP, that is, whether humans possess a theory of mind. The legal variant of this concern is whether the information about the mind stored within law forms a theory. The importance of this issue for law should be clear by now. Firstly, if the information about the mind stored within law does not form a theory of mind – for example, if it is just a set of loosely connected, shallow platitudes – then there could never be any serious impact of cognitive science on law – at least as far as the folk-psychological content of law goes.

4.4.1 Is There a Theory of Mind Within Law?

The issue at stake is whether law's 'theory of mind' consists of everyday platitudes, or whether it is more nuanced. As already mentioned, this has been a matter of controversy in the dispute between the theory-theorists, who claimed that FP is information-rich, and the simulationists who claimed that FP is information-poor. Simulationists attempted to show how FP is possible without people having a sophisticated conceptual repertoire which they use to explain, predict or manipulate behaviour. Although there are cases when people mind-read without deploying such a conceptual framework, in the case of law I think it is safe to say that it contains a rather nuanced set of beliefs about the mind.

The simulationists' rationale for the proposal that mind reading does not require theorizing about minds has arisen, *inter alia*, because people tend to have difficulties with spelling out the psychological principles they find plausible, especially principles of a more sophisticated kind. What is more, people are able to solve complex mind-reading tasks on the fly, which makes the assumption that they use abstract folk-psychological laws even more dubious. However, these simulationists' objections miss their target as far as folk-psychologizing within law is concerned. First of all, the law's conceptual framework contains, explicitly, various folk-psychological notions. So there are no significant difficulties in actually spelling out the folk-psychological principles which law finds plausible. Examples of the folk-psychological principles present within law include the following: 'coercion or ignorance limit the ability to practically deliberate', 'emotions limit the ability to practically deliberate', 'people have the capacity to act with intent' or 'people can have various motivations when they act'. These principles are easily discerned when one studies, for example, the conditions of legal responsibility in criminal law and tort law.

What is more, everyday psychological concepts such as knowledge, will, intent or motive have been with us for a few thousand years already (Aristotle, 2000, *passim*). It is true that lawyers are not fond of the topic of psychological states because it is difficult to reliably ascribe them on the basis of behavioural and circumstantial evidence. On the other hand, few would deny that law should require us to take into account the psychological states of the person who has committed a crime. What is more, in many cases, law introduces psychological distinctions which are subtle enough to assume that they are not universally known. A good example here may be the vast legal-dogmatic literature pertaining to the nature of intent. Different criminal law systems recognize that there are various types of intent with which a crime can be committed, such as direct or indirect as well as conditional and unconditional intent. It is implausible to claim that this psychological knowledge stored within law is of an everyday kind. Many folk psychologists – at least those who are not lawyers, psychologists or philosophers – would most probably have difficulties in distinguishing between these types of intention by relying on their own psychological knowledge. In such cases, knowledge about the mind stored within law can be more plausibly regarded as a development of the folk-psychological conceptual framework.

On the other hand, the legal-specific distinctions between intentional states are only that: developments of FP. Once introduced, they seem to make sense for non-lawyers and they do not require any profound break with FP. For instance, many folk psychologists who did not study law may have difficulties arriving at the distinction between direct and oblique intent by themselves. But after they are introduced to this distinction, it will most probably be clear to them that we should differentiate between acts committed with the intent to bring about a particular consequence – that is, acts committed with direct intent – and acts committed without a direct intent of bringing about a particular consequence, in the case of which their consequences could be foreseen, but were ignored by the perpetrator. A perpetrator who shoots to kill has a direct intent of killing their victim. A perpetrator who shoots to hurt their victim, but actually kills them may be judged to have an indirect intent of killing if, for instance, it will be proved that it was indifferent to them whether the victim would survive. The need to distinguish between these types of intent is, at the core, moral: direct intent seems to us as more blameworthy than oblique intent.

The observation that there is a considerable amount of information about the mind within law counters the standard simulationist objection to the claim that people use a complex theory of mind to explain behaviour. In some cases the simulationists are right, but not in the case of law. What is more, there is also the issue that when FP is used in the legal context, the explanation of behaviour is explicit, complex and laborious. In the legal context, proving that the person was in some particular state of mind when they acted may require a rather elaborate line of argumentation – especially if this particular state of mind is of importance in the legal proceedings. At least from the phenomenological perspective, in such cases mind reading looks more like theorizing than simulating.

Before making the attempt at the reconstruction of the folk-psychological conceptual framework present within law, two preliminary remarks are in order. First of all, despite the fact that when mind reading is engaged in a legal context it looks more like theorizing than simulating, it does not follow that there is a theory of mind stored somewhere in law which is composed of general psychological laws. Theorizing may also be viewed as building a model – that is, a simple, hypothetical structure – to explain some complex, real-world phenomenon. This is the sense of 'theorizing' that I have in mind when I claim that in the legal context mind reading resembles theorizing about the mind. Secondly, I will attempt to reconstruct only the basic features of the model of mind present within law. This model can be further developed in different areas of law depending on the particular needs of legal theory or practice in the particular legal branch.

4.4.2 *Theory of Mind Within Law*

There is a broad consensus amongst legal philosophers that the basic feature of law's outlook on the mind is that its machinery allows us to reason practically, that is, to rationally deliberate about what we ought to do (Alexy, 1989, pp. 211–20; Shapiro, 2002, p. 402; Bertea, 2015, p. 55; Morse, 2015, p. 40; Alces, 2018, p. 8). Practical deliberation in the legal context requires taking legal rules as its premises. This includes knowing what these rules require or how they are connected with other rules of both a legal and non-legal type. For example, within jurisprudence, many regard the relationship between law and practical reason as a matter of orthodoxy and seek to explain how legal rules can be reasons for action, that is, how they could influence deliberations of a practical reasoner. That people are responsive to reasons is also an important feature of various doctrinal theories, for example, the doctrines pertaining to holding people legally responsible. Interestingly, the concept of practical reason has been investigated by philosophers since ancient times and these investigations belong to the best examples of how FP has been used to understand human behaviour (Aristotle, 2000, *passim*).

Let us attempt to reconstruct the model of mind required to account for practical deliberation. It will also be the model of the mind assumed within law. I will call it 'The Model of the Practical Mind' (MPM). A survey of the literature on the relationship between law and practical reason suggests that there are several core components of this model. First of all, MPM includes two types of intentional states which correspond to desires and beliefs. On any account of practical reason, a person capable of deliberating what they should do, also needs to have a desire to do something. Without such a motivation, there would not be anything to practically deliberate about. I might think that by becoming a lawyer I will be able to help other people, but without the desire to help other people, this thought alone will not move me to act. But desire alone is not enough to be a practical reasoner. We also need to be able to think about how to fulfil our desires. In order to do this, we need to have beliefs about how the world is. So beliefs and desires are reasons for action – either together or individually. My further considerations will not depend on the issue of whether it is the combination of beliefs and desires which forms a reason or action or whether beliefs and desires are individually reasons for action.

Further core components of MPM are the capacity to act in the light of reasons and the capacity to act on the grounds of reasons. The former is the capacity to be aware of one's reasons for action. When a person is aware of their beliefs and desires, they can reflect on them and find some of them to be persuasive. For example, when I claim that someone bought a computer because it had the best price/performance ratio, we mean that they were aware that the computer had the best price/performance ratio and they came to the conclusion that this was the appropriate reason to buy it. Acting on the grounds of reason consists of being motivated by reasons. When I claim that someone bought a computer because it had the best price/performance ratio, I not only mean that they were aware that the computer had the best price/performance ratio and came to the conclusion that this was the appropriate reason to buy it, but also that their action was motivated by this reason.

The distinction between acting in the light of reasons and on the grounds of reasons is useful because sometimes these abilities can come apart. For instance, because some people have access to their beliefs and desires, they are able to appropriately weigh those reasons, but when it comes to actual action, these reasons fail to motivate them. Imagine a person who realizes that the computer has the best price/performance ratio, comes to the conclusion that this is the reason which, for them, trumps other reasons for action, but still buys a different computer – a more expensive and less advanced machine manufactured by a fashionable company.

It is a received view amongst theorists of practical reason that only persons who are capable of acting in the light of reasons and on the grounds of reasons can make genuine decisions. Many thinkers claim that decision making requires the capacity to deliberate about reasons for action and to then find some of them persuasive (Velleman, 1992, p. 466; Wallace, 1999, p. 219).

There is at least one more core component of MPM: the principle of rationality. According to MPM both the capacity to act in the light of reasons and to act on the grounds of reasons are somehow sensitive to this principle. There are numerous incarnations of the principle of rationality and all of them determine how beliefs and desires should be interconnected. For instance, a well-known version of such a principle includes the claim that beliefs form a web which is held together by logical implication (Quine & Ullian, 1978, p. 25). On this view, if we see that a particular sentence is false, we should disbelieve this sentence or change our other beliefs. Being capable of appropriately weighing one's reasons for action requires grasping such principles.

4.5 COGNITIVE SCIENCE AND THE RELATIONSHIP BETWEEN LAW AND FOLK PSYCHOLOGY

Besides the claim that according to the folk-psychological conceptual framework present within law people are practical reasoners, there is perhaps little more that can be said about the relationship between law and FP which would not be controversial. Even so, virtually all of the core components of MPM have been vigorously discussed within philosophy and cognitive science. One of the most important themes of these discussions pertains to the issue of how we should understand these components. As we already know, doubts have been expressed concerning the very existence of intentional states such as beliefs and desires. What is more, some philosophers and scientists claim that our capacities to act in the light of reasons and on the grounds of reasons are significantly limited (Wilson, 2002, pp. 44–64; Wegner, 2002, pp. 2–28). Not to mention the growing literature according to which our minds are not as sensitive to the principle of rationality as is usually assumed (Kahneman, 2011, *passim*). In turn, the very notion of practical reason can be called into question.

As a result, we can differentiate between three stances towards the possible impact of cognitive science on the relationship between law and FP. The three stances are autonomy, revision and integration. Proponents of autonomy claim that no such impact is possible. Revisionists argue that law will change considerably under this scientific pressure. Finally, supporters of integration claim that a third way is possible: that law can absorb much of what cognitive science will throw at it, although some changes in its legal-psychological conceptual framework are to be expected.

We have already mentioned that there are two important concerns pertaining to FP. One is whether people have a theory of mind. The legal variant of this concern is whether the information about the mind stored within law forms a theory. I have answered in the affirmative to this question and so do the proponents of revision and integration. The case is not clear with autonomists. They tend to disagree with this claim, but they usually understand the relevant theory as a set of sentences about unobservable mental entities which describe how the mind operates. But I will attempt to show that their view can be aligned with the 'model' understanding of the theory of mind.

Another important concern pertaining to FP is whether the theory of mind present within law corresponds to reality. Because autonomists disagree with the claim that the information about the mind stored within law forms a theory, for them the question of whether this theory corresponds to reality does not arise (that is, if we agree with their understanding of what the theory of mind consists in). Therefore, this question is the subject matter of the dispute between revisionists and integrationists. Revisionists argue that even if there is some sort of correspondence between FP and reality then it is at best weak. According to revisionists, we may expect that for the purposes of law this correspondence will turn out be too weak for FP to survive without major modifications.

Integrationists argue, on the other hand, that there is a strong correspondence between FP and reality. They think that, at least for the purposes of law, this correspondence is strong enough and we should not expect a revolution in law's outlook on how the mind works. What we should expect are some refinements in the legal conceptual apparatus pertaining to the mind. So, at the bottom, the difference between revisionism and integrationism is a difference in degree rather than in kind.

4.5.1 *Autonomy*

Proponents of the autonomy of the relationship between law and FP in connection to the findings of cognitive science think that lawyers and cognitive scientists are at cross purposes. The latter aim to explain or predict human behaviour in the most comprehensive manner. The former aim to understand behaviour only to the extent of making this understanding appropriate for legal assessment. Understanding behaviour in a legal context is often equated with its rationalization, that is, an explanation which is transparent to reasons. For instance, explaining behaviour by means of an appeal to the activity of the synapses is not transparent to reasons as the person does not make a decision in the light and on the grounds of this activity. Such activity is introspectively inaccessible. Autonomists understand reasons as somehow influencing thought and behaviour, but they think of them as different types of causes in comparison to the causes which feature in empirical explanations. The uniqueness of reasons explanation boils down to the fact that they invoke an understanding of people as rational.

The autonomy view is somewhat popular in the discussion pertaining to the relationship between law and cognitive science. A variant of this position is defended by two legal scholars, Michael Pardo and Dennis Patterson, who discuss 'neurolaw' – an emerging field in the family of legal sciences (Pardo & Patterson, 2013). Proponents of neurolaw argue that cognitive science – especially neuroscience – will have a significant impact on law. But Pardo and Patterson argue that our folk-psychological conceptual framework is independent from scientific findings. Their main argument is that the correct way to use this framework is determined by behavioural criteria (Pardo & Patterson, 2013, p. 4). We know when to ascribe beliefs and desires because we can observe that people behave as if they had beliefs and desires. For instance, when I observe that the person reaches for a bottle of water, opens it and drinks from it I am justified in thinking that they were thirsty and desired to drink some water. Cognitive science, on the other hand, deals with psychological or neurobiological mechanisms which underpin the explained behaviour. By postulating particular psychological or neurobiological mechanisms, we may account for a desire to drink water in scientific terms, but Pardo and Patterson claim that it is literally absurd to ascribe to these mechanisms the desire to drink water. Still, cognitive science can provide evidence that in certain situations some folk-psychological concepts, such as the concepts of belief or desire, apply. Pardo and Patterson do not claim, therefore, that science is irrelevant for the law. There are cases in which it will provide better evidence pertaining to the mental states of the person than the folk-psychological inquiry.

Pardo and Patterson's argument is of an a priori nature: they claim that concepts of intentional states only apply at the level of the whole person. They do not apply at the level of scientific explanation which deals with sub-personal mechanisms operating at the level of the brain. To apply concepts of intentional states at the sub-personal level is to commit a mereological fallacy, that is, to ascribe the features of the whole persons to their parts (e.g. 'A resonator neuron *prefers* inputs having certain frequencies that resonate with the frequency of subthreshold oscillations of the neuron'; Izhkevich, 2007, p. 3). This fallacy is of a logical or conceptual nature.

Pardo and Patterson are right to underscore the importance of precision when psychological predicates are used. Firstly, some cognitive scientists tend to use psychological predicates in a loose manner, especially in those of their works that are aimed at a popular audience (Figdor, 2018). This tends to cause confusion because if psychological vocabulary is used analogically, it is often not clear on what grounds we can use these terms in novel, scientific contexts. It is often left to the reader to conjecture what is the feature of the brain or the mind which justifies the applicability of a particular psychological concept.

What is more, Pardo and Patterson plausibly claim that there is a difference between the folk-psychological level of behaviour explanation and its scientific counterpart. There is something to be said for the fact that behaviour can be explained on various levels of generality – from folk psychological to neurobiological – depending on the needs of the person doing the explaining. As we have seen, different types of behaviour explanations can co-exist and be, at least to some extent, autonomous, and this is a powerful argument for functionalism. That there is such a similarity between functionalism and Pardo and Patterson's position is not a coincidence, because adherents of both positions admit that they have their roots in the Aristotelian idea that things can be classified by what they do (Putnam, 1975, pp. 435–9; Pardo & Patterson, 2013, p. 44). So, in various everyday situations, folk-psychological explanations will suit our needs just fine. That is, we will not require knowledge about the physical nature of intentional states to account for a particular behaviour in folk-psychological terms. To a certain extent, this appears to be the case with behaviour explanations required in the legal context. When we observe that the behaviour of a person does not diverge from a certain standard, from the legal perspective we will be justified in assessing their behaviour with the use of MPM. In such a situation we will not need to inquire into the details of the activity of their mind or brain.

Be that as it may, Pardo and Patterson's position is considerably more at odds with the idea of scientific explanation in comparison to functionalism. This is because their position is paired with the above-mentioned mereological argument, which appears to preclude any changes in our folk-psychological conceptual apparatus under the influence of scientific findings. Functionalism, on the other hand, is open-ended in this regard and most functionalists agree that not only can different levels of explanations co-exist, but also that it is worthwhile to pursue the issue of how phenomena at various levels are related (Marr, 2010).

What is more, despite Pardo and Patterson's rejection of the claim that FP is a theory (Pardo & Patterson, 2013, p. 31), their understanding of what it takes for FP to be a theory of mind is limited. These authors claim that when we use language to mind-read we do not postulate that entities such as beliefs and desires exist. They propose that when we use language to mind-read we are involved in a linguistic practice, not in a theoretical exercise. When we are involved in a linguistic practice, our language is like a tool with which we do things and not describe them. But this is an overly restrictive understanding of what a theoretical exercise amounts to, one reminiscent of what the theory-theorists and simulationists had in mind when they discussed the theory of mind. In line with Pardo and Patterson's account, we can explain the linguistic practices pertaining to FP by postulating that people have a model of the mind, albeit one of a behavioural nature. The model does not postulate that intentional states are real and unobservable entities, but rather that we understand the terms for intentional states behaviourally. So it appears that Pardo and Patterson's account actually allows – or even presupposes – that FP is a theory, albeit a theory of a behavioural nature. But behavioural explanations of the mind lead to many difficulties. Such attempts have been, to a large extent, discredited and superseded by cognitive explanations which include appeals to unobservable entities (Greenwood, 2008). There is also evidence which undermines the claim that our folk-psychological network is insulated from scientific findings. An instructive example of an valuable interaction between FP and cognitive science pertains to the concept of memory.

What is even more interesting is that memory is explicitly discussed by Pardo and Patterson in the context of their main thesis (Pardo & Patterson, 2013, pp. 102–5). They claim that it is nonsensical to ascribe memories to the brain, since only people can remember. But the facts diverge from this conceptual conclusion, as it was the study of brain lesions which led scientists to differentiate between different types of memory, such as semantic, episodic long-term, short-term and working memory. Scientific evidence suggests that distinct parts of the brain are correlated with these types of memories. Memory provides a revealing example of the explanatory strategy of contemporary science. It is not that the folk-psychological concepts are explained away – for they are still prominent in the mechanical explanations of behaviour – but they are developed according to the evidence provided by science. Such conceptual changes pertaining to memory are not at the margins of interest for lawyers. The assessment of our capacities for remembering can play a crucial role in a legal setting. This is because these conceptual changes impact MPM – in particular they impact our understanding of the abilities to act in the light of and on the grounds of reasons. From this perspective, Pardo and Patterson's conceptual conservatism appears misguided.

In general, we should always be wary of a priori considerations which conclude with claims about the boundaries of scientific explanation. It has become the norm that psychological predicates – such as preferring, interpreting or choosing – are used in novel ways to describe parts of the brain or even particular neurons. It happens not only in popular scientific writing, but also in peer-reviewed papers – including Nobel-prize-winning works (Figdor, 2018, p. 94). But if we agree with Pardo and Patterson, then it appears that we have to conclude that the growth of scientific knowledge about the mind is paired with the growing conceptual confusion of cognitive scientists as to the object of their inquiry: and this is implausible. We associate scientific developments with an increase in our understanding of the world, not a decrease in it.

It appears to be the case that with the evolution of cognitive science new rules of semantic applicability for FP terms can emerge which do not pertain to the capacities which make a human being a person. The novel usage of psychological predicates does not have to be ad hoc. It may be grounded in discoveries of both the qualitative and quantitative similarities between persons and sub-personal phenomena (Figdor, 2018, pp. 12–60). For instance, it has been proposed that creatures which are able to learn by trial and error have minds (Dennett, 1996, p. 92). Such learning consists of the reinforcement of actions paired with favourable consequences. What is interesting is that organisms very different from humans can learn in this way. For example, pigeons can be trained to press a bar to receive food. It does not seem to be absurd to describe such pigeons as remembering how they should behave and choosing the correct behaviour, for they are able to differentiate between important features of their external environment, albeit to a lesser extent than we are.

4.5.2 Revision

Revisionists argue that FP is, at least to a large extent, a false theory of mind. What is more, its falsity will have a serious impact on law. This position is in many ways similar to the already mentioned eliminativism. The difference is that proponents of revision do not argue for a complete elimination of the folk-psychological conceptual apparatus from law. An example of revisionism can be found in a paper by two psychologists, Joshua Greene and Jonathan Cohen (2004).

Greene and Cohen raise two important issues in the context of the relation between the legal-psychological conceptual framework and the conceptual apparatus of neuroscience. The first is that the understanding of the mind by neuroscientists is mechanistic and thus incompatible with FP. The second is that this incompatibility may have serious implications for law. These implications are not direct, however, but mediated through the impact which neuroscience may have on our understanding of agency and responsibility. To explain why neuroscience will have an impact on our concepts of agency and responsibility, we can refer to the dependence of these concepts on MPM and the fact that it is MPM which is threatened by neuroscience. Although Greene and Cohen do not refer to MPM, their discussion explicitly pertains to the threat neuroscience poses to our self-understanding as being capable of rational choices which are grounded in our beliefs and desires (Greene & Cohen, 2004, p. 1781). Agency depends on MPM because agents are just entities, the behaviour of which can be adequately explained by reference to their reasons for action, that is, their beliefs and desires. So agents should have minds which are explained by invoking MPM. And responsibility depends on MPM because only agents can be responsible for their behaviour.

The driving idea behind mechanistic explanation – preferred by cognitive scientists to explain the sub-personal phenomena – is that complex phenomena can be explained by reference to how their parts work (Craver, 2007, pp. 2–9). It is a type of causal explanation, that is, mechanisms are understood to be physical phenomena that consist of parts coming into contact with each other. As our scientific knowledge grows, we find more basic, simpler mechanisms which allow us to explain more complex mechanisms. For instance, in neuroscience, which is perhaps a paradigmatic example of a mechanistic science, the brain is understood to be a complex mechanism. Its activity is explained at various, interconnected levels. The topmost level is that of the whole brain, and then there are the cellular, molecular, and atomic levels. Revisionists understand this explanatory strategy as posing a direct threat to FP because they think that it will considerably limit the explanatory range of FP or even make FP explanatorily idle (Greene & Cohen, 2004, pp. 1781–2).

However, the greater reliability and precision of scientific explanations in comparison to FP is not the only reason why we should expect that FP will lose its grip on law. Greene and Cohen also argue that scientific evidence suggests that FP explanations are unreliable to begin with. In particular, they refer to the work in cognitive science which suggests that FP behaviour explanations are confabulatory (Wegner, 2002, p. 146). That is, at least sometimes when people provide such explanations of their behaviour, these reports are false. Notice that confabulations are not merely false memories. Confabulations are false beliefs which tend to be made up on the spot and have very little or nothing to do with actual memories. For instance, it may seem to us that we consciously will our actions and it is our conscious will which is causally responsible for these actions, but – in reality – the actual causal mechanism responsible for the action operates without us being aware of it. The existence of such confabulations may be used as an example that FP makes empirical commitments – for example, that we consciously will our actions and it is our conscious will which is causally responsible for these actions – and that these commitments may be false.

What are the revolutionary consequences for law which such empirical findings may bring? Greene and Cohen claim, for instance, that such findings will change the way we think about punishment. The change will consist of abandoning the retributivist justification of punishment – according to which we punish criminals because they deserve it – in favour of its consequentialist counterpart. According to the consequentialist proposal, we should punish criminals because of the benefits which the punishment brings. The received view is that the retributivist – to justify that people deserve punishment – needs a strong understanding of our capacities of practical deliberation. According to the strong understanding of the capacity of practical deliberation, we have the capacity to weigh reasons for action and influence the desires which motivate us to act. This strong understanding of practical reason is at odds with the scientific outlook on persons, which highlights the great extent to which people are determined in their actions. On the other hand, the consequentialist needs only a weak understanding of our capacities of practical deliberation, according to which we have the capacity to weigh reasons for action, but we cannot influence the desires which motivate us to act. On the weak understanding of practical reason, the weights of the reasons are already assigned when we reason what to do. This notion of practical reason appears to be more in line with scientific evidence.

Revisionism is a tempting position towards the FP–law–cognitive science relationship. An overview of the dispute pertaining to this relationship reveals that revisionism is perhaps the most tempting for cognitive scientists or scientifically oriented thinkers. They are probably the most aware of the extent to which our common-sensical understanding of the world – including our minds – is at odds with how the world actually is. And, in connection to the scientific understanding of the mind, there are serious doubts pertaining to the usefulness of FP. But it appears that revisionists — by undermining the usefulness of FP for law — do not fully appreciate the difference between the scientist's pursuit of theoretical knowledge and the practical goals of the participant in the legal practice.

The consequences of law's practical nature for the FP–law–cognitive science relationship may be illustrated by underscoring the fact that law is an artefact. This artefact is designed to influence behaviour. On the whole, the more efficient law is in influencing behaviour, the better an artefact it is. This observation is important for our purposes because investigations into artificial systems lead to the conclusion that in many cases whether the artefact will achieve its goal depends on only a few characteristics of the environment in which it operates (Simon, 1996, p. 8). This is especially the case with well-designed artefacts which are homeostatic, that is, they are to a large extent insulated from the environment. Homeostatic systems maintain an invariant relation between the artefact and its goal, which is 'independent of variations over a wide range of parameters that characterize the outer environment' (Simon, 1996, p. 20). One could argue that particular legal systems are homeostatic in this sense as they appear to achieve their goal of influencing behaviour despite the fact that their outer environments vary. The variations pertain, for instance, to the moral, political, religious or social outlooks of the people whose behaviour the law influences. This suggests that law can be similarly insulated from the variations in the scientific environment in which it operates — although the extent of this insulation is a matter of dispute. But FP which is present in law — particularly MPM, which forms its core — seems to be flexible enough to withhold a lot of scientific pressure. This is perhaps due to the fact that MPM latches onto only the most general features of behaviour and leaves unexplained many of its details which are of interest for scientists. To substantiate this claim, one can refer to the above-mentioned considerations of the functionalists.

What is also characteristic of revisionism is that its proponents tend to overstate the consequences of empirical findings. Let us assess one broad type of such evidence: the findings put forward by Daniel Wegner in his much-discussed book *The Illusion of Conscious Will* (Wegner, 2002). What Wegner claims is understood by revisionists such as Greene and Cohen as a powerful argument against FP. In general, Wegner's goal is to argue for the claim that our conscious willing is epiphenomenal, that is, it lacks any causal role in how the action is produced. This claim is at odds with MPM, as one of the components of this model is the capacity to act on the grounds of reasons. So MPM entails that our conscious deliberations causally influence our actions. To reach his goal, Wegner discusses empirical evidence for the hypothesis that our conscious experience of action initiation and the actual action initiation may come apart. That is, we can act without experiencing action initiation and we can experience action initiation when we do not act. Wegner thinks that the evidence for this dissociation undermines the claim that our conscious deliberations have a direct causal influence on our actions.

But this is too hasty. First of all, the dissociation of two cognitive systems does not entail that there is no causal connection between them. For instance, our perceptual systems are sometimes dissociated from what we take ourselves to perceive. If I take my hand from a bowl of cold water, a warm object will feel cool to my touch. But this dissociation should not lead me to the conclusion that there is no causal connection between what I perceive and what I experience. Other things being equal, if I take an object to be warm, it will, in fact, be warm. Rather, the evidence which Wegner puts forward suggests that sometimes there is no causal connection between the experience of action initiation and actual action initiation.

This leads us to another issue pertaining to the evidence for the above-mentioned dissociation: to what extent it undermines the causal connection between the experience of action initiation and actual action initiation. Despite Wegner's fascinating examples as to when this causal connection appears to be broken – such as hypnosis, Ouija-board spelling, automatic writing or various psychological disorders –the cases in which there is no such connection appear to be rare occurrences. What is more, some even suggest that Wegner's account of the experience of conscious will entails that such experiences will be veridical (Bayne & Pacherie, 2015, p. 226). On this account, people experience themselves as causally influencing their actions when the contents of their thoughts prior to these actions are consistent with these actions and when they are not aware of any influences on their action which would undermine their agency. But this condition is also satisfied when people's practical deliberations do, in fact, influence their actions.

The last difficulty for revisionists such as Greene and Cohen is that there appear to be limitations to the possible changes in our understanding of agency and responsibility. These limitations are not conceptual – as the autonomist would like to think – but empirical, that is, they pertain to our biological nature. Namely, it is the understanding of persons through the lens of MPM which justifies praising or blaming them for their actions. Only the doings of agents capable of having good or bad intentions, and correct or incorrect beliefs appear to be the appropriate target of moral evaluation. This is because we are moved, so to speak, by behaviour explanations which cite reasons in a way that allows these behaviours to be evaluated. And we are not moved in such a way by behaviour explanations citing, for example, biological causes. Moral emotions appear to play an important role in determining whether we find particular actions good or bad (Strawson, 1962, p. 6). In light of this, the malleability of our emotional dispositions limits the malleability of our understanding of agency or responsibility. But emotional dispositions are not something which we can change freely.

4.5.3 Integration

A person with an integrationist view on the impact of scientific findings on the relationship between law and FP will resist the autonomists' claim, according to which anyone involved in the project of explaining how facts about the organization of behaviourally complex organisms – and facts about our actual practices of interpretation and ascription of propositional attitudes are connected – is deeply mistaken. They will also oppose revisionists' doubts as to the overall usefulness of FP for law. They will think that behaviour explanations put forward by FP are, in many ways, as important as scientific explanations of behaviour – particularly for legal purposes. The main difficulty for this view is to find a solution to the problem of how these two types of explanation can be interconnected. Revisionists will tend to resist searching for a solution to this problem, because they will regard any attempts to find the conceptual link between FP and cognitive science as desperate. Integrationists, on the other hand, will not only think that finding such a link is possible in principle, but also that to find it, one needs to look at the available evidence.

One of the proponents of integrationism is Stephen Morse. He claims that despite the fact that the FP presupposed by law is, in principle, open for revision, we should not expect significant changes within law from scientific findings pertaining to how the mind functions (Morse, 2015, p. 42). His reason for this claim is that, first of all, with the current state of our scientific knowledge about the mind or the brain it is difficult to say anything precise about the possible impact of cognitive science on law. For instance, cognitive science is interested in the features of mechanisms underlying human mental capacities as such, whereas law is usually interested in the mental capacities of a particular person. It is not obvious how much can we say about the causes of a particular behaviour on the basis of a more general scientific evidence pertaining to the whole group of people of which the particular person is a member.

But Morse also entertains a more general and future-oriented threat to the law's folk-psychological outlook of the person. He notices that there is a tension between the mechanistic explanation of the mind and the brain provided by cognitive science and the FP explanation of behaviour. He claims that it is difficult for the former to account for acting on the basis of reasons, which is the mode of explanation distinctive to FP. Still, he remains optimistic about the future of FP within law. He thinks it is superior to cognitive science in accounting for the features of behaviour which matter for law, that is, for the evaluation of behaviour in terms of how it is related to our values. As we have noticed, such evaluations make sense if we view people through the lens of MPM – as agents acting on reasons.

The argument underlining the role of MPM in connecting behaviour explanation to values is a powerful one. It indicates how our theoretical concerns pertaining to knowing how the world is can be limited by our practical concerns pertaining to what we should do. This observation is important for our purposes, as the relationship between law and values is rich and complex. It is difficult to deny that not only does moral evaluation often play a role in legal evaluation, but that it often should play such a role. So if we adopt the mechanistic account of behaviour – which is often understood not to be transparent to reasons – we will cripple our moral and legal evaluation practices.

But there is a substantial argument against integrationism. Namely, the revisionist will claim that the integrationist puts too much hope in the usefulness of FP. The revisionist will claim that the evidence for what our practical deliberations look like is, to a large extent, introspective and that such evidence is famously unreliable (Wegner, 2002, *passim*). Integrationists reason as follows: it is clear that I sometimes reason what to do and my reasonings influence my doings. Others behave similarly to me, so most probably they also reason what to do and their reasonings influence their doings. But, as we have noticed, it is not at all clear to what extent my reasonings influence my doings. As a consequence, it is not clear to what extent others' reasonings influence their doings. Not to mention the issue that it is not at all clear to what extent our practical considerations are, in fact, rational. It is perhaps true that, at least on the basis of the current scientific evidence, we are unable to limit MPM to a great extent, but we may expect that we will be able to do so in the future.

The integrationist will agree with the revisionist that law will change under scientific pressure, but they will also think that these changes will not be revolutionary. They will think this because they will view FP as getting important things right about how the mind works. But if FP gets something right about how the mind works, then FP should not be autonomous of cognitive science. That is, if FP makes empirical commitments and these empirical commitments – to an important extent – hold, then we should expect that these commitments can be translated to the language of cognitive science. So the challenge for the integrationist is to put their name to the test and to propose how FP could be integrated with cognitive science. If such an integration is impossible, the tension between FP and cognitive science will play into revisionist hands.

Fortunately for the integrationist, there appears to be some evidence at least for a local integration of FP and cognitive science. We have already mentioned how scientific findings influenced the changes to the folk-psychological concept of memory. Similar changes appear to be taking place in regard to the folk-psychological concept of belief. The received view pertaining to beliefs is that children younger than four years old do not understand what beliefs are, and there is a large body of empirical evidence for this claim. Much of this evidence comes from studies on false-belief tasks, yet recently it has been suggested that even children younger than two years old behave as if they understood what beliefs are (Onishi & Baillargeon, 2005, p. 256). This study was based on a non-linguistic version of the false-belief task, focused on measuring the eye movement of participating children. This evidence has led some researchers to conclude that children younger than two are able to track such simple, lower-level, non-linguistic belief-like states (Apperly & Butterfill, 2009, pp. 961–3). What is more, some researchers think that when the children reach the age of four, the belief-like tracking system does not transform into a system tracking complex, higher-level, and linguistic beliefs. Instead, both systems remain operative. The consequence of this for our understanding of belief is that we should differentiate between two types of intentional states which track truth, since they have different features and different consequences for action (Gendler, 2008, pp. 637–45). But FP treats both state types as one and the same type of state, that is, belief.

What does the integrationist have in mind when they claim that cognitive science will change law, but the changes in question will be moderate? For instance, they might think that the changes will pertain to some conceptual tools which we use to assess legal responsibility. According to one such proposal, the so-called 'reasonable person standard' – used to determine negligence in criminal and tort law – is a good candidate for such a modification (Dahan-Katz, 2013, pp. 148–52). The reasonable person standard consists in hypothesizing what a hypothetical reasonable man would do in the situation of the person whose legal responsibility is at issue. The problem is that the capacities for practical deliberation of the model person – as it is constructed by particular judges – may be superlative in comparison to the capacities for practical deliberation of the person whose legal responsibility is at issue. In such cases, law seems to break the 'ought implies can' principle, according to which we have a legal obligation to perform an action only if it is possible for us to perform this action. Traditionally, this objection has been countered by stating that only in the case of the unfortunate few – who are, in fact, unable to reach the expected standard in their practical deliberations – is this principle broken. But the empirical science suggests that the limitations in our reasoning are far greater than we ordinarily think. So it might be the case that more than the unfortunate few are negatively affected by use of the reasonable person standard. This calls for a revision of how this standard is used in legal practice.

4.6 CONCLUSION

The discussion about the law–FP–cognitive science relationship is still in its infancy and there are many problems which remain unresolved. Some of them are of a philosophical nature – such as the ontological status of the entities postulated by FP – and as such they may be particularly difficult to solve. But there are also problems in this area which seem to be more in our grasp, such as the cognitive and biological machinery underpinning FP. We should expect that as our scientific knowledge about these issues grows, it will enable us to see the philosophical issues pertaining to FP in a more nuanced and insightful way. This should, in turn, lead to a better assessment of the impact of these issues on law.

As for the influence of cognitive science on the future of the relationship between law and FP, at the moment it is difficult, if not outright impossible, to outline its contours in any detail. So we should take the views presented above – that is, autonomy, revision and integration – with a pinch of salt and remember that their claims hinge, to a large extent, on the future development of our scientific knowledge about the mind. In particular, they hinge on the extent of the actual discrepancy between the scientific and the folk-psychological understanding of ourselves. This variable is perhaps the most important one within the law–FP–cognitive science framework, but also the most difficult to speculate about. Yet if we decide to entertain the risky speculation about what the future may hold for the law–FP–cognitive science framework, I think that we will continue to observe the growing, albeit piecemeal, influence of cognitive science on the folk-psychological content within law.

REFERENCES

Alces, P. (2018). *The Moral Conflict of Law and Neuroscience*. Chicago and London: The University of Chicago Press.
Alexy, R. (1989). *A Theory of Legal Argumentation*. Oxford: Clarendon.
Apperly, I., & Butterfill, S. (2009). Do Humans Have Two Systems to Track Beliefs and Belief-Like States? *Psychological Review* 116(4), 953–70.
Aristotle. (2000). *Nicomachean Ethics*. Cambridge: Cambridge University Press.
Bayne, T., & Pacherie, E. (2015). Consciousness and Agency. In J. Clausen & N. Levy (eds.), *Handbook of Neuroethics*. Dordrecht: Springer, pp. 211–30.
Bertea, S. (2015). A Foundation for the Conception of Law as Practical Reason. *Law and Philosophy* 34, 55–88.
Churchland, P. (1981). Eliminative Materialism and the Propositional Attitudes. *Journal of Philosophy* 78, 67–90.
Craver, C. (2007).*Explaining the Brain: Mechanisms and the Mosaic Unity of Neuroscience*. Oxford: Oxford University Press.
Dahan-Katz, L. (2013). The Implications of Heuristics and Biases Research on Moral and Legal Responsibility: A Case Against the Reasonable Person Standard. In N. Vincent (ed.), *Neuroscience and Legal Responsibility*. Oxford: Oxford University Press.
Davidson, D. (1984). *Inquiries into Truth and Interpretation*. Oxford: Oxford University Press.
Dennett, D. (1978a). Intentional systems. In D. Dennett, *Brainstorms*. Montgomery, VT: Bradford, pp. 3–22.
Dennett, D. (1978b). Beliefs about Beliefs. *Behavioral and Brain Sciences* 1, 568–70.
Dennett, D. (1991). Real Patterns. *Journal of Philosophy* 88, 27–51.
Dennett, D. (1996). *Kinds of Minds: Toward an Understanding of Consciousness*. New York: Basic Books.
Figdor, C. (2018). *Pieces of Mind: The Proper Domain of Psychological Predicates*. Oxford: Oxford University Press.
Fodor, J. (1987). *Psychosemantics*, Cambridge, MA: MIT Press.
Gendler, T. (2008). Alief and Belief. *The Journal of Philosophy* 105(10), 634–63.
Godfrey-Smith, P. (2005). Folk Psychology as a Model. *Philosophers' Imprint* 5(6), 1–16.
Goldman, A. (2006). *Simulating Minds: The Philosophy, Psychology, and Neuroscience of Mindreading*. Oxford: Oxford University Press.
Gopnik, A., Meltzoff, A., & Kuhl, P. (1999). *The Scientist in the Crib: What Early Learning Tells Us About the Mind*. New York: HarperCollins.
Greene, J., & Cohen, J. (2004). For the Law, Neuroscience Changes Nothing and Everything. *Philosophical Transactions of the Royal Society of London* 359, 1775–85.
Greenwood, J. (2008). *A Conceptual History of Psychology*. New York: McGraw-Hill.

Humphrey, N. (1976). *The Social Function of Intellect*. In P. P. G. Bateson & R. A. Hinde (eds.), *Growing Points in Ethology*. Cambridge: Cambridge University Press, pp. 303–17.

Izhikevich, E. (2007). *Dynamical Systems in Neuroscience: The Geometry of Excitability and Bursting*. Cambridge, MA and London: MIT Press.

Kahneman, D. (2011). *Thinking, Fast and Slow*. New York: Farrar, Straus and Giroux.

Knobe, J. (2005). Theory of Mind and Moral Cognition: Exploring the Connections. *Trends in Cognitive Sciences* 9(8), 357–9.

Knobe, J. (2014). Free Will and the Scientific Vision. In E. Machery & E. O'Neill (eds.), *Current Controversies in Experimental Philosophy*. New York and London: Routledge, pp. 69–85.

Lewis, D. (1972). Psychophysical and Theoretical Identifications. *Australasian Journal of Philosophy* 3(50), 249–58.

Maibom, H. (2003). The Mindreader and the Scientist. *Mind & Language* 18(3), 296–315.

Malle, B. (2004). *How the Mind Explains Behavior: Folk Explanations, Meaning and Social Interaction*. Cambridge, MA: MIT Press.

Malle, B., & Nelson, S. (2003). Judging Mens Rea: The Tension between Folk Concepts and Legal Concepts of Intentionality. *Behavioral Sciences and the Law* 21(5), 563–80.

Marr, D. (2010). *Vision: A Computational Investigation into the Human Representation and Processing of Visual Information*. Cambridge, MA: MIT Press.

Marshall, J. (1968). *Intention in Law and Society*. New York: Funk and Wagnall.

Mollo, D. (2017). Content Pragmatism Defended. *Topoi*, https://doi.org/10.1007/s11245-017-9504-6.

Morse, S. (2015). Criminal Law and Common Sense: An Essay on the Perils and Promise of Neuroscience. *Faculty Scholarship*. Paper 1609. http://scholarship.law.upenn.edu/faculty_scholarship/1609.

Nichols, S., & Stich, S. (2003). *Mindreading: An Integrated Account of Pretence, Self-Awareness, and Understanding Other Minds*. Oxford: Clarendon Press.

Onishi, K. H., & Baillargeon, R. (2005). Do 15-Month-Old Infants Understand False Beliefs? *Science* 308(5719), 255–8.

Pardo, M., & Patterson, D. (2013). *Minds, Brains and Law. The Conceptual Foundations of Law and Neuroscience*. Oxford: Oxford University Press.

Premack, D., & Woodruff, G. (1978). Does the Chimpanzee Have a Theory of Mind? *Behavioral and Brain Sciences* 1, 515–26.

Putnam, H. (1975). *Mind, Language and Reality*. Cambridge: Cambridge University Press.

Quine, W. V. O., & Ullian, J. S. (1978). *The Web of Belief*. New York: McGraw-Hill Education.

Sellars, W. (1956). Empiricism and the Philosophy of Mind. *Minnesota Studies in the Philosophy of Science* 1, 253–329.

Shapiro, S. (2002). Laws, Plans, and Practical Reason. *Legal Theory* 8(1), 387–441.

Simon, H. (1996). *The Sciences of the Artificial*. Cambridge, MA: MIT Press.

Strawson, P. (1962). Freedom and Resentment. *Proceedings of the British Academy* 48, 1–25.

Tomasello, M. (2003). *Cultural Origins of Human Cognition*. Cambridge, MA: Harvard University Press.

Velleman, J. (1992). What Happens When Someone Acts? *Mind* 101(403), 461–81.

Wallace, R. J. (1999). Three Conceptions of Rational Agency. *Ethical Theory and Moral Practice* 2(3), 217–42.

Wegner, D. (2002). *The Illusion of Conscious Will*. Cambridge, MA: Bradford Books.

Wilkes, K. (1984). Pragmatics in Science and Theory in Common Sense. *Inquiry* 27(4), 339–61.
Wilson, T. (2002). *Strangers to Ourselves: Discovering the Adaptive Unconsciousness*. Cambridge, MA and London: The Belknap Press.
Wimmer, H., & Perner, J. (1983). Beliefs about Beliefs: Representation and Constraining Function of Wrong Beliefs in Young Children's Understanding of Deception. *Cognition* 13, 103–28.

5

Law and the Cognitive Science of Ordinary Concepts

Kevin Tobia

5.1 INTRODUCTION

Folk psychology is at the root of 'the legal understanding of the human mind – that is, how the human mind is conceptualized within, for example, criminal law, tort law, contract law or jurisprudence'. This is the central thesis of Professor Kurek's insightful chapter on law, cognitive science, and folk psychology (Kurek, Chapter 4 this volume).

What is 'folk psychology?' In Kurek's terms, it is 'the common-sense understanding of the human mind'. Thus, the claim is that the common-sense understanding of the mind is central to law's understanding of the mind. I will refer to this as the *folk law thesis*.

This chapter agrees wholeheartedly. In fact, I contend that the folk law thesis extends more broadly: Laypeople's common-sense understandings, or 'ordinary concepts', are at the root of *many* important legal concepts – ones about the mind, like INTENT and KNOWLEDGE, but also a host of other central legal concepts including CONSENT, REASONABLENESS and CAUSATION.

As a complement to the preceding chapter, this chapter presents some very recent empirical work in cognitive science that suggests that ordinary concepts are importantly related to legal concepts. The broader conclusion is that cognitive scientists can make significant progress in understanding legal cognition – and law itself – by studying the ordinary cognition of people with no special legal training.

To build its case, this chapter proceeds with several examples. First, it introduces recent empirical work that supports the narrow version of the folk law thesis (about folk psychology and law). Recent studies have found that ordinary people track law's subtle distinction between knowledge and recklessness, suggesting an important relationship between the legal concepts of KNOWLEDGE and RECKLESSNESS and the ordinary ones. As another example, recent work suggests that the legal concept of acting INTENTIONALLY shares several (surprising) features of the ordinary concept.

The next three sections argue that the folk law thesis extends beyond folk psychology. Recent studies of CONSENT, REASONABLENESS and CAUSATION reveal surprising ways in which the legal concept flows from the corresponding ordinary concept. The final section concludes by indicating further examples in support of the folk law thesis and raising questions for future research.

5.2 FOLK PSYCHOLOGY: KNOWLEDGE, RECKLESSNESS, INTENT

Various legal rules and standards turn on the attribution of mental states: from capacity requirements in contract law, to the division between intentional and non-intentional torts, to criminal law *mens rea*. Across these diverse legal domains, key concepts include KNOWLEDGE, RECKLESSNESS and INTENT. Recent work in psychology and cognitive science has discovered various important features of the corresponding *ordinary* concepts, such as features of the non-legal concept of INTENT (e.g. Malle & Nelson, 2003). The folk law thesis contends that the legal concept shares some of those features. But this is an open empirical question: Does the legal concept share features of the ordinary one?

One recent set of studies assessed this question with respect to the concept of acting intentionally. This is a concept that plays a role in criminal law and tort law, amongst other legal areas. Building on work on the ordinary concept of intentional action (e.g. Knobe, 2003), Kneer reports that ordinary people are sensitive to the *severity* of a side effect when judging whether it was produced intentionally.[1] Imagine that someone performs an act that produces a good consequence C and bad side effect S, but the person did not *desire* for S to occur; Did they intentionally cause S? Kneer and Bourgeois-Gironde (2017) find that people judge that S was intentionally produced as the badness of S becomes more severe.

In an experiment, Kneer and Bourgeois-Gironde (2017, p. 143) presented one of two versions of an outcome (minor or severe) to a sample of thirty-two French judges:

> The mayor of a small beach town is approached by his advisor who says: 'We could build a new highway connection. This would make car traffic much more efficient. However, there would be [minor/severe] adverse effects on the environment. During construction, the animals in the construction zone will [be disturbed/die]. This is [only temporary/not a temporary condition], [everything goes/things will not go] back to normal once construction is finished.' The mayor responds: 'I don't care at all about the environment. All I care about is making car traffic as efficient as possible. Let's build the new highway connection.' They build the new highway connection. The animals in the zone are [temporarily disturbed/die]. [Everything goes/Things do not go] back to normal after construction is finished.

In both cases, the judges were asked to rate whether the mayor *intentionally* harmed the environment. When the outcome was more severe, mean ratings were significantly higher (almost 2 points on a 7-point scale; Cohen's d = 1.06).

---

[1] See M. Kneer (n.p.), 'Guilty Minds and Biased Minds' (unpublished article).

Kneer and Bourgeois-Gironde interpret this as evidence that legal judgements of intentional action are severity-sensitive. If this severity-sensitivity feature is part of the concept,[2] this finding counts in favour of the folk law thesis. The ordinary concept of acting intentionally is severity-sensitive, and the legal concept inherits this property.[3]

As another example, consider the subtle legal distinction between knowledge and recklessness in criminal law. In the United States, criminal culpability requires proof of the *actus reas* (broadly speaking, the act requirement) and *mens rea* (broadly speaking, the mental-state requirement). *Mens rea* is the difference between accidental killing and various degrees of criminal homicide. And *mens rea* turns, in large part, on the application of legal concepts like KNOWLEDGE and RECKLESSNESS. For example, many state criminal codes follow the Model Penal Code, which distinguishes between four different mental states, of increasing culpability: negligence, recklessness, knowledge and purposefulness. Different guidelines and laws elaborate these legal concepts in various ways, but a key question remains: Are these entirely distinctive legal concepts, or do they in some way draw from the corresponding folk concepts (e.g. the ordinary concept of KNOWLEDGE or RECKLESSNESS)?

Vilares et al. (2017) set out to address this question with an impressive neuroscientific experiment, evaluating whether attributions of knowledge and recklessness are associated with different brain states and whether one can predict (with only brain-imaging data) which of those two states a person is in. They conducted an fMRI study involving a 'contraband scenario'. Participants evaluated different scenarios in which they could carry a suitcase, which might have contraband in it, through a security checkpoint. The probability that the suitcase had contraband varied across different scenarios – in some scenarios participants were completely sure that the suitcase had contraband ('knowledge condition') and in others, there was merely a risk that the suitcase had contraband ('recklessness conditions').

The experiment indicated that participants' evaluation of the two states (knowledge, recklessness) were associated with different brain regions. Moreover, Vilares et al. could use the fMRI data to predict (out of sample) which scenario participants faced, at rates greater than chance. This provides evidence that the legal concepts are, in part, running parallel to an ordinary distinction (but cf. Shen et al., 2011). After all, the fMRI participants had not been to law school or otherwise learned about the *legal* concepts of KNOWLEDGE and RECKLESSNESS. Those legal concepts are, at the very least, sensible to laypeople in a way that calls for explanation. One natural explanation is that the legal concepts of KNOWLEDGE and RECKLESSNESS are actually founded on the ordinary (or folk-psychological) notions.

---

[2] Kneer and Bourgeois-Gironde interpret severity-sensitivity as a *bias*; on their view, the correct application of INTENT would not be sensitive to severity. Whether this finding reflects a bias or conceptual competence is a matter of great debate (cf. Knobe, 2003), and it cannot be treated fully here. Note, however, that even on the bias account, there is a striking similarity between ordinary and legal cognition.

[3] But see Tobia 'Experimental Jurisprudence' (unpublished manuscript). https://papers.ssrn.com/sol3/papers.cfm?abstract_id=3680107

Both of these studies provide some initial evidence for the folk law thesis: Legal concepts share some of the features of the corresponding ordinary concept, including surprising and subtle features. The next three sections consider the folk law thesis outside of the realm of folk psychology (e.g. KNOWLEDGE). It turns to recent work on the concept of CONSENT, REASONABLENESS and CAUSATION.

5.3 CONSENT

In law, 'consent turns a trespass into a dinner party; a battery into a handshake; a theft into a gift; an invasion of privacy into an intimate moment; a commercial appropriation of name and likeness into a biography' (Hurd, 1996). Legal consent is, in Hurd's words, a 'magical' concept. But is it an entirely *distinctive* legal creation? Or, are some of legal consent's features drawn from the ordinary concept?

An impressive experimental study of the ordinary notion of consent uncovered some surprising features (Sommers, in press; see also Sommers & Furth-Matzkin, 2019). One is that laypeople view consent as consistent with some forms of deception. In an experiment, Sommers (in press) provided participants with scenarios in which a person agrees to do something after being deceived about an important aspect of the arrangement.:

> Ellen and Frank meet in a night class and have several dates. Ellen makes it clear that she refuses to sleep with married men. When asked, Frank lies and says that he is not married. Ellen agrees to sleep with Frank.

Respondents evaluated a consent statement, 'Did Ellen give consent to sleep with Frank?', on a scale from 0 ('Not at all') to 100 ('Very much'). Average ratings were about 77, and only 12 per cent of participants gave a rating lower than 50 (the scale midpoint).

Some philosophers may find this unsurprising: Consent is referentially opaque. As Onora O'Neill (2001) put it: 'The central philosophical weakness of relying on informed consent ... is that consent is a propositional attitude, so referentially opaque: consent is given to specific propositions describing limited aspects of a situation, and does not transfer even to closely related propositions.'

If consent were referentially opaque, that would lead to well-known substitution problems. For example, consider *belief*: It can be true that (a) Lois Lane *believes* Superman is strong and also that (b) Lois Lane *does not believe* Clark Kent is strong (even though Superman and Clark Kent are the same person). In a similar way, perhaps, Ellen might (a) *consent* to sleep with Frank but (b) *not consent* to sleep with a married man (even though Frank is a married man). Of course, an important question remains: what explains which aspects are consented to and which are not?

Sommers (in press) argues that part of the answer here involves essentialism: consent covers the more essential elements, but not more tangentially related elements. Intriguingly, Sommers argues, this folk 'commonsense consent' actually tracks the *legal* distinction between fraud in the factum and fraud in the inducement. The former pertains to the nature of the activity itself, while the latter pertains to more unrelated or inessential matters. Here again, this would be consistent with the folk law thesis: the legal concept of CONSENT inherits important properties from the ordinary concept. If so, this supports a surprising implication: Further empirical study of the *ordinary* notion of consent can actually provide deep insight into the legal concept.

5.4 REASONABLENESS

As further evidence for the folk law thesis, consider the concept of REASONABLENESS. From the first year of American law school, torts classes ask what kind of precautions would be taken by 'the reasonable person'; contracts classes estimate the 'reasonable time' in which a contract offer remains open; criminal law considers what 'reasonable provocations' would mitigate murder to manslaughter; and constitutional law elaborates 'reasonable suspicions' and 'reasonable expectations of privacy'.

So what is reasonableness? A series of experimental studies assessed how ordinary people – that is, potential jurors – make reasonableness judgements. Drawing on important work on the cognitive science of NORMALITY (Bear & Knobe, 2017), Tobia (2018) predicted that laypeople apply reasonableness as a hybrid notion, one that reflects a mixture of statistical and prescriptive norms. For example, tort law decisions about 'reasonable care' reflect both norms about *typical* care and norms about *ideal* care. Law's so-called 'reasonable person', is neither the statistically average person, nor the perfectly ideal person; rather, they are a mixture of both.

To assess this hypothesis, experimental participants were assigned to one of three groups: average, ideal or reasonable. In the average group, participants provided their judgement of the 'average' quantity across various domains. For example, they were asked to provide their view of the 'average' number of weeks that a criminal trial is delayed, the 'average' number of days that a contract offer remains open, and so on. The 'ideal' group provided their views of ideal quantities, for example the 'ideal' number of weeks that a criminal trial is delayed. The 'reasonable' group answered what is a 'reasonable' quantity for each domain. Across various domains, a striking pattern emerged. The mean reasonable quantity was typically intermediate between divergent average and ideal quantities. For example, the reasonable number of weeks' delay before a criminal trial (10) fell between the judged average (17) and ideal (7). These findings suggest that reasonableness judgments reflect both statistical and prescriptive considerations.

The experiments suggest that the ordinary concept of REASONABLENESS has this 'hybrid' feature, but does the legal concept? Legal historian Simon Stern (2017) argues that the true origin of the 'reasonable person' reflects such a 'blend of normative and descriptive features'. In legal philosophy, there has been much debate *between* purely descriptive and purely normative views of reasonableness (e.g. Miller & Perry, 2012). But perhaps reasonableness is neither simply averageness, nor pure virtuousness. In other words, each side of that debate is focused on an important aspect of reasonableness. Moreover, various elaborations of reasonableness like the 'ideal average prudent man' (Holmes, 1881) might be best understood not as gesturing to an ideal person, nor to an average one, but rather to a reasonable one, understood as a hybrid.

Other recent work has found important differences between the folk concepts of *reasonableness* and economic *rationality* (Grossman et al., 2020). While lay judgements of what is legally reasonable are affected by consideration of what most people *would* do in the circumstance, they are not affected by consideration of what would be economically efficient in the circumstance (Jaeger, 2021; cf. Jaeger, Levin & Porter, 2017). Other work has found further evidence consistent with the 'hybrid' theory of reasonableness. Tobia, Nielsen, and Stremitzer (2021) studied lay assessment of how a 'reasonable physician' would use AI precision medicine tools. Lay judgement of the 'reasonable physician' was predicted by judgement about the 'average' and 'ideal' physicians.

One benefit of the cognitive science of ordinary concepts is that it provides new tools to make progress on these legal-theoretical questions, facilitating the experimental study of concepts. But other benefits come from cognitive scientific theory. In this case, the cognitive science of normality as a 'hybrid concept' (Bear & Knobe, 2017) opened new possibilities in theorizing legal reasonableness. If the folk law thesis is right, this inspiration from cognitive scientific theory should occur frequently: Ordinary concepts are at the root of legal concepts, and so discoveries about ordinary concepts will facilitate discoveries about legal ones.

5.5 CAUSATION

As a brief final example, consider the concept of CAUSATION. There has been an impressive array of experimental work on ordinary and legal judgements of causation (e.g. Greene & Darley, 1998; Solan & Darley, 2001; Cushman, 2008; Macleod, 2019; Tobia & Mikhail, 2021). The terrain is too vast to cover in detail here. But for the purposes of this chapter, consider just one example of a recent empirical finding about the ordinary concept: 'causal superseding' (Kominsky et al., 2015).

'Causal superseding' is the effect by which, when two agents produce an outcome, people judge one agent to be less causal when the other agent violates a norm. Consider Kominsky et al.'s (2015) 'Bartlett bookend' case. They presented experimental participants with two versions of a story about pairs of bookends. In both versions, Bill's wife, Sue, leaves town for the weekend. She calls Bill and says that she just saw a bookend called a 'Bartlett bookend', which she will get tomorrow for the 'left side of our bookshelf'. In the *morally good* version of the story, Bill buys a right-side Bartlett bookend from a friend. In the *morally bad* version of the story, Bill steals a right-side Bartlett bookend from his friend. Then, at the end of the story (in both versions), Sue arrives home with the left-side bookend, and the couple has a pair of Bartlett bookends. Experimental participants rated their agreement with the statement, 'Sue caused them to possess the paired set of bookends.' They evaluated Sue as less causal in the morally bad version, where Bill steals the bookend. Kominsky et al. (2015) interpret this as evidence that Bill's bad action 'supersedes' Sue's causality.

This is just one of several features that experimental cognitive scientists have discovered about the ordinary concept of CAUSATION (see generally Lagnado & Gerstenberg, 2017). But here again, we can ask: Does the legal concept actually share those features? Is the legal concept of CAUSATION predicated on the ordinary concept (as the folk law thesis would have it), or is the legal concept largely dissimilar?

In an article on proximate causation in tort law, Knobe and Shapiro (in press) contend that, 'legal judgments of proximate cause are based, at least for the most part, on people's ordinary concept of causation'. To support this claim, they articulate a formal model of the pattern of ordinary judgements of causation, one that explains surprising features like causal superseding. Then, they survey all of the cases on intervening causation and concurrent causation in a well-known torts handbook (Prosser, 1986), arguing that the analysis supports the claim that the legal concept is the ordinary concept.

Again, this is but one of many intriguing features of the ordinary concept of CAUSATION, and future work would do well to investigate further the relationship between the ordinary concept and law's concept (or concepts) of CAUSATION. But here again, the folk law thesis gains some initial support. Even subtle and surprising features of the ordinary concept, like causal superseding, seem to characterize the legal notion.

5.6 CONCLUSION

This brief chapter has developed an initial framework for the 'folk law thesis', the claim that many central legal concepts share features of the corresponding ordinary concept. It also began to make the case for the truth of this thesis with respect to psychological concepts like KNOWLEDGE and INTENT, but also other legal concepts like CONSENT, REASONABLENESS and CAUSATION.

The discussion here only scratches the surface. Empiricists have conducted similar work on many other important legal concepts, including IDENTITY (e.g. Mott, 2018; Earp, Latham & Tobia, in press), OWNERSHIP (e.g. Friedman & Neary, 2008) and LAW itself (e.g. Donelson & Hannikainen, in press). Moreover, this chapter has focused primarily on experimental survey methods. But other methods play a similar role in studying ordinary and legal concepts, including neuroscientific methods (see, e.g., Vilares et al., 2017) behavioural methods (e.g. Sommers & Bohns, 2018) and other empirical methods, such as corpus linguistics (e.g. Sytsma et al., in press).[4]

---

[4] Additionally, this chapter has focused on law and the cognitive science of ordinary concepts. But there is much other important work in law and psychology, including work on responsibility, culpability and liability (e.g. see Robinson & Darley, 1995); eyewitness testimony (e.g. Loftus, 1996); intuitions about

Yet, the brief survey here provides evidence that ordinary concepts are at the heart of a diverse array of legal concepts. This opens up a set of new and promising empirical research questions. For each legal concept, what are the features of the corresponding ordinary concept – and what, if any, are the distinctive features of the legal concept?

The chapter has focused mostly on these empirical questions. But the folk law thesis opens an equally vast range of new and important normative questions. For each feature of the ordinary concept, we can – and should! – ask a corresponding normative question: *should* the legal concept have this or that feature? Should legal INTENT be severity-sensitive; should legal CONSENT be compatible with some forms of deception; should legal REASONABLENESS be a hybrid of statistical and normative considerations? In this way, the cognitive science of ordinary concepts is not only a useful part of legal psychology, but also a critical part of legal theory and jurisprudence.[5]

REFERENCES

Bear, A., & Knobe, J. (2017). Normality: Part Descriptive, Part Prescriptive. *Cognition* 167, 25–37.

Cushman, F. (2008). Crime and Punishment: Distinguishing the Roles of Causal and Intentional Analyses in Moral Judgment. *Cognition* 108(2), 353–80.

Donelson, R., & Hannikainen, I. (in press). Fuller and the Folk: The Inner Morality of Law Revisited. In T. Lombrozo, J. Knobe, & S. Nichols (eds.), *Oxford Studies in Experimental Philosophy*, vol. 3. Oxford: Oxford University Press.

Earp, B., Latham, S. R. & Tobia, K. (in press). Personal Transformation and Advance Directives: An Experimental Bioethics Approach. *American Journal of Bioethics*.

Friedman, O., & Neary, K. (2008). First Possession Beyond the Law: Adults' and Young Children's Intuitions About Ownership. *Tulsa Law Review* 83, 679.

Greene, E. J., & Darley, J. M. (1998). Effects of Necessary, Sufficient, and Indirect Causation on Judgments of Criminal Liability. *Law and Human Behavior* 22(4), 429–51.

Grossmann, I., Eibach, R., Koyama, J., & Sahi, Q. (2020). Folk Standards of Sound Judgment: Rationality Versus Reasonableness. *Science Advances* 6.

Guthrie, C., Rachlinski, J. J., & Wistrich, A. J. (2007). Blinking on the Bench: How Judges Decide Cases. *Cornell Law Review* 93, 1–44.

Hans, V. (1992). Jury Decision Making. In Dorothy K. Kagehiro & William S. Laufer (eds.), *Handbook of Psychology and Law*. New York: Springer-Verlag, pp. 56–76.

Holmes, O. W. H. (1881). *The Common Law*. London: Macmillan.

Hurd, H. M. (1996). The Moral Magic of Consent. *Legal Theory* 2, 121–46.

Jaeger, C. B. (2021). The Empirical Reasonable Person. *Alabama Law Review* 72.

---

blame (e.g. Solan, 2002, 2005, 2009) and justice (e.g. Tyler, 1994); jury decision making (Hans, 1992); motivated reasoning (e.g. Kahan et al., 2015); heuristics (e.g. Guthrie, Rachlinski & Wistrich, 2007); unconscious racial bias (e.g. Rachlinski et al., 2008); other biases (e.g. Solan, Rosenblatt & Osherson, 2008); and interpretation (e.g. Struchiner et al., in press; Tobia, in press).

[5] For further elaboration of this view of 'experimental jurisprudence' see, for example, Macleod (2019) and Tobia, 'Experimental Jurisprudence' (unpublished article).

Jaeger, C. B., Levin, D. T., & Porter, E. (2017). Justice Is (Change) Blind: Applying Research on Visual Metacognition in Legal Settings. *Psychology, Public Policy, and Law* 23(2), 259–79.

Kahan, D. M., Hoffman, D., Evans, D., et al. (2015). Ideology or Situation Sense: An Experimental Investigation of Motivated Reasoning and Professional Judgment. *University of Pennsylvania Law Review* 164, 349–439.

Kneer, M., & Bourgeois-Gironde. (2017). Mens Rea Ascription, Expertise and Outcome Effects: Professional Judges Surveyed. *Cognition* 169, 139–46.

Knobe, J. (2003). Intentional Action and Side Effects in Ordinary Language. *Analysis* 63, 190–94.

Knobe, J., & Shapiro, S. (in press). Proximate Cause Explained: An Essay in Experimental Jurisprudence. *University of Chicago Law Review*.

Kominsky, J. F., Phillips, J., Gerstenberg, T. et al. (2015). Causal Superseding. *Cognition* 137, 196–209.

Lagnado, D. A., & Gerstenberg, T. (2017). Causation in Legal and Moral Reasoning. In M. R. Waldmann (ed.), *The Oxford Handbook of Causal Reasoning*. Oxford: Oxford University Press, pp. 565–601.

Loftus, E. F. (1996). *Eyewitness Testimony*. Cambridge, MA: Harvard University Press.

Macleod, J. A. (2019). Ordinary Causation: A Study in Experimental Statutory Interpretation. *Indiana Law Journal* 94, 957–1029.

Malle, B. F., & Nelson, S. E. (2003). Judging Mens Rea: The Tension Between Folk Concepts and Legal Concepts of Intentionality. *Behavioral Sciences & the Law* 21(5), 563–80.

Miller, A. D., & Perry, R. (2012). The Reasonable Person. *New York University Law Review* 87, 323–92.

Mott, C. (2018). Statutes of Limitations and Personal Identity. 2 *Oxford Studies in Experimental Philosophy* 243.

O'Neill, O. (2001). Informed Consent and Genetic Information. *Studies in History and Philosophy of Biological and Biomedical Sciences* 32, 689–704.

Prosser, W. L. (1986). *Prosser and Keeton on Torts*, 5th ed. St Paul, MN: West Publishing.

Rachlinski, J. J., Johnson, S. L., Wistrich, A. J., & Guthrie, C. (2008). Does Unconscious Racial Bias Affect Trial Judges. *Notre Dame Law Review* 84, 1195–1246.

Robinson, P. H., & Darley, J. M. (1995). *Justice, Liability, and Blame: Community Views and the Criminal Law*. Boulder, CO: Westview Press.

Shen, F. X., Hoffman, M. B., Jones, O. D., et al. (2011). Sorting Guilty Minds. *New York University Law Review* 86, 1306–60.

Solan, L. M. (2002). Cognitive Foundations of the Impulse to Blame. *Brooklyn Law Review* 68, 1003–29.

Solan, L. M. (2005). Where Does Blaming Come From. *Brooklyn Law Review* 71, 939–1029.

Solan, L. M. (2009). Blame, Praise, and the Structure of Legal Rules. *Brooklyn Law Review* 75, 517–43.

Solan, L. M., & Darley, J. M. (2001). Causation, Contribution, and Legal Liability: An Empirical Study. *Law and Contemporary Problems* 64(4), 265–98.

Solan, L., Rosenblatt, T., & Osherson, D. (2008). False Consensus Bias in Contract Interpretation. *Columbia Law Review* 108, 203–29.

Sommers, R. (in press). Commonsense Consent. *Yale Law Journal*.

Sommers, R., & Bohns, V. K. (2018). The Voluntariness of Voluntary Consent: Consent Searches and the Psychology of Compliance. *Yale Law Journal*, 129, 2232–2324.

Sommers, R., & Furth-Matzkin, M. (2019). Consumer Psychology and the Problem of Fine Print Fraud. *Stanford Law Review* 72, 503–60.

Stern, S. (2017). R v. Jones (1703). In P. Handler, H. Mares & I. Williams (eds.), *Landmark Cases in Criminal Law*. Oxford: Hart, 59–79.

Struchiner, N., Hannikainen, I. R., & de Almeida, G. (in press). An Experimental Guide to Vehicles in the Park. *Judgment and Decision Making*.

Sytsma, J., Bluhm, R., Willemsen, P., & Reuter, K. (in press). Causal Attributions and Corpus Analysis. In E. Fisher (ed.), *Methodological Advances in Experimental Philosophy*. London: Bloomsbury Press.

Tobia, K. P. (2018). How People Judge What Is Reasonable. *Alabama Law Review* 70, 293–360.

Tobia, K. P. (in press). Testing Ordinary Meaning. *Harvard Law Review* 134.

Tobia, K. P., & Mikhail, J. (2021). Two Types of Empirical Textualism. *Brooklyn Law Review*.

Tobia, K. P., Nielsen, A., & Stremitzer, A. (2021). When Does Physician Use of AI Increase Liability? *The Journal of Nuclear Medicine*.

Tyler, T. (1994). Psychological Models of the Justice Motive: Antecedents of Distributive and Procedural Justice. *Journal of Personality and Social Psychology*, 67, 850–863.

Vilares, I., Wesley, M., Ahn, W., et al. (2017). Predicting the Knowledge–Recklessness Distinction in the Human Brain. *Proceedings of the National Academy of Sciences*, 114, 3222–7.

II

Ontology and Epistemology

6

Cognitive Science and the Nature of Law

Corrado Roversi

6.1 INTRODUCTION

Law is not simply a matter of rules: it is also a domain of facts and objects. There are professors of legal theory; Parliament enacted a statute; Italy is part of the European Union; that is a traffic light; this is my passport. These facts, and these objects, are complex. They are clearly dependent on rules – rules about universities, norm-enacting procedures, states, and traffic. Moreover, their existence depends on acts, events and artifacts: a student may receive a grade in legal theory because the professor gave an assessment of his knowledge during an exam; someone acquires the age of majority after reaching a predetermined age; what I have in my pocket is my passport, for it has the makings of one (it is a compact booklet bearing official insignia and a photo of someone who looks like me, along with stamps, signatures, dates, addresses, and other markers of "passportness"). Explaining these facts – their nature and structure, and more in general, the nature of law – is a crucial problem of jurisprudence and is a special case of the general philosophical problem of the metaphysics of social phenomena, discussed by the philosophical discipline that now goes by the name of "social ontology."

There is a relevant and quite intuitive sense in which social facts can be assumed to depend on the mental states of individuals.[1] One could wonder about *which* individuals – members of the community at large or officials? – or about whether individuals suffice – should we postulate a collective spirit or mind? – and of course about whether other elements are necessary – contextual elements, historical considerations, power, and so on. However, in the end social facts depend necessarily, and at least partly, on mental states. If there were no human beings, or if human beings were incapable of having symbolic representations, legal and social facts could not exist. The features of this dependence, and the kinds of mental states

---

[1] Throughout the chapter, I will use technical metaphysical terms like "depend" and "ground" purposely in a naïve way, simply to convey an idea of fundamentality. It is not within the scope of this chapter to enter into the difficult metaphysical problems connected with these notions when applied to law. Dedicated discussions can be found in (Epstein, 2015; Chilovi & Pavlakos, 2019; and Plunkett, 2019).

involved, are two separate questions – the first metaphysical, the second psychological. The point, however, is that these questions are deeply intertwined. For this reason, legal metaphysics is inevitably an interdisciplinary research connected with cognitive psychology: it is not possible to have a clear idea of the nature of legal facts without understanding the cognitive underpinnings of the mental states those facts depend on.

In this chapter, I will adopt this interdisciplinary approach and try to outline a picture, however tentative and incomplete, of the psychological problems and findings that are relevant for research in the metaphysics of law. This chapter is based on two separate assumptions, which I will put forward as my analytical framework. These assumptions are drawn from research in social and legal metaphysics and will be presented by highlighting that research. The first assumption has already been mentioned: legal facts are a subset of social facts; hence, legal metaphysics is a subset of social metaphysics. For this reason, most of the first part of this chapter will deal with the relation between cognitive-psychological research and social metaphysics in general, not with the metaphysics of law specifically. The second thesis is that legal institutions are peculiar social institutions that put in place a framework consisting of sanctions, along with the authority to define, apply, and enforce shared rules of conduct in a formal way, namely, in terms of legal validity. Here, I provide a definition of legality – of what makes an institution legal. However, as we will see, this definition will be framed in the weakest sense possible, that is, without bringing a specific conception of law into play, or at least, hopefully, without falling into the legal-theoretical pitfalls one can encounter when attempting to formulate a view about the "nature" of law.

The analytical framework presented here will make it possible to distinguish two aspects of law, each corresponding to one of the two theses: one is the law's *root* in collective acceptance, the other is its *structure*, namely, a framework of sanctions and power/authority. Both these aspects ultimately trace back to cognitive mechanisms. The discussion is organized accordingly. Section 6.2 deals with the root of law, Section 6.3 with its structure, and for each of them I will first present its conceptual and theoretical background and then describe the connected cognitive-psychological studies and topics of research. It is important to set up this twofold treatment from the outset – theoretical first, then empirical – because otherwise the reader may find some difficulty in connecting the theoretical discussion with the ensuing presentation of psychological findings. Finally, in Section 6.4, I will summarize the overall picture.

6.2 THE ROOT OF LAW

6.2.1 *First Thesis: Legal Facts Are a Subset of Social Facts*

The first thesis, here taken as a working assumption, is that legal facts are a subset of social facts. Hence, in order to explain what legal facts are, we need to explain both the general features of social facts and the special features of law as a social fact. Law regulates interpersonal relationships and thus cannot play a role if not within a social group. I will assume that social facts are themselves grounded, at least partly, in the mental states of human beings. I take these assumptions to be quite intuitive and in a sense conceptual. To be sure, the label "social" could apply to animals that are not capable of having complex mental states, but this is not the kind of society that can insightfully be placed in the background of law such as we find it among human beings. Human society requires human mental states to exist; this is all we have to take for granted. And human mental states have contents: they refer to something and are thus instances of human "intentionality," a term which in philosophy denotes precisely the capacity to have something as object and content. For example, if we believe that it will rain, if we want to be somewhere else, or if we intend to take an exam, all these mental states involve kinds of intentionality.

In what follows, and for analytical purposes, I will make a distinction between ideal-typical layers of complexity in human society based on the kind of intentional states involved and the way in which these states are interrelated. In particular, I will distinguish four levels of sociality, levels 0 through 3. Level 0 is the baseline of sociality, that is, acting together; level 1 is a fundamental element, the acceptance of norms; level 2 is a specific thing we can do together, namely, attribute a status; and, finally, level 3 combines levels 1 and 2 in the attribution of a status through social norms. In the passage from level 0 to level 3 the creation of social facts is made possible. I will be using this framework for the entire chapter, so it is important that we bear that in mind. Let us then see how it works in detail.

Intentions, conceived as a specific instance of intentionality, are crucially important in understanding social facts. Consider this example:

1) Yesterday we cooked our dinner together.

This is a case in which an action is ascribed not to an individual but to a group; it is thus a social action. And, just as in the case of individual actions, it makes sense to ask whether the action was intentional, and here it does indeed seem reasonable to suppose that it was. But then another question emerges: is the intention behind a collective action different from an individual intention? There are several reasons to suppose so: Our collective intention to cook our dinner cannot be fruitfully analyzed as a sum of individual intentions. Suppose I walk into the kitchen with the intention of cooking a meal for myself, and my wife does the same for her meal, and then we eat at the same time and in the same place: would this count as "cooking together"? The answer is no: my wife is not cooking together with me; she is simply cooking her meal at the same time as me. Hence, at least a certain degree of interconnection among the participants' intentions and actions is necessary for a collective intention and action to be in place. (A similar example, involving parkgoers, can be found in Searle, 2002.) This collective action, supported by a collective intention, is what I will call "level 0 sociality": basic joint action.

The actual structure of the interconnections behind level 0 sociality is much debated in the current literature on collective intentionality. Some authors (among whom Michael Bratman, Seumas Miller, and Kirk Ludwig) believe that collective intentionality can be explained by relying on a minimal framework of individual intentions, *plus* a series of special correlations among them (Bratman, 1992; Miller, 2001), or in any case by relying on notions that are already in use in our understanding of individual intentions and actions (Ludwig, 2016). Others (among whom John Searle and Raimo Tuomela) think instead that a specific mode of intentionality is also needed: Intentions, on this view, can be held either individually or collectively (in the "we-mode," to use Tuomela's expression: Tuomela, 2013). Searle, in particular, maintains that collective intentions, and more generally collective intentionality, are "biological primitives" of human beings (Searle, 1995, 2010).

Apart from collective intentions, there is another kind of collective intentionality that is crucial to understanding social phenomena: collective acceptance. Consider this case:

2) At today's meeting we decided that members of the association should adhere to a formal dress code when attending monthly meetings.

Here a collective intention is at play, as in the case of cooking together, but in this case the collective intention has to do with the creation of a rule that all the members of a given group are made aware of and asked to abide by. This is what I will call "level 1 sociality," namely, a situation where a social norm is introduced. There is an important distinction to be made here between the introduction of a norm and its continuing endorsement. The introduction of a norm can very well be an instance of joint intention and action, and so can be explained at level 0. The endorsement of the norm – the process through which the norm is "kept in place" as effective – is instead based on an intentional state that differs from collective intention, namely, collective acceptance. Collective acceptance is weaker than collective intention, because it assumes a weaker sense of cooperation by members of the group. Some members of the association will resent this rule, and certainly will not feel they can heartily endorse it. In some cases, they will even end up "forgetting" the rule, and in those cases the rule will be enforced by others by recourse to soft kinds of sanctioning, like quipping and chuckling or gossiping, or else to formal punishment, like expulsion. Indeed, Searle (2010), Tuomela (1995, 2013), and Gilbert (1989) all clarify that, in the case of acceptance, the we-mode and collective character will allow for a weaker sense of cooperation, and Searle, in particular, maintains that it can be compatible with a set of individual intentions coupled with mutual beliefs.

Consider now this example:

3) At today's meeting we decided that Mr. Pink is the founder of the association.

Here, a more specific kind of collective intention and action is considered: we decide to attribute a status according to which something must be collectively considered as something else, and this "something else" has relevant normative consequences for the group. This is what I will call "level 2 sociality": the attribution of a status. As in the case of social norms, status attribution involves collective acceptance. In this particular example, members of the association accept that Mr. Pink is the founder and that they should behave accordingly, as by conferring some rights and powers on him. And, as in the case of social norms, these members are not expected to be necessarily enthusiastic about it, or even to know what the status entails in practical detail. They should simply have a disposition to behave according to the attributed status.

Levels 1 and 2 can be combined. Consider this final example:

4) At today's meeting we decided that all presidents of the association who have served in that capacity for at least five years are to be recognized as honorary founders of the association.

Here, too, a status is attributed, but through a general rule. Members of the association do not know who will become honorary founder, but they collectively accept the rule by way of which this status is attributed. This rule does not state who the honorary founders are here and now, but frames the conditions for identifying them in all situations, across different possible worlds so to speak. This is what I will call "level 3 sociality": status attributions through social norms. The distinction between levels 2 and 3 is that in the first case the group simply attributes a status to a specific entity, and people go along with this attribution, whereas in the second case the group accepts a rule, which is constitutive of the concept of a status in *defining* its conditions of applicability, and that rule assigns the status to different persons depending on circumstances. Moreover, the distinction between levels 1 and 3 is that the latter requires collective endorsement not simply of a social norm, but of a norm that "creates" a new kind of institutional entity. Level 3 includes *constitutive* rules in Searle's sense, namely, rules under which something "brute" (X) "counts as" something "institutional" (Y) having a status and a normative import, in Searle's (1995, 2010) terms: having a "status function" and "deontic powers."

It should be clear that level 3 plays a particularly important role in the social phenomenon we call "law." Status attribution is a form of attribution of social meaning, and law is one kind of such attribution: In law, internal legal concepts such as "owner" are created by using rules to specify the way in which these statuses can be accorded, on the one hand, and the normative consequences of these statuses, on the other (Hage, 2018, ch. 2). Indeed, this kind of analysis shows how legal facts are connected with the creation of symbolic statuses in general, among which are fictions, games and rituals. Kendall Walton (1990), for example, argues that fictional truths in the context of "games of make-believe" depend on "principles of generation" that determine the coming into being of fictional facts on the basis of "props," and indeed the mechanism is very similar to that of constitutive rules connecting "brute" facts with "institutional" facts.[2] As Amie Thomasson (1999) shows, fictions are particular cases of artifacts, and some recent approaches in legal theory have argued that the reality of social institutions can be traced to the general human capacity for building artifacts. According to the so-called "artifact theory of law" (Crowe, 2014; Burazin, 2016, 2018; Ehrenberg, 2016; Roversi, 2016, 2019; Burazin et al., 2018) law is a genre of abstract rule-based artifacts, namely, artifacts built to enable interaction among human agents and that work if the underlying rules are collectively accepted. Legal artifacts in particular are meant by political authority to hold generally and to shape the community members' normative reasons for action.

We now have the theoretical underpinnings of the first thesis, which is that legal facts are a subset of social facts. The overall picture that emerges from this account is that law is ultimately rooted in four distinct and progressively more complex layers of sociality, moving from joint action to symbolic status attributions by way of social norms. Of course, there are significant objections and important alternative views in social ontology and in the social sciences (Epstein, 2018). A game-theoretic approach, for example, will explain institutions without requiring rules or acceptance but rather calling for individual strategic preferences and behavioral regularities (see Lewis, 1969; Ullman-Margalit, 1977; Bicchieri, 2006; among others). A more sociological approach will define institutions as sets of rules aimed at reducing uncertainty by stabilizing the expectations of individuals (see, for example, Parsons, 1935; North, 1990; and Hodgson, 2006). Significant work has also been done to merge these two last accounts (Hindriks & Guala, 2015). One could also object, on a more general note, that the background of sociality as depicted on this approach is too "irenic": overly focused on cooperation, while glossing over the basic conflicts that lie at the core of any society (see, for example, Fittipaldi, in press, with a focus on jural emotions). But I cannot here argue for the merits of the four-level approach: As mentioned in the introduction, the theoretical underpinnings of this chapter are assumed as an analytical framework. Hence, how compelling this systematization of the cognitive-psychological elements will seem as a framework within which to analyze legal reality will depend on the degree to which we share the underlying assumptions. Regardless, however, the approach will at least give us a clearer idea of how we might want to complement the picture.

---

[2] Incidentally, tracing the roots of law to status attributions similar to fictions is a strategy that finds some common ground with the legal philosophers who have looked most deeply at the way legal institutions emerge from collective psychological processes, namely, the so-called "psychologistic" legal realists traceable to Scandinavian and Polish-Russian legal realism, and none more so than Axel Hägerström, Karl Olivecrona, and Leon Petrażycki (see Hägerström, 1917, 1941; Petrażycki, 1955; Olivecrona, 1971; see also in this regard Pattaro, 2016 and Fittipaldi, 2016).

6.2.2 The Cognitive Structure of Collective Intentionality and Acceptance: Joint Action

Let us focus on level 0 of sociality: joint action. As mentioned above, there are several different models for the analysis of joint action developed by contemporary social ontology: I will take three of these models as a starting point for discussion. The first model, which is Michael Bratman's (1992) analysis of shared cooperative activities, is exclusively individualistic: It involves only individual intentions (ones that I, as an agent, can have); but these intentions take a "we" as their content ("*I* intend that *we* j") and are interconnected by way of mutual knowledge. The second model is that of John Searle's (1995, 2010) collective intentionality. Here we are at the opposite end of the spectrum relative to Bratman's model. In fact, Searle's model assumes that intentions are primitively held in the plural mode, as a "we." On Searle's view, an individual could even have a collective intention on her own, as a "brain-in-a-vat," given that she is biologically and neurologically framed to have intentions in the plural form. But, of course, joint action is possible only when intentions framed in this way are shared among different persons. Finally, the third model combines elements from the last two: this is Raimo Tuomela's (2013) conception. Here, joint action is indeed the outcome of an interconnection of intentions held by individuals – hence collective intentions could not be had by one person alone, as in Searle's case – but these intentions are not framed in the same way as individual intentions are in Bratman's theory. Rather, Tuomela singles out the concept of "we-mode we-intention," which is a slice of a joint intention that someone can have not simply as an individual but rather as the member of a group ("As a member of this group, I intend that *p* like the other members").

The capacity for joint action and joint intention is crucial in accounting for the specificity of human sociality, as opposed to that of other animals, including the great apes. Now, of course, the kind of cognitive abilities required to engage in joint intentional actions depend on which model you take as your starting point, either Bratman's minimalistic model or Searle's strong collectivist view or Tuomela's "middle way." But there is at least a minimal set of progressively stronger cognitive conditions that must be met in all these three models: participants must be able to (1) have intentions, (2) understand the intentions of other participants, and (3) coordinate their own actions with those of others according to a more or less explicitly shared plan geared toward a common goal. Whether the great apes can meet all these conditions is contested. According to some scholars, chimpanzees and bonobos have significant mind-reading abilities and can meet conditions (1) and (2); they can even sympathize with groupmates and help them, and they can keep their own impulses under control when at risk, but they cannot (3) share a plan and cooperate in working toward a common goal (Tomasello et al., 2005, p. 676; Dubreuil, 2010, pp. 55–58; Gallotti, 2012; Tomasello, 2016). In particular, although chimpanzees and bonobos show some kind of cooperation in group hunting for monkeys, they do not clearly show a capacity to act interdependently, that is, as agents acting under a single plan: They mostly act individually, each doing the same thing, at best taking into account the actions of others (for example, "one individual begins the chase, and then others go to the best remaining locations in anticipation of the monkey's attempted escape" so as to increase their own chance of taking the prey for themselves: Tomasello, 2016, p. 27). And, in case of group defense, the great apes "mob" their enemies, showing no sophisticated forms of cooperation (ibid., p. 23). Other scholars instead argue that there are indeed signs of sophisticated forms of cooperation among chimpanzees, such as supporting the status of others, acting strategically (see de Waal, 1998, pp. 31–32, 197–199), and differentiating roles when group hunting (Boesch, 2002). It is clear, however, that as considerable as the cooperation abilities one can observe in great apes may be, they are magnified and brought to an entirely new level of complexity in humans.

Human children are clearly capable of dyadic interaction and responsiveness with their caregiver since birth. From the age of six months, they can share a goal and do something together with their caregiver to achieve that goal, and from the age of twelve to fifteen months, they can actively interact with their caregiver, coordinating individual plans and actions (Tollefsen, 2004; Tomasello et al., 2005, pp. 681–683). On the one hand, this last capacity involves the ability to interpret the emotions of others and adjust one's behavior on that basis (distinctive capacities for emotional sharing, like emotion detection, mood contagion, and empathy likely play an important role in building joint action; Michael, 2011). On the other hand, it involves a greater ability than primates have to share perceptual space and perceptual attention: a capacity for joint *attention*, which develops at an earlier stage than joint *intention* (Tomasello & Carpenter, 2005, ch. 5; Dubreuil, 2010, pp. 57–58). Subsequently, at the age of four to five years, human children on that basis develop full-fledged perspective taking in the background of a robust theory of mind, namely, an understanding of others in terms of their thoughts and beliefs as well as an understanding of the fact that others' beliefs may differ from their own (Tollefsen, 2004, p. 81). In adults, attention sharing is embodied, in the sense that on the basis of gaze direction and head and body orientation, individuals can figure out what another is seeing as if they were seeing it themselves (Becchio et al., 2013). Moreover, the actions of another agent are represented and have an impact on their own actions, even if there is no strict need for coordination (Sebanz, Knoblich, & Prinz, 2003). Finally, it seems that human adults simulate the actions of others on the basis of an understanding of their *task*, and that they act accordingly, as part of their conceptualization of a given social situation (Sebanz, Knoblich, & Prinz, 2005). Electrophysiological evidence can be found in Sebanz et al. (2006) and in Tsai et al. (2006), but see Vesper et al. (2010, p. 1000).

Some authors conjecture that this set of abilities can be based on the multimodal capacity of mirror neurons, in which motor and sensory properties coexist. See, for example Becchio and Bertone (2004, p. 131), Tollefsen (2004, p. 95), and Sebanz et al. (2003), but skepticism about this approach has been raised in Pacherie and Dokic (2006). This multimodality makes it possible to understand the action of *others* in our group on the same cognitive basis we rely on when *we* engage in that action. Hence, there is a connection here to the idea of *roles* that (a) are all distinctly necessary in carrying out the plan, (b) are to a significant extent interchangeable, and (c) can be performed by me or my partner depending on the circumstances. Thus, at the core of human cooperation lies the triadic system according to which "I" and "you" act according to a role under the activity that "we" are doing together, a structure of roles that is geared toward a shared goal (Tomasello et al., 2005, 2016).

Whether this interpretation supports Bratman's model or Tuomela's or Searle's is an open question. On the one hand, Bratman's model seems to require a complex set of interrelated intentions along with recursive representations of others' beliefs, a structure that has been argued to entail a cognitive load too great to explain joint actions in small children (Tollefsen, 2004; Michael, 2011; Pacherie, 2011; Butterfill, 2012; Gallotti, 2012). On the other hand, if humans can have representations as if they were in the place of another, and if this capacity is built into our neural structures, our model will have to postulate some hardwired capacity to process actions in a collective, intersubjective modality, thereby at least lending some support to Tuomela's idea of a distinctive, we-oriented way of having mental content, if not to Searle's stronger model of we-intentions as primitive modalities of our brain. The cognitive relevance of "we-representations" is also shown by the so-called "GROOP effect" (Tsai, Sebanz, & Knoblich, 2011), according to which adult human beings increase their capacity to perform an action when they perceive others performing the same action, but only if there is an equal number of performing actors and observed actors. This effect can be interpreted to imply that there is a distinctively "group-oriented" way of representing action when someone is part of a group.

Hence, level 0 sociality (joint action) can be traced to a distinct ontogenetic process in human individuals, that is, a process that all humans go through in their development. It has been conjectured that this ontogenetic development could map onto a phylogenetic development – an evolutionary development of the human species – and could thus point to an emergence of these cognitive capacities in species under the *Homo* genus, giving them an evolutionary edge over other species. With the emergence of *Homo habilis* (2 million years ago) came a progressive process of self-regulation: Interpersonal relations grounded in dominance and competition had to change, because cooperation was the only option in competing for food in a natural environment made particularly difficult by climatic changes. In particular, cooperative joint action in its most primitive form was rendered necessary by two activities that secured a competitive advantage for humans in gathering food: the first was cooperative group hunting of big animals by males, which ensured access to large amounts of meat but also required accurate planning; the second was cooperative breeding of children by females, which gave mothers some time to gather resources (Tomasello, 2016, ch. 3). These developments in turn prompted anatomical and neurological changes, which in further turn led to even greater cooperation: The enlargement of the brain, and in particular of medial prefrontal cortex, which made mind reading and perspective taking possible, meant that it would take longer for the brain to develop in children: this in turn meant that pregnancy and birth would be more painful for the mother (because the child's head is bigger), which strengthened the need for cooperation in giving birth to, raising, and protecting the offspring. Moreover, this kind of cooperative attitude ultimately led to a reduced dimorphism between males and females by comparison with other species, such as chimpanzees or gorillas (Dubreuil, 2010, pp. 80–83). Finally, greater competition in food gathering required greater flexibility in changing context and environments, and thus greater risks, which could be taken only if cooperatively shared within a group (ibid., pp. 68–70). The first migrations out of Africa, which can be attested at least for *Homo erectus* (1.8 million years ago), should therefore be considered in light of an improved capacity for joint action. Level 0 of sociality was a crucial and necessary tool that human animals had to develop in order to survive.

6.2.3 *Joint Commitment, Social Norms, Rights, and Duties*

There is a further notion we need to take on board if we are to fully understand the structure of joint action and the passage to a fully normative framework, namely, the notion of joint commitment introduced by Margaret Gilbert (1989, 2014). On Gilbert's conception, which can be grouped with Searle's and Tuomela's collectivist conceptions of collective intentionality, the construction of a "plural subject" requires a sort of original communicative (though not necessarily linguistic) act through which the partners agree to undertake a joint activity and commit to acting accordingly. This means, in particular, that they will be mutually supportive in performing the activity the group is to carry out, and that they will not drop their commitment without justification. I will try to show how, from this original sense of commitment, early humans could have evolved full-fledged social norms.

Commitment was a crucial element of cooperative group hunting as early as at the time of *Homo heidelbergensis* (700,000 to 300,000 years ago). In experimental settings, reproducing the features of stag hunting – a game where cooperation is needed to get the best payoff, but a lesser payoff can also be obtained through noncooperative behavior – children solve cooperation problems through communicative gestures, whereas great apes in the same setting do not. Thus, it can be conjectured that this element made possible the "cooperative" leap in early humans. Nonlinguistic communicative offers of cooperation were made on the unspoken understanding that the prey would be shared equally, and if uncooperative members sought to gain a bigger share, they would be excluded from the practice, in such a way that they could no longer exploit the prey (Tomasello, 2016, pp. 65–67, 70–72). Indeed, commitments have a crucial place in ensuring the predictability of others' behavior in cooperative activities and so in stabilizing expectations (Konvalinka et al., 2010; Bolt & Loehr, 2017). Through commitments, cooperative agents fulfill roles that are connected with tasks, and it is crucial to joint activity that these tasks be coordinated and that a monitoring process be in place for detecting errors (Vesper et al., 2010).

The element of commitment as part of joint action is understood by human children even as preschoolers. Warneken and Tomasello (2009) show that already at the age of fourteen months, infants who are engaged in a collaborative activity attempt to reengage the partner when the interaction stops abruptly. Three-year-old children engaged in joint activities based on an explicit commitment show particular expectations toward fellow children (Gräfenhain et al., 2009), and they are also less likely to yield to the temptation of giving up (Michael, Sebanz, & Knoblich, 2016a, p. 4). Finally, Hamann, Warneken, and Tomasello (2012) and Gräfenhain, Carpenter, and Tomasello (2013) found evidence to show that three-year-old children are supportive of their partners in activity and help them even when they themselves have already earned their reward.[3]

In early humans, having a reputation for being a cooperative agent could mean having better chances of survival, and of course cooperative agents had access to better support, which in its own turn implied a higher success rate in reproduction: In this sense, human cooperation could be a mechanism of social evolution (Haidt, 2012, ch. 7, quoting Trivers, 1971; cf. Trivers, 1985), an instance of pure biological cooperation, progressively enriched through cultural means in the development of species under the *Homo* genus (see Birch, 2017, p. 34 and ch. 8). At first, commitment was purely instrumental, and it would arise from an *external* source, when a cooperative fellow member would protest the noncompliance of others. Normative notions can in this sense be said to have first emerged as a second-person morality, meaning that they initially took the form of judgments that others would make of our cooperative attitude, and the assurance we would give others of our own cooperative attitude, and this was functional to building the framework for mutual compliance (Tomasello, 2016, pp. 67–70, 73–75; Darwall, 2006). It was basically a matter of mutual expectations.

---

[3] In a sense, the function of commitments in carrying out joint activities at such an early stage is mysterious from the standpoint of instrumental rationality, because there is nothing to ensure that others will actually live up to the commitment (Michael & Pacherie, 2015). Moreover, some studies show that children under the age of nine have difficulties fully grasping the moral significance of commitments and the conditions under which commissive speech acts give rise to commitments (Astington, 1988; Mant & Perner, 1988). For this reason, some have conjectured that while children at three years of age have only a minimal normative notion of commitment, this normative notion is already at work in joint action starting at the age of two, where it is connected with the emergence of social emotions. Children develop the ability to commit and protest when others fail to comply with a commitment: This is part of their ability to share emotions with others and avoid negative emotions, an ability they exercise without any prudential calculus, that is, without calculating the risk they incur for failing to keep their commitment or for protesting when others do not, and without being able to predict when others might comply or not (Michael & Pacherie, 2015, p. 111).

It has been argued by Michael et al. (2016a, p. 9) that at the age of two, children are already sensitive to others' expectations and have expectations about others when trying to achieve a goal. Thus, the default mode at that stage is to expect help and give help if expected. Only in further development do children understand that they should not have expectations in all cases and that commitment in the strict sense arises only under more definite circumstances, and this holds even when humans observe joint action from the outside. When action is highly coordinated, a perception of commitment arises independently of whether an explicit commitment was signaled or otherwise understood to have been made (Michael, Sebanz, & Knoblich, 2016b). Moreover, experimental game theory seems to support the view that there is in humans a default mode that consists in fulfilling others' expectations.[4]

What humans wound up developing with the construction of joint commitments was thus a second-person basic morality based on the actual commitment and expectations of other participants. But, over and above that, they also wound up developing normative notions endowed with a higher degree of objectivity. Agents whose offer to cooperate was accepted *deserved* their share of prey. At the same time, they had a *duty* to act according to what had been agreed to, which in turn meant that they had a *role* that they *had to* fulfill, failing which they would have been *guilty* of breaking their commitment. All these elements were connected with expectations and with emotions of aggressiveness if these commitments were to go unfulfilled (Fittipaldi, in press). This coupling of roles and rights – roles with associated duties that had to be fulfilled, and rights to reap the ensuing benefit – thus came to be a crucial coordination-smoother (Vesper et al., 2017): Tasks were structured in the interaction, and errors corrected by other participants in the activity. Personal identity gradually became social, that is, it came to be grounded in a cooperative role. Starting at three years of age, human children feel a responsibility to communicate to the adults they are interacting with that they are willing to give up a joint game and shift to another one. They also make some amends for breaking their commitment to participate in the joint activity they and their fellow participants (their "we") are doing together (Gräfenhain et al., 2009, 1436ff.). This independent feeling of responsibility could thus be imagined to have developed in early humans, perhaps as the result of internalizing others' protests when their expectations were not fulfilled. The idea of a collective notion, *we*, gave place to the idea that duties

---

[4] Studies have shown that participants in joint action persist longer when they perceive cues from other participants that they, too, are contributing to the action (Skezely & Michael, 2018). When people are asked to invest in anonymous public good situations (where all participants can contribute to a pool of resources which will then be evenly divided among them), they will be more generous in giving if they see images of eyes (Francey & Bergmüller, 2012). Finally, in anonymous one-shot dictator games (in which one person gets to choose how to split a sum, and the respondent cannot refuse that offer), people tend to give away less money if they find themselves in a "double-blind" setting, namely, when they know that the experimenter will not know how they have chosen to behave (Camerer, 2003, pp. 62–63).

were not directly dependent on the protests of others, but were instead grounded in shared, quasi-objective grounds: in what *we* are doing together. Someone could develop a sense of guilt even when others did not protest (Tomasello, 2016, 73–75).

Roles ultimately came to be detached from particular agents. They could be fulfilled by anyone capable of performing the related tasks and fulfilling the attendant duties, and willing to access the related rights. The plural subject formed by two or more individuals who shared an original agreement gradually evolved into a group, defined by means of imitation and similarity – a shared culture – rather than being defined by actual and personal contact (ibid., pp. 88–90). Second-person morality based on joint commitments and direct contact evolved into a system of fixed moral conventions that applied to all the members of the group (ibid., pp. 96–97). This is where level 0 sociality advanced to level 1: joint action gave place to social norms by way of joint commitments. The development of social norms is commonly taken to be a distinctive feature of humans, though here, too, the assumption is far from uncontested.[5]

Four elements come into play in the progression toward full-fledged normativity in humans: (i) loyalty to the group as motivation for following norms, (ii) legitimation within the group as justification for those norms, (iii) the idea of a normative duty as distinct from a merely prudential reason for action, and hence (iv) an objectivizing of norms as standards that hold good independently of personal interests (Tomasello, 2016, pp. 122–126). Among these elements, a tension between two poles can be identified: at one end is the *strategic* consideration that group membership was necessary to one's own survival; at the opposite end, a *disinterested* recognition of norms as objective entities. The tension was solved through the device of normative identity: I am what I am because I am a member of this group, which means that I abide by those norms because those norms are objective in the same way as I am objective (ibid., pp. 105–107, 111–115).

An important role in this process of normative objectification may have been played by the development of language. First, because language was among the main conventional practices through which the boundaries of a group were defined, and second, because through language it became possible to hypostatize norms in such a way that they could exist independently of any specific personal relationship (ibid., 102–103).[6] This process of objectification was needed as a way to strengthen

---

[5] See the interesting observations on "animal norms" and on "evolutionary precursors of social norms" in Lorini (2018) and Rohr, Burkart, & van Schaik (2011), respectively, as well as the studies on "natural normativity" in De Waal (2014) and on nonhuman "naïve normativity" in Andrews (2009, 441ff.; 2015, pp. 55, 59 62).

[6] A shared language plays a role in defining normative behavior: There is an important linguistic factor at work in human children when they select someone they will trust (Kinzler, Shutts, DeJesus, & Spelke, 2009; Kinzler, Corriveau, & Harris, 2011), as well as when they learn by imitation (Buttelmann, 2013), and when norms are conveyed to novices as entities endowed with an objective force (Göckeritz, Schmidt, & Tomasello, 2014, pp. 88, 91–92). The role of language, however, should not be overplayed, since it is possible for norms to have been initially conceptualized as "crypto-types," that is, simply as

compliance, and the effectiveness of social norms in ensuring conformity and cooperation was a crucial factor in determining evolutionary success among groups (Richerson & Boyd, 2005).

The same relation between prudential elements and the objectivization of norms can also be appreciated from an ontogenetic point of view. The construction of groups on the basis of behavior patterns and imitation is a crucial factor for the development of norms in children, and indeed human children are much more concerned with the social aspect of imitation than are the great apes (Carpenter, 2006): On the one hand, children tend to imitate actions without appearing to consider the causal efficiency of the relevant behavior (Horner & Whiten, 2005);[7] on the other hand, they are more flexible than chimpanzees in adopting and imitating new techniques, showing an enhanced capacity for cumulative cultural learning (Whiten et al., 2009, pp. 2425–2426; Haun, Rekers, & Tomasello, 2014).[8] Groups define the boundaries of normative imitation: A central aspect of the motivation to comply with social norms in humans lies in the prudential element connected with reputation within the group, as well as in conformity, and reputational concerns in children are already in place by the age of five (Shaw, Li, & Olson, 2013). Experiments in behavioral economics show that personal reputation (along with punishment) is a crucial factor that agents take into account when deciding whether to cooperate, and to what extent, in public-goods games (Rockenbach & Milinski, 2006, p. 722), and this conclusion is supported by neurological data.[9] But normativity does not arise only in connection with a specific preoccupation with our own reputation, but also arises from a disinterested (un-self-centered) perspective: Unlike great apes, as early as the age of three human children intervene to punish others for their deviant behavior, and to protect the rights of others, even when they are not directly affected by that behavior (Rossano, Rakoczy, & Tomasello, 2011; Vaish, Missana, & Tomasello, 2011). Young children can also appreciate the connection between social norms and social cooperation in various contexts, so much so that they grasp quite early how norms are connected with a deeper layer of cooperativeness even in competitive settings (Schmidt, Hardecker, & Tomasello, 2016).

Much work has been done investigating the question of whether social norms are completely culturally determined or whether a core of common cross-cultural traits can be found. Children aged four to five can understand that some norms are more relative, conventional, and culturally determined than others, and they understand

---

patterns of reaction to the behavior of others (Sacco, 2007, ch. 8), which patterns (or norms) constituted emerging practices of social organization and positioning (Lawson, 2012, 2016, pp. 373ff.).

[7] This leads to an unnecessary over-imitation, which children consider to be normative (Kenward, 2012; Lyons & Keil, 2013; Whiten, 2013), and which may even require them to sacrifice a previously successful strategy (Haun & Tomasello, 2011).

[8] On the role of imitation in basic normativity see also Brożek (2013).

[9] It has been shown, in particular, that feelings of guilt and embarrassment (the latter more specifically) activate the medial prefrontal cortex, which is at the core of cognitive social-integration processes (Takahashi et al., 2004, p. 971).

that norms regulating physical assault are less conventional (Turiel, 1983; but see Kelly et al., 2007). In an extensive study Haidt (2012, ch. 7) shows that a set of moral foundations can be identified that is transcultural in essence and is only specified on cultural grounds, two examples being social norms based on taboos connected with a universal sense of disgust (elicited by dangerous or unhealthy behaviors) and norms supporting cooperation through fairness. Studies with children show that a common and transcultural conception of fairness is already present in preschoolers, and that cultural parameters become relevant only thereafter (House et al., 2013, p. 14590; Tomasello, 2016, pp. 116–117). However, studies in behavioral economics have also shown that, conversely, considerations of fairness can be dramatically influenced by specific normative and cultural framings (see Dubreuil, 2010, pp. 28–31).

So at work in norm-following is a commixture of cultural and cross-cultural factors, and this connection can be hardwired in our brain as a co-activation of emotional and social areas. Typically, norm-following raises the fear of being punished and hence activates areas related to negative emotions (*anterior insula*), but also cortical areas related to the inhibition of selfish reactions (dorsolateral prefrontal cortex), risk assessment in cooperation (frontal ventro-medial cortex), and social and emotional integration (orbitofrontal cortex) (see Dubreuil, 2010, pp. 46–47). For this reason, it can be conjectured that the development and reorganization of the cortical areas, starting from the prefrontal cortex, was connected with the increase in brain size that can be found in *Homo heidelbergensis*, and that in the mid-Pleistocene this led to long-term cooperative games and then, ultimately, to the emergence of social norms. The normative revolution in humans – level 1 sociality – would on this theory be a result of neurological modifications (see also ibid., pp. 88–90).

6.2.4 *Symbolic Artifacts, Status Attribution, and Games of Make-Believe*

We have seen how the passage from level 0 sociality (joint action) to level 1 (social norms) is made cognitively possible by the development of a sense of joint commitment, first from a second-person perspective and then, within a group, from a third-person perspective. The next step in sociality is the advancement to level 2, namely, the attribution of statuses. As an example of joint cooperation and commitment, let us consider someone having the status of chief, judge, or king. This passage is made possible by symbolization, under which something or someone (a physical object, an event, a person) can count as, or stand for, something else (an object with normative value, an event in an ideal domain, a role connected with an honorific, religious, or normative status).

From a cognitive point of view, the attribution of statuses has three requirements. First, a capacity to understand that the same thing can be seen in different ways, hence a capacity to understand and perceive in a multimodal way (the relevant person will be seen both as a person and as the chief). Second, a capacity to understand the mental states of others, hence an ability for perspective taking (others have beliefs; they have the same beliefs as I do about the chief). Third, and connected with the first two, a capacity to understand that different perspectives can entail different, possibly false, beliefs (if others have beliefs, they can act on beliefs that are different from mine and that I take to be false).

It has been conjectured that these three cognitive abilities – multimodality, full-fledged perspective taking, and the capacity to understand false beliefs – were the core elements in the cognitive evolution of *Homo sapiens* between 300,000 and 100,000 years ago, and are related to the expansion of the temporal and parietal cortices and the resulting structural reshaping and globularization of the human cranium (Dubreuil, 2010, pp. 117–118; see also Lieberman, McBratney, & Krovitz, 2002; Bruner, Manzi, & Arsuaga, 2003).[10] While level 1 sociality (social norms) emerged out of an increase in brain size, as observed in *Homo heidelbergensis*, level 2 of sociality (status attribution) could have emerged out of a functional reorganization without further expansion in brain size, as observed in *Homo sapiens* (Dubreuil, 2010, pp. 120–121). The most important behavioral changes that can be connected to this cognitive development lie in the construction and use of signs and artifacts having either an ornamental or a ritual value, a development that took place in the Middle Stone Age, as attested by the presence of red ochre in connection with burial sites, or perforated shells used as ornaments in Northern Africa (ibid., p. 109; see also Hovers et al., 2003; Vanhaeren et al., 2006) or the shell beads with residues of ochre found in the Blombos Cave in South Africa (Dubreuil, 2010, pp. 110–111; see also Henshilwood et al., 2004; d'Errico et al., 2005). The use of bones or shells as objects of symbolic or aesthetic value presupposes an ability to move from the purely concrete substratum to a more abstract level, and also an ability to consider one's own perspective on an object in relation to that of others, for the purpose of sharing that perspective as the background against which to attribute value (Dubreuil, 2010, p. 131, 136).

There is some evidence that the great apes can show a certain degree of multimodality when dealing with objects, for example by using replicas and scale models as sources of information (Kuhlmeier & Boysen, 2002). It is not clear, however, that the great apes have the ability to extend this multimodality on a collective level, considering status attribution as a group factor. This requires a high degree of mind-reading capacities, among which that of attributing beliefs to others which can possibly conflict with our own – an attribution, and hence an understanding, of false beliefs.

Studies in human ontogenesis show that the full-fledged perspective taking and mind reading required for level 2 sociality are capacities that emerge in human

---

[10] Indeed, contemporary studies based on neuroimaging show that the processing of false beliefs is connected with the junction between the temporal and parietal cortices (Dubreuil, 2010, p. 129; see also Aichorn et al., 2006; Perner et al., 2006; Saxe & Kanwisher, 2003).

children around the age of four or five (but they are based on more primitive forms of attention sharing that, as we have seen, form the background to level 0). At that age children can inhibit their own cognition to the point of activating an alternative and conflicting one, and, more in particular, they understand that when they share attention over an object they can have divergent and conflicting perspectives over it (see Carlson & Moses, 2001; Wellman, Cross, & Watson, 2001; Carlson, Mandell, & Williams, 2004; for a cross-cultural perspective, see also Liu, Wellman, & Tardif, 2008). Moreover, even though a full-fledged theory of mind emerges at age four or five, a basic ability to attribute beliefs to others and construct alternative views can be found even in the first year in human infants (Baillargeon et al., 2013, pp. 88–89), and by the age of fifteen months children show signs of surprise if someone's behavior is inconsistent with the belief they have attributed to that person (Onishi & Baillargeon, 2005). Some authors have argued that these are distinctively human abilities that great apes do not share (see Tomasello & Moll, 2013, pp. 81–85), but more recent findings raise many doubts about that conclusion (Krupenye et al., 2016; De Waal, 2016).

These capabilities make it possible for there to be situations in which members of a group share a two-level conception of objects. To use Searle's well-known formula, "let's assume together that this X counts as Y in this context C." The whole mechanism of status attribution from an ontogenetic point of view is connected with the activity of joint pretense, namely, collectively pretending that something is something else. The psychology behind pretend-play is therefore crucial in this regard. We previously saw that, from an ontogenetic perspective, a distinction is to be drawn between a basic capacity for joint attention and intention, which human children develop from twelve to fifteen months of age, and a full-fledged theory of mind, which they develop at the age of four or five. This two-step process finds a parallel in the development of pretend-play. From the time children are two years old, they learn how to engage in these kinds of games on an imitative basis (Rakoczy, Tomasello, & Striano, 2005a, 2005b), and they also show an awareness of the normative structure of pretend-play connected with the notion of joint commitment, as by protesting if others do not act consistently with the shared principles of generation (Rakoczy, 2008; Rakoczy, Warneken, & Tomasello, 2008). Moreover, of course, starting at age two, children learn the most basic system of statuses, namely, language, an "institution" in which things (sounds) count as something else (words with a meaning). At this stage, however, the attribution of a second, symbolic status to objects is practiced but not conceptualized: Young children are not aware of the fact that the dual nature of objects in pretend-play depends on collective beliefs (Kalish, 2005, pp. 249–50; Rakoczy & Tomasello, 2007, p. 131). As mentioned, doing so requires developing the concept of belief as well as the perspective taking abilities entailed by the understanding of false beliefs that children develop at age four to five. This is also the age at which children develop metalinguistic awareness and hence grasp the structure of status attribution in semantics (Doherty & Perner, 1998). Phylogenetically, behavior innovations typical of *Homo sapiens* can be connected with the development of semantics through an enhancement of phonological working memory, which is instrumental in using recursive syntax and hence in constructing sentences about semantics (Dubreuil, 2010, pp. 124–125).

The passage from joint pretending to understanding the dual, symbolic structure of status attribution – and hence to conceptualizing the "X counts as Y" structure – is conducive to level 3 sociality, where status attribution becomes the content of a norm. It is not just *this* stone that under certain circumstances counts as an apple in this game, but *any* stone will do so as well ("for every X, X will count as Y in context C"). We saw that at least two passages are necessary for the emergence of social norms on level 1: (1) objectivization, namely, the perception of norms as something that can be considered from a third-person perspective (hence independently of our actual involvement), and (2) an earnest appreciation of their "weightiness," namely, an awareness that these norms are constitutive of membership in the group and are thus of fundamental importance in our social setting. At level 3, these two elements result in an understanding of institutional entities as objective artifacts, which can be grouped under categories and that are supported by social norms and collective intentions because the group considers them to be important (they are not "just games").

Artifacts in general come with an in-built normativity and teleology of usage that children learn by imitation and can already make explicit at preschool stage (German & Johnson, 2002; Kemler Nelson, Holt, & Egan, 2004). This exemplifies a phenomenon called "functional fixedness," namely, a difficulty in deviating from normal use, presumably because there is at play a process that categorizes objects into kinds, yielding a system of concepts organized around functional knowledge (Vaesen, 2012, p. 206). Institutional objects having a status function are categorized by children as standard artifacts from the age of four or five, and they are conceptualized as having the same kind of objectivity that ordinary artifacts have. For this reason, the idea that the function of institutional objects can change when intentions in a community change is only understood by older children (eight to nine years old) (Noyes, Keil, & Dunham, 2018). Objectivity is therefore the original cognitive phenomenon in institutional artifacts, despite their mind-dependent nature. A crucial role is played here by the analogy with standard artifacts, because when it comes to other sorts of conventions, children understand their mind-dependent nature even at preschool age (Noyes & Dunham, 2017). Hence, with institutional objects, the group-dependent objectification in terms of norms merges with a group-independent objectification in terms of kinds of artifacts. Indeed, human adults conceptualize institutional artifacts as being typically opposed to social objects while being more similar to standard artifacts, be they abstract or concrete (Roversi, Borghi, & Tummolini, 2013). This conclusion can find some support even from the phylogenetic point of view. When symbolic artifacts originally emerged in human activities, they were organized in the same way as ordinary, functional artifacts. In the Blombos Cave in South Africa – where the richest collection of bone tools from the Middle Stone Age has been found and the most compelling evidence of the emergence of symbolic behavior in Homo sapiens has been gathered – shell beads have been found that were organized in clusters of two to seventeen, and all the elements of each cluster presented similar physical and functional features (Dubreuil, 2010, pp. 110–111).

Even though the pretend-play mechanism finds its cognitive root very early in human children, the passage from pretend-play to more "serious" institutional games occurs later. In this sense, games of make-believe can be interpreted as a bridge between a safe dimension, where the basics are learned in a closed and personally restricted context, to a properly social dimension, where the elements of life within the relevant group are acquired (Rakoczy, 2007, pp. 129–131). Here, the problem of proper interaction among agents shifts from the game-playing setting to the "normal" setting, and this requires an understanding of social roles.

From the perspective of cognitive development, social roles are inherently connected with norms. Young children (aged four to five) preferably connect social roles with normative properties rather than with psychological or behavioral ones, even when these roles are novel for them (Kalish & Lawson, 2008, pp. 588ff.), and preschoolers predict individual behavior by way of norms rather than by way of psychological motives (Kalish & Shiverick, 2004; see also, more in general, Kalish, 2013). Hence, the normative framework connected with roles is the preferred original framework by which to understand social reality, and allegiance within a group has an important impact in attributing social categories (Rhodes, 2013). The first status children take very seriously, and in a cross-cultural way, is gender: preschoolers see gender as a fundamental social category (Rhodes & Gelman, 2009) connected with normative considerations that play a crucial role in their life (though their strength can vary depending on the behavior taken into consideration: see Blakemore, 2003). Another possible bridge between pretend-play and more "serious" games is ownership, which is the first serious institution children engage in. Already at age two, children recognize that owning something goes beyond having it at their disposal; toddlers expect reciprocity in sharing; and young children treat stealing as a violation (Kalish, 2005, p. 256; see also Rossano et al., 2011): Conflicts over property is one of the most fundamental sources of conflict among children, in part because – and this is distinctively human – young children conceive it as something that can change and be contested, which means that they recognize the status-based character of ownership quite early on (Kalish, 2005, p. 256). This complex human understanding of ownership can find a cognitive ground in a more basic instinct of possession, which for evolutionary reasons is present in many animals (Stake, 2006). Other "serious" institutional statuses relevant for law concern authority, responsibility, and punishment, and we will look at their cognitive underpinnings in Section 6.3.2.

6.3 THE STRUCTURE OF LAW

6.3.1 Second Thesis: Legal Institutions Formally Organize Sanctions and Authority

We have thus far discussed the theoretical and psychological implications of the first thesis about the metaphysics of law, stating that if we are to understand the structure and conceptualization of legal facts, we have to understand basic social facts such as joint action, joint commitment, the emergence of social norms, and the nature of status attribution. The second theoretical thesis elaborates on the first by defining some peculiarities of law within the social domain. It states that law is a normative organization of sanctions and authorities. According to H. L. A. Hart's classic picture, law in its proper sense comes into being when (primary) rules of conduct within a given community are supplemented with (secondary) norms conferring the power to create and apply primary rules as well as specifying their conditions of validity (Hart, 1994). This model finds a parallel in Hans Kelsen's view of legal systems as dynamic systems, namely, systems of norms whose objective validity rests on the fact that they have been produced by an act qualified by a higher-order norm (Kelsen, 1992), or in the more recent view of Scott Shapiro, where norms conceived as plans are created by people empowered by meta-plans (Shapiro, 2011). A possible alternative conceptualization of law is that of Theodor Geiger (1964, p. 168), who insists on regulation under a centralized mechanism for social reaction when social norms are deviated from. But even this conceptualization assumes the creation of an authority to regulate social sanctions. The point is that giving someone the power to modify norms and make decisions, as well as distinguishing between valid and invalid norms, implies conferring a status. Hence, in all these pictures and according to the second thesis, law finds its roots in level 3 of sociality (status attribution through social norms).

Even though this thesis is quite minimal, it finds several possible – and quite traditional – counterarguments. First, it could be argued that organizing sanctions and defining authorities is not peculiar to law. For example, the religious and moral systems adhered to by a sect can define their own kind of sanction and authority without, strictly speaking, being law-making authorities. Second, and conversely, social norms can be enforced within groups without authority, as when in small social groups deviants are excluded from the group or marginalized by way of shared disapproval. So it seems that in assuming this thesis, we are not introducing necessary conditions for something to count as law, nor any sufficient ones: We are not really going after the essential features of law.

There are good reasons for accepting this conclusion and still maintaining that the second thesis can be fruitful. Indeed, one could argue that the very endeavor of trying to define the essential features of law by way of conceptual analysis will inevitably bump up against counterexamples, given the artifactual, historical, and context-dependent nature of its object (Leiter, 2011; Schauer, 2012, 2015; Tamanaha, 2017a). In this sense, the very metaphysics of law would imply that it is impossible to posit a priori essential features. Moreover, given these shifting boundaries, the considerations just made can be considered not as counterexamples but rather as features of the development of law over the course of history. It is true that religious and moral rules can in some contexts bear some legal traits and, indeed, this is one of the main reasons why, from a historical and anthropological point of view, these domains have shown significant overlap in most communities and cultures. On the other hand, it is also true that there can be an informal law without hierarchies. However, apart from bands of hunter-gatherers and small groups, the regulation of social life by way of a legal framework has in most cases required some degree of hierarchy. And where there is hierarchy, there is also status. One could weaken the Hartian requirement of secondary rules of change – rules conferring the power to create other rules – when considering societies based only on customary norms, but even in those cases there will at least be, first, authorities to apply and enforce the customs, and second, an idea of *the* law, that is, the definition of a set of norms that are valid in a given context or are laid down by a certain authority. We will therefore have both authority and validity.

Notice that legal pluralism is not a counterexample to the second thesis. It has been argued that a state-centric model is too parochial to account for legal domains across different periods and contexts, and that in several contexts – and over significant periods of time, as in the case of Europe before the advent of nation-states – law was grounded not in a single source but rather on several, and possibly competing, sources (Tamanaha, 2017b). The second thesis, however, does not assume a monistic, state-centric perspective in this regard. Even in a pluralistic setting, the different sources of authority have their own normative organization of authority, sanctions, and validity. In these contexts, however, law does not have a single, unified meta-institution claiming supremacy over all others and validating them as legal or extralegal.

In a sense, the second thesis is quite minimal from a functionalist perspective as well. Apart from a generic purpose of social regulation, the most peculiar trait of law lies not in its point but in its structure. In this sense, the second thesis is quite Hartian in its inspiration (it focuses not on the ends which law serves, but on its means; Green, 2010), and here the Nietzschean skepticism about overly comforting, ahistorical functionalistic dreams seems well placed: "Today it is impossible to say precisely why people are actually punished: all concepts in which an entire process is semiotically concentrated defy definition; only something which has no history can be defined" (Nietzsche, *On the Genealogy of Morality*, II, 13, p. 53 in the English edition). Legal structures can serve different purposes depending on the situation, ranging from the very broad objective of social utility or coordination to the specific aim of serving highly technical, and self-referential, bureaucratic needs created by the organizations that law itself makes possible, even passing through the mere enforcement of needs based on domination (Tamanaha, 2017b, pp. 46ff., ch. 4). Of course, legal institutions can simply be instruments of brute dominion, something that cannot be captured by a view of legal ontology based purely on collective acceptance (Canale, 2014, pp. 310–312). However, despite the Hartian-inspired insistence on structural elements, the second thesis takes coercion to be an important, if not central, feature of legal organizations. This, of course, does not entail a strong view about coercion as the content or background of all legal norms properly so called. It rather entails a point about legal systems and legal institutions considered as a whole. There can be legal norms not supported by sanctions, and of course there can be legal norms that do not have any kind of sanction as their content, but the general phenomenon of law within a given community must regulate sanctions in some way, because this is the way in which legal regulation achieves social organization (Schauer, 2015; Himma, 2018).

Finally, the second thesis is quite neutral when it comes to a legal system's legitimacy and the specific features of a legal system's sources of validity. It will be helpful to qualify the second thesis by taking up Joseph Raz's (1979) view that legal authority claims legitimacy in a way that imparts a sort of peremptory, exclusionary character to the kinds of reasons it provides us with. This qualification, however, does not mean that, on the second thesis, legal authority actually *does* have legitimacy or that it actually provides exclusionary reasons. Rather, it entails only that there is a claim in place, which means that legal authority typically comes with a story about its ultimate legitimation. The peculiar features of this story depend, once more, on context. Moreover, authority is based on status attribution, but the second thesis makes no claim that a legal system's sources of validity must be organized hierarchically. There can be law even without a formalized and single system of norms, a model that indeed is quite recent in the development of legal history (Tamanaha, 2017b). Accordingly, the second thesis does not commit us to any description of the rule of recognition or of the basic norm at the core of the legal system. It can be that a basic norm transcendentally justified as a precondition for legal science is nothing more than an arbitrary postulate, or that deriving a rule of recognition from the social practice of officials is a category mistake. These legal-theoretical problems have no direct impact on the second thesis. As noted, the thesis is minimal, and it suffices for our purposes.

6.3.2 *The Psychology Behind Legality: Authority, Sanction, Validity*

The second thesis makes it possible to draw a map of the possible cognitive-psychological topics that are relevant for the metaphysics of legality – where the term *legality* is used not evaluatively but descriptively, as the domain of things in the world that are legal or pertain to law. The first topic is the *psychology of authority*. As noted, the typical status in the domain of law is the one connected with empowerment: the power to create and modify, apply and interpret, or simply enforce legal norms. The second topic is the *psychology behind punishment and sanction*, because coercion is indeed a typical outcome of law enforcement. The third topic is the *psychology behind the concept of validity*. Even if law is not necessarily connected with the idea of a system based on a highly formalized organization of sources, legal norms – as well as legal entities, legal roles, and legal institutions in general – come with a distinction between valid and invalid, or at least borderline, instances. It is therefore crucial to understand the cognitive process through which these distinctions are made. Clearly, it is here impossible to offer a complete description or even an overview of psychological research in all these fields. What I will do instead is draw a sort of conceptual map: From these general topics, I will extract the problems in relation to which psychological research can give a crucial contribution, thus establishing a set of connections between legal metaphysics and cognitive psychology. In this way, legal theorists will have a picture of which kinds of psychological studies can be relevant in working on the nature of law, and cognitive psychologists will have an idea of where their research can have an impact on our understanding of legality.

Let us then start with authority. From a phylogenetic perspective, institutional structures defining authoritative roles came into play when social groups grew bigger – when bands of hunter-gatherers evolved into tribes, then chiefdoms, then primitive kingdoms (Dubreuil, 2010, pp. 147–157) – and the cognitive costs of sanctioning other members of the group became too high. In this situation, it simply became impossible for every member of the group to have a complete outlook on all the other members. On the one hand, chiefs and leaders became the main representatives of subgroups and guaranteed for the trustworthiness of the less salient members. On the other hand, they acquired a progressively increasing power to coerce and sanction deviant members of their subgroups, this by way of norms that empowered them to do so: norms of competence, secondary norms in Hart's sense, and hence norms for status attribution (Dubreuil, 2010, pp. 164ff.).

Of course, authoritative roles implied hierarchies. In this regard, it has been argued that the evolution of mankind has a distinctively U-shaped trajectory (Boehm, 1999, ch. 6; Dubreuil, 2010, pp. 91–92). Ape-like hierarchies based on dominance and bullyism were reversed as early as with *Homo erectus* and *Homo heidelbergensis* because, as we saw, competition for resources under conditions of survival required joint action, reciprocity, and substantial equality between potential contributors to cooperative group hunting and childrearing.[11] But later, on that basis, more evolved kinds of hierarchies grounded in status attribution and symbolic behavior emerged in *Homo sapiens* – complex formal structures for dominance

---

[11] Of course, this statement needs to be qualified to the extent that social relationships in great apes are described as based not on "brute" dominance but on a "formal" dominance predicated on acceptance (De Waal, 1998, ch. 2).

which chimpanzees could never have evolved and which are a human universal (a political feature of what has been called the "universal people"; Brown, 1991).

This kind of inequality required justification, and indeed justification was given on the basis of cultural factors, typically on cosmological/magical grounds. The sorcerer justifies the leaders' power as functional to the good of the whole group (Fiske, 1991, pp. 14, 42–49, on "authority ranking"; Sacco, 2007, ch. 6 and 9; Dubreuil, 2010, pp. 181–185; Tamanaha, 2017b, ch. 4) and builds an ideal of purity and holiness whose violation provokes disgust among the group's members (Haidt, 2012, ch. 7; Tomasello, 2016, pp. 131–132). Hence, two necessary elements of the cognitive machinery of authority are suggestion and identification with the group, alongside the mere fear of sanction. The latter is a distinct element that cannot be grouped with the other two, which by contrast required greater cognitive capacities, such as a capacity to take the perspective of the group as a whole, and a stronger episodic memory so as to remember the main narrative the group is acting on (Dubreuil, 2010, pp. 170–174).

Indeed, experiments conducted within the paradigm provided by Stanley Milgram (1974) show that even a weak authoritative nudge has a strong effect on compliance, and this effect is even greater when the request is justified, but not if the request is formulated as an explicit order (Burger, 2009; Karakostas & Zizzo, 2016). In these experiments, subjects were requested to harm someone by delivering potentially lethal electric shocks "for the sake of science." When it comes to the content of these possible justifications, an important role is played by considerations of social identity, which particularly means identifying with a group's endeavor as depicted by those who hold positions of leadership. In Milgram's case, this endeavor is the scientific enterprise (Reicher, Haslam, & Smith, 2012), but considerations of social identity have also been applied to Philip Zimbardo's famous Stanford prison experiment (Haney, Banks, & Zimbardo, 1973a, 1973b), where participants selected to play the role of prison guards showed an impressive escalation in cruelty after only six days of the experiment (Haslam, Reicher & van Bavel, 2019). In obedience to authority, therefore, identification with the group is the active counterpart to passive conformity: Being an active participant in the group's endeavor becomes an integral part of the construction of personal identity (Tomasello, 2016, pp. 62–63, 105–107). Of course, a role is also played by passive elements. Apart from the mere fear of sanction, there is the tendency to submit to a sort of "sacred" superiority that can very well find its ontogenetic roots in paternal/maternal authority, the first, original authority in children experience (Sacco, 2017, pp. 131–133), and one that, as early as 1930, Jerome Frank famously connected with the authority of law (Frank, 1930). Hence, the psychology of deference to adult authority in children, as well as the analysis of the cognitive underpinnings of mere habits – in this case habits of obedience – are topics in developmental psychology that may be relevant to the ontology of legal authority.[12]

---

[12] For an overview of these questions on a cross-cultural approach, see Harris and Corriveau (2013). See also (Kalish & Cornelius, 2007) arguing that preschool children tend to conflate obligations with an authority's desires; and, of course, Piaget (1997) on how children perceive the authority of adults. From a legal-realistic perspective, see Fittipaldi (2012, ch. 3).

Authority can be interpreted as a high-level and quite recent cognitive phenomenon from a phylogenetic perspective, given its connection to group identification, status attribution, and justification. The disposition to sanction behavior in human agents has much deeper, and more ancient, cognitive roots. These lie in the basic emotions of rage and disgust located in the anterior insula (Sanfey et al., 2003) and in the pleasure of reward located in the caudate nucleus when the punishment is altruistic (De Quervain et al., 2004, p. 1256).[13] Rage is a typical animal reaction to unexpected damage and goal frustration (Haidt, 2003), and humans are no exception, showing an emotional reaction based on outrage when they are directly influenced by the actions of others that can be harmful or violate trust. An important role in supporting cooperation is played by rage and punishment in the form of revenge. Public-goods games with the ability to punish free-riders show that free-riders are heavily punished, and that punishment has a big disciplining effect (Fehr & Gächter, 2000a, 2000b). However, there is a strong psychological tendency to overestimate the damage received in revenge and to underestimate the damage done, for which reason personal revenge will typically result in an escalation of violence (Shergill et al., 2003). Human beings are consequentialist calculators when it comes to crimes in general and in judging punishments in the abstract, but they are emotional deontological retributivists when that crime affects them directly (Greene, 2008). For this reason, delegation of punishment to a third, neutral power can keep the escalation in check, and indeed it will hinder the tendency to react, but this effect will depend on the extent to which the power is perceived to be legitimate (Pinker, 2011, pp. 772–773; Hermann, Thoni, & Gächter, 2008).

Apart from rage, disgust is another emotion that serves as a foundation for punishment or, more in general, for reaction to violations of norms. Of course, the specific conditions that elicit disgust are culturally determined, but it has been argued that disgust as a basis for normative reactions can be seen as a universal and could even serve an evolutionary role (Haidt, 2012, ch. 7, section 5). Moreover, unlike other primates, humans show indignation even when norms are violated in ways that do not directly affect them, though in this case the motivation to exact sanctions is less strong (Fehr & Fischbacher, 2004), and in large groups third-party punishment is necessarily delegated and hence organized around institutions (Hoffman, 2014, ch. 7).

Experiments in behavioral economics show that the degree of punishment in humans is modulated by expectations. Strong punishment is triggered, and moral rage in particular, when the behavior of others exceeds a threshold of unfairness that one can expect. Even if punishment exacted under the threshold will still be considered justifiable, it will typically be weaker and less likely, and its likelihood will decrease over time (see Van Winden, 2007, pp. 43ff. Dubreuil, 2010, pp. 23–27). Anger can in this regard be argued to have a cross-cultural recalibrating effect, that is, a specific evolutionary role in increasing the chances that a conflict will be resolved in favor of the angry individual (Sell et al., 2017), and indeed there is a high degree of cross-culturality both in the propensity to

---

[13] On the neurological underpinnings of violence in humans, see also Pinker (2011, ch. 8).

punish wrongdoers and in ranking the seriousness of some core crimes and the blameworthiness of those who commit them (see Robinson & Kurzban, 2007; but compare Hermann et al., 2008 on cross-cultural variations).

In law, authority, powers, and sanctions are organized according to conceptual structures. In a typical legal syllogism, the second premise qualifies some fact, act, or event according to a legal concept, and the first premise qualifies a norm as legally valid or applicable. The basic cognitive process that is called for in this kind of reasoning is conceptual qualification, or categorization, understood as the general ability to recognize instances as tokens of a general type (Pattaro, 2005, pp. 13ff.; Ehrenberg, 2016, ch. 2, Section D). Therefore, it is not surprising that, from a phylogenetic point of view, the qualification of legal roles and events by way of statuses emerged only when humans developed an enhanced linguistic working memory capable of formulating and communicating meta-representations, namely, representations about meaning and conceptual content (Coolidge and Wynn, 2007, 2009, ch. 11; Dubreuil, 2010, pp. 123–125). From an ontogenetic perspective, even though young children tend to understand categories in general as natural kinds, they are also capable of understanding that some categories are conventional and that they can be constructed in different ways depending on the goal one is aiming to achieve (Kalish, 1998).

For these reasons, theories of categorization will necessarily have a crucial impact on the metaphysics of law, and the specific kind of theory of categorization that will prove to be useful will depend on the legal-theoretical approach taken. In principle, formalistic normativism seems tied to a rule-based, definitional, and hence classic theory of categorization. Legal concepts are defined through a set of essential features set forth in rules (Winter, 2001, ch. 4). To that classic theory one could also connect Searle's idea of constitutive rules in the form "X counts as Y in C." To the extent that our explanation of legality departs from such a formalistic approach, other theories of categorization can become relevant. These range from prototype theories (Rosch & Mervis, 1975; Rosch, 1978; Lakoff, 1987), in which some features are connected with prototypical exemplars and conceptual boundaries are shaded, to a more extreme exemplar-based view on which concepts are represented through particular instances (Medin & Shaffer, 1978; Nosofsky & Palmeri, 1997; Wills, Inkster, & Milton, 2015).

When dealing with the legal qualification of facts, acts, and events, contextual considerations will be extremely relevant, hence a situated conceptualization theory of categorization like that proposed by Lawrence Barsalou (2016) can provide significant insights into the cognitive underpinnings of this crucial mechanism of legal reasoning. More to the point, a prototype theory seems well suited to explain the process of assessing whether legal acts are typical or atypical (Passerini Glazel, 2005).[14] When it comes to the process of assessing legal validity for the purposes of stating the first, normative premise in legal decisions, the kind of cognitive theory one proceeds from will also depend on the kind of legal system in question. In a common-law system, a theory of categorization in

---

[14] See also (Fittipaldi, 2013, pp. 78–80) on prototype theory and legal interpretation in general.

terms of prototypical precedents and shaded boundaries seems well suited to account for the typical flexibility that kind of system requires (Winter, 2001, ch. 6). At the same time, civil-law systems, built around a strict system of sources of law, seem to be more adequately explained in terms of a rule-based and definitional model. But, again, much depends, here too, on the kind of theoretical attitude we take to judicial reasoning in general, whether formalistic or antiformalistic. From an antiformalistic perspective, the categorization of a norm as valid is not distinct from an interpretation of textual provisions. A norm is valid if it is the outcome of judicial interpretation, and interpretation depends at least on (a) the content of the norm itself, (b) the content of the norms that make those provisions formally valid, and (c) the content of the principles that make or do not make that norm substantively valid. This process involves a complex interweaving of linguistic categorizations that can call for definitions, rules, prototypes, and exemplars. Indeed, even on a more general level, recent research in the psychology of categorization has advanced hybrid models in which category learning seems to be influenced by both rules and exemplars (Thibaut, Gelaes, & Murphy, 2018).

The problem of legal validity and of legal categorization can also be addressed from the point of view of the "embodied cognition" paradigm, that is, proceeding from the assumption that cognitive processing can be grounded in sensory-motor perception (Lakoff & Johnson, 1980; Barsalou, 1999, 2008; Borghi & Pecher, 2011).[15] From this perspective, the question of how legal concepts are processed becomes an instance of a more general problem of embodiment, namely, the problem of how abstract concepts can be based on sensory-motor patterns or whether they can instead be traced to more linguistic forms of social elaboration (Borghi & Binkofski, 2014). Recent experimental research has been conducted – and is currently ongoing at the University of Bologna – on how to define the peculiar features of legal concepts within the "embodied cognition" paradigm (Roversi, Pasqui & Borghi, 2017). The problem of how theories of embodied cognition can explain legal concepts is particularly relevant because this paradigm makes it possible to assess the weight of subjective, mind-dependent, and social considerations relative to more objective, concrete, and physically determined features (or even spatial, geometric considerations).[16]

6.4 CONCLUSION

In this chapter, I have provided a model for the metaphysics of law and tried to show how studies in cognitive psychology may have a crucial bearing on this topic. In order to do so, I presented two theses about legal metaphysics, the first being that legal facts are a subset of social facts, and hence that legal metaphysics is a special case of social metaphysics, and the second that legal facts are the outcome of rules that organize sanctions and authority in a formal way. I elaborated on the first thesis

---

[15] An important study that applies extensively the embodied cognition paradigm, and in particular the theory of conceptual metaphors, to property is Larsson (2017).
[16] See for example Costa & Bonetti (2016) with regard to religious concepts.

FIGURE 6.1A Sociality

by distinguishing among four different and ideal-typical levels of society (levels 0 through 3): (0) joint action and joint commitment, (1) social norms, (2) status attribution, (3) status attribution through social norms. For each level, I gave a picture of the relevant cognitive underpinnings, from both a phylogenetic and an ontogenetic point of view. I then proceeded with the second thesis about the nature of legality and I explained how it can be consistent with several legal-theoretical approaches. In general, the second thesis is a very weak thesis about legality, coherent with both source-monism and source-pluralism. It is not aimed at positing essential properties that make legality necessarily peculiar within the social domain. Given this background, I gave some suggestions about the cognitive-psychological research topics that are relevant for the questions of authority, sanctions, and validity. The outcome of this presentation is summarized in the two graphs below (see Figures 6.1a and b).

Obviously, the theses presented here cannot be considered an answer to the question of the nature of law from a psychological point of view. In a sense, the picture I have drawn is not even a presentation of the state of the art in "legal metaphysics and

FIGURE 6.1B Legality

cognitive psychology," because a field so described has yet to be established. This is meant to be an initial proposal and an initial picture – tentative, provisional, and certainly incomplete – of the many different topics, problems, and strands of research in legal theory and cognitive psychology that appear to intertwine in the effort to understand the nature of law and of legal entities. My hope is that this classic and millenary endeavor can make further progress by working together conceptual-philosophical theories and empirical-psychological studies, in a way that is not different from what has already happened, and is now happening, in other fields of philosophy.

REFERENCES

Aichhorn, M., Perner, J., Kronbichler, M., Staffen, W., & Ladurner, G. (2006). Do Visual Perspective Tasks Need Theory of Mind? *NeuroImage* 30, 1059–1068.
Andrews, K. (2009). Understanding Norms Without a Theory of Mind. *Inquiry* 52, 433–448.
Andrews, K. (2015). The Folk Psychological Spiral: Explanation, Regulation, and Language. *The Southern Journal of Philosophy* 53, 50–66.

Astington, J. W. (1988). Children's Understanding of the Speech Act of Promising. *Journal of Child Language* 15, 157–173.
Baillargeon, R., He, Z., Setoh, P. et al. (2013). False-Belief Understanding and Why It Matters. In M. Banaji & S. Gelman (eds.), *Navigating the Social World: What Infants, Children, and Other Species Can Teach Us*. Oxford: Oxford University Press, pp. 88–95.
Barsalou, L. W. (1999). Perceptual Symbol Systems. *Behavioural Brain Sciences* 22, 577–660.
Barsalou, L. W. (2008). Grounded Cognition. *Annual Review of Psychology* 59, 617–645.
Barsalou, L. W. (2016). Situated Conceptualization: Theory and Application. In Y. Coello & M. H. Fischer (eds.), *Perceptual and Emotional Embodiment. Vol. 1, pp. Foundations of Embodied Cognition*. London and New York: Routledge, pp. 11–37.
Becchio, C., & Bertone, C. (2004). Wittgenstein Running: Neural Mechanisms of Collective Intentionality and We-mode. *Consciousness and Cognition* 13, 123–133.
Becchio, C., Del Giudice, M., Dal Monte, O., Latini-Corazzini, L., & Pia, L. (2013). In Your Place: Neuropsychological Evidence for Altercentric Remapping in Embodied Perspective Taking. *Social Cognitive and Affective Neuroscience* 8, 165–170.
Bicchieri, C. (2006). *The Grammar of Society*. Cambridge: Cambridge University Press.
Birch, J. (2017). *The Philosophy of Social Evolution*. Oxford: Oxford University Press.
Blakemore, J. E. O. (2003). Children's Beliefs about Violating Gender Norms: Boys Shouldn't Look Like Girls, and Girls Shouldn't Act Like Boys. *Sex Roles* 48, 411–419.
Boehm, C. (1999). *Hierarchy in the Forest: The Evolution of Egalitarian Behaviour*. Cambridge, MA: Harvard University Press.
Boesch, C. (2002). Cooperative Hunting Roles among Taïe Chimpanzees. *Human Nature* 13, 27–46.
Bolt, N. K., & Loehr, J. D. (2017). The Predictability of a Partner's Actions Modulates the Sense of Joint Agency. *Cognition* 161, 60–65.
Borghi, A., & Binkofski, F. (2014). *Words as Social Tools: An Embodied View on Abstract Concepts*. Berlin: Springer.
Borghi, A., & Pecher, D. (2011). Introduction to the Special Topic Embodied and Grounded Cognition. *Frontiers in Psychology* 2, 1–3.
Bratman, M. (1992). Shared Cooperative Activities. *The Philosophical Review* 101, 327–341.
Brown, D. E. (1991). *Human Universals*. New York: McGraw-Hill.
Brożek, B. (2013). *Rule-Following: From Imitation to the Normative Mind*. Kraków: Copernicus Center Press.
Bruner, E., Manzi, G., & Arsuaga, J. L. (2003). Encephalization and Allometric Trajectories in the Genus *Homo*: Evidence from the Neanderthal and Modern Lineages. *Proceedings of the National Academy of Sciences* 100, 15335–40.
Burazin, L. (2016). Can There Be an Artefact Theory of Law? *Ratio Juris* 29, 385–401.
Burazin, L. (2018). Legal Systems as Abstract Institutional Artifacts. In L. Burazin, K. E. Himma, and C. Roversi (eds.), *Law as an Artifact*. 112–35. Oxford: Oxford University Press.
Burazin, L., Himma, K. E., & Roversi, C. (eds.) (2018). *Law as an Artifact*. Oxford: Oxford University Press.
Burger, J. (2009). Replicating Milgram: Would Still People Obey Today? *American Psychologist* 64, 1–11.
Buttelmann, D. (2013). Selective Imitation of In-Group Over Out-Group Members in 14-Month-Old Infants. *Child Development* 84, 422–428.
Butterfill, S. (2012). Joint Action and Development. *The Philosophical Quarterly* 62, 23–47.
Camerer, C. (2003). *Behavioral Game Theory: Experiments in Strategic Interaction*. Princeton, NJ: Princeton University Press.

Canale, D. (2014). Is Law Grounded in Joint Action? *Rechtstheorie* 45, 289–312.
Carlson, S. M., & Moses, L. J. (2001). Individual Differences in Inhibitory Control and Children's Theory of Mind. *Child Development* 72, 1032–1053.
Carlson, S. M., Mandell, D. J., & Williams, L. (2004). Executive Function and Theory of Mind: Stability and Prediction from Age 2 to 3. *Developmental Psychology* 40, 1105–1122.
Carpenter, M. (2006). Instrumental, Social, and Shared Goals and Intentions in Imitation. In S. J. Rogers & J. H. G. Williams (eds.), *Imitation and the Social Mind: Autism and Typical Development*. New York and London: The Guilford Press.
Chilovi, S., & Pavlakos, G. (2019). Law Determination as Grounding: A Common Framework for Jurisprudence. *Legal Theory* 25, 53–76.
Coolidge, F. L., & Wynn, T. (2007). The Working Memory Account of Neanderthal Cognition: How Phonological Storage Capacity May Be Related to Recursion and the Pragmatics of Modern Speech. *Journal of Human Evolution* 52, 707–10.
Coolidge, F. L., & Wynn, T. (2009). *The Rise of Homo sapiens: The Evolution of Modern Thinking*. Chichester: Wiley-Blackwell.
Costa, M., & Bonetti, L. (2016). Geometrical Factors in the Perception of Sacredness. *Perception* 45(11), 1240–1266.
Crowe, J. (2014). Law as an Artifact Kind. *Monash University Law Review* 40, 737–757.
Darwall, S. L. (2006). *The Second-Person Standpoint: Respect, Morality, and Accountability*. Cambridge, MA: Harvard University Press.
de Quervain, D. J. F., Fischbacher, U., Treyer, V., et al. (2004). The Neural Basis of Altruistic Punishment. *Science* 305, 1254–1258.
De Waal, F. (1998). *Chimpanzee Politics: Power and Sex among Apes*, 2nd revised ed. Baltimore, MD: Johns Hopkins University Press.
De Waal, F. (2014). Natural Normativity: The "Is" and "Ought" of Animal Behaviour. *Behaviour* 151. 185–204.
De Waal, F. (2016). Apes Know What Others Believe. *Science* 354, 39–40.
Doherty, M., & Perner, J. (1998). Metalinguistic Awareness and Theory of Mind: Just Two Words for the Same Thing? *Cognitive Development* 13, 279–305.
Dubreuil, B. (2010). *Human Evolution and the Origins of Hierarchies: The State of Nature*. Cambridge: Cambridge University Press.
d'Errico, F., Henshilwood, C., Vanhaeren, M., & van Niekerk, K. (2005). *Nassarius kraussianus* Shell Beads from Blombos Cave: Evidence for Symbolic Behaviour in the Middle Stone Age. *Journal of Human Evolution* 48, 3–24.
Ehrenberg, K. (2016). *The Functions of Law*. Oxford: Oxford University Press.
Epstein, B. (2015). *The Ant Trap: Rebuilding the Foundations of the Social Sciences*. Oxford: Oxford University Press.
Epstein, B. (2018). Social Ontology. *The Stanford Encyclopedia of Philosophy*. https://plato.stanford.edu/entries/social-ontology/
Fehr, E., & Fischbacher, U. (2004). Third Party Punishment and Social Norms. *Evolution and Human Behavior* 25, 63–87.
Fehr, E., & Gächter, S. (2000a). Fairness and Retaliation: The Economics of Reciprocity. *Journal of Economic Perspectives* 14, 159–181.
Fehr, E., & Gächter, S. (2000b). Cooperation and Punishment in Public Good Experiments. *The American Economic Review* 90, 980–994.
Fiske, A. P. (1991). *Structures of Social Life: The Four Elementary Forms of Human Relations*. New York: Free Press.
Fittipaldi, E. (2012). *Everyday Legal Ontology: A Psychological and Linguistic Investigation within the Framework of Leon Petrażycki's Theory of Law*. Milan: LED.

Fittipaldi, E. (2013). *Conoscenza giuridica ed errore: Saggio sullo statuto epistemologico degli asserti prodotti dalla scienza giuridica.* Rome: Aracne.

Fittipaldi, E. (2016). Leon Petrażycki's Theory of Law. In E. Pattaro & C. Roversi (eds.), *Legal Philosophy in the Twentieth Century: The Civil Law World. Tome 2, Main Orientations and Topics.* Berlin: Springer, pp. 443–503.

Fittipaldi, E. (in press). Petrażycki's Puzzle of Jural Emotions: Bridging the Psychological Theory of Law with Modern Social and Psychological Sciences. In E. Fittipaldi & A.J. Treviño (eds.), *The Living Legacy of Leon Petrażycki.* London: Routledge.

Francey, D., & Bergmüller, R. (2012). Images of Eyes Enhance Investments in a Real-Life Public Good. *PLoS ONE* 7, e37397.

Frank, J. (1930). *Law and the Modern Mind.* New York: Brentano's.

Gallotti, M. (2012). A Naturalistic Argument for the Irreducibility of Collective Intentionality. *Philosophy of the Social Sciences* 42, 3–30.

Geiger, T. (1964). *Vorstudien zu einer Soziologie des Rechts.* Neuwied am Rhein & Berlin: Luchterhand. (1st ed. 1947.)

German, T. P., & Johnson, S. C. (2002). Function and the Origins of the Design Stance. *Journal of Cognition and Development* 3, 279–300.

Gilbert, M. (1989). *On Social Facts.* Princeton: Princeton University Press.

Gilbert, M. (2014). *Joint Commitment: How We Make the Social World.* Oxford: Oxford University Press.

Göckeritz, S., Schmidt, M. F. H., & Tomasello, M. (2014). Young Children's Creation and Transmission of Social Norms. *Cognitive Development* 30, 81–95.

Gräfenhain, M., Behne, T., Carpenter, M., & Tomasello, M. (2009). Young Children's Understanding of Joint Commitments. *Developmental Psychology* 45, 1430–1443.

Gräfenhain, M., Carpenter, M., & Tomasello, M. (2013). Three-Year-Olds' Understanding of the Consequences of Joint Commitments. *PLoS ONE* 8, e73039.

Green, L. (2010). Law as a Means. In P. Cane (ed.), *The Hart-Fuller Debate in the Twenty-First Century.* Oxford: Hart Publishing, pp. 169–188.

Greene, J. D. (2008). The Secret Joke of Kant's Soul. In W. Sinnott-Armstrong (ed.), *Moral Psychology. Vol. 3. The Neuroscience of Morality: Emotion, Brain Disorders, and Development.* Cambridge, MA: The MIT Press, pp. 35–79.

Hage, J. (2018). *Foundations and Building Blocks of Law.* Maastricht: Eleven International Publishing.

Hägerström, A. (1917). *Till frågan om den objektiva rättens begrepp. I. Viljeteorien.* Uppsala: Akademiska Bokhandeln/ Leipzig: Harrassowitz.

Hägerström, A. (1941). *Der römische Obligationsbegriff im Lichte der allgemeinen römischen Rechtsanschauung. II.* Uppsala: Alqvist & Wiksell.

Haidt, J. (2003). The Moral Emotions. In R. J. Davidson, K. R. Scherer, & H. H. Goldsmith (eds.), *Handbook of Affective Sciences.* Oxford: Oxford University Press, pp. 852–870.

Haidt, J. (2012). *The Righteous Mind: Why Good People Are Divided by Politics and Religion.* London: Penguin.

Hamann, K., Warneken, F., & Tomasello, M. (2012). Children's Developing Commitments to Joint Goals. *Child Development* 83, 137–145.

Haney, C., Banks, C., & Zimbardo, P. G. (1973a). Interpersonal dynamics in a simulated prison. *International Journal of Criminology and Penology* 1, 69–97.

Haney, C., Banks, C., & Zimbardo, P. G. (1973b). *Naval Research Reviews: A Study of Prisoners and Guards in a Simulated Prison.* Washington, DC: Office of Naval Research.

Harris, P. L., & Corriveau, K. H. (2013). Respectful Deference: Conformity Revisited. In M. Banaji & S. Gelman (eds.), *Navigating the Social World: What Infants, Children, and Other Species Can Teach Us.* Oxford: Oxford University Press, pp. 230–234.

Hart, H. L. A. (1994). *The Concept of Law*, 2nd ed. Oxford: Clarendon. (1st ed. 1961.)

Haslam, S. A., & Reicher, S. D., & Van Bavel, J. J. (2019). Rethinking the Nature of Cruelty: The Role of Identity Leadership in the Stanford Prison Experiment. *American Psychologist* 74, 809–822.

Haun, D. B. M., Rekers, Y., & Tomasello, M. (2014). Children Conform to the Behaviour of Peers; Other Great Apes Stick With What They Know. *Psychological Science* 25, 2160–2167.

Haun, D. B. M., & Tomasello, M. (2011). Conformity to Peer Pressure in Preschool Children. *Child Development* 82, 1759–1767.

Henshilwood, C. S., d'Errico, F., Vanhaeren, M., van Niekerk, K., & Jacobs, Z. (2004). Middle Stone Age Shell Beads from South Africa. *Science* 384, 404.

Hermann, B., Thoni, C., & Gächter, S. (2008). Antisocial Punishment Across Societies. *Science* 319, 1362–1367.

Himma, K. E. (2018). The Conceptual Function of Law: Law, Coercion, and Keeping the Peace. In L. Burazin, K. E. Himma, & C. Roversi (eds.), *Law as an Artifact.* Oxford: Oxford University Press, pp. 136–159.

Hindriks, F., & Guala, F. (2015). Institutions, Rules, and Equilibria: A Unified Theory. *Journal of Institutional Economics* 11, 459–480.

Hodgson, G. M. (2006). What Are Institutions? *Journal of Economic Issues* 15, 1–23.

Hoffman, M. B. (2014). *The Punisher's Brain: The Evolution of Judge and Jury.* Cambridge: Cambridge University Press.

Horner, V., & Whiten, A. K. (2005). Causal Knowledge and Imitation/emulation Switching in Chimpanzees (*Pan troglodytes*) and Children. *Animal Cognition* 8, 164–181.

House, B. R., Silk, J. B., Henrich, J. et al. (2013). Ontogeny of Prosocial Behaviour across Diverse Societies. *Proceedings of the National Academy of Sciences of the United States of America* 110, 14586–91.

Hovers, E., Ilani, S., Bar-Yosef, O. & Vandermeersch, B. (2003). An Early Case of Color Symbolism Ocher Use by Modern Humans in Qafzeh Cave. *Current Anthropology* 44, 491–522.

Jones, O. D., & Kurzban, R. (2010). Intuitions of Punishment. *The University of Chicago Law Review* 77, 1633–1640.

Kalish, C. (2005). Becoming Status Conscious: Children's Appreciation of Social Reality. *Philosophical Explorations* 8, pp. 245–262.

Kalish, C. W. (1998). Natural and Artifactual Kinds: Are Children Realists or Relativists About Categories? *Developmental Psychology* 34, 376–391.

Kalish, C. W. (2013). Status Seeking: The Importance of Roles in Early Social Cognition. In M. Banaji & S. Gelman (eds.), *Navigating the Social World: What Infants, Children, and Other Species Can Teach Us.* Oxford: Oxford University Press, pp. 216–219.

Kalish, C. W., & Cornelius, R. (2007). What Is to Be Done? Children's Ascriptions of Conventional Obligations. *Child Development* 78, 859–878.

Kalish, C. W., & Lawson, C. A. (2008). Development of Social Category Representations: Early Appreciation of Roles and Deontic Relations. *Child Development* 79, 577–593.

Kalish, C. W., & Shiverick, S. M. (2004). Rules and Preferences: Children's Reasoning about Motives for Behavior. *Cognitive Development* 19, 410–416.

Karakostas, A., & Zizzo, D. J. (2016). Compliance and the Power of Authority. *Journal of Economic Behaviour and Organization* 124, 67–80.

Kelly, D., Stich, S., Haley, K., Eng, S., & Fessler, D. (2007). Harm, Affect, and the Moral/conventional Distinction. *Mind and Language* 22, 117–131.

Kelsen, H. (1992). *Introduction to the Problems of Legal Theory*. Trans. by S. Paulson and B. L. Paulson. Oxford: Clarendon Press.

Kemler Nelson, D. G., Holt, M. B., & Egan, L. C. (2004). Two- and Three-Year-Olds Infer and Reason about Design Intentions in Order to Categorize Broken Objects. *Developmental Science* 7, 543–549.

Kenward, B. (2012). Over-Imitating Preschoolers Believe Unnecessary Actions Are Normative and Enforce Their Performance by a Third Party. *Journal of Experimental Child Psychology* 112, 195–207.

Kinzler, K. D., Corriveau, K. H., & Harris, P. L. (2011). Children's Selective Trust in Native-Accented Speakers. *Developmental Science* 14(1), 106–111.

Kinzler, K. D., Shutts, K., DeJesus, J., & Spelke, E. S. (2009). Accent Trumps Race in Guiding Children's Social Preferences. *Social Cognition* 27, 623–634.

Konvalinka, I., Vuust, P., Roepstorff, A., & Frith, C.D. (2010). Follow You, Follow Me: Continuous Mutual Prediction and Adaptation in Joint Tapping. *The Quarterly Journal of Experimental Psychology* 63, 2220–2230.

Krupenye, C., Kano, F., Hirata, S., Call, J., & Tomasello, M. (2016). Great Apes Anticipate that Other Individuals Will Act According to False Beliefs. *Science* 354, 110–114.

Kuhlmeier, V. A., & Boysen, S. T. (2002). Chimpanzees (*Pan troglodytes*) Recognize Spatial and Object Correspondences Between a Scale Model and Its Referent. *Psychological Science* 13, 60–63.

Lakoff, G. (1987). *Women, Fire, and Dangerous Things: What Categories Reveal About the Mind*. Chicago and London: The University of Chicago Press.

Lakoff, G., & Johnson, M. (1980). *Metaphors We Live By*. Chicago: University of Chicago Press.

Larsson, S. (2017). *Conceptions in the Code: How Metaphors Explain Legal Challenges in Digital Times*. Oxford: Oxford University Press.

Lawson, T. (2012). Ontology and the Study of Social Reality: Emergence, Organisation, Community, Power, Social Relations, Corporations, Artefacts and Money. *Cambridge Journal of Economics* 36, 345–385.

Lawson, T. (2016). Comparing Conceptions of Social Ontology: Emergent Social Entities and/or Institutional Facts? *Journal for the Theory of Social Behaviour* 46, 359–399.

Leiter, B. (2011). The Demarcation Problem in Jurisprudence: A New Case for Scepticism. *Oxford Journal of Legal Studies* 31, 663–677.

Lewis, D. (1969). *Convention: A Philosophical Study*. Cambridge, MA: Harvard University Press.

Lieberman, D. E., McBratney, B. M., & Krovitz, G. (2002). The Evolution and Development of Cranial Form in *Homo sapiens*. *Proceedings of the National Academy of Sciences* 99, 1134–1139.

Liu, D., Wellman, H. M., & Tardif, T. (2008). Theory of Mind Development in Chinese Children: A Meta-Analysis of False-Belief Understanding Across Cultures and Languages. *Developmental Psychology* 44, 523–531.

Lorini, G. (2018). Animal Norms: An Investigation of Normativity in the Non-Human Social World. *Law, Culture, and the Humanities* 2018, 1–22. https://doi.org/10.1177/1743872118800008

Ludwig, K. (2016). *From Individual to Plural Agency. Collective Action I*. Oxford: Oxford University Press.

Lyons, D. E. & Keil, F. C. (2013). Overimitation and the Development of Causal Understanding. In M. Banaji & S. Gelman (eds.), *Navigating the Social World: What Infants, Children, and Other Species Can Teach Us*. Oxford: Oxford University Press, pp. 145–149.
Mant, C. M., & Perner, J. (1988). The Child's Understanding of Commitment. *Developmental Psychology* 24, 343–351.
Medin, D. L., & Shaffer, M. M. (1978). Context Theory of Classification Learning. *Psychological Review* 85, 207–238.
Michael, J. (2011). Shared Emotions and Joint Action. *Review of Philosophy and Psychology* 2, 355–373.
Michael, J., & Pacherie, E. (2015). On Commitments and Other Uncertainty Reduction Tools in Joint Action. *Journal of Social Ontology* 1, 89–120.
Michael, J., Sebanz, N., & Knoblich, G. (2016a). The Sense of Commitment: A Minimal Approach. *Frontiers in Psychology* 6, Article 1968.
Michael, J., Sebanz, N., & Knoblich, G. (2016b). Observing Joint Action: Coordination Creates Commitment. *Cognition* 157, 106–113.
Milgram, S. (1974). *Obedience to Authority: An Experimental View*. London: Harper and Row.
Miller, S. (2001). *Social Action: A Teleological Account*. Cambridge: Cambridge University Press.
Nietzsche, F. (2006). *On the Genealogy of Morality*, ed. K. Ansell-Pearson. Cambridge: Cambridge University Press.
North, D. (1990). *Institutions, Institutional Change and Economic Performance*. Cambridge: Cambridge University Press.
Nosofsky, R. M., & Palmeri, T. J. (1997). An Exemplar-Based Random Walk Model of Speeded Classification. *Psychological Review* 104, 266–300.
Noyes, A., & Dunham, Y. (2017). Mutual Intentions as a Causal Framework for Social Groups. *Cognition* 162, 133–142.
Noyes, A., Keil, F. C., & Dunham, Y. (2018). The Emerging Causal Understanding of Institutional Objects. *Cognition* 170, 83–87.
Olivecrona, K. (1971). *Law as Fact*, 2nd ed. London: Stevens.
Onishi, K. H., & Baillargeon, R. (2005). Do 15-Month-Old Infants Understand False Beliefs? *Science* 308, 255–258.
Pacherie, E. (2011). Framing Joint Action. *Review of Philosophy and Psychology* 2, 173–192.
Pacherie, E., & Dokic, J. (2006). From Mirror Neurons to Joint Actions. *Cognitive Systems Research* 7, 101–112.
Parsons, T. (1935). The Place of Ultimate Values in Sociological Theory. *International Journal of Ethics* 45, 282–316.
Passerini Glazel, L. (2005). *La forza normativa del tipo: teoria della categorizzazione e pragmatica dell'atto giuridico*. Macerata: Quodlibet.
Pattaro, E. (2005). *A Treatise of Legal Philosophy and General Jurisprudence*, Vol. 1, *The Law and the Right: A Reappraisal of the Reality that Ought to Be*, ed. E. Pattaro. Berlin: Springer.
Pattaro, E. (2016). Axel Hägerström at the Origins of the Uppsala School. In E. Pattaro and C. Roversi (eds.), *Legal Philosophy in the Twentieth Century: The Civil Law World. Tome 2, Main Orientations and Topics*. Berlin: Springer, pp. 319–363.
Perner, J., Aichhorn, M., Kronbichler, M., Staffen, W., & Ladurner, G. (2006). Thinking of Mental and Other Representations: The Roles of Left and Right Temporo-parietal Junction. *Social Neuroscience* 1, 245–258.

Petrażycki, A. (1955). *Law and Morality*, ed. N. S. Timasheff. Cambridge, MA: Harvard University Press.

Piaget, J. (1997). *The Moral Judgment of the Child*. New York: Free Press. (1st ed. 1932.)

Pinker, S. (2011). *The Better Angels of Our Nature: Why Violence Has Declined*. New York: Viking.

Plunkett, D. (2019). Robust Normativity, Morality, and Legal Positivism. In D. Plunkett, S. J. Shapiro & K. Toh (eds.), *Dimensions of Normativity: New Essays on Metaethics and Jurisprudence*. Oxford: Oxford University Press, pp. 105–136.

Rakoczy, H. (2007). Play, Games and the Development of Collective Intentionality. *New Directions for Child and Adolescent Development* 115, 53–67.

Rakoczy, H. (2008). Taking Fiction Seriously: Young Children Understand the Normative Structure of Joint Pretence Games. *Developmental Psychology* 44, 1191–1205.

Rakoczy, H., & Tomasello, M. (2007). The Ontogeny of Social Ontology: Steps to Shared Intentionality and Status Functions. In S. L. Tsohatzidis (ed.), *Intentional Acts and Institutional Facts*. Berlin: Springer, 113–137.

Rakoczy, H., Tomasello, M., & Striano, T. (2005a). On Tools and Toys: How Children Learn to Act on and Pretend with "Virgin" Objects. *Developmental Science* 8, 57–73.

Rakoczy, H., Tomasello, M., & Striano, T. (2005b). How Children Turn Objects into Symbols: A Cultural Learning Account. InL. Namy (ed.), *Symbol Use and Symbol Representation*. New York: Erlbaum.

Rakoczy, H., Warneken, F., & Tomasello, M. (2008). The Sources of Normativity: Young Children's Awareness of the Normative Structure of Games. *Developmental Psychology* 44, 875–881.

Raz, J. (1979). *The Authority of Law: Essays on Law and Morality*. Oxford: Oxford University Press.

Reicher, S. D., Haslam, A., & Smith, J. R. (2012). Working Toward the Experimenter: Reconceptualizing Obedience within the Milgram Paradigm as Identification-Based Followership. *Perspectives on Psychological Science* 7, 315–324.

Rhodes, M. (2013). The Conceptual Structure of Social Categories: The Social Allegiance Hypothesis. In M. Banaji & S. Gelman (eds.), *Navigating the Social World: What Infants, Children, and Other Species Can Teach Us*. Oxford: Oxford University Press, pp. 258–262.

Rhodes, M., & Gelman, S. A. (2009). A Developmental Examination of the Conceptual Structure of Animal, Artifact, and Human Social Categories across Two Cultural Contexts. *Cognitive Psychology* 59, 244–274.

Richerson, P. I., & Boyd, R. (2005). *Not by Genes Alone. How Culture Transformed Human Evolution*. Chicago and London: The University of Chicago Press.

Robinson, P. H., & Kurzban, R. (2007). Concordance and Conflict in Intuitions of Justice. *Minnesota Law Review* 91, 1829–1907.

Rockenbach, B., & Milinski, M. (2006). The Efficient Interaction of Indirect Reciprocity and Costly Punishment. *Nature* 444, 718–723.

Rohr, C. R., von, Burkart, J. M., & van Schaik, C. P. (2011). Evolutionary Precursors of Social Norms in Chimpanzees: a New Approach. *Biology and Philosophy* 26, 1–30.

Rosch, E. (1978). Principles of Categorization. In E. Rosch & B. B. Lloyd (eds.), *Cognition and Categorization*. New Jersey: Hillsdale, pp. 27–48.

Rosch, E., & Mervis, C. B. (1975). Family Resemblances: Studies in the Internal Structure of Categories. *Cognitive Psychology* 7, 573–605.

Rossano, F., Rakoczy, H., & Tomasello, M. (2011). Young Children's Understanding of Violations of Property Rights. *Cognition* 121, 219–227.

Roversi, C. (2016). Legal Metaphoric Artefacts. In J. Stelmach, B. Brozek, & Ł. Kurek (eds.), *The Emergence of Normative Orders*. Krakow: Copernicus Center Press, pp. 215–280.
Roversi, C. (2019). Law as an Artefact: Three Questions. *Analisi e Diritto* 2, 41–68.
Roversi, C., Borghi, A. M., & Tummolini, L. (2013). A Marriage Is an Artefact and Not a Walk that We Take Together: An Experimental Study on the Categorization of Artefacts. *Review of Philosophy and Psychology* 4, 527–542.
Roversi, C., Pasqui, L., & Borghi, A. M. (2017). Institutional Mimesis: An Experimental Study on the Grounding of Legal Concepts. In J. Stelmach, B. Brożek, & Ł. Kurek (eds.), *The Province of Jurisprudence Naturalized*. Warsaw: Wolters Kluwer, pp. 130–153.
Sacco, R. (2007). *Antropologia giuridica*. Bologna: Il Mulino.
Sanfey, A. G., Rilling, J. K., Aronson, J. A., Nystrom, L. E., & Cohen, J. D. (2003). The Neural Basis of Economic Decision-making in the Ultimatum Game. *Science* 300, 1755–1758.
Saxe, R., & Kanwisher, N. (2003). People Thinking About Thinking People: The Role of the Temporoparietal Junction in Theory of Mind. *NeuroImage* 19, 1835–1842.
Schauer, F. (2012). On the Nature of the Nature of Law. *Archiv für Rechts- und Sozialphilosophie* 98, 457–467.
Schauer, F. (2015). *The Force of Law*. Cambridge, MA: Harvard University Press.
Schmidt, M., Hardecker, S., & Tomasello, M. (2016). Preschoolers Understand the Normativity of Cooperatively Structured Competition. *Journal of Experimental Child Psychology* 143, 34–47.
Searle, J. R. (1995). *The Construction of Social Reality*. New York: The Free Press.
Searle, J. R. (2002). Collective Intentions and Actions. In J. R. Searle, *Consciousness and Language*. Cambridge: Cambridge University Press, 90–105. (1st ed. 1990.)
Searle, J. R. (2010). *Making the Social World*. Oxford: Oxford University Press.
Sebanz, N., Knoblich, G., & Prinz, W. (2003). Representing Others' Actions: Just Like One's Own? *Cognition* 88, 11–21.
Sebanz, N., Knoblich, G., & Prinz, W. (2005). How to Share a Task: Corepresenting Stimulus-Response Mappings. *Journal of Experimental Psychology* 31, 1234–1246.
Sebanz, N., Knoblich, G., Prinz, W., & Wascher, E. (2006). Twin Peaks: An ERP Study of Action Planning and Control in Coacting Individuals. *Journal of Cognitive Neuroscience* 18, 859–870.
Sell, A., Sznycer, D., Al-Shawaf, L., et al. (2017). The Grammar of Anger: Mapping the Computational Architecture of a Recalibrational Emotion. *Cognition* 168, 110–128.
Shapiro, S. (2011). *Legality*. Cambridge, MA: Harvard University Press.
Shaw, A. W., Li, W., & Olson, K. R. (2013). Reputation is Everything. In M. Banaji & S. Gelman (eds.), *Navigating the Social World: What Infants, Children, and Other Species Can Teach Us*. Oxford: Oxford University Press, pp. 220–224.
Shergill, S. S., Bays, P. M., Frith, C. D., & Wolpert, D. M. (2003). Two Eyes for an Eye: The Neuroscience of Force Escalation. *Science* 301, 187.
Skezely, M., & Michael, J. (2018). Investing in Commitment: Persistence in a Joint Action Is Enhanced by the Perception of a Partner's Effort. *Cognition* 174, 37–42.
Stake, J. E. (2006). The Property "Instinct." In S. Zeki and O. Goodenough (eds.), *Law and the Brain*. Oxford: Oxford University Press, pp. 185–204.
Takahashi, H., Yahata, N., Koeda, M., et al. (2004). Brain Activation Associated with Evaluative Processes of Guilt and Embarrassment: An fMRI Study. *NeuroImage* 23, 967–974.
Tamanaha, B. (2017a). Necessary and Universal Truths about Law? *Ratio Juris* 30, 3–24.
Tamanaha, B. (2017b). *A Realistic Theory of Law*. Cambridge: Cambridge University Press.

Thibaut, J.-P., Gelaes, S., & Murphy, G. L. (2018). Does Practice in Category Learning Increase Rule Use or Exemplar Use – or Both? *Memory and Cognition* 46, 530–543.
Thomasson, A. (1999). *Fiction and Metaphysics*. Cambridge: Cambridge University Press.
Tollefsen, D. (2004). Let's Pretend! Children and Joint Action. *Philosophy of the Social Sciences* 35, 75–97.
Tomasello, M. (2016). *A Natural History of Human Morality*. Cambridge, MA: Harvard University Press.
Tomasello, M., & Carpenter, M. (2005). The Emergence of Social Cognition in Three Young Chimpanzees. *Monographs of the Society for Research in Child Development* 70, 1–131.
Tomasello, M., Carpenter, M., Call, J., Behne, T., & Moll, H. (2005). Understanding and Sharing Intentions: The Origins of Cultural Cognition. *Behavioural and Brain Sciences* 28, 675–735.
Tomasello, M., & Moll, H. (2013). Why Don't Apes Understand False Beliefs? In M. Banaji & S. Gelman (eds.), *Navigating the Social World: What Infants, Children, and Other Species Can Teach Us*. Oxford: Oxford University Press, pp. 81–87.
Trivers, R. (1971). The Evolution of Reciprocal Altruism. *Quarterly Review of Biology* 46, 35–37.
Trivers, R. (1985). *Social Evolution*. Menlo Park: Benjamin/Cummings Pub.
Tsai, C.-C., Kuo, W.-J., Jing, J.-T., Hung, D. L., & Tzeng, O. J.-L. (2006). A Common Coding Framework in Self-Other Interaction: Evidence from Joint Action Task. *Experimental Brain Research* 175, 353–362.
Tsai, C.-C., Sebanz, N., & Knoblich, G. (2011). The GROOP Effect: Groups Mimic Group Actions. *Cognition* 118, 138–143.
Tuomela, R. (1995). *The Importance of Us: A Philosophical Study of Basic Social Notions*. Stanford: Stanford University Press.
Tuomela, R. (2013). *Social Ontology*. Oxford: Oxford University Press.
Turiel, E. (1983). *The Development of Social Knowledge: Morality and Convention*. Cambridge: Cambridge University Press.
Ullman-Margalit, E. (1977). *The Emergence of Norms*. Oxford: Clarendon Press.
Vaesen, K. (2012). The Cognitive Bases of Human Tool Use. *Behavioural Brain Sciences* 35, 203–262.
Vaish, A., Missana, M., & Tomasello, M. (2011). Three-Year-Old Children Intervene in Third-Party Moral Transgressions. *British Journal of Developmental Psychology* 29, 124–130.
Vanhaeren, M., d'Errico, F., Stringer, C. et al. (2006). Middle Paleolithic Shell Beads in Israel and Algeria. *Science* 312, 1785–1788.
Van Winden, F. (2007). Affect and Fairness in Economics. *Social Justice Research* 20, 35–52.
Vesper, C., Abramova, E., Bütepage, J. et al. (2017). Joint Action: Mental Representations, Shared Information and General Mechanisms for Coordinating with Others. *Frontiers in Psychology* 7, Article 2039.
Vesper, C., Butterfill, S., Knoblich, G., & Sebanz, N. (2010). A Minimal Architecture for Joint Action. *Neural Networks* 23, 998–1003.
Walton, K. L. (1990). *Mimesis as Make-Believe*. Cambridge, MA: Harvard University Press.
Warneken, F., & Tomasello, M. (2009). Varieties of Altruism in Children and Chimpanzees. *Trends in Cognitive Science* 13, 397–402.
Wellman, H. M., Cross, D., & Watson, J. (2001). Meta-Analysis of Theory-of-Mind Development: The Truth about False Belief. *Child Development* 72, 655–684.
Whiten, A. (2013). Social Cognition: Making Us Smart, or Sometimes Making Us Dumb? Overimitation, Conformity, Nonconformity, and the Transmission of Culture in Ape and Child. In M. Banaji and S. Gelman (eds.), *Navigating the Social World: What Infants, Children, and Other Species Can Teach Us*. Oxford: Oxford University Press, pp. 151–154.

Whiten, A., McGuigan, N., Marshall-Pescini, S., & Hopper, L. M. (2009). Emulation, Imitation, Over-imitation and the Scope of Culture for Child and Chimpanzee. *Philosophical Transactions of the Royal Society* 364, 2417–2428.

Wills, A. J., Inkster, A. B., & Milton, F. (2015). Combination or Differentiation? Two Theories of Processing Order in Classification. *Cognitive Psychology* 80, 1–33.

Winter, S. L. (2001). *A Clearing in the Forest: Law, Life, and Mind*. Chicago and London: The University of Chicago Press.

7

The Architecture of the Legal Mind

Bartosz Brożek[*]

If one were to peruse the long list of important legal philosophers, I would argue that it would be difficult to find even one who had not contributed to the discussion pertaining to the nature and limits of legal cognition. What does it mean to know the law? What are the methods of reasoning utilised by lawyers? Is legal thinking based on logic? Is there specialised legal logic? Does intuition play any role in the thinking of judges? How should one justify a legal decision? For centuries, these questions and the like have shaped the debates in legal epistemology. This is far from surprising, given the importance of law for our interactions and social structure, and the law's direct impact on the lives of individuals. A thorough understanding of the essence and limitations of legal thinking constitutes the backbone of any serious reflection on the law.

This kind of reflection has been firmly embedded in philosophical argumentation from the outset, mainly based on common-sense observations and practical considerations, but also metaphysical theories. Once again, it is not surprising since this is how epistemology in general has developed. The situation has changed in the last seventy years with the rise of experimental psychology, neuroscience and, more generally, cognitive science. It transpired that our old ways of thinking about the architecture of the mind and the mechanisms behind human cognition were essentially flawed. In particular, we had become overly attached to the view of a rational human being which always makes informed and conscious decisions. Meanwhile, empirical observations and clever experiments strongly suggest that our decisions are, more often than not, unconscious and emotion-driven. If this is even half true, epistemology – including legal epistemology – should also be considered from the perspective of the cognitive sciences: it should be, as W. V. O. Quine suggested, naturalised (see Quine, 1969).

To a certain extent, legal philosophers have taken note of this suggestion. In particular, considerable effort has been devoted to the experimental research and

---

[*] Professor of Law and Philosophy, Jagiellonian University, Kraków, Poland. This chapter has been written with the support of research grant no. 2017/27/B/HS5/01407 funded by the National Science Center.

philosophical argumentation connected to intuitive decision making in law.[1] It is difficult to escape the conclusion, however, that the research in question provides no comprehensive picture of legal thinking. There seems to be no overarching naturalistic framework, where unconscious intuitive decisions would fit together with legal argumentation or sophisticated legal conceptual schemes. Legal epistemology has been naturalised only partially, and in a somewhat erratic way.

How might one go about changing this situation? It would be impossible to simply go step by step and consider each and every conception of legal thinking in light of the findings of the cognitive sciences – were this to be done, then this chapter would become a hodgepodge of more or less interconnected claims, mutually inconsistent theories and conjectures. A thorough examination of them all would require a thick volume rather than a relatively short chapter. Therefore, a different strategy is called for here. Instead of providing a historically informed account of legal epistemology filled with references to the cognitive sciences, I am forced to adopt an approach which is perhaps unusual for a handbook. I will offer an argument which aims to substantiate the following three claims:

1) Legal thinking consists in the interaction between three mental mechanisms: intuition (unconscious decision making), imagination (mental simulation) and thinking in language (theory-construction).
2) Legal epistemology has largely neglected the role of imagination in legal thinking, while it is imagination that provides 'the missing link' between unconscious decision making and thinking in language.
3) The picture of the legal mind which embraces intuition, imagination and language provides an explanation of the enduring and seemingly inconsistent threads in legal epistemology.

Since my argument requires a rough historical and conceptual background, I will begin with a more general overview of the existing theories in legal epistemology, distinguishing between formalism, dialecticism, coherentism and intuitivism. I will highlight the fact that these four philosophical stances offer different and sometimes mutually inconsistent perspectives on legal thinking. Subsequently, I will analyse the three mechanisms at play in all types of reflection, including legal thinking: intuition, imagination and thinking in language. I will try to explain what stands behind these labels, and argue that a lawyer cannot limit themselves to only some of these mechanisms in their cognitive efforts. Moreover, I will venture to depict how the mechanisms in question interact in, and what they contribute to legal decision making. In this context, I will put special emphasis on the role of imagination, explaining how it provides a link between intuition and language.[2]

---

[1] See the references in Section 7.2 of the present chapter.
[2] The architecture of the legal mind described in this chapter is elaborated further in my book (Brożek, 2020).

7.1 THEORIES OF LEGAL REASONING

Legal epistemology, that is the systematic reflection on cognition in law, is one of the most highly developed branches of legal philosophy. Over the last 150 years, a vast number of works have been devoted to topics such as legal reasoning, legal logic and the rationality of legal decisions. In this brief chapter, it would be extremely difficult to provide an outline of even the most important achievements of this field. Instead, one should perhaps restrict oneself to some justified simplifications which will serve to highlight the aspects of legal epistemology which are important from the perspective of research conducted in cognitive science.

Arguably, theories of legal reasoning can be divided into four types: formalism,[3] dialecticism, coherentism and intuitivism. The first of these positions is that the essence of the reasoning carried out by lawyers is the use of special forms of thinking, and in particular deduction, or logically valid schemes of reasoning (see MacCormick, 1994). Highlighting any thinkers who actually subscribe to the 'pure' form of formalism, however, is problematic; this view has been subjected to a number of fierce attacks, regardless of whether it can be ascribed to a particular person or not. Perhaps the most famous of these attacks was carried out by Roscoe Pound in his lecture on 'Mechanical Jurisprudence' which was published in the *Columbia Law Review* in 1908. Pound argued that legal reasoning cannot be limited to the logical or 'mechanical' application of legal rules to specific facts (of which the use of deduction is paradigmatic); in this sense, the law does not resemble the more precise sciences, such as mathematics, where – at least in the common-sense understanding of these sciences – new truths can be discovered by means of deriving deductive conclusions from axioms and other previously derived truths.[4] Pound was joined by a number of other legal philosophers, such as Chaïm Perelman, who believed that the essence of legal reasoning lies not in deduction but valuation (cf. Perelman, 1955). It is worth noting, however, that the attacks on formalism were directed in most cases against an imaginary and incredibly naïve position, a straw man as it were. Those who propose the application of logic in law do not claim that legal thinking amounts to the application of simple deductive rules, nor do they insist that they need necessarily be the rules of the classical logic. Mature formalism is the view according to which formal structures *organise* legal cognition, without over-applying them to encompass any and all conclusions drawn in the process of applying and interpreting the law (see Prakken, 1997, Brożek, 2004; Stelmach & Brożek, 2006, ch. 2). There is ample room in the mind of the lawyer for both value judgements and a formal framework.

---

[3] 'Formalism' is also one of the fundamental stances in the philosophy of mathematics, claiming that all mathematics can be reduced to logic. I do not use the term in this sense here.

[4] A careful reading of Pound's essay suggests that his attack is levelled against the use of deductive logic in legal thinking. However, one must remember that at the time when Pound was composing his argument the contemporary formal logic, which today also encompasses various non-deductive systems, was only *in statu nascendi*.

Dialecticism is the view that legal thinking is primarily discursive: decision making in law calls for the comparison of differing arguments for competing solutions.[5] Perhaps the two most important dialectical concepts of legal reasoning were developed by Robert Alexy and the aforementioned Chaïm Perelman. For Alexy, whose theory is based on Kantian practical philosophy, a legal decision can be considered rational if it could be the result of a discussion conducted according to certain rules, such as 'No speaker may contradict him or herself', 'Every speaker may only assert what he or she actually believes' or 'Everyone who can speak may take part in discourse' (Alexy, 1989, pp. 188, 193). The catalogue of the rules of discourse proposed by Alexy is an extremely broad one, since it encompasses dozens of different rules which apply to the general practical discourse as well as those specific to legal discourse. At the heart of this conception is not the notion that the lawyer must adhere to these rules in their reasoning rather than any others, but rather the observation that the settlement of legal problems is only possible in a dialectical structure, within the framework of which competing arguments for alternative and often contradictory solutions may be deliberated. The rules of discourse constitute a procedural criterion for comparing these arguments, and the fact that many of them are 'embodied' in the actual legal discourse makes it impossible to formulate all of them by means of a priori considerations alone (see Alexy, 1989, pp. 189, 193; see also Brożek, 2008). The idea that legal reasoning is based on the comparison of arguments is also the basis for the concept proposed by Chaïm Perelman. In contrast to Alexy, however, Perelman does not claim that legal thinking must meet certain idealised Kantian standards.[6] Perelman argues that, in practice, a particular audience (such as a judge, jury, etc.), which is bound up in various psychological prejudices and private interests, will determine which arguments are stronger and thus which decision shall be considered justified (see Perelman & Olbrechts-Tyteca, 1958).

Coherentism is yet another group of theories that try to capture the structure of legal reasoning. In this approach, solutions to legal problems that 'fit' the broader context of legal knowledge – that is, not only legal provisions and precedents but also dogmatic considerations, the broadly understood legal tradition and even moral standards or dominant political views – are considered appropriate (justified). In continental philosophy, the coherentist approach is characteristic of legal hermeneutics. In the works of philosophers such as Hans-Georg Gadamer or Arthur Kaufmann, legal thinking is depicted as having a circular structure. The first reaction to a specific legal case is pre-understanding; it is a provisional solution, by definition imperfect, that 'appears' in the mind of a judge or lawyer. Pre-understanding is only the beginning of the cognitive process, in which a specific

---

[5] A more detailed analysis leads to distinguishing between procedural and non-procedural accounts of dialecticism. For the sake of simplicity, I do not explore this distinction (cf. Hage, 2000).
[6] It must be observed, however, that Perelman's conception also exhibits an idealised dimension in the concept of the universal audience; there, Perelman's view becomes quite close to Alexy's.

case is referred to the entire legal tradition, and in particular to the direct 'background knowledge' (precedents, legal norms, dogmatic theories); if the pre-understanding 'fits' it, it is 'confirmed', if not – it is modified (see Kaufmann, 1986; Stelmach, 1991). Ronald Dworkin presents a similar concept of thinking in law that is derived from a different philosophical tradition. The idea of 'law as interpretation' which he proclaimed not only emphasises specific legal decisions being rooted in a long and complex tradition, but also draws attention to the dynamics of legal thinking, one which is a continuous 'game' between a concrete case and background legal knowledge (Dworkin, 1986; see also Hage, 2013) .

One may also delineate those conceptions of legal reasoning which stress the role of intuition in solving legal problems and these may be grouped together under the banner of intuitivism. Judge Joseph Hutcheson or, to a certain extent, Leon Petrażycki, claimed that the basis of legal decisions, especially in hard cases, is a certain type of feeling which Hutcheson termed a *hunch*. The working mechanism of a hunch is not transparent, in the sense that we are not conscious of the processes which lead to the manifestation of this particular feeling. A useful hunch is what characterises a good lawyer: the more of an expert they are, the better the 'feeling' they are likely to have in relation to the case at hand. One may thus conclude that the intuitive thinking of the kind described by Hutcheson is an effect of training: a legal hunch needs to be developed, it is something we acquire with experience. Recognising intuition as the main source of legal decisions does not mean, however, that other forms of legal cognition such as deduction or imagination do not play a role in legal thinking. They remain in thrall to a hunch, helping to shape it or justify a decision which has been taken on the basis of the unconscious intuitive mechanism (see Hutcheson, 1929; Petrażycki, 2011).

I would not like to claim that formalism, dialecticism, coherentism and intuitivism represent completely separate strands in legal epistemology. It is easy to show that advocates of coherentism and dialecticism do not resign from the application of formal methods or that dialectical elements can be discerned in coherentism. One may even argue that there are other methods of thinking at play in intuitivism aside from intuition, although they play a secondary, if not servile, role to unconscious mental processes. I would claim, however, that all four approaches to legal reasoning have distinct 'epistemological accents' which represent different aspects of legal thinking.

It should also be stressed that conceptions of legal thinking, even those grouped together under the four headings identified, can differ significantly from one another. In particular, some of them have a descriptive character (they attempt to answer the question of how lawyers really think) while others are normative (addressing the matter of how lawyers should think). Formal models are normative as a rule, while dialectical ones may be normative (such as Alexy's) or descriptive (as one may interpret Perelman's theory of the particular audience). Coherentism, whether in the form of legal hermeneutics or according to Dworkin, may also be both normative or descriptive. Intuitivism is usually regarded as a description of the actual processes of legal cognition, but this does not prevent one from deriving normative postulates on the basis of the intuitionist view of legal cognition, albeit solely in relation to the shaping of legal hunches.

In this context, the fact that both descriptive and normative concepts of legal thinking assume a certain vision of the mechanisms responsible for cognition in law is crucial. Formalism assumes that the legal mind is able to carry out complex arguments with the use of logical schemes of reasoning; dialecticism holds that a lawyer is able to compare various arguments leading to contradictory conclusions in accordance with some normative criterion; coherentism claims that the legal mind is able to 'integrate' a particular case into a broad background of knowledge; while intuitivism believes that it has the ability to unconsciously find solutions to legal problems.

This observation gives rise to an interesting question. It transpires that the above-described conceptions sometimes have radically different visions of the architecture of the legal mind. At the same time, these conceptions are extremely durable – formalism, dialecticism, coherentism and intuitivism are not only historical epistemological positions but ones which continue, in one form or another, to be defended to this day. This is perhaps surprising, especially considering how radically different these theories are and the variations in the assumptions on which they are based. It seems that the explanation of this state of affairs is the following: traditional approaches to legal thinking only encapsulate some aspects of the cognitive processes at play in solving legal problems, never all of them. The architecture of the legal mind is far more complex than it is assumed to be by formalism, dialecticism, coherentism and intuitivism taken by themselves. My claim is that it consists of three interwoven mechanisms: intuition, imagination and thinking in language. The remaining part of this chapter is devoted to a detailed presentation and defence of this claim.

7.2 INTUITION

The word 'intuition' is derived from the Latin *intueri*, to look at, consider. Until the eighteenth century, it was used exclusively to describe a certain mental phenomenon of 'looking at' things with the 'eye of the soul' (*The Oxford English Dictionary*, 1989). With time, however, it began to be used in a different sense – initially in philosophy and theology and then in other fields – which was far removed from its etymological origins. Today, the term intuition is usually used to mean thinking which is not preceded by reasoning, a form of direct knowledge, or adopting a conviction that may not be entirely justifiable (*The Oxford English Dictionary*, 1989). The semantic peregrinations of the term 'intuition' may easily become the source of powerful misunderstandings and conceptual confusion. There is talk, for example, of the existence of analytical intuition, especially in relation to spheres of knowledge such as mathematics or logic; or about phenomenological intuition, or the ability to capture what is essential in the phenomena that 'manifest themselves' in our consciousness (Stelmach, 2013). Without wishing to belittle or denigrate these notions of intuition, I will focus solely on its psychological understanding in the considerations which follow.

What, then, is intuition in the psychological understanding? Given the multifarious conceptions of intuitive understanding to be found in modern cognitive sciences, it is difficult to rely on the formulation of any one, single and concrete definition of 'intuition'. In any case, this would be a short-sighted tactic, one which easily leads to gross oversimplifications and erroneous conclusions. It seems eminently more reasonable to try to characterise intuitive understanding in a more general way in order to indicate some of its typical features. There seems to be a degree of agreement amongst psychologists that intuition is an unconscious mechanism. This is not unconscious in the Freudian sense, but rather concerns the kind of mental processes that, although they are carried out beyond our conscious control, may potentially be processed consciously. Another feature of intuitive understanding is its speed (Bargh & Morsella, 2008). In contrast to slow, conscious deliberation, intuition provides its answers instantly – it is an immediate response to the problem before us. This speed can be explained by the fact that the functioning of intuition is based on affective processes. An intuitive judgement is an emotional reaction to a situation, to an encountered problem, for example. Although there is no consensus as to the shape of the neural mechanism which corresponds to such reactions, there are some persuasive models. Perhaps the most famous of these is Antonio Damasio's somatic marker hypothesis. Damasio formulated his hypothesis while researching the social decision-making process amongst patients with damage to their ventromedial prefrontal cortex. Such patients typically behave in an 'asocial' manner, despite being able to function normally in intellectual terms (functions such as memory, language or perception are within the expected norms); they cannot, however, use their emotions and feelings adequately enough so as to manage their behaviour. Damasio explains this phenomenon by proposing that such patients have impaired access to so-called somatic markers. In situations in which a complex decision-making process has to be undertaken, a normally functioning brain activates somatic states that 'categorise' the possible ways of acting into good or bad categories. This information is used (consciously or unconsciously) by the body and allows us to take the course of action that is best for us (see Damasio, Tranel, & Damasio, 1991).

Importantly, somatic markers develop hand in hand with the experience that we acquire in social interactions: they are something which are learned rather than an innate ability. The mechanism of somatic markers allows us to make unconscious, intuitive decisions that may also be rational:

The quality of one's intuition depends on how well we have reasoned in the past; on how well we have classified the events of our past experience in relation to the emotions that preceded and followed them; and also on how well we have reflected on the successes and failures of our past intuitions. Intuition is simply rapid cognition with the required knowledge partially swept under the carpet, all courtesy of emotion and much past practice. (Damasio, 2006, pp. xviii–xix)

Damasio emphasises an important point here: good intuition is the result of training derived from our past experiences. This fact is of great importance for the discussion of intuitive decisions in areas such as law. The average Joe Bloggs, one who has not undergone the requisite legal training, will be unable to quickly and accurately resolve even relatively simple legal problems. At the same time, an experienced lawyer, one who possesses the proper education and many years of legal practice under his belt, would be in a much better situation: intuition will usually provide him with the correct solution. In other words, an experienced lawyer is an expert in his field, as is the doctor with the requisite experience or the installer of parquet flooring who has been laying wooden floors for years. In their case, expert knowledge – concerning respectively legal issues, the diagnosis and treatment of people, and laying parquet floors – has been 'swept under the carpet of consciousness' by means of long-term training and practice: it has become intuitive.

The image of intuition which emerges from the above analyses is a mechanism that is unconscious (the processes which lead to the formulation of a solution to a given problem take place unconsciously, and this response appears to come 'from nowhere'); fast (in comparison to conscious reasoning); automatic (intuitive judgements occur spontaneously and cannot be intentionally controlled); and founded on experience (intuition is based on the knowledge acquired by means of our interactions with the environment). Yet this rapid processing comes at a certain price. Research from psychologists, and particularly Amos Tversky and Daniel Kahneman, has shown that trusting our intuitive judgements may lead to systematic errors (see Kahneman, 2011). Such errors occur as a result of the workings of a number of mechanisms on which intuition is based. The first would be the so-called anchoring effect, which manifests itself when people make numerical estimates. When they do so, they are often unaware that they are influenced by certain numbers – the aforementioned 'anchors' – which do not necessarily have any relation to the problem under consideration. In their seminal study, Tversky and Kahneman asked participants to estimate what percentage of countries belonging to the UN were African ones. Prior to this, however, they had been asked to say whether this figure was greater or smaller than the number which featured on a Wheel of Fortune. The latter had been constructed in such a way that it always fell on either the number 10 or 65. It transpired that participants for whom the needle pointed to number 10 on the Wheel of Fortune estimated on average that 25 percent of the countries belonging to the UN were African. Those who had 65, however, opted for a significantly higher average percentage – 45 per cent. This research and similar studies suggest that our intuitive judgements may depend to a large extent on incidental and irrelevant information, including numerical (see Tversky & Kahneman, 1974, p. 1128).

The anchoring effect is also at work in law. Guthrie, Rachlinski and Wistrich presented a group of judges with the following case. The plaintiff had been hit by a truck belonging to the defendant. It was found that the accident had been caused by faulty brakes; moreover, the accused had not performed the necessary routine inspections of their trucks. After the accident, the plaintiff was hospitalised for several months, and ever since had been a wheelchair user. He had previously worked as an electrician, a highly regarded one, with a large group of regular customers. In the lawsuit he demanded compensation for his lost earnings, the coverage of his medical bills and compensation for his suffering. However, he did not specify the exact amount that he demanded from the defendant. The task of the judges participating in the experiment was to determine the amount of compensation due to the plaintiff. The subjects were divided into two groups: one received the above description of the facts, while in the second group, the description was supplemented by the information that the defendant had requested the claim be rejected due to the fact that the plaintiff's damages did not exceed $75,000 and thus his case should be considered by a lower court. This application by the defendant was patently unfounded since the losses suffered by the plaintiff clearly exceeded $75,000. It transpired, however, that adding this number to the information pertaining to the description of the facts had a significant impact on the average amount of damages awarded by participants in the experiment. While the first group was willing to award the plaintiff an average amount of $1,249,000, the second group of judges – apparently 'anchored' by the figure of $75,000 – awarded an average of $882,000 (Guthrie, Rachlinski, & Wistrich, 2001).

In their ground-breaking work, 'Judgment under Uncertainty: Heuristics and Biases', Tversky and Kahneman (1974) showed two other types of systematic error which intuitive reasoning can lead to, the first stemming from the application of representativeness heuristic. Participants in Kahneman and Tversky's study had to order in terms of probability the likelihood of certain future prospects for a young woman, Linda, who is '31 years old, single, outspoken, and very bright. She majored in philosophy. As a student, she was deeply concerned with issues of discrimination and social justice, and also participated in anti-nuclear demonstrations.' The scenarios which they were asked to judge were the following: (a) Linda is active in the feminist movement; (b) Linda is a psychiatric social worker; (c) Linda is a member of the League of Women Voters; (d) Linda is a bank teller; (e) Linda is an insurance salesperson; (f) Linda is a bank teller and active in the feminist movement. Kahneman and Tversky were shocked to learn that *all* of the participants in the experiment thought it more likely that Linda would be a bank teller active in the feminist movement than just a bank teller (see Kahneman, 2011, p. 156ff.). This is an evident error, since the probability of these two independent events is necessarily lower than just one of them. The explanation of this error lies in the notion that intuition is based on the representativeness heuristic: the attributes displayed by Linda are representative of an activist in a feminist movement and not those of a bank teller and this is why this future scenario exerted such a strong effect that it caused participants to ignore one of the fundamental rules of probability.

This type of error is also manifested by lawyers in relation to legal problems. In one study, lawyers were asked to assess the chances of a certain case (*Jones v. Clinton*) ending in one of the following ways: court sentence, dismissal, settlement, withdrawal and so on. One option, however, was 'an outcome other than a judicial verdict'. It turned out that the respondents estimated that the probability of a settlement was greater than the chances of the case ending 'in an outcome other than a judicial verdict', in a situation where the latter includes the former together with other solutions (dismissing the claim, withdrawal, etc.) (Peer & Gamliel, 2013, p. 116). It can be presumed that this mistake stems from the fact that certain features of the *Jones v. Clinton* case are representative of disputes that usually end in a settlement; however, there are no representative features of cases that are resolved 'in an outcome other than a judicial verdict'.

Another type of error indicated by Kahneman and Tversky stems from the use of the availability heuristic. This helps us to assess the probability of a certain kind of phenomena based on how easily we recall cases of their occurrence. For example, if an English user is asked if there are more words starting with the letter 'r' or having the letter 'r' in the third place, they usually indicate – incorrectly – the first eventuality, probably because it is easier to recall those words in which 'r' is the first letter (cf. Tversky & Kahneman, 1974, p. 1127). This type of error can also be committed – in the context of professional activity – by a lawyer. Let us consider a concrete example (Reyes, Thompson, & Bower, 1980). Participants in an experiment received a description of a court case concerning a car accident caused by someone under the influence of alcohol. The description included the arguments of both the prosecutor and the defender, with the difference being that half of the respondents were given material in which the case for the prosecution was presented in a lively manner, one that was rich and full of particulars, while the defence's arguments were formulated in more abstract language. The other group of respondents received the opposite. It transpired that when asked to deliver a verdict immediately on the case at hand, the participants did not differ in their judgements; however, when the question was repeated after 48 hours, the respondents showed a tendency to decide in favour of the party which had presented the argument using more lively language and with more particulars. In other words, those who had the opportunity to become acquainted with the suggestive version of the prosecution's position were willing to condemn the defendant, while those who had read the more fluid version of the defence were more likely to acquit him (Reyes et al., 1980). This effect was explained by the operation of availability heuristics – it is easier to recall a lively and florid description of an event than one which uses abstract language full of technical formulations or statistics.

Alongside the already mentioned errors associated with the operation of the anchoring effect, representativeness and availability heuristics, the literature indicates other phenomena which cause intuitive reasoning to lead us astray, including in the legal context. They are, amongst others, hindsight bias, the framing effect and egocentric bias (see McCaffery, Kahneman, & Spitzer, 1995; Langevoort, 1998; Hastie, Schkade, & Payne, 1999).

Does this mean that a lawyer cannot trust his intuition? An affirmative answer to this question would constitute a grave misunderstanding. One may venture the thesis that the errors described in the literature in making legally relevant decisions – committed both by laypeople and those with a legal education and many years of experience as judges or lawyers – say more about the nature of the tasks set for participants of experiments, rather than the (un)reliability of intuitive reasoning per se. Let us consider for a moment some of the cognitive mechanisms described by Kahneman and Tversky, for example the availability heuristic. When someone asks the question of which city – Chicago or Baltimore – is bigger, we would answer Chicago without thinking. The reason for this is simple: Chicago is more 'available', we have heard a lot about it, we know it is a metropolis with a long tradition, while 'Baltimore' is only a name for most of us, without any hidden, extensive knowledge. Let us note that such a mental shortcut is quite reasonable – the bigger of the cities will be the one we have heard about more often, one which is described in popular culture as the capital of blues and jazz, as Capone's criminal stomping ground, one with the Sears Tower in the background and as the city of Michael Jordan and the Chicago Bulls.

The same applies to other 'mental shortcuts' on which our intuitive judgements are based. For example, the representativeness heuristic supplies us with hints based on certain patterns or prototypes: if a given situation is sufficiently similar to typically dangerous circumstances, our intuition will tell us that we should exercise caution. If someone exhibits the typical characteristics of a friendly and nice person – they are smiling, helpful and polite – we will intuitively judge that they are not a threat to us. Yet, of course, in both cases we may be mistaken. A 'dangerous' situation may turn out to be a joke played on us by our friends (especially if they are cognitive scientists: it may be a joke that exploits our intuitive reactions), while the friendly stranger may be a psychopathic murderer. The fact is that such mistakes happen relatively rarely. They will only become frequent and systematic in relation to problems that themselves are atypical, at least from the perspective of the evolution of the human mind. This would, for example, be the case when we attempt to tackle issues that require statistical analysis. In other words: intuition is a very useful cognitive mechanism that usually provides us with helpful, albeit imperfect, tips on how to solve the problem we are presented with.

It must be stressed once again that good intuition is the result of experience and training. From someone who has had little to do with the law, we cannot expect accurate, intuitive judgements regarding legal problems, just like someone who knows almost nothing about laying parquet floors cannot rely on their intuition about how best to restore an old oak parquet floor. In this sense, it may be said that legal intuition exists. However, this is by no means a mysterious ability: a lawyer has legal intuition in the same way that a mathematician has mathematical intuition and a doctor has a medical one. They use the same neuronal architecture, but in each case it is filled – by means of years of education and experience – with different content.

7.3 MENTAL SIMULATION

Let us now consider the role played by mental simulation in legal thinking. People, and most likely also other animals (see Byrne, 1988), have the ability to imagine objects and situations, to 'play them over' in their own minds. There is a very convincing evolutionary explanation for this skill. Mental simulations allow us to prepare for future events, significantly reducing the cost of acting in the world. To put it briefly: it's better to die in the imagination than in reality. Instead of risking our lives, we can imagine a number of different ways of hunting a potentially dangerous animal and thus avoid at least some of the mistakes that we could otherwise have made. Instead of risking our reputation, we can mentally 'play over' several versions of a speech we are meant to give to an important and demanding audience, and eliminate at least some of the potential reasons for public humiliation.

Perhaps most importantly, research conducted in recent years using brain imaging technology clearly shows that mental simulations use the same neuronal circuitry which activates when we perceive an object or perform an action. For example, if I imagine a hammer, the same circuits in the brain that are responsible for seeing the hammer are activated; if I mentally simulate hammering a nail into the wall, the same groups of neurons are active as if I were actually performing this operation. (Of course, these activations may be weaker during simulations than when an actual action or observation takes place.) Furthermore, some behavioural experiments seem to confirm the theses formulated above. Most of them are connected with the so-called Perky effect: imagining something can interfere with the perception of actual objects. For example, if someone imagines a certain object at the bottom of a blank screen, they will notice that a new image has appeared in the same place only after a certain delay; if, however, the image is placed at the top of the screen, the delay will not take place (Bergen, 2012, p. 26ff.).

An important feature of mental simulations is that they are multimodal: they can simultaneously include visual, auditory, kinaesthetic and even emotional elements. When we imagine a triangle, we probably use only those areas of the brain that are responsible for visual perception. However, when we make a mental simulation of a dog, it will probably be more than a static image of a Labrador or a King Charles Spaniel. In all likelihood, we will 'see' a dog in action (wagging its tail, barking, begging for food), and everything will be 'underpinned' with positive or negative emotions.

Research also shows that there exists an important relationship between the ability to perform mental simulations and to use language (Bergen, 2012, *passim*). When we hear or say the word 'hammer', the same areas are activated in our brains which are responsible for seeing a hammer or using it for something, as well as those which are used for imagining these things. This conclusion is derived from the results of research using both brain imaging and behavioural tasks. Let us consider an example. In one experiment, a screen and three buttons were used: grey, black and white. Pressing and holding the grey button caused a sentence to appear on the screen. If the sentence was a meaningful one, the task of the participant was to let go of the grey button and instead press the black one which was closer to the participant. If the sentence was nonsensical, the participant should press the white button. It turned out that if a meaningful sentence – regardless of whether it was declarative or imperative – described an action involving movement towards the body, participants gave their answers faster than in cases where the sentence described the movement in the opposite direction (Bergen, 2012, pp. 78–9). This means that the understanding of the contents of these sentences had to be based on an appropriate simulation. If what the sentence said was incompatible with the movement that the participant had to perform (the sentence concerned the movement 'from' the body, and it was meaningful, so one had to press the button closer to the body), this resulted in a slower reaction. Dozens of studies have been carried out using this experimental paradigm. All of them – as well as studies using neuroimaging and those based on observational analysis of the behaviour of people with damage to certain parts of their brains – clearly indicate that:

> people perform perceptual and motor simulation while they're processing language. They do so using the same parts of the brain they use to perceive the world and execute actions. Moreover, when specific aspects of embodied simulation are hindered, people have more trouble processing language about those specific aspects of perception or action. And finally, when brain regions dedicated to action or perception are damaged or temporarily taken offline, people have more trouble processing language about the specific perceptual or motor events it encodes. Taken together, all this evidence makes a pretty compelling case that embodied simulation plays a functional role in language understanding. (Bergen, 2012, p. 238)

What is more, it should be stressed that the mental simulations related to understanding language do not have to be conscious processes. Quite the contrary: behavioural research on this issue – such as the experiment described above – shows that the mental simulations of the sentences read usually 'play out' on an unconscious level.

The conception of the understanding of language based on simulation, however, encounters a serious problem – the processing of abstract language. When we read the sentence 'Peter smashed the iPhone belonging to Adam', it is easy to understand how the situation described therein can be recreated in the imagination. Consider, however, another sentence: 'Peter destroyed the movable property belonging to Adam.' It is far from clear what kind of mental simulation may accompany the understanding of this statement. A cursory review of research carried out in recent years only provides clues as to the role of the imagination in the processing of such abstract expressions as 'movable property' (Bergen, 2012, p. 209ff.). Firstly, a number of experiments have been devoted to linguistic metaphors. These studies suggest similar conclusions to the conceptions dealing with concrete language processing. For example, people reading the sentence 'The rates climbed' and given the task of deciding whether it is a meaningful one, press the (correct) button which is higher up faster, and slower if the button is located lower down. Secondly, more abstract sentences, such as 'You radioed the message to the policeman', also interfere with our motor functions, suggesting that some mental simulations using motor neurons play a role in the understanding of such sentences. Thirdly, it can be assumed that simulations associated with understanding abstract language will show considerable individual differences. Reading that Peter destroyed the movable property belonging to Adam, person A can imagine one particular object, and person B another or even some indistinct shape which can hardly be considered to be an object belonging to the correct category. Fourthly, it seems very likely that the mental simulations accompanying the processing of abstract language will be less detailed than those by which we understand concrete language. Although there is no reason to claim that mental simulations are the only neuronal phenomena associated with the understanding of language expressions, it can be assumed with a high degree of certainty that they are a key element in this process (Bergen, 2012, pp. 210ff.).

Let us now consider the role played by mental simulation in legal thinking. In light of the previous findings, it seems that two of its functions should be indicated in this respect: the heuristic and the hermeneutic. In its heuristic function, the role of mental simulation is to evoke intuitions or – possibly – lead to their (re)shaping. As noted above, mental simulations are multimodal in nature: they may include visual, auditory and motor, but also emotional aspects. If we mentally simulate a certain situation – for example the behaviour of a person – our intuition, shaped by many years of experience, provides us with a preliminary assessment of this behaviour. When I imagine that someone commits a robbery while in full possession of their faculties, severely beating an old lady and stealing from her, my intuition will provide me with a clearly negative assessment of this act. If, in turn, I make a mental simulation of the behaviour of a mother who steals bread in order to feed her children, my intuition will probably supply me with a different assessment, one which is certainly not so unambiguous.

Of course, such intuitive assessments are moral ones: from a moral point of view, the beating and robbing of an old woman leads to condemnation, while stealing bread in order to feed one's starving children to less condemnatory conclusions. Yet the same mechanism is also at play in legal thinking. When judges reconstruct a state of affairs on the basis of the available evidence, they perform a mental simulation of the event in question, and usually do so unconsciously. Such a simulation triggers intuitions which have been developed over many years of training and experience in the settlement of legal cases. In this way, the judge is able to adequately classify the defendant's behaviour and to recognise that it has – or does not have – the hallmarks of a particular type of offence. Of course, it may also transpire that the reconstruction leads to the manifestation of 'conflicting' intuitions; we are then confronted with something that some legal philosophers have termed 'a hard case'.[7]

Mental simulation may also be used to shape and determine appropriate intuitive reactions. Indeed, it is used in this manner in the lecture hall. In order to understand and be able to reasonably apply the complicated provisions of a corporate tax act, a student needs to do more than just carefully read the relevant provisions. The effective lecturer will help to facilitate this process, highlighting the various examples – frequently similar to one another – in which the norms of tax law find application.

In some cases, it is necessary to develop not only new intuitions, but also to work to rid ourselves of our old ones, those which are based on the 'folk' understanding of the social world. A good example is the legal discussion about the status of omission as an act in the Polish criminal law (cf. Kulesza, 2007). The thesis that omission constitutes an act is difficult to understand for someone who sticks to a common-sense framework. Changing this attitude calls for the 're-education' of our intuition, and a good way to do this is to utilise various mental simulations in order to see how refraining from a particular action may be considered to be an act from the point of view of criminal law.

Mental simulations also have a hermeneutic function: they allow us to understand linguistic expressions and so, in the legal context, the provisions of laws and other normative acts, the content of judicial decisions and doctrinal theories. As I emphasised above, however, this is a far from easy task, since legal regulations are formulated in very abstract language. For an illustration of this point, let us compare two pieces of legislation. The first of these is a casuistic norm from the *Code of Hammurabi*: 'If any one steal cattle or sheep, or an ass, or a pig or a goat, if it belong to a god or to the court, the thief shall pay thirtyfold therefor; if they belonged to a freed man of the king he shall pay tenfold; if the thief has nothing with which to pay he shall be put to death' (Harper, 1904). Even though this provision has a somewhat

---

[7] Of course, this is only one way in which hard cases may be understood in law (see Stelmach, 2003, p. 38).

complicated logical structure, the notions at play in it are relatively concrete ones. It is easy to understand what are mental simulations of events such as the theft of a sheep, pig or goat, and thus how the simulations can help in understanding the norm in question. The situation changes when we consider a more abstract regulation, such as Article 278 §1 of the Polish Criminal Code: 'Whoever, with the purpose of appropriating, wilfully takes someone else's movable property, shall be subject to the penalty of deprivation of liberty for a term of between 3 months and 5 years.'[8] What would constitute the mental simulation of 'with the purpose of appropriating, wilfully takes someone else's movable property'?

When dealing with such abstract regulations, we are faced with three potential courses of action (see Brożek, 2011). The first of these may be described as *exemplification*, and this relies on consciously mentally simulating an event which is a case of 'wilfully taking someone else's movable property' (positive exemplification), or is not (negative exemplification). We might imagine, for example, that John, taking advantage of Peter's lapse of concentration, steals his mobile phone; or we could think of a situation where Stacey, like on April Fool's Day every year, wants to play a trick on her work colleague and so takes her purse and hides it in the pocket of another colleague. In the first case, we would have no doubts as to the fact that a theft had taken place while in the second, it is clear that the provisions of Article 278 have not been breached. The problem is that, the more abstract the regulation, the more difficult it is to imagine the different kinds of potential situations that might fall under its provisions. Moreover, the more abstract the regulation, the more it tends to produce borderline cases that are difficult to classify as either positive or negative exemplifications. Let us assume, for example, that Adam has downloaded the latest computer game from the Internet for free; or that Joe hooks up the electricity network in his flat to the meter responsible for regulating electricity use in the whole building. Are these cases in which someone 'wilfully takes someone else's movable property'?

The second procedure that facilitates the understanding of abstract legal provisions is paraphrase. This leads to the claim that the interpreted utterance is synonymous (in the given context) with another statement. For example, by using doctrinal theories and previous legal cases, it can be argued that the provision of Article 278 that 'whoever, with the purpose of appropriating, wilfully takes someone else's movable property, shall be subject to the penalty of deprivation of liberty for a term of between 3 months and 5 years' is (contextually) equivalent to the following norm: 'Whoever removes unlawfully a material object that is separated, can be subject to business trading, possess a business value, and is not immovable, from a person already holding it, is subject to the penalty of deprivation of liberty from 3 months to 5 years' (see Zoll, 2016, p. 30). This paraphrase also uses many abstract

---

[8] The English translation of the Polish Criminal Code is taken from www.imolin.org/doc/amlid/Poland_Penal_Code1.pdf.

concepts such as 'material object', 'possession', 'being subject to business trading' or 'possessing business value' – yet still allows for some solutions to be formulated at the level of mental simulations. For example, it would lead to the conclusion that the imagined situation in which Adam downloads the latest computer game for free from the Internet will not constitute a violation of Article 278 §1, because the computer program is not a 'separate material object'. In other words, the paraphrases of legal provisions formulated by judges as well as in legal doctrine do not have to be less abstract than the original; their task is to facilitate the process exemplification, whether positive or negative.

Thirdly, the interpretation of a legal text may take the form of embedding the given provision (or its paraphrase) in a broader context. Context plays a selective role here: it allows certain paraphrases to be regarded as acceptable and others as unacceptable. For example, in Article 115 of the Polish Penal Code there is a legal definition which states that 'A movable item or chattel refers also to Polish or foreign currency or other means of payment and a document which entitles one to a sum of money or includes the obligation to pay principal, or interest, share in the profits or a declaration of participation in a company or partnership.' This definition excludes any formulations that do not recognise money or other means of payment as movable items, as being admissible paraphrases of Article 278 §1 of the Penal Code. In other words, if we assume that the provisions of the Penal Code should be consistent (and this is one of the basic assumptions of the interpretation of law), we must at least strive to ensure that our understanding of these provisions does not contain contradictions. Therefore, any paraphrase of the interpreted provision should be avoided if it is incompatible with another provision or its previously accepted paraphrase.

Taking these three mechanisms of interpreting the provisions of law into account – namely exemplification, paraphrase and embedding – it is easy to see that the linguistic interpretation, especially that of abstract language, has a dual nature. On the one hand, it relies on a simulation of interpreted statements, although the greater the level of linguistic abstraction, the more extensive and indeterminate the scope of possible simulations will be. When we attempt to understand what is meant by the formulation 'If a citizen steals a sheep then the restoration should be thirtyfold', we may obviously imagine numerous competing situations, but these simulations will be similar to one another; when we interpret the regulation 'whoever wilfully takes someone else's movable property shall be subject to the penalty of deprivation of liberty for a term of between 3 months and 5 years', we may make use of many very different mental simulations, including such cases where we may have justified doubts as to whether they constitute an instance of 'wilfully taking someone else's movable property'. The interpretation of abstract statements is aided by the fact that we consider them to be part of a larger theoretical structure, which – as we assume – is at least non-contradictory, if not entirely coherent. This permits us to make the appropriate paraphrase or to embed the interpreted expression in a broader context.

At this level, the purely formal relationships of the interpreted provision (or its paraphrase) with other regulations play a key role. Thus, the processes of paraphrasing and embedding are aimed at determining a more precise space for mental simulations. It can therefore be said that the interpretation of law – like the interpretation of all abstract statements – consists of a kind of 'game' between mental simulations (exemplifications) and formal or quasi-formal operations on sentences (embedding), where an auxiliary function is performed by paraphrase.

In cognitive science, this dual nature of linguistic understanding is best expressed by the so-called dual coding theory, the first version of which was developed by A. Paivio (2013). According to this conception, language expressions are processed by our minds in two ways: analogously (with the help of so-called imagens, which from the perspective of the theory of embodied cognition can be described as certain mental simulations shaped in the mind by means of its interaction with its environment), and symbolically (with the help of the so-called logogens or the linguistic code). The word 'dog' is associated with a certain imagen (or collection of imagens) which enables us to imagine or mentally simulate a dog when we say, hear or read the word; but the word is also coded into our brains with the help of a corresponding logogen which – on the one hand – is associated with our 'dog imagen(s)' but also – one the other – it has numerous connections and associations with other logogens. The more abstract the language, the weaker and less defined the relationship between the logogens and imagens is likely to be. The terms 'justice', 'Hilbert space' or '*statio fisci*' are associated in numerous ways with different notions at the level of the linguistic code level, but it is hard to believe that they would conjure up the same imagens in different people. One person might imagine 'justice' as Themis, with her blindfold and scales, while another might envisage a concrete event in which justice was manifested, and yet another might have no associations whatsoever with the use of that particular word.

7.4 THINKING IN LANGUAGE

When posing the question of what language gives to thinking, it is difficult to provide a simple answer which would not meet with disagreement. The effect that it has is so important and complex that some philosophers have been inclined to accept that we think only – or almost exclusively – in language. Already in the *Theaetetus*, Plato had Socrates claim that thinking is 'a conversation that the soul carries on with itself, whatever it takes into consideration'. On the other hand, it is necessary to bear in mind that:

> there are many different modes of organised, complicated and highly sophisticated thinking ... for which there are certainly no words: not only the composer composing music in his head, or a music teacher evaluating nuances of a performance on the violin, but a motor-racing driver perceiving and seizing unexpected

opportunities in the course of a race, and thereby changing his prepared strategy; a football coach working out a new and subtle manoeuvre; the choreographer of a Broadway show considering various possibilities for a new dance number involving several soloists and a large chorus; or someone selecting paintings for an exhibition from a larger body of competent work. In all these activities the decisive considerations are things for which there are no words. (Magee, 1997, pp. 83-4)

Thinking in language does not use up all of our cognitive capacities, but there is no doubt that the emergence of language fundamentally changed how people think. Research by evolutionary and cognitive scientists suggest that this happened in at least three ways. Firstly, language unified our cognitive apparatuses. This is easily demonstrated by means of intercultural research devoted to the linguistic categorisation of the world: people using different languages see the world and explain human behaviour in different ways, although the scope of this influence remains open to question. Let us consider the fascinating case of understanding the intentions and mental states of other people. In the Philippine tribal language of Llongot, there is a word *rinawa* (Lillard, 1998) which is perhaps best translated as 'mind'. The problem lies in the fact that *rinawa* not only refers to thoughts and feelings but also encompasses different social contexts, such as fertility or health. *Rinawa* is possessed not only by people since it is also ascribed to animals and plants. As a result, when trying to understand the actions of other people, representatives of the Llongot tribe not only focus on convictions and desires, but also take into account the social and external relations which may supply the subject with reasons for their actions (Lillard, 1998, p. 12).

However, one does not need to conduct a wide-ranging study of indigenous languages to find similar ways of conceptualising human behaviour. It has been noted, for example, that members of Asian societies typically explain behaviour by means of reference to situational factors, while representatives of Western cultural groups tend to focus more on personal factors (cf. Morris & Peng, 1994). In the Chinese paper *World Journal* an article was published on a mass murder in which attention was paid to the fact that the perpetrator had recently been fired from his job, that his replacement was an enemy of his and that a similar murder had taken place a few months earlier in Texas. Reporters for *The New York Times*, when describing a similar event, focused on the fact that the perpetrator had earlier displayed a predilection for violence and was a fan of martial arts, while also showing his mental instability (Morris & Peng, 1994).

This and other examples – which concern the perception of space and time, colours or emotions – unambiguously show that we see and perceive the world within a conceptual framework which is rooted in our language. As a result, users of the same language will have more similar conceptual schemes than people belonging to different cultures. This is the unifying function of language: it makes us think in similar categories.

This is related to the second way in which language affects thought: through the use of language our cognitive efforts may become joint ventures. We can share the discoveries that we have made and deal with complex problems together. It is difficult to imagine how this would be possible without language on any larger scale. This 'publicisation' of thought also permits its objectivisation: we can discuss the ideas that have been proposed by others, test them and subject them to criticism, proposing improvements or alternative solutions. Therefore, it can be argued that rationality was born together with the emergence of language, and that human attempts to conceptualise the world have acquired the characteristics of systematic reflection striving for objective decisions.

The third dimension of the influence of language on thought is equally important. Language allows us to consider and reflect upon issues that cannot otherwise be grasped. It suffices to say that the creation of modern science, the emergence of complicated normative systems or the development of technology would not have been possible without the existence of a tool such as language. 'Language, like the beaver's dam, is a collectively constructed trans-generational phenomenon. But human language, unlike the beaver's dam, provides our species with a distinctive, general purpose cognitive niche: a persisting, though never stationary, symbolic edifice whose critical role in promoting thought and reason remains surprisingly ill-understood' (Clark, 2005, p. 257). Without language, we would have been unable to learn nature's secrets, to have conducted any joint ventures on a large scale, or to live in large, well-organised societies.

Obviously, legal language also fulfils these three functions. Those who have been educated in a legal culture possess similar conceptual systems and, as a result, treat the legally relevant aspects of reality in the same way. Legal language also facilitates common and objectivised consideration of legal problems and thus opens the way to new conceptual categories: perceiving new phenomena and problems and constructing theories in response to these new challenges.

The unification of conceptual apparatus, objectivisation and the creation of new cognitive categories are not the only things that language can give us, especially in those areas which call for abstract and highly systematic reflection. Let us, therefore, look at the three more 'specialised' functions that language plays in legal thinking: abstraction, theorising and dialogisation.

In order to understand abstraction in law, it is worth returning to the *Code of Hammurabi* mentioned above. One can find a number of regulations therein related to theft such as:

> 7. If any one buy from the son or the slave of another man, without witnesses or a contract, silver or gold, a male or female slave, an ox or a sheep, an ass or anything, or if he take it in charge, he is considered a thief and shall be put to death.
>
> 8. If any one steal cattle or sheep, or an ass, or a pig or a goat, if it belong to a god or to the court, the thief shall pay thirtyfold therefor; if they belonged to a freed man of

the king he shall pay tenfold; if the thief has nothing with which to pay he shall be put to death.

14. If any one steal the minor son of another, he shall be put to death.

25. If fire break out in a house, and some one who comes to put it out cast his eye upon the property of the owner of the house, and take the property of the master of the house, he shall be thrown into that self-same fire. (Harper, 1904)

The level of detail with which various forms of theft are described in this catalogue is striking. The theft of goods belonging to a temple or ruler is one thing, and the theft of property belonging to one's fellow citizens is quite another; the appropriation of gold or silver and that of farm animals is treated in a different manner too; and there is a special criminal category – which is punished in a special way – namely the theft of property from a fire. The regulations in the *Code of Hammurabi* are therefore casuistic: they distinguish between very similar events. Let us compare them to the regulations contained in the Polish Penal Code:

> Article 278. §1. Whoever, with the purpose of appropriating, wilfully takes someone else's movable property, shall be subject to the penalty of deprivation of liberty for a term of between 3 months and 5 years.

Setting aside the relevant cultural differences (such as the fact, for example, that slavery no longer exists in Poland), it may be ventured that Article 278 of the Penal Code encompasses all of the regulations mentioned in the *Code of Hammurabi* (and many others). This article is, put simply, much more abstract. What do we gain from the utilisation of such abstract notions as 'movable property'? It seems that by adopting such abstract notions, we simplify our image of the world. 'Movable property' is a category which encompasses the greatest possible diversity of such objects. We are not interested in whether they are small or large, whether they have been made or are the products of nature. The notion of movable property is 'blind' to many of the features of the situations being assessed but, as a result, it is relatively easy to use. Imagine what would happen if the Penal Code had separate provisions for the theft of more specific items, for example apples produced in the EU, whose weight does not exceed 100 grams and which are not entirely pale red in colour; blue-coloured bicycles which have been repaired in a certain workshop on Starowiślna Street in Kraków; phones manufactured in China between 15 and 20 January 2016, and so on. Such an ultra-casuistic regulatory system would be very difficult to apply. The use of abstract concepts introduces order into this system and simplifies it to the extent that we are able to use it efficiently.

The careful reader will have noticed, however, that the notions which feature in the *Code of Hammurabi* are also somewhat abstract. For example, one of the articles refers to a 'goat', without specifying its age, sex or health. Of course, a 'goat' is less abstract than 'movable property', since the latter is 'blind' to more of the features of the situations being assessed. This shows that abstraction is a matter of degree and is conditioned by the emergence of language. Each and every concrete linguistic concept (with the exception of the special case of proper names) is to a certain extent an abstraction, since by using them we ignore a whole range of the attributes of other things or events.

It should also be remembered that a certain price is paid for the simplicity of such abstract conceptual systems. More abstract expressions require far more interpretive efforts than formulations that use relatively specific words. In an extreme case, if the legal system consisted of only one or a few very general and abstract provisions, it would probably be completely useless. Imagine, for example, that a legal order contains only one norm: 'Do good and avoid evil.' It can be argued that this provision would not play any role in court decision making – everything would be a matter of interpretation here, and further rulings would be based on previous decisions, not a general norm. It turns out, therefore, that abstraction has its limits, and it is determined by the cost – both cognitive and economic – of the interpretation and application of law. Too abstract a legal system would not be useful, since it would not allow even simple cases to be decided unequivocally; a too concrete and casuistic one would also be useless, since it would be impossible to cognitively master it, and thus effectively use it.

The second way in which language supports thinking is by means of theorising. It is only through language that it is possible to construct and analyse complex theories describing selected fragments of physical and social reality: to establish logical relations between their elements and draw more concrete conclusions from them. Modern criminal law provides a good example of how the theorisation mechanism works. The provisions of the special part of the Penal Code, for example the above-quoted Article 278 §1, do not constitute the sole basis for determining criminal liability.

In order to convict someone of a crime such as theft, we should also take into consideration the provisions of the general part of the Code, which specify the conditions for assigning criminal responsibility in all types of crimes. Thus, according to Article 1 of the Penal Code, 'penal liability shall be incurred only by a person who commits an act prohibited under penalty, by a law in force at the time of its commission', while 'a prohibited act whose social consequences are insignificant shall not constitute an offence' and 'the perpetrator of a prohibited act does not commit an offence if guilt cannot be attributed to him at the time of the commission of the act'. Also, a crime cannot have been committed if any of the grounds excluding unlawfulness or guilt are present: necessary defence (Article 25); averting an immediate danger (Article 26); conducting a cognitive, medical, technical or economic experiment (Article 27); justified error (Articles 28–30); or serious mental illness, brain damage or other mental factors which lead to grounds of diminished responsibility in terms of actions or behaviour (Article 31). In the general part of the Penal Code, the legislator also defines the forms and stages of the committing of a crime: perpetration, instigation, aiding, preparing, attempting and accomplishing. The points regulating these issues are in a way 'factored out' – they refer to all types of prohibited acts described in the special part of the Code. They therefore define the structural elements that are common to all possible crimes. The same applies to other branches of law. For example, the provisions of the Civil Code regarding contracts, in addition to the regulation of specific types of contracts, such as sale, rental, lending, loan or commission, also include general solutions defining the structure of any kind of contract which is legally acceptable.

Thanks to theorising, our knowledge about the world – for example about attributing criminal or civil liability – can be unified to a considerable extent. To understand what unification concerns, let us consider a completely different field of knowledge, that of physics. Prior to the discoveries of James Clerk Maxwell in 1861, electricity and magnetism were explained using two different, unrelated theories. Maxwell, however, noticed and expressed in a precise mathematical form that electricity and magnetism were two kinds of the same phenomenon – electromagnetism. The emergence of quantum mechanics and subsequent discoveries made it possible to attempt another unification: that of electromagnetism with weak interactions in the form of so-called quantum field theory. Contemporary physicists are now attempting to take the next steps on the path to the unification of all basic physical interactions in one theory: they want to combine the theory of electroweak interactions with quantum chromodynamics into a single grand unified theory, which in turn could be combined with the general theory of relativity into a theory of everything. Such steps will help to foster a better understanding of the world, but

> the kind of understanding provided by science is global rather than local. Scientific explanations do not confer intelligibility on individual phenomena by showing them to be somehow natural, necessary, familiar, or inevitable. However, our overall understanding of the world is increased; our total picture of nature is simplified via a reduction in the number of independent phenomena that we have to accept as ultimate. (Friedman, 1974, p. 18)

One may understand unification in every field of reflection in a similar manner. If the Penal Code did not contain a general part, with uniform principles of criminal law for the entire legal system, we would be condemned to a casuistic, unrelated consideration of many different types of crimes. The criminal-law image of the world would be far more fragmentary, with a correspondingly less coherent understanding of penal law institutions. Just as abstraction allows us to ignore the various aspects of reality that are irrelevant from the perspective of the goals of law, so theorising ensures order in the legal conceptual system. Of course, striving for unification at all costs can lead to unfortunate consequences. One may wonder, for example, if it would be beneficial to introduce identical standards for the assessment of behaviour (the same understanding of agency, forms of committing an offence, guilt, etc.) in criminal law and civil liability, or quite the opposite. For example, this type of unification entails the removal of strict liability from civil law, something which seems to be an undesirable consequence. Thus, as in the case of abstraction, there is a kind of trade-off between the degree of unification of the legal system – and, hence, its simplicity of use and intelligibility – and other values.

Finally, let us look at the third way in which language shapes legal thinking: through dialogisation. The ability to use language to formulate more or less complex theories facilitates the creation of alternative solutions to problems, of means of comparing and criticising them. The importance of this feature of thinking in language is difficult to overestimate. The theories and conceptualisations of the world accepted by us have many hidden assumptions that we are unable to recognise by means of the analysis of the claims alone (see Feyerabend, 1993). If I see a table in the full light of day, I can say with certainty that it is of a brown colour. If I see a different table at dusk, and this picture evokes similar colour impressions, I will probably say that it 'seems' to be brown. This is a natural way of expressing oneself, but it is based on very strong, unconscious assumptions. In particular, it tacitly acknowledges that the perception of objects under 'optimal' conditions (for example, in the correct lighting conditions) allows us to know their 'real' properties.

At the same time, it is an illusion stemming from the fact that the mind usually functions in a particular type of environment. If we mainly lived in semi-darkness, then a table seen in these conditions would always be brown, and the one perceived in the full light would only 'appear to be' brown (Feyerabend, 1993, pp. 21–2). In order to understand this, however, we must question what we accept in a non-reflective way. As Paul Feyerabend puts it: 'how can we possibly examine something we are using all the time? ... How can we discover the kind of world we presuppose when proceeding as we do?' (see Feyerabend, 1993, p. 22). His answer is the following: 'we need a dream-world in order to discover the features of the real world we think we inhabit' (see Feyerabend, 1993, p. 22). In other words, in order to obtain a full understanding of a given theory, with all of its underlying assumptions, we have to be able to contrast it with alternative theories, sometimes even evidently false ones. This is also true in legal thinking, and at every level, from the law-making process, through dogmatic considerations to court trials. Thinking which relies on the simultaneous contemplation of alternative theories can also fulfil an important heuristic function, even suggesting better ways of solving the problems at hand. The contradictions that we perceive within a theory, as well as the non-correspondence between theories, constitute the fuel for human creativity. Finally, it should be noted that comparing alternative theories may also serve to justify our own statements. A solution that emerges triumphant from a contest between alternative suggestions has far greater legitimacy than one formulated in a 'dialogical vacuum'. This is particularly important in fields such as law, where other criteria, such as verification or falsification, are not available for use in our justifications.

7.5 CONCLUSION

I have argued in the above considerations that legal thinking, just like any other form of systematic reflection, uses three mental mechanisms: intuition, imagination (mental simulations) and thinking in language. An appropriately trained intuition, based on emotional responses, acting rapidly and beyond our conscious control, usually provides acceptable, albeit not always optimal answers to emerging questions. Imagination, or more precisely, mental simulation, serves as a kind of link between intuition and thinking in language. On the one hand, it performs a heuristic function, allowing the activation of the appropriate intuitions; on the other, it also has a hermeneutic function, enabling us to understand the abstract language of legal provisions and to consider legal doctrine. In turn, thinking in language provides us with the required level of abstraction and theorising (unification), simplifying and harmonising the legal image of the world, and thus making it applicable to the often extremely complex problems that a lawyer encounters in his or her professional life. Once again, it should be stressed that legal thinking is inconceivable without the interaction between these three mechanisms.

Of course, not everyone will use their intuition, imagination and thinking in language in the same way, and certainly not in all cases. On the one hand, differences in cognitive styles will matter. Those referred to in psychology as verbalisers will tend to rely mainly on thinking in language; in turn, the visualisers will reach for their imagination and mental simulation more frequently (see Kozhevnikov, 2007). On the other hand, the actual use of a mental mechanism will also depend on the type of problem under consideration. Simple, 'algorithmic' legal cases will be solved quickly and effortlessly, relying on the hints afforded by intuition. Hard cases, in which the hints of intuition are unclear or contradictory, will require the use of mental simulation and abstract theory. Also, conducting dogmatic considerations cannot be limited to the use of intuition alone. The analysis of abstract legal regulations cannot be made without complex interpretative procedures, aided by the imagination and the development of a theory, and particularly the comparison of alternative solutions to the problem under consideration.

In closing, let us note that the conception of legal thinking outlined in this chapter explains the enduring nature of four very different, and often conflicting, visions of legal reasoning: intuitivism, formalism, coherentism and dialecticism. These theories – regardless of whether they are descriptive or normative – place an emphasis on some aspects of the architecture of the legal mind while ignoring others. Intuitivism exaggerates the role of unconscious decision-making processes; formalism is blind to the benefits stemming from the use of intuition and imagination, limiting legal thinking to language; coherentism and dialecticism act in a similar manner. By this I do not mean that I consider these ideas to be wrong; I rather argue that the structure for legal thinking that they assume is one which is far from complete.

REFERENCES

Alexy, Robert. (1989). *A Theory of Legal Argumentation*. Oxford: Clarendon Press.
Bargh, J. A., & Morsella, E. (2008). The Unconscious Mind. *Perspectives on Psychological Science* 3(1), 73–9.
Bergen, Benjamin. (2012). *Louder Than Words*. New York: Basic Books.
Brożek, Bartosz. (2004). *Defeasibility of Legal Reasoning*. Kraków: Zakamycze.
Brożek, Bartosz. (2008). *Rationality and Discourse: Towards a Normative Model of Applying Law*. Warsaw: Wolters Kluwer.
Brożek, Bartosz. (2011). Beyond Interpretation. In J. Stelmach & R. Schmidt (eds.), *Krakauer-Augsburger Rechtsstudien: Die Grenzen der rechtsdogmatischen Interpretation*. Warsaw: Wolters Kluwer, pp. 19–28.
Brożek, Bartosz. (2020). *The Legal Mind: A New Introduction to Legal Epistemology*. Cambridge: Cambridge University Press.
Byrne, Richard W. (1988). The Early Evolution of Creative Thinking: Evidence from Monkeys and Apes. In Steven Mithen (ed.), *Creativity in Human Evolution and Prehistory*. London, Routledge, pp. 110–24.
Clark, Andy. (2005). Word, Niche, and Super-Niche: How Language Makes Minds Matter More. *Theoria* 54, 255–68.
Damasio, Antonio. (2006). *Descartes' Error*. London: Vintage.
Damasio, A. R., Tranel, D., & Damasio, H. (1991). Somatic Markers and the Guidance of Behaviour: Theory and Preliminary Testing. In H. S. Levin, H. M. Eisenberg, A. L. Benton (eds.), *Frontal Lobe Function and Dysfunction*. New York: Oxford University Press, pp. 217–29.
Dworkin, Ronald. (1986). *Law's Empire*. Cambridge, MA: Belknap Press.
Feyerabend, Paul. (1993). *Against Method*. London & New York: Verso.
Friedman, Michael. (1974). Explanation and Scientific Understanding. *The Journal of Philosophy* 71(1), 5–19.
Guthrie, C., Rachlinski, J. J., & Wistrich, A. J. (2001). Inside the Judicial Mind. *Cornell Law Review* 86, 778–830.
Hage, Jaap. (2000). Dialectical Models in Artificial Intelligence and Law. *Artificial Intelligence and Law* 8, 137–72.
Hage, Jaap. (2013). Three Kinds of Coherentism. In M. Araszkiewicz, J. Šavelka (eds.), *Coherence: Insights from Philosophy, Jurisprudence and Artificial Intelligence*, Law and Philosophy Library, vol. 107. Dordrecht: Springer, pp. 1–32.
Harper, Robert. (1904). *The Code of Hammurabi*. Chicago: The University of Chicago Press.
Hastie, R., Schkade, D. A., & Payne J. W. (1999). Juror Judgments in Civil Cases: Effects of Plaintiff's Requests and Plaintiff's Identity on Punitive Damage Awards. *Law and Human Behavior* 23, 445–70.
Hutcheson, Joseph C., Jr. (1929). Judgment Intuitive. The Function of the Hunch in Judicial Decisions. *Cornell Law Review* 14(3), 274–88.
Kahneman, Daniel. (2011). *Thinking, Fast and Slow*. New York: Farrar, Straus and Giroux.
Kaufmann, Arthur. (1986). Vorüberlegungen zu einer juristischen Logik und Ontologie der Relationen: Grundlegung einer personalen Rechtstheorie. *Rechtstheorie* 17 (3), 257–76.
Kozhevnikov, Maria. (2007). Cognitive Styles in the Context of Modern Psychology: Toward an Integrated Framework of Cognitive Style. *Psychological Bulletin* 133(3), 464–81.
Kulesza, Jan. (2007). O pojmowaniu zaniechania w polskiej nauce prawa karnego. *Czasopismo Prawa Karnego i Nauk Penalnych* XI(2).

Langevoort, Donald C. (1998). Behavioral Theories of Judgment and Decision-Making in Legal Scholarship: A Literature Review. *Vanderbilt Law Review* 51, 1499–1540.

Lillard, Angeline. (1998). Ethnopsychologies: Cultural Variations in Theories of Mind. *Psychological Bulletin* 123, 3–32.

MacCormick, Neil. (1994). *Legal Reasoning and Legal Theory*. Oxford: Oxford University Press.

Magee, Bryan. (1997). *Confessions of a Philosopher*. New York: Random House.

McCaffery, E. J., Kahneman, D., & Spitzer, M. L. (1995). Framing the Jury: Cognitive Perspectives on Pain and Suffering Awards. *Virginia Law Review* 81(1341), 1341–1420.

Morris, M., & Peng, K. (1994). Culture and Cause: American and Chinese Attributions for Social and Physical Events. *Journal of Personality and Social Psychology* 67(6), 949–71.

The Oxford English Dictionary. (1989). 2nd edition. Oxford: Oxford University Press.

Paivio, Allan. (2013). *Mind and Its Evolution: A Dual Coding Theoretical Approach*. New York: Lawrence Erlbaum Associates Publishers.

Peer, E., & Gamliel, E. (2013). Heuristics and Biases in Judicial Decisions. *Court Review* 49 (2013), 114–18.

Perelman, Chaïm. (1955). How Do We Apply Reason to Values? *Journal of Philosophy* 52(26), 797–802.

Perelman, Chaïm, & Olbrechts-Tyteca, L. (1958). *Traite de l'argumentation: La nouvelle rhetorique*. Paris: Pressess Universitaires de France.

Petrażycki, Leon. (2011). *Law and Morality*. New York: Routledge.

Pound, Roscoe. (1908). Mechanical Jurisprudence. *Columbia Law Review* 8, 605–23.

Prakken, Henry. (1997). *Logical Tools for Modelling Legal Argument*. Dordrecht: Kluwer Academic Publishers.

Quine, Willard Van Orman. (1969). Epistemology Naturalized. In Willard Van Orman Quine, *Ontological Relativity and Other Essays*. New York: Columbia University Press.

Reyes, R. M., Thompson, W. C., & Bower, G. H. (1980). Judgmental Biases Resulting from Differing Availabilities of Arguments. *Journal of Personality and Social Psychology* 3, 2–12.

Stelmach, Jerzy. (1991). *Die Hermeneutische Auffassung der Rechtsphilosophie*. Ebelsbach: Verlag Rolf Gremer.

Stelmach, Jerzy. (2003). *Kodeks argumentacyjny dla prawników*. Kraków: Zakamycze.

Stelmach, Jerzy. (2013). *Uporczywe upodobanie*. Olszanica, Poland: BOSZ.

Stelmach, J., & Brożek, B. (2006). *Methods of Legal Reasoning*. Dordrecht: Springer.

Tversky, A., & Kahneman, D. (1974). Judgment under Uncertainty: Heuristics and Biases. *Science* 185(4157), 1124–31.

Zoll, Andrzej (ed.). (2016). *Kodeks karny. Część szczególna. Tom III*. Warsaw: Wolters Kluwer.

8

The Psychology of the Trial Judge

Morris B. Hoffman[*]

Despite the fact that psychologists have been plying their trade in judicial waters for almost a century, and even after behavioral economists joined the fun in the early 1980s, there remains a relative paucity of research into the psychology of judging. There are lots of reasons for this, both theoretical and practical.

On the theoretical side, judicial decision making in many respects just doesn't fit comfortably into traditional psychological, and especially economic, analyses. Judges are generally insulated from market incentives (but see Posner, 1993; and Epstein, Landes, & Posner, 2013), have specialized training that uniquely emphasizes obedience to precedent, and, at least in Anglo-American systems, rely almost entirely on the information produced by advocates. Some scholars have even suggested that legal reasoning may be a unique kind of decision making to which some ordinary psychological insights may not apply (Schauer & Spellman, 2017).[1]

Research into the psychology of judging also faces daunting empirical challenges, including the ever-present problem of designing ecologically valid experiments. Subjects awarding hypothetical damages or imposing hypothetical prison sentences, even when those subjects are judges, are arguably operating in different psychological states than judges making decisions in real cases. Judging is also a specially constrained kind of decision making, not just because of the requirements of precedent and the reliance on advocacy but also because of limitations on whether the judge even has the authority to make a decision (jurisdiction) and what kinds of information may be presented (rules of evidence), not to mention the substantive law into which proof of any legal claim must fit, the different standards which that

---

[*] District Judge, Second Judicial District, State of Colorado; Member, John D. and Catherine T. MacArthur Foundation Research Network on Law and Neuroscience; Research Fellow, Gruter Institute for Law and Behavioral Research; Adjunct Professor of Law, University of Denver. I thank Jaap Hage, not just for inviting me to make this contribution, but especially for including the psychology of judging in this big topic of Law and Mind. I also thank my friend Bill Pizzi and my former MacArthur colleague Jed Rakoff for their cogent comments on prior drafts of this chapter.

[1] The law has had its own meta-controversies over the nature of law and of judicial decision making, in the form of the jurisprudential battles between natural law theorists, positivists, realists, and normativists (Aharoni & Hoffman, in press).

proof must meet, and the party on whom the burden of proof rests. There are also unique data-gathering challenges with judges, both in experimental and observational work. Judges tend to be less enthusiastic than undergraduates when it comes to volunteering for behavioral experiments. Academic access to state and federal judicial databases can also be difficult, and even after researchers gain access to judicial data the real trouble begins: many legal decisions are not made in open court on the record, but rather take the form of written legal opinions crafted over time in the privacy of judges' chambers and with untraceable assistance from law clerks.

For all of these reasons, the psychology of judicial decision making remains an understudied field with many more unanswered questions than answered ones. To be sure, there seems to have been an upswing of interest in recent years, beginning with Klein & Mitchell's *The Psychology of Judicial Decision-Making* (Klein & Mitchell, 2010). But compared to the psychology of juror decision making, the psychology of judge decision making remains a relatively ignored stepchild.

This chapter is intended to summarize what is known about the psychology of the trial judge. It is organized in three parts. The first section examines the question of whether the general insights of psychology and behavioral economics can be applied to trial judges, or whether, by virtue of their special training and experience or some other reason, trial judges are different. The second section surveys the relatively scant behavioral literature on judging and places it in the larger context of nonjudge decision making. It does so by considering four well-studied "heuristics," or cognitive shortcuts that allow people to make quick, intuitive decisions with little or no deliberation, but that can sometimes also result in errors in reasoning. The four heuristics considered are: anchoring, hindsight, compromise and contrast, and representativeness. The third section finishes the chapter with a series of reflections about specific challenges I've thought about over the twenty-nine years I've been a trial judge, coupled with a few suggestions about how the system might better accommodate some of those challenges.

Before we begin, a few comments are in order about what I've intentionally left out. Because I am a trial judge, this chapter is devoted to the psychology of the trial judge, and therefore ignores the work that has been done in analyzing the psychology of appellate judges, including the decisions of the United States Supreme Court (see Wrightsman, 2010). Trial judges are just a small part of a much larger adjudicative process, with many players and many interacting psychologies, but that broader picture is also beyond of the scope of this chapter. I've therefore excluded any separate psychological consideration of litigants, lawyers, witnesses, and jurors, as well as their interactions with each other and with trial judges. There is an extensive literature on group decision making generally (see Kerr & Tindale, 2004) and jury decision making in particular (see MacCoun, 1984; Peter-Hagene & Salerno, 2019), as well as a growing interest in the judge/juror interaction represented by judges' written jury instructions (see Vidmar & Hans, 2007), all of which is excluded. There has been some study of the application of behavioral economics to the rules of evidence (see Vars, 2014), and of litigation as a game-theoretic and behavioral undertaking (see Robbennolt, 2014), all of which is also excluded.

There are well-developed models of general decision making that fall roughly into two large camps: coherence-based reasoning (see Simon, 2004) and storytelling (see Pennington & Hastie, 1991). Discussion of these two models is likewise beyond the scope of this chapter, although I do touch a bit on the storytelling model when I raise what I call "the light bulb problem" in Section 8.3.

The four heuristics discussed in Section 8.2 are only a small part of a long list of heuristics identified by thousands of studies over the last several decades (see Keren & Wu, 2015).[2] Limiting the chapter to just these four was a decision driven in part by considerations of space and focus, but also because the four selected heuristics seemed to me to have the most traction with trial judging.

Finally, readers steeped in the theory of behavioral economics will recognize that by looking only at heuristics, the chapter leaves out two other broad categories of departures from classical economic rationality: departures from "motivational rationality" and from "consequentialist morality" (see Teichman & Zamir, 2014).

8.1 ARE TRIAL JUDGES DIFFERENT?

Does legal training and experience inoculate trial judges from common cognitive errors to which lay people are prone? So far, there is no general answer to this question. Judges seem less prone to some kinds of errors in some kinds of domains, but just as bad as everyone else in other domains. This is hardly surprising. Many studies have examined in many different occupational contexts the general question of whether well-recognized irrationalities can be trained out of people, or at least muted, by education, experience, or even targeted learning, and the results of those studies are decidedly mixed. Some techniques reduce (but never seem to eliminate) some kinds of cognitive biases, others don't seem to have any effect, and still others make things worse (Zamir, 2017).

There have been a handful of studies aimed specifically at whether trial judges behave differently than nonjudges in legally relevant circumstances. In a famous experiment in the early 1990s, researchers investigated the extent to which trial judges and laypeople follow instructions to disregard information (Landsman & Rakos, 1994). This is something jurors and judges are regularly called upon to do at various points in the process – at trial, for example, if evidence is inadvertently disclosed to jurors and the judge directs them to disregard it. In this particular experiment, the researchers found that in the context of a hypothetical products

---

[2] These include availability, loss aversion/risk seeking, framing effects, omission bias, the endowment effect, sunk costs/escalating commitment, and confirmation bias (Zamir, 2017).

liability case, judges (Ohio state trial judges) and nonjudges had an equally difficult time disregarding information about a prior product recall which they were instructed to disregard (a whopping 25 percent of both judges and nonjudges were unable to disregard the information).

Different researchers obtained similar results in criminal contexts. In these experiments, judges had difficulty ignoring information they had been directed was inadmissible and must be ignored, including prior criminal convictions, conversations protected by the attorney–client privilege, and the sexual history of rape victims. But there was one important and puzzling exception: judges were much better at ignoring inadmissible confessions than other kinds of information (Wistrich, Guthrie, & Rachlinski, 2005), perhaps because judges think they know something about the coercion and trickery that can produce false confessions.

As we will see in Section 8.2.4, ordinary subjects are quite poor at some kinds of Bayesian reasoning, meaning the ability to update conditional probabilistic information with new information, especially information about base rates. But in one experiment by Guthrie, Rachlinski, and Wistrich (2001), judges were much better than the general population at working through a series of conditional probabilities involving links in a chain of caused harm.

Specializing in a particular judicial domain looks like it doesn't help. Bankruptcy judges were no better than their nonspecialized colleagues or nonjudges at resisting many cognitive biases (Rachlinski, Guthrie, & Wistrich, 2007).

The spottiness of judges' abilities to overcome some common cognitive biases is perhaps nowhere more evident than in the context of racial bias. In one experiment, judges' implicit racial bias did not correlate to any disparate sentencing treatment of black and white defendants, but only when race was subtly suggested. When the race of the defendant was made explicit, judges seemed to overcompensate – those with higher implicit biases against black defendants treated them better than similarly situated white defendants (Rachlinski, Johnson, Wistrich, & Guthrie, 2009).

Evidence from actual sentencing is no more enlightening. Some studies of the impact of the defendant's race in the context of departures from the federal sentencing guidelines seemed to show that federal judges imposed harsher sentences on black and Hispanic defendants than on white ones (see Mustard, 2001). But other studies showed that the seriousness of the crimes was accounting for most of these differences (Blumstein, 1982). Still other studies have shown that, within the population of black defendants, the degree of their "Afrocentric features" seems to have a significant impact on sentence lengths (Pizzi, Blair, & Judd, 2004).

When one throws in the race of the judge, things get even murkier. In the Rachlinski, Johnson, Wistrich, and Guthrie (2009) experiment mentioned above, when the race of the defendant was made explicit, black judges, but only black judges, showed biases in sentencing that correlated to their implicit biases. The researchers suggest that black judges were less worried about appearing biased, and therefore did not compensate, causing their implicit biases to be expressed.

An early study by Uhlman (1978) suggested that black judges are much more lenient than white judges in sentencing black defendants. A 1990 study found no sentencing differences between black and white judges (Spohn 1990). In a more comprehensive study, researchers in 2001 looked at actual criminal sentences imposed by Pennsylvania judges statewide between 1991 and 1994, and discovered that black judges were somewhat more likely than their white colleagues to sentence both black and white defendants to incarceration, but found no differences in the lengths of those sentences (Steffensmeier & Britt, 2001). But when a researcher reexamined the Pennsylvania data, and looked only at cases that went to trial (thus eliminating the discretion-narrowing impacts of plea bargaining), he found black judges were more lenient than white judges, both in their likelihood of imposing incarceration and in their average length of sentence (Johnson, 2006).

The effects of the judge's race in civil cases are a little clearer, though they seem to impact only one discrete domain of civil cases: those involving allegations of discrimination based on race or sex. In those limited kinds of cases, it appears black judges rule more favorably for plaintiffs than do white judges when it comes both to pretrial motions (Boyd, 2016) and actual outcomes when the case is tried to the judge (Chew & Kelley, 2009).

Age and gender have similarly confusing effects. It appears well settled that men are sentenced more harshly than similarly situated women (Desantts & Kayson, 1997), and younger defendants more harshly than similarly situated older ones (Smith & Hed, 1979). But what about the age and gender of the judge? Nonjudge subjects generally get more punitive as they age (Brillon, 1983), and men are generally more punitive than women (Gault & Sabini, 2000). But it is not at all clear that these effects translate into differences in sentencing.

Early studies of the sentencing impacts of the judge's gender showed little difference between male and female judges (Kritzer & Uhlman, 1977; Gruhl, Spohn, & Welch, 1981). But a later study by Spohn (1990) showed female judges were considerably harsher than their male colleagues, sentencing defendants to an average of four years more incarceration. In an even more recent study, researchers found a three-way interaction between the judge's age and gender, and the seriousness of the case. For serious "high harm" cases only, younger (<54 y. o.) female judges sentenced much more harshly than their male or older female colleagues (Hoffman, Shen, Iyengar, & Krueger, 2020).

The lesson in all of this is that the extent to which judges' training and experience inoculate them from some of the cognitive biases exhibited by non-judges remains largely an open question. We simply do not have enough experimental or real-world data to answer this question, either broadly or across different legal contexts.

8.2 FOUR HEURISTICS THAT MAY BE IMPACTING TRIAL JUDGES

A "heuristic" is a cognitive shortcut, likely built into our brains by evolution, that allows us to make certain kinds of quick decisions without spending too much time cogitating about them. Our ancestors may never have survived to produce us if they had brains that spent time mulling over whether the snake under that log was actually poisonous or not. In this section we consider four well-studied heuristics and their application to the psychology of judging. Readers will see that not much is offered in terms of suggestions for dealing with the biases these heuristics produce. That's in part because much more needs to be learned about these heuristics in judicial settings, but also because some of the heuristics – especially anchoring and hindsight bias – seem impervious to debiasing strategies.

8.2.1 Anchoring

When people are presented with a number before they make numerical guesses about an unknown, the number presented can have dramatic effects on their judgment. In their famous 1974 paper on anchoring, Kahneman and Tversky presented subjects with a random number between 1 and 100, then asked them (a) whether the percentage of African countries in the UN was higher or lower than the presented number and (b) to guess about the actual percentage. The random number had enormous effects on subjects' guesses. Subjects presented with the random number of 10 on average answered that 25 percent of UN countries are African; subjects presented with the random number of 60 answered that 45 percent of UN countries are African (the correct answer at the time of the study was 29 percent) (UN Membership, 1974).

The anchoring effect can have pervasive everyday impacts, most notably in pricing. That 40 percent sale price anchors all of us to the presale price, and makes the sale price look good even if the item was originally overpriced by more than the discount. I remember that when I was a teenager working summers at a retail store that shall remain nameless, we occasionally had "sales" where the boss would direct us first to double the item's price and then to make signs that announced the price was being slashed by 40 percent.

The anchoring effect is a potential problem whenever uncertain evaluations are reduced to a quantitative judgment. The judicial system is strewn with such circumstances, including the judge's or jury's determination of damages in civil cases, *additur* and *remittitur* (processes by which a judge can increase or decrease a jury's award of civil damages), the determination of the reasonableness of costs and attorney fees to be awarded to a successful litigant, and, perhaps most significantly, criminal sentencing.

There have been a few anchoring experiments with judges, all of which show that we are just as susceptible to the anchoring effect as anyone else. In one of the first such studies, Guthrie, Rachlinski, and Wistrich (2001) asked 167 federal magistrate judges to estimate damages in a personal injury case arising out of a traffic accident. Half of them were given a not-so-subtle anchor by being informed the defendant had also filed a motion to dismiss for failure to meet the $75,000 jurisdictional threshold for federal courts, despite the fact that the scenario unambiguously showed that the hypothetical plaintiff suffered considerably more than $75,000 in damages. The anchored group awarded an average of $882,000 compared to $1,249,000 for the unanchored group. These results mirror an extensive literature showing that nonjudge experimental subjects (Chapman & Bornstein, 1996), as well as jurors in actual cases (Diamond, Rose, Murphy, & Meixner, 2011), exhibit strong anchoring effects when a damage number is suggested by lawyers in opening or closing arguments, although with real cases there also seems to be a ceiling above which a suggested number by the plaintiff's lawyer, and a floor below which a number suggested by the defense, become perceived as outrageous and their effects counterproductive (Diamond, Rose, Murphy, & Meixner, 2011).[3]

When one side suggests a high number and the other a low one, these suggestions seem to create a kind of double-anchor situation that powerfully drives judgments to the middle (see Chien, Huang, & Shaw, 2005). Part of this anchoring to the mean is explained by the compromise effect, discussed in Section 8.2.3.

These results show that suggestions about damages can have enormous anchoring effects on judges in those relatively rare cases where the trial is to the judge and not to a jury. But more concerning is criminal sentencing, which in federal courts and almost all state courts is performed by the judge and not the jury. Are lawyers' suggestions about the length of a criminal sentence likely to anchor the ultimate sentence? Almost certainly.

There have only been a handful of sentencing anchoring experiments, but they all show significant anchoring effects. In one, German judges read a criminal scenario and were asked to impose a hypothetical sentence. After reading the scenario but before imposing the hypothetical sentence, each judge was asked to roll a die with just two numbers on it – 3 and 9. They were then asked whether they would impose a sentence greater or less (in months) than the number on the die, and finally asked for the specific sentence they would impose. The anchoring effect was significant: those who rolled a 3 imposed an average sentence of 5 months; those who rolled a 9 imposed an average sentence of 8 months (Englich, Mussweiler, & Strack, 2006).

What if anything should the system do to address these kinds of effects? Unfortunately, it looks like not much can be done. Experiments have shown that the anchoring effect is very difficult to overcome, even when subjects are forewarned about it or are incentivized against it (Chapman & Johnson, 2002; Englich, Mussweiler, & Strack, 2006), and even when, as we have seen, the anchor itself is

---

[3] Interestingly, damage caps seem to have the perverse effect of increasing both the amount and variability of awards in low-severity cases, but not changing the amount or variability of damages in medium- and high-severity cases (Saks et al., 1997; Robbennolt, 1999).

patently incorrect (Guthrie, Rachlinski, & Wistrich, 2001) or known to be random (Englich, Mussweiler, & Strack, 2006).

We probably could not prohibit lawyers from suggesting sentence lengths in their arguments, without violating the defendant's rights to counsel and to be heard at sentencing. Maybe these effects could be blunted if the judge goes into every sentencing hearing, as I try to do, with an explicit presumptive number in mind (Bennett, 2014), although the risk there is that our presumptive number will itself become the anchor and we will be impervious to cogent arguments to depart significantly from it. Other scholars have suggested tactics that lawyers might use to dampen the impact of anchoring effects on judges, including the suggestion that defense lawyers must *always* suggest a low sentence to counter a high sentence suggested by the prosecution (Stein & Drouin, 2018).

In federal courts, where the sentencing guidelines generate a point sentence, and in state courts with similar sentencing architectures, the guideline number itself becomes an anchor. This is seen most clearly in a natural experiment occasioned by the US Supreme Court's decision in 2005 holding that the federal sentencing guidelines, which until that decision were thought to be virtually mandatory,[4] are in fact just advisory.[5] A comparison of federal sentences imposed before 2007, when the guidelines were thought to be virtually mandatory, and those imposed after 2007, when the guidelines were just advisory, shows comparable degrees of departure, both in frequency and amount (Bennett, 2014). The guidelines are anchoring federal sentencing. Of course, proponents of guidelines would argue that the anchoring effect is exactly what was intended – we don't want judges departing too wildly from the guideline because the whole purpose of guidelines is to help produce similar sentences for similarly situated defendants. But there have also been critics of the anchoring effects of the federal guidelines, who argue that the effects are so strong that federal judges have become unwilling to depart from them even in cases where they should depart, and even after the guidelines have been made merely advisory (Bennett, 2014).

The sentencing anchoring problem may be just as acute in nonguideline jurisdictions, where legislatures generally divide crimes into classifications and set a presumptive sentencing range for each class. For example, in my state, Colorado, the widest presumptive range is 8 to 24 years for what are called Class 2 felonies, which include crimes like racketeering and second-degree murder. Legislatures of course have the right, and indeed the obligation, to impose these

---

[4] Trial courts could depart from the guideline number, but not without making specific findings justifying the departure.
[5] *United States* v. *Booker*, 543 US 220 (2005). Since its decision in Booker the Court has had a few occasions to describe the extent to which the guideline number is something more than merely advisory but something less than virtually mandatory. See *Gall* v. *United States*, 522 US 38 (2007). This problem has its origins in the fact that in the federal system criminal sentences may be appealed, so the question becomes to what extent may appellate courts alter the trial court's sentence, whether it imposed a guideline sentence or departed from the guideline.

ranges, but the ranges themselves are probably having significant double-anchoring effects on sentencing judges in the sense that we are being driven to the mean. Again, perhaps that is not an unintended effect, and in fashioning these ranges maybe legislatures are expressly intending to drive judges to the mean.

A similar anchoring risk comes not from guidelines or legislative ranges but from plea-bargaining lawyers. There is a common practice in state courts (which I do not permit in my court) called "sentence bargaining" or "sentence concessions," in which the defendant and the prosecution agree not only to the crime to which the defendant will plead, but also to the sentence he will receive. The agreed-to sentence could be either an explicit point sentence (e.g., twelve years) or a range within which the judge retains discretion to impose a point sentence (e.g., ten to twenty-four years). In the case of a negotiated range, all the same anchoring-to-the-mean considerations apply, though those ranges will often be narrower than the legislative ones.

8.2.2 Hindsight Bias

People tend to overestimate the probability of an event once the event has occurred. If you've ever been hit by lightning, your guess about the probability of being hit will be much greater (and much more inaccurate) than that of those who have never been hit.[6] This bias is not limited to personal experience. In a famous experiment, Baruch Fischhoff (1975) gave subjects summaries of different events from history, gave several different possible outcomes for each event, and asked subjects to assign probabilities to those different outcomes. For example, one of the stories was about General Hastings' campaign against the Gurkas in India in 1814. The narrative provided certain information about the situation, and then asked subjects to assign probabilities to four outcomes: British win; Gurkas win; military stalemate with a peace treaty; or military stalemate without a peace treaty. The control group got just the unfinished stories. The other groups were told the actual historical outcomes of one of the four stories. On average, the subjects who were told the actual historical outcome substantially inflated (roughly doubled) their probability estimates for that outcome.

By the way, if your reaction to that last experiment was that subjects were not being irrational but in fact were rationally updating their knowledge based on new facts, you are committing your own version of the hindsight bias. By asking the subjects to assess the likelihood of various outcomes, the subjects were in effect being asked to go back in time and tell researchers what their predictions would have been *without* the new information. The new information should therefore have been

---

[6] This is probably an example of two heuristics – the hindsight bias and our struggles with Bayesian reasoning, the latter of which is discussed in Section 8.2.4.

irrelevant to that assessment, but it seems so salient that we are simply unable, or too lazy, to ignore it.

In addition to this inevitability phenomenon ("It had to happen"), researchers have identified two other related drivers of hindsight bias: (1) faulty memory about our probability assessments before the event ("I said it would happen"); and (2) exaggerated beliefs in our ability to predict ("I knew it would happen") (Roese & Vohs, 2012). These latter two effects can be impressive. In a 1991 study, researchers asked college students to predict whether the Senate would confirm Clarence Thomas to the Supreme Court, and 58 percent predicted it would. After the confirmation, and one month after their predictions, *the same students* were asked simply to report on their earlier predictions, and the number saying they had predicted confirmation jumped up to 78 percent (Dietrich & Olson, 1993).

The "it had to happen" leg of hindsight bias is particularly significant to the law. Court cases *always* examine facts after they have occurred, and judges and jurors are frequently asked to go back in time and examine prospectively the likelihood of the events unfolding as they did. For example, jurors are asked in virtually every negligence case whether defendants should have foreseen that their behavior would injure the plaintiffs; indeed, that is part of the definition of being negligent. But because jurors already know that the defendant's actions did in fact harm the plaintiff (assuming they believe the plaintiff's testimony and any other evidence about the injuries and their cause), hindsight bias makes it very difficult for jurors to imagine that harm, once caused, may nevertheless have been unforeseen. The same is true in criminal cases where defendants are charged not with intentionally causing harm but with recklessly or negligently disregarding the risk that their actions would harm the victim.

Judges are also regularly called upon to make similar *ex post* judgments about *ex ante* probabilities. For example, we are often asked to assess whether police officers had probable cause to conduct a search or make an arrest – that is, whether the officer's antecedent judgments about the likelihood of a crime having been committed were reasonable. But we always make that assessment after the fact, under the shadow of the large, looming, and impossible-to-ignore fact that in every such case the officer's suspicion proved to be justified. We don't see the cases, at least in the criminal courts, where the officers' guesses turned out to be wrong – for example, where there were no drugs in the backpack.

Much work, both experimental and observational, has been done confirming that the hindsight bias plays a pervasive role in these ubiquitous kinds of after-the-fact legal judgments about pre-event probabilities. For torts, see Kamin & Rachlinski (1995); for search and seizure, see Rachlinski, Guthrie, & Wistrich (2011). Judges don't seem to be any better than nonjudges at resisting the siren of hindsight. Guthrie, Rachlinski, and Wistrich (2001) asked their subject federal magistrate judges to make predictions about the outcome of an appeal of a hypothetical case. Those who were told an outcome were substantially more likely (72 percent more likely!) to match their prediction to the outcome than had they not known about the outcome.

The hindsight bias seems almost as hard to cure as the anchoring effect. Neither educating subjects about it (Wood, 1978) nor incentivizing them not to engage in it (Hell et al., 1988) has any effect. There are a few studies that suggest hindsight bias could be reduced by changing the structure of the decision-making problem, including forcing subjects to consider other outcomes (see Arkes, Faust, Guilmette, & Hart, 1988). But none of these techniques eliminates hindsight bias entirely (Kamin & Rachlinski, 1995).

Debiasing hindsight in specific legal contexts has garnered some attention, although all of it has focused on jurors and all of it has been shown to be ineffective. In their 1995 paper, Kamin and Rachlinski showed that express directions by a hypothetical judge, cautioning subjects against the hindsight bias and urging them to consider alternative *ex ante* outcomes, had no significant effect. Others have suggested that in negligence cases liability could be bifurcated from damages – one jury determines whether the defendant was negligent, and only if it says yes does a different jury then determine the amount of damages – though even they admit bifurcation will not eliminate hindsight bias entirely (Wexler & Schopp, 1989). In fact, it is not clear to me how bifurcation will help at all: the first jury will know that harm occurred, and that outcome will affect their judgment about negligence; the second jury will implicitly know that the defendant has already either admitted negligence or been determined to be negligent, and that outcome will affect the damage trial. Of course, even if there were some debiasing benefits from bifurcation, those benefits might well be outweighed by the costs of conducting two jury trials in a significant number of tried civil cases.

8.2.3 *Compromise and Contrast Effects*

When people decide between two options, adding a third might make them switch to the third, but it should not, as a matter of pure logic, change their preference as between the original two. If you are trying to decide between ordering spaghetti or a hamburger for lunch, and you settle on the hamburger, discovering that fish is also an option might cause you to switch from hamburger to fish, but it should not cause you to switch your preference of hamburger over spaghetti. But in fact adding a third option regularly changes people's preferences between the first two. Psychologists traditionally distinguish between two forms of this phenomenon, depending on whether the third option falls generally between the other two in quality and stimulates a compromise effect, or whether it is inferior or superior to the original options and creates a contrast effect (Teichman & Zamir, 2014).

For instance, when consumers were asked to state a preference between a low- and medium-priced camera, they split roughly equally between them. But when the option of a high-priced camera was added, 72 percent of the consumers preferred the medium-priced camera (Simonson & Tversky, 1992). The addition of a high-priced or high-quality choice drives a significant number of people to switch from their original low-cost/low-quality choice to what is now the medium choice. The compromise/contrast effect might be viewed as a kind of double anchoring to the mean: if people had unlimited discretion to pick items at any price range between the two offered choices, those two offered choices would tend to drive them to the mean. When they only have those two offered choices, and then are suddenly presented with a third option, they jump at the choice nearer the mean.

Adding an inferior option has a similar effect – it pulls people who had originally chosen one option to what is now a middle option. Thus, when facing the choice between a pen and six dollars, only 36 percent of subjects picked the pen. But when an inferior pen was added to the mix, that number jumped to 46 percent (Simonson & Tversky, 1992).

These context dependencies are almost certainly having significant impacts in the legal system. Jurors in criminal cases are told at the beginning of every criminal case that their task will be to decide whether the prosecution has proven the defendant's guilt, thus creating two options. But in a significant number of criminal cases the jury is later told by the trial judge during jury instructions that they must also decide whether the prosecution has proven a lesser offense. Although judges are not deciding these issues, we do have to deal with them in the context of sentencing. It is quite possible that in sentencing a defendant for a lesser offense judges are unconsciously being pulled by the compromise/contrast effect to a longer sentence because the defendant was also accused of a more serious offense. Of course, the pull may also go in the other direction, if the sentencing judge focuses on the fact that the defendant could have been acquitted entirely.

In the end, these context effects may depend on the judge's own assessment of the strength of the case, in a sort of echo effect that itself acknowledges the jury's context effects. If the judge thinks the case was strong, he or she might conclude that the jury's conviction only of the lesser offense was a compromise verdict, and that the defendant is lucky he is not facing a sentence on the original more serious charge, and thus sentence him more harshly. If the sentencing judges think a case was weak, they might view the jury's compromise verdict as a gift to the prosecution, and sentence the defendant less harshly.

Civil cases are even more ripe for compromise verdicts as between liability, compensatory damages, and punitive damages. Jurors and judges being asked to award compensatory damages in cases where the evidence of negligence is weak, might decide the defendant is not liable. But when those same judges or jurors are faced with a third option – punitive damages – that option might pull them toward a compromise of finding the defendant negligent but not awarding punitive damages.

There is surprisingly little experimental literature on compromise verdicts. Kelman, Rottenstreich, and Tversky (1996) gave nonjudge subjects a homicide scenario and asked them to pick between different levels of murder. When picking just between manslaughter and murder, 47 percent chose manslaughter and 53 percent murder. But when a more serious option was added – "murder with aggravating circumstances" – only 19 percent chose manslaughter, 39 percent murder, and 42 percent murder with aggravating circumstances.

These same investigators saw the same compromise/contrast effects with sentencing. Nonjudge subjects asked to sentence a hypothetical defendant to either jail or probation became much more willing to give probation if a less-serious third option (fine) were added (Kelman, Rottenstreich, & Tversky, 1996). Rachlinski and Jourden (2003) obtained similar experimental results when subjects were asked not about the kind of punishment but rather about the length of the sentence.

There is a fairly large observational literature about compromise verdicts in real cases, both criminal and civil, generally showing that jurors seem regularly to compromise when given the opportunity (Pietrantoni, 2017; Abramowicz, 2001). Indeed, criticisms of compromise verdicts is one line of argument used in favor of non-unanimous verdicts (Bouton, Llorente-Saguer, & Malherbe, 2018).

There is a much smaller empirical literature examining whether the compromise/contrast effect applies to actual judges, but by all indications it does. In one of the two studies on this issue, researchers found that Pennsylvania state criminal judges regularly exposed to lower-gravity crimes sentenced more harshly than those regularly exposed to higher-gravity crimes (Leibovitch, 2016). Perhaps this argues in favor of a robust rotational system where judges do not sit hearing the same kinds of cases for too long, and specifically against those jurisdictions (Philadelphia, for example) that have judges who try nothing but murder cases.

In the other study, researchers examining asylum decisions by US immigration judges found a "gambler's fallacy" effect – a short string of decisions in one direction appeared to influence these judges to buck that string in the next decision (Chen, Moskowitz, & Shue, 2016). I'm not sure what can be done about the gambler's effect, except maybe to educate judges in some fundamentals of probability, and in particular to convince them that fairly long strings of heads (or tails) can and do happen in random coin tosses.

8.2.4 Representativeness

Most of us are pretty poor probabilistic reasoners. For instance, we tend to undervalue probabilistic information compared to identical information presented in the form of natural frequencies. Telling subjects that 1 percent of a million people have some trait tends to cause people to think the trait is rarer than if we say 10,000 out of 1 million people have it (Tversky & Kahneman, 1974; Thompson & Schumann, 1987). There is an extensive literature showing that at least in some contexts many of our difficulties with probabilistic reasoning vanish when the problem is recast from probability into the language of natural frequency (see Hertwig & Gigerenzer, 1999).

But even when considering natural frequencies, we often have difficulties understanding probabilistic information. For example, in a game where you win if you are able to pick a red jellybean out of a jar while blindfolded, would you rather use a jar with 10 beans, one of which is red, or a jar with 100 beans seven of which are red? Although the probability in the first case (10 percent) is higher than in the second case (7 percent), subjects regularly prefer the second case (Slovic, Finucane, Peters, & MacGregor, 2002). We seem riveted by the number of red beans, and blinded by the number of nonred ones.[7]

These are just two examples of the many kinds of difficulties we seem to have with probabilistic reasoning. The particular probabilistic failing I consider here is called "the representativeness heuristic," a term coined by Dan Kahneman and Amos Tversky (1972) to connote our tendency to conflate the representativeness of information with its probability. It is also sometimes called the "base-rate problem," "base-rate neglect," or "the problem of Bayesian reasoning."

When we use information to make categorical judgments (such as whether a graduate student who is smart, uncreative, and a poor writer is more likely to be in computer science than in the humanities), we tend to ground those judgments on our assessment of whether the information is representative of the category (computer scientists tend to be smart, uncreative, and poor writers compared with humanities students). We tend to disregard the representativeness of the categories themselves (there were, at the time of this study, three times more graduate students in the humanities than in computer science) (Kahneman & Tversky, 1973). This can lead us to spectacularly erroneous conclusions in many different circumstances. Moreover, in some of those circumstances the representativeness heuristic seems virtually impossible to debias, even when we are told about it and even when we are experts in an area and should know better.

The most famous example is probably the Monty Hall paradox. At the end of the old TV game show *Let's Make a Deal*, the host, Monty Hall, would ask a contestant to pick one of three doors. One door has a fabulous prize, two have duds. We can all agree the contestant has a 1/3 chance of getting the prize and a 2/3 chance of getting one of the duds. Monty knows where the real prize is (that's the key), and after the contestant selects a door, Monty opens up one of the two unselected doors to reveal one of the duds. At this point Monty asks the contestants whether they would like to switch their pick to the other unselected door. Should they?

Almost everyone presented with this question, including many mathematicians, responds that it doesn't matter. Most say that the chance of winning was 1/3 before Monty opened the other door and remains 1/3 afterwards; a few say it is now 1/2 since there are two remaining doors and we know one has the real prize in it. But under either of these views switching won't matter (Tierney, 1991). But in fact switching

---

[7] This effect could also be driven by the differences between the way we tend to perceive future risks and future benefits (or what the behavioral economists would call loss aversion and risk seeking), a framing problem outside the scope of this chapter.

makes a huge difference – contestants who switch double their chance from 1/3 to 2/3. Why? This is easy to prove using Bayes' theorem for discrete probabilities, but, precisely because of the power of this heuristic, it is much harder to explain in words. It has to do with the fact that Monty knows where the real prize is, and he chose not to open the door the contestant did not pick.[8]

The representativeness heuristic can wreak havoc across many disciplines because it can impair our assessments of cause and effect. The law is regularly faced with these questions of causation; for example, whether a given product caused a certain disease in a given plaintiff. Epidemiological evidence that Bendectin doubles the risk of birth defects can sound awfully powerful in court, but it tells only part of the story. If the rate of birth defects in the general population (the base rate) is only 0.001 to start with, then the real causation argument is that this given plaintiff's risk went from 0.001 to 0.002. Understood in this way, the question of whether the Bendectin caused the birth defect in this particular plaintiff arguably becomes much more difficult.[9] The hindsight bias kicks in here too, because of course our particular plaintiff *did* have birth defects.

There have been several studies exploring the representativeness effect in jurors, but only a few looking at it in judges. All show robust, but perhaps not incurable, base-rate biases.

Bar-Hillel (1980) conducted what is probably the most famous representativeness experiment in a forensic context. She provided nonjudge subjects with a narrative about a hit-and-run caused by a taxicab. She also told them that the town has only two taxicab companies – the Blue Company and the Green Company – and that an eyewitness was 80 percent sure the taxi was green. But she also gave the subjects key base-rate information – that 85 percent of the city's taxis are blue and 15 percent green. She then asked subjects to estimate the likelihood that the taxi culprit was green. Subjects tended to focus on the witness's reliability and ignore the base-rate information, and thus their average answer was 80 percent (the correct answer, taking into account the base rate that only 15 percent of the taxis are green, is 41 percent[10]).

Are judges just as bad at ignoring base rates? It doesn't appear so. Guthrie, Rachlinski, and Wistrich (2001) gave their federal magistrate judges a task similar

---

[8] This becomes clearer if we reframe the problem using a deck of cards, with the task being trying to find the ace of spades. The contestant picks one card, then Monty reveals the fifty other cards that are not the ace of spades, leaving one card hidden. The contestant clearly should switch from his original pick, which had a 1/52 chance of being the ace of spades, to Monty's hidden card, which has a 51/52 chance of being the ace of spades.

[9] This ultimate question not only implicates the problem of base rates but also raises the broader question of using group data to make judgments about individuals. Scholars have dubbed this the G2i problem (group to individual), and there is a growing literature exploring it (see Faigman, Monahan, & Slobogin, 2014).

[10] The calculation is: the chance taxi is green = (the chance the witness was right and it was green) ÷ (chance witness was wrong and it was blue + chance that witness was right and it was green) = (80% × 15%)/((20% × 85%) + (80% × 15%)) = 12/(12 + 17) = 12/29 = 0.41.

to the blue and green taxi task, this time using a hypothetical involving the risk that a warehouse worker would be injured by a negligently secured barrel. They gave the judges the two main probabilities necessary to calculate this risk – that a negligently secured barrel will break loose and that such a barrel will then injure a worker. But they also gave the judges a base rate by informing them how often barrels were in fact negligently secured. At least in this context, the judges were significantly better than Bar-Hillel's nonjudges at integrating the base rate into their calculations (40 percent of the judges got the correct answer).

These results suggest that, at least when the base-rate problem is not as hidden as in the Monty Hall paradox, judges and maybe even jurors might be able to be educated about base rates. Lawyers should be calling experts who can explain the often-profound impact of base rates, but of course that will require lawyers themselves to appreciate that impact.

There are some obvious criminal applications of the representativeness bias, although I am unaware that those applications have been the subject of any experiments or observational studies. The base-rate problem can rear its ugly head whenever considering predictive issues like whether a charged defendant released on bond will return to court, or whether a convicted defendant should be released early on parole. Judges and parole officials could be terribly wrong if they rely only on professional assessments of a given defendant's comparative risk if they don't also factor in the base rates of that risk. Would you release a prisoner on parole if you were convinced he was 10 percent less likely to reoffend than the average prisoner, if the base recidivism rate were 80 percent?

8.3 SOME OBSERVATIONS FROM THE BENCH

8.3.1 *The Trial Penalty*

There are lots of data showing that, controlling for the seriousness of the conviction and the defendant's criminal history, judges sentence criminal defendants more harshly after a trial than after a guilty plea (see McCoy, 2005). Many commentators have argued that this so-called "trial penalty" proves that judges are penalizing criminal defendants for exercising their right to trial, and there may be some truth to that. Many trial judges, especially in state court systems, are facing significant docket pressures that make going to trial feel like a luxury we simply cannot regularly afford.

On the other hand, it seems reasonable to give a defendant some credit for taking responsibility by pleading guilty and saving the state the time and expense, and the victim the angst, of a trial. Indeed, the federal sentencing guidelines formally recognize that a defendant who "clearly demonstrates acceptance of responsibility" is entitled to a downward departure (United States Sentencing Guidelines, 2019). Whether the *amount* of the observed trial penalty is fully justified by this rationale is open for debate.

But I think there is another, much more significant, psychological phenomenon driving the trial penalty. When defendants plead guilty, the facts of the crime are presented in a rather emotionally flat fashion. Most trial judges simply allow defendants to respond to the charged language, which itself is often composed of unemotional legalese, by saying the single word "guilty." Judges who allow defendants to waive the factual basis – that is, who do not require defendants to admit to the facts behind the charges to which they are pleading guilty – hear only that single word "guilty" in terms of a defendant admitting what happened.

Sure, most sentencing judges are armed with substantial information about the crime itself – at least the charged crime – in the form of affidavits in support of the arrest warrant, probable cause statements, testimony from any preliminary hearing, and descriptions of the offense in presentence investigation reports. But this stream of information suffers from two significant defects: first, it is of limited help when a defendant pleads guilty to an offense less serious than the one charged (and this is almost always the case with plea bargains); and, most importantly for our purposes here, the information is often not very emotionally salient.

It is one thing to hear a defendant say the word "guilty" when responding to a charge, say, of rape, or even reading about the rape in documents, and quite another to spend days hearing about the rape and the suffering it inflicted on the victim. I suspect the bulk of the trial penalty comes simply from that difference. Is that a good thing? Yes, but only up to a point.

No matter our approach to sentencing, all judges would probably agree that at least in theory, and in a perfect world, the more details we know about the crime the more just the sentence is likely to be. Indeed, for this very reason I do not allow criminal defendants in my courtroom to waive the factual basis. Before I accept guilty pleas the defendants have to look me in the eye and tell me exactly what they did (in fact, I regularly require them to admit the facts of the original charge, especially when they are pleading guilty to a fictitious lesser charge). But I have also come to believe that there is a point at which too much emotionally laden information can distort sentences.

There is a significant amount of research, including most recently some neuroimaging studies, suggesting that when we engage in third-party punishment (that is, punish people whose wrongs did not injure us directly but injured third parties), we engage in a two-step process: first we blame, then we impose punishment (Buckholtz et al., 2015; Krueger & Hoffman, 2016). In experimental contexts, subjects express "blame" by being asked, for example, to state how "blameworthy" a given criminal scenario is and to order various scenarios by "blameworthiness" (Robinson & Kurzban, 2007). Punishment, by contrast, is elicited by asking subjects how much punishment they would inflict on a hypothetical criminal, for example, by indicating the amount of the punishment on a scale of 0 to 9 (0 being no punishment, 9 being the most punishment the subject can imagine) (Buckholtz et al., 2008; Shen et al., 2011).

Blame seems to be driven by our assessment of only two factors: the amount of the harm and the wrongdoer's intent (accidental, intentional, or something in between) (Shen et al., 2011; Krueger & Hoffman, 2016). Blame appears to be a more deeply rooted, emotionally laden response than punishment. That response is extraordinarily stable across demographics and between individuals in the same demographics; we all blame pretty much the same, because we all assess harm and the wrongdoer s intent pretty much the same (Robinson & Kurzban, 2007).

Punishment, by contrast, is a more complex evaluation that depends on a host of facts beyond the mere amount of harm to the victim and the wrongdoer's intent, including virtually everything about the crime and the history of the criminal and the victim. Because there are so many facts that make up that contextual picture, and also because the assessment and weight we give to these extra-blame facts seem to vary greatly across demographics and indeed between individuals within similar demographics, we see wide variations in punishment decisions (Albanese, 1984).

Some researchers have hypothesized that the roots of this two-step process lie in older forms of second-party punishment – where we (and indeed many other animals) retaliate against those who harm us (Hoffman, 2014; Aharoni & Hoffman, in press). In this model, our quicker, more emotional blame reaction in third-party contexts has its roots in second-party punishment; we blame as if we were the victim. Our third-party punishment decisions, by contrast, are ordinarily cooler, and require us to consider all the circumstances surrounding the crime, the criminal, and the victim, because third-party punishment, though essential to our evolution, was extraordinarily costly while only indirectly beneficial.

I mention all of this because I have often felt during a sentencing hearing, especially if it was a particularly heinous crime causing significant harm, that I might be engaging in second-party punishment rather than third-party punishment. I might be taking the victim's point of view to such an extent that I might be retaliating instead of punishing. My sentence might be being driven only by the amount of the harm and the defendant's intention. And I suspect all trial judges are more likely to do that if we've sat for days listening to the dirty details of the crime than in the rarified confines of a guilty plea.

I don't have any particularly brilliant suggestions to avoid slipping into second-party punishment, just the obvious ones: judges who feel overcome with anger during sentencing hearings should probably take a break; before putting that sentence number in their mind as suggested above to avoid getting anchored by the lawyers' arguments, judges should try to read something about the defendants' lives that might make them seem more like people and less like monsters; and judges should remember there are reasons we don't let victims impose sentences.

8.3.2 Forgiveness and Apology

During several noncapital first-degree murder sentencings (where in my jurisdiction the sentence is mandatory life without parole), I've observed the following rather extraordinary phenomena. Defendants remain unmoved by the surviving victims' statements, sometimes even smirking, while everyone else in the courtroom (including me) is close to tears. But if a family member of the victim says that he or she forgives the defendant (and this happens more than you might think), the defendant breaks down into tears. This is the first professional clue I had about the power of forgiveness.

Whenever we sentence criminals, we feel the pull of forgiveness in lots of different forms. Mental health and other professionals may tell us how it was that the defendant came to the point of committing this crime; the defendant and others may tell us he learned his lesson and poses no future risk to society, and the victims themselves may ask for forgiveness. Even the hardest retributivist cannot resist the pull of these calls for forgiveness, and indeed study after study in all kinds of contexts show that while we are punishing animals by nature, we are also primed to forgive (see McCullough & van Oyen Witvliet, 2001). That's probably because third-party punishment was so evolutionarily costly compared to its indirect benefits: if we could have some assurance that wrongdoers' risks of committing future harms were low enough, we'd all be better off keeping them in the fold (Hoffman & Goldsmith, 2004; Hoffman, 2014). I suspect that's why, when I am in the middle of a criminal sentencing and ready to impose a certain sentence, the amount of that sentence almost always drops a little if the victim expresses forgiveness, even when I know the defendant deserves the higher sentence.

Apology is the wrongdoer's signal that his future risks are low enough to justify forgiveness, and we also seem primed to accept apologies. There is a large literature showing that apologies can have effects in many different contexts, though those effects tend to be smaller than the effects of forgiveness, especially when the wrong was intentional and the harm high (see Bennett & Earwaker, 2010). In the right contexts, though, and especially if the wrongdoer seems sincere, apologies can have big impacts.

For example, retrospective studies of medical malpractice patients showed that a substantial number of them claim they would not have sued had the doctor explained and apologized for the poor outcome (Vincent, Young, & Phillips, 1994). Mock jurors are likewise much more forgiving of doctor error when the doctor apologizes (Bornstein, Rung, & Miller, 2002). Indeed, these studies have driven some changes in the laws of some states that now exclude such apologies from being introduced in medical malpractice trials.

Apology seems just as powerful in criminal law. I regularly find myself at a sentencing hearing feeling my presumptive sentence edge downward when a defendant apologizes, sometimes even when I suspect the defendant's apology is insincere. Though I also admit that a palpably insincere apology occasionally has the opposite effect, I also must admit that I have low confidence in my ability to distinguish sincere apologies from insincere ones.

Although there has been a considerable amount of work done on the impact of forgiveness and apology in legal contexts, the neural correlates of forgiveness have remained unexamined. It is therefore unclear whether forgiveness works at the blame or punishment levels, both, or neither. If it turns out that forgiveness and apology do their work at the blame level and not at the punishment level, then this would explain why these phenomena are so powerful and seem to affect our punishment judgments even in the face of our conscious sense that they should not.

8.3.3 Beliefs in Free Will

I often have two different thoughts when sentencing defendants: "What species are they?" and "There but for the grace of God go I." Some crimes are so horrendous that we cannot imagine that any human would commit them. Others seem like norm violations any of us could commit if pushed. Truth be told, I have occasionally had these two seemingly incompatible thoughts simultaneously, about a single defendant.

Part of what underlies these two thoughts may be two ways to think about norm violations. We can focus on the crime itself, and therefore on the punishment required before the defendant can come back into the social fold. Or we can focus on the criminals, and on the forces in their environments that drove them to commit the crimes. I generally think of myself as focusing on the crime and not the criminal, but have to admit that during the course of a sentencing hearing my thoughts so often vacillate between the two that I doubt I am "focusing" on either.

For many years I didn't give too much thought to what might be going on with these two vacillating perspectives; I just fought my battle with them in virtually every difficult sentencing. Then I stumbled on an entire cottage industry in psychology that measures people's belief in free will and then tries to correlate that belief to attitudes and behaviors. I now suspect that these two perspectives that so often fight for my attention when I sentence criminals (and, I assume, for the attention of my colleagues when they sentence) are probably related to conflicting feelings about free will. If you have a strong belief in free will, the notion that someone's environment would have driven them to commit crimes will probably garner much less of your attention than the crime itself, an act committed by a presumptively responsible moral agent.

Researchers have developed a question-based instrument to measure beliefs in free will. The first one was called the FAD, which stands for "Free Will and Determinism" (Viney, Waldman, & Barchilon, 1982). There have been several versions of FAD, each one getting increasingly more sophisticated. The original FAD measured these beliefs in two dimensions, one along a free-will axis and one along a determinism axis, and plotted a subject's score in the plane defined by those two axes. It was an elegant measure of what philosophers call compatibilism – the idea that free will and responsibility are not incompatible with a deterministic universe. The FAD measures how far from full compatibilism subjects land (in the two-dimensional version, how far from the x = y axis). The FAD has since undergone several iterations, including increasing the number of its dimensions (see the FAD-Plus used in Paulus & Carey, 2011); other researchers have proposed an entirely new instrument to measure beliefs in free will, which they call the Free Will Inventory (Nadelhoffer et al., 2014).

Regardless of the instrument used, the idea is that people's measured beliefs in free will sometimes correlate to their attitudes and even behaviors, in many different contexts. For example, strong beliefs in free will are highly predictive of things like job performance (Stillman, Baumeister, & Vohs, 2010) and success in school (Feldman, Chandrashekar, & Wong, 2016). And of course while these studies do not distinguish cause from effect (after all, success might cause beliefs in free will, not vice versa), experimentally weakened beliefs in free will (by the use of deterministic prompts) cause subjects to behave more antisocially and aggressively (Vohs & Schooler, 2008), suggesting there may be aspects of these beliefs in free will that are in fact driving our attitudes and behaviors.

There have been a handful of studies looking at the effects that beliefs in free will have on punishment, but they are decidedly mixed. Some showed that strong beliefs in free will increased punishment amounts (a result that seems intuitive) (Viney, Waldman, & Barchilon, 1982), some showed no effect (Viney, Parker-Martin, & Dotten, 1988), and one old study showed that people with strong beliefs in free will actually punished *less* (Nettler, 1959).

This mystery may have been solved recently when researchers considered how the seriousness of the hypothetical offense may be mediating the interaction between beliefs in free will and punishment amounts (Krueger, Hoffman, Walter, & Grafman, 2014). They found that for low-harm crimes only, subjects with strong belief in free will punished more harshly than subjects with weak belief in free will. But when harms are high, belief in free will have no effect. As the authors put it, when harms are high, everyone acts like they believe in free will. It's only when the harms, and stakes, are low that judges' belief in free will seems to matter. Judges who are libertarians (that's the word philosophers use to describe people with strong beliefs in free will) really hammer that shoplifter, while the determinists treat him with kid gloves, but the rapists and murderers tend to get the same treatment from both judicial extremes and from everyone in between.

These insights probably won't change the way judges sentence (though they certainly could change the way appointing authorities select judges). But it is interesting to contemplate that judicial struggles between the primacy of the crime and the primacy of the criminal may have deeper philosophical roots in our ambivalence about free will.

8.3.4 The Light Bulb Problem

A federal judge before whom I often practiced had a quirk that everyone who spent any time in his courtroom quickly discovered. Although he always paid great attention to the testimony of witnesses, often asking his own questions, there came a point in almost every hearing or bench trial when this judge would put his head down and never look up. We all knew what he was doing – he had decided the matter and was writing his ruling.

Once I became a judge I also felt the pull to start writing my order – or at least an outline of an oral ruling – as soon as it seemed to me that I understood the case. And there is almost always a moment in any trial or hearing when the light bulb goes off and I say to myself, "Aha, *this* is what's going on." Once the light bulb goes off there are tremendous pressures to start preparing the decision.

But there is a considerable storytelling literature, including in forensic contexts, showing not only that people impose narratives on evidence but also that once they construct those narratives they tend not to pay attention to, and therefore forget, evidence that does not fit with the narrative (see McGregor & Holmes, 1999). Whoever was representing the defense before this particular judge tried to get their best witness on first, because we all knew that once that head went down he was simply not listening to other witnesses.

Deciding cases too soon is a huge problem for jurors, magnified by the artificially linear nature of the adversary process. Jurors not only have information dribbled out to them one question at a time, they hear only from one side first. This is a real challenge, which I try to deal with by actually talking to jurors about it explicitly, in both civil and criminal jury trials.

I don't know if there is anything else we can do to help jurors avoid the light bulb problem, but I've thought about how I can avoid it as a judge. One strategy I've considered is to issue a written order in every case, which by its very nature takes a longer time than ruling orally from the bench, thus giving more time for the flash of the bulb to dim. But the cost of doing that includes delay, not to mention the problem that judicial memories will fade along with, and maybe even faster than, the flash of the bulb.

The moment I think I understand what's going on in a case, I intentionally try to put that picture out of my mind. That hardly ever works. I've also experimented with presenting the case to my law clerks as soon as the bulb lights up, taking the (presumptively) losing side's perspective. That seems to help a little. I have also promised myself never to succumb to the temptation of drafting orders or even outlines of orders while the case is still going on, though the flash of the light bulb is still there, and presumably infecting my decision, when I later get around to the oral or written ruling.

I don't have any bright ideas about the light bulb problem, but I do think it is something that judges and academics need to spend more time pondering.

8.4 CONCLUSION

Trial judges, just like electricians and plumbers, are prone to numerous kinds of faulty reasoning. Unlike the tasks of plumbing and wiring, however, the trial process itself seems especially vulnerable to cognitive bias. The entire judicial system is about making present judgments about past actions, and is therefore a giant hindsight bias waiting to happen. Complex judgments that are collapsed into quantitative conclusions – how much money to award a plaintiff or how many years of prison to impose on a criminal – are ripe for anchoring and context biases. A system that regularly requires judges and jurors to engage in probabilistic reasoning is asking for lots of trouble.

My own experiences as a trial judge suggest that academics may want to spend more time exploring, and trial judges more time reflecting on, the way the emotional gain of the trial itself may be affecting our sentencing decisions; on the impact our own endogenous feelings about free will, as well as the exogenous impacts of forgiveness and apology, might be having on our judicial decisions, and on the way our storytelling natures may be shaping those decisions.

Having said all of that, I don't mean to join the ranks of those handwringing over the frailties of human decision making generally, or more particular claims that our justice system is more often wrong than right. On the contrary, I am more amazed than ever at the ability of our adjudicative systems to find truth and do justice (Hoffman, 2007), knowing that they are populated with decision makers prone to such a large array of serious and largely incurable cognitive failures.

In this regard I agree with those psychologists and behavioral economists who have called for a dose of perspective when it comes to heuristics and biases (see Posner, 1998; Gigerenzer & Todd, 1999). Heuristics and biases are interesting and important phenomena to uncover and understand, but they are still a tiny part of our decision-making toolbox. We have spent the last 500,000 years getting pretty good at making all kinds of judgments, especially social judgments about one another, which is really what the adjudicative part of the legal system does. We should not lose sight of that central rational core in our hunt for irrationality at the peripheries.

REFERENCES

Abramowicz, M. (2001). A Compromise Approach to Compromise Verdicts. *California Law Review* 89(2), 231–314.

Aharoni, E., & Hoffman, M. (in press). Evolutionary Psychology, Jurisprudence, and Sentencing. In T. Shackelford (ed.), *Handbook of Evolutionary Psychology*. Thousand Oaks, CA: SAGE Publications.

Albanese, J. S. (1984). Concern about Variation in Criminal Sentences: a Cyclical History of Reform. *Journal of Criminal Law and Criminology* 75, 260–271.

Arkes, H. R., Faust, D., Guilmette, T. J., & Hart, K. (1988). Eliminating the Hindsight Bias. *Journal of Applied Psychology* 72(2), 305–307.

Bar-Hillel, M. (1980). The Base-Rate Fallacy in Probability Judgments. *Acta Psychologica* 44, 211–233.
Bennett, M. (2014). Confronting Cognitive "Anchoring Effect" and "Blind Spot Bias" in Federal Sentencing: a Modest Solution for Reforming a Fundamental Flaw. *Journal of Criminal Law and Criminology* 104(3), 489–534.
Bennett, M., & Earwaker, D. (2010). Victims' Responses to Apologies: the Effects of Offender Responsibility and Offense Severity. *Journal of Social Psychology* 134(4), 457–464.
Blumstein, A. (1982). On the Racial Disproportionality of United States' Prison Population. *Journal of Criminal Law and Criminology* 73, 1259–1281.
Bornstein, B. H., Rung, L. M., & Miller, M. K. (2002). The Effects of Defendant Remorse on Mock Juror Decisions in a Malpractice Case. *Behavioral Sciences and the Law* 20(4), 393–409.
Bouton, L., Llorente-Saguer, A., & Malherbe, F. (2018). Get Rid of Unanimity Rule: the Superiority of Majority Rules with Veto Power. *Journal of Political Economy* 126(1), 107–149.
Boyd, C. L. (2016). Representation on the Courts? The Effects of Trial Judges' Sex and Race. *Political Research Quarterly* 69(4), 788–799.
Brillon, Y. (1983). Fear of Crime an Punitive Attitudes Among the Elderly. *Criminologie* 36 (1), 7–29.
Buckholtz, J. W., Asplund, C. L., Dux, P. E., et al. (2008). The Neural Correlates of Third-Party Punishment. *Neuron* 60, 930–940.
Buckholtz, J. W., Martin, J. W., Treadway, M. T., et al. (2015). From Blame to Punishment: Disrupting Prefrontal Cortex Activity Reveals Norm Enforcement Mechanisms. *Neuron* 87 (6), 1369–1380.
Chapman, G. B., & Bornstein, B. H. (1996). The More You Ask the More You Get: Anchoring in Personal Injury Verdicts. *Applied Cognitive Psychology* 10(6), 519–540.
Chapman, G. B., & Johnson, E. J. (2002). Incorporating the Irrelevant: Anchors in Judgments of Belief and Value. In T. Gilovich, D. Griffin, & D. Kahneman (eds.), *Heuristics and Biases: the Psychology of Intuitive Judgment*. Cambridge: Cambridge University Press, pp. 120–138.
Chen, D. L., Moskowitz, T. J. & Shue, K. (2016). Decision Making Under the Gambler's Fallacy: Evidence from Asylum Judges, Loan Officers, and Baseball Umpires. *The Quarterly Journal of Economics* 131(3), 1181–1242.
Chew, P., & Kelley, R. (2009). The Myth of the Color-Blind Judge: an Empirical Analysis of Racial Harassment Cases. *Washington University Law Review* 86, pp. 1117–1166.
Chien, Y. L., Huang, C. J., & Shaw, D. (2005). A General Model of Starting Point Bias in Double-Bounded Dichotomous Contingent Valuation Surveys. *Journal of Environmental Economics and Management* 50(2), 362–377.
Desantts, A., & Kayson, W. A. (1997). Defendants' Characteristics of Attractiveness, Race, and Sex and Sentencing Decisions. *Psychological Reports* 81(2), 679–683.
Diamond, S. S., Rose, M. R., Murphy, B., & Meixner, J. (2011). Damage Anchors on Real Juries. *Journal of Empirical Legal Studies* 8(1s), 148–178.
Dietrich, D., & Olson, M. (1993). A Demonstration of Hindsight Bias Using the Thomas Confirmation Vote. *Psychological Reports* 72(2), 377–378.
Englich, B., Mussweiler, T., & Strack, F. (2006). Playing Dice With Criminal Sentences: the Influence of Irrelevant Anchors on Experts' Judicial Decision Making. *Society for Personality and Social Psychology* 32, 188–200.
Epstein, L., Landes, W. M., & Posner, R. A. (2013). *The Behavior of Federal Judges: A Theoretical and Empirical Study*. Cambridge, MA & London: Harvard University Press.

Faigman, D. L., Monahan, J., & Slobogin, C. (2014). Group to Individual (G2i) Inference in Scientific Expert Testimony. *University of Chicago Law Review* 81(2), 417–480.
Feldman, G., Chandrashekar, S. P., & Wong, K. F. E. (2016). The Freedom to Excel: Belief in Free Will Predicts Better Academic Performance. *Personality and Individual Differences* 90, 377–383.
Fischhoff, B. (1975). Hindsight Is Not Equal to Foresight: the Effect of Outcome Knowledge on Judgment Under Uncertainty. *Journal of Experimental Psychology: Human Perception and Performance* 1(3), 288–299.
Gault, B. A., & Sabini, J. (2000). The Roles of Empathy, Anger, and Gender in Predicting Attitudes Toward Punitive, Reparative, and Preventative Public Policies. *Cognition and Emotion* 14(4), 495–520.
Gigerenzer, G., & Todd, P. M. (1999). *Simple Heuristics that Make Us Smart*. New York: Oxford University Press.
Gruhl, J., Spohn, C., & Welch, S. (1981). Women as Policymakers: the Case of Trial Judges. *American Journal of Political Science* 25(2), 308–322.
Guthrie, C., Rachlinski, J. J., & Wistrich, A. J. (2001). Inside the Judicial Mind. *Cornell Law Review*, 86, 777–830.
Hell, W., Gigerenzer, G., Gauggel, S., Mall, M., & Müller, M. (1988). Hindsight Bias: an Interaction of Automatic and Motivational Factors? *Memory and Cognition* 16(6), 553–538.
Hertwig, R., & Gigerenzer, G. (1999). The "Conjunction Fallacy" Revisited: How Intelligent Inferences Look Like Reasoning Errors. *Journal of Behavioral Decision Making* 12(4), 275–305.
Hoffman, M. B. (2007). The Myth of Factual Innocence. *Chicago-Kent Law Review* 82(2), 663–690.
Hoffman, M. B. (2014). *The Punisher's Brain: the Evolution of Judge and Jury*. New York: Cambridge University Press.
Hoffman, M. B., & Goldsmith, T. H. (2004). The Biological Roots of Punishment. *Ohio State Journal of Criminal Law* 1(2), 627–641.
Hoffman, M., Shen, F., Iyengar, V., & Krueger, F. (2020). The Intersectionality of Age and Gender on the Bench: Are Younger Female Judges Harsher with Serious Crimes? *The Columbia Journal of Law and Gender* 40(1), 128–165.
Johnson, B. (2006). The Multilevel Context of Criminal Sentencing: Integrating Judge- and County-Level Influences. *Criminology* 44(2), 259–298.
Kahneman, D., & Tversky, A. (1972). Subjective Probability: a Judgment of Representativeness. *Cognitive Psychology* 3(3), 430–454.
Kahneman, D., & Tversky, A. (1973). On the Psychology of Prediction. *Psychological Review* 80(4), 237–251.
Kahneman, D., & Tversky, A. (1974). Judgments Under Uncertainty: Heuristics and Biases. *Science* 184(4157), 1124–1131.
Kamin, K., & Rachlinski, J. J. (1995). Ex Post ≠ Ex Ante. *Law and Human Behavior* 19(1), 89–104.
Kelman, M., Rottenstreich, Y., & Tversky, A. (1996). Context-Dependence in Legal Decision Making. *Journal of Legal Studies* 25, 287–318.
Keren, G., & Wu, G. (2015). A Bird's-Eye View of the History of Judgment and Decision-Making. In G. Keren & G. Wu (eds.) *The Wiley Blackwell Handbook of Judgment and Decision Making*. Chichester: John Wiley & Sons, pp. 1–40.
Kerr, N. L., & Tindale, R. S. (2004). Group Performance and Decision Making. *Annual Review of Psychology* 55, pp. 623–655.

Klein, D. E., & Mitchell, G. (2010). *The Psychology of Judicial Decision-Making*. New York: Oxford University Press.

Kritzer, H. M., & Uhlman, T. M. (1977). Sisterhood in the Courtroom: Sex and Judge and Defendant in Criminal Case Disposition. *Social Science Journal* 14, 366–379.

Krueger, F., & Hoffman, M. (2016). The Emerging Neuroscience of Third-Party Punishment. *Trends in Neurosciences* 39(6), 499–501.

Krueger, F., Hoffman, M., Walter, H., & Grafman, J. (2014). An fMRI Investigation of the Effects of Belief in Free Will on Third-Party Punishment. *Social, Cognitive, and Affective Neuroscience* 9(8), 1143–1149.

Landsman, S., & Rakos, R. F. (1994). A Preliminary Inquiry Into the Effect of Potentially Biasing Information on Judges and Jurors in Civil Litigation. *Behavioral Sciences* 12(2), 113–126.

Leibovitch, A. (2016). Relative Judgments. *Journal of Legal Studies* 45(2), 281–330.

MacCoun, R. J. (1984). Experimental Research on Jury Decision-Making. *Science* 244, 1046–1050.

McCoy, C. (2005). The Trial Penalty and Plea Bargaining Reform. *Criminal Law Quarterly* 50, 67–107.

McCullough, M., & van Oyen Witvliet, C. (2001). The Psychology of Forgiveness. In C. R. Snyder & Shane J. Lopez (eds.), *The Handbook of Positive Psychology*. New York: Oxford University Press, pp. 446–458.

McGregor, I., & Holmes, J. G. (1999). How Storytelling Shapes Memory and Impressions of Relationship Events Over Time. *Journal of Personal and Social Psychology* 76(3), 403–419.

Mustard, D. B. (2001). Racial, Ethnic, and Gender Disparities in Sentencing: Evidence from the US Federal Courts. *Journal of Law and Economics* 44, 285–314.

Nadelhoffer, T., Shepard, J., Nahmias, E., Sripada, C., & Thompson-Ross, L. (2014). The Free Will Inventory: Measuring Beliefs About Agency and Responsibility. *Consciousness and Cognition* 25, 27–41.

Nettler, G. (1959). Cruelty, Dignity, and Determinism. *American Sociological Review* 24, 375–384.

Paulus, D. L., & Carey, J. M. (2011). The FAD-PLUS: Measuring Lay Beliefs Regarding Free Will and Related Constructs. *Journal of Personality Assessment* 93(1), 96–104.

Pennington, N., & Hastie, R. (1991). A Cognitive Theory of Juror Decision Making: the Story Model. *Cardozo Law Review* 13, 519–557.

Peter-Hagene, L. C., & Salerno, J. M. (2019). Jury Decision Making. In N. Brewer & A. Bradfield-Douglass (eds.), *Psychological Science and the Law*. New York: Guilford, pp. 338–366.

Pietrantoni, G. (2017). Jury Deliberation. *The Review: a Journal of Undergraduate Student Research* 18. https://fisherpub.sjfc.edu/ur/vol18/iss1/7

Pizzi, W. T., Blair, I. V., & Judd, C. M. (2004). Discrimination in Sentencing on the Basis of Afrocentric Features. *Michigan Journal of Race and Law* 10, 327–354.

Posner, R. A. (1993). What Do Judges and Justices Maximize? (the Same Thing Everybody Else Does). *Supreme Court Economic Review* 3, 1–41.

Posner, R. A. (1998). Rational Choice, Behavioral Economics, and the Law. *Stanford Law Review* 50, 1551–1575.

Rachlinski, J. J., Guthrie, C., & Wistrich, A. J. (2007). Heuristics and Biases in Bankruptcy Judges. *Journal of Institutional and Theoretical Economics* 163, 167–186.

Rachlinski, J. J., Guthrie, C., & Wistrich, A. J. (2011). Probable Cause, Probability, and Hindsight. *Journal of Empirical Legal Studies* 8, 72–98.

Rachlinski, J. J., Johnson, S., Wistrich, A., & Guthrie, C. (2009). Does Unconscious Racial Bias Affect Trial Judges? *Notre Dame Law Review* 84, 1195–1246.
Rachlinski, J. J., & Jourdan, F. (2003). The Cognitive Components of Punishment. *Cornell Law Review* 88, 457–485.
Robbennolt, J. K. (1999). Anchoring in the Courtroom: the Effects of Caps on Punitive Damages. *Law and Human Behavior* 23, 353–373.
Robbennolt, J. K. (2014). Litigation and Settlement. In E. Zamir & D. Teichman (eds.), *The Oxford Handbook of Behavioral Economics and the Law*. Oxford: Oxford University Press, pp. 623–642.
Robinson, P. H., & Kurzban, R. (2007). Concordance and Conflict in Intuitions of Justice. *Minnesota Law Review* 91, 1821–1907.
Roese, N. J., & Vohs, K. D. (2012). Hindsight Bias. *Perspectives on Psychological Science* 7(5), 411–426.
Saks, M., Hollinger, L., Wissler, Evans D., & Hart, A. (1997). Reducing Variability in Civil Jury Awards. *Law and Human Behavior* 21(3), 243–256.
Schauer, F., & Spellman, B. (2017). Analogy, Expertise, and Experience. *University of Chicago Law Review* 84, 249–268.
Shen, F. X., Hoffman, M. B., Jones, O. D., Greene, J. D., & Marois, R. (2011). Sorting Guilty Minds. *New York University Law Review* 86, 1306–1360.
Simon, D. (2004). A Third View of the Black Box: Cognitive Coherence in Legal Decision Making. *University of Chicago Law Review* 71, 511–586.
Simonson, I., & Tversky, A. (1992). Choice in Context: Tradeoff Contrast and Extremeness Aversion. *Journal of Marketing Research* 29(3), 281–295.
Slovic, P., Finucane, M., Peters, E., & MacGregor, D. (2002). Rational Actors or Rational Fools: Implications of the Affect Heuristic for Behavioral Economics. *Journal of Behavioral and Experimental Economics* 31(4), 329–342.
Smith, E. D., & Hed, A. (1979). Effects of Offenders' Age and Attractiveness on Sentencing by Mock Jurors. *Psychological Reports* 44(3), 691–694.
Spohn, C. (1990). The Sentencing Decisions of Black and White Judges: Expected and Unexpected Similarities. *Law and Society Review* 24(5), 1197–1216.
Steffensmeier, D., & Britt, C. L. (2001). Judges' Race and Judicial Decision Making: Do Black Judges Sentence Differently? *Social Science Quarterly* 82(4), 749–764.
Stein, C. T., & Drouin, M. (2018). Cognitive Bias in the Courtroom: Combating the Anchoring Effect Through Tactical Debiasing. *University of San Francisco Law Review* 52, 393–428.
Stillman, T. F., Baumeister, R. F., & Vohs, K. D. (2010). Personal Philosophy and Personal Achievement: Belief in Free Will Predicts Better Job Performance. *Social Psychological & Personality Science* 1, 43–50.
Teichman, D., & Zamir, E. (2014). Judicial Decision-Making: a Behavioral Perspective. In E. Zamir & D. Teichman (eds.), *The Oxford Handbook of Behavioral Economics and the Law*. Oxford: Oxford University Press, pp. 664–702.
Thompson, W. C., & Schumann, E. L. (1987). Interpretation of Statistical Evidence in Criminal Trials. *Law and Human Behavior* 11(3), 167–187.
Tierney, J. (1991). Behind Monty Hall's Doors: Puzzle, Debate, and Answer? *The New York Times*, July 21, 1991.
Uhlman, T. M. (1978). Black Elite Decision Making: the Case of Trial Judges. *American Journal of Political Science* 22(4), 884–895.
United Nations (1974). *Growth in United Nations Membership 1945–Present*. www.un.org/en/sections/member-states/growth-united-nations-membership-1945-present/index.html
United States Sentencing Guidelines (2019), §3E1.1 (Acceptance of Responsibility).

Vars, F. E. (2014). Evidence Law. In E. Zamir & D. Teichman (eds.), *The Oxford Handbook of Behavioral Economics and the Law*. Oxford: Oxford University Press, pp. 703–718.

Vidmar, N., & Hans, V. P. (2007). *American Juries: the Verdict*. Amherst, NY: Prometheus, pp. 158–168, 175–176, 236–240, 260–262.

Vincent, C. A., Young, M., & Phillips, A. (1994). Why Do People Sue Doctors? A Study of Patients and Relatives Taking Legal Action. *Lancet* 343, 1609–1613.

Viney, W., Waldman, D. A., & Barchilon, J. (1982). Attitudes Toward Punishment in Relation to Beliefs in Free Will and Determinism. *Human Relations* 35, 939–949.

Viney, W., Parker-Martin, P., & Dotten, S. (1988). Belief in Free Will and Determinism and Lack of Relation to Punishment Rationale and Magnitude. *Journal of General Psychology* 115, pp. 15–23.

Vohs, K. D., & Schooler, J. W. (2008). The Value of Believing in Free Will: Encouraging a Belief in Determinism Increases Cheating. *Psychological Science* 19, 49–54.

Wexler, D. B., & Schopp, R. F. (1989). How and When to Correct for Juror Hindsight Bias in Mental Health Litigation: Some Preliminary Observations. *Behavioral Sciences & the Law* 7, 485–504.

Wistrich, A. J., Guthrie, C., & Rachlinski, J. J. (2005). Can Judges Ignore Inadmissible Evidence? The Difficulty of Deliberately Disregarding. *University of Pennsylvania Law Review* 153, 1251–1345.

Wood, G. (1978). The Knew-It-All-Along Effect. *Journal of Experimental Psychology: Human Perception and Performance* 4, 345–353.

Wrightsman, L. S. (2010). *The Psychology of the Supreme Court*. Oxford: Oxford University Press.

Zamir, E. (2017). Law and Behavioral Economics. In M. Sellers & S. Kirste (eds.), *Encyclopedia of the Philosophy of Law and Social Philosophy*. New York: Springer, pp. 1–11.

9

Institutional Design and the Psychology of the Trial Judge

Adi Leibovitch[*]

9.1 INTRODUCTION

The psychological research of judicial behaviour and decision making has evolved markedly over the last few decades. While we are still far from developing a full empirical account of what is happening 'inside the judicial mind' (Guthrie, Rachlinski & Wistrich, 2001), substantial progress has been made as studies have gradually expanded in scope and methodology. In particular, an increasing number of studies strive to better capture the unique conditions that are relevant to judicial behaviour. For instance, researchers have moved to conduct laboratory experiments with expert subject pools, including judges and legal professionals (for an overview see, e.g., Rachlinski & Wistrich, 2017), more realistic settings (Spamann & Klöhn, 2016), and more sophisticated methods, looking not only at the final outcome reached but also at elements of the decision-making process, such as the order in which judges approach various documents and how much time they devote to reading them (Liu, Klöhn & Spamann, 2019). Researchers have also deployed the random assignment of cases to judges in order to isolate causal psychological mechanisms in real-world judicial decisions – documenting how differences in case attributes can lead to context-dependent decisions in criminal (Leibovitch, 2016) and asylum cases (Chen, Moskowitz & Shue, 2016), and how judicial decisions may change in response to emotional shocks (Eren & Mocan, 2018).

Alongside growing methodological sophistication, scholars have also started to make headway on the manifold ways in which the psychology of judicial decision making may be intertwined with wider institutional design aspects (Leibovitch, 2016, 2017; Schauer & Spellman, 2017). This new paradigm highlights the ways in which cognitive biases and heuristics can lead not only to transient effects on decisions but can also affect judgements in more systematic and prolonged ways. At its roots is the understanding that the expertise and repeat experience that characterize judges can lead to the creation of schemas and baselines which judges employ when making

---

[*] Assistant Professor, the Hebrew University of Jerusalem, Faculty of Law. I thank Jaap Hage, Doron Teichman, and Eyal Zamir for their helpful comments.

decisions in individual cases. The institutional capacity of the courts and the applicable rules of procedure and evidence can foster different decision-making environments, thereby changing the schemas created and nudging judicial decisions in a particular direction.

In Chapter 8, Judge Hoffman emphasizes how judicial decision making, like human decision making in general, is susceptible to various cognitive biases. This chapter complements that discussion by extending from the individual trial judge to the characteristics of the court in which she operates, and reviews the connection between institutional design and the psychology of judging through three prominent examples. The first section discusses how because of context-dependent decision making, the assignment of jurisdiction and types of cases across courts can change the substantive outcomes reached by the courts. The second section draws attention to the tension between the human tendency to retributivism and the rehabilitative goals set by problem-solving or treatment-oriented courts, and how this tendency may be responsible for some of the unintended consequences of specialized courts. The third section reviews the accumulating findings regarding the difficulty of disregarding irrelevant or inadmissible evidence, and discusses how these could inform the applicable rules of evidence governing trials. As this is a developing field of research, throughout the discussion I also highlight some of the limitations of existing evidence and offer new avenues for future research on these topics.

9.2 CONTEXT DEPENDENCE AND CASE ASSIGNMENTS

People's judgements and decisions are affected by the context in which they are made. One of the most studied manifestations of context dependence in legal decision making is the contrast effect – the enhanced or diminished perception of a case feature as a result of successive or simultaneous exposure to another case of lesser or greater value in the same dimension (Zamir & Teichman, 2018, pp. 76–9, 532–5).

The impact of the contrast effect on the decisions of jurors and judges has been studied in laboratory settings both within and across cases. In Chapter 8, Judge Hoffman discusses how, within cases, attorneys can prompt decision makers to prefer a certain option by manipulating the menu of options presented for them to choose from. For example, researchers have found that parties to civil disputes can induce settlements by presenting the opposing party with two settlement options, one of which is clearly inferior to the other (Kelman, Rottenstreich & Tversky, 1996; Guthrie, 2003), and that in hypothetical criminal cases, adding a more extreme option to the menu of charges brought by the prosecution, or adding an inferior sentencing option to the sentences recommended by the prosecutor, can affect the choice of conviction charge and sentence amongst the other constant options, due to the compromise effect (Kelman et al., 1996).

But the contrast effect plays an even greater role in judicial decision making. The contrast effect can change judgements not only through its effect on the weighing of possible case outcomes directly, but also by influencing the evaluation of evidence presented within a case. In a lab experiment conducted with state trial judges, Rachlinski, Wistrich, and Guthrie (2013) found that judges assessed the credibility of expert witnesses more favourably when lawyers presented an additional expert with similar, albeit notably weaker, credentials. The additional expert's inferior credentials made the first expert appear much more qualified by comparison.

In addition – and this will be my focus in this section – the contrast effect can also result from the comparison across cases. Lab experiments with lay subjects have repeatedly shown that a legal claim or case is on average evaluated as more serious when assessed after a case that is viewed as relatively mild, and as less serious when encountered after a more egregious one. The comparison appears to alter both how a decision maker morally evaluates the severity of wrongful conduct (Parducci, 1968; Pepitone & DiNubile, 1976), and the decision regarding the appropriate level of punitive damages (Kahneman, Schkade & Sunstein, 1998; Sunstein, Kahneman & Schkade, 1998; Sunstein, Kahneman, Schkade & Ritov, 2002) or criminal sentences (Pepitone & DiNubile, 1976; Rachlinski & Jourden, 2003; Rodríguez & Blanco, 2016).

Traditionally, this line of research has focused on the problems presented by the contrast effect for decision making by juries. Studies were conducted with lay subjects, attributed the erratic nature of the decision outcomes to jurors' lack of exposure to other cases against which they can form their evaluations of the severity of behaviours and penalties, and speculated that judges could outperform juries because, unlike jurors, they encounter multiple and varying sets of cases (Kahneman et al., 1998; Sunstein et al., 1998; Sunstein et al., 2002; Rachlinski & Jourden, 2003). More recent studies, however, have demonstrated that judges are similarly susceptible to the contrast effect.

Because of their broader perspective, judges' decisions can be coloured by comparison of a particular case to the contours of the other cases in their caseloads. This can, under certain conditions, lead to greater coherence in judicial decision making. For example, because judges ordinarily view cases involving varying types of harms while jurors view one case in isolation, judicial decisions of damage awards can portray more granular differentiation across types of harm than those of juries, and thereby present a better fit between the gravity of behaviours and legal outcomes (Eisenberg, Rachlinski & Wells, 2002). But the relative comparison across the cases in judges' caseloads can also lead to adverse consequences. This is demonstrated by two studies from 2016 that take advantage of the random assignment of cases to judges to evaluate the impact of disparate exposure to various case characteristics on judicial decisions in real cases.

First, there could still be some arbitrariness in judicial decisions as a result of immediate sequential comparisons within the caseload. Chen, Moskowitz, and

Shue (2016) studied decisions by US judges in refugee asylum cases and found that the order in which cases were heard on a given day significantly affected the likelihood of granting an asylum request. Judges were more likely to deny asylum after granting asylum to the previous applicant, and the effect was stronger after a streak of consecutive grant or denial decisions than after a single such decision. The authors estimate that, if not for this bias, about 2 per cent of judges' decisions would have been reversed.

Second, judicial exposure to other cases in their caseloads may be a source of more systematic bias vis-à-vis these cases. Leibovitch (2016) focused on this kind of more systematic effect by looking at the accumulated exposure of trial judges in Pennsylvania's Courts of Common Pleas to criminal cases of differing degrees of severity. While under random assignment of cases judges are expected to see a similar composition of cases in the long run, there could be considerable variation in the severity of cases allocated to each judge in the short run, including during the first period following their appointment to the bench. Using a matched sample of judges that were randomly located at different ends of the caseload distribution, Leibovitch found that with regard to similar cases, judges who had initially been exposed to milder offences ordered incarceration sentences that were approximately 25 per cent longer, and were three to four times more likely to find aggravating circumstances or to depart above sentencing guidelines recommendations, than judges who had been previously exposed to more serious offences.

The finding that judges compare a particular case to the other cases before them has important policy implications. To be clear, the relative evaluation of cases has justified doctrinal and practical roots.[1] These include the principles of proportionality and marginal deterrence, the development of rules through case law and precedents, the desire for equitable treatment and the need to guard against arbitrariness and to assess the reasonableness of particular decisions. All these considerations call for assessing whether the circumstances of particular cases justify a harsher, more lenient or equal penal response.

The problem is that existing research on context dependence indicates that judicial evaluations of blameworthiness or deservedness are done not in relation to the entire possible spectrum of human behaviour, but to the limited spectrum that judges view on a regular basis. Judges in courts with different jurisdictions, in specialized courts, and even in divisions within a court, may have quite different cases on their dockets. If judicial decisions are based on the relative within-docket evaluation, then when caseloads differ case outcomes will differ as well. Indeed, qualitative and quantitative evidence from courts of limited jurisdiction seem to reflect such a pattern. Paradoxically, courts that specialize in relatively less serious

---

[1] For a comprehensive discussion of the role of relative comparisons and analogical reasoning in legal decision making and their interaction with judicial expertise, see Schauer and Spellman (2017).

crimes, such as misdemeanour courts or juvenile courts, are likely to treat the mild offences on their docket more harshly than generalist courts (Leibovitch, 2017).

More work remains to be done in order to improve our understanding of how context dependence influences judicial decision making in general, and how it interacts with the design of courts of limited jurisdiction and court divisions in particular. To date, most studies of context dependence in legal decision making have focused on decisions by laypersons (and mainly on decisions regarding sentences and damage awards, but not so much on other types of legal decisions). But taking the recent evidence regarding decisions by judges (Chen et al., 2016; Leibovitch, 2016) together with the documented trends and unintended consequences in courts of limited jurisdiction (Leibovitch, 2017), suggests it could be fruitful to turn more attention to the relationship between the composition of judicial dockets and the substantive outcomes judges reach.

9.3 THE HUMAN INCLINATION TO RETRIBUTIVISM AND SPECIALIZED COURTS

Moral philosophy is dominated by the distinction between consequentialism – assessing the desirability of actions solely by their outcomes – and deontology – subjecting the justification of actions to moral constraints, duties and rights (Zamir & Medina, 2010, pp. 41–2). The choice of moral theory underpinning legal rules can lead to very different determinations regarding the desirability and magnitude of sanctions. In criminal law, this is the question of which penal goals should be at the forefront of sentencing: retribution, or the consequentialist goals of deterrence, rehabilitation or incapacitation. When determining appropriate sentences or punitive damages, implementing a deterrence paradigm, for example, would lead one to focus on the likelihood of imposing liability and sanctions, while under a retributive framework weight would be granted to the wrongfulness of the behaviour and the culpability of the wrongdoer.

Many psychological studies show that most people reason, and behave, as moral deontologists (for a review see Zamir & Teichman, 2018, pp. 97–101). In legal settings as well, when asked to decide on punitive damages or criminal sentences, people's decisions are affected by the perceived outrageousness of the behaviour (Baron & Ritov, 1993; Kahneman et al., 1998; Sunstein et al., 1998, 2002; Darley, Carlsmith & Robinson, 2000; Carlsmith, Darley & Robinson, 2002), but not by the probability of detection (Sunstein, Schkade & Kahneman, 2000; Carlsmith et al., 2002; Baron & Ritov, 2009; Ouss & Peysakhovich, 2015), the publicity of the event (Baron & Ritov, 1993, Carlsmith et al., 2002) or the anticipated impact on future behaviour (Baron & Ritov, 1993; Darley et al., 2000). This is true for laypersons and professional judges alike (Baron & Ritov, 1993, 2009).

Furthermore, not only is deontology the penal theory of choice, people's judgements reflect deontological considerations even when they are asked to decide on compensatory damages. Unlike punitive damages, awards of compensation should presumably only reflect the actual harm suffered, not the culpability of the offender. Yet, Hans and Ermann (1989) find that people award higher compensatory damages for medical expenses and for pain and suffering when they find the wrongdoer's behaviour more reckless and more morally wrong, even though their judgements of the magnitude of harm suffered are the same. Similarly, Baron and Ritov (1993) show that even when people are asked to separately decide on both penalties and compensation, people award greater compensation for the same harm when the harm is caused by commission rather than by omission or misfortune.

The inclination towards retribution seems to be so pervasive that it shapes decisions of punishments even when people are specifically instructed to adhere to a consequentialist theory. In a series of experiments by Carlsmith, Darley and Robinson, subjects were asked to sentence various cases from three perspectives. First, participants were presented with the different offences and circumstances and simply asked to decide on the appropriate punishment. Then, participants were asked to re-evaluate their judgements from a just-deserts perspective as well as from a deterrence (in Carlsmith et al., 2002) or an incapacitation (in Darley et al., 2000) perspective. The findings consistently demonstrate that the primary determinate of criminal sentences is just deserts: Participants' intuitive initial judgements of the appropriate punishment were similar to their judgements under the retributive orientation, but differed from their judgements under the consequentialist orientation. Furthermore, when explicitly instructed to punish based on incapacitation considerations, participants' decisions on punishments were affected both by the likelihood of recidivism and by the seriousness of the offence (Darley et al., 2000). When asked to consider only deterrence in their determination, not only did participants' judgements continue to reflect the seriousness of the offence, they remained unaffected by the probability of detection (influencing individual deterrence) and the degree of publicity of the crime (influencing general deterrence). Instead, the instruction to apply deterrence led to increased harshness and participants ratcheted up the punishment (Carlsmith et al., 2002).

One clear implication of these findings for the criminal justice system regards the question of which penal justifications should be at the forefront in light of these psychological insights. Some legal scholars argue that criminal law should follow people's moral judgements and reflect the preference for a retributive penal theory. Proponents of this approach posit that aligning the law with people's moral intuitions is not only more fair, but from a consequentialist perspective can also improve respect for the law and law-abiding behaviour (e.g., Robinson & Darley, 1997; Tyler & Darley, 2000; Darley & Alter, 2013). Critics of this approach, on the other hand, have highlighted the fact that a consequentialist justification of retribution may be unrealistic, because with regard to many areas of law people lack intuitions or knowledge regarding the content of law; and even tautological, since people's opinions themselves can be shaped by law and social interventions (e.g., Zamir &

Teichman, 2018, pp. 438–40). This discourse focuses on law compliance by people as the subjects of the law. A related question, however, that did not receive similar attention is, how should criminal law adjust to the fact that such moral views could also be reflected in the judgements ordered by the judges asked to apply the law?

One area of law in which the tension between deontological and consequentialist justifications for punishment is particularly prominent is the establishment of problem-solving courts. The proliferation of specialization in the courts has brought with it an increased movement to establish therapeutic and treatment-oriented courts, focused on court-supervised rehabilitation-oriented treatment programmes in lieu of criminal sanctions. Scholars have long warned, however, that '[t]he most serious vice of sanctioning systems that were associated with the rehabilitative ideal was their tendency to distort the definition of just proportion in punishment' (Zimring, 1993, p. 813). Indeed, qualitative and quantitative evidence from specialized courts suggests that treatment-oriented courts, such as juvenile courts or drug courts, often take an unintended punitive turn, with emphasis on accountability and just-deserts sentencing, contrary to the mission of these courts (Leibovitch, 2017). If this tendency is rooted in the human difficulty in ignoring retributive sentiments, this may offer further support to the calls to reconsider the operation of specialized courts, and to develop instead a non-carceral social approach that is distinctly separated from the classical criminal justice system (e.g., Bowers, 2008; McLeod, 2012). Severing the tie between decisions on supervised treatment and the adjudicative criminal process could elevate the reliance on penal rationales in such decisions, and the central role of retribution amongst them. Alternatively, this tendency may highlight the desirability of a very specific type of specialized court – placing greater emphasis on the selection and training of judges that are genuinely committed to the rehabilitative ideal, and on the implementation of alternative procedures and monitoring of decisions to ensure that these ideals are in fact implemented. It is also possible that this issue involves not only the psychology of the judge, but also the psychology of the prosecutor. In many courts, cases need to be diverted to specialized courts. It is generally the prosecutor who decides which cases are suitable for diversion, often as part of a conditional plea bargain – and such decisions might be affected by retributive inclinations as well.

The exploration of the tension between the human tendency towards retribution and the implementation of consequentialist goals in the court system thus seems a valuable avenue for future studies. The experimental findings have focused on the comparison between deontology and consequentialist theories of deterrence and incapacitation, but not on the choice between just deserts and rehabilitation, and with few notable exceptions (Baron & Ritov, 1993, 2009) were mostly conducted with laypersons. Further research may examine how the inclination towards retributivism actually affects judges and prosecutors, as well as other relevant professionals, such as parole boards or probation officers, focusing specifically on intuitions regarding rehabilitation. Future research may also explore possible ways to counter retributive intuitions, such as testing the efficacy of framing the intervention as of a social or criminal nature.

9.4 THE IMPACT OF IRRELEVANT OR INADMISSIBLE INFORMATION AND THE RULES OF EVIDENCE

Other notable features of institutional design in US courts are the possibility to have a case decided by a judge or a jury, and the rules of evidence governing each type of trial. As Judge Hoffman's main focus is on the question of whether trial judges are different from laypersons, it seems fitting to conclude with this area of law where, despite findings of similar biases in the decisions made by judges and juries, the differences in the rules applicable to them are striking. The law of evidence is generally perceived as targeting lay jurors, who may suffer from various cognitive failings, and therefore should be shielded from certain evidence, such as evidence that may inflame prejudice, that is unreliable or that has low probative value. When judges sit without juries, they often disregard many rules of evidence or interpret them loosely, preferring to allow more evidence to be considered and to move from questions of admissibility to questions of weight (Schauer, 2006).

Underlying this practice is the belief that judges are less prone to the cognitive biases and heuristics we worry about being prevalent amongst jurors – because of their legal training and expertise, their better understanding and appreciation of the rationales underlying exclusionary rules and their greater experience in hearing testimonies, evaluating evidence and finding facts (e.g., Wistrich, Guthrie & Rachlinski, 2005; Schauer, 2006). It turns out, however, that there is not much existing data to support the belief that judges can outperform jurors. Experience, for example, as the discussion of context effects above demonstrates, can not only mitigate bias but also create it, and judges as repeat players may thus simply exhibit different biases from jurors.[2] It is also unclear whether experience without feedback regarding the correctness of decisions can improve decision making. Judges hear multiple cases, but usually get no reliable feedback as to whether their (or a jury's) determinations of fact are accurate, and thus have no mechanism by which to evaluate the reliability of the fact-finding rules that they use. By virtue of hearing many cases judges may be more consistent than jurors, but absent feedback there is no reason to believe those consistent findings are closer to the truth than those of juries (Robinson & Spellman, 2005; Spellman, 2007).[3]

[2] For instance, it was shown that experienced jurors are more likely to convict, and tend to recommend more severe sentences, than first-time jurors (for an overview of the literature, see Himelein, Nietzel & Dillehay, 1991). Based on these findings, Robinson and Spellman (2005) suggest that judicial experience over many trials, or faith in the legal system, may also lead judges to have greater initial belief in the guilt of the defendant than jurors.
[3] In addition, scholars have also noted the different institutional settings in which jurors and judges operate. For example, with regard to jurors' decision making it was shown that group deliberation can improve the ability to disregard inadmissible evidence (e.g., Kerwin & Shaffer, 1994; London &

Empirical findings indeed show that experts in general, and judges in particular, are subject to many cognitive biases and heuristics.[4] Furthermore, studies suggest that experts tend to overestimate their own cognitive abilities, the power of their professional skills and the reliability of their judgements (Zamir & Teichman, 2018, pp. 114–17). Specifically with regard to the inability to disregard irrelevant information, alongside the extensive research on jurors' difficulty with disregarding inadmissible evidence (e.g., Steblay et al., 2006; Spellman & Schauer, 2014), a few studies conducted with real judges demonstrate that judges suffer from a similar problem.

A seminal study by Landsman and Rakos (1994) directly compared the decisions reached by judges and laypersons in an experiment involving a hypothetical product liability case. Participants in the experiment were assigned to one of three conditions: no exposure to biasing material, exposure to a judicial decision to exclude the material and exposure to a judicial decision to admit the material. Strikingly, the instruction to disregard the inadmissible information resulted in verdicts similar to those under the exposure condition rather than under the no-exposure condition. This was true for judges and jurors alike. Despite their legal training, judges were similar to laypersons in that they did not disregard the legally impermissible facts in rendering a verdict, and consequently were more likely to find the defendant liable.

The same phenomenon has been repeatedly demonstrated for many types of inadmissible evidence. A series of experiments by Wistrich, Guthrie, and Rachlinski (2005) with state judges as subjects included hypothetical cases with different types of inadmissible information: prior demands disclosed during a settlement conference; conversations protected by attorney–client privilege; sexual history of an alleged rape victim; prior criminal convictions of a plaintiff; and information that the government promised not to rely on at sentencing hearing. Regarding all of those, judges were generally unable (or, perhaps, unwilling) to avoid being influenced by the inadmissible evidence of which they were aware. The information influenced judges' decisions on verdicts, sentences and damage awards, even when judges were reminded, or even ruled themselves, that the information was inadmissible.

Interestingly, one type of case in which inadmissible information did not have a significant effect on judges' verdicts was when the information was a confession

---

Nunez, 2000). While judges might enjoy advantages as experienced repeat players, with regard to the evaluation of evidence the independent decision making characterizing bench trials, rather than the group decision making characterizing jury trials, might be a disadvantage (Robinson & Spellman, 2005; Wistrich, Guthrie & Rachlinski, 2005).

[4] Judges, for example, were found to exhibit susceptibility to the contrast effect (Rachlinski et al., 2013; Leibovitch, 2016); anchoring (Guthrie et al., 2001; Englich, Mussweiler & Strack, 2006; Rachlinski, Guthrie & Wistrich, 2006, 2007; Guthrie, Rachlinski & Wistrich, 2009; Rachlinski, Wistrich & Guthrie, 2015); framing (Guthrie et al., 2001, 2009; Rachlinski et al., 2006, 2007); hindsight bias (Guthrie et al., 2001, 2007, 2009); and order effects (Guthrie et al., 2001; Rachlinski et al., 2015).

extracted by violating the defendant's right to counsel (Wistrich et al., 2005).[5] It is likely, however, that the judges in this experiment did not truly ignore the inadmissible confession, but rather heavily discounted the weight they granted to that information by weighing the cost of suppression against the degree of police misconduct. In a following experiment, the same group of authors found that the gravity of police misconduct and the severity of the crime at issue significantly affect the extent to which judges grant weight to inadmissible confessions in their verdicts. When the police engaged in a relatively minor violation of a defendant's rights, even though judges suppressed the confession they were nevertheless more likely to convict the defendant. When the police misconduct was more severe, the impact of the inadmissible confession on judges' willingness to convict depended on the severity of the crime. For a less serious crime, grave police misconduct reduced judges' willingness to convict. But when the defendant had committed murder, judges were less willing to punish the same police misconduct with lower conviction rates and were consistently more willing to convict (Rachlinski et al., 2013).

The impact of inadmissible information can also extend beyond the effect of relying on that information in the decision. Research demonstrates that when people try to disregard inadmissible evidence – even when it is clear that the information they are asked to ignore is substantively foundationless and uninformative, is struck or withdrawn for neutral reasons and has no bearing on the reliability attributed to any party – they may exhibit a tendency to overcorrect, becoming more likely to rule in favour of the opposite side (Guttel, 2004). While studies to date on this question were only conducted with lay subjects (presenting yet another opportunity for future research on judges), their findings are illuminating on how difficult it is for the human mind to truly ignore – rather than weight, balance or overcompensate – information to which it has been exposed. Multiple studies, dealing with both criminal (Schul & Goren, 1997; Sommers & Kassin, 2001) and civil case scenarios (Hatvany & Strack, 1980; Guttel, 2004), presented subjects with a case involving various evidence, including an incriminating testimony that was later debunked. Participants introduced to the additional debunked testimony did not merely ignore that piece of unprobative evidence – they actually became more likely to rule in favour of the defendant than subjects never exposed to the evidence to begin with.

---

[5] In addition, unlike determinations of verdicts, one area in which evidence suggests judges might be better able to ignore irrelevant information is when they are asked to determine whether probable cause exists, and therefore whether to admit evidence uncovered during a search conducted without a warrant. Experimental findings suggest that judges exposed to the evidence produced by a search appear to be subject to hindsight bias with regard to their abilities to assess the likely outcome of the search, but not with regard to their legal judgements on whether there was probable cause to conduct the search (Wistrich et al., 2005; Rachlinski, Guthrie & Wistrich, 2011). It is possible that the fact that judges actually have experience with deciding on search warrants *ex ante* allows them to better evaluate the evidence from the same perspective when they are requested to decide on the constitutionality of a search *ex post*.

The influence of inadmissible information on legal judgements – whether by the continued consideration of the excluded information, or by overcorrecting in the opposite direction – is a source of concern for the legal system. At the same time, the judicial inclination in bench trials to admit evidence and decide on its weight later makes judges even more susceptible to this phenomenon than jurors who were never exposed to the information in the first place. Interestingly, in common law countries in which the jury is in decline, scholars note a commensurate decline in the law of evidence as well (Schauer, 2006). Yet the accumulating findings reviewed above – including from experiments conducted with real judges – may support the calls to reconsider this trend and the lax evidentiary rules that apply to bench trials.

9.5 CONCLUSION

The study of the connection between judicial psychology and institutional design is still at its nascent stage. As scholars are starting to scratch the surface on these topics, there are many more relevant questions to be investigated than those reviewed above, and much greater depths to delve into on the questions reviewed. This chapter does not purport to cover all relevant intersections between psychological insights and the institutional design of the courts. Rather its aim is to complement Judge Hoffman's discussion of the psychology of the trial judge by highlighting the possible role of procedures and institutions in perpetuating, exacerbating or creating cognitive biases in judicial decisions. It is not only that the trial process itself is especially vulnerable to cognitive biases and heuristics – for example, because of the need to make judgements about past events (opening the door to hindsight bias), or to transform evaluations of harm to dollar amounts or years in prison (which is sensitive to anchoring and contrast effects). The trial process is also particularly susceptible to systematic biases because of the structure of adversarial proceedings and of the courts where they are conducted. Parties, judges and policy makers who understand these biases and their anticipated direction can have better chances of achieving their goals. Obliviousness, on the other hand, can lead to unintended consequences – offering a windfall to better informed repeat players, and potentially even undermining the goals of the legal system itself (as reflected in the examples from specialized courts).

Future research should continue to devote more attention to the institutional aspects of the courts system, and their interaction with psychological biases. Scholars could trace the methodological developments we have seen in the law and psychology literature more generally by using more realistic experimental settings, and especially ones which are attentive to the varying and nuanced institutional conditions that characterize the different types of judicial decisions and court environments that judges operate in. Further research could also follow in the footsteps of studies building on the random assignment of cases to judges as a source of natural experiments, enabling the testing of more behavioural theories and mechanisms in the field. More generally, bridging together qualitative and quantitative field evidence with lab experiments would allow a more holistic picture to emerge of the systematic trends manifested in the courts and of the potential psychological mechanisms underlying them.

REFERENCES

Baron, J., & Ritov, I. (1993). Intuitions About Penalties and Compensation in the Context of Tort Law. *Journal of Risk and Uncertainty* 7, 17–33.

Baron, J., & Ritov, I. (2009). The Role of Probability of Detection in Judgments of Punishment. *Journal of Legal Analysis* 1(2), 553–90.

Bowers, J. (2008). Contraindicated Drug Courts. *UCLA Law Review* 55, 783–835.

Carlsmith, K. M., Darley, J. M., & Robinson, P. H. (2002). Why Do We Punish? Deterrence and Just Deserts as Motives for Punishment. *Journal of Personality and Social Psychology* 83 (2), 284–99.

Chen, D. L., Moskowitz, T. J., & Shue, K. (2016). Decision Making Under the Gambler's Fallacy: Evidence from Asylum Judges, Loan Officers, and Baseball Umpires. *The Quarterly Journal of Economics* 131(3), 1181–1242.

Darley, J. M., & Alter, A. L. (2013). Behavioral Issues of Punishment, Retribution, and Deterrence. In E. Shafir (ed.), *The Behavioral Foundations of Public Policy*. Princeton: Princeton University Press, pp. 173–205.

Darley, J. M., Carlsmith, K. M., & Robinson, P. H. (2000). Incapacitation and Just Deserts as Motives for Punishment. *Law and Human Behavior* 24(6), 659–83.

Eisenberg, T., Rachlinski, J. J., & Wells, M. T. (2002). Reconciling Experimental Incoherence with Real-World Coherence in Punitive Damages. *Stanford Law Review* 54 (6), 1239–72.

Englich, B., Mussweiler, T., & Strack, F. (2006). Playing Dice with Criminal Sentences: the Influence of Irrelevant Anchors on Experts' Judicial Decision Making. *Personality and Social Psychology Bulletin* 32(2), 188–200.

Eren, O., & Mocan, N. (2018). Emotional Judges and Unlucky Juveniles. *American Economic Journal: Applied Economics* 10(3), 171–205.

Guthrie, C. (2003). Panacea or Pandora's Box? The Cost of Options in Negotiation. *Iowa Law Review* 88(3), 601–54.

Guthrie, C., Rachlinski, J. J., & Wistrich, A. J. (2001) Inside the Judicial Mind. *Cornell Law Review* 86(4), 777–830.

Guthrie, C., Rachlinski, J. J., & Wistrich, A. J. (2007). Blinking on the Bench: How Judges Decide Cases. *Cornell Law Review* 93(1), 1–44.

Guthrie, C., Rachlinski, J. J., & Wistrich, A. J. (2009). 'The Hidden Judiciary': an Empirical Examination of Executive Branch Justice. *Duke Law Journal* 58(7), 1477–1530.

Guttel, E. (2004). Overcorrection. *Georgetown Law Journal* 93(1), 241–84.

Hans, V. P., & Ermann, M. D. (1989). Responses to Corporate Versus Individual Wrongdoing. *Law and Human Behavior* 13(2), 151–66.

Hatvany, N., & Strack, F. (1980). The Impact of a Discredited Key Witness. *Journal of Applied Social Psychology* 10(6), 490–509.

Himelein, M. J., Nietzel, M. T., & Dillehay, R. C. (1991). Effects of Prior Juror Experience on Jury Sentencing. *Behavioral Sciences & the Law* 9(1), 97–106.

Kahneman, D., Schkade, D., & Sunstein, C. (1998). Shared Outrage and Erratic Awards: the Psychology of Punitive Damages. *Journal of Risk and Uncertainty* 16(1), 49–86.

Kelman, M., Rottenstreich, Y., & Tversky, A. (1996). Context-Dependence in Legal Decision Making. *The Journal of Legal Studies* 25(2), 287–318.

Kerwin, J., & Shaffer, D. R. (1994). Mock Jurors Versus Mock Juries: the Role of Deliberations in Reactions to Inadmissible Testimony. *Personality and Social Psychology Bulletin* 20(2), 153–62.

Landsman, S., & Rakos, R. F. (1994). A Preliminary Inquiry Into the Effect of Potentially Biasing Information on Judges and Jurors in Civil Litigation. *Behavioral Sciences and the Law* 12, 113–26.

Leibovitch, A. (2016). Relative Judgments. *The Journal of Legal Studies*, 45(2), 281–330.

Leibovitch, A. (2017). Punishing on a Curve. *Northwestern University Law Review* 111(5), 1205–80.

Liu, Z., Klöhn, L., & Spamann, H. (2019). Precedent and Chinese Judges: an Experiment. *American Journal of Comparative Law*.

London, K., & Nunez, N. (2000). The Effect of Jury Deliberations on Jurors' Propensity to Disregard Inadmissible Evidence. *Journal of Applied Psychology* 85(6), 932–9.

McLeod, A. M. (2012). Decarceration Courts: Possibilities and Perils of Shifting Criminal Law. *Georgetown Law Journal* 100(5), 1587–1674.

Ouss, A., & Peysakhovich, A. (2015). When Punishment Doesn't Pay: Cold Glow and Decisions to Punish. *The Journal of Law and Economics* 58(3), 625–55.

Parducci, A. (1968). The Relativism of Absolute Judgments. *Scientific American* 219(6), 84–93.

Pepitone, A., & DiNubile, M. (1976). Contrast Effects in Judgments of Crime Severity and the Punishment of Criminal Violators. *Journal of Personality and Social Psychology* 33(4), 448–59.

Rachlinski, J. J., & Wistrich, A. J. (2017). Judging the Judiciary by the Numbers: Empirical Research on Judges. *Annual Review of Law and Social Science*, 13, 203–29.

Rachlinski, J. J., Wistrich, A. J., & Guthrie, C. (2013). Altering Attention in Adjudication. *UCLA Law Review*, 60(6), 1586–1619.

Rachlinski, J. J., Wistrich, A. J., & Guthrie, C. (2015). Can Judges Make Reliable Numeric Judgments: Distorted Damages and Skewed Sentences. *Indiana Law Journal* 90(2), 695–740.

Rachlinski, J. J., Guthrie, C., & Wistrich, A. J. (2006). Inside the Bankruptcy Judge's Mind. *Boston University Law Review* 86(5), 1227–66.

Rachlinski, J. J., Guthrie, C., & Wistrich, A. J. (2007). Heuristics and Biases in Bankruptcy Judges. *Journal of Institutional and Theoretical Economics* 163(1), 167–86.

Rachlinski, J. J., Guthrie, C., & Wistrich, A. J. (2011). Probable Cause, Probability, and Hindsight. *Journal of Empirical Legal Studies* 8, 72–98.

Rachlinski, J. J., & Jourden, F. (2003). The Cognitive Components of Punishment. *Cornell Law Review* 88(2), 457–85.

Robinson, P. H., & Darley, J. M. (1997). Utility of Desert. *Northwestern University Law Review* 91(2), 453–99

Robinson, P. H., & Spellman, B. A. (2005). Sentencing Decisions: Matching the Decisionmaker to the Decision Nature. *Columbia Law Review* 105, 1124–61.

Rodríguez, G., & Blanco, S. (2016). Contrast Effect on the Perception of the Severity of a Criminal Offence. *Anuario de Psicología Jurídica* 26(1), 107–13.

Schauer, F. (2006). On the Supposed Jury–Dependence of Evidence Law. *University of Pennsylvania Law Review* 155(1), 165–202.

Schauer, F., & Spellman, B. A. (2017). Analogy, Expertise, and Experience. *University of Chicago Law Review* 84(1), 249–68.

Schul, Y., & Goren, H. (1997). When Strong Evidence Has Less Impact than Weak Evidence: Bias, Adjustment, and Instructions to Ignore. *Social Cognition* 15(2), 133–55.

Sommers, S. R., & Kassin, S. M. (2001). On the Many Impacts of Inadmissible Testimony: Selective Compliance, Need for Cognition, and the Overcorrection Bias. *Personality and Social Psychology Bulletin* 27(10), 1368–77.

Spamann, H., & Klöhn, L. (2016). Justice Is Less Blind, and Less Legalistic, than We Thought: Evidence from an Experiment with Real Judges. *The Journal of Legal Studies* 45(2), 255–80.

Spellman, B. A. (2007). On the Supposed Expertise of Judges in Evaluating Evidence. *University of Pennsylvania Law Review* 156(1), 1–9.

Spellman, B. A., & Schauer, F. (2014). Law and Social Cognition. In D. E. Carlston (ed.), *The Oxford Handbook of Social Cognition*. Oxford University Press, pp. 829–50.

Steblay, N., Hosch, H. M., Culhane, S. E., & McWethy, A. (2006). The Impact on Juror Verdicts of Judicial Instruction to Disregard Inadmissible Evidence: A Meta-Analysis. *Law and Human Behavior* 30(4), 469–92.

Sunstein, C. R., Kahneman, D., & Schkade, D. (1998). Assessing Punitive Damages (with Notes on Cognition and Valuation in Law). *Yale Law Journal* 107(7), 2071–2153.

Sunstein, C. R., Kahneman, D., Schkade, D., & Ritov, I. (2002). Predictably Incoherent Judgments. *Stanford Law Review* 54(6), 1153–1215.

Sunstein, C. R., Schkade, D., & Kahneman, D. (2000). Do People Want Optimal Deterrence? *The Journal of Legal Studies* 29(1), 237–53.

Tyler, T. R., & Darley, J. M. (2000). Building Law-Abiding Society: Taking Public Views About Morality and the Legitimacy of Legal Authorities into Account When Formulating Substantive Law. *Hofstra Law Review* 28(3), 707–40.

Wistrich, A. J., Guthrie, C., & Rachlinski, J. J. (2005). Can Judges Ignore Inadmissible Information? The Difficulty of Deliberately Disregarding. *University of Pennsylvania Law Review* 153(4), 1251–1345.

Zamir, E., & Medina, B. (2010). *Law, Economics, and Morality*. New York: Oxford University Press.

Zamir, E., & Teichman, D. (2018). *Behavioral Law and Economics*. New York: Oxford University Press.

Zimring, F. E. (1993). Drug Treatment as Criminal Sanction. *University of Colorado Law Review* 64(3), 809–26.

10

Bias at the Surface or the Core? A Comment on the Psychology of the Trial Judge

Eyal Aharoni

Is judicial decision making steeped in cognitive bias? And which way does it lean in the perennial rivalry between emotion and reason? In "The Psychology of the Trial Judge," Chapter 8 in this volume, Morris Hoffman draws on a studious reading of the scientific literature and on his real-world experience as a trial judge to examine these difficult questions. In this commentary, I attempt to raise some additional questions that stem from his analysis, as applied to the legal justification for criminal punishment.

By way of background, the question of judicial bias represents a long-standing debate between two formidable opponents: The rationalist perspective argues that reason plays the leading role in moral judgment (Turiel, 1983; May, 2018) whereas decision bias is a supporting actor at best. The implication of this perspective is that education and expertise should tend to reduce decision bias. The intuitionist account makes the opposite case – that emotion leads, while reason plays little to no causal role. Like an emotional dog with a rational tail, it would be a mistake to think the tail is the primary driver of the dog's trajectory (Haidt, 2001). If human decision making is fundamentally emotional and intuitive, decision bias, even among legal experts, would tend to be far-reaching and relatively immutable.

So, which is it? Ultimately, Hoffman's analysis resists this dichotomy, favoring instead a more nuanced narrative between these extremes. That narrative acknowledges that even expert judges may not be immune to various cognitive biases, but expertise does seem to afford at least some protection. So let's not throw the baby out with the bath water, says Hoffman, because beneath the veneer of psychological biases lies a basically rational core.

To evaluate this conclusion, it might help to deconstruct the question into two forms. The weak form asks whether judges are in some ways affected by bias. The answer here is a decisive yes. There is ample empirical evidence of this, which Hoffman characterizes fairly. Scholars simply disagree about how much they are affected, and that question will be directly informed by further research, as Hoffman rightly acknowledges.

The strong form asks whether judicial decision making, being an expression of human decision making more generally, is fundamentally rational or emotional and intuitive. This is a much harder question to answer, and it is where Hoffman's interpretation might be slightly more optimistic than my own. One reason for my reluctance about claims of judicial rationality lies in the observation that we, as a society, do not have a clear conceptual understanding of why we punish criminals, and this lack of understanding makes it effectively impossible to punish rationally. There is, of course, a rich history of scholarship on the legal justifications for punishment, namely deontological theories of retribution and consequentialist theories of behavior control, with retribution recognized as the dominant justification in current US law (American Law Institute §1.02(2), 2017). But this framework is deeply flawed, and these flaws pose additional challenges for the prospect of a rational law.

To defend this proposition, let us review what rationality means in this context. To engage in *rational* decision making implies, at the very least, some strategic attempt to optimize a behavior with respect to some conceivable goal state. For example, if it is important to me that my child gets good grades, then hiring a tutor might count as a rational strategy in the pursuit of my goal. (Certainly, there are other definitions of rationality, such as that of logical reasoning or the pursuit of self-interest, but these forms of rationality exhibit even higher standards than means–goal rationality.) At minimum, being goal-directed necessitates a prospective relationship between the means and the end. But this is exactly the opposite of what deontological theories of retribution prescribe. Instead, these theories assert that violators deserve punishment for what they did, regardless of its bearing on future behavior (Packer, 1968). So, being explicitly retrospective in nature, what observable goal state is retribution designed to optimize for?

To obviate my point, there is an illustrative case of a Denver teen, Darrell Havens, who was paralyzed from the neck down after being shot by a police officer during the theft of a car. He would never be able to steal a car again, and yet he was sentenced to 20 years in prison. (The total taxpayer burden was estimated to the tune of $4 million, had his sentence not been cut short by an apparent suicide; Prendergast, 2017.) And for what – to set an example that "if you're thinking about using paralysis as a way to get away with crime, you better think twice?" Surely, there are better examples by which to send a deterrent message to society.

When people do bad things but are no longer dangerous, and when their example does not lend itself to a clear deterrent message, most people still demand punishment – but we have a hard time articulating why (Aharoni & Fridlund, 2011). Our retributive impulses do not seem ruffled by the fact that no amount of punishment can actually change the past. Instead, theories of retribution offer rhetoric about expressing condemnation for its own sake, or as a means to restoring a moral balance (Kant, 1998; Duff, 2001), but they do not clearly define what a moral balance is let alone how or when it has been restored (see Hart, 2008; Greene, 2014). This deontological hand-waving confirms to me that retribution, as acknowledged by some of its own proponents, is not goal-directed at all. And if it is not goal-directed, it is fundamentally incompatible with the enterprise of rationality. The implication is that participants in criminal justice institutions are carrying out the bidding of enigmatic, emotionally charged motivations that make insistent demands for the delivery of harm to others yet offer no clear goal definition or way to optimize for some goal. So, I worry that when we punish on retributive grounds, we are using the offender as a scapegoat to help us manage our own evasive and intractable moral emotions. I worry that retributive sentiments are expressions of psychological bias.

If the desire for retribution itself is a bias, then bias does not just grow at the periphery of our criminal punishment system – it is at the core. Granted, there are other (i.e., consequentialist) justifications to lean on. But neither legal theory nor practice offer ways for us to reconcile conflicts between the two types of justifications. They seem fundamentally incompatible, and the law lacks a higher-order theory prescribing when one should override the other. So, how can we expect judges to punish rationally, if we cannot even provide them with a coherent answer to the basic question: What is the primary goal of the punishment?

This is where it becomes instructive to consider, from a scientific perspective, how human decision making developed into its current form. Research in the evolutionary sciences has begun to uncover quite specific answers to the question of what goals our retributive motivations are optimized to serve. After examining these descriptive reasons, we as a society can more cogently evaluate whether we endorse or condemn them.

To make sense of retributive behavior, we need to consider the environment in which our modern minds adapted. In that environment, our ancestors didn't have state police forces and prison facilities, so they needed efficient, interpersonal solutions for managing threats and leveraging social relationships for their own benefit. Indeed, people who were motivated (by retributive emotions) to punish transgressors could have derived a variety of fitness advantages, whether by deterring or directly incapacitating one's oppressor, or deterring opportunistic onlookers, for example. Through these mechanisms, the expression of a strong commitment to punish transgressors can advertise the punisher's social capital, discourage future threats, and facilitate cooperation, as Hoffman and others have contended (Trivers, 1971; Frank, 1988; Fiddick, Cosmides, & Tooby, 2000; Fehr & Gächter, 2002; Price, Cosmides, & Tooby, 2002; Fehr & Fischbacher, 2004; Petersen et al., 2010; Krasnow et al., 2012; Aharoni & Fridlund, 2013; Hoffman, 2014; Krasnow et al., 2016; Delton & Krasnow, 2017; Pedersen, McAuliffe, & McCullough, 2018).

Owing to these advances in evolutionarily informed scholarship, we can, for the first time, articulate clear, observable (albeit descriptive) goals to be achieved by retributive punishment. Notice that these goals have a striking resemblance to the standard consequentialist justifications for punishment like deterrence and incapacitation, except for a key difference: emotion. According to evolutionary theories of punishment, punitive emotions like moral outrage (which are irrelevant by traditional consequentialist accounts) evolved because they provided a computationally inexpensive way of motivating punishment behavior. In ancestral environments, as with retaliatory actions observed in other animals (e.g., Clutton-Brock & Parker, 1995), you shouldn't have to deliberate your way to a punishment decision; that would be far too slow and costly. Retributive emotions solved that problem using automation. From an evolutionary perspective, this feature makes retributive motives begin to sound an awful lot like a strategic bias.

If retributive punishment decisions are fundamentally biased, is that necessarily a bad thing? If it evolved to reduce threats and increase cooperation, isn't that just the kind of bias we need in our justice system? Yes and no. Certainly, we can take inspiration from the scientific research on punishment, and ask whether we want to optimize punishment for evolved goals. Some of these (like incapacitation and deterrence) seem like legitimate societal goals to me, while others (like jockeying for social status) do not. But therein lies a major caveat in the extent to which we ought to lean on our retributive biases as guides to punishment: they evolved to benefit *individuals*, not societies. Indeed, research on our ancestors' darker behaviors have obviated the conclusion that traits that have conferred reproductive advantages to individuals – such as adultery, child maltreatment, and homicide – are a poor guide for a functional and moral *society* (Daly & Wilson, 1988). So, if we embrace retribution in criminal punishment, I submit that we carry a burden to prove that it is not doing more harm than good to society.

Ultimately, debates about the justification for punishment have much to learn from ongoing research and scholarship. Traditional notions of these justifications (namely the deontological versus consequentialist theories) are at a stalemate. At first glance, scientific perspectives on the evolution of our motivations for punishment might seem to complicate that relationship even more. Since discoveries about our ancestral heritage are purely descriptive, they cannot, by themselves, justify how we ought to live.

Yet, in addition to providing an explanation for why human beings seek retribution, research on our evolved psychology of punishment can be of use in another important way: it provides a new framework for unifying rival legal theories. This framework suggests that retributive and consequentialist motives for punishment are not orthogonal as legal philosophy would suggest – they are just different levels of analysis for describing a single psychological phenomenon. When a moral violation evokes strong feelings of moral outrage, these feelings evolved precisely because they motivated our ancestors to act on them, and such actions conferred important benefits upon punishers, such as protection from future harm. So, ironically, retribution is a proximate representation of an evolved psychology whose ultimate function was consequentialist (Cushman, 2015; Aharoni & Hoffman, 2020). Once endowed with the impulse to punish, you need not be conscious of the advantageous function of the impulse in order to benefit from it. You just need to submit to the impulse. Retributive theorists seem to be in the business of providing post hoc justifications for this impulse whereas consequentialist theorists require that any justification for such an impulse must explicitly fulfill a legitimate prospective goal. So when retributive and consequentialist theorists talk past each other, they may be simply engaging in different levels of analysis of the same phenomenon. Understanding the relationship between these levels can obviate the differences between the goals targeted by our intuitive impulse to punish and those targeted by our modern social values.

Scholars have argued that we can leverage this newfound scientific knowledge to make clearer, more goal-directed, collective decisions (Jones, 2000). For example, if we were to collectively decide that the dominant goal of punishment should be to protect public safety, then we don't need to argue about whether it is moral to assign lengthy prison terms to quadriplegic car thieves. Instead, we could conclude that this action is not an efficient means to our collective goal. Indeed, it could siphon away scarce funds from the punishment of more dangerous individuals. But if we never question the legitimacy of our retributive impulses, we have no way to prevent them from getting the better of us.

Asking whether judges are biased has both a short answer and a long one. The short answer, on which Hoffman and I closely agree, is: sure, kind of. The long answer – about which thoughtful minds can disagree – taps a much deeper question about the present and proper roles of emotion and reason in our justice system. Evolutionary scholarship casts doubt on the integrity of the folk psychology on which the law is based, but it also offers the law a powerful tool for reconciling the historically incompatible justifications for punishment by showing that what feels like a retributive impulse in the proximate sense might have design features for fulfilling particular fitness goals for our ancestors. Our foremost goal as a society, in my view, should be to decide, with the aid of rigorous research and scholarship, when we are better off fulfilling those evolved goals and when we are better off protecting ourselves from them.

REFERENCES

Aharoni, E., & Fridlund, A.J. (2011). Punishment Without Reason: Isolating Retribution in Lay Punishment of Criminal Offenders. *Psychology, Public Policy, and the Law* 18(4), 599–625.

Aharoni, E., & Fridlund, A. J. (2013). Moralistic Punishment as a Crude Social Insurance Plan. In T. Nadelhoffer (ed.), *The Future of Punishment* (pp. 213–229). New York: Oxford University Press.

Aharoni, E., & Hoffman, M. B. (2020). Evolutionary Psychology, Jurisprudence, and Sentencing. In T. Shackelford (ed.), *The SAGE Handbook of Evolutionary Psychology* (pp. 221–242). London: SAGE Publications.

American Law Institute. (2017). *Model Penal Code*. Philadelphia, PA: The American Law Institute. https://archive.org/stream/ModelPenalCode_ALI/MPC

Clutton-Brock, T. H., & Parker, G. A. (1995). Punishment in Animal Societies. *Nature* 373 (6511), 209–216.

Cushman, F. (2015). Punishment in Humans: From Intuitions to Institutions. *Philosophy Compass* 10(2), 117–133.

Daly, M., & Wilson, M. (1988). *Homicide*. New Brunswick, NJ: Transaction Publishers.

Delton, A. W., & Krasnow, M. M. (2017). The Psychology of Deterrence Explains Why Group Membership Matters for Third-Party Punishment. *Evolution and Human Behavior* 38(6), 734–743.

Duff, A. (2001). *Punishment, Communication, and Community*. New York: Oxford University Press.

Fehr, E., & Fischbacher, U. (2004). Third-Party Punishment and Social Norms. *Evolution and Human Behavior* 25(2), 63–87.

Fehr, E., & Gächter, S. (2002). Altruistic Punishment in Humans. *Nature* 415(6868), 137–140.

Fiddick, L., Cosmides, L., & Tooby, J. (2000). No Interpretation Without Representation: the Role of Domain-Specific Representations and Inferences in the Wason Selection Task. *Cognition* 77(1), 1–79.

Frank, R. H. (1988). *Passions Within Reason: the Strategic Role of the Emotions*. New York: W. W. Norton & Co.

Greene, J. D. (2014). *Moral Tribes: Emotion, Reason, and the Gap Between Us and Them*. New York: Penguin.

Haidt, J. (2001). The Emotional Dog and Its Rational Tail: a Social Intuitionist Approach to Moral Judgment. *Psychological Review* 108(4), 1024–1052.

Hart, H. L. A. (2008). *Punishment and Responsibility: Essays in the Philosophy of Law*. Oxford: Oxford University Press.

Hoffman, M. B. (2014). *The Punisher's Brain: the Evolution of Judge and Jury*. New York: Cambridge University Press.

Jones, O. D. (2000). Time-Shifted Rationality and the Law of Law's Leverage: Behavioral Economics Meets Behavioral Biology. *Northwestern University Law Review* 95, 1141–1205.

Kant, I. (1998). Kant's Groundwork of the Metaphysics of Morals. In P. Guyer's (ed.), *Critical Essays on the Classics*. Lanham, MD: Rowman and Littlefield. (Original work published in 1785.)

Krasnow, M. M., Cosmides, L., Pedersen, E. J., & Tooby, J. (2012). What Are Punishment and Reputation For? *PLOS ONE* 7(9), e45662.

Krasnow, M. M., Delton, A. W., Cosmides, L., & Tooby, J. (2016). Looking Under the Hood of Third-Party Punishment Reveals Design for Personal Benefit. *Psychological Science* 27(3), 405–418.

May, J. (2018). *Regard for Reason in the Moral Mind*. Oxford: Oxford University Press.

Packer, H. (1968). *The Limits of the Criminal Sanction*. Stanford, CA: Stanford University Press.

Pedersen, E. J., McAuliffe, W. H., & McCullough, M. E. (2018). The Unresponsive Avenger: More Evidence that Disinterested Third Parties Do Not Punish Altruistically. *Journal of Experimental Psychology: General* 147(4), 514.

Petersen, M. B., Sell, A., Tooby, J., & Cosmides, L. (2010). Evolutionary Psychology and Criminal Justice: A Recalibrational Theory of Punishment and Reconciliation. In H. Høgh-Oleson (ed.), *Human Morality & Sociality: Evolutionary & Comparative Perspectives*. New York: Palgrave Macmillan.

Prendergast, A. (2017, April 27). The Strange Death of Darrell Havens, Prisoner Who Battled the System. *Westword*. www.westword.com/news/darrell-havens-paralyzed-prisoner-who-battled-the-system-has-died-9006082

Price, M. E., Cosmides, L., & Tooby, J. (2002). Punitive Sentiment as an Anti-Free Rider Psychological Device. *Evolution and Human Behavior* 23(3), 203–231.
Trivers, R. L. (1971). The Evolution of Reciprocal Altruism. *The Quarterly Review of Biology* 46(1), 35–57.
Turiel, E. (1983). *The Development of Social Knowledge: Morality and Convention.* Cambridge: Cambridge University Press.

III

Legal Doctrine and Cognitive Sciences

11

Private Law and Cognitive Science

Przemysław Pałka[*]

11.1 INTRODUCTION

Imagine a beach in Cuba. Amidst the calming sound of the sea, gentle gusts of wind, and a pleasant smell of coconuts, Melanie and Nikolas are experiencing the warmth of the coral sand. It no longer burns their feet; the afternoon is about to turn into evening. "Just in case" – says Melanie, urging Nikolas to apply some more sun cream – "we are not used to the sun yet!" The two spent the last week swimming in the crystal-clear water, drinking mojitos, dancing, laughing, and smoking cigars. Melanie, a corporate lawyer from New York, and Nikolas, an aspiring legal scholar from Berlin, have discovered a way to earn large sums of money by mostly chilling at the beach. I have learned their secret. In the next few pages, I am going to share it with you.

Well, of course, I am not. The previous paragraph exemplifies some findings of cognitive science. To get your point across, grasp the audience's attention. To grasp their attention, tell a short story (Vaughn, 2012). Make the characters relatable, invoke the senses, and promise something exciting. This knowledge, even if not always backed by scientific publications, is common to marketers, salespersons, or negotiators. The people whose job it is to make you buy something, want something, or agree to something know a lot about human psychology and behavior. Arguably, they know much more than the lawmakers did, when forging the foundations of private law centuries ago; and more than legal scholars know even today. Does it matter? I argue that it does.

This chapter addresses the question of how cognitive science can inform the theory and practice of private law. I propose seeking the answer along two dimensions. First, cognitive science challenges the presuppositions about human beings enshrined in the law. Lawyers often employ notions like "meeting of minds," "free will," or "expression of intention." Contract and tort law presupposes a lot about persons' reactions to incentives, the ability to reason and to make decisions.

[*] Assistant Professor at the Future Law Lab, Jagiellonian University, Visiting Fellow at the Information Society Project at Yale. Visiting Fellow at the Information Society Project at Yale.

A discipline seeking understanding of human cognition can help evaluate the correctness of these, often implicit, assumptions. Moreover, as a source of knowledge about human psychology and behavior, cognitive science can serve as a resource for rule-makers, both of the rules enshrined in (state) law and in privately drafted contracts. When trying to empower consumers by imposing new information duties on traders, attempting to guide people's behavior through private fines, or drafting a contract that the other party is supposed to (not) understand and accept, lawyers benefit from the knowledge created within cognitive science. When critically assessing private law from these two perspectives, conceptual and practical, cognitive science can help lawyers refine their understanding of what human beings *are* – what qualities they have and how they behave in various situations.

Second, cognitive science can help us understand the changing nature of the private law society (Böhm, 1966) in the digitally mediated, cognitively driven marketplace (Zuboff, 2019). Private law presupposes not only certain features of natural persons, but also the types of actions they undertake, types of relations they engage in, and types of objects they control. These elements, in turn, are contingent upon the state of technology, culture, and science. Currently, new types of activities are occurring, like micro-targeted behavioral advertising (Mik, 2016); and new types of commodities, like humans' attention (Wu, 2017; Newman, 2019) and future conduct (Zuboff, 2019) are forming objects of private law relations. These transformations result directly from the application of cognitive insights by corporations, and their will to develop new knowledge about people's preferences and behavior. Consumers' growing reliance on technology, paired with developments in data analytics techniques (Alpaydin, 2016), expand the locus of the creation of "cognitive knowledge" from universities to corporations (Lustig, 2017). Firms operating online can continuously "experiment" with human subjects (Kramer, Guillory, & Hancock, 2014), yet remain free of (formalized) ethical duties and incentives to publish their results. Along this dimension, cognitive science can help private lawyers understand what private persons (humans and firms) *currently do*, and update the law's conceptual framework and axiological backbone, to account for these changes.

The genre of a research handbook dictates the style of presentation in this chapter. I want it to be a valuable resource for both private law scholars wishing to incorporate insights and methods of cognitive science in their work, and for cognitive scientists wanting to study the law and the law-affected human practices. Moreover, I want it to be useful regardless of the jurisdiction and the specificity of local private law doctrines. For these reasons, I include numerous citations to the existing literature, but seldom directly challenge the views I invoke. In addition, I prioritize breadth over depth in terms of the problem presentation and leave the reader with questions instead of arguing for any specific normative solutions.

The chapter consists of three sections. Section 11.2 clarifies my understanding of "private law" and "cognitive science," as well as offering an overview of the literature that could be qualified as representing the emerging field of (private) law and cognitive science. Section 11.3 explains how private law presupposes various characteristics of human beings, demonstrates what these presuppositions are, and shows how cognitive science can help scrutinize them. I show how the law presupposes the *homo legalis privatus* to have free will and intentions, rationally guiding her behavior to pursue these intentions, and understanding the consequences of her actions to a degree sufficient to hold her responsible for them. I scrutinize these assumptions in the light of what cognitive sciences tell us about human behavior, and show how one's assessment will differ depending on the role one believes private law to play in our society. I also exhibit how these findings can be used instrumentally, to make contracts more readable and information conferring more effective. Section 11.4 maps the transformations in the private law society triggered by the development and application of cognitive science, demonstrates what novel elements exist in the cognitively driven world, and scrutinizes the role played by private law in these changes.

11.2 MEET THE FIELD: CONCEPTUAL CLARIFICATIONS AND THE STATE OF THE ART

To begin, let me introduce and clarify the concepts of "private law" and "cognitive science," as well as provide a bird's-eye overview of the scholarly field of (private) law and cognitive science.

By "private law" I mean the legal and social rules and institutions structuring and governing the relations between formally equal persons: property, contract, and tort law, as well as economic regulations shaping market conduct (Micklitz, 2009). I will not pay attention to dispute resolution, that is, adjudication of private law cases in courts or via arbitration.[1] Instead, I will focus on the ways these rules shape social life, how transformations in social life challenge these rules, and the role that cognitive science is, and could be, playing in these processes.

By "cognitive science" I mean a social effort aimed at understanding how humans think and behave. In this sense, I employ both notions quite liberally. In "cognitive" science I include behavioral studies (treating brains/minds as "black boxes"), cognitive neuroscience (trying to "peek inside" those boxes), psychology, anthropology, evolutionary biology, philosophy, and anything else that might be illuminating. Similarly, by "science," I mean not only the "proper" endeavors of scholars working at universities and publishing in peer-reviewed journals, but also the knowledge amassed by private corporations and trading communities. The reason for this (potential over-)inclusiveness is that when dealing with novel phenomena, striving

---

[1] Litigation, evidence, and cognitive science make up a fascinating, but different, area of inquiry. It encompasses questions like the role of bias and prejudice and adjudication, strength of evidence based on memory, novel types of possible evidence, and so on. These questions are common to all types of judicial proceedings, not just the civil procedure.

at terminological purity might cost us missing something unexpectedly fundamental outside the established drawers.

11.2.1 *Private Law*

The term "private law" belongs to the basic legal vocabulary of European lawyers, but might seem far from natural to Americans and nonlegal scholars.[2] Moreover, the discipline itself is currently undergoing rapid transformations, and so one cannot assume that a consensus exists even amongst those who consider themselves private law scholars. To avoid misunderstandings and unwarranted assumptions, I want to address two issues at the outset: (i) what branches of law can the term *"private* law" refer to?; (ii) what dimensions of social reality can be designated by the term "private *law"*? I do so primarily to clarify what I mean by these terms and why I do so, without the pretense of "solving" any exciting scholarly disputes, or arguing for "the correct" viewpoint.

First: what branches of law make up the "private" law part? The simplest definition involves enumeration: traditionally, *"private* law" encompasses the rules of property, contract, and tort.[3] In continental Europe, these areas are governed by civil codes, while the Anglophones refer to them as "common law," given these rules' judiciary origin. Disputes arising about property, contract, and tort are adjudicated within civil procedures (as opposed to criminal or administrative ones). One could say that "private" law is the body of law governing relations between formally equal persons (individuals and corporations[4]). "Public" law, on the other hand, governs the functioning of public authorities, and the relations between individuals and these authorities (like criminal law, administrative law, and constitutional law). The distinction dates back to Roman times (Mousourakis, 2015), and as far as books (in Europe) are concerned, it has stood the test of time.

However, the world consistently refuses to align itself with the neat typologies of black-letter lawyers. Think about the legal relations you have with other humans and corporations. When you buy clothes, food, or books, you act as a consumer, within the realm of consumer law. Labor law governs your relationship with your employer or workers. The contents of your telephone, banking, energy, and insurance contracts stem from the regulations and decisions of various administrative agencies.

---

[2] One should note that, ever since the legal realist movement in the first half of the twentieth century, many American scholars have openly challenged the usefulness of the private/public law distinction, and as a result, do not even employ the term.

[3] Many would also include family law, inheritance law, and rules on unjust enrichment. Note that "private" law thus understood is still state administered. We do not mean *privately created* rules (though we do not exclude them), but rather state-backed rules governing relations between legally equal persons.

[4] By "corporations" I mean both private entities like for-profit firms and nonprofit foundations and associations, and public bodies exercising their *dominio*, as opposed to *imperio*. In this sense, when a police department purchases paper for its printers, it is treated as a private person for the purposes of the law.

Probably, you seldom conclude a "pure" contract of sale, as envisioned by the civil codes. Similarly, the limitations on the exercise of property rights often stem from regulations (environmental law, food law, zoning laws, etc.). For these reasons, paradoxically, one cannot grasp the full content of contract/property/tort norms by focusing solely on these branches of law. All this has led some scholars to expand the meaning of "private" law to *"regulatory* private law," encompassing both the traditional triad of property, contract, and tort, and the administrative norms shaping the market and social relations (Micklitz, 2009). In this chapter, I adhere to this view, and to account for rules, principles, and concepts foundational for the private law society in the twenty-first century, employ the term *"private* law" in a broader, inclusive manner.

Second: what elements of social reality are we talking about when invoking the term private "law"? The classical view, still pervasive in the European scholarship, concentrates primarily on *norms* (rules and principles) and their *sources* (legislation and judicial decisions). From this perspective, private law scholarship is a domain of humanities: philosophy and interpretation, taking as an object of its study (i) texts and (ii) abstract entities, "created" by these texts, like rules, principles, and concepts. A private law scholar might ask positive questions (What is the content of the law?), explanatory questions (Why is it the way it is, what led to its adoption?), or normative questions (Is this law good, could it be better?), but she will still focus on what she can read, or imagine while reading. Law, thus understood, is an intellectual system, presupposing a particular structure of the reality it aims to govern. This is a valid and important perspective, and I adopt it in many places throughout this chapter. Nevertheless, limiting one's analysis solely to legal texts on one hand, and norms and concepts on the other, leaves out a significant portion of the legal reality.

Private law is a domain of everyday life, not just the lawyerly treatises. Individuals constantly conclude contracts, exchange goods, provide and receive services, injure others, and get injured themselves. Relations amongst persons exist not (only) because law constitutes them, but primarily because social life gives rise to them. Hence, to appreciate the insights that a(n empirical) discipline like cognitive science[5] can offer to private law, one needs to concentrate on the empirical aspects of the law's domain: real-world *practices* and *phenomena* of advertising, trespassing, contracting, and so on. This expansive view, sociological in nature, compels us to include in the scope of inquiry not just the "law-in-action," that is, what judges and other officials do; but primarily *what persons do*: how contracts get concluded, what do they stipulate, what commodities get traded, and so on. Therefore, when speaking of "private *law*" in this chapter, I refer not only to norms, concepts, and institutions of black-letter law, not only to the practices of the officials, but also to the practices of persons themselves.

---

[5] Cognitive science, just like legal scholarship, includes both philosophical reflections and empirical findings. I explain this in more detail in Section 11.1.2.

11.2.2 *Cognitive Science and (Private) Law*

Cognitive science is an "interdisciplinary study of mind and intelligence" (Thagard, 2018), concerned with perception, emotions, attention, decision making, and behavior (Passingham, 2016). As an interdisciplinary endeavor, it employs the methods of philosophy, neuroscience, biology, evolutionary psychology, anthropology, and social science. Cognitive scientists are interested in a diverse set of questions, and study themes like, amongst others, free will (Balaguer, 2014); relations between brain and mind (Passingham, 2016); cognitive biases (Kahneman, 2011); consciousness; creativity; or persuasion. Various competing communities of discourse exist within cognitive science itself; many of them have views on what types of questions and methods belong inside and outside of the field. Without taking sides in these debates, I adopt a broad and inclusive understanding of the term.

What fascinates many scholars about cognitive science is its merger of philosophy and humanities with empirical data and natural sciences. The unexpected encounter of centuries-old-questions (Do humans have free will? Is it possible to think rationally? How should we understand the relationship of body and mind?) with modern experimental methods and sophisticated tools like fMRI brain imaging (Passingham, 2016) brings with it a refreshing breeze that blows both into the dusty libraries of philosophers and the sterile laboratories of hard scientists. Certain questions that intrigue philosophers sometimes require that data be consulted, while many empirical findings collected via experiments need to be interpreted with philosophical sensitivity, caution, and diligence. I discuss several examples of such questions, regarding free will and culpability, in the next subsection (Section 11.3.4).

Moreover, the types of questions posed by cognitive science can be illuminating, almost by definition, to any discipline concerned with humans doing things, thinking about things, or trying to make a decision. In *Thinking, Fast and Slow*, Daniel Kahneman (2011) recalls how, after he published "Judgment under Uncertainty: Heuristics and Biases" (Tversky & Kahneman, 1974) with Amos Tversky, they were both surprised at the breadth of its reception:

> Our article attracted much more attention than we expected, and it remains one of the most cited works in social science ... Scholars in other disciplines found it useful, and the ideas of heuristics and biases have been used productively in many fields, including medical diagnosis, legal judgment, intelligence analysis, philosophy, finance, statistics and military strategy. (Kahneman, 2011)

Once one notices that our presuppositions about human thinking and behavior not only might be wrong, but actually can be productively tested and refined, broad application of cognitive science should no longer come as surprising. One of many disciplines that have benefited from its encounter with cognitive science is law.

The dialogue between cognitive science and law is not exactly a new endeavor. As an anecdotal example: back in 1989, George Lakoff presented a paper titled "Cognitive Science and the Law" (1989) at the Yale Law School Legal Theory Workshop.[6] Since then, numerous articles and books have been published, though not necessarily in dialogue with one another. Several communities of discourse have emerged, amongst them law and psychology (Bartol & Bartol, 2019; Granhag et al., 2016; Miller & Bornstein, 2016; Sales & Krauss, 2015); law and neuroscience (Brożek, 2017a; Blitz, 2017; Jones, Schall, & Shen, 2014; Hirstein, Sifferd, & Fagan, 2018; Patterson & Pardo, 2016; Pardo & Patterson, 2013); law and artificial intelligence (Sartor, 2006; Hage, 2011); and behavioral law and economics (Sunstein, 2000; Rachlinski, 2009; Zamir & Teichman, 2018). The subjects and questions tackled within these discourses range from judicial legal reasoning (Brożek, 2019) to cognitive biases (Fruehwald, 2018), from subjects of liability and culpability to applications in specific areas of law, like criminal law, antidiscrimination law, family law, and others. All these efforts can illuminate the law as "cognitive science" broadly understood, though it would be a stretch to say that "law and cognitive science" has already become an established scholarly field in its own right.

Regarding private law and cognitive science, the most robust contributions have been offered within the field of behavioral law and economics. Classic works include studies by Williamson (1989), Jolls, Sunstein and Thaler (1998), and Kaplow and Shavell (2009). More recently, Oren Bar-Gill authored an insightful monograph, titled *Seduction by Contract*, exploring various ways in which psychological, behavioral, and cognitive processes play in consumer markets (Bar-Gill, 2012). An entire handbook devoted to research methods in consumer law has been published, drawing heavily from behavioral insights (Micklitz, Sibony, & Esposito, 2018).

The success of this angle is hardly surprising, given both the popularity of law and economics as a discipline and the fact that economics has traditionally been the most outspoken discipline regarding the assumptions it makes about humans (see Section 11.3.1). However, one should bear in mind that, as is the case with many disciplines with evaluative ambitions, behavioral law and economics has an underlying political project, or at least assumes a set of implicit normativities. The focus on "efficiency" or "consumer welfare" tacitly crawls into the supposedly "scientific" considerations, sometimes blinding us to the other goals pursued by the private law (see Section 11.3.3). Hans Micklitz has made a strong argument for caution in this sphere (Micklitz, 2018).

In addition to behavioral law and economics, the literature one could label as private law and cognitive science has been growing under the labels of the

---

[6] G. Lakoff. *Cognitive Science and the Law*. Unpublished manuscript, hard copy archived in the Yale Law School Library, 1989.

psychology of tort law (Shuman, 1994; Robbennolt & Hans, 2016) as well as, indirectly, in various philosophical accounts of contract law (Benson, 2001; Kraus, 2002).

The literature surveyed here is, at the same time, broad and not fully representative. Obviously, there is more to discover, once one dives deeper into the debates within a particular community of discourse. My goal so far has been to give the reader an overview of the "menu" and to highlight the works I consider fundamental or most interesting. Having done so, without making claims to be right or fully comprehensive, I would like to move to two substantive dimensions where I believe cognitive science can inform the theory and practice of private law. In the following sections, I will show how cognitive science can help challenge the presuppositions about humans engrained in the legal discourses and serve as a resource to private rule-makers; and help us understand new types of activities that persons engage in and new types of objects that persons enter into private law relations over. Let us start with the presuppositions.

11.3 COGNITIVE SCIENCE AND PRIVATE LAW'S PRESUPPOSITIONS ABOUT HUMANS

Law is a normative creature, instructing people on how to behave, and in a sense telling a story about how the world *should* be. However, like any normative system, the law is also a repository of assumptions and presuppositions about how the world *is*. These presuppositions stem from our joint experiences of social life, from culture and philosophy, and have made their way into the law through the lawmakers' vision of the world, broadly understood. As with any assumptions, they might be true or false, useful or harmful. However, making the assumptions explicit does not belong to the traditional legal methodology. Law and lawyers seldom *make assumptions*, they rather *hold presuppositions*.[7]

In this section, I bring some of these presuppositions to the fore and reconstruct the qualities of a human agent presupposed by private law: *homo legalis privatus*. I show how the law assumes her to have a free will and intentions, to act rationally in accordance with these intentions, and to understand the consequences of her actions to a degree sufficient to hold her responsible for these actions. I scrutinize these assumptions in the light of the findings of cognitive science and show how, even though they are not untrue, human cognition is much more complicated than an unabridged version of these qualities. I further discuss the role these assumptions play in private law and argue that whether we should assess their *usefulness* or *correctness* will depend on one's normative take on private law's role in the society. I further take a closer look at three fundamental aspects of *homo legalis privatus*: free

---

[7] "Making an assumption" is a conscious act, while "holding a presupposition," is an unconscious state. In other words, assumptions are always explicit, while presuppositions are implicit. They can be made explicit, and then they become assumptions.

will, rationality, and culpability. The section finishes with a discussion of several examples of how cognitive science can be used to increase the effectiveness of private rule-making: contract drafting, consumer disclosure, and guiding behavior through private fines.

11.3.1 Homo Economicus *and* Homo Legalis Privatus

If you have ever taken an introductory class in microeconomics, you are familiar with the concept of *homo economicus* – the economic human. Homo economicus is perfectly rational, self-interested, and utility/profit-maximizing. She has a fixed set of preferences, which she can always order coherently. Microeconomic models are stories about economic humans. If a more affordable alternative is available, economic humans will switch to it. If the cost goes up, the amount of purchases goes down. If we put a price on some harmful activity, the occurrence of this activity will become less frequent. In this view, human behavior is mostly predictable. And if it is predictable, it can be modified, to a certain extent.

Those assumptions are not entirely in line with our everyday experience. One can easily point to situations suggesting that humans are not perfectly rational, and much more complex than self-centered profit maximizers. The existence of fair-trade coffee or volunteering would suggest that people care about other things than profit, or at least understand "utility" in much broader terms. On-the-spot purchases that we later regret suggest that not all our decisions are well thought through. An economist's answer to these objections would be that economists do not claim that humans *factually are* like this; they rather *assume* that humans *act as if they were*, to construct models. If a model has high explanatory and predictive power, that is, if people end up behaving the way economists thought they would, their *actual* features or motivations are irrelevant. And it just so happens that assuming that people are economical leads to the high predictive power of many economic models. The claim that economic models always have high predictive power is not entirely accurate, hence the booming field of behavioral economics (Thaler, 2016). However, what I want to draw the reader's attention to is that traditional economic theory: (i) makes assumptions about humans, (ii) in an explicit manner, (iii) to increase the explanatory and predictive power of economic models.

The traditional legal approach is different. If you ask a contract lawyer about his assumptions about *homo legalis privatus* – a private law human, a member of the private law society – there is a chance is that he will not be able to answer. If you are dealing with an American, she might describe someone akin to the economic human, given the omnipresence of law and economics in the US scholarship. However, a continental colleague might look startled. The lack of a clear answer stems not from the fact that the law does not contain assumptions or construct models. Rather, we are not used to making them explicit and critically scrutinizing them. We often simply presuppose a set of facts about human beings and the world.

Possibly, these presuppositions are correct, or at least useful. However, to assess that, we should bring them to the fore.

How to go about making these assumptions explicit? One can start by looking at provisions expressing particular norms, and ask: "What factual claims are presupposed by a given (normative) statement?" (Levinson, 1983). Consider a simple example. A sentence: *"Children must not eat ice cream before dinner"* expresses a norm, but also contains several assumptions about the real world. For example, it holds ontological commitments to the existence of children and ice cream; a prediction that children *might* want to eat ice cream, and judgment that children *are capable* of refraining from eating ice cream, despite having an urge to do so. These statements might strike you as too obvious to mention, as they are obviously true. However, consider an example at the other extreme: *"Whenever a person sees a unicorn, he or she must refrain from breathing for an hour."* Such a norm would presuppose existence of unicorns, and humans' ability to stop breathing for an hour. Both of which are, clearly, not true. Hence, it is possible for a meaningful sentence expressing an imperative statement to presuppose factual statements which are untrue. As the law is a product of our common experience of reality, it probably will seldom contain presuppositions that are flatly false. However, it might contain some that are questionable.

Provisions expressing legal norms can be analyzed in the same way as the two examples in the previous paragraph. Below, I consider a few private law examples, concerned with capacity for performing juridical acts, with the conditions for successful concluding of contracts, and with stipulating what actions should be treated as torts. I take them from the Polish Civil Code, as this is the legal act that I am most familiar with. However, one can repeat the same exercise regarding other legal systems, and the results should not differ significantly. This is due not only to the fact that many Western private law systems have common roots (Gordley, 2006) but also to the fact that our image of the world has been shaped by transnational phenomena like science and philosophy. Let us take a closer look at four examples of private law norms containing presuppositions about humans.

First, consider the capacity for legal actions. In Western liberal democracies, every human being enjoys a legal personality, that is, the quality of being the subject of one's own rights and duties (Brożek, 2017b). However, not everyone (in particular, not children and persons with mental disabilities) enjoys the ability to perform juridical acts (ger. *Rechtsgeschäfte*, fr. *actes juridiques*) in one's own name (Hage, 2011). As a rule, the Polish Civil Code attributes full capacity for juridical acts to all persons of eighteen years or older. However, it also states:

> Art 13.1: A person ... might be legally incapacitated, if due to mental illness, mental underdevelopment, or any other type of mental disorder, in particular substance addiction, he or she is unable to control [lit. direct] his or her behavior.[8]

---

[8] Translation by the author.

Therefore, the Code assumes that *unless* an adult suffers from a mental disorder, he or she *can control his or her behavior*. A human being, in this view, understands the reality around her, can make decisions, and understands the meaning and the consequences of these decisions. These abilities are so crucial to the proper functioning of a society based on private law that, once a person loses them, the law provides for a mechanism of limiting one's legal capacity to perform juridical acts. Moreover, this norm presupposes that somewhere around the date of their eighteenth birthday, a person generally become more capable of controlling their behavior than before.[9] Regardless of whether those assumptions are factually correct or not, their existence can be made explicit.

Second, consider two articles of the Polish Civil Code, governing the activity of performing a juridical act (concluding contracts, preparing wills, etc.), and the directive for contracts' interpretation, respectively:

> Art. 60: ... The will of a person engaging in a juridical act can be expressed by any behavior of that person, if only it expresses his or her will sufficiently clearly ("declaration of intent").
>
> Art. 65.2: When interpreting contracts, one should inquire into the joint intention and goal of the parties, rather than their literal formulation.

These two provisions presuppose that human beings: have will(s) and intentions, and can express these intentions through their behavior, including through language. They also assume that persons can achieve a common understanding of their intentions, but that they sometimes fail to express this understanding in an unambiguous manner. They assume that the common intention can be retroactively established, and compared with the literal meaning of a contract. According to this image of the world, human cooperation involves negotiations of a *common goal and intention* by individuals who themselves have motives of their own, direct their behavior according to their will, and express their intentions about the future states of affairs.

Third, the Polish Civil Code foresees circumstances when an action that could look like the conclusion of a contract (or a performance of a different juridical act, like preparing a will) should not be treated as one. Consider the following provisions:

> Art. 82: A declaration of intent shall be null and void if expressed by a person who, for any reason, could not make a decision and express his or her will consciously and freely. This applies in particular to mental illness, mental disability, or any other, even temporary, distortion of mental faculties.

---

[9] The assumption that a person's ability to understand and direct their behavior changes profoundly on the date of their eighteenth birthday would obviously not be true. There are good reasons for the existence of this rule, having to do, amongst others, with the protection of minors and legal certainty. The persons' legal status of capacity should not be confused with their psychological status of rationality. However, from a purely formalistic perspective, the Code presupposes that as a matter of general rule: persons younger than eighteen are not capable of fully controlling their behavior, while people that are eighteen or older (subject to exceptions) are.

> Art. 87: Whoever made a declaration of intent under the influence of an unlawful threat ... may evade the legal consequences of that declaration, if the circumstances indicate that they may have been afraid that they or another person may be in serious danger to their person or their property.

First, by studying these "exceptional," states of affairs, we can discover what the Code treats as the rule, namely that adults can consciously make decisions and freely express their will. At the foundation of the Code's vision of private law lies a presupposition that persons understand the world and the consequences of their actions, and upon this understanding act as free agents making choices about their legal situations. This is so crucial that a lack of these faculties, even if temporary, can render a contract null and void. Second, in addition to the need for "internal" freedom of will, the Code also makes it possible to annul contracts concluded under coercion. Note, however, the gradation of circumstances rendering contracts null and void – a lack of "mental faculties" necessary to act freely renders a declaration of intent null and void as a matter of law, while external coercion gives one a right to seek annulment.

Fourth, consider the basic provision establishing tortuous liability in the Polish Civil Code:

> Art. 415: Whoever, culpably [lit. through his, or her, fault], has done harm to another, is obliged to remedy [lit. repair] that harm.

This norm, apart from adhering to the most basic principle of corrective justice (Weinrib, 2012), also contains a set of presuppositions about the world. First, that humans can harm one another. Second, that the harms can be remedied somehow. Third, and crucially – that persons can be held *responsible* for their actions. That *fault* can be ascribed to an individual. This matters greatly, both in terms of practice, and in terms of theory. From the Code's point of view, human beings are not like machines reacting to stimuli, but moral agents, who have the capacity to control their actions to such a high degree that, when directing their actions at harming another, they can be deemed normatively culpable of doing so.

The Code contains many more norms based on presuppositions about humans – that they can deceive one another, pretend to make promises, err with respect to the facts, and so on. My goal in this section (and chapter) is not to reconstruct a full picture of a "private law human," but rather to (i) demonstrate that the law *presupposes* such a picture; (ii) provide its general sketch; (iii) suggest that it might be counterfactual. Based on the analysis up to this point, let us see what qualities, in general, our *homo legalis privatus* has.

11.3.2 Homo Legalis Privatus vs. Homo Sapiens

The private law human – an abstract entity, a model agent presupposed by the law – has free will and intentions; can express them and understand others' expressions;

can control her behavior, regarding both choosing to contract and to harm others, and as a result, can be held responsible for her choices. She is rational, both in the sense of understanding the meaning and the consequences of her actions, and in the sense of acting in accordance with the goals and principles she adopts. She is both an economic actor and a normative agent. These qualities might be absent in case of "any mental disorder/ distortion of mental faculties," but as a matter of rule, are common to all humans. According to private law, at least.

What does cognitive science tell us about these presuppositions?

Put simply: these assumptions are *not untrue*, but the *full truth* is significantly more complicated. Cognitive science teaches us that actual humans possess these qualities to a varying and sometimes limited degree, cautions us against adopting strong binaries (e.g. perfectly rational vs. irrational), and provides tools to test specific assumptions. It demonstrates not only that humans are different from one another, but also that the same person can be more rational/conscious/understanding when rested and happy than when tired and stressed about work. It explains how and why the simple binaries – like free will vs. determinism, perfect rationality vs. irrationality, or full ability vs. inability to direct one's actions – render us unable to explain many real-life situations.

Daniel Kahneman, in his *Thinking Fast and Slow* (2011), a book summarizing his lifetime's work with Amos Tversky, proposes to conceptualize human cognition as metaphorical cooperation between System 1 and System 2. System 1 is responsible for quick, intuitive, and automatic judgments, requiring little time and mental effort – fast thinking. System 2 is the logical, deliberative, and conscious "agent" in human mental processes, taking a lot of time and energy – slow thinking. According to Kahneman, most human decisions, judgments, and activities are undertaken by System 1. It is responsible for "naturally automatic" processes, like breathing; acquired skills that become automatic (like moving your eyes when reading, moving your fingers when typing on a keyboard or playing instruments); and mental operations that we often conduct (like simple addition or deciding whether to take an umbrella by looking at the sky). System 2 is the one that comes into play whenever no mental shortcuts (intuitions, heuristics, habits) are available.

To understand this relationship, consider a hypothetical example. Imagine going to a new supermarket, where you do not know what types of goods are being offered, nor where they are located. Shopping there for the first time will take quite some mental effort: you will need to compare prices and quality of goods you have not seen before, look for the things you need, and you might change your mind when seeing yet another product. If you are listening to a podcast upon entering, you will turn it off – System 2 needs to be fully concentrated on the task. The fiftieth time you shop there, most of your movements and choices will be automatic, and you might be able to handle a phone conversation or listening to an audiobook at the same time. All human activity could be understood as an attempt to optimize our actions by gradually reassigning them from System 2 to System 1.

However, System 1 often makes mistakes. Kahneman and many others (Fruehwald, 2018) have demonstrated the existence of so-called "cognitive biases," that is, mistakes humans are prone to make under some conditions. For example, when assessing a price of a product, we might be misled if a much higher "initial" price (for example, $99.99) is displayed next to the new, lower (but still too high) price (ONLY $39.99!). We will assess not the *actual* value of the product, but the *supposedly new* price in comparison to the old one.

Moreover, System 2 is not a super-computer either. There is only a limited amount of work it can handle at the same time. Christopher Chabris and Daniel Simons (2011) describe an experiment where participants watched a video of two groups passing basketballs and were asked to count how many times one group passed the ball, while ignoring the other group. The video also featured a person in a gorilla costume entering the scene, banging their chest, and leaving. The experiment found that many people concentrated so much on the task of counting passes that they literally did not notice the gorilla. This finding indicates that when we focus our attention on something, we might completely ignore some other elements, even if it is fully "available" to our perception.

Importantly, the mistakes committed by Systems 1 and 2 are *inherent* and *natural* to human thinking. Our inability to fully understand the world around us, or to always act in the ways corresponding with our goals and principles (instead of based on emotions or impulses), is the typical human condition. On top of these limitations, obviously, we might be suffering from other "distortions of mental faculties." However, to get back to presuppositions enshrined in the Polish Civil Code, a person "who does not suffer from any distortion of mental faculties" is not "able to control her behavior." Rather, she is able to control her behavior to a certain degree, subject to cognitive biases, and provided that she can concentrate on the task at hand.

In other words, private law's presuppositions about human beings are not entirely correct. We seem to presuppose the existence of an agent who is constantly able to exercise their System 2 capacities to the fullest. Such situations *do* occur, but they do not always occur, and one could argue that their occurrence is an exception rather than a rule. "This is interesting" – one might say – "but does it really matter? And if so, why?" To answer this question, we might have to ask two more fundamental ones: "Why does private law hold presuppositions about humans?" and "What is it that private law tries to achieve?"

11.3.3 What Threshold: Truth or Usefulness? Or: Does Private Law Aim to Guide Behavior?

Why does private law hold presuppositions about humans? Leaving aside the purely linguistic reasons for this,[10] one should ask: what is the goal of private law? What is it

---

[10] It might be impossible to formulate imperative statements that do not contain descriptive presuppositions.

that, as a society, we want to achieve by building our shared lives around the institutions of property, contract, and tort? Why do we choose to rely on private relations amongst formally equal persons, and not, for example, on a centrally planned economy or an aristocratic society where one's status dictates one's possessions, occupation, and relation toward others? Economics, as a discipline, makes assumptions about humans to increase the explanatory and predictive power of their models. Economists are less interested in whether their assumptions are true than whether they are useful for explaining reality. Neuroscience, on the other hand, tries to establish causal links between activations in various parts of a brain and human experience. Natural scientists will often seek the truth, rather than a useful fiction. What is it that private law, not as a scholarly discipline, but as a shared experience of practices enabled by norms, is doing for us?

Two general types of answers are available: consequentialist (we rely on private law because it brings about certain desirable results) and deontological (we rely on private law because it is a morally right thing to do, regardless of consequences). In other words, one could either claim that the role of private law is basically to guide human behavior, if not through direct commands, than by endowing persons with property and providing institutions for resource (contract) and risk (tort) allocation (Posner, 2011). Or, equally plausibly, one could claim that the role of private law is precisely *not* to guide behavior, but rather to delegate choices on what to do to the individuals themselves. The former view, best exemplified by the field of economic analysis of law, looks at the law instrumentally and will judge it based on how well it fares in leading us to the desired outcome. It is within this logic that in *The Law of the Horse* Lawrence Lessig (1999) wrote: "As the Legal Realists spent a generation teaching, and as we seem so keen to forget: contract law is *public* law" (emphasis original). The latter view, typical for Europeans, would see the private law society as a value in itself (Böhm, 1966), and be less concerned with its societal impact, and more with the actual realization of the autonomy of private persons.

The difficulty is that both justifications hold at the same time. Or, to be less extreme: Both viewpoints seem to be necessary to fully explain why the Western liberal democracies all decided to build their shared social lives on the institutions of private law. However, the roles of presuppositions about humans in both logics – *usefulness* in behavioral models' construction, and *truth* in the quest of fully grasping the complexities of the human condition – are different, and not always fully alignable. Consider some examples.

In a complex society, with a significant division of labor, we need to allocate the scarce resources somehow. We care about efficiency, both in the sense of maximizing overall wealth and in the sense of assigning resources to those who need/make the best use of them. However, it is impossible to make a list of all available goods and all the existing demands – the nature of this type of knowledge proves to be local, dispersed, and time-dependent (Hayek, 1945). You know what kinds of things you need and that you can contribute, I know what I need and can contribute. You need potatoes now, I need a bike within a week. I know that my uncle just had a bountiful potato harvest and needs workers to help him. I also know that my neighbor broke his hip and will be selling his bike. I can tell my unemployed friend about the work opportunity, you can buy the food, and I can purchase the bike. Decisions and transactions like this occur all the time, every day, and it would be literally impossible to aggregate this knowledge and distribute goods through a central plan. Hence, the state grants the people property rights and the competence to contract about labor and goods to *make them signal the knowledge and to engage in exchanges*. To choose optimal rules of contract, and to enact food- and bike-safety regulations ensuring overall health without stifling commerce, we do not need to know much about how people really are. We just need assumptions that will increase the explanatory and predictive power of our models. For, within this view, rules are like models – the lawmaker, when pondering changing them, will inquire into the changes' consequences on individual behavior.

However, at the same time, we would be cautious to strip people of their property or the right to contract once their behavior becomes inefficient. We might want to ponder various mechanisms to "nudge" them to behave more efficiently (Thaler & Sunstein, 2008), but there is something fundamental about everyone's right to own assets and to choose where to work and what to do with the fruits of their labor. Ever since John Locke, many people in Western societies have held the view that everyone *deserves* to own property and enjoy the autonomy of choice. If we follow this line of thinking, a hypothetical situation where people *do* behave efficiently but cannot really exercise actual choices and freedom, becomes morally problematic. Within this view, where the goal of private law is not to guide anyone's behavior, but rather to endow persons with full and conscious choices and autonomy, it very much matters whether they *actually* understand their decisions and pursue their subjective, personally defined goals and intentions. Within this view, private law norms allow the state to step back and delegate the normative choices to private law humans. The law only facilitates human conduct by granting powers (Hage, 2013), but does not prescribe how these powers should be used, let alone what citizens ought to do in general.

Similarly, one can think of tort law from both perspectives. In modern society, people can engage in certain inherently risky activities, like driving cars. There is a benefit to having traffic – people and goods can move around efficiently – but there is also an inherent risk – accidents will occur, some people will lose their health, and some will lose lives. If we institute a liability regime where people need to compensate those that they harm, they will adjust their behavior to the optimal level of care (Calabresi, 1965). On the individual level, if I know that I must compensate someone I harm through my negligent behavior, I will act with more care (the law would assume). In this sense, tort law is about guiding people's behavior – do not harm others, and if the harm is inherent in the activity, exercise caution. However, at the same time, we believe in the value of corrective and restorative justice. Regardless of whether the financial transfer is efficient, or what the broader societal implications are, we believe that if someone was harmed, she should be compensated. Seen from this perspective, private law does not say: "do not engage in activity X," but rather "if you chose to do X, be ready to own your action and accept the consequences." Tort law is both about guiding behavior *and* about leaving decisions entirely to the persons concerned.

One should bear this inherent tension in mind when trying to evaluate the private law's presuppositions about humans through the findings of cognitive science. Some assumptions might be untrue (for example, that when people sign contracts, they have read them) but useful. Before jumping to conclusions on how to change the law, in order to make it better reflect the human condition, one should carefully assess the role a particular presupposition plays in the broader picture.

With this in mind, let us take a closer look at two sets of particular presuppositions. First, I would invite the reader to ponder three fundamental assumptions about persons: that they have free will, that they are rational, and that they can be held responsible for their actions. Then, I will look at how challenging some specific assumptions can be useful in the process of rule-making (if one wishes to guide behavior through private law rules) and contract drafting.

11.3.4 Fundamentals: Free Will, Rationality, Culpability

Free will might be the most central feature of the *homo legalis privatus*. Its importance is so great that (in some jurisdictions) contracts (and other juridical acts) concluded by a person who "was not able to act consciously and freely, even temporarily" are null and void *ex lege*. The significance of free will for the law should not come as a surprise in the Western world which, for good or for bad, has been forged in relationship Christianity, which treats the free will of humans as the fundamental quality of persons in its metaphysics. The question of whether humans are *actually* free has bothered philosophers for centuries now, with elaborate arguments offered for both affirmative and negative answers (Balaguer, 2014). All this amplified the shock everyone experienced when Benjamin Libet (1993) published his experimental findings supposedly proving that free will is an illusion.

In a neuroscientific experiment, Libet asked people to perform a simple task (pushing a button) and to also report the time when they made the decision to do so. Simultaneously, he measured the activation levels in the parts of the brain responsible for making the decision. He found that the brain activation occurred 300 milliseconds *before* persons experienced making the decision to press the button. One way to look at this finding is to claim that our experience of free will is simply a post hoc rationalization of an exogenous decision "taken" by our brain. Libet himself did not argue for such a strong position, but added that, even though decisions might be independent of our will, we still retain the capacity to "veto" our brain and refrain from undertaking the action (Libet, 1993). Others argued against these interpretations of his findings, pointing out that the activation levels of a brain should not be equated with "brain deciding," but rather "getting us ready to decide" (Passingham, 2016). The societal reception of this experiment sparked a renewed interest in the intersections between hard science and philosophy, forcing many to reconsider the interpretation of experimental data within (implicit) metaphysical frames (Mele, 2014). Nevertheless, results like this should make us pause and ask us to at least clarify what is it exactly that we mean when assuming that actions of humans are "free" for the purposes of private law.

The theme of free will is linked to the question of human rationality. "Rationality" can mean different things, from "understanding our actions and their consequences," to "acting based on cold reasoning rather than emotions," to "aligning our choices with professed goals and values," to "adopting utility-maximizing as the goal." Findings of scholars like Kahneman (analyzed in Section 11.3.2) put into question the presupposition that any of these features (even if present in humans) are unconditional. "Fast thinking," leading us to tortious actions or purchases we later regret, is a natural element of the human condition. Acting upon emotions, or making mistakes, does not mean that humans are never rational. Rather, it means that our idea of rationality might have been an ideal never fully occurring in the real world. Should this be a reason to modify the assumptions of private law? It depends on how we see its role in society.

The problem of culpability best exemplifies the tensions between presuppositions and reality, and between private law's goal of guiding behavior and of only facilitating the actions of persons choosing their own goals. Should we treat humans as agents responsible for their actions? On the one hand, one could argue that their actual features do not matter for this question. If, through behavioral studies, we can prove that tort law *does* have an impact on individual conduct, and having to compensate for causing harm *does* serve as a deterrent, it really is of no importance whether humans actually make free and rational decisions to act or to refrain from acting. What matters is that the policy goal is achieved. However, if what we care about is the culpability of particular persons, and the question of whether they, in the light of what cognitive science teaches us, *really deserve* to be held liable, their mental states and processes might be *all* that we care about. Taking both views to the extreme could lead us to exactly opposite results: whenever mental disorders are absent, culpability is always a useful assumption and should be employed; and, since we can (almost) never actually be sure whether a person made a fully free and conscious decision, holding persons responsible for their actions is always unjust.

Since private law is a matter of everyday life, societies do not have the luxury to leave questions like these to philosophers and scholars alone. Some version of an answer to this question is always given by the current state of private law. This answer impacts individuals' lives and social relations. The more prudent way of using cognitive science to question the fundamental presuppositions that private law holds about individuals seems to be to follow its own insights: embrace the complexity and avoid strong binaries. Instead of asking: "Do people have free will? Are people rational? Can they be held responsible for their actions?" we should try to square the competing visions of private law's role in our societies with the empirical findings. There will be no one, correct answer to the question: "What features of humans should private law assume?" A range of equally good answers (on top of many bad ones, of course) will always exist, and will depend on normative choices taken by both scholars theorizing the problem and the societies living it.

"That's all interesting" – you might think again – "but *really*, does it matter? Or are we just talking about concepts that, in the end, have no bearing on everyday life?" I am tempted to argue that, paraphrasing a famous line by J. M. Keynes,[11] nothing has as much influence on everyday life as general concepts about human nature. That, however, is a subject for another paper. Let me then move to three concrete examples on how the findings of cognitive science can help with private rule-making: contract drafting, consumer empowerment through disclosure and information duties, and trying to use private fines as a means of steering behavior.

11.3.5 Cognitive Science and Private Law-Making

Imagine you are drafting a contract. Let us assume you want the other party to comprehend it fully. For example, it might be a nondisclosure agreement, carefully outlining what types of information she is (not) allowed to share with others. Or, it might be a specification of an intricate piece of work you are procuring. Generally, when dealing with professional entities, the law assumes that signing a contract is equal to having read and understood it. If the signee breaches, she will have to compensate. However, you suspect this might not always be the case. Imagine a situation in which your preference for nonbreach is high (because you want to minimize a chance of judicial proceedings or the other party is highly skilled, but not solvent enough to cover the damages of a breach); and you have reason to assume that if the breach occurs, this will result from a misunderstanding. What you want to achieve is a contract design that maximizes the other party's understanding. Cognitive science, dealing with attention, perception, and comprehension, is a valuable resource in this regard. Daniel Kahneman reports how simply bolding a part of a text makes readers concentrate on it (Kahneman, 2011). Moreover, legal-design researchers studying contract comprehension have empirically demonstrated how rearranging the form, sequence, and visual layout of contracts can increase the

---

[11] "The ideas of economists and political philosophers, both when they are right and when they are wrong are more powerful than is commonly understood. Indeed, the world is ruled by little else. Practical men, who believe themselves to be quite exempt from any intellectual influences, are usually slaves of some defunct economist." See John Maynard Keynes (1936), *The General Theory of Employment, Interest and Money*. Keynes wrote about economics, but his insight is equally powerful regarding philosophy, law, and political theory.

speed of reading and contract comprehension (Passera, 2015). Stefania Passera measured understanding of the same contract arranged in different ways, and found that "visual display of information (visually perceptible information design solutions in terms of layout, typography and iconic language) is necessary, in addition to a logical structure of the text, in order to make the meaning of contract clauses clearer to readers" (Passera, 2015). This finding has a double significance for contract drafters. First, adding elements like pictures or graphs might make a contract look less serious, but increase the chances of comprehension. Second, the understandability of a contract can be empirically tested. If a party has a strong preference for contract understanding, cognitive science offers the tools to compare how well various models fare.

However, one needs to be aware that this approach can be a double-edged sword. A bad-faith business which needs to meet transparency requirements, but at the same time wishes to keep some information hidden in the "fine print," might also use cognitive science to achieve an equilibrium point between seeming clarity and factual noncomprehension. This is not to mention entities that might explicitly try to design hard-to-understand contracts, exploiting the assumption the law makes about professional parties. Nevertheless, even here cognitive science might provide tools for better understanding the strategies of bad-faith contractors.

Second, consider consumer-oriented disclosure duties as an example of private law trying to minimize the factual information asymmetry between formally equal parties. These duties concern, for example, statements of risk given to consumers buying financial products ("Investing in X-type funds comes with a risk of loss"), nutritional boxes found on food products ("a serving of this product contains 20 per cent of an average persons' daily need for sugar"), or privacy policies ("we collect and use your data for the purposes of improving our services"). Those duties are usually imposed by consumer law in situations where the lawmakers assume that individuals might need to know something in order to make a fully informed decision, while the businesses will not have an incentive to provide this information unprompted. Informational boxes on cigarette packets ("Smoking causes cancer") or warnings read at the end of commercials for pharmaceutical products ("Before using this product, consult your doctor") are another example of the same trend.

According to Omri Ben-Shahar and Carl Schneider, mandated disclosure is one of the most prominent, while at the same probably least useful, regulatory tools in consumer law (Ben-Shahar & Schneider, 2014). Sometime in the past, we assumed that if consumers "have" more information, they will make more "reasonable" or at least more "informed" market decisions. The problem, however, is that simply making some information available to consumers does not mean that they will read it. Moreover, even if they read it, that does not mean that they will comprehend it; and even if they comprehend it, that does not mean that they will be able to take it into account while making a complex decision (Solove, 2013). The assumption that making information available will lead to reasonable consumer choices is particularly strong in American consumer privacy law, where consumers' acceptance of a "privacy policy" when interacting with online traders is equated with their "choice" of a certain level of privacy in exchange for an optimal price (Pałka, 2020). As Ben-Shahar and Schneider argue, certain types of knowledge are so specialized, and decisions so complex (which type of financing of a mortgage to choose? What cancer treatment to purchase?) that they should be taken away from the market and placed in the hands of specialists. At the same time, they argue, the existence of disclosure duties, paired with the belief in the value of individual choice, and the presumption that humans are able to comprehend and reason on the basis of the disclosed information, takes responsibility away from regulators who, instead of trying to solve complex problems, simply say that they "trust the choices of people."

Such problems persist in consumer financial products, food, and pharmaceuticals. These findings have led some scholars to argue against disclosure as a means of regulation (Ben-Shahar & Schneider, 2014). Those are valid criticisms, especially when treating disclosure as the *primary* regulatory tool. However, cognitive science can be of help with increasing the understandability of existing disclosure mechanisms. We could experiment with various forms of information conferring, and scientifically test how well they fare. For example, we could try to play with the color, location, and font of certain vital pieces of information. Or, we could try to see if the tone of voice with which warnings are read affects comprehension, and if so, require a particular standard. Or, we could ponder using more visual forms of information conferring (sugar cubes on soda cans, for example). The fact that persons have trouble comprehending a lot of information might be a reason to regulate more, while at the same time should not be the reason to give up on conferring information at all.

Consumer law, and in general the "behavior modification" part of private law, demonstrates that not all presuppositions about humans engrained in law are "descriptive" in nature; some are political. Consider the debate that European private lawyers are having about the image of the consumer that the law does, and should, adopt (Leczykiewicz & Weatherhill, 2016). Should we imagine a consumer to be "reasonable," or "vulnerable," or "well-informed"? Such a decision has far-reaching normative consequences. However, it will not only be based on how consumers "actually are," but also on our political choices regarding the types of protection we want the law to offer.

Third, consider the problem of using private fines as a means of influencing behavior. We tend to assume that if the cost of a specific activity goes up, this activity will occur less often. However, this might not always be the case. In a famous study of Israeli day-care centers, Gneezy and Rustichini (2000) tested the impact of monetary fines on behavior. Parents were supposed to pick up their children from day care at a specific hour, but many of them often came late. In some of the day-care centers, a fine was introduced for picking up children after hours. Instead of arriving on time more often, the parents started coming late more often and simply paid the fine.

When the fine was dropped, their behavior did not return to the pre-fine levels. The authors explained this phenomenon by suggesting that whereas coming late (and so forcing a teacher to stay longer at work) was seen as a social wrong before the fine's introduction, upon the introduction of the fine, parents started treating this as a price. The logic shifted, from a social relation to a market transaction. As surprising as this finding was, it offers us a valuable lesson: sometimes, if people can pay for inflicting a wrong on someone else, they will choose to do so, even if they would refrain from doing so when they do not need to compensate.

This can be helpful when trying to minimize the undesirable behavior of clients. For example, when people call a taxi and make the driver wait, imposing a fine might be a less successful deterrent than sending a text reading "Being late is impolite; you are wasting someone else's time now." Or, if we want people not to use pencils on the pages of books checked out from the library, instead of fining them, we might include a description of a librarian who, instead of helping other readers, must now sit there with an eraser. Or, instead of fining people who drop litter in parks, put up signs there showing sad people sitting on a grass lawn full of cans. Again, the lesson is twofold: contrary to our assumptions, increasing the monetary costs might not necessarily lead to a decrease in some behavior; and alternative strategies (like those outlined above) can be experimentally tested, either as parts of scholarly studies or simply by using them and observing the impact.

11.4 COGNITIVE SCIENCE AND NEW TYPES OF GOODS AND PRIVATE LAW RELATIONS

Up until now, I have analyzed how private law could critically scrutinize its presuppositions about humans with the help of cognitive science. However, the vision of the world presupposed by private law consists not just of actors, but also the types of relations they engage in, the types of activities they undertake, and the types of objects they control and trade. The reality of everyday life in the private law society has been rapidly transforming over the last couple of decades, largely due to the development of cognitive knowledge by private corporations. Meanwhile, private law is still trying to make sense of the world using concepts and categories developed in a different era. Granted, many of them are useful, but to comprehend the world governed by private law in its entirety, an update may be necessary. And cognitive science can help us with this update.

Consider what the building blocks of the private law society are, as assumed by the law. Private persons (humans and corporations) own property, conclude contracts, and (sometimes) harm one another. When they conclude contracts, one of them usually makes an offer, and another one will negotiate and/or accept it. Sometimes they will conclude a contract of labor or for a service; sometimes they sell and/or license goods. The goods they control are tangible objects (movables and immovables, or chattels and realty) and intangible entities. Intangibles can be further divided into rights, company shares, intellectual property (works, inventions, trademarks), and other types. Whenever making offers, persons should not deceive one another – they are required to provide true information, or otherwise risk the consequences stipulated in rules regulating unfair commercial practices.

What is missing from this picture, if we compare it to our shared experience of everyday life? First, knowledge. The law assumes that knowledge about the world and about market actors is generally available to the public, and in situations where it is not, it requires market actors to disclose that knowledge (see the previous section). Second, advertisements. Classic private law almost does not notice ads, and if forced to classify them somehow, usually treats them as "invitations to make an offer." Third, private coercion. Law assumes that the only entity which can legitimately force persons to do something is the state. However, as we shall see, big chunks of consumer markets rely on the business model of behavior modification. In the next two subsections I would like to show how cognitive science can help us understand two new phenomena: the emergence of "private cognitive science" and of "cognitive goods" currently traded as commodities.

11.4.1 The Emergence of the "Private Cognitive Science"

George should not have stayed at the party that long. And he probably should not have drunk that one last beer. Or three. Now, awoken by the deafening sound of the alarm clock he forgot to turn off, he is lying in bed, too tired to get up, yet too restless to fall back asleep. George grabs his smartphone, opens a social media app, and scrolls mindlessly through the feed featuring photos of his friends, news stories, and Star Wars memes. Suddenly, he sees a video ad – marked as one, though gently incorporated into the whole experience – of a mouthpiece robotic toothbrush. Attractive and well-rested-looking people place the device in their mouths, and proceed to do something else with their hands – text a friend, make tea, or just relax on a sofa – while this fantastic product, by itself, provides them with the experience of clean teeth and a fresh mouth. "That's exactly what I need right now" – thinks George while tapping on the ad. His smartphone autofills the address and the credit card number, and in less than two minutes, George becomes the owner of a robotic mouthpiece toothbrush, on its way to his place with "free" one-day delivery.

Consider what is familiar in this story and what is novel, from the private law perspective. Some company invents a new product and tries to market it skillfully – nothing new. A consumer engages in a long-distance purchase, without examining the product first – the law grants him protection (Luzak, 2014). He does not even have to call anyone, only taps his smartphone – this we might consider an important change, though arguably quantitative rather than qualitative. The ad he sees is specifically tailored to him, at this very moment – this is where our focus should sharpen.

Though audience segmentation in marketing has become an established practice (Draper & Turow, 2017), the ability to fine-tune the timing, form, and content of an ad to maximize the chance of a *single* purchase is a qualitative shift in how the advertisement business operates. Not only are the ads based on data about a particular consumer, seen against the data about everyone else (Pałka, 2020), but also, companies can continuously experiment with the timing, form, and context of the ads they display, through trial-and-error procedures. It is possible to show an ad with a pink font to a random selection of 1,000 people, and with a blue font to another random 1,000, and see how this change affects their behavior. The ad-delivery systems have become their own feedback providers, capable of assessing the success and failure of a given strategy in real time. The online marketplace is, in a way, the biggest laboratory a cognitive scientist could ever dream about. Corporations have constructed an environment where they can conduct studies on both consumer behavior, and those consumers' emotions and thoughts.

In 2014, Facebook's core science team published a paper summarizing the effects of an experiment conducted on a group of 689,003 platform users, titled *Experimental Evidence of Massive-Scale Emotional Contagion Through Social Networks* (Kramer et al., 2014). The researchers demonstrated, on the basis of a sample of 0.7 million people (*sic*!) that emotions are contagious, that based on what users see on their news feeds their feelings will change, and that this process can be consciously directed by the team running the platform. This paper was not only a contribution to cognitive science but also a show of strength by Facebook. Amidst criticism, the company's executives apologized for not obtaining properly informed consent from the experiment's participants, although they argued that this had been consistent with their terms of use and privacy policies (Gibbs, 2014). Nevertheless, the lesson learned by Facebook was not to stop engaging in these experiments; the lesson was to stop publishing the results, or conceptualizing them as "science."

Cognitive scientists, when experimenting on humans, need to abide by codes of ethics, secure the informed consent of participants, and in most cases obtain approval from an ethics committee. A private corporation testing its ability to engage in "successful marketing" faces no such requirements. Clearly, there are rules on what is not allowed in advertising, but the threshold pertains to the potential "misleading" nature of commercial communications (Howells, Micklitz, & Wilhelmsson, 2016). One could argue that the personal data protection law enacted in the European Union (EU) (the General Data Protection Regulation, or GDPR) places significant constraints on traders, who now need to obtain consent for such practices as a matter of law, regardless of whether they call their activities "research" or not. However, the extent to which the GDPR will really affect corporate behavior is yet to be seen, with no spectacular changes having happened within the first two years of its application. As we begin the third decade of the twenty-first century, the largest entities capable of conducting cognitive experiments are not universities, but corporations; and their primary intentions are not "contributions to a field," but making money.

11.4.2 Markets in the "Cognitive Goods": Our Thoughts and Behavior

The emergence of "private cognitive science," paired with the promise of high returns upon its "application" in product design and marketing, is tacitly transforming the digital marketplace, that is, the very domain of private law's governance. The trade concerning new types of "commodities" is booming and power relations are shifting. Private law both played a role in the creation of this world and could be one of the tools used to tame its negative effects. Let us first take a closer look at the phenomena, and then ponder their relation to private law.

First, the value of data about individual behavior is growing. As we have seen, such information can improve the accuracy of online advertising. Since the more information a company has, the better results it will deliver, and the more time a user spends on the platform, the more ads he or she will see, there exists an incentive to make users spend as much time on the platform as possible. Researchers have demonstrated how, in order to act upon these incentives, corporations deliberately design their products to be addictive (Balkin, 2018; Lanier, 2018). This design, in turn, will be more effective given the data corporations can collect about the time users spend using their services, depending on various engagement strategies. Hence, the circle closes. There is value in data, so companies collect them whenever they can; and if they cannot obtain them themselves, they have reasons to buy them. As a result, markets in personal data emerge (Draper, 2019), data that, for a cognitive scientist, would look like research material.

Second, we begin to appreciate the market value of human attention. Online giants like Facebook or Google now act as "attention merchants," to use a phrase coined by Tim Wu in his tremendous account of the history of the marketing industry (Wu, 2017). With direct communication channels linked to our smartphones, and the ability to experiment and to make us into addicts, these firms continually refine their "knowledge" about grasping attention, in order to later sell it as a commodity. In this view, users of Facebook and Google are not so much customers, as the "product" sold to the real clients, that is, other corporations (Williams, 2018). Legal scholars have begun to reflect upon the relationship between attention and law, also from the perspective of property and contract (Newman, 2019). The legal scholarship could tremendously benefit from engaging with the work of cognitive scientists aimed at understanding how human attention works, while cognitivists might discover yet another venue in which to apply the results of their basic research.

Third, once in possession of users' data, their attention, and the ability to influence their thoughts and behavior, online companies began trading these thoughts and that behavior as commodities too. Obviously, no one would explicitly characterize the service in these words, but effectively, this is what is happening. As far back as 2014, Jonathan Zittrain was theorizing how Facebook could "flip" the results of an election (Zittrain, 2014). By modifying what users (do not) see on their feeds, the company will probably not be able to turn liberals into conservatives, or vice versa; but it might be able to convince supporters of one political party to stay at home instead of going to vote. Not all of them, not even a majority of them; but just enough (2 percent? 4 percent?) to change the ultimate result. Two years later, in the aftermath of the Cambridge Analytica scandal, we realized that precisely this had happened in the American election which, contrary to almost all predictions, elevated Donald Trump to the presidency (Rosenberg, Confessore, & Cadwalladr, 2018), and in the United Kingdom where, by a close margin, the Brits voted to leave the European Union. It was not that Facebook itself supported one political option over the other in any way. However, it created a tool, based on data collection, attention sales, and refined marketing experiments, which was later exploited by a company working for the Trump and Leave campaigns.

Soshana Zuboff has proposed a theory of an economy where this type of business model is allowed to flourish as "surveillance capitalism" (Zuboff, 2019). In her view, the most accurate classification of the business model based on data collection, attention grasping, and monetizing both through revenues from micro-targeted behavioral advertising is to see it as a "market in behavioral futures." Statistically speaking, the owner of an ad delivery system can promise that X amount of people will act in the way wanted by the advertiser (purchase a product, change their mind on a certain issue, go to vote, or stay home). Since this future behavior is no longer a matter of uncertainty but probability (Knight, 2012), even before the actual revenues occur, it can be traded as a security, akin to any other stock.

All these changes occur because tech companies are developing their "private cognitive science." To fully appreciate them, lawyers need to rely on methods and insights from cognitive science. And for cognitive scientists to theorize them properly, they need to understand the role played in these changes by private law.

Even though classic private law does not "see" human behavior, emotions, and thoughts as "property," it indirectly contributed to the emergence of these markets. Contract law serves as a legitimizing tool for practices that, otherwise, we could deem unethical or borderline illegal. When criticized for its 2012 experiment, Facebook apologized, yet claimed that everything it had done was lawful, since the users had previously accepted the terms of service and privacy policies stipulating that the company had the right to engage in this type of behavior. And, legally speaking, they were correct. One could imagine challenging these contracts as unconscionable in the United States, or as containing unfair contractual terms in the EU (Loos & Luzak, 2016; Micklitz, Pałka, &

Panagis, 2017), but as of today, no binding case law or direct legislation makes them clearly unlawful.

Property law, on the other hand, contributed to the emergence of "private cognitive science" by refraining from stepping in. Since "data" are not treated as anyone's property, upon capture, companies do not fear individual challenges to data collection and usage. Julie Cohen calls this the "biopolitical public domain," where anyone with factual capabilities is legally allowed to use data about individual behavior (Cohen, 2019). It just so happens that the only types of entity possessing such abilities are tech companies, controlling the algorithms and contracts which govern the platforms.

Understanding the legal strategies employed by companies to justify their engagement in "private cognitive science" seems to me to be a step we should take before engaging in any prescriptive arguments on how to change the law. Many such suggestions have already been offered, including calls to treat those companies as "information fiduciaries," with obligations akin to those of doctors or researchers (Balkin, 2015); recognizing the de facto property status of personal data and granting individuals some *erga omnes* effective rights in such data (Purtova, 2015); moving away from individual consent and contract, toward full-fledged regulation (Pałka, 2020); or treating data provision as labor, worthy of proper remuneration and (potentially) labor protections (Posner & Weyl, 2018).

However, even though there might be reasons to act quickly, there are never reasons to act hastily. Understanding how "private cognitive science" transforms the digital marketplace, either for its own sake or as a first step toward suggesting a comprehensive legislative response, will be one of the most fertile grounds for collaboration between (private) law scholars and cognitive scientists. Those dealing in our emotions, thoughts, and behavior are skilled legal and cognitive "engineers." Their efforts should be met with equally interdisciplinary expertise.

11.5 CONCLUSION

Neither Melanie nor Nikolas have actually discovered any secrets about making money on the beach. Not directly, at least. Relying on their intuition, not backed by scientific publications, albeit supported by the general experience of young lawyers and other professionals, they went to Cuba to "recharge their batteries," relax, so that upon their return to New York and Berlin, their work might become more efficient. Cognitive science, understood in one way or another, has a lot of insights to offer legal scholars and practitioners.

In this chapter, I have argued that cognitive science can help us scrutinize the assumptions about human beings tacitly made in law, as well as help us draft more effective rules, in form and in content. The image of a human presupposed by private law – *homo legalis privatus* – is someone with free will, consciously directing her behavior to align with adopted goals and intentions, and understanding the consequences of her actions to such an extent that she might be held responsible for concluded contracts and committed torts. Cognitive science does not compel us to deem any of these assumptions *untrue* or *incorrect* – but it does invite more caution when adopting strong binaries and assuming that humans always perform at the peak of their capacity. How to assess these presuppositions (in other words: what the findings of cognitive science mean for law) will depend on one's normative view of the role of private law in our societies. Those seeing private law as an instrument for guiding behavior might concentrate on whether these assumptions are *useful* for increasing the explanatory power of models and rules' effectiveness in steering private conduct. Those concentrating on private law's deontological character might be more interested in whether these assumptions are *true*, and whether they best reflect the human condition as it actually is. Given that private law, in reality, serves several functions at the same time, it will be up to individual researchers – including the reader! – to argue for the position they deem most important. In the meantime, cognitive science can help us on the micro-scale, showing how to increase (or decrease) readability of contracts, how to best inform consumers about features of consumer products and the risks associated with them, or how to guide behavior through privately drafted rules and/or signals.

I have also drawn the reader's attention to the emergence of a novel phenomenon – "private cognitive science" – partly caused by, and partly demanding response from, private law. Cognitive science not only teaches us more about what humans *are*, but also enables private corporations to engage in new types of activities (micro-targeted behavioral advertising) and has led to the emergence of new types of objects of private law relations (human thoughts, emotions, and future behavior).

Whatever research path we take, I am certain that countless illuminating discoveries await us. Dozens of questions remain unanswered, and many more unasked. Should we succeed, the theoretical advancements and societal benefits could be significant. That is, of course, assuming that anyone will read them. Which might be tricky, in an era of omnipresent addictive distractions, developed with the help of cognitive science and given a green light by private law. Feel free to tweet about it!

REFERENCES

Alpaydin, E. (2016). *Machine Learning: The New AI*. Cambridge, MA: MIT Press.
Balaguer, M. (2014). *Free Will*. Cambridge, MA: MIT Press.
Balkin, J. M. (2015). Information Fiduciaries and the First Amendment. *UCDL Review*, 49, 1183.
Balkin, J. M. (2018). *Fixing Social Media's Grand Bargain*. Hoover Working Group on National Security, Technology, and Law, Aegis Series Paper (1814).
Bar-Gill, O. (2012). *Seduction by Contract: Law, Economics, and Psychology in Consumer Markets*. Oxford: Oxford University Press.

Bartol, C. R., & Bartol, A. M. (2019). *Psychology and Law: Research and Practice*. Los Angeles: SAGE.
Ben-Shahar, O., & Schneider, C. E. (2014). *More Than You Wanted to Know: The Failure of Mandated Disclosure*. Princeton, NJ: Princeton University Press.
Benson, P. (2001). *The Theory of Contract Law: New Essays*. Cambridge: Cambridge University Press.
Blitz, M. J. (2017). *Searching Minds by Scanning Brains: Neuroscience Technology and Constitutional Privacy Protection*. Cham: Springer.
Böhm, F. (1966). Privatrechtsgesellschaft und Marktwirtschaft. *ORDO: Jahrbuch Für Die Ordnung von Wirtschaft und Gesellschaft* 17, 75–151. www.jstor.org/stable/23742267.
Brożek, B. (2017a). Neuroscience and the Ontology of Law. *Polish Law Review* 3(1).
Brożek, B. (2017b). The Troublesome "Person." In *Legal Personhood: Animals, Artificial Intelligence and the Unborn*. Cham: Springer, pp. 3–13.
Brożek, B. (2019). *The Legal Mind: A New Introduction to Legal Epistemology*. Cambridge: Cambridge University Press.
Calabresi, G. (1965). The Decision for Accidents: An Approach to Nonfault Allocation of Costs. *Harvard Law Review*, 78(4), 713–745.
Chabris, C. F., & Simons, D. (2011). *The Invisible Gorilla: And Other Ways Our Intuitions Deceive Us*. Chicago: Harmony.
Cohen, J. (2019). *Between Truth and Power: The Legal Constructions of Informational Capitalism*. New York: Oxford University Press.
Draper, N. A. (2019). *The Identity Trade: Selling Privacy and Reputation Online*. New York: NYU Press.
Draper, N. A., & Turow, J. (2017). Audience Constructions, Reputations, and Emerging Media Technologies. In Roger Brownsword, Eloise Scotford, and Karen Yeung (eds.), *The Oxford Handbook of Law, Regulation and Technology*. Oxford: Oxford University Press.
Fruehwald, E. S. (2018). *Understanding and Overcoming Cognitive Biases for Lawyers and Law Students: Becoming a Better Lawyer Through Cognitive Science*. San Bernandino, CA: CreateSpace.
Gibbs, S. (2014, July 2). Facebook Apologises for Psychological Experiments on Users. *The Guardian*. www.theguardian.com/technology/2014/jul/02/facebook-apologises-psychological-experiments-on-users
Gneezy, U., & Rustichini, A. (2000). A Fine Is a Price. *The Journal of Legal Studies* 29(1), 1–17.
Gordley, J. (2006). *Foundations of Private Law: Property, Tort, Contract, Unjust Enrichment*. Oxford: Oxford University Press.
Granhag, P. A., Bull, R., Shaboltas, A., & Dozortseva, E. (eds.). (2016). *Psychology and Law in Europe: When West Meets East*. Boca Raton, FL: CRC Press.
Hage, J. (2011). A Model of Juridical Acts: Part 1: The World of Law. *Artificial Intelligence and Law* 19(1), 23–48.
Hage, J. (2013). Juridical Acts and the Gap Between Is and Ought. *Netherlands Journal of Legal Philosophy* 42, 50.
Hayek, F. A. (1945). The Use of Knowledge in Society. *The American Economic Review* 35(4), 519–530.
Hirstein, W., Sifferd, K., & Fagan, T. (2018). *Responsible Brains: Neuroscience, Law, and Human Culpability*. Cambridge, MA: MIT Press.
Howells, G., Micklitz, H. W., & Wilhelmsson, T. (2016). *European Fair Trading Law: The Unfair Commercial Practices Directive*. Abingdon: Routledge.

Jolls, C., Sunstein, C. R., & Thaler, R. (1998). A Behavioral Approach to Law and Economics. *Stanford Law Review*, 50, 1471–1550.

Jones, O. D., Schall, J. D., & Shen, F. X. (2014). *Law and Neuroscience*. New York: Wolters Kluwer Law & Business.

Kahneman, D. (2011). *Thinking, Fast and Slow*. London: Allen Lane.

Kaplow, L., & Shavell, S. (2009). *Fairness Versus Welfare*. Cambridge, MA: Harvard University Press.

Keynes, J. M. (1936). *The General Theory of Employment, Interest and Money*. London: Macmillan.

Knight, F. H. (2012). *Risk, Uncertainty and Profit*. North Chelmsford: Courier Corporation. (Reprint of the first edition, 1921.)

Kramer, A. D., Guillory, J. E. & Hancock, J. T. (2014). Experimental Evidence of Massive-Scale Emotional Contagion Through Social Networks. *Proceedings of the National Academy of Sciences* 111(24), 8788–8790.

Kraus, J. S. (2002). Philosophy of Contract Law. In Jules L. Coleman, Kenneth Einar Himma, & Scott J. Shapiro (eds.), *The Oxford Handbook of Jurisprudence and Philosophy of Law*. Oxford: Oxford University Press.

Lanier, J. (2018). *Ten Arguments for Deleting Your Social Media Accounts Rights Now*. New York: Henry Holt and Company.

Leczykiewicz, D., & Weatherill, S. (eds.). (2016). *The Images of the Consumer in EU Law: Legislation, Free Movement and Competition Law*. Oxford: Bloomsbury Publishing.

Lessig, L. (1999). The Law of the Horse: What Cyber Law Might Teach. *Harvard Law Review* 113, 501.

Levinson, S. C. (1983). *Pragmatics*. Cambridge: Cambridge University Press.

Libet, B. W. (1993). Neuronal vs. Subjective Timing for a Conscious Sensory Experience. In *Neurophysiology of Consciousness: Contemporary Neuroscientists* (Selected Papers of Leaders in Brain Research). Boston, MA: Birkhäuser, https://doi.org/10.1007/978-1-4612-0355-1_8

Loos, M., & Luzak, J. (2016). Wanted: A Bigger Stick. On Unfair Terms in Consumer Contracts With Online Service Providers. *Journal of Consumer Policy* 39(1), 63–90.

Lustig, R. (2017). *The Hacking of the American Mind: The Science Behind the Corporate Takeover of Our Bodies and Brains*. Harmondsworth: Penguin.

Luzak, J. A. (2014). To Withdraw or Not to Withdraw? Evaluation of the Mandatory Right of Withdrawal in Consumer Distance Selling Contracts Taking Into Account Its Behavioural Effects on Consumers. *Journal of Consumer Policy* 37(1), 91–111.

Mele, A. (2014). *Free: Why Science Hasn't Disproved Free Will*. Oxford: Oxford University Press.

Micklitz, H. W. (2009). The Visible Hand of European Regulatory Private Law – The Transformation of European Private Law from Autonomy to Functionalism in Competition and Regulation. *Yearbook of European Law* 28(1), 3-59.

Micklitz, H. W. (2018). The Politics of Behavioural Economics of Law. In H. W. Micklitz, A. L. Sibony, & F. Esposito (eds.), *Research Methods in Consumer Law: A Handbook*. Cheltenham: Edward Elgar Publishing.

Micklitz, H. W., Pałka, P., & Panagis, Y. (2017). The Empire Strikes Back: Digital Control of Unfair Terms of Online Services. *Journal of Consumer Policy* 40(3), 367–388.

Micklitz, H. W., Sibony, A. L., & Esposito, F. (eds.). (2018). *Research Methods in Consumer Law: A Handbook*. Cheltenham: Edward Elgar Publishing.

Miller, M. K., & Bornstein, B. H. (2016). *Advances in Psychology and Law*. Cham: Springer.

Mik, E. (2016). The Erosion of Autonomy in Online Consumer Transactions. *Law, Innovation & Technology* 8(1), 1–38.

Mousourakis, G. (2015). *Roman Law and the Origins of the Civil Law Tradition*. Berlin: Springer.

Newman, J. M. (2019). *Attention and the Law*. SSRN: https://papers.ssrn.com/sol3/papers.cfm?abstract_id=3423487

Pałka, P. (2020). Data Management Law for the 2020s: The Lost Origins and the New Needs. *Buffalo Law Review* 68(2).

Pardo, M. S. & Patterson, D. M. (2013). *Minds, Brains, and Law: The Conceptual Foundations of Law and Neuroscience*. Oxford, UK: Oxford University Press.

Passera, S. (2015). Beyond the Wall of Text: How Information Design Can Make Contracts User-Friendly. In *International Conference of Design, User Experience, and Usability*. Cham: Springer, pp. 341–352.

Passingham, R. (2016). *Cognitive Neuroscience: A Very Short Introduction*. Oxford: Oxford University Press.

Patterson, D. M., & Pardo, M. S. (2016). *Philosophical Foundations of Law and Neuroscience*. Oxford: Oxford University Press.

Posner, R. (2011). *Economic Analysis of Law*. New York: Aspen Publishers.

Posner, E. A., & Weyl, E. G. (2018). *Radical Markets: Uprooting Capitalism and Democracy For a Just Society*. Princeton, NJ: Princeton University Press.

Purtova, N. (2015). The Illusion of Personal Data as No One's Property. *Law, Innovation and Technology* 7(1), 83–111.

Rachlinski, J. J. (2009). *Behavioral Law and Economics*. Cheltenham: Edward Elgar.

Robbennolt, J. K., & Hans, V. P. (2016). The Psychology of Tort Law. In M. K. Miller & B. H. Bornstein (eds.), *Advances in Psychology and Law*, Vol. 1. Cham: Springer, pp. 249–274.

Rosenberg, M., Confessore, N., & Cadwalladr, C. (2018). How Trump Consultants Exploited the Facebook Data of Millions. *New York Times*. www.nytimes.com/2018/03/17/us/politics/cambridge-analytica-trump-campaign.html

Sales, B. D., & Krauss, D. A. (2015). *The Psychology of Law: Human Behavior, Legal Institutions, and Law*. Washington, DC: APA.

Sartor, G. (2006). Fundamental Legal Concepts: A Formal and Teleological Characterisation. *Artificial Intelligence and Law* 14(1–2), 101–142.

Shuman, D. W. (1994). The Psychology of Compensation in Tort Law. *University of Kansas Law Review* 43, 39.

Solove, D. J. (2013). Introduction: Privacy Self-Management and the Consent Dilemma. *Harvard Law Review* 126(7), 1880–1903.

Sunstein, C. R. (2000). *Behavioral Law and Economics*. Cambridge: Cambridge University Press.

Thagard, P. (2018). Cognitive Science. *Stanford Encyclopedia of Philosophy*. https://plato.stanford.edu/entries/cognitive-science/.

Thaler, R. (2016). *Misbehaving: The Making of Behavioral Economics*. New York: W. W. Norton & Company.

Thaler, R. H., & Sunstein, C. R. (2008). *Nudge: Improving Decisions About Health, Wealth, and Happiness*. Harmondsworth: Penguin.

Tversky, A., & Kahneman, D. (1974). Judgment Under Uncertainty: Heuristics and Biases. *Science* 185(4157), 1124–1131.

Vaughn, L. B. (2012). Feeling at Home: Law, Cognitive Science, and Narrative. *McGeorge Law Review* 43, 999.

Weinrib, E. (2012). *Corrective Justice*. Oxford: Oxford University Press.
Williams, J. (2018). *Stand Out Of Our Light: Freedom and Resistance in the Attention Economy*. Cambridge: Cambridge University Press.
Williamson, O. E. (1989). Transaction Cost Economics. *Handbook of Industrial Organization 1*, 135–182.
Wu, T. (2017). *The Attention Merchants: The Epic Scramble to Get Inside Our Heads*. New York: Vintage.
Zamir, E., & Teichman, D. (2018). *Behavioral Law and Economics*. New York: University Press.
Zittrain, J. (2014). Facebook Could Decide an Election Without Anyone Ever Finding Out: the Scary Future of Digital Gerrymandering – and How to Prevent It. *New Statesman America*. www.newstatesman.com/politics/2014/06/facebook-could-decide-election-without-anyone-ever-finding-out
Zuboff, S. (2019). *The Age of Surveillance Capitalism: The Fight for a Human Future at the New Frontier of Power*. New York: Profile Books.

12

Private Law and Cognitive Science: A Methodological Commentary

Bartosz Brożek and Marek Jakubiec

12.1 INTRODUCTION

The relationship between cognitive science and the law is a complex and relatively unexplored one, and this assessment applies in particular to private law. While a significant number of studies have been devoted to the evidence law or criminal law as seen through the prism of neuroscience and experimental psychology (Aharoni et al., 2008; Morse, 2015), little has been said in this context on contract law or torts. In his chapter, Przemysław Pałka (Chapter 11 in this volume) sheds light on some aspects of the influence of the cognitive science on private law. As we generally agree with his main claims, in the following commentary we would like to focus on one of the problems addressed by Pałka, which – in our opinion – needs further philosophical elaboration: the descriptive layer of private law and its relation to the view of human decision making as portrayed by the cognitive sciences. There are two interrelated issues here: the presuppositions of legal norms and the relationship between legal and scientific "images of man." Because of the nature of these problems, this commentary is made from the perspective of philosophy and methodology, rather than legal doctrine or cognitive science.

12.2 THE PRESUPPOSITIONS OF PRIVATE LAW

Normative expressions do not directly describe anything; their aim is to regulate human behavior. However, one can hardly imagine a legal rule which does not implicitly assume some descriptive claims concerning, for instance, the human behavioral patterns, causal chains, and innumerable basic beliefs we are driven by. Nevertheless, it is unclear how one should depict the relation between the descriptive and the normative content of rules. An application of the theory of presuppositions, as alluded to by Pałka, seems a potential solution here.

We will put aside the multifaceted philosophical debate concerning the character of presuppositions. Instead, we will adopt a very general characterization of presuppositions: a sentence A presupposes a sentence B if and only if whenever A is meaningful, B is true.[1] For example, the sentence "The Polish Civil Code is well structured" would be meaningless if there were no Civil Code in Poland, that is, the sentence "The Polish Civil Code exists" were false.

The application of this definition to (legal) rules comes with some intriguing twists. Let us consider the following provision of the Polish Civil Code: "Article 415. Whoever by a fault on his part causes damage to another person is obliged to remedy it." What are the presuppositions of this sentence? Arguably, the sentence is only meaningful if there exist persons, damages, and ways of remedying them. However, such existential presuppositions are ultimately trivial. When uncovering the descriptive layer of legal rules, something else is much more important. For example, the cited provision of the Polish Civil Code speaks of *causing* damage *by a fault* on one's part. This expression speaks of a mechanism of decision making and action. On the one hand, it assumes that people are capable – through their action – of causing damage to other people. On the other hand, it also speaks of doing so "by one's fault," suggesting that there are various (at least two) ways of acting, which may lead to damage being caused to someone else, and one of them is associated with fault.

Of course, the presuppositions of Article 415 do not constitute a complete description of the mechanisms of human decision making and acting. In order to obtain a more comprehensive picture thereof, one needs to contemplate the presuppositions of other provisions of the Civil Code. For example, Article 60 says that "the intention of a person performing a legal act may be expressed by any behavior of that person which manifests his intention sufficiently," which presupposes that people are capable of forming intentions. In turn, Article 82 reads: "A declaration of intent made by a person who, for any reason, is in a state which precludes the conscious or free making of a decision and declaring of intent is invalid," which presupposes that people can make their decisions both consciously and freely.

Such presuppositions, in contradistinction to existential ones, may be deemed *nomothetic*. They can only be reconstructed on the basis of an entire cluster of legal rules (provisions) – as opposed to a single sentence – and they describe the laws (causal or statistical) governing – in our case – human decision making and behavior. And so, the Polish law presupposes (at least) that people are capable of forming intentions in a free and conscious way, and act upon these intentions to cause

---

[1] In the traditional approach to presuppositions championed by Strawson (1950), this definition is slightly different: a sentence A presupposes a sentence B iff whenever A is true or false, B is true. We have adopted a more general and – admittedly – much more vague definition. There are two reasons to do so. On the one hand, there are doubts whether rules may be ascribed truth or falsehood (and hence it may be argued that they cannot have presuppositions in the Strawsonian sense). On the other hand, it is intuitively obvious that rules *do* presuppose some descriptive content. For analytical purists, who might find our solution somewhat lacking, we suggest taking advantage of the "OUGHT implies CAN" principle, which is clearly one of the cornerstones of private law (*impossibilium nulla obligatio est*). On this approach, one does not consider the (Strawsonian) presuppositions of legal rules (such as "Whoever by a fault on his part causes damage to another person is obliged to remedy it"), but of modal-alethic sentences that follow from them according to "OUGHT implies CAN" (in our case: "Whoever by a fault on his part causes damage to another person can/is able to remedy it").

changes in their environment. Also, the Polish civil regulations assume that this is not the only way in which people may act: clearly, unconscious and/or coerced behavior is considered possible, as well as acting without intention.

12.3 TWO IMAGES OF MANKIND

As we have tried to argue above, the set of presuppositions of private law may serve as the basis for reconstructing the legal "image of mankind," that is, a "theory" of how human beings make their decisions and act. This "theory" is expressed with the use of a particular conceptual scheme (it may, for example, take advantage of such concepts as "conscious," "free," "intention," "declaration of intent," "fault," etc.). Crucially, the concepts in question and the interconnections between them depict the mechanism of human decision-making processes, and thus of the motives and causes for acting in one way rather than other (Hage, 2019).

Let us briefly consider the following example. In Polish law, a contract is binding when a concordant intent to execute it has been expressed by all the parties. A further analysis of the relevant provisions of the Polish Civil Code, as well as their presuppositions and doctrinal considerations, reveals that "expressing one's intent" is understood as rational and voluntary (Brożek, 2015). It is assumed that a party is able to make free and conscious decisions in a purely rational manner. In other words, emotional and unconscious factors do not in principle influence the decision-making processes. Of course, there are exceptions such as – unsurprisingly – being in a state which precludes the conscious or free making of a decision. Yet this only reinforces the point that the basic tenets of the legal "image of mankind" are deeply rooted in the principles of rationalism and voluntarism. Anything different from free, conscious, and rational choice is treated as an aberration.

Meanwhile, the "image of mankind" and of human decision making as painted by contemporary cognitive science is quite different. It is believed that the overwhelming majority of our daily decisions are unconscious and based on emotional mechanisms: Through social training, supported by appropriate emotions, we learn fast, unconscious responses to typical situations (Damasio, 1994). Of course, we also make conscious, reasoned decisions, but this happens relatively rarely, in unusual situations.

Prima facie, it seems that these two pictures of human decision-making processes, one coming from private law and the other drawn by cognitive sciences, are incompatible. Let us consider in more detail whether this is really the case and, if so, what are the consequences of such a situation. First and foremost, one needs to determine whether there in fact is an inconsistency between the two "images of man." It may be pointed out that the law uses a completely different conceptual scheme than the cognitive sciences. Neuroscientists and psychologist do not take advantage of typically legal concepts such as "internal will" or "the meeting of minds." Moreover, when they use the same words, they may ascribe a different meaning to them than lawyers do. A case in point is the concept of "free will" or "free decision." As we have indicated above, (Polish) private law is based on a general assumption that people act with free will. There has been a lot of (celebrated, but also contested) research in the cognitive sciences which suggests that free will does not exist. But are lawyers and cognitive scientists talking about the same thing in this case? In the law, free will is *assumed* (and not precisely defined), and attention is focused on the circumstances under which the decision-making process is *not* free (e.g., when the intent is declared under coercion). In other words, the concept of free will is introduced in a *negative* way. In the cognitive sciences, and in particular in the famous experiments of Benjamin Libet, an operational definition of free will is adopted (i.e., that a free action is an action in which the conscious act of deciding precedes any physiological processes required for the execution of the action). Libet's experiments (Libet, 1985), as is well known, have determined that *some* physiological processes associated with the execution of an action (i.e., the appearance of the so-called readiness potential) may be registered *before* a subject becomes aware of their decision to act in a given way. It may therefore be argued that Libet had a different concept of "free will" or "free action" than the one assumed in private law. But if the concepts are different, there is no place for inconsistency: What the cognitive sciences say is not in contradiction with the presuppositions of private law.

This sounds like a simple solution, but it does not bring us very far, or even far enough for our purposes. Of course, from a purely logical point of view, a contradiction may occur only between sentences expressed in the same language; if the concepts differ and consequently so do the languages, no contradiction may arise. However, when one is dealing with two different languages, there are no logical relations between them whatsoever. They constitute completely isolated conceptual frameworks. In the context of our considerations, it means that the two "images of man," one outlined by the cognitive sciences, and the other presupposed by the law, cannot even be compared. This sounds like a formal trick rather than a satisfactory solution. One can clearly see that even if the concepts of free will in the law and in the cognitive sciences are different, they *do* have something in common. To deny this is to live in a "schizophrenic" and highly fragmented world. Even if there is no one-to-one correspondence between the conceptual scheme of the law and of the cognitive sciences, there may exist some *translation rules*, enabling the expression of (a part) of one of the two images of man in terms of the other. It is no simple task to establish such (partial) translation rules: It requires considerable methodological awareness and caution. Arguably, however, it is where interesting issues between the law and the cognitive sciences lie. To say that the legal image of mankind has nothing in common with the scientific image of mankind is an artificial maneuver which saves us substantial cognitive effort, but at the same time leaves us with a less-than-perfect understanding of the world. To say that the two images can easily be compared is simply not true. What is interesting lies in between these two positions.

There is one more point we would like to stress. The above analysis assumes that there is one, uniform legal image of human decision making (even if relativized to a particular legal system) and one view of human action stemming from the cognitive sciences. The truth is much more complex. In the law, the same set of legal provisions may give rise to different, often competing interpretations. For example, the provisions of the Polish Civil Code pertaining to legal acts (such as entering into a contract) are accounted for in two diametrically different ways. The *theory of will* places the emphasis on the processes occurring in one's mind: A contract is legally binding if all the parties have had the required intent to enter it. On the other hand, the *theory of declaration* is not interested in the actual mental processes: What matters is whether the behavior of the contracting parties may be construed (from the perspective of an average and neutral external observer) as amounting to entering into a contract. On the first reading, the law is based on very strong presuppositions regarding "the image of mankind"; on the second, the emphasis is placed upon the way people behave and their minds are treated like "black boxes" – the mechanisms behind our decision making are opaque.

Similar observations may be made in relation to the cognitive science. There is no unique, uniform image of decision making agreed upon by psychologists and neuroscientists. Of course, there are clearly discernible tendencies, such as the acknowledgment of the importance of unconscious processes or the emphasis on the role of emotions in the human mental life (Damasio, 1994; Morsella & Bargh, 2008). However, once we wade into the details, the accounts may differ considerably. For example, conscious reasoning may be treated as a way to justify our emotion-driven actions *ex post factum* or as a genuine factor in the decision-making process.

Thus, rather than being faced with images of man, we have to consider a multitude of them, ones which come from both the legal and the scientific side of the debate. However, we do not think this is an obstacle to an attempt to enrich the doctrine of private law with some insights from the cognitive sciences. On the contrary: The abundance of theories and perspectives makes the entire enterprise even more exciting and potentially fruitful.

REFERENCES

Aharoni, E., Funk, C., Sinnott-Armstrong, W., & Gazzaniga, M. (2008). Can Neurological Evidence Help Courts Assess Criminal Responsibility? Lessons from Law and Neuroscience. *Annals of the New York Academy of Sciences* 1124, 145–160.

Brożek, B. (2015). O naturalizacji prawa (On the naturalization of law). In J. Stelmach, B. Brożek, Ł. Kurek, & K. Eliasz (eds.). *Naturalizacja prawa: Interpretacje*. Warsaw: Wolters Kluwer.

Damasio, A. (1994). *Descartes' Error: Emotion, Reason, and the Human Brain*. New York: Putnam Publishing.

Hage, J. (2019). Autonomy, Reason and Bias in Contract Law. In A. Waltermann, D. Roef, J. Hage, & M. Jelicic (eds.), *Law, Science, Rationality*. The Hague: Eleven International Publishing.

Libet, B. (1985). Unconscious Cerebral Initiative and the Role of Conscious Will in Voluntary Action. *The Behavioral and Brain Sciences* 8, 529–539.

Morse, J. (2015). *Neuroscience, Free Will, and Criminal Responsibility*. Faculty Scholarship (Paper 1604) http://scholarship.law.upenn.edu/faculty_scholarship/1604.

Morsella E., & Bargh J. (2008). The Unconscious Mind. *Perspectives on Psychological Science* 3(1), 73–79.

Strawson, P. (1950). On Referring. *Mind* 59, 320–344.

13

Responsibility, Liability, and Retribution

Jaap Hage and Antonia Waltermann

13.1 RESPONSIBILITY AND LIABILITY

13.1.1 *The Roles of Responsibility and Liability*

On his way to bring his five-year old daughter Susan to school, John is driving his car through the quiet outskirts of his hometown. Suddenly, Susan starts making unexpected noises, so John turns to the back of the car to see what is going on. It is nothing serious – but while John is trying to figure out what is going on, a pedestrian, Geraldine, crosses the street. Because he is not paying attention, John notices Geraldine too late. He cannot brake in time and hits Geraldine with his car. Fortunately, Geraldine survives the accident, but not without injuries which require hospitalisation. Even though he was distracted by his young daughter, John is still responsible for not braking in time, and he is liable for at least part of Geraldine's medical costs. Moreover, John is responsible for violating traffic rules and, as a consequence, he is liable to be fined.

As the short story above illustrates, the notions 'responsibility' and 'liability' play important roles in law. John's responsibility for not braking in time and the ensuing liability for damages illustrate their role in private law, in particular the law of torts. His responsibility for violating the rules of traffic law and the ensuing liability to be fined illustrate a similar role for these notions in criminal law. In both cases, John's liability depends on his responsibility for what he did. This relationship between liability and responsibility – with liability depending on and being a consequence of responsibility – is typical for a retributivist view on liability: an agent is liable for damages or liable to be punished because they deserve it.[1] This central role of desert is characteristic of retributivism.

This retributivist view of liability has been relatively unproblematic for a long time. In recent decades, however, this has begun to change. The nature of responsibility has become a hotly debated issue in moral and legal philosophy (e.g. Hart, 1968; Feinberg, 1970; White, 1985; Fischer & Ravizza, 1993; Kenneth, 2001; Lucy,

---

[1] In this chapter, we will apply the convention that an author uses the pronouns that reflect her or his own gender. In the case of this co-authored chapter, this means that male and female pronouns are used interchangeably.

2007; Sinnott-Armstrong & Nadel, 2011; Vincent, 2013; Sinnott-Armstrong, 2014). Moreover, the dependence of liability on responsibility has become questionable. One of the reasons why the notion of responsibility has been problematized is because of the increasing insights into the causes of human behaviour that the flourishing of the cognitive sciences has brought about. The debate whether human beings can ever be responsible for their actions is as old as debates about the truth of determinism. It has been topical since the cognitive sciences have provided evidence of how this alleged determination is – literally – embodied (Greene & Cohen, 2004).

The central topics of this chapter are whether responsibility exists and whether law – in particular criminal law – should base liability on responsibility and responsibility on retribution. These questions have received considerable attention in recent decades, and it is not our aim to summarize these extensive debates.[2] Instead, we want to briefly present the main lines of the debates and then examine whether – and if so, how – the different positions within the debate can be reconciled.

In this examination, a central role is reserved for a social practice we call the 'practice of agency' and the tension between two different ways of looking at the world around us, namely the phenomenological and the realist way. Before we can consider a possible reconciliation, however, we first want to introduce and disambiguate the central notions of responsibility and liability and explain why retributivism plays such an important role in the arguments surrounding these notions. Section 13.1.2. of this chapter will specify what we mean by 'responsibility'; Section 13.1.3. distinguishes two forms of liability, civil and criminal. Criminal liability can be justified by reference to consequentialism or retributivism, which are introduced in Section 13.1.4. Retributivism makes presuppositions that go hand in hand with free will libertarianism, one of the positions in the debates. We outline this position in Section 13.2, before turning to the arguments against it in Section 13.3. Section 13.4 describes compatibilism as an attempt to reconcile opposing positions – free will libertarianism, retributivism, and the phenomenological way of looking at the world on the one hand, and hard determinism, no responsibility, and the realist perspective on the other. In Section 13.5, we examine whether compatibilism can succeed in reconciling these positions, and whether such a reconciliation is desirable. We conclude in Section 13.6.

13.1.2 *Responsibility*

The term 'responsibility' is ambiguous. For instance, Hart (1968, pp. 211–12) famously distinguished between four forms of responsibility. Sometimes, the word

---

[2] Good recent overviews can be found in the work of Kane (2002, 2005) and online (Caruso, 2018; Talbert, 2019; O'Connor & Franklin, 2020).

'responsible' is used as a synonym for 'liable'. For instance, it is possible to say that John is responsible for the damage suffered by Geraldine. A different use of 'responsible' makes the word stand for accountability, as when we say that Harry was not responsible for what he did because he was suffering from severe paranoia at the time of the act. The plural 'responsibilities' can be used for the set of duties attached to a particular role, as when we say that the responsibilities of an airplane pilot are manifold.

The notion of responsibility that is at stake in this chapter is closely connected to the notion of agency. We can ascribe an action to an agent by claiming that the agent is responsible for the action. For instance, 'Louise is responsible for the theft' can be used to say that Louise is the one who stole something. Sometimes, agency goes hand in hand with blame or praise for the agent, based on his performing the action. The relation between being considered the agent of some action and deserving praise or blame for the action is so close that we sometimes refuse to call a person responsible for an action if she has an excuse. (From here on, we will ignore praise, because it is less relevant for criminal liability.) For instance, if Alan was blackmailed and under that influence committed theft, we do not blame him for doing so, and this absence of blame is reflected in an unwillingness to call Alan responsible for the theft. Perhaps Alan stole, but the blackmailer is responsible. Moreover, this absence of responsibility will then generally[3] be translated into an absence of legal liability: Alan is not criminally liable, because he is not responsible for his action.

In this chapter, we will use the word 'responsible' for the combination of being both the agent and the proper target for blame.

13.1.3 *Liability*

As the brief case at the start of this chapter has already illustrated, the law recognizes at least two kinds of liability. The first kind is the liability to compensate damage; the second kind is the liability to be punished. As the first kind of liability primarily plays a role in private law, more in particular in tort law and in contract law, we will call this kind 'civil liability'.[4] In law, punishment is a reaction to crime, and therefore we will call the liability to be punished 'criminal liability'.

Civil liability is the obligation of a legal subject – often a natural person, but it can also be a non-human entity such as a company or a state – to compensate the damage suffered by another legal subject. If the damage was caused by an unlawful action for which the former legal subject can be blamed, we speak of 'fault liability'. In the case

---

[3] The relation between responsibility and legal liability depends on the law of a particular jurisdiction. Therefore, it is hard to make statements about this relation that are true without exceptions.
[4] Liability for damages also plays a role in connection to administrations and states. Some would see this as evidence that liability for damages also plays a role in administrative and in international law. Others see this as a reason why private law also deals with administrations and states. For present purposes, this does not matter.

described above, John's liability for Geraldine's damage is an example of this. Fault liability can also arise in a contractual setting, where the unlawful behaviour consists in defaulting on one's contractual obligation. For example, if Firm A sold 10,000 widgets to Firm B, but does not deliver in time, Firm A commits contractual default, which is unlawful. If the debtor can be blamed for the non-compliance, this is also a case of fault liability.[5] Fault liability in civil law is an example of liability dependent on responsibility: an agent was at fault (that is, responsible) and therefore liable.

Fault liability is no longer the only – or even main[6] – form of civil liability. The requirement that the liable legal subject can be blamed for her action was the standard on the European continent until far into the twentieth century. Since then, however, there has been a gradual shift since towards more strict liability, in order to provide the victim of wrongfully caused damage with legal protection and for reasons of economic efficiency.[7] This shift from fault liability to a stricter form of liability illustrates the increasing role of consequentialist considerations in civil liability.

For example, a legal subject may, under certain circumstances be civilly liable for damage caused by other persons, such as employees, pupils, or children, and in that case we have a stricter form of liability, as this liability may also exist if the liable subject cannot be blamed for causing the damage.[8] A legal subject may also be liable for damage caused by events that she could not have prevented, and in which no person acted. If, because of a heavy storm, tiles fall off a well-maintained roof, and a passer-by is hurt, the possessor of the building may be liable for the damage, even if he was in no way involved in the accident. However, the possessor would not be responsible for causing the damage in such a case. This is a case of liability without responsibility, exemplifying civil liability based on consequentialist considerations (Van Dam, 2014, section 1001 f.; Hage, 2017b; Smits, 2017, ch. 3).

In criminal law, meanwhile, liability is still more strongly related to and dependent on responsibility. Criminal liability is a precondition for punishment. If somebody commits a crime and if this has been established officially, it is possible for an official to impose a sanction on this person. If this possibility exists, we speak of 'criminal liability'. Although there are a few exceptions, criminal liability typically presupposes that the criminal is considered responsible and blameworthy for the crime (Fletcher, 2007, pp. 298–339; Blomsma & Roef, 2019b, p. 207). The punishment is then considered to be 'deserved' by the criminal. For instance, John violated the traffic rules and therefore deserves having to pay a fine. Firm C intentionally provided the tax service with incorrect information about its profits and in that way

---

[5] For historical reasons that go back to Roman law, it is customary to distinguish between contractual and tort liability. However, fault liability and also stricter forms of liability in contract and tort law are so similar that the historical distinction seems outdated.
[6] This depends on the legal system in question, which makes generalized statements difficult.
[7] In the common law, this shift has not been as prevalent.
[8] The liability is called 'stricter', rather than 'strict', as it may be a condition for vicarious liability that the person who caused the damage could be blamed for what he did.

dodged taxes. The firm therefore also deserves to be fined. In both cases, the liability and the actual punishment based on it are seen as a way to redress a wrong from the past; punishment is considered as a kind of retribution.

As the brief discussion above illustrates, criminal and civil liability differ from each other: criminal liability typically requires the responsibility of the criminally liable person, while civil liability is – certainly in the civil law tradition – often a form of stricter liability, which does not require personal responsibility. This difference between criminal and private law can be explained by the different functions liability fulfils in private and criminal law. Civil liability moves damage from the person who suffered it in the first place to the agent that caused it. Whether this is a good idea depends on the interests of all involved parties, including the person who originally suffered the damage. This means that the interests of the person who becomes liable may have to be sacrificed to the interests of the person who suffered the damage. Criminal liability causes additional 'damage', not only for the person who will be punished, but also for society, which must enforce the punishment. This damage is added to the 'damage' of the crime. Whether this additional damage is justified depends on the interests of society as a whole.

In the rest of this chapter, we will focus on criminal liability, which typically presupposes personal responsibility. Much of the argument, however, is also relevant for fault liability in private law.

13.1.4 *Justification and Explanation of Liability*

In criminal law, there are two main ways to justify criminal liability: consequentialist and retributivist. On a consequentialist approach, the imposition of criminal sanctions is justified by the alleged positive effects of doing so. These effects include the prevention of criminal behaviour through incapacitation or deterrence, reparation of the harm done through crimes, or the rehabilitation of criminals. On a retributivist approach, the imposition of criminal sanctions is justified by the fact that the criminal deserved his punishment because he is responsible for what he did. One factor that plays a role in determining what a criminal deserves is the damage caused by the crime. For instance, genocide deserves a greater punishment than speeding on the highway, and armed robbery deserves a greater punishment than the mere possession of a gun without a permit. Other factors are whether the crime was committed intentionally and the motive for the crime: was it the desire to harm, or merely self-interest?

So far, we have looked at the relationship between responsibility and liability primarily from a normative perspective: what justifies liability? In this connection, retributivism holds that if a person is responsible for some action, this is why she is liable. If we look at the relationship between responsibility and liability from a (cognitive) scientific perspective, however, the question arises whether and to what extent responsibility explains (rather than justifies) why we hold persons liable.

More in particular, do the reasons that people adduce to justify their imposition of liability also explain their behaviour?

Carlsmith (2008) found that when people are asked for reasons why they punish, they often mention consequentialist reasons (e.g. deterrence). However, when asked to judge a number of cases that reflected alternatively consequentialist or retributivist reasons for punishing, they imposed punishments in a manner consistent with a retributivist approach to punishment. For instance, they were motivated by the seriousness of the crime, or by the mental state of the agent, more than by the expected (dis)advantages of punishment. This – and much other research[9] – indicates that retributivist motives play an important role in the decision whether or not to punish. This role is bigger than people think when they reflect on their own reasons for punishing. Retributivist motives, which focus on the responsibility of an agent, may provide a better explanation for the imposition of punishment on this agent than consequentialist ones.

This is an important observation when it comes to debates about the relationship between responsibility and liability. On the one hand, it shows that discussions about responsibility are not merely an academic exercise, but touch upon an important social practice. On the other hand, it shows that scientific findings that question the role of responsibility in attributing liability may have to overcome an important hurdle if they are to influence our social practice, namely the (unconscious) retributivism underlying practices of punishment.

Our natural inclination towards retributivism at first glance seems to be a reason to base responsibility on retribution and liability on responsibility, but this has been called into question. Before we consider the criticism raised against retributivism and retribution as a reason for punishment, we will examine what the retributivist position entails more closely. We do this in Section 13.2, which outlines the position on one side of the debate, namely free will libertarianism. In Section 13.3, we turn to the other side of the debate – hard determinism – looking at the reasons why retributivism and related positions have been called into question and criticized. Historically, the criticism has been framed in terms of determinism and the idea that if determinism is true, there should be no responsibility. As we will see, the argument lost some of its attraction during the twentieth century, when doubts were cast on the universal truth of determinism. However, it has a worthy successor in a related argument about control and agency. Determinism claims to refute free will because it allegedly means that an agent has no control over his actions. The argument from control states that irrespective of the truth of determinism, an agent still has no control over his actions and therefore still has no free will. The argument from control is dealt with at the end of Section 13.3.

---

[9] For a more extensive overview of relevant research, see Section 9.3 of Leibovitch, Chapter 9 in the present volume.

Compatibilism seems to offer a solution in the form of a compromise – or rather: compatibility – between the two conflicting positions. In Section 13.4, we first offer a description of compatibilism, before examining in Section 13.5 whether it really is a solution for the conflict between the libertarian and the hard determinist position.

13.2 FREE WILL LIBERTARIANISM AND RETRIBUTIVISM

In the example at the beginning of this chapter, John has the choice between, on the one hand, paying attention to traffic and complying with the rules of traffic law, and, on the other hand, looking back to see what his daughter is doing, thereby violating the rules. It seems that John could do either, although not both at once, and that he can freely choose which course of action to take. It depends on his will what he will do. This is the idea of free will: an agent has several courses of action open to him, it depends on his will what he will do, and the agent is free to choose. This view of human beings as free agents who are responsible for their actions has been the predominant view, despite (philosophical) challenges in the form of determinism. Running ahead of our argument slightly, determinism denies that agents have more than one option available to them. It is the view that, given the laws of nature, any exhaustive set of states of affairs can only be followed by one particular sequence of new states of affairs (see Figure 13.1). If determinism is true, an agent has, at any given time, only one option available to him. This means that determinism is incompatible with free will as analysed above.

Illustrating this, in Figure 13.1, circles represent exhaustive sets of states of affairs – the whole universe – at a particular moment in time, and the arrows represent all the transitions allowed by the set of all laws of nature. This figure represents determinism because every circle, which represents the complete universe at one particular moment, is followed in time by precisely one other circle.[10] This other circle is 'determined' by its predecessor in combination with the laws of nature.

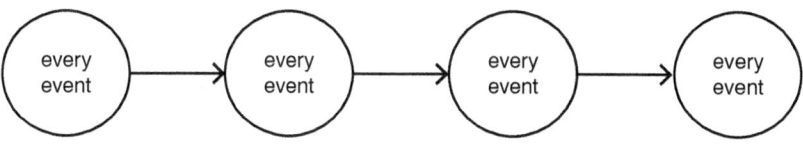

FIGURE 13.1 Determinism

---

[10] In Figure 13.1, every circle is also preceded by one other circle. That is, as far as determinism is concerned, a coincidence. It is compatible with determinism that different universes at time t determine the same universe at time t+1. That would be represented as two different circles pointing to the same follow-up circle.

Retributivism and responsibility based on retributivism presuppose free will. An agent is free to choose from amongst options and because of this, the agent deserves blame if he chooses wrong. The view that defends free will in light of the determinist challenges has become known as 'free will libertarianism'[11] and has recently been defended by Chisholm (1982), O'Connor (1995), and Kane (1996). There are two main strands of free will libertarianism: indeterminism and agent causation. The first denies that determinism is true and typically invokes as reason that quantum physics, which describes entities and events on a micro-level, is in its prevalent interpretation probabilistic and indeterminist (Hodgson, 2002). The traditional counterargument here is that the probabilities and their resulting indeterminacy on the micro-level, if they exist, are cancelled out in macro-phenomena such as neurons and their functioning. That would mean that from a certain level of size on, including the level of actions, determinism would still hold.

13.2.1 Agent Causation

The second strand of free will libertarianism is a modern form of mind/body-dualism, which goes under the name of 'agent causation'. When we speak of causation, we often do so to ascribe some fact to an action or other event. In common parlance, we typically attribute the status of cause to events and, as a special case, to actions. For instance, the cause of the economic recession in 2020 was the Covid-19 pandemic; the death of Hattie Carroll was caused by William Zanzinger, who hit Hattie with his cane.[12] This last example illustrates that an action can be the cause of an (other) event, but that, at the same time, the agent can also be seen as the cause. This is a typical example of agent causation. Since events, actions and agents are, logically speaking, individuals, and since individuals as such cannot be caused – although their existence can be caused – causal chains can only *start* with agents. This suggests that agents and their actions can be the beginnings of causal chains, but not intermediate links in causal chains. That would mean that agents can start new causal chains, which will somehow interact with existing ones and influence the future that seemed to be determined. Seemingly, agents and their actions can interrupt the causal chains that existed, and this makes room for the existence of free will.

If agent causation is to be a reason why free will exists, the step must be made from an agent being the cause of an action to the free will of the agent playing an essential role in this process. The line of argument would then be something like the following:

1) An agent has free will.
2) This will causes the agent to perform an action.
3) The action was caused by the agent, exercising his free will.

---

[11] This free will libertarianism should be distinguished from libertarianism as a radical liberal political philosophy (Boaz, 1997).
[12] Inspired by the lyrics of the Bob Dylan song 'The Lonesome Death of Hattie Carroll'.

13.2.2 *Free Will and Responsibility*

Free will matters for responsibility under this view because agents are responsible only if they have free will (O'Connor & Franklin, 2020). John, from our case above, is liable to be punished because he is responsible for not paying attention to traffic and violating traffic rules, and he is responsible because he exercised his free will by turning around, thereby causing the accident that injured Geraldine. John is the agent who caused the accident and he is therefore responsible for the accident. Because he is responsible (which includes being blameworthy), he deserves punishment (and to allow for punishment, criminal liability is imposed). Free will libertarianism, agent causation, and responsibility based on retributivism fit together. We have already seen that human beings have a natural inclination towards retributivism. Similarly, we have a natural tendency to consider ourselves and others as agents with free will (Greene & Cohen, 2004).

This position makes intuitive sense and of the two main justifications for criminal liability, retribution seems the more natural approach. We have an inclination to punish wrong behaviour, because the wrongdoer 'deserved' to be punished. We are psychologically inclined to base criminal liability on the responsibility of the agent for what she did. Given this, why have the positions retributivism entails been increasingly problematized?

13.3 ARGUMENTS AGAINST RETRIBUTIVIST PUNISHMENT

The argument against retributivist punishment is often framed in terms of free will and determinism. People can only be blameworthy and responsible for their behaviour if they have free will. Since – it is assumed in this argument – all events in the universe, including human behaviour, are determined by physical laws, people do not have free will and cannot be responsible. Criminal liability presupposes responsibility, which presupposes blameworthiness, which presupposes free will, which presupposes the falsity of determinism (Strawson, 1962). If determinism is true, there should be no criminal liability based on retribution.

As indicated in the previous section, determinism holds that any exhaustive set of states of affairs can only be followed by one particular sequence of new states of affairs, meaning that an agent does not have different options available between which she can freely choose. In this section, we first consider determinism in more detail, delineating it from fatalism (Sections 13.3.1 and 13.3.2), before turning to the arguments against retributivism (Sections 13.3.4 and 13.3.5).

13.3.1 *Fatalism*

Determinism should be distinguished from fatalism, which claims that no matter what action an agent takes, a particular consequence will always result. The difference between determinism and fatalism is that determinism allows that an action can influence the future. For example, whether Jane buys a ticket in the lottery can make a difference for the question of whether she will become a millionaire soon. It is not under her control whether she will buy a ticket, but her action can make a difference for what happens in the future. Fatalism, on the contrary, assumes that your present actions do not make a difference for (some particular aspect of) the future.[13] For instance, whether Jane buys a lottery ticket or not, she will not soon become a millionaire anyway (see Figure 13.2). Determinism is relevant for the free will issue, as it claims that an agent has at any time only one option open. Fatalism is not relevant for the freedom of the will, because it does not address the issue what an agent can(not) do.[14]

Figure 13.2 assumes that determinism is false: the leftmost circle has more than one possible successor. It represents fatalism as both alternative successors lead to the same final result, which is apparently unavoidable. In the example about the lottery the leftmost circle represents the situation before Jane decides whether to buy a ticket, the two successor circles represent the situations that she bought, or did not buy, a ticket, and the final circle represents the fact that Jane did not become a millionaire.

Fatalism as such does not require determinism; it allows that a particular state of the universe has more than one possible continuation. However, all the possible continuations have one or more elements in common and these elements occur whatever an agent does.

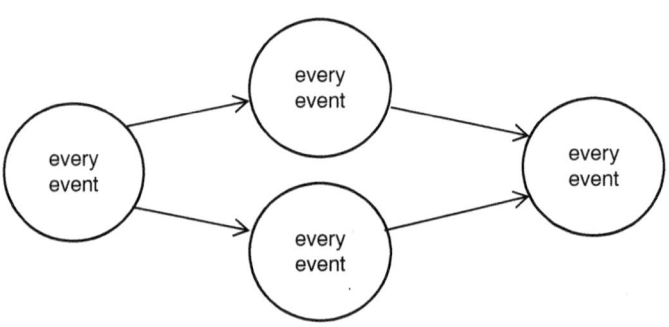

FIGURE 13.2 Fatalism

[13] This definition of fatalism differs from the definition given by Bernstein (2002), which reads that every fact, given that it is what it is, could not have been otherwise. In terms of dyadic modal logic: N(P|P). The drawback of this latter definition is that it does not mention actions, while fatalism is a view on the causal inefficacy of actions.

[14] Actually, this is not completely true. Some actions are defined in terms of their consequences. An example would be committing a murder. If the victim will not die, no matter whether the agent fires the pistol, it is not open to the agent whether or not to kill the victim. However, even in cases like this, fatalism does not answer the question of whether the agent can fire the pistol.

13.3.2 What Must Be the Case and What an Agent Can Do

Running ahead of our argument about compatibilism, we want to point out already here that there is a difference between what is necessarily the case concerning an action (e.g. 'it is necessarily the case that Beatrix shoots Henry') and what the agent of that action can(not) do (e.g. 'Beatrix cannot do anything but to shoot Henry'). Determinism holds that given the laws of nature, only one sequence of exhaustive states of affairs can follow a given exhaustive state of affairs. The later states are necessary, given the state from which they originate. Determinism as such does not say anything about what an agent can do. Perhaps this seems a strange remark. Suppose that, at some moment t+1, Beatrice decides to pull the trigger and to shoot Henry, and suppose also that determinism is true. Then, given the universe as it actually was just before Beatrice pulled the trigger (at t) and given the laws of nature, is it necessarily the case that Beatrice pulls the trigger at t+1? Any fact that occurs after t is necessary, given the exhaustive set of facts at t. Beatrice pulling the trigger is one of them, and that was necessary too: it could not have been otherwise, given the situation at t. So, it seems to follow that Beatrice could not do anything other than pulling the trigger.[15]

Yet this does not follow logically. The sentence that at time t+1, Beatrice had to (could not do anything but) pull the trigger does not follow from the sentence that it is necessarily the case that at time t+1, Beatrice pulled the trigger. The former sentence deals with ability, or the lack thereof, of Beatrice, while the latter sentence deals with Beatrice's actual behaviour and the necessity thereof.[16] As we will point out in Section 13.4.3, both abilities and necessities are defined in our social practices, and it depends on those practices, not on logic, whether the necessity of the state of affairs that a person acts in a particular way implies that this person lacked the ability to do something else. So, theoretically, it is possible that Beatrice necessarily pulled the trigger (necessity of a state of affairs), but that she could have refrained from doing so (ability to refrain from that action).

13.3.3 Three Positions

The threat that determinism poses to the existence of free will and to the possibility of holding people responsible for what they have done has met with three main kinds

---

[15] The difference between what actions necessarily take place and what an agent can(not) do is central in the debate between compatibilists and those incompatibilists who adhere to the so-called consequence argument. See (Van Inwagen, 1995) and the discussion in (Kane, 2005, chapter 3).

[16] The difference becomes immediately clear if we formalize the example. The sentence that it is necessarily the case that Beatrice pulled the trigger would be formalized as N (Pulled_trigger(Beatrice)). The sentence that Beatrice had to (could not do anything but) pull the trigger would be formalized as ~Could(Beatrice, refrain_from (pull_trigger)).

Of course, other formalizations are possible. However, it would be a challenge to find a formalization which *both* does justice to the natural language formulations of the two propositions – the one about what is necessarily the case and the other about what an agent can do – *and* exhibits a logical relation between the two sentences.

of reaction: free will libertarianism, hard determinism, and compatibilism. We have already considered the first, free will libertarianism, above. The second, hard determinism, accepts the determinist threat and its consequences: we cannot hold people responsible for an action if the responsibility is based on the alleged fact that they were free to perform the action or to refrain from it. Either the notion of responsibility should be given up, or – if we want to maintain it – we should use it for consequentialist reasons but give up retributivism. For instance, holding people responsible for what they do, even if they do not deserve it, may lead to better behaviour and a better society (see also Section 5.5). Hard determinism and its implications have recently been advocated by, amongst others, Smilansky (2000, 2002), Peereboom (2001, 2014), and Caruso (2012).

The third kind of reaction is to argue that determinism and free will, or determinism and responsibility, are compatible with each other. This view has become known as 'compatibilism', or 'soft determinism' (Kane, 2005, p. 22) and has recently been defended by, amongst others, Dennett (1984), Dworkin (2011), and Morse (2013). We will turn to compatibilism in Section 13.4 to examine whether it offers a solution between the conflicting positions of free will libertarianism and hard determinism. In the following, we will first consider the arguments hard incompatibilists bring against free will libertarianism and retributivism.

13.3.4 Libet's Experiments

Free will libertarianism – at least the strand of it that argues for agent causation – holds that

1) An agent has free will.
2) This will causes the agent to perform an action.
3) The action was caused by the agent, exercising his free will.

The correctness of this line of argument has been tested empirically by a series of experiments conducted under the responsibility of Libet (1985, 2011). To make this test possible, Libet had to find a measurable correlate of the will, and to that purpose he used the conscious experience of the intention to act.[17] It was already known that an increase of the brain's electrical activity, called the 'readiness potential', preceded voluntary finger-flexing movements (Kornhuber & Deecke, 1965). That neural activity precedes voluntary movement is not very surprising. What Libet wanted to find out is the timing of brain processes in relation to the conscious intention to initiate the movement.

The set-up of Libet's experiment was essentially as follows: subjects were instructed to perform a simple and predefined bodily movement, such as flexing

---

[17] Much of the following text on Libet's experiments is based on an unpublished text written by our colleague David Roef. We thank David for allowing the use of his text. Of course, we remain responsible for the resulting argument.

one's finger or wrist, whenever they felt the urge or wish to do so, while at the same time taking note of the time when the urge or wish to move took place. During this process, EEG-measurements were taken to record the readiness potential. This allowed the experimenters to compare the timing of the onset of the conscious intention with the timing of the readiness potential.

The main finding of the experiment was that the readiness potential precedes the occurrence of the conscious intention to move by about 330 ms (milliseconds) and the onset of the movement itself by about 530 ms. Interestingly, the awareness of moving also precedes the actual movement in time. The following timeline was adapted from Wegner (2002, 53):

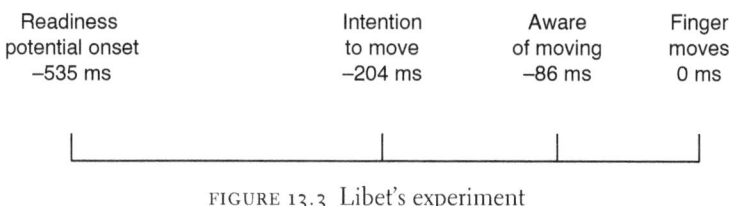

FIGURE 13.3 Libet's experiment

Libet derived two conclusions from the experiments. The first conclusion is that the conscious intention to move cannot be the *original* cause of action because it comes too late in the neuropsychological sequence. The second claim is that the conscious intention does not initiate the bodily movement, because it could only do this if it preceded, or at least coincided with the readiness potential (Libet, 1985).

If the activation of the readiness potential plays a causal role in producing an action and if the conscious will to perform this action only sets in after the readiness potential was activated, the conscious will cannot be the original cause of the action or initiate it. This finding seems to overthrow at least a simple view of how a person's consciousness decides about an action and then as a result of this decision starts a brain process which in the end leads to the muscular events that are an essential aspect of an action.

Libet's findings are one of the many building blocks of an extended argument presented by Wegner (2002), with the conclusion that human behaviour is not caused by a conscious will. Wegner's conclusion is that 'the experience of conscious willing action occurs as the result of an interpretive system, a course-sensing mechanism that examines the relations between our thoughts and actions and responds with "I willed this" when the two correspond appropriately' (Wegner, 2002, p. 317). If Wegner is correct, the main reason to believe in free will, namely that we experience having it, is misguided. Perhaps we experience having free will, but this free will experience is not an experience of anything outside the experience itself.

13.3.5 The Elusive 'I'

Libet's results have received so much attention because they are often interpreted as being relevant for responsibility. This is, for example, reflected in the title of a book on the impact of Libet's research, which reads *Conscious Will and Responsibility* (Sinnott-Armstrong & Nadel, 2011). People tend to see themselves as agents with a central role for their conscious will that is manifested in the intention to act. They assume that they are persons, typically self-referred to as 'I'. They also assume that persons are continuous in time, that they have – but are not identical to – bodies, and that they are often – but not continuously – conscious of themselves and of their bodies and surroundings. If a person acts, it is this 'I' that acts and if actions are performed intentionally, this 'I' has the relevant intention.

Descartes (1641) assumed that this 'I' was an independent substance, a 'thinking thing' (*res cogitans*). He opposed it to the human body. That would be an independent extended thing, a *res extensa*. These assumptions lead to the now unpopular dualism between mind and body and raises the difficult question of how the mind and the body can interact. If we reject Cartesian mind/body-dualism, the alternative seems to be to find a place for the mind in the body. There are two main ways to do this, called 'identity theories' and 'epiphenomenalism' respectively.

Identity theories hold that mental phenomena are identical to states of the body, typically of the brain. Mental phenomena are another aspect of brain states (Smart, 2017) – a mental state is how a brain state is experienced. In some, or perhaps all, of these experiences an 'I' plays a role as the subject of the experience. According to identity theorists, it also holds for these experiences that they are the counterparts, in the sense of different aspects, of brain states. If mental states are brain states, they can exert causal influences, such as making a muscle contract, to the same extent that their identical brain states can. Figure 13.4 depicts this graphically. A circle represents a combined mental/physical state, and the arrows between the circles represent causal relations between these combined mind/brain states. The lines dividing the circles do not represent a separation between two parts, but a distinction between two aspects of the same 'thing'.

A main function, perhaps *the* main function of identity theories, is to explain how mental causation (Maslen, Horgan & Daly, 2009; Robb & Heil, 2019) is possible. How can mental states exert a causal influence on the body? The answer of identity theories is

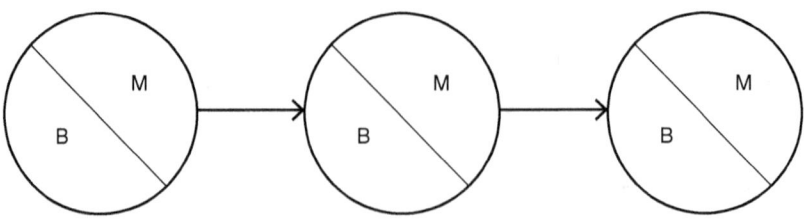

FIGURE 13.4 Identity of mind (M) and brain (B)

that the mental states are at the same time bodily states and that they exert this influence in their role of bodily (brain) states. Assume, for instance, that some brain state is experienced as the desire to drink a beer, that the brain state causes William's muscles to contract, which leads in turn to William's body moving. These effects can also be described as William going to the fridge and taking a beer. Does it make sense to describe this course of events as William's desire to drink a beer causing him to go to the fridge and take a beer? According to identity theorists, this makes sense. According to epiphenomenalists, it does not, because all the causal work is performed by the bodily states, and the mental states might just as well not have existed.

Epiphenomenalism is the view that mental events are caused by physical events in the brain but have no effects upon any physical events (McLaughlin, 1994; Robinson, 2019). The relation between brain states and mental states has been compared to that between a steam locomotive and the plumes of steam it ejaculates, respectively. The state of the locomotive at time t influences the state at time t+1, and each state goes together with a steam cloud, but the clouds do not influence the movement of the locomotive. Similarly, brain state b1 at time t1 goes together with mental state m1 (also at time t1). Brain state b2 at time t2 goes together with mental state m2 (at time t2). State b1 causally influences b2, but no causal connections start from a mental state: neither from a mental state to another mental state, nor from a mental state to a brain state. This is depicted in Figure 13.5, where rectangles represent brain states and circles represent mental states. The horizontal arrows represent causal relations, and the vertical lines indicate what mental state goes together with some particular brain state.

Epiphenomenalists do not try to find a role for mental causation; they deny that mental causation is possible. If epiphenomenalism is adopted, there is no place for an 'I' as a mental phenomenon in the explanation of actions. Of course, it remains possible to ascribe an action to a person, and to admit that this person experiences

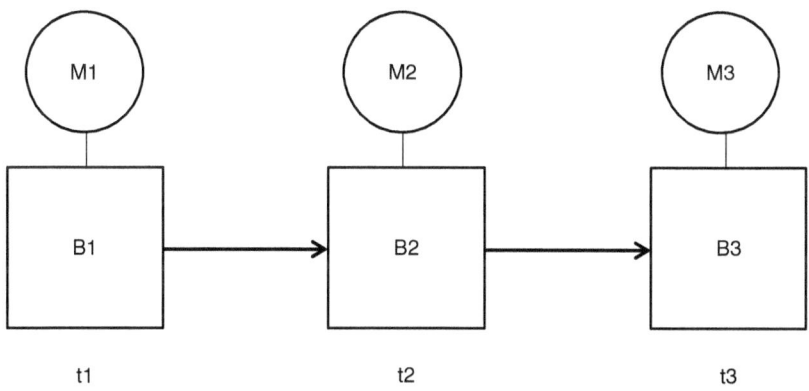

FIGURE 13.5 Epiphenomenalism

herself as 'I', but this is then nothing other than a mere mode of speaking. This 'I' has no place in the causal processes that lead to actions or other events. For the same reason, intentions as mental states have no causal influence. The events that are called actions may be accompanied or preceded by mental events such as intentions to act, but these intentions play no causal role in the generation of the actions.[18] Libet's experiments are fully compatible with this epiphenomenalist view.

If it is assumed that mental states are identical to bodily states – for instance brain states – the prospects for finding an 'I' that acts and that initiates bodily movements seem better. It is 'only' necessary to find a part of the brain, or a brain state, that embodies this 'I' and that realizes conscious experiences, including intentions to act, and that initiates intentional actions. The problem is that such a brain part or brain state has never been found. Moreover, the Libet experiments seem to show that there are at least some intentional actions that are not initiated by a brain state that also embodies the relevant intention to act. If there are *some* intentional actions that are not initiated by a brain state that also embodies the intention, it seems at least possible that *no* intentional action is initiated in that way.

13.3.6 From Free Will Libertarianism vs. Hard Determinism to Compatibilism

The libertarian theory of agent causation requires that there is an agent, an 'I', from which actions originate. This very notion of an 'I' that can represent a person or other agent is problematic. If an 'I' is identified with a substance that is conscious, there is a problem with the discontinuity of consciousness. Does the 'I' stop existing if a person is dreamlessly sleeping, or in a coma? If it does, how does the 'I' of an earlier stream of consciousness relate to the 'I' of a later conscious experience? Is it the same 'I', and if so, what makes it the same (Metzinger, 2011; Strawson, 2011)? Questions like these are hard to answer, and perhaps they do not even make sense and are 'empty questions' (Parfit, 1984).

Nevertheless, most people tend to experience themselves as continuous in time, and as agents who decide about their actions, who plan and perform many of those actions intentionally, who have reasons for what they are doing, and who let these reasons influence what they do. These experiences underlie our social practice of holding people responsible for their actions and making them liable for (some of) the consequences. The problem seems to be that these experiences and the social practices that build on them are hard to reconcile with the results of science and the philosophical theories that elaborate on these scientific insights. In Section 13.5, we will return to this apparent conflict, but before doing so, we want to turn to compatibilism, the third position in the debate surrounding responsibility, determinism, and free will.

---

[18] Contrary to what is claimed in Searle (1983, pp. 83f.).

13.4 COMPATIBILISM

The philosophical discussion about determinism and free will is highly technical. The notion of determinism needs to be defined in terms of states of affairs or events (or a combination of both) and invokes the idea of necessity, which itself is not very transparent either. The phrase 'free will' has only a limited use in common parlance. Moreover, this use – for example 'She did this out of her own free will' – stands for voluntariness, which is not the same as the philosophical notion of free will (Van Inwagen, 1995). This raises the sceptical question of whether the philosophical discussion has much practical relevance, and even whether it should have such relevance.

This approach, which starts from the question of why we are bothered by determinism, takes a central place in the work of Dennett (1984, 2003). Dennett lists a number of reasons why people may be worried about determinism. They include the ideas that if determinism is true, we are like prisoners robbed of the freedom to do what we want, or like persons whose will is manipulated by a nefarious neurosurgeon; or otherwise, that people are otherwise the playthings of external forces, or like automata who merely mechanically follow behavioural patterns imprinted in us, and so on (Dennett, 1984, pp. 7–12). Slightly less evocatively, but more systematically, Kane lists objections that compatibilists adduce against determinist critics of free will. He does so under two headings: the determinist critics misrepresent (1) freedom as absence of determinism, while it should be absence of (relevant) constraints; (2) determinism as a constraint, while it is a form of necessity.[19]

Compatibilism about determinism and free will has its basis in this scepticism about determinism as a criticism of free will and responsibility. In one variant, compatibilism holds that it is reasonably possible to hold somebody responsible for her actions, even if she lacks free will. In a second variant, it holds that an agent can have free will, even if determinism is true (McKenna & Coates, 2020).

To substantiate compatibilism, it is possible to refer to our social practices, as they are known to us through our intuitive judgements about being free or responsible. These practices may be moral, and then the determinist criticism of free will and responsibility should be tested against our moral intuitions. The practices may also be legal, in which case our law is the touchstone for evaluating theories about free will and responsibility. In the two following subsections, we will briefly discuss two

---

[19] *Digression on necessity and constraints.* Arguably, all necessity is the result of *some* constraint(s). For example, the sentence 'It does not rain if it is not the case that it rains' is made necessarily true by the constraints of logic. Or, it must be the case that a particular bachelor is unmarried because of the constraints of semantics (Hage, 2016). However, it does not follow from the fact that something is necessarily the case, without a gloss referring to a point of view, that it was constrained *in a particular way*. Moreover, a particular constraint may make that something is necessarily the case, or that something necessarily happens, but the constraint is not identical to this necessity. The necessity of a particular logical truth is not the same as the logical rule that makes it necessary.

examples. The first one deals with the relation between determinism and moral responsibility; the second one with the relation between, on the one hand, determinism and free will and, on the other hand, legal responsibility and liability.

13.4.1 *Frankfurt on Moral Responsibility*

In a series of articles (amongst others Frankfurt, 1969, 1971, and 1983), Frankfurt developed a theory of freedom of the will. In this theory, he tried to overcome the problem that determinism poses for the requirement of alternate possibilities. We have already seen that the availability of alternate possibilities for action is one of the two requirements that are often assumed for the existence of free will, the other requirement being that the action an agent performs is 'up to her'. Frankfurt claims that the requirement of alternate possibilities can be dropped and replaced by the requirement that a person not only wills her action, but also has a second-order volition that she wills what she first-order wills. If this requirement is met, the person wholeheartedly endorses her action, and then she can be said to have acted out of her free will.

For instance, if an alcoholic drinks another bottle of gin and wanted to do so, his addiction may have stood in the way of his free will. The alcoholic did not want to want another bottle of gin, although he actually (first-order) wanted to drink another one. If this second-order volition is lacking, the alcoholic does not wholeheartedly want to drink another bottle of gin. In a sense he is forced to do so by his addiction. The force is in this case a force that influences his first-order will, which is therefore not free.

However, if an alcoholic completely endorses her alcohol-centred life and wants to want to drink more, her will is free. In that case, it is wholly up to her if she drinks another bottle of gin. So, where originally it was assumed that there are two requirements for the existence of free will, namely the existence of alternate possibilities and that her actions are 'up to the agent', now there is only one requirement left. This requirement, that a person wholeheartedly accepts her own will, can be seen as an alternative formulation of the requirement that an action is 'up to the agent'.

Let us ignore the question of whether Frankfurt's analysis of free will is correct,[20] choosing to focus on the method that Frankfurt implicitly applies instead. This method is to test imaginary cases against the reader's intuition. The example about the alcohol addict is a case in point. How do we know that the ordinary addict lacks free will, precisely because of his addiction? We have no sense to detect free will if we encounter it. Somehow, we just 'know' that the will of addicts is not free and that

---

[20] There are many papers addressing this issue. For an overview of some of them, see Kane (2002, pp. 281–334). One issue is whether second-order volition suffices for the will to be free. Is it not also necessary to have similar third- and higher-order volitions? This discussion is similar to the discussion of infinite regress in connection with constructivist facts. See Hage (Chapter 2 in the present volume).

their addictions compel them to 'will' things that they do not 'really' will. Moreover, we know in the same way that the typical addict does not 'really' (second-order) will to satisfy his addiction.

Not only do we know this, but we also know that others know the same. We would be surprised if others claimed that an ordinary addict, one who has not voluntarily chosen to be addicted, is happy with his first-order desires. It is part of the very notion of an addict that he does not endorse his first-order desires; the ability to refer to such people who lack the relevant second-order desires is the very purpose for which we have the term 'addict' in our vocabularies (Hage, 2018, pp. 39–40). We do not need empirical enquiries and we can normally rely on our intuitions to determine whether a person has free will. This is so, we venture, because during our socialization process we have been introduced to a social practice in which we distinguish between persons with ordinary volitions and persons who are addicted, and in which we distinguish between persons with and without free will. So, when we use our intuitions to test theories about when free will is present or absent, we try to systematize a social practice which is already present.

In this chapter, we have used Frankfurt's approach to the free will discussion as an example, both because Frankfurt's view has been very influential on that discussion, and also because his work is illustrative for much research that is done on moral responsibility and its requirements. The method that Frankfurt employs is used in much research on free will and responsibility, in particular in research that leads to compatibilist outcomes. Frankfurt formulated theories about the nature of free will and tested these theories against our intuitions about specific cases. These intuitions are more or less taken at face value. If the research method is based on systematizing moral intuitions, it is not done to question these intuitive judgements on a large scale. Researchers explore our social practice as it actually is, without proposing far-reaching alternatives for how we should see responsibility and free will in our daily lives. The following presentation of the views of Morse provides a good illustration of this with regard to law.

13.4.2 Morse on Legal Responsibility and Liability

In law, the relevant social practice to analyse is positive law itself. The question of how to see determinism, free will, responsibility, and liability in law is answered by the law. In a relatively recent article, Morse has done the relevant study for the criminal law in common law systems (Morse, 2013). Here we will mostly confine ourselves to quoting phrases from the article in question and adding some comments. All the italics in the quotations are the present authors' (JH & AMW), and footnotes are omitted.

> 'The state may imprison people in the criminal justice system if they *deserve punishment* for crimes they have committed, and it may civilly commit dangerous people if they are not responsible agents . . .'

> 'Virtually all criminals are rational responsible agents, and according to the dominant story, the deprivation imposed on them – punishment – is premised on considerations of desert.'

Here we see a sharp distinction between criminal and private law. Criminal law is deemed essentially retributivist, while private law may be based on consequentialist considerations, such as prevention. Moreover, the reason why criminals are punished is that they deserve punishment, and they deserve punishment because they are rational and responsible agents. Here we encounter the idea of reasons-responsiveness that is by many considered the ground for holding people responsible for what they do and, in criminal law, for punishing them.

> 'The law presupposes the folk-psychological view of the person and behaviour. . . . *folk psychology considers mental states fundamental to a full explanation of human action*. Human behaviour cannot be adequately understood if mental state causation is completely eliminated.'
>
> 'We are practical reasoners, the sort of creatures that can act for and respond to reasons. *The law does not treat persons generally as nonintentional creatures of mechanical forces of nature*. As a system of rules and standards that guides and governs human interaction, law tells citizens what they may and may not do . . .'

The concepts that are used in criminal law are those used by folk psychology. They deal with mental states, and not with, for instance, neurons or readiness potentials. Morse claims that these folk-psychological concepts are essential for a proper understanding of human behaviour. This claim is supported by the function of law which addresses people as users of guiding reasons (rather than as objects determined by physical forces). This is, again, the idea of reasons-responsiveness.

> '. . . if the agent lacks a requisite mental state, the agent is not also prima facie criminally responsible and must be acquitted outright of the crime requiring that mental state.'
>
> 'Mens rea terms, such as intention, purpose, knowledge, recklessness . . . and negligence . . . have their ordinary language, common-sense meanings. No degree of commitment or rationality is included in the definitions of mens rea.'

Mens rea is an essential condition for most, if not all, crimes, and the different forms of *mens rea* are psychological situations.[21] There is no (implicit) reference to the possession of free will. Moreover – and we do not include quotations to illustrate this, but Morse claims it – the affirmative defences through which a defendant can prevent punishment even though he is prima facie responsible for a crime, are defined by the law in plain categories such as insanity, or self-defence, without

---

[21] It is open to discussion whether negligence is really a mental condition. Perhaps it is better described as a kind of unlawful behaviour that was performed unintentionally. With some good will, this lack of intention may be seen as the mental condition that satisfies the *mens rea* requirement. Cf. Blomsma and Roef (2019a, p. 195).

reference to philosophical doctrines about determinism, or actions 'being up to the agent'. This suggests that the free will discussion as it is conducted in the philosophical literature is not relevant for the law as it actually is.

Is this something we should be willing to accept? According to Morse it is, because

> ordinary people are intuitive compatibilists, and my hunch is that even the most committed hard incompatibilists actually live as if they were compatibilists. Finally, ... it seems clear that interpersonal life would be exceptionally impoverished if concepts of responsibility, including genuinely deserved praise or blame, were extirpated from our lives, even assuming that this is possible. If people came to be treated as objects to be manipulated rather than full agents, much that we most treasure would be lost.

Apparently, our actual social practice is so attractive that we should stick to it, irrespective of whether it is based on a sound image of humankind. It is what it is, and it is good (enough).

Morse's argument contains two main lines. The first line relates the legal reasons on whether to hold people responsible for their behaviour to the reasons in the philosophical discourse and finds that they are by and large disconnected. The law does not presuppose the absence of determinism, the presence of free will, or an action 'being up to the agent'. To the extent that the law implicitly works with these notions, it does so by assuming that these conditions are fulfilled, unless the contrary is shown by means of one of a limited number of exceptions that are explicitly allowed by the law. Legal debates do not deal with the philosophically big issues, but with the exceptions allowed by the law such as absence of *mens rea*, or presence of insanity, or duress.

The second line deals with the (im)possibility and undesirability of abandoning our actual social practice. Morse admits that our actual social practice of punishing those who committed crimes for the reason that they deserved punishment is not yet perfect. However, he does not see any fundamental flaws, but merely imperfections in what is basically good. So, there is no need for large-scale modification of our practice of criminal law, and Morse suggests that, even if this were needed, it would be impossible to accomplish. This suggestion echoes the views of Peter Strawson (1962), who claimed that we are not able to replace our actual social practice of holding people responsible and having moral emotions with an instrumental one which treats people as elements of physical reality rather than as responsible persons.

13.4.3 The Practice of Agency

Compatibilists typically take as their starting point our present social practice of holding people responsible for their actions. This practice makes no claims about big philosophical issues such as determinism, free will, and actions 'being up to the agent'. Rather, it deals with common-sense notions such as intellectual disability, insanity, addiction, duress, momentary confusion, and so on. Although it is possible to relate these common-sense notions to the philosophical issues, we tend not to do so in our daily practices. We typically do not excuse people for the reasons that they lacked free will, or that their behaviour was determined by past events and the laws of nature. We do so because they acted under duress, or that they are mentally handicapped. This difference creates the impression that our actual practice is compatible with any answers to the big philosophical questions. Is this impression correct? We will discuss this question by means of two examples relating to determinism.

The case of Esther. Esther received a good education from her parents. One of the things they told her is that it is wrong to discriminate against people because of their ethnic or religious background. They informed Esther that history contains several examples of peoples that were slaughtered precisely because of such discrimination, and that there were dictators who encouraged or even initiated this. It would have been better if these dictators had never lived.

Esther took her parent's words to heart. When she turned thirty, a racist politician rose to power in her country. Esther decided that it would be better to kill the potential dictator now, while it was still possible, rather than wait until the politician had enough power to become invulnerable and start a genocide against people with Esther's ethnic background. Esther shot the politician dead, was arrested, and brought to trial.

Esther's advocate argued that Esther should be excused of the crime of murder because of her upbringing and because of her fears. The court did not accept this defence, however. It argued that, apart from the killing, Esther was a normal person, and that an anti-racist upbringing or an unjustified fear for genocide could not excuse a political murder. Neither Esther's advocate, nor the court mentioned anything about Esther being determined (in the philosophical sense) to kill the politician.

The case of Harry. Harry was an ordinary boy until his early twenties. At that age he started to become afraid and suspicious of what people in his environment were doing. He consulted his physician, who referred Harry for psychiatric treatment. However, the mental health services in Harry's country suffered from underfinancing. They had a large backlog of work, and the waiting time for even having an intake conversation with a qualified mental health care worker was more than a year.

During this year, Harry's condition worsened considerably. He came to believe that a politician who had risen to power in his country would become a dictator and would start a war against neighbouring countries. Harry decided that it would be better to kill the potential dictator now, while it was still possible, rather than to wait until the politician had enough power to become invulnerable and start these wars. He shot the politician dead, was arrested, and brought to trial.

Harry's advocate argued that Harry should be excused of the crime of murder because of his mental condition. The court accepted the insanity defence, ordered that Harry would receive treatment for his mental illness, but did not penalise Harry for the murder. Neither Harry's advocate, nor the court mentioned anything about Harry being determined (in the philosophical sense) to kill the politician.

These two cases have in common that a set of circumstances brought a person to commit a political murder. In Esther's case, these circumstances were not recognized as a valid excuse and Esther was convicted for the murder. In Harry's case, the circumstances were recognized as an excuse and Harry was not convicted, although he was committed for medical treatment.

What circumstances count as an excuse is determined by the legal system in question, which in this respect often follows pre-existing social practices. People who commit crimes for merely putative justifications are typically not excused, while people who do so because of what is recognized as a mental illness are excused. That is how society operates, and the law reflects this social practice.

As compatibilists argue, these social practices do not refer to the philosophical issue of determinism but deal on a case-to-case base with the circumstances that may constitute an excuse. Non-compatibilists may argue that implicitly, these social practices nevertheless reject determinism. What counts as an excuse may be based on an implicit view on what an agent can or cannot avoid. Apparently, society assumes that persons like Esther can refrain from political murders, while persons like Harry cannot.

The hard determinists claim, however, that determinism – or, rather, the facts and physical laws to which the doctrine of determinism refers – makes that nobody can help anything they do. Society wrongly distinguishes between Esther's and Harry's case: if there is a reason to excuse Harry, there is also a reason to excuse Esther.

The compatibilist can rebut that society does not consider determinism relevant for what an agent can do. Indeed, underlying the justification of criminal sanctions is a theory of what agents can do or avoid. This theory, so claims the compatibilist, does not depend on whether determinism is true; it is also part of our social practice (Hage, 2017a).

The picture that arises is that of a complex social practice, which uses a set of interrelated concepts, such as action, agent, intention, negligence, blameworthiness, justification, excuse, ability, necessity, responsibility, liability, cause, effect, voluntariness, force, and duress. However, this practice does not deal with free will or determinism. We will call this social practice the *practice of agency*, because of the central role that actions, agents, and responsibility play in it. The practice of agency defines its own concepts and, as compatibilists argue, it does so with little regard for big philosophical issues such as determinism, free will, and the foundation of responsibility. Because the concepts used in the social practice of agency are defined in this practice, independent of the philosophical issues, the philosophical debate and the social practice seem worlds apart. The social practice uses notions that, in the eyes of philosophers, only make sense against the background of determinism and free will. Insanity or duress are relevant in the eyes of these philosophers because they are signs of determination and lack of free will. However, these same philosophers neglect the issues that our social practice deals with. They are lost in the 'big issues' such as determinism and free will and overlook that in society, the 'minor' topics such as insanity or duress are more relevant than these bigger issues. This conceptual distance gives rise to the belief that our practice of agency is compatible with the philosophical theories, even if these philosophical theories are inconsistent between themselves. This would mean that the practice of agency can be continued without worrying about the issues raised by some philosophers. Compatibilism, it seems, is able to reconcile retributivism and responsibility based on retributivism, and the philosophical arguments.

That conclusion does not follow, however. Even if adherents of the existing social practice, such as Morse, could show that their practice is not vitiated by philosophical theories, this leaves open the issue whether the practice of agency as such is justified. Perhaps, Peter Strawson is right in assuming that we are not able to abandon our practice of agency and perhaps Morse is right in claiming that our practice is not so bad that it requires to be abandoned. However, those are as yet unsubstantiated assumptions.

13.5 IS COMPATIBILISM THE SOLUTION?

The central question which this chapter has wrestled with is whether criminal liability can and should be based on retribution. The previous sections have discussed this question from the perspectives of three main positions in the debate. The first position, free will libertarianism, rejects determinism and holds that free will exists, that agents are responsible and deserve punishment for wrong actions, and that criminal liability based on responsibility is possible. The second position, hard indeterminism, is that determinism makes free will impossible, that free will is a necessary condition for responsibility and criminal liability, and that therefore the truth of determinism makes criminal liability based on responsibility impossible. The third position is compatibilism. Its many variants share the idea that the philosophical debates on determinism, free will, and responsibility deal with other issues than our actual social practice, that the outcome of the philosophical debate therefore does not affect this practice, and that determinism and the absence of free will are therefore compatible with criminal responsibility and liability.

Our aims in this chapter were to present the main lines of the debate surrounding responsibility and free will, given their relevancy for the question of whether criminal liability should be based on responsibility and responsibility on retributivism, and to examine whether the different positions within the debate can be reconciled. So far, we have considered free will libertarianism and hard indeterminism as two opposing sides of the debate, and compatibilism as a possible form of reconciliation between the two. In the following section, we want to examine whether compatibilism can succeed at this reconciliation.

13.5.1 *Internal and External Questions*

In order to examine whether compatibilism succeeds in reconciling the different positions of the debate, it is necessary to gain more distance from the details of the main positions, in order to obtain a suitable perspective on the continuing debate. In a conceptually illuminating article, Mackor (2013) distinguishes between four kinds of questions that can be asked about the relevance of the cognitive sciences for legal responsibility. There are two 'internal questions'. One concerns the issue of whether the neurosciences can change the conditions that our social practice uses for assuming responsibility. For instance, should we still consider addiction as a reason why the addict is not responsible? The other addresses the issue of whether the neurosciences can be of help in answering the question of whether in a particular case the conditions, as they are actually used, have been fulfilled. For instance, did the brain tumour actually make it impossible for the defendant to act on his knowledge of right and wrong?

There are also two 'external questions', which deal with the viability of our social practice of holding people responsible as a whole. One of them concerns the issue of whether our social practice is based on false presuppositions, for instance the presupposition that agents have free will. The other addresses the question of whether our social practice promotes its own purpose, for instance the purpose of preventing crime.

The questions addressed in this chapter are typical external ones. The existence of free will and responsibility are allegedly presuppositions of our practice of agency, although compatibilists deny this. The question of whether our practice of agency is worthy to be rescued from the criticism may be answered on the basis of the purpose of this practice, and is also external. This section returns to these questions as questions about the tenability (presuppositions) and the desirability (purpose) of our actual practice of agency. We will start with another look at the presuppositions by distinguishing the phenomenological and the realist view of the world.

13.5.2 *The Phenomenological and the Realist View*

When we grow up, we learn to live in a meaningful world. Already at a young age, we identify objects in the world around us, and these objects have colours and smells, they are beautiful or ugly, quiet or noisy, hard or soft, kind or unkind, heavy or light, and so on. In this first stage, we do not distinguish between what and how the objects around us are and how we experience them: they are assumed to be as we experience them.

At some moment, we start to distinguish between the objects and their characteristics as they are 'in themselves' and how they appear to us. The stick that seemed to be bent when standing in water turns out to be straight if taken out of the water. The colours that we see turn out to be different for colour-blind people. Moreover, it becomes possible to raise philosophical questions, such as whether a tree that falls in a forest without living beings around makes a sound.[22]

The insight that we can distinguish between how things are 'in themselves' and how they appear to us is not new. A famous example from antiquity is the cave simile that Plato presented in his dialogue about Justice and the State (*The Republic*, 514A-520A). The simile tells us about people who are fettered in a cave, where they can only see shadows of real things. One of them manages to escape from the cave and learns what the real world, illuminated by the sun, looks like. When he returns to the cave and tells the others what the real world is like, the others do not believe him and ultimately, they even kill the enlightened adventurer. Today, scientists who tell us that the real word is very different from how it appears to us do not run a big risk of being killed, but the resistance against their views takes different forms, including the opinion that for our daily lives, we can ignore their findings.

Let us call the view that assigns a central role to how we experience the world the 'phenomenological view' (Smith, 2018). This phenomenological view can be opposed to the view that aims at knowledge of the world as it is in itself, independent of our experience or knowledge of it. Let us call this the 'realist view', borrowing the term 'realist' from the usage of that word current in philosophical ontology (Miller, 2019). Unavoidably, human knowledge starts from how we experience the world. This is the perspective with which individual human beings grow up. Arguably, a similar development has taken place in the development of humankind, as is evidenced in Plato's cave simile. Much of modern science aims at collecting and systematizing knowledge about the world as it exists independent of our experience of it. Our mental phenomena, including our mental states and including the meanings we attach to the world that we experience, change from being a window to the world into objects of knowledge, analogous to the objects in the 'real world' (in the philosophical-technical sense). Rather than taking the world-as-experienced, our 'life-world' in phenomenological jargon (Gallagher, 2012, pp. 159–64), for granted, as happens in the phenomenological view, the realist view of the world tries to account for the world as it really (mind-independently) is.[23] As the experiences that are caused in human perceivers by the external world are also seen as parts of the real world, they become phenomena that need explanation, just like other parts of the real world. Realist science aims to explain the external world as well as the

---

[22] See the discussion in the *Wikipedia* encyclopaedia: https://en.wikipedia.org/wiki/If_a_tree_falls_in_a_forest.

[23] We ignore, for the purposes of this paper, questions of philosophy of science relating to whether it is possible to account for the world as it really is, how much theory is involved in scientific enterprises, and so on.

experiences created by this world, and the relations between them (e.g. how can we explain vision?).

We can also take the realist approach when it comes to our experiences of ourselves. For Descartes, a person's experience of himself as thinking was sufficient evidence to derive that there was a thinking substance. Logically speaking, however, it is impossible to derive the existence of a thinking substance from the existence of an experience with 'I think' as propositional content.[24] As there is no other clear support for the existence of an 'I' apart from the I-aspect of our conscious experiences, the realist approach to human existence may be the cause of the vanishing 'I' that was discussed in Section 13.3.5.

In Section 13.3, we encountered the argument that if determinism is true, there is no free will because of a lack of alternate courses of action. If determinism is false, there is no free will either, because then it is not 'up to the agent' what course of action she will take. So, apparently, the absence of free will follows from both determinism and indeterminism and the determinism issue is not relevant for the existence of free will. Nevertheless, it is the discussion of determinism that shows us why there is no free will. At this stage in our argument, we can explain why determinism is irrelevant to the issue of free will – no matter whether determinism is true, there is no free will – while at the same time showing why the discussion of determinism is relevant. The discussion of determinism and its relevance for free will takes the free will issue out of the phenomenological domain and puts it in the realist domain. In the realist discourse, the phenomenological ability to choose what course of action to take becomes the realist possibility that the development of the world in time takes a particular direction. As soon as this shift in the kind of discourse has taken place, free will has become problematic, either because of a lack of alternate actions, or because the agent does not determine the course of events (or because there is no agent at all). The recent results of the cognitive sciences are therefore not relevant for the existence of free will in the sense that they show that free will does not exist. They are relevant because they are an extra step in the discourse shift from phenomenological to realist.

13.5.3 Reductionism

The effects of this step from phenomenology to realism are further strengthened by a development in the sciences. The sciences strive for explanatory parsimony by trying to derive more specific laws from more general ones (Curd & Cover, 1998, pp. 903–1047). For example, theories about the motion of the planets are derived from a general theory of gravitation, which is in turn derived from the general theory of relativity and the curvature of space/time. This development goes hand in hand with

---

[24] For logicians: It is not possible to derive from $\exists e(e = \text{experience}(<\text{jaap thinks}>))$ that $\exists p(p = \text{jaap} \& \text{Thinks}(p))$. The text between '<' and '>' represents the propositional content of the experience. Cf. (Quine, 1976).

a reduction of the entities in more specific and concrete theories to entities in more general and more abstract theories. The entities in modern physics become increasingly further removed from the entities in the meaningful world in which we live.[25]

This development towards reduction of the elements of our 'life-world' to elements that are so far removed from our experienced world that they have become unrecognizable makes it difficult, if not impossible, for people to live in the world as physics describes it. Herein lies the cause of the alleged impossibility, pointed out by Peter Strawson, that we live in a world in which human beings are treated as mere objects. (Apparently, he still assumed that the world about which physics talks contains human beings, rather than collections of subatomic particles, or only 'fields'.) The replacement of the discourse about the human 'life-world' with a discourse about the entities in the latest physical theories may well be impossible for most human beings. Moreover, as Morse pointed out, such a replacement may go at the cost of what we highly value in inter-human relations.

13.5.4 The Possibility of Compatibilism

This supports the compatibilist solution: why not use the two kinds of discourse side by side? Apparently, we can talk both about the chemical reactions that make our muscles contract, and about one person catching another person who almost fell. These are just two perspectives, used to describe the 'same' event in the world. If physics prefers the one level of description, while humans prefer the other level for their mutual relations, nothing seems to be wrong.

A popular metaphor in this connection is that of different kinds of maps that represent the same area, for instance a map of waterways and a map of industrial activities. The different maps give us different information about the same area, and the information of the one map cannot be reduced to the information provided by the other map, but one could be superimposed on the other or they could be combined into a new, more detailed map without contradiction. As long as the information provided by the maps is consistent, there is nothing wrong. However, if the maps contain inconsistent information, for instance because the one map portrays a lake exactly where the other maps shows an industrial plant, roads included, they cannot be used together, and there is good reason to assume that at least one of the maps must contain errors.

The same holds for different perspectives on action. If the one perspective provides us with a story about chemical reactions in a pack of neurons, while the other perspective talks about a person pondering a difficult decision, it must be possible to combine these two perspectives if they are to deal with 'the same thing'.

However, the consistency of two perspectives on the same thing must allow the perspectives to be perspectives on 'the same thing'. This kind of consistency, which

---

[25] Moore (2018) discusses different varieties of reductionism and their relevance for responsibility.

deals with different aspects of the same thing, is not the same as the consistency of theories that deal with different topics and which for that reason cannot contradict each other, just as two maps of entirely different areas cannot contradict each other. Another example of the latter would be the way in which theories about the opening times of cinemas in Paris and about the best way to maximize the lifetime milk production of a cow are consistent. These two topics have nothing to do with each other, and that is precisely the point of this example: theories that deal with topics that have nothing to do with each other will typically be consistent in that they do not (and cannot) contradict each other.

It is more difficult to achieve consistency of theories that deal with 'the same thing'. Yet, that is the kind of consistency that is required for the tenability of compatibilism. A neurophysiological theory should be consistent with a theory about belief formation, or about the choice for an action. More is required, however: if compatibilism is to become plausible, the neurophysiological theory and the folk-psychological theories should not merely be consistent with each other about belief and action, it should also be made plausible that they are theories of 'the same thing'. This requires either that the entities in the phenomenological/folk-psychological account can be reduced to entities in the realist account, or that there is a neutral third way of identifying entities into which both accounts can be translated.[26] Moreover, ideally it should also be possible to explain the folk-psychological theories on the basis of the neurophysiological ones[27]: why do particular brain states and brain events lead to particular beliefs or actions?

We find that the contrast between, on the one hand, a phenomenological/folk-psychological perspective on human action – which we see reflected in free will libertarianism – and, on the other hand, a realist/reductionist perspective – which we see reflected in hard determinism – cannot easily be overcome by stating that the perspectives talk about different things and are therefore consistent and compatible. A successful compatibilist reconciliation of the two perspectives asks for more, including at least an account of how the two perspectives are perspectives on 'the same thing'. Such an account is at present still lacking, and part of the worries of non-compatibilists is that such an account will turn out to be impossible. Whether this worry is justified is still an open question. Impossibility is hard to prove.

13.5.5 The Desirability of Compatibilism

Either compatibilism is tenable in the sense that it can be made plausible that the phenomenological/folk-psychological account of mental phenomena and actions deals with 'the same thing' as the realist/reductionist account, or it is not. In both

---

[26] For lawyers: this is the philosophical counterpart of the demand for a *tertium comparationis* in the theory of comparative law (Michaels, 2006).
[27] Theoretically, it would also be acceptable if the neurophysiological states and events could be explained on the basis of the folk-psychological ones, but that seems (even more) unlikely.

cases, it is possible to plead for the co-existence of the two kinds of discourse, albeit that the plea is (even) more attractive if compatibilism is tenable. However, if we assume that there is no place for blame or responsibility in the realist/reductionist account, the continuation of the phenomenological/folk-psychological account cannot be based on the fact that it best fits with the blameworthiness and responsibility of agents. If the traditional account is to co-exist with the modern scientific account, it must be justified on non-retributivist grounds. In practice, this would mean that we need a consequentialist justification for retribution in criminal law.[28]

Rawls (1955) famously argued that the social practice – he called it an 'institution' – of criminal law should be justified through its positive consequences. These might, for example, be the prevention of criminal behaviour through incapacitation or deterrence, reparation of the harm done through crimes, or the rehabilitation of criminals. At the same time, individual cases of punishment could be justified with retributivist reasons: the rules defining criminal liability may require blameworthiness as a condition for criminal liability. This would fit with the practice described by Carlsmith (2008) that people who must justify punishment in general often do so by means of consequentialist reasons, while actual punishing behaviour seems to be motivated by retributivism.

The Rawlsian solution seems to provide an attractive way out of the retributivist/consequentialist dilemma in criminal law. It remains to be seen, however, whether this way out really works. That it is theoretically possible to give a consequentialist justification for a retributivist social practice does not yet prove that this consequentialist justification can actually be given. Whether that is the case depends on the actual consequences of retributivism. And precisely here, we can count on the cognitive sciences for new insights.

13.6 CONCLUSION

In this chapter we have considered the debates in criminal law theory about responsibility and liability, and how the use of these notions is threatened by determinism, or by the lack of agent control. These debates have been mainly philosophical, although they have been influenced by the upcoming physical sciences with their increasing explanatory power and, quite recently, findings from the cognitive sciences, including the experiments of Libet.

The main positions in these debates have been (1) libertarianism, which defends a central role for agents and their free will, (2) hard incompatibilism, which denies the existence of free will and the possibility of responsibility or liability based on desert, and (3) compatibilism, which argues that our actual social practice does not

---

[28] It is somewhat akin to an atheist pleading for the promotion of (civil) religion because it has such attractive consequences (cf. Rousseau, 1762, book IV, chapter 8).

depend on any philosophical position and can therefore co-exist with both libertarianism and hard incompatibilism.

We have tried to describe the different positions in the debate in a fair manner. Moreover, in the penultimate section we have tried to explain the continuing debates by means of a distinction between the phenomenological/folk-psychological way of looking at the world in general and agency in particular, and the realist/reductionist perspective. In doing so, we have reformulated the core business of compatibilism. The central question is no longer whether free will is compatible with determinism, or whether responsibility is compatible with the non-existence of free will. It has become whether, and to what extent, the realist/reductionist perspective on the world and on agency is compatible with the phenomenological/folk-psychological perspective. The cognitive sciences operate precisely in the border area between (folk-)psychological phenomena that need to be explained, and realist theories that are often used to provide the explanations. It seems, therefore, that the successfulness of the cognitive sciences will determine the successfulness of this new form of compatibilism.

REFERENCES

Bernstein, Mark. (2002). Fatalism. In Kane, 2002, pp. 65–81.
Blomsma, Jeroen, & Roef, David. (2019a). Forms and Aspects of Mens Rea. In Johannes Keiler & David Roef (eds.), *Comparatible Concepts of Criminal Law*. Cambridge: Intersentia, pp. 177–205.
Blomsma, Jeroen, & Roef, David. (2019b). Justifications and Excuses. In Johannes Keiler & David Roef (eds.), *Comparatible Concepts of Criminal Law*. Cambridge: Intersentia, pp. 207–51.
Boaz, David (ed.). (1997). *The Libertarian Reader*. New York: The Free Press.
Carlsmith, Kevin M. (2008). On Justifying Punishment: The Discrepancy between Words and Actions. *Social Justice Research* 21, 199–137.
Caruso, Gregg D. (2012). *Free Will and Consciousness*. Lanham, MD: Lexington Books.
Caruso, Gregg D. (2018). Skepticism About Moral Responsibility. In Edward N. Zalta (ed.), *The Stanford Encyclopedia of Philosophy* (Spring 2018 Edition). Retrieved from https://plato.stanford.edu/archives/spr2018/entries/skepticism-moral-responsibility/
Chisholm, Roderick M. (1982). Human Freedom and the Self. In Gary Watson (ed.). *Free Will*. Oxford: Oxford University Press, 24–35.
Curd, Martin, & Cover, J. A. (eds.). (1998). *Philosophy of Science*. New York and London: W.W. Norton & Company.
Dennett, Daniel C. (1984). *Elbow Room. The Varieties of Free Will Worth Wanting*. Cambridge, MA: MIT Press.
Dennett, Daniel C. (2003). *Freedom Evolves*. London: Penguin Books.
Descartes, René. (1641). *Meditations Metaphysique*, 1st ed. Paris: Larousse.
Dworkin, Ronald. (2011). *Justice for Hedgehogs*. Cambridge, MA: Harvard University Press.
Feinberg, Joel. (1970). *Doing and Deserving*. Princeton, NJ: Princeton University Press.

Fischer, John Martin, & Ravizza, Mark (eds.) (1993). *Perspectives on Moral Responsibility*. Ithaca, NY: Cornell University Press.
Fletcher, George P. (2007). *The Grammar of Criminal Law. Volume One: Foundations*. Oxford: Oxford University Press.
Frankfurt, Harry G. (1969). Alternate Possibilities and Moral Responsibility. *Journal of Philosophy* 45, 829–39.
Frankfurt, Harry G. (1971). Freedom of the Will and the Concept of a Person. *Journal of Philosophy* 68, 5–20.
Frankfurt, Harry G. (1983). What Are We Morally Responsible For. In Leigh S. Cauman & S. Morgenbesser (eds.), *How Many Questions? Essays in Honor of Sidney Morgenbesser*. Indianapolis, IN: Hackett.
Gallagher, Shaun. (2012). *Phenomenology*. Basingstoke: Macmillan.
Greene, Joshua, & Cohen, Jonathan. (2004). For the Law, Neuroscience Changes Nothing and Everything. *Philosophical Transactions of the Royal Society B: Biological Sciences* 359, 1781–85.
Hage, Jaap. (2017a). The Compatibilist Fallacy. *Revus* 32, 97–118.
Hage, Jaap. (2017b). Tort Law. In Jaap Hage, Antonia Waltermann, & Bram Akkermans (eds.), *Introduction to Law*, 2nd ed. Cham: Springer, pp. 109–28.
Hage, Jaap. (2018). *Foundations and Building Blocks of Law*. Den Haag: Eleven International Publishing.
Hart, H. L. A. (1968). *Punishment and Responsibility. Essays in the Philosophy of Law*. Oxford: Clarendon Press.
Hodgson, David. (2002). Quantum Physics, Consciousness and Free Will. In Kane, 2002, pp. 85–110.
Kane, Robert. (1996). *The Significance of Free Will*. Oxford: Oxford University Press.
Kane, Robert (ed.). (2002). *The Oxford Handbook of Free Will*. Oxford: Oxford University Press.
Kane, Robert. (2005). *A Contemporary Introduction to Free Will*. Oxford: Oxford University Press.
Kenneth, Jeannette. (2001). *Agency and Responsibility*. Oxford: Clarendon Press.
Kornhuber, K., & Deecke, L. (1965). Hirnpotentialänderungen bei Willkürbewegungen und passiven Bewegungen des Menschen: Bereitschaftspotential und reafferente Potentiale. *Pflügers Archiv für die gesamte Physiologie des Menschen und der Tiere* 284, 1–17.
Libet, B. (1985). Unconscious Cerebral Initiative and the Role of Conscious Will in Voluntary Action. *Behavioral and Brain Sciences* 8, 529–66.
Lucy, William. (2007). *Philosophy of Private Law*. Oxford: Oxford University Press.
Mackor, Anne Ruth. (2013). What Can Neuroscience Say About Responsibility? Taking the Distinction Between Theoretical and Practical Reason Seriously. In Vincent, 2013, pp. 53–83.
Maslen, Cei, Horgan, Terry, & Daly, Helen. (2009). Mental Causation. In Helen Beebee, Christopher Hitchcock, & Peter Menzies (eds.), *The Oxford Handbook of Causation*. Oxford: Oxford University Press, pp. 523–53.
McKenna, Michael, & Coates, D. Justin. (2020). Compatibilism. In Edward N. Zalta (ed.), *The Stanford Encyclopedia of Philosophy* (Spring 2020 Edition). https://plato.stanford.edu/archives/spr2020/entries/compatibilism/
McLaughlin, Brian P. (1994). Epiphenomenalism. In Samuel Guttenplan (ed.), *A Companion to the Philosophy of Mind*. Oxford: Blackwell, pp. 277–88.
Metzinger, Thomas. (2011). The No-Self Alternative. In Shaun Gallagher (ed.), *The Oxford Handbook of The Self*. Oxford: Oxford University Press, pp. 279–96.

Michaels, Ralph. (2006). The Functional Method of Comparative Law. In M. Reimann & R. Zimmerman (eds.), *The Oxford Handbook of Comparative Law*. Oxford: Oxford University Press, pp. 339–82.

Miller, Alexander. (2019). Realism. In Edward N. Zalta (ed.), *The Stanford Encyclopedia of Philosophy* (Winter 2019 Edition). https://plato.stanford.edu/archives/win2019/entries/realism/

Moore, Michael. (2018). 'Nothing But a Pack of Neurons': The Moral Responsibility of the Human Machine. In Bebhinn Donelly-Lazarov (ed.), *Neurolaw and Responsibility for Action*. Cambridge: Cambridge University Press, pp. 28–70.

Morse, Steven J. (2013). Common Criminal Law Compatibilism. In Vincent, 2013, pp. 27–52.

O'Connor, Timothy. (1995). Agent Causation. In Timothy O'Connor (ed.), *Agents, Causes & Events, Essays on Indeterminism and Free Will*. Oxford: Oxford University Press, pp. 173–200.

O'Connor, Timothy, & Franklin, Christopher. (2020). Free Will. In Edward N. Zalta (ed.). *The Stanford Encyclopedia of Philosophy* (Spring 2020 Edition). https://plato.stanford.edu/archives/spr2020/entries/freewill/

Parfit, Derek. (1984). *Reasons and Persons*. Oxford: Clarendon Press.

Peereboom, Derk. (2001). *Living Without Free Will*. Cambridge: Cambridge University Press.

Peereboom, Derk. (2014). *Free Will, Agency and Meaning in Life*. Oxford: Oxford University Press.

Quine, W. V. (1976). Quantifiers and Propositional Attitudes. In W. V. Quine (ed.), *The Ways of Paradox and Other Essays* (revised and enlarged edition). Cambridge, MA: Harvard University Press, pp. 185–96.

Rawls, John. (1995). Two Concepts of Rules. *Philosophical Review* 64, 3–32.

Robb, David, & Heil, John. (2019). Mental Causation. In Edward N. Zalta (ed.), *The Stanford Encyclopedia of Philosophy* (Summer 2019 Edition). https://plato.stanford.edu/archives/sum2019/entries/mental-causation/

Robinson, William. (2019). Epiphenomenalism. In Edward N. Zalta (ed.), *The Stanford Encyclopedia of Philosophy* (Summer 2019 Edition). https://plato.stanford.edu/archives/sum2019/entries/epiphenomenalism/

Rousseau, Jean-Jacques. (1762). *Du contrat social*. Marc Michel Rey: Amsterdam.

Searle, John R. (1983). *Intentionality: An Essay in the Philosophy of Mind*. Cambridge: Cambridge University Press.

Sinnott-Armstrong, Walter. (ed.). (2014). *Moral Psychology, Volume 4: Free Will and Moral Responsibility*. Cambridge, MA: MIT Press.

Sinnott-Armstrong, Walter, & Nadel, Lynn. (eds.) (2011). *Conscious Will and Responsibility*. Oxford: Oxford University Press.

Smart, J. J. C. (2017). The Mind/Brain Identity Theory. In Edward N. Zalta (ed.),*The Stanford Encyclopedia of Philosophy* (Spring 2017 edition). https://plato.stanford.edu/archives/spr2017/entries/mind-identity/.

Smilansky, Saul. (2000). *Free Will and Illusion*. Oxford: Oxford University Press.

Smilansky, Saul. (2002). Free Will, Fundamental Dualism, and the Centrality of Illusion. In Kane, 2002, pp. 489–505.

Smits, Jan M. (2017). *An Advanced Introduction to Private Law*. Cheltenham: Edward Elgar Publishing.

Strawson, Peter. (1962). Freedom and Resentment. *Proceedings of the British Academy*, 48, 1–25.

Strawson, Galen. (2011). The Minimal Subject. In Shaun Gallagher (ed.), *The Oxford Handbook of The Self*. Oxford: Oxford University Press, pp. 253–78.

Talbert, Matthew. (2019). Moral Responsibility. In Edward N. Zalta (ed.), *The Stanford Encyclopedia of Philosophy* (Winter 2019 Edition). https://plato.stanford.edu/archives/win2019/entries/moral-responsibility

Van Dam, Cees. (2014). *European Tort Law*, 2nd ed. Oxford: Oxford University Press.

Van Inwagen, Peter. (1995). When Is the Will Free? In Timothy O'Connor (ed.), *Agents, Causes & Events, Essays on Indeterminism and Free Will*. Oxford: Oxford University Press, pp. 219–38.

Vincent, Nicole A. (ed.). (2013). *Neuroscience and Legal Responsibility*. Oxford: Oxford University Press.

Wegner, Daniel M. (2002). *The Illusion of Conscious Will*. Cambridge, MA: The MIT Press.

White, Alan R. (1985). *Grounds of Liability: An Introduction to the Philosophy of Law*. Oxford: Clarendon Press.

14

Guilt in Criminal Law: Guilt in Us or in the Stars?

Mikołaj Małecki and Marek Sławiński

The fault, dear Brutus, is not in our stars,
  But in ourselves
             W. Shakespeare, *Julius Caesar*, Act I, Scene II, ll. 148-9

14.1 INTRODUCTION: THE QUESTION OF GUILT

The words above are those that Cassius addresses to Brutus in order to convince him to take part in the plot against Caesar. Neither blind fate nor the providence of the gods or the stars explain why Caesar has gained so much power in the Roman Republic. The fault lies with those who allowed Caesar to act, therefore the fault will also be on the part of Cassius and Brutus if they remain passive. While pondering the future of the Roman state, the characters in Shakespeare's drama raise a very important question, namely, where does the fault lie? In us or in external circumstances over which we often have no influence? Questions like these are of great significance, not only to philosophy but also to criminal law (see Filar, 2011, p. 65).

Before we proceed to the proper consideration of this topic, a brief explanation of the terminology is necessary.

In the Shakespeare quote above, Cassius uses the word 'fault', while the title of this article not only employs the term 'guilt' but does so in a somewhat unusual manner, stating that guilt is 'in something or someone'. Given the respective meanings both words have in ordinary and legal language,[1] one might be curious as to the topic we

---

[1] English dictionaries typically indicate three basic meanings for each of those words. For 'fault': (1) weakness or unattractive feature, (2) mistake, failure, or misfortune in someone's action, and (3) responsibility or fact of being responsible for such an act. For 'guilt': (1) a feeling of worry or shame for doing something wrong, (2) fact of committing a crime or wrongdoing, and (3) responsibility for such an act (for example, see McIntosh, 2013; Simpson & Weiner, 1989). Both words thus cover a wide spectrum of objects, including feelings, features of a person, their acts, and the notion of responsibility. Reference to legal language increases this number by adding technical meanings, specifically tailored to the content of given legal provisions or judicial decisions.

intend to discuss here. The short answer is that the subject of our investigation is one of the conditions that must be met in order to impose criminal liability, namely, the requirement to establish that the prohibited act committed by the perpetrator is culpable. We refer to the above-mentioned condition of criminal liability by means of the term 'guilt', thus using this word in a technical sense which is different from its ordinary meaning. Choosing between 'guilt' and 'fault' may seem arbitrary, but the language issues concerning the selection of the appropriate English word are of secondary importance here.[2] The subject of this study is one of the theoretical concepts used in continental criminal law, and our aim is to present and characterize it. Because of that, direct attention is given to the content of the concept in question rather than the words used to label it.

The word 'guilt' can be understood in criminal law in two general ways. One of them has already been mentioned above, namely that guilt is the requirement to establish that the prohibited act committed by the perpetrator is culpable. This meaning can be called *narrow* or *essential* because it refers to guilt as to one of the necessary conditions of criminal liability. The second meaning of the term in question is closely related to the intuitions of common language. When we say that someone is guilty of a crime (e.g. murder or theft), it means that this person has committed an unlawful act and is responsible for it. In other words, the guilt here is synonymous with the fact of being liable for a crime. The provisions regulating criminal procedure typically refers to this meaning. A good example is the principle of the presumption of innocence, according to which the accused is presumed to be innocent until proven guilty.[3] Guilt in this sense does not refer to one of the conditions of criminal liability but to the liability as such. In this context, 'to prove guilt' simply means to prove that a perpetrator committed a crime for which he or she is liable. This understanding of guilt can be called *broad* or *procedural*.

As we can see, the judicial formula that someone has been found guilty can be understood in two ways. On the one hand, as the recognition that all the conditions required to held perpetrator liable for a crime have been established; on the other, as a recognition that one specific condition of criminal liability has been established, namely, that the perpetrator committed a culpable act. Therefore, guilt and being guilty can be understood very broadly, in a procedural manner (as the fact of being criminally responsible for a certain act), or narrowly, in an essential manner (as only one of the necessary premises of criminal liability). Our further considerations in this article will only be aimed at the essential meaning of guilt, as this is the subject of the theories of guilt that we want to discuss.

[2] Both terms can be found in the criminal law literature as translations of the concept discussed in this paper.
[3] See for example Article 6 section 2 of the Convention for the Protection of Human Rights and Fundamental Freedoms (also known as the European Convention on Human Rights): 'Everyone charged with a criminal offence shall be presumed innocent until proved guilty according to law', and Article 48 section 1 of the Charter of Fundamental Rights of the European Union: 'Everyone who has been charged shall be presumed innocent until proved guilty according to law.'

The connection between guilt and criminal liability is firmly rooted in the minds of continental criminal law scholars, as reflected by the commonly accepted maxims: *nullum crimen sine culpa* (no crime without guilt), or *nulla poena sine culpa* (no punishment without guilt), which are often directly expressed in legal provisions or employed by the courts in their reasoning. Emphasizing the importance of the issue of guilt for various areas of human life, Jacob Chwast stated: 'If there were no guilt there would be no ethics, no morality, no religion, and no law; indeed, there would be anarchy' (Chwast, 1964, p. 58). In fact, as a matter of principle, if there were no guilt, there would be no criminal liability. However, as we have stated above, guilt is only one of the conditions required to impose this liability. Because of that, it is necessary to precisely determine what guilt is, and how it can be attributed to the perpetrator. Answers to those questions are given by *the theories of guilt*.

While guilt is unquestionably treated by continental criminal law scholars as a necessary condition of criminal liability, all other issues related to this concept, even the most basic and fundamental ones, are highly disputed. The existence of different theories of guilt is a good example of this situation. What is guilt? How can we attribute it to a perpetrator? What are the circumstances that eliminate the possibility of this attribution? (for example see Greenawalt, 1986, pp. 89–108) These are just some of the questions that have been a constant topic of inquiry for continental criminal law scholars for a long time now.[4] Shakespeare's statement can serve as an illustration of a search which is aimed at unfolding the elusive nature of the concept in question. According to Cassius, the guilt is in us, not in the stars, because we act or remain passive. Therefore, a man should not blame other people or external factors for his or her own actions. To put it simply, we are the masters of our own fate. In consequence, to find guilt, we should not look up at the stars but deep into ourselves. This short exposition of Cassius's reasoning shows that the issue in question raises many important topics along the way, such as the deterministic or indeterministic nature of the world around us, human agency, free will, or the psychological traits required to attribute guilt. Therefore, the problem of guilt can not only be approached from different points of view in criminal law, but also provides a good opportunity for an interdisciplinary discussion between law, philosophy, and the cognitive sciences.[5]

Inspired by Shakespeare's quote, we will look closely at Cassius's question, albeit slightly rephrased for the purposes of this article as '*where does the guilt lie?*' This marks the starting point of our considerations, from which we will venture into discussion between the two most representative theories of guilt in continental criminal law: the psychological (in Section 14.2) and the normative (in Section 14.3). This discussion will be supplemented (in Section 14.4) with remarks

---

[4] It is worth noticing that some of these issues are discussed in common law systems as well (see Corrado, 1991, pp. 465–97).
[5] An example of such an interdisciplinary discussion can be seen in Hörnle (2016, pp. 1–10).

concerning two other theories, the functional and the imputative, that further develop some of the issues raised by the psychological and normative approach.

Can cognitive science help in the assessment of given theories of guilt, especially by pointing out their problems, advantages, and disadvantages? Such a perspective seems intriguing, but it needs to be noted that the application of this type of research to the considerations made in criminal law is not a simple task. We are dealing here with two different fields of study, each with its own respective methodology and terminology, thus resulting in differences of approach to the same subject matter. Our main point of interest is criminal law with its theories of guilt. During our discussion, however, we will highlight some of the problems that might be interesting from the cognitive perspective. This will allow us to compare how criminal law and cognitive science approach different aspects of the issue of guilt. For the purposes of this paper, we will especially focus on the following four aspects:

i) What is guilt and how can we describe it?
ii) What allows us to say that someone is guilty?
iii) How can we distinguish guilt from other concepts related to criminal liability (e.g. human agency, volition)?
iv) How is the concept of guilt (or can it be) applied by the court during the assessment of the criminal liability of the accused?

In all of those aspects, it is possible to point out specific tensions between the intuitive understanding of guilt and the more specific, typically legal one. Our intuitions seem to be closer to an understanding of guilt that situates this phenomenon in ourselves (and perhaps even identifies it with one of our mental states). In contrast, criminal law not only employs sophisticated concepts that are hard to grasp, but more importantly tends to separate guilt from our everyday and easy-to-grasp mental experiences. When considered from such a perspective, guilt presents itself as something unfamiliar, as something that, referring to the Shakespeare quote, is in the stars. Because of that, we will sum up our considerations by presenting a view that aims to reconcile those two perspectives by focusing on the protective function of guilt (Section 14.5).

14.2 PSYCHOLOGICAL THEORIES OF GUILT: GUILT IN US

Historically, the psychological approach was the earliest method to define guilt in modern continental criminal law. The name of this theory (or, in fact, group of theories) reflects its basic premise, according to which guilt is identified as a *psychological fact*, namely, *a state of the perpetrator's mind*. One of the most prominent features of those theories is the usage of the terms 'intentional guilt' (to indicate wrongful intent) and 'unintentional guilt' (to indicate a lack of wrongful intent).

Traditionally, continental criminal law was oriented towards the objective elements of a crime, such as the wrongful behaviour of a perpetrator, causation, or the harmfulness of an act. During the Enlightenment period, the tendency to individualize and subjectivize criminal liability began to be more prominent. This change in the approach to criminal law led to the formulation of the first psychological theories of guilt. The next impulse for those theories came in the nineteenth century, with the rapid development of psychology, which offered valuable insights into the human mind and scientific terminology to describe psychological phenomena, such as consciousness, volition, motivation, and knowledge. The employment of those results by continental criminal law scholars opened up new perspectives for theoretical concepts of guilt. An awareness of one's situation and behaviour, one's attitude towards the attempted or committed act, one's willingness to cause harm, or mistakes in the perception of reality, and other characteristic features of a perpetrator acquired significant importance for the assessment of criminal liability.

The basic statements of the psychological approach were formulated in German criminal law theory. As early as the eighteenth century, Christoph Karl Stübel claimed that the essence of guilt lies in the fact that a perpetrator wants to commit a criminal act, for example, he or she wants to kill someone, or take someone else's belongings. This wrongful intent exhausts the notion of guilt and justifies the application of punishment. What to do with situations in which a perpetrator has no such intent? Consider the following example. John overslept and is now late for work. Because of that, he decided to drive as fast as he could, even if this would mean exceeding the speed limit a few times. Unfortunately, on a sharp turn, he lost control of the vehicle and hit a bus stop, injuring three people as a result. What response can the theory in question give to such cases? Can John be held criminally liable for the traffic accident which resulted in three injuries? According to Stübel, the mental state of our perpetrator can be described by two elements. First, by the behaviour that John was willing to perform, and second, by John's awareness of the possible consequences of his behaviour. We know that John decided to do two things: to drive to work and exceed the speed limit. The first is a legally permitted action, while the second constitutes a breach of traffic rules. Therefore, he was willing to break the law, but only by the violation of speed limits and nothing more. Based on this, we ask the question of whether John was aware of the possibility that his behaviour could result in a traffic accident with people injured. The degree of the foreseeability of the consequences of an undertaken behaviour depends on the circumstances of a given situation and the characteristic features of the agent; thus, this degree may vary, even be absent altogether. For Stübel, if the perpetrator was completely unaware that the performed action might result in criminal harm, then he or she cannot be punished for a crime but only for a misdemeanour or a petty offence (of course, if his or her behaviour constitutes such a misdemeanour or petty offence).[6] In our example, the answer to the question of John's guilt depends on whether he was aware that the speeding could result in a traffic accident and the subsequent injuries.

The most renowned adherent of the psychological approach was Paul Johann Anselm von Feuerbach. He formulated his own theory of guilt on the basis of the so-called psychological coercion thesis. The idea behind it is as follows. Legal provisions make sense only when they can influence the behaviour of their addressees. Let us take, for example, the legal provision that prohibits jaywalking. Its purpose is to ban a certain type of pedestrian behaviour in traffic. In other words, it sets a requirement for pedestrians to refrain from crossing the street outside of specially marked areas. Because of that, it can be said that this provision enforces a kind of coercion. Of course, the ban on jaywalking can be efficient only if two conditions are met. First, its addressees must know of its existence and its content, that is they must know that the law prohibits jaywalking. Second, addressees must be aware of their factual circumstances in order to be able to adapt their behaviour to the relevant legal provisions. The first condition concerns knowledge about the law in force, the second knowledge about the facts relevant to this law. In this context, guilt is understood by Feuerbach as a deliberate violation of a legal provision by a perpetrator who has knowledge of the contents of this provision. In other words, it is an intentional breach of the law, the content of which is known to us (Feuerbach, 1798, p. 61; see Zoll, 1984).

Subsequent criminal law scholars took over the assumptions of the psychological approach and developed them further. For example, another German scholar, Robert von Hippel, clarified the psychological theory by distinguishing two mutually related aspects of guilt: intellectual and volitional. The first is the perpetrator's knowledge of the situation which he or she is currently in (e.g. knowledge of the fact that a certain person has a significant amount of money), the second is the desire to cause a criminal effect (e.g. to take this money). Therefore, guilt is understood as a knowledge of the existing situation accompanied by a desire to commit the prohibited act. This theory is also called the theory of will (Hippel, 1908, p. 378).

The above presentation gives us a good glimpse of the psychological theories of guilt. Let us now turn to the assessment of their advantages and disadvantages. The primary merit of the psychological approach to the issue of guilt is the emphasis on subjective and individual features of the perpetrator, such as motivation, volition, and knowledge.[7] Those factors give us better and more detailed insight into the mind of a person that has committed a crime. In consequence, the assessment of criminal liability and the imposition of penalties can be done in a more accurate way.

---

[6] Reconstruction of Stübel's theory is based on Loffler (1895, p. 210f.).
[7] These factors are usually addressed in common law tradition as part of the notion of *mens rea* (see Heller, 2009, p. 317).

However, psychological theories are not free of their own shortcomings. First of all, they do not cope well with *unintentional acts*. We have seen some problems with this issue while discussing Stübel's theory of guilt. Let us explore this topic further by considering the following example. A car driver did not notice a give way sign and entered an intersection while convinced of his or her priority. At the same time, another vehicle was coming from the priority road. In consequence, the cars crashed into each other, and the force of the collision was so severe that all of the passengers in the second car died. Can it be established, on the grounds of psychological theories, that the driver who was falsely convinced of his or her priority committed a culpable act? He or she did not have any blameworthy attitude towards violating traffic rules, and did not even realize that there was going to be a traffic accident because of his or her actions. Quite the opposite; he or she was convinced that everything that he or she did was in accordance with those rules. The psychological theory of guilt leads to the conclusion that guilt cannot be attributed to a perpetrator in this situation, and thus no criminal liability can be imposed. Such consequences do not seem to be acceptable for two main reasons. First, absolution of criminal liability in the case of a perpetrator whose behaviour caused the death of two people seems to be in clear contradiction with our common intuitions about the appropriate response to socially harmful acts. Second, such a solution poses a serious risk of abuse, especially in situations where the perpetrator of an accident could falsely claim that he or she did not notice a road sign, and the other available evidence would not allow a judge to discern the truth.

The inability to successfully attribute guilt in cases of unintentional acts is not the only problem here. The psychological theories do not offer us a satisfactory description and explanation of unintentionality. Therefore, if we do not know what an unintentional act really is, how can we attribute criminal liability in such cases? The psychological theories only tell us that in cases of unintentional acts a perpetrator is not fully aware of his or her behaviour. In other words, a cognitive deficit of some sort exists on his or her side. However, we do not know what to do with this deficit. One possible reply is to say that, in cases of unintentional actions, guilt cannot be established, and thus a perpetrator cannot be held criminally liable. Such a conclusion is consistent with the basic premises of psychological theories, but not with our sense of justice.

Is there any possibility for psychological theories of guilt to avoid these two problems? Let us consider the following solutions:

i) Extended concept of guilt that encompasses the lack of intent.
ii) Assumption that guilt is based on the objective features of the perpetrator's behaviour, including carelessness and violation of the rules of conduct required by the law.

iii) Concept of pre-guilt, which allows us to establish guilt based on the perpetrator's psychological experiences that took place prior to the performance of a prohibited act.[8]
iv) Adoption of the fiction of guilt in the case of unintentional acts.
v) Resignation from treating guilt as a necessary condition of criminal liability, thus making it possible to impose this liability without establishing guilt.

Proposition no. (i) is prone to result in incoherence because it assumes that two opposing psychical phenomena – the intention to do something, and lack of such an intention – should be called guilt. If the psychological theories adhere to the claim that guilt is wrongful intent, then they cannot embrace the unintentional acts under the same notion. Proposition no. (ii) equals resignation from the psychological approach to criminal liability. Establishing guilt on the basis of the objective features of the perpetrator's behaviour has nothing to do with his or her state of mind. Proposition no. (iii) is unacceptable because it does not refer to the mental state of the perpetrator during the time of the prohibited act.[9] Proposition no. (iv) is fundamentally inconsistent with the basic purpose of the psychological approach to the issue of guilt, namely placing more emphasis on the subjectivization and individualization of criminal liability. Instead, we are presented here with a fictional assumption. Because of that, this proposition seems to be an attempt to bypass the problem of unintentional acts rather than a solution to it. Finally, proposition no. (v) equates to the resignation of the principle of guilt in the cases of unintentional acts. Such a claim is in clear opposition to the one that guilt is one of the conditions required for the attribution of criminal liability. Therefore, none of those propositions can be deemed satisfactory on the grounds of the psychological approach.

The problems with unintentional acts did not overwhelm the psychological theories of guilt. However, another attack has been launched, this time aimed at the central assumption of those theories, namely the claim that guilt is a psychological fact.

A good example of this line of argumentation is the case of the imprisoned cavers (see Fuller, 1949, pp. 616–45; D'Amato, 1980, pp. 467–85). Four cave explorers are trapped in an underground cave with a limited amount of food and water, and no prospect of a quick rescue. To avoid starvation, they draw straws in order to decide who will be killed and eaten. Help comes a few days after this gruesome act, and only three explorers are rescued.

Based on the assumptions of the psychological approach, the cavers are guilty because they committed the intentional act of murdering another man. They knew

---

[8] For example, in the case of a physician carrying out a negligent medical procedure, the essence of guilt would consist of the intention of not studying diligently a subject which the physician had taken classes in during their medical studies years earlier. This intentional negligence in acquiring medical knowledge (pre-guilt) resulted in an incorrect diagnosis.

[9] In the given example, pre-guilt refers only to the preparation for exams during medical studies in the past, not to actions undertaken currently.

what they were doing and wanted to do this. However, there is one important feature of their intent; namely that they decided to kill another in the hope of saving themselves. Should they be held liable for the crime of murder when their motivation was to save their own lives at the expense of another person's? This question seems vital for the imposition of criminal liability because it directly addresses the fundamental issues concerning justice. However, the psychological theories of guilt do not seem to notice it. For them, the fact that the cave explorers decided to kill their fellow constitutes a wrongful intent. This approach seems too simple for the moral (and legal) dilemma that we have here. As the critics of these theories have pointed out, it is necessary to distinguish between facts relevant for criminal liability (such as an act committed by a perpetrator, his or her intellectual condition during performance of this act, and volition) and the normative evaluation of those facts. What is more important is the question of whether the intent of the cave explorers can be deemed wrongful. In other words, we should focus here not only on the *description* of relevant facts, but also on their *evaluation*. To say that something is wrong is not to describe, but to evaluate.

This critique leads to another issue with the theories in question. Let us look at the following line of argumentation. Some of the legal provisions describing crimes mention the intent with which they are committed, while some of them do not require such intent, but only recklessness or negligence. As we have said before, on the basis of the psychological approach, intent (which is a psychological phenomenon) is treated as guilt. Therefore, each time it is established that the perpetrator acted intentionally, his or her guilt is also established. This leads to two problems. First, what is guilt in the case of crimes that do not require intent? We have already discussed this issue above. Second, if the guilt is identical with intent, then why use both terms in criminal law? By establishing intent, we are at the same time establishing guilt, and by establishing guilt we are simply confirming the prior attribution of intent. If there is no difference between those two concepts, then, in fact, we have only one concept that is referred to by two different names. On the grounds of the language used, this leads to unnecessary ambiguity and renders one of those terms redundant. On the grounds of the used concepts, it deflates the structure of the crime because a prohibited act that is guilty is identical with a prohibited act that is intentional. This poses a serious *methodological drawback* to the theories in question (see Zoll, 2003, p. 84).

Let us return to the case of the trapped cave explorers. If we would like to free them from criminal liability because of the unusual situation in which they found themselves, we need to have an adequate legal concept. The assessment that they had an intent to kill another person is clearly not enough. The intentions of the cavers deserve understanding and proper *justification*. That is why the German criminal law scholar and critic of psychological theory, James Goldschmidt, distinguished two separate issues: the desire to commit an act that should not be committed (*Wollen des Nicht-sein-Sollenden*), and the determination of whether the perpetrator should or should not want it at all (*nicht-sein-sollendes Wollen*) (see Goldschmidt, 1913, pp. 129–96, 224–9; Achenbach, 1974, p. 85).

This critique of the psychological theory of guilt is also aimed at the relatively naïve understanding of psychology to which this theory refers. It can be said, of course, that the description of someone's act in terms of psychological theories is a natural and straightforward choice. Let us consider the following example. When we say, 'someone wanted to do something wrong, and then did it', we are already treating this person as responsible for what has happened. Such a statement indicates two things: (1) the relationship between the agent and his or her act, and (2) a desire on the part of that person to commit this act. Therefore, it is easy to identify guilt with this second element, namely, with an intentional attitude towards one's behaviour. In most situations we can say 'You are guilty, because you wanted to do what you did', and it will be completely clear what we are talking about. Even more, we will find that this statement is in perfect accordance with our typical intuitions about moral right and wrong. However, if we look at this seemingly straightforward picture in more detail, some things start to blur. Our common way of speaking about people and their actions confers hidden presuppositions. One of them is the free will of an agent. By saying 'Someone wanted to do something wrong, and then did it', we are tacitly implying that this person had an area of freedom. Common experience shows us that we can act or refrain from doing so, even in situations in which we have a specific desire for this act. In other words, we have the ability to choose whether to follow our intentional attitudes or not. Free will, intentional attitudes, or the possibility to make rational decisions are notions that we implicitly employ in our everyday life in our perceptions of others, as well as of ourselves (see Brożek & Jakubiec, 2017, pp. 296–7). However, as cognitive sciences show us, concepts such as will (and accompanying mental states) are much more intricate and complex than our common intuitions about them (see Chapter 4 in this volume, by Kurek). Therefore, folk psychology (and its concepts, to which psychological theories of guilt tend to refer) are in need of substantial revision and need to take into account the current state of research on the human mind offered by cognitive science (see Greene & Cohen, 2004; Hörnle, 2016).

14.3 NORMATIVE THEORIES OF GUILT: GUILT IN THE STARS

Let us return for a moment to the quote from Shakespeare. If the psychological approach to the issue of guilt places the concept in question in us, then its opponents – the normative theories – transfer it to the stars. This means that the guilt is somehow located outside of us. But what does this mean exactly?

Richard Frank is considered to be a founder of the normative approach to the issue of guilt (see Achenbach, 1974, p. 99). The main idea of this theory lies in the concept called *chargeability*, that is, the possibility of accusing the perpetrator that he or she did not act in compliance with the obligations imposed by legal norms. We take the perpetrator's act in its entirety (that is as a socially harmful, intentional or unintentional act) and ask the question: was it possible to require from a perpetrator, at the moment in which he or she was acting, that he or she act in accordance with the law? As we can see, the notion of chargeability relies on the normative assessment of the perpetrator's act in terms of his or her ability to comply with the obligations imposed by legal norms.

If the answer is positive, then we can attribute guilt to the perpetrator's act because he or she had the possibility of acting in accordance with the law. If the answer is negative, this means that there are some other circumstances resulting in the perpetrator's inability to act in accordance with the law, thus preventing the attribution of guilt (see Graf zu Dohna, 1905, pp. 304–24; Freudenthal, 1922, p. 7; Welzel, 1969, p. 180). Therefore, guilt is a result of the assessment made from the normative point of view.

The name of the discussed theory is not accidental. When we talk about guilt in terms of chargeability, we abandon the sphere of facts and direct our eyes towards the sphere of legal obligations. In other words, we move from the sphere of *Sein* to the sphere of *Sollen*. The essence of guilt is not exhausted by the unlawfulness of an act or by the specific mental relation of the perpetrator to this act, but by the conclusion that such an act should not be committed in the first place (see Heinitz, 1926; Marcetus, 1928; Goldschmidt, 1930; Schaffstein, 1933). The category of chargeability applies to all types of prohibited acts, both intentional and unintentional. The process of examining criminal liability goes through two phases: the descriptive and the normative. The descriptive phase refers to the description of the actual event which consists of the prohibited act committed by a given perpetrator. Because the attribution of criminal liability is something more than a simple description of reality, the next phase (the normative one) consists of the normative evaluation of a factual event (see Schaffstein, 1933; Heinitz, 1926; Marcetus, 1928; Goldschmidt, 1930).

Of the many variants of the normative theories of guilt, two are the most representative (see Glaser, 1934, p. 4):

i) *The complex normative theory* (or eclectic theory) which postulates that the perpetrator's mental attitude has two functions in the process of establishing criminal liability. On the one hand, it constitutes a subjective element of the prohibited act (such as intent or lack of it), on the other, it is the element of guilt. Therefore, guilt is understood here as a *chargeable mental attitude* towards the committed act. The adherents of this theory state that the mental attitude of a perpetrator cannot be separated from its normative evaluation. If someone, for example, was acting with intent, then this particular state must also be reflected by the normative assessment of the committed act. In other words, the intent or lack of it are important for the question of facts and for the question of evaluation. This theory employs the same terminology as the psychological approach, namely 'intentional guilt' and 'unintentional guilt'.

ii) *The pure normative theory* separates the mental attitude of a perpetrator from the issue of guilt. The intentionality or unintentionality are the elements of the description of a prohibited act. They are objective features of the world and a question concerning facts. Guilt, however, is something entirely different. It is only an allegation based on the assessment of whether a given perpetrator had the objective ability to act in accordance with the law. Therefore, the mental state of the perpetrator is established only as a matter of fact, and guilt is established only as a matter of normative evaluation (see Maurach & Zipf, 1983, p. 440; Kindhäuser, 2005, p. 134). The adherents of this theory propose a change in terminology by swapping the predicate with the argument: instead of 'intentional guilt' or 'unintentional guilt' one should use the concept of 'intentional act' or 'unintentional act', which can be assessed as guilty or not.

The complex normative theory is an attempt to combine the findings of psychological theories with the normative approach. The dual function attributed to the mental state of a perpetrator (as an element of a prohibited act and as an element of guilt) helps to avoid the methodological objection raised against the psychological theories, namely, that there is no real distinction between the mental state of a perpetrator and the concept of guilt. The adherents of the complex normative theory agree that there is only one phenomenon in question here, namely the psychological fact of the perpetrator's having a particular state of mind. They also agree that this phenomenon in the process of attributing criminal liability is analysed twice, however, each time different aspect of it is considered. First, we simply establish facts, that is the actual mental status of a perpetrator at the time of his or her behaviour. Secondly, we evaluate this status from the perspective of legal provisions that provide obligations which were breached by a perpetrator's actions.

The pure normative theory of guilt is even better at avoiding the inconsistencies of the psychological approach. There is only one concept of guilt that is inherently consistent. The notions of 'intentional guilt' or 'unintentional guilt' which combine facts with normative evaluations are rejected. Also, there is no need to search for a specific solution in order to explain guilt in the case of unintentional acts. Regardless of the state of mind of the perpetrator, guilt is attributed in the same way.

In the case of the intentional act, guilt is the assessment that the perpetrator decided to commit a prohibited act while having the option to refrain from doing so. However, in a given situation, there may exist justifying circumstances such as insanity, the state of necessity, a so-called abnormal motivational situation, a significant mistake as to the circumstances excluding liability, and so on. If one of them occurs, then the possibility of attributing guilt will be excluded. Let us go back to the case of cave explorers who have killed and eaten their fellow companion. If we can say that in the situation in which they found themselves they should not have decided to kill another person, then we can also attribute guilt. If not, then they cannot be charged for their intent of killing another man. This type of consideration requires reference to values.

As we can see, two levels of analysis are clearly separated here: determination of the facts, including the murder and intention to cause death, and the *moral/normative evaluation* of that act in terms of the possibility of acting in conformity with the law (see Goldschmidt, 1913, pp. 129f., 224f.).

In the case of the unintentional act, guilt is also understood as the assessment that the perpetrator decided to commit a prohibited act while having the option to refrain from doing so. However, the characteristics of such an act are different from those of the case of an intentional one. Unintentionality means that the perpetrator has no intent to commit a prohibited act but still does so due to the lack of carefulness required in the given circumstances. It is important to distinguish two situations here, one in which the perpetrator is aware that the undertaken behaviour carries a risk of harm, and a second in which such an awareness is completely absent. In the first case, the unintentional act is chargeable either on the basis of the perpetrator's belief, which turned out to be erroneous, that no harmful consequences would follow from his or her action, or on the basis of undertaking his or her action despite having the awareness of the risk. In the second case, the unintentional act is chargeable based on a failure to anticipate the consequences of an undertaken action which could have been foreseen if he or she had acted with the diligence required in those circumstances (see Jescheck, 1972, pp. 313–14).

According to the normative theories of guilt, the behaviour of a car driver who unintentionally causes a road accident is chargeable, as is the behaviour of someone who intentionally kills another person. In both cases, it is possible to establish guilt which will be understood in the same way, namely, as a normative evaluation that a perpetrator decided to violate the law instead of acting in accordance with it. However, the basis on which guilt is established is different in each of those cases. In the first situation, the charge of guilt refers to features such as the perpetrator's negligence or carelessness during the performance of obligations imposed on him or her as on a traffic participant. Therefore, it is the absence of awareness, or an insufficient degree of it, resulting in the absence of a proper mental attitude towards the undertaken behaviour that is the basis for the attribution of guilt in such cases. In the second situation (murder), the charge refers to an actual desire to cause a human death. The presented differences in the grounds on which guilt is established allow a judge to differentiate the punishment imposed accordingly.

The discussed examples lead us to the conclusion that the concept in question for the normative theories of guilt is not something 'in us', but rather in the stars, that is in the normative system used to assess our behaviour. The achievement of the normative approach is the recognition of the heterogeneous nature of the conditions of criminal liability because some of them refer to facts, while others resort to normative evaluation. This distinction has an impact on criminal procedure as well. If the mental state of the perpetrator and the issue of guilt are two separate elements constituting criminal liability, then both should be proven separately in the course of evidence proceedings in a criminal trial. From the determination that the perpetrator was acting with intent, it does not immediately follow that it is possible to attribute guilt. On the other hand, the very fact of acting unintentionally does not automatically exclude guilt. Therefore, the application of the basic insights made by the normative approach to guilt strengthens the possibility of obtaining the resolution of a case that is individualized.

From the perspective of cognitive science, the normative theories of guilt make an important categorical shift. The sphere of facts concerning the course of the mental processes of a perpetrator can be studied and described in terms of modern neuroscience and philosophy of mind (see Jescheck, 1972, pp. 313–14). Therefore, it is the domain of expert specialists in a given field of knowledge. Evidence provided by neuroscience is admissible in the course of a criminal trial and should be taken into consideration by the court (see Małecki & Zyzik, 2014, p. 167f.). The sphere of the legal evaluation of the act in question belongs to the authorities, for example, the judge who gives the verdict, or the prosecutor who files the indictment. It is not the facts that ultimately burden or excuse the perpetrator, but the extent of the duty which the perpetrator violated by committing a crime. The assessment of whether the perpetrator can be accused of having violated the law belongs to the essence of justice (von Liszt & Schmidt, 1922, p. 209f.).

Normative conceptions of guilt are not free from their own drawbacks. These weaknesses have their source in three issues:

1) The assumption of free will.
2) The temptation to objectify human freedom and to generalize guilt in the practical application of law by employing various types of normative models used to assess certain types of behaviour.
3) The possibility that the need to punish the perpetrator will be the basic argument when determining the issue of his or her guilt.

(1) Normative theories of guilt are based on the assumption of free will,[10] however, legal scholars rarely consider how this assumption is understood. In other words, free will is taken for granted in legal discourse. This is not the case for philosophy or the cognitive sciences, where various approaches and theories of free will can be highlighted. Without going into details here, we will limit ourselves to mentioning only two of them. The first, which can be called the classic or libertarian approach, understands free will as one's possibility of acting differently. The second approach (compatibilism) demands somewhat less from the notion in question, thus free will is simply the ability to act according to one's intentions. It is worth noticing that the

---

[10] See the presentation and discussion of various positions concerning this issue from the perspective of criminal law (Singer, 2003, p. 58f; Hillenkamp, 2015, p. 30f.; Barczak-Oplustil, 2016, p. 182f.).

employment of this last approach by the normative theory of guilt would allow it to be more resistant to critical remarks (see Dennett, 2006). Without getting into the philosophical disputes about the existence of free will as such, adherents of normative theories of guilt quite universally admit that freedom of decision is the basic condition for charging the perpetrator that he or she did not act in accordance with the law. This thesis, however, is now being questioned due to achievements in neuroscience and neurobiological studies of the human brain. It is one of the most actively explored and analysed issues in criminal law today (Stühler, 1999, p. 26; Prinz, 2003; Merkel, 2008, p. 5; Detlefsen, 2006, pp. 278f.; Herzberg, 2012, p. 58).

(2) The normative theories of guilt are prone to the temptation to objectify the criteria for the attribution of guilt. Such an objectification is of practical importance because it offers operational criteria that can help in the application of law. This leads to the development of various normative models of a reasonable citizen, of a reasonable participant in legal transactions, of a reasonable physician, and so on, which are employed as the basis for the process of the evaluation of the perpetrator's behaviour. The main problem is that those models are usually characterized by features that the actual perpetrator does not have or did not have when the prohibited act was committed. In extreme cases, it can even transpire that no real person would be able to meet those standards. Guilt in the normative sense certainly cannot be reduced to the comparison of a perpetrator's act with such an objective model, because guilt is understood as a charge addressed individually to the specific perpetrator of a specific act. Without denying the practical need for the usage of normative models, it should be remembered that in the case of guilt, we are dealing with a premise of criminal liability which in its essence should be personalized and individualized. Actual behaviour often escapes typical generalizations.

Therefore, in the process of imposing criminal liability, courts should also consider the *individual*, *specific*, and *subjective* features of a perpetrator in question so as not to impose requirements that would be impossible for him or her to realize in the given circumstances of the committed act (see Barczak-Oplustil, 2005, p. 84f.). In other words, instead of relying on overly abstract generalizations, the judge should examine the decision-making processes, psychophysical condition, and motives of a given perpetrator. With this modification, the normative approach to guilt in continental criminal law can be reconciled with the findings of the biological sciences (see Kurek, 2018, p. 119f.).

(3) The placement of guilt in the stars generates a new problem which, referring to Shakespeare's quote, can be called 'the shooting stars'. What we have in mind here are the modifications of the normative approach which identify guilt with a particularistic need to punish the perpetrator. These positions are sometimes called *functional theories of guilt*. The advantage of the psychological theory of guilt is the ontological justification of the concept in question. Guilt is recognized as the mental state of a perpetrator. By situating guilt in the realm of normative

assessment, the normative approach creates a risk of arbitrariness in determining guilt (see Stomma, 1947, p. 11). First of all, the answer to the essential question for establishing guilt – was it possible for the perpetrator to decide to act in accordance with the law? – is in itself prone to arbitrariness, depending highly on the reference to certain values and way in which they are understood. The same can be said about the determination of the scope of legal duties which should be obeyed by a perpetrator in the case of unintentional acts. The answers to those questions can be highly influenced by the current demands of political needs. This risk is especially significant in cases that draw high public interest and media coverage, such as violent or sexual crimes.

Therefore, the functional theories of guilt reverse the vector of implication: in the classical scheme, the need for punishment results from the guilt attributed to the perpetrator; for the adherents of functional theories, it is exactly the opposite; the guilt results from the *need to punish*.[11] This approach opens the way for penal populism, the instrumental use of law as an instrument to manage social emotions, and poses a high risk of the infringement of basic human rights, such as the right to a fair trial, or the presumption of innocence. On the other hand, the functional theory of guilt can be useful for explaining the grounds for the responsibility of autonomous agents (e.g. self-trade programmes on the stock market, 'intelligent' thermostats, 'intelligent' weapons, or self-driving cars).[12] If a need for the legal responsibility of the autonomous agents arises, the functional theory of guilt will be ready with its response: 'It is not a problem. They are guilty' (because they should bear the consequences of what they did).

14.4 IMPUTATIVE THEORY OF GUILT: FROM THE STARS TO US

A continuation of the ideas developed by the normative concepts of guilt is to be found in a relatively new approach that can be called the imputative conception of guilt. This approach is based on the integration of various results obtained by the normative approach and is faithful to the basic thesis of normativism: guilt is a normative evaluation (see Małecki, 2019, p. 105f.).

The starting point for the theory in question is the close analysis of the fundamental idea behind the normative approach, namely, situating guilt outside of the perpetrator. This is how the Polish criminal law scholar, Stefan Glaser, commented on this:

> At first glance, it may seem strange that a person's guilt should not be in her head, but in other people's heads. However, one should realize [the following]: the statement that the perpetrator, in a culpable manner, committed an unlawful act

---

[11] For a presentation of the functional theories of guilt see Roxin (1974, pp. 171f.; 1979, p. 279ff.); Jakobs (1983, pp. 394f.; 1976, pp. 12f.); Joecks (2012, pp. 26–8).

[12] For analysis of the responsibility of autonomous agents see Hage (2017, pp. 255f.).

that corresponds to the statutory essence of the prohibited act, refers to a specific state of affairs in the perpetrator; however, this state of affairs is also assessed by this statement as an occurrence due to which the perpetrator should be charged. And only this assessment of value raises psychological event to the concept of guilt. (Glaser, 1934, p. 10)

As we can see, Glaser is talking here about *two different events*: the prohibited act, with the accompanying mental state of its perpetrator, and the evaluation that the perpetrator is guilty. The act of the perpetrator becomes a crime when the court finds him or her liable (this is what Glaser calls 'raising a psychological event to the concept of guilt'). This moment, of declaring that someone is liable, can be used to return guilt back from the stars. By stating that a given perpetrator is found guilty (in a procedural meaning) and thus liable for a committed crime, guilt (in its essential meaning) materializes itself in the form of a particular charge made against a given perpetrator in the real world.

To explain this notion of guilt, imputative theory employs the philosophical concept of possible worlds.[13] The world in which the prohibited act took place (possible world W_1) is different from the world in which the assignment of guilt (in essential meaning) and attribution of liability take place (possible world W_2). Let us take a closer look at those worlds and the relation between them. The charge of guilt (in its essential meaning) is made by a conventional entity (e.g. a judge, a jury) in a possible world W_2 and is addressed to the perpetrator as he or she presents him or herself at precisely this moment. The reason why this charge of guilt is made is the perpetrator's behaviour conducted earlier, in possible world W_1. The conventional charge of guilt and the perpetrator's behaviour cannot ever be simultaneously a part of the same possible world. A judge doesn't assess the prohibited act during the time of its commission, and the perpetrator doesn't commit this act during the trial. Therefore, there exists a relation between W_1 and W_2 which enables us to attribute guilt (in its essential meaning) to the perpetrator. In consequence, this attribution in W_2 leads to the imposition of criminal liability (guilt in the procedural meaning) and to the creation of new obligations and duties addressed specifically to the perpetrator, namely, to serve his or her sentence. However, those obligations are imposed for the future. In other words, they will be realized by the convicted perpetrator in another possible world, W_3.

To summarize, the attribution of guilt (in its *essential* meaning) is undertaken because of a historical event that occurred in world W_1. This event influences (because of the criminal trial and judicial assessment) the current legal situation of the perpetrator in the actual world W_2, and is aimed at affecting the future possible world of W_3.[14] because the perpetrator who has been found guilty needs to feel the burden of punishment. As we can see from this exposition, the charge of guilt (in the

---

[13] On the notion of possible worlds see Lewis (1986).
[14] Imputational theory thus refers to the criminological idea of retributarianism (see Dancing-Rosenberg & Dagan, 2019, p. 129f.).

essential sense) is always made in regard to other possible worlds. This distinction has not been sufficiently explained by the traditional normative theories, which tend to centre only on the concept of guilt and thus ignore the issue of the attribution of guilt to the given perpetrator for his or her act. The imputative conception of guilt, in general, does not change the meaning of guilt developed by normative theories, but it supplements this meaning by including the ontological circumstances of the attribution of guilt in a given criminal trial.

The presented approach refers to the so-called *relational conception of guilt* developed by Wojciech Patryas, according to which the concept of 'guilt' is the name of the set whose elements are given by following condition: 'subject X has committed culpable act C at time t'. The relation allows us to establish that guilt occurs between the subject who produced a certain state of affairs at a specific time, and this state of affairs (see Patryas, 1988, p. 192f.). The imputative approach is not only interested in the relation between the perpetrator and his or her act, but also in the relation between this perpetrator and the subject who is assessing this act and thus attributing guilt.

The imputative theory of guilt can be summarized by the Latin maxim: *nullum crimen sine culpa imputatione*. The classic maxim which we referred to in the introductory part, *nullum crimen sine culpa* (no crime without guilt), does not specify where we should locate guilt (in us or in the stars) and at what moment guilt occurs. The perpetrator of a criminal act is burdened by this act, that is by the act which was committed in the past (in the possible world W_1). However, this is not enough in the context of criminal liability because the fact of committing this act must be established by the court in another possible world W_2. At precisely the moment the evaluation is made, guilt will be attributed to a perpetrator (hence the term 'imputation' added in the maxim quoted above).

Guilt is not attributed in a vacuum or to a perpetrator as he or she was at the time when a prohibited act was committed. The court assigns guilt to a perpetrator as he or she presents himself or herself at the *time of sentencing*. This action is aimed at shaping the future legal situation of this perpetrator because it imposes new duties and obligations resulting from the punishment, such as the obligation to pay a fine, deprivation of liberty, or prohibition from operating vehicles. As a result, the imputative approach distinguishes between the chargeability *in potentia*, characteristic of normative theories, and the chargeability *in actu*. Therefore, the idea of this approach is not about the possibility of charging the perpetrator that he or she should have acted differently (i.e. in accordance with the law instead of violating it) but about the possibility of accusing him or her during the assessment of the prohibited act of not having obeyed the legal provisions and that he or she should now bear the burden of guilt and imposed penalties. This requires taking a whole range of circumstances into account, not only from the past (i.e. the time of committing the prohibited act) but also the actual ones, affecting a fair assessment of the possibility of incurring a burden of guilt by a given perpetrator. If the perpetrator as he or she is 'here and now' is not fit to be burdened with a charge of guilt, then the perpetrator should not be held criminally liable.

The imputative approach draws attention to the need to consider the current *condition* of the perpetrator accused of committing a prohibited act. It cannot be disregarded whether the perpetrator is able to understand the message addressed to him or her by means of the attribution of guilt and whether he or she is able to suffer the ailments associated with this attribution. For this reason, we can distinguish two types of circumstances excluding the assignment of guilt:

i) *First-degree exculpatory circumstances* – these are circumstances accompanying a prohibited act and appearing during the time of its realization (e.g. insanity during the time of an act, mistake as to the legal assessment of an act, state of necessity).

ii) *Second-degree exculpatory circumstances* – these are circumstances that appear after the time of act and can justify its perpetrator by excluding the possibility of the attribution of guilt. They include voluntary prevention of the consequences of a prohibited act, self-denunciation, reparation of damage, positive change in the perpetrator's way of life, personality change of the perpetrator, state of health that renders perpetrator unable to be burdened with criminal liability, and the passage of time.[15]

The advantage of the imputative theory is in its holistic, retrospective and prospective approach to the attribution of guilt in criminal law. It also better suits the procedural reality because it takes into account the factual and legal circumstances in which the assessment in question takes place. Because of that, we return from distant stars of normativism to a particular perpetrator.

The imputative theory of guilt opens the possibility of taking advantage of various information concerning the perpetrator such as intellectual and emotional conditions, past diseases or brain injuries. For this reason, this approach to guilt offers new possibilities of integration between criminal law and cognitive science, especially in the field of analysing *personal identity* (see Williams, 1956/1957, pp. 229–52; Dennett, 1976; Mohapatra, 1983; Parfit, 1984, *passim*; Shoemaker & Swinburne, 1984, p. 144; McCall, 1990, p. 177; Olson, 1997, *passim*; Noonan, 2003; Belzer, 2005, pp. 126–64; Kind, 2015, pp. 47–50).

One can argue that the imputative approach uses the procedural conception of guilt rather than the essential one. However, for this argument to succeed, it needs to be demonstrated that, on the basis of the imputative theory, there is no difference between the notions of guilt and criminal liability. This does not seem to be the case. It is clearly stated that guilt is understood here as one of the necessary conditions of criminal liability, beside the wrongfulness of a prohibited act or its social harmfulness. Normative assessment, which is the essence of this approach to guilt, is

---

[15] On the passage of time in the context of the punishment see Douglas (2019, pp. 335–58).

therefore not concerned with any other features of the perpetrator's prohibited act than its culpability. From this we can see that the concept of guilt used here is narrower than the concept of criminal liability. It is guilt in its essential meaning as the failure to act in accordance with the law. The fact that the attribution of guilt is made in certain procedural conditions (because it must be done in such a manner) does not change its essence (see Małecki, 2019, p. 51f.).

The imputative theory, however, seems to be more complicated than the psychological or normative ones. The psychological approach offers us a simple answer to the question of guilt: 'You have done something wrong that you wanted to do.' The normative approach (in its pure form) is a bit more elaborate, but still simpler than the imputative one. According to normative theory: 'You have done something wrong in a situation in which you could have acted in accordance with the law.' The imputative approach is the most complicated one: 'You have done something wrong in the past, namely, you have violated the law in a situation in which you could have acted in accordance with the law, and because of that act in the past, you are now burdened by the consequences of this act.'

14.5 CONCLUSIONS: FUNCTIONS OF STARS

The above presentation of the most notable concepts of guilt in continental criminal law can be summarized in the form of the following table.

Definitions of guilt

Theory	Definition of guilt
Psychological	Psychological fact which consists of the state of the perpetrator's mind at the time of the act
Complex Normative	Chargeable mental attitude towards the committed act
Pure Normative	Pure charge based on the assessment that a perpetrator had the objective possibility of acting in accordance with the law
Functional	Need for punishment in a particular case
Imputative	Charge referred to the time when the assessment of the prohibited act was made

First, each of the discussed concepts highlights different aspects of criminal liability. The psychological theories emphasize the role of mental state of the perpetrator. Normativism organizes the premises of responsibility, delineating the area of factual findings and the area of free judicial assessment related to the charge of guilt. The functional approach reminds us of the social function of the law and the significance of convicting an offender for a crime. The imputative approach describes the ontological mechanism of attributing guilt to the perpetrator.

Second, none of the indicated concepts originated on the basis of findings concerning the functioning of the human mind. In other words, what we have here are theories construed only for the purposes of criminal law, without interdisciplinary aspirations. However, as we have tried to show, each of these concepts is open for further studies and analyses.

Third, different theories of guilt differ in their susceptibility to being integrated with scientific theories. The functional approach to guilt seems most resistant to this integration because in extreme cases it may completely ignore substantive arguments and scientific evidence, giving primacy to the social need to punish the perpetrator. Pure normativism offers some space to take into account the results of neurobiological research, both in terms of factual findings (the psychological experience of the perpetrator) and normative conditions (the degree of requirements addressed to the perpetrator can be agreed with the broadly understood condition of the perpetrator's mind). The continuation of this trend in the imputative theory draws attention to the need to take into account the current condition of the perpetrator at the time of the attribution of guilt. Therefore, this theory creates the opportunity to employ neuroscientific evidence, providing information about the current psychophysical condition of a particular offender in court.

However, from the cognitive science point of view, the theories presented have two main weaknesses. Either they assume an explanation of psychological mechanisms that is incompatible with the current state of knowledge about the human mind, or they are becoming less understandable to the average addressee of legal provisions, as they move away from folk psychology. The latter results in a tension between the common understanding of guilt and the legal theories and definitions of this concept. The departure from the psychological theories of guilt creates the opportunity to employ a more specialized analysis. However, this creates the risk of 'flying away into the stars', that is to move so far away from social intuitions about guilt that the proposed theories and definitions are completely incomprehensible for anyone other than legal scholars or cognitivists. As Bartosz Brożek and Marek Jakubiec point out:

> Thus, for example, the rule which says that 'A person commits a criminal offence if he or she acts with intention, recklessness, or negligence' is replaced with 'A person commits a criminal offence if he or she has an elevated blood pressure in prefrontal cortex, motor cortex, basal ganglia and cerebellum', while the rule 'A person who acts in self-defence is not criminally liable' becomes 'A person whose oxytocin level is elevated is not criminally liable'. It is not difficult to observe that such radical changes to the conceptual foundations of the legal system would result in complete chaos. The new law would be totally incomprehensible. (Brożek & Jakubiec, 2017, p. 299)

The same objection can be made to some claims of the normative theory of guilt, including the formulation of various normative models of reasonable citizens. Consider the following example: Eve is looking after her three-year-old son Adam. The child is sitting quietly in the room. Eve goes out to the kitchen. During this time, Adam goes out onto the balcony, climbs the railing and falls off. Of course, we can build a model of a 'good mother' that would prevent such a result. But how many times have parents lost sight of their children, or left them alone, especially if they are playing quietly in a room and there is no indication that they might do something unexpected?

The explanation of criminal liability in this case must use the simple categories which are *socially understandable*. Even if we conceptually move in the area of the strict categories adopted by cognitive sciences, even if we rationalize the described case in the normative categories or in motivational terms we will be forced to reduce ourselves to the level of simple categories of psychologism. This is very important for substantiating a decision imposing criminal liability when the court must explain its rationale to the public. The court should use the simplest categories understandable to the recipient, and these certainly include colloquially understandable experiences: intentions, motivations, and so on. This is especially important in the case of misdemeanours or minor offences, when a body applying the law is often a non-professional judge, police officer, or even a civil servant. In such situations, the legal provisions should be as simple as possible to both the addressee of those provisions, and the entity that enforces it. This comprehensibility of the legal text contributes to the mutual understanding of the parties involved in the procedure of the application of law, and helps to fulfil the *social functions* of criminal law.

This leads us to the following question: is there another possibility to consider guilt, besides its placement in us or in the stars as discussed above? It seems that an important factor that could be taken into account are the functions of law. They seem especially important in the case of criminal law, which employs the most severe sanctions that the law has to offer. In this context, the appropriate understanding of guilt can play two roles:

i) It makes it possible to explain to the perpetrator and society why a given person is or is not criminally liable
ii) It protects citizens against the arbitrariness of the authority which has the apparatus of coercion at its disposal.

The second point seems the most important for criminal law. Guilt can be seen as one of the mechanisms that *protect* the citizen against the abuse of power by the state. The need to establish guilt in order to impose criminal liability gives a degree of protection against instrumental treatment (e.g. in hope of achieving a specific political effect).

The idea that the attribution of legal liability depends on a requirement of establishing that the committed act is culpable does not limit itself to criminal law. Other branches of law, such as civil law, commercial law, or administrative law, also refer to this concept and employ it in their own provisions. Of course, in each case the concept in question can be (and often is) understood in a slightly different manner that is adjusted to the characteristic features of the type of social relations regulated by a given branch of the law. However, despite all those differences, it can be generally stated that the concept in question expresses one of the principles according to which legal liability can be conceived.

If the relation between guilt and liability is not an exclusive feature of criminal law, then why does it receive so much attention from criminal law scholars? The short answer is that the issue of guilt holds a distinguished position in criminal law. While in other branches of law it is possible to employ a legal liability that is not based on this condition, in the case of criminal law (at least continental criminal law) such a possibility is excluded as a matter of principle. It follows from the general idea of what criminal law is and what its function is supposed to be. In general, criminal law describes the most severe, harmful, or dangerous types of behaviour that are undesirable from an individual or social point of view. If someone commits such an act and this is proven before the court, then certain types of sanctions can be imposed. Those sanctions are usually aimed at the deprivation or limitation of the most important goods of the individual (e.g. life, freedom, or assets). Because of the degree of harmfulness of a prohibited act and the severity of punishment, all important aspects of the perpetrator and its act need to be properly identified and evaluated before rendering the judgement. This is not only the case of the evidential standard (which is important in its own right) but also of the elements required to constitute criminal liability. The latter concerns the issue of guilt. The assessment of the culpability of an act is seen by criminal law scholars as one of necessary conditions that must be met before applying such a severe type of legal liability as the criminal one. Because of this fact, this requirement is often directly expressed in legal provisions, thus emphasizing its importance. It can be found in criminal codes and even in constitutions. Therefore, guilt is recognized as one of the most important principles of criminal law and a crucial prerequisite of the imposition of criminal liability.

The protective function of guilt weakens the arguments of that legal constructions are often too complex in nature and incompatible with folk psychology. Legal language uses many terms in the context of a specific, technical meaning. For example, legal provisions sometimes precisely define how certain phrases should be understood for the purposes of a given branch of law. The concept of guilt is treated by criminal law scholars in precisely the same way. This departure from the colloquial meaning can be seen as an advantage. By constructing the technical meaning of the term 'guilt', criminal law can *guarantee* additional protection for citizens and the extension of their right to a fair trial. If guilt is separated from the everyday notion of wrong or evil, then it is separated from the risk of evaluation on the basis of such broad and vague concepts, which differ from person to person.

Therefore, locating guilt in the stars can be seen as a solution aimed at ensuring the protection of citizen's rights. For this idea to work, we need stable and *general standards* of criminal liability, standards which are not susceptible to frequent and particular transformations depending, inter alia, on political short-sighted interests. For a better illustration of this point, consider the following example.

Let us suppose that, in a given civil-law-system country, speeding is considered a crime, but only a mild financial penalty can be imposed for it. Because it is a crime, each case must be tried before the court and the regulations of criminal procedure normally apply.[16] At some point in time, the legislature deems this way of handling the problem of speeding as being overly troublesome. In response, a new law is enacted, stating that cases of speeding would from now on be adjudicated by special traffic commissions with the application of the administrative procedure. The financial nature of sanctions is maintained but their amount is raised significantly. What we have here is a change in the legal liability regime: from the criminal to a new one that is administrative in nature. It is easy to see a close similarity between those two mechanisms. Both are aimed at combating the same type of unwanted social behaviour, both use the same type of sanctions (i.e. financial ones), and both serve as a punishment for what the perpetrator did, as well as a preventive measure against subsequent acts of this kind.

However, there are three major differences that cannot be ignored. First, instead of court, all cases are adjudicated by the administrative body. Second, if speeding is no longer subject to criminal liability but rather administrative liability, then other elements than in the case of crime need to be established to impose such a liability. Precisely because of this point, it is possible to exclude the requirement of guilt (as well as other requirements that are unique for a crime) from the argumentation as it is not a necessary element of administrative liability. It is easy to see what consequences follow from such a change if we consider our example. Without the requirement of guilt, the imposition of liability would be based only on a simple fact of committing the behaviour indicated. No additional circumstances would be taken into consideration. Imagine two people, one who speeds only for the thrill of the ride, and another who just wants to quickly get his or her relative to the hospital. From the objective point of view, both are violating the speed limit, but the second person is doing so for a reason we would probably be willing to accept. Treating them in the same way may appear to be inconsistent with our basic intuitions regarding justice. This shows how important the requirement of guilt is to the proper evaluation of human behaviour. Third, there are differences in procedural regulations. In place of criminal procedure (with its evidential standard) we have the administrative one. International and domestic laws usually provide a set of guarantees specifically tailored for those accused in a criminal trial. In case of other types of

---

[16] For simplicity's sake, let us suppose that there is no other way of dealing with cases of speeding, such as the possibility for the police to issue a ticket.

liability, especially administrative ones, such regulations are mostly absent. Therefore, the problem of determining which legal provisions are subject to criminal liability is strongly connected with the issue of *human rights*.[17]

As we can see from this short exposition, the question of whether a given legal liability can be called criminal or otherwise is not just an academic inquiry concerning how to divide and organize a system of law. Because it is a different topic (and quite a broad one), we cannot discuss it any further here.[18] It suffices to say that the concept of guilt presents itself as one of the important factors that can help ensure an adequate standard of human rights. For this reason, it can be stated that in any case of provisions that establish a type of liability that can be assessed as criminal, the requirement of guilt should be present.

The history of the theories of guilt in criminal law, as can be said referring to Cassius's sentence, has come full circle: from 'guilt in us' (guilt described in *psychological* terms) through 'guilt in the stars' (*normative* and *functional* approach) to 'guilt in us' in a sense given by a *imputative* theory of guilt. However, stars – understood as the standards of criminal liability – are needed in each of those theories, if guilt is to serve its *protective function*.

REFERENCES

Achenbach, H. (1974). *Historische und dogmatische Grundlagen der Strafrechtssystematischen Schuldlehre*. Berlin: Schweitzer.

Barczak-Oplustil, A. (2005). Sporne zagadnienia istoty winy w prawie karnym. Zarys problemu (Disputable Issues of the Essence of Guilt in Criminal Law. Outline of the Problem). *Czasopismo Prawa Karnego i Nauk Penalnych* (Journal of Criminal Law and Penal Studies), 9(2) 79–96. https://czpk.pl/dokumenty/zeszyty/2005/zeszyt2/Barczak-Oplustil_A-Sporne_zagadnienia_istoty_winy_w_prawie_karnym._Zarys_problemu-CZPKiNP_2005-z.2.pdf

Barczak-Oplustil, A. (2016). *Zasada koincydencji winy i czynu w Kodeksie karnym* (Principle of Coincidence of Guilt and Act in Criminal Code). Kraków: Krakowski Instytut Prawa Karnego Fundacja (Kraków Institute of Criminal Law Foundation).

Belzer, M. (2005). Self-Conception and Personal Identity: Revisiting Parfit and Lewis with an Eye on the Grip of the Unity Reaction. *Social Philosophy and Policy* 22(2). 126–64. www.cambridge.org/core/journals/social-philosophy-and-policy/article/selfconception-and-personal-identity-revisiting-parfit-and-lewis-with-an-eye-on-the-grip-of-the-unity-reaction/4E60FA91894DD65FC00B8343BC3E0FE7

We would like to thank Professor B. Brożek and Dr Ł. Kurek for their valuable comments on an earlier version of this paper.

This article is a result of the research project 'A New Model of Law of Contraventions. Theoretical, Normative, and Empirical Analysis' financed by the National Science Centre (grant OPUS 14, no. 2017/27/B/HS5/02137).

[17] See the judgement of the European Court of Human Rights in the case of *Sergey Zolotukhin* v. *Russia* (application no. 14939/03).

[18] See on that matter the Recommendation No. R (91) 1 of the Committee of Ministers to Member States on Administrative Sanctions issued by the Council of Europe.

Brożek, B., & Jakubiec, M. (2017). On the Legal Responsibility of Autonomous Machines. *Artificial Intelligence and Law* 25, 293–304. https://link.springer.com/article/10.1007/s10506-017-9207-8

Chwast, J. (1964). The Social Function of Guilt. *Social Work* 9(2)(April), 58–63. https://academic.oup.com/sw/article-abstract/9/2/58/1942722?redirectedFrom=fulltext

Corrado, M. (1991). Notes on the Structure of a Theory of Excuses. *The Journal of Criminal Law and Criminology*, 82(3)(Autumn), 465–497.

D'Amato, A. (1980). The Speluncean Explorers – Further Proceedings. *Stanford Law Review*, 32, 67–485.

Dancing-Rosenberg, H., & Dagan, N. (2019). Retributarianism: A New Individualization of Punishment. *Criminal Law and Philosophy* 19, 129–147.

Dennett, D. (1976). Conditions of Personhood. In A. Oksenberg-Rorty (ed.), *The Identities of Persons*. Berkeley, Los Angeles, London: University of California Press.

Detlefsen, G. (2006). *Grenzen der Freiheit – Bedingungen des Handelns – Perspektive des Schuldprinzips*. Berlin: Duncker & Humblot GmbH.

Douglas, T. (2019). Punishing Wrongs From the Distant Past. *Law and Philosophy* 38. 335–358. https://link.springer.com/article/10.1007/s10982-019-09352-8

Feuerbach, A. (1798). *Revision der Grundsätze und Grundbegriffe des peinlichen Rechts*. Chemnitz: Erfurt.

Filar, M. (2011). Umyślność faktyczna czy umyślność prawna? (Factual or Legal Intent?) In J. Majewski (ed.), *Umyślność i jej formy. Pokłosie VII Bielańskiego Kolokwium Karnistycznego* (Intentionality and its Forms. The Results of VII Bielany Criminal Law Colloquium). Toruń: Towarzystwo Naukowe Organizacji i Kierownictwa. Dom Organizatora.

Freudenthal, B. (1922). *Schuld und Vorwurf im geltenden Strafrecht*. Tübingen. J. C. B. Mohr.

Fuller, L. L. (1949). The Case of the Speluncean Explorers. *Harvard Law Review* 62(4). 616–45. www.jstor.org/stable/1336025?origin=crossref&seq=1

Glaser, S. (1934). *Normatywna nauka o winie* (Normative theory of guilt). Warsaw. Drukarnia Rolnicza. www.wbc.poznan.pl/dlibra/publication/287312/edition/236735/content

Goldschmidt, J. (1913). *Der Notstand, ein Schuldproblem: mit Rücksicht auf die Strafgesetzentwürfe Deutschlands, Oesterreichs und der Schweiz*. Vienna: Manz Juristische Gesellschaft.

Goldschmidt, J. (1930). *Normativer Schuldbegriff*. Tübingen: J. C. B. Mohr.

Graf zu Dohna, A. (1905). *Die Elemente des Schuldbegriffs*. Stuttgart: Stuttgart Union Deutsche Verlagsgesellschaft.

Greenawalt, K. (1986). Distinguishing Justifications from Excuses. *Law and Contemporary Problems* 49(3), Responsibility (Summer), 89–108.

Greene, J., & Cohen, J. (2004). For the Law, Neuroscience Changes Nothing and Everything. *Philosophical Transactions of the Royal Society of London* 359(1451), 1775–1785.

Hage, J. (2017). Theoretical Foundations for the Responsibility of Autonomous Agents. *Artificial Intelligence and Law* 25, 255–271. https://link.springer.com/article/10.1007/s10506-017-9208-7

Heinitz, E. (1926). *Das Problem der materiellen Rechtswidrigkeit*. Breslau: Schletter.

Heller, K. J. (2009). The Cognitive Psychology of Mens Rea. *Journal of Criminal Law and Criminology* 99, 317–379.

Herzberg, R. D. (2012). Setzt strafrechtliche Schuld ein Vermeidenkönnen voraus? *Zeitschrift für die gesamte Strafrechtswissenschaft* 124(1), 12–63.

Hillenkamp, T. (2015). Hirnforschung, Willensfreiheit und Strafrecht – Versuch einer Zwischenbilanz. *Zeitschrift für die gesamte Strafrechtswissenschaft* 127(1), 10–96.

Hippel, R. (1908). *Vorsatz, Fahrlässigkeit, Irrtum.* In Karl v. Birkemeyer (ed.). *Vergleichende Darstellung des Deutschen und Ausländischen Strafrechts, Allgemeiner Teil,* III. Berlin: Liebmann.
Hörnle, T. (2016). Guilt and Choice in Criminal Law Theory – A Critical Assessment. *Bergen Journal of Criminal Law and Criminal Justice,* 4(1), 1–24. https://boap.uib.no/index.php/BJCLCJ/article/view/1023/942
Jakobs, G. (1976). Schuld und Prävention. In Series: *Recht und Staat in Geschichte und Gegenwart,* No. 452/453. Tübingen. J. C. B. Mohr.
Jakobs, G. (1983). *Strafrecht, Allgemeiner Teil.* Berlin & New York: De Gruyter.
Jescheck, H. H. (1972). *Lehrbuch des Strafrechts, Allgemeiner Teil,* 2nd ed. Berlin. Duncker und Humblot,
Joecks, W. (2012). *Strafgesetzbuch: Studienkommentar.* Munich: Beck.
Kind, A. (2015). *Persons and Personal Identity.* Cambridge: Polity Press.
Kindhäuser, U. (2005). *Strafgesetzbuch, Lehr- und Praxiskommentar.* Baden-Baden: Nomos.
Kurek, Ł. (2018). The Image of Man in Criminal Law and Cognitive Sciences. In B. Brożek, Ł. Kurek, & J. Stelmach (eds.), *Law and Cognitive Sciences.* Warsaw: Wolters Kluwer Polska.
Lewis, D. K. (1986). *On the Plurality of Worlds.* Oxford: Blackwell.
Loffler, A. (1895). *Die Schuldformen des Strafrecht.* Leipzig: Hirschfeld.
Małecki, M. (2019). *Przypisanie winy. Podstawy teorii ekskulpantów* (The Attribution of Guilt. The Fundaments of Exculpatory Circumstances Theory). Kraków. Krakowski Instytut Prawa Karnego Fundacja (Kraków Institute of Criminal Law Foundation).
Małecki, M., & Zyzik, R. (2014). Poczytalność i wina psychopaty w świetle ewolucyjnych koncepcji genezy psychopatii (Sanity and psychopath's guilt in light of the evolutionary concepts of the origin of psychopathy). *Ruch Prawniczy, Ekonomiczny i Socjologiczny* (Journal of Law, Economics and Sociology) 76(3), 161–74. https://pressto.amu.edu.pl/index.php/rpeis/article/view/1799
Marcetus, K. (1928). *Der Gedanke der Zumutbarkeit und seine Verwendung in den amtlichen Entwürfen eines Allgemeinen Deutschen Strafgesetzbuches von 1925 und 1927.* Breslau: N.p.
Maurach, R. & Zipf, H. (1983). *Strafrecht, Allgemeine Teil.* Heidelberg: Müller.
McCall, C. (1990). *Concepts of Person: An Analysis of Concepts of Person, Self and Human Being.* Aldershot and Brookfield: Gower.
McIntosh, C. (ed.) (2013). *Cambridge Advanced Learner's Dictionary.* Cambridge: Cambridge University Press.
Merkel, G. (2008). Hirnforschung, Sprache und Recht. In H. Putzke et al. (eds.), *Strafrecht zwischen System und Telos, Festschrift für R. D. Herzberg zum 70. Geburtstag.* Tübingen: Mohr Siebeck.
Mohapatra, K. P. (1983). *Personal Identity.* Cuttack: Santosh Publications.
Noonan, H. W. (2003). *Personal Identity.* London & New York: Routledge.
Olson, E. T. (1997). *The Human Animal: Personal Identity without Psychology.* New York: Oxford University Press. .
Parfit, D. (1984). *Reasons and Persons.* Oxford: Clarendon Press.
Patryas, W. (1988). *Interpretacja karnistyczna. Studium metodologiczne* (Criminal Law Interpretation. A Methodological Study). Poznań: Wydawnictwo Naukowe Uniwersytetu im. Adama Mickiewicza (Adam Mickiewicz University in Poznań Press).
Prinz, W. (2003). Der Mensch ist nicht frei. *Das Magazin des Wissenschaftszentrum Nordrhein-Westfalen,* 2, 8–20.

Roxin, C. (1974). 'Schuld' and 'Verantwortlichkeit' als strafrechtliche Systemkategorie. In H. Jäger, C. Roxin, & H-J. Burns (eds.) *Grundfragen der gesamten Strafrechtswissenschaft – Festschrift für Heinrich Henkel zum 70. Geburtstag am 12 September 1973*. Berlin & New York: Walter de Gruyter.

Roxin, C. (1979). Zur jüngsten Diskussion über Schuld, Prävention und Verantwortlichkeit im Strafrecht. In A. Kaufmann, G. Bemmann, D. Krauss, & K. Volk (eds.), *Festschrift für Bockelmann*. Munich: Beck.

Schaffstein, F. (1933). *Die Nichtzumutbarkeit als allgemeiner übergesetzlicher Schuldausschliessungsgrund*. Leipzig: Scholl.

Shoemaker, S., & Swinburne, R. (1984). *Personal Identity*. Oxford: Blackwell.

Simpson, J., & Weiner, E., eds. (1989). *The Oxford English Dictionary*. Oxford: Clarendon Press.

Singer, W. (2003). *Ein neues Menschenbild? Gespräche über Hirnforschung*. Frankfurt am Main: Suhrkamp.

Stomma, S. (1947). Fikcja winy (Fiction of Guilt). *Państwo i Prawo* (The State and The Law), 10, 11–26.

Stühler, H. (1999). *Die actio libera in causa de lege lata und de lege ferenda: Eine Analyze von Rechtsprechung und Literatur verbundene mit einem Gesetzgebungsvorschlag*. Würzburg: Ergon Verlag.

von Liszt, F., & Schmidt, E. (1922). *Lehrbuch des deutschen Strafrechts*. Berlin: Berlin Vereinigung Wiss. Verl.

Welzel, H. (1969). *Das Deutsche Strafrecht: Eine systematische Darstellung*. Berlin: Walter de Gruyter.

Williams, B. (1956/1957). Personal Identity and Individuation. *Proceedings of the Aristotelian Society* 57, 229–252.

Zoll, A. (1984). Der Einfluß der Feuerbachschen Teorie auf die polnische Strafrechtswissenschaft. *Wissenschaftliche Zeitschrift der Friedrich-Schiller-Universität* 4, 507–515.

Zoll, A. (2003). Dyskusja poświęcona art. 9 k.k. (Discussion on the Article 9 of Polish Criminal Code). *Czasopismo Prawa Karnego i Nauk Penalnych* (Journal of Criminal Law and Penal Studies), 7(1), 84–92. https://czpk.pl/dokumenty/zeszyty/2003/zeszyt1/Dyskusja_nad_prezydenckim_projektem_nowelizacji_Kodeksu_Karnego_-_Dyskusja_w_Krakowie-CZPKiNP_2003-z.1.pdf

15

The Insanity Defense

Gerben Meynen[*]

15.1 INTRODUCTION

The insanity defense dates back to ancient times and it is a component of many criminal justice systems. It seems that many have been intrigued by this defense, one which touches upon a variety of enigmatic subjects, such as severe crimes, fairness, free will, retribution, and the reliability of psychiatric expert testimony (Meynen, 2016). In this chapter, key questions regarding the defense will be considered. Should insanity be part of our legal system? What should be the criterion for legal insanity? Can neuroscience help to assess a defendant's sanity? As legal insanity lies at the interface of law and psychiatry, we will have to consider both legal and psychiatric matters. Since we are interested in the foundations of legal insanity, we will have to take moral philosophy into account as well.

The outline of the chapter is as follows. In Section 15.2, we consider arguments pro and con the insanity defense as an element of our criminal law system. This implies addressing certain challenges of insanity assessments, such as the fact that it concerns a *past* mental state, and the fact that defendants may malinger (faking bad) or hide their symptoms (faking good). In Section 15.3, we will look in more detail at several legal standards for insanity such as the *M'Naghten Rule* and the *Model Penal Code* test. I will suggest that the criterion for insanity must include both an epistemic (knowledge) and a control component. In Section 15.4 we discuss the idea that the defense relies on the possibility that a mental illness may compromise a person's *free will*. We will conclude that the notion of "free will" provides a partial justification for legal insanity at best. In the fifth section, we concisely discuss the burden of proof, in particular the threshold of proof. In Section 15.6, the ethics of forensic psychiatric assessment and testimony about a defendant's insanity will be considered. Since the forensic psychiatric evaluation does not take place in a doctor–patient relationship, the ethical context is also different from the standard healthcare setting. In Section

---

[*] Prof. G. Meynen, forensic psychiatry, Willem Pompe Institute for Criminal Law and Criminology and Utrecht Centre for Accountability and Liability Law (UCALL), Utrecht University, the Netherlands, and Dept. of Philosophy, Humanities, VU University Amsterdam, the Netherlands.

15.7 we examine whether new neuroscientific developments involving "mind reading" could support insanity evaluations in the future.[1]

15.2 AN ELEMENT OF OUR LEGAL SYSTEM

In our everyday lives, we may well excuse people for their behavior because of a mental disorder. For instance, we may not blame our friend John for skipping our birthday party because he has social anxiety disorder. We may feel that given his extreme anxiety in social situations, his absence should be excused. In other words, exculpation because of mental illness is a normal societal phenomenon. The insanity defense reflects such a practice in criminal law.

The defense is often justified referring to *morality*. Slobogin, for instance, writes: "A person with severe mental disability, like the person who acts in self-defense or who causes harm accidentally, does not deserve the moral condemnation associated with criminal punishment."[2] Yet, even though criminal law often reflects moral notions and intuitions, there are specific issues to consider within the context of criminal law, a domain of our society where the stakes tend to be (very) high.

One crucial issue is *evidence*. In everyday contexts of moral praise and blame, we do not (always) require specific proof. We informally *assume* that John's social anxiety was the reason that he skipped the party. We don't need actual or formal proof that he suffers from a social anxiety disorder and that it was this disorder that made him skip the party – we won't ask for a doctor's certificate. The criminal law context is different, however. Society, in general, won't excuse a defendant charged with a serious crime, unless there is sufficient *proof* to support such an exculpation. Now, regarding the insanity defense, several qualms[3] have been raised about the reliability of the evidence. In fact, *many* aspects of the insanity defense are (heavily) debated and legal insanity is presumably one of the most debated topics in criminal law.[4] For heated discussions to occur, in general, two things are required: *difference of opinion* and *relevance* – without relevance, nobody would be bothered by the differences of views. Apparently, many people feel that insanity is relevant – and there is no shortage of differences of opinion either. We will consider some of the issues under debate.

The first worry concerns the fact that legal insanity relies on a psychiatric assessment made some time after the delinquent act took place. Since the insanity assessment focuses on the moment of the delinquent act, it is an examination in *retrospect*. Often, the legally relevant act has taken place weeks or even months ago.

---

[1] On topics discussed in this chapter, see also Meynen (2016, 2019, 2020a, and 2020b).
[2] Slobogin (2018). See also Morse, in a section entitled "The moral basis of the defence of legal insanity": "The insanity defence is grounded in long-recognised legal and moral principles and on routinely admissible evidence" (Morse, 2016, p. 241).
[3] For these and further qualms and responses to them see Meynen (2016).
[4] Slobogin (2018) writes, "The insanity defense is perhaps the most widely discussed doctrine in criminal law."

How reliable is information retrospectively gathered about such a past event? For instance, the defendant's condition at the moment of the examination may be completely different from his mental state at the time of the act. At the time of the act, he may have been delusional and under the influence of alcohol and drugs. At the moment of examination, however, he may be sober and his delusion may have disappeared. What does the psychiatric mental state examination *now* tell us about the defendant's state of mind at the time of the offense?

A second qualm concerns the fact that a defendant may not always be a reliable source of information. Apart from the possibility that the defendant is honestly mistaken or lacks specific memories about the event, there is the risk of malingering (faking symptoms of an illness) or faking good (hiding symptoms of a disease). The defendant may prefer a certain outcome of the psychiatric insanity assessment and deliberately provide information that, in his opinion, increases the chance of that desired outcome. The clear and present danger of faking on the part of the defendant could further decrease the reliability of insanity examinations.

A third argument against the insanity defense concerns the fear that as a result of the availability of the insanity defense, deterrence is diminished. Criminal law serves different goals, and one of them is deterrence – trying to keep people from committing crimes because of the fear of punishment. The insanity defense may convey the message that even if it has been proven that you committed a serious crime, you could still get away with it.

Yet, replies can be formulated to each of the three worries. First, as far as the retrospective nature of the assessment is concerned, we should note that criminal law generally deals with past events, and, more specifically, with mental states during or preceding those events. Criminal law is not only interested in a person's behavior, but also in issues like intent and ignorance, which refer to the realm of the mind. Was the harm deliberately inflicted, or was it merely accidental? These aren't minor issues in criminal law; on the contrary, these are core questions for juries and judges. And establishing these mind-related phenomena may even be more challenging than determining the presence of a severe mental illness at the time of the crime. According to Morse and Bonnie (2013, p. 493) "[t]he severe mental disorder that is necessary for practical support of an insanity defense is in most cases easier to prove than ordinary *mens rea*." In fact, the differences between negligence, recklessness, acting knowingly, or acting purposefully may well be subtler than the presence or absence of a mental illness at the time of the crime.

In addition, psychiatrists routinely perform assessments of past mental states and conditions. For instance, when diagnosing a major depressive disorder, it is important to exclude the possibility that the patient is suffering from bipolar disorder. In order to find out whether or not a patient has a bipolar disorder, a psychiatrist will ask about earlier manic and hypomanic states. Hypomanic states are episodes lasting at least four days, characterized by elevated mood, increased energy, and reduced need of sleep – but milder than manic episodes (American Psychiatric Association, 2013).

Patients may not even notice that they have such episodes, and psychiatrists sometimes have to *retrospectively* establish whether such episodes occurred by asking specific questions about the behavioral changes that may have occurred intermittently in the past. It is clinically important to find out, for at least two reasons. First, for people with bipolar disorder, another type of treatment is generally more appropriate: a mood stabilizer (instead of an antidepressant). Second, a person with bipolar disorder may not respond well to antidepressants; this type of medication may induce a manic episode. This is just one example of a backward-looking psychiatric assessments. Still, we could object to this reply that the assessment of insanity concerns a rather short period of time in the past, for example, last November 27th, around 23:00 h, the time the crime was committed. Was the person psychotic at *that* moment in time? This may be more difficult than retrospectively assessing a period of four days or more.

A response to the second objection to the insanity defense – that faking is a danger – is that psychiatrists are well aware of this risk, and that they actively try to detect signs of faking or malingering. For instance, they are on the alert regarding inconsistencies in the defendant's account, but also regarding inconsistencies between the account and other information sources, such as police reports and medical records. In addition, tools have been developed to assess the risk of malingering in an individual, the SIMS (Structured Inventory of Malingered Symptomatology) is an example (van Impelen, Merckelbach, Jelicic, & Merten, 2014). Also, in some cases, neuroimaging may provide additional information. An example is a Dutch attempted extortion case. On the *Judicial System Netherlands* website, we read about the defendant, an elderly man:

> Several behavioral experts have assessed the defendant. They conclude that the defendant suffers from frontotemporal dementia, behavioral subtype. As a result of this condition, according to the experts, the defendant had hardly any moral awareness of his actions. The defendant was guided by – childlike – sentimentality. He did not realize the consequences of his actions and he lacked empathy for the victims. It is very unlikely that the defendant can *fake* his brain disorder, this is *evident from* the MRI scan and PET scan that were shown during the session and assessment by the behavioral experts.[5]

His criminal responsibility was considered to be strongly reduced.[6] Clearly, neuroscience will not always be helpful in corroborating findings relevant for the question of legal insanity (see Section 15.7).

---

[5] Emphasis added, own translation. www.rechtspraak.nl/Organisatie-en-contact/Organisatie/Rechtbanken/Rechtbank-Midden-Nederland/Nieuws/Paginas/Veroordeling-voor-poging-afpersing-familie-De-Mol.aspx For the case itself: ECLI:NL:RBMNE:2015:4866

[6] Instead of the dichotomy sanity/insanity, at the time of this verdict, five grades of criminal responsibility/legal insanity were in use in the Netherlands: responsible, somewhat diminished responsibility, diminished responsibility, strongly diminished responsibility, complete legal insanity (Meynen, 2016).

There is no denying that psychiatric (and psychological) assessment often strongly relies on a patient's or defendant's own account (Meynen, 2020b).[7] As Linden writes:

> Psychiatry is the oddball of medical disciplines because it has almost no tests that positively aid the diagnosis of a particular disease. Where diagnostic tests are applied, such as neuroimaging, these normally serve to exclude other, "organic" causes for the reported symptoms and observed behavioural abnormalities. Although behavioural changes feature prominently in the diagnosis of some mental disorders, particularly those with childhood onset (autism, attention deficit/hyperactivity disorder, conduct disorder), most classic psychiatric diseases are largely diagnosed on the basis of patients' self-report. (Linden, 2012)

Suppose that a defendant states that he heard a voice (an auditory hallucination) commanding him to commit the crime he is charged with, and that the command could not be disobeyed. Hearing voices is a quite common psychopathological phenomenon, and we know that in some cases these voices may order the patient to perform certain actions. In a minority of these cases, the patient cannot but obey such an order. In a small percentage of these cases, finally, obeying the order constitutes a crime. But how do we know that *this* defendant actually heard such a commanding voice? The *defendant* must inform the psychiatrist about the occurrence at the time of the crime. If another person would also have heard that same voice, then, by definition, it would no longer be a hallucination. And, crucially, how does the psychiatrist know that the voice's command was irresistible? Again, basically, the defendant must tell him. Clearly, there may be some corroborating evidence, such as documentation from psychiatrists who had treated him earlier, which might show that the patient sometimes hears voices, or a witness, but the medical record doesn't tell whether a voice was heard at the time of the crime. There may be a witness who heard the patient talking to someone, while there was nobody there, which can be considered indicative of the presence of a voice to which the defendant was talking aloud. But no other person can testify about the force of the actual voice – if heard – at the moment of the crime. This is just to illustrate that, to a large extent, the psychiatrist has to rely on the defendant's own account. The patient's own account, however, need not be reliable. As already mentioned, faking, malingering are dangers. As Resnick and Knoll write, "command auditory hallucinations are easy to fabricate" (Resnick & Knoll, 2005).

One might ask at this point: can one ever be completely sure about the defendant's mental state as far as it is relevant to an insanity plea? Well, we may not even have to answer that question, because criminal law – and legal insanity only exists within the realm of criminal law – does *not require* that insanity be established with absolute certainty. Many legal systems define a specific threshold of proof for insanity. In the United States this may be "clear and convincing evidence" or "by a preponderance of the

---

[7] Even though, in many cases, additional evidence is available that the behavioral expert should take into account as well. See on this issue and what follows also Meynen (2019).

evidence."[8] Suppose the latter is the case, then the evidence supporting the insanity plea has to be stronger than the evidence indicating that the person was sane. Such a threshold of proof is far from absolute certainty. This means that one can still support legal insanity as an element of a legal system, even if one feels that 100 percent certainty about this issue is impossible.

15.3 CRITERIA FOR LEGAL INSANITY

In many legal systems, a criterion for legal insanity has been formulated. In this section we discuss three types of them, and we will also consider a jurisdiction in which a criterion for legal insanity has not been defined (the Netherlands).

15.3.1 M'Naghten and the Model Penal Code Test

The most influential legal criterion or standard in the Western world is the M'Naghten Rule:

> At the time of committing the act, the party accused was laboring under such a defect of reason, from disease of the mind, as not to know the nature and quality of the act he was doing; or if he did know it, that he did not know what he was doing was wrong.[9]

This criterion has, in practice, the following components:[10]

1) the presence of a mental disorder . . .
2) resulting in . . .
3) not knowing *what* the defendant was doing or not knowing that what he was doing was *wrong*.

So, if the person knows what he is doing and that it is wrong, an insanity defense cannot be successful. What counts is the influence of a disorder on the defendant's knowledge. This is not unreasonable, in the sense that ignorance is often an exculpatory factor in criminal law – just as long as the lack of knowledge is not culpable.

As said, many aspects of the insanity defense are under debate. Now which are important topics regarding the M'Naghten Rule? The first[11] topic is that many feel that it is too restrictive. Since Aristotle, two issues are taken to be relevant to

---

[8] See also Scott and Resnick (2016) on expert testimony in the United States: "The psychiatrist will then be asked to describe his examination of the patient. He will be asked whether he has formed an opinion with reasonable medical certainty regarding the legal issue. The term 'reasonable medical certainty' simply means that there is a 51% or greater probability that a conclusion is correct, in most states."
[9] Or M'Naghten Rules (plural). M'Naghten's Case, 10 Cl. & Fin. 200, 8 Eng. Rep. 718 (H.L. 1843).
[10] Slightly different from Meynen (2016, p. 15).
[11] For a discussion of the two issues that are discussed in this section (control and wrongness), see also Meynen (2020a).

responsibility and blameworthiness: peoples' knowledge *and* their control. In criminal law, if a person knows that what she is doing is harmful to another person – and therefore wrong – but she couldn't help doing it, for example, because another person forced her at gunpoint to do it, she may well be exculpated. The reason is that she was *coerced* to act as she did, and, in that sense, not in control. M'Naghten, however, only reflects the epistemic component, not the control (or coercion) element. This would not be a problem if mental illnesses could not affect a person's control, but they can.

Arguably, the best example of such an influence on control is the already mentioned type of command hallucination: a voice, which cannot be disobeyed, orders the person to act. The person may well know that what the voice tells her to do is wrong, but she cannot help but comply. Now should we hold a defendant who could not act otherwise than she did because of a psychopathological phenomenon (the occurrence of which is beyond her control) criminally responsible for the act? Apparently, many jurisdictions feel that she should be exculpated – considered legally insane – because these jurisdictions have an insanity standard that, often besides an epistemic element, includes a control or "volitional" prong (Simon & Ahn-Redding, 2006). The Model Penal Code (American Law Institute 1985) test, used in the United States,[12] is an example:

> a person is not responsible for criminal conduct if at the time of such conduct as a result of mental disease or defect he lacks substantial capacity either to appreciate the criminality (wrongfulness) of his conduct or to conform his conduct to the requirements of the law.

The inability to conform one's conduct to the requirements of the law is the MPC's formulation of the control element. Another example is Article 88 of the Italian Penal Code:

> A person who committed a criminal act is not considered responsible if at the time of the commission of the criminal act he was incapable of *understanding* the significance of his act or *control* his conduct, by reason of insanity. (Ferracuti & Roma, 2008, p. 84, emphasis added)

In China, the two components are reflected in article 18 of the criminal law:

> A mentally ill person who causes dangerous consequences at a time when he is *unable to recognize or unable to control* his own conduct is not to bear criminal responsibility after being established through accreditation of legal procedures; but his family or guardian shall be ordered to subject him to strict surveillance and arrange for his medical treatment. When necessary, he will be given compulsory medical treatment by the government. (Zhao & Ferguson, 2013, p. 639, emphasis added)

---

[12] Even though most US states have M'Naghten, Scott and Resnick (2016).

Yet in law, it is not only a question of whether a person who acted on a commanding voice should be exculpated in theory; a relevant issue is also whether such a control-problem can be reliably established in a court of law. Morse does not believe that control issues can be sufficiently reliably assessed, at least not in the realm of criminal law. He writes (1985, p. 817):

> There appears to be a prima facie case for a compulsion branch of the insanity defense, but is it persuasive and would the test be workable? If or to what degree a person's desire or impulse to act was controllable is not determinable: there is no scientific test to judge whether an impulse was irresistible or simply not resisted. At best, we may develop a phenomenological account of the defendant's subjective state of mind that will permit a common sense assessment of how much compulsion existed.

Again, we are confronted with an essential tenet of criminal law compared to morality: the emphasis on the reliability of the *evidence*. Even if from a moral (theoretical) perspective, control would be relevant, evidentiary worries may still hinder the inclusion of a control prong in an insanity standard.

Interestingly, Morse writes that "[a]t best, we may develop a phenomenological account of the defendant's subjective state of mind that will permit a common sense assessment of how much compulsion existed." But how different is that from establishing a delusion from which a defendant may suffer? A delusion is also a subjective phenomenon. In fact, almost all core symptoms of mental illness are subjective phenomena, to which we have only indirect access. We cannot hear the commanding voice as we cannot see the delusion or its content. Elsewhere, I have tried to explain why the control issue may be harder to establish, arguing that a crucial issue is stability over time (Meynen, 2016). Delusions tend to be more or less stable over time, while control problems tend to come and go. For example, when a person had the delusion that the CIA was persecuting her on Tuesday and on Thursday, she most probably had the same delusion on Wednesday, 3:26 p.m. (the moment of the crime). But a voice may be heard on Tuesday 1:23 p.m. and on Thursday 8:27 a.m. – without having been heard on Wednesday at all. More precisely, a voice may be there on Tuesday and Thursday and its command may have been easily resistible, but on Friday, the command may be irresistible. Control problems tend to fluctuate. So, regarding control issues, there is often a discontinuity over time. Still, even though in general control assessments may be more challenging, in my view, in principle, it is possible to reach the burden of proof (at least on a balance of probabilities) that the person acted because of an auditory hallucination.

There is another issue regarding the M'Naghten Rule, which does not concern the absence of an element, but rather its interpretation. It concerns the last word of the Rule: *wrong*. How should the wrongness be understood? Basically, there are two approaches: the first is the interpretation as *legal* wrongfulness, the second is *moral* wrongfulness.[13] The first interpretation is, in practice, quite strict. Generally, the legal wrongfulness will work in cases of delusionally presumed *self-defense*. For instance, Peter has the delusion that his longtime friend, Tom, is involved in a conspiracy against him and that he is going to attack him any moment. When Peter notices that his friend's hand goes into his pocket, he is certain that this is the moment that Tom will strike, and Peter immediately decides that, to save his own life, he should attack first. Peter seriously harms his longtime friend Tom. Clearly, Peter honestly believed that he was acting in self-defense and that, therefore, his action was *legally* justified – self-defense being a justification. M'Naghten works well in this case. Note that the moral interpretation works as well: Peter believes that his action is morally justified, too, as he acted to defend himself against an imminent attack (self-defense is recognized as a justification both in the moral and legal realm).

But there is another type of cases in which the legal interpretation does not work well. A mother suffers from a postpartum psychosis and she delusionally believes that her newborn baby will go to hell unless she kills her (which will make her go to heaven). The mother knows that killing one's child constitutes a crime, but her delusion about her child's eternal suffering in hell "overrides" the importance of legal considerations. According to the legal interpretation of "wrong," this mother is not insane: she knows what she is doing (killing her child) and knows this is legally wrong. *Morally*, however, she honestly believes she is doing the right thing: saving her child. Cases in which a mother kills her own child because of a delusion are amongst the most tragic insanity cases. These mothers may still know that killing one's child constitutes a crime. But they may also feel that their act was not morally wrong, but, instead, morally required. The type of cases in which the legal interpretation does not "work," but the moral interpretation does, tend to involve God, Satan, demons, etcetera – in general, the supernatural.[14] In such cases, in my view, the insanity defense should also be possible.

15.3.2 *Psychosis at the Time of the Crime*

Arguably the most well-known recent insanity case – even though the defendant was eventually considered sane – is the Norwegian Breivik case. On July 22, 2011, Anders Breivik killed 77 people, amongst whom many were youngsters. Breivik's sanity was evaluated by two pairs of psychiatrists (Melle, 2013). The first pair concluded that he was psychotic at the time of the crime and suffering from schizophrenia, specifically of the paranoid type. The second pair, however, concluded that he was not psychotic

---

[13] Morse favors the moral interpretation: "To the extent that an outcome might turn on moral versus legal wrong, the former should be preferred because it is more action guiding and provides a better fit with the underlying rationale for the defence" (Morse, 2016).
[14] See on moral vs. legal wrongness also Ligthart, Kooijmans, and Meynen (2018) and Meynen (2020a).

at the time of crime. The presence of psychosis was crucial for insanity in Norway, as article 44 Norwegian General Civil Penal Code §44 stated,

> A person who was psychotic or unconscious at the time of committing the act shall not be liable to a penalty. The same applies to a person who at the time of committing the act was mentally retarded to a high degree.[15]

A peculiar aspect of this insanity criterion is that the mere presence of a psychosis at the time of the crime is sufficient for legal insanity.[16] No *influence* – either in terms of knowledge or control – has been specified. In addition, a *specific type* of disorder is required. Whereas M'Naghten needs a "disease of the mind" – which could, in principle, be any disease of the mind – this criterion is very precise. The type of disorder, psychosis, does not seem to be unreasonable. According to Slobogin (2017), "the typical mental disorder associated with insanity is psychosis." So, if one would have to select one type of disorder for the insanity defense, the best option is most probably psychotic illness.

Meanwhile, the question is whether it is justified to restrict the insanity defense merely to psychotic illness. Couldn't other serious disorders – depression, a manic episode, dementia – lead to situations in which a person is no longer responsible? That is one type of concern: isn't this standard too restrictive? The other concern is that this standard may, at the same time, be too broad and inclusive, because *all* people who are psychotic at the time of the crime are deemed legally insane. Is that justified? Some people have chronic psychotic features; is it reasonable to never hold such a person responsible for any crime he or she might commit? That doesn't appear to be the case. There may well be choices that the person can make more or less "independent" of the illness. In fact, never considering psychotic people responsible for crimes committed could lead to stigmatization of psychotic people as "irresponsible" fellow citizens. If they cannot take responsibility for their criminal actions, one might start to wonder, should we still consider them autonomous decision makers in other areas of life? For instance, are they still competent to make decisions about their treatment? According to Welie and Welie (2001, p. 129, emphasis added), "Competence is the patient's ability to make a choice about the various medical interventions offered to her by the caregiver, and to bear *accountability* for that choice." So, people may ask: If psychotic people are never held accountable in the court of (criminal) law, should we still consider them competent to make healthcare decisions?

Yet, there is an evidentiary advantage provided by this legal standard. As we have seen, it may be really challenging to assess the impact of a disorder on a person's behavioral control. How to establish the exact impact of a voice on a person's

---

[15] Quote taken from the English translation of the Breivik verdict, Lovdata TOSLO-2011–188627-24E. Notably, the Norwegian criterion for insanity has recently changed; see Gröning et al. (2020) for a discussion. Psychosis is no longer central.

[16] On the Norwegian test see also J. Bijlsma (2018).

behavior? A psychosis-standard does not require the establishment of such a link; psychiatrists can just determine the presence of a psychotic disorder (with hallucinations), without having to specify its exact influence on a particular action.

15.3.3 No Criterion

Even though many jurisdictions have specified the criteria for insanity, not all have done so. In the Netherlands, legal insanity is a component of the criminal justice system, but no standard has been specified (Bijlsma, 2016). More precisely, Dutch criminal law stipulates that: "Anyone who commits an offence for which he cannot be held responsible by reason of the mental disorder, psychogeriatric condition, or intellectual disability, is not criminally liable" (Kooijmans & Meynen, 2017, adapted because terminology has recently changed). This article merely states that *if* a person is not responsible for an offense due to a mental disorder, he *cannot be punished*. In forensic psychiatric practice this leads to a situation in which the evaluators have to build their own arguments as to why a defendant should – or should not – be considered legally insane (in the Netherlands, experts are asked to provide explicit advice regarding the issue of legal insanity). In other words, behavioral experts have to interpret the legal concept – insanity – without legal guidance. Also, the judges lack such legal guidance, and, as Bijlsma has convincingly shown, this has resulted in diverging interpretations of the same concept in legal practice (Bijlsma, 2016).

Recently, a Dutch Court of Appeal, in the absence of a clear legal criterion, formulated its own criterion. Part of it was that "it must be plausible that the defendant's actions were not (partly) motivated by real, non-pathological motives." In other words, the actions should be purely based on pathological motives. This, however, does not appear to be a helpful criterion (Ligthart et al., 2018). For instance, the mother who tries to save her newborn baby from eternal suffering is, at least in part, motivated by love for her child (see Section 15.3.1). In fact, it is the nonpathological love for her baby *combined with* the pathological phenomenon (a delusion about eternal suffering if the child is not killed) that results in the tragedy. Also, in cases of delusional self-defense (see Section 15.3.1) the criterion offered by this Court of Appeal is unhelpful. A person who defends himself against an imagined (delusion-based) attacker acts partially on nonpathological motives: self-defense is not a pathological phenomenon at all. So, requiring merely pathological motives for a successful insanity defense is not a helpful and realistic criterion for legal insanity. In fact, one could argue that not having a clear criterion for legal insanity may lead to courts that – understandably – improvise to define a criterion. This may not only result in inequality of justice, but also in suboptimal criteria for insanity.

It has been argued that a Dutch criterion has to be developed (Bijlsma, 2016; Ligthart et al., 2018). However, opinions differ as to the question of who should develop such a criterion. Bijlsma suggests that the Dutch Supreme Court could define the standard, while others have argued that, given its importance, the legislator – parliament – should take responsibility for defining the criterion for legal insanity (Ligthart et al., 2018).

Finally, I briefly mention an issue related to the standard, which concerns the possibility of *grades* of responsibility. Often, the dichotomy of sane versus insane is employed: does the criterion apply, or doesn't it? Yet some jurisdictions use a grade in the middle: diminished or partial responsibility, and thus the criterion may be partially fulfilled. For instance, several European states have diminished responsibility, and thus a graded concept (Salize & Dressing, 2005, p. 62). The Netherlands, until recently, had no fewer than five grades of responsibility (see footnote 6). Recently, Bijlsma and Meynen have argued that whether or not diminished responsibility is useful depends on the characteristics of a legal system (Bijlsma & Meynen, 2018). For instance, in the Netherlands the judges have considerable freedom regarding the sentence and the issues they may or may not take into account, and the category "diminished responsibility" does not really add to or limit the possibilities. More specifically, judges may take the influence of a mental disorder into account in their sentencing irrespective of the "label" of diminished responsibility. Yet, in other legal systems, the formal category may be useful, and in such jurisdictions it may, therefore, be advisable to add such a legal category.

15.4 FREE WILL

In Section 15.3, we considered several insanity standards, and, as it became clear, they differ across jurisdictions. But we may also ask on a conceptual level: Why is it that mental disorders undermine a person's criminal responsibility in the first place? In other words, what justifies the insanity defense? Many have argued that the justification is that such illnesses may compromise free will.[17] For instance, Allan (2018) writes: "In many legal jurisdictions, the insanity defense applies when it is judged that the accused is dispossessed of their free will." Apparently, the underlying assumption is that free will is foundational for criminal responsibility (Parmigiani et al., 2017; Wright, 2014), and that mental disorders affect this basis for responsibility.

The problem with this justification of the insanity defense is that it makes it vulnerable to skepticism about free will. Free will is one of the most frequently discussed topics in the history of philosophy (Kane, 1998). The main issue concerns the question of the compatibility of free will and determinism. For various reasons, people believe – and have believed – that our world or cosmos is determined. Determinism, broadly conceived, is the idea that the future is fixed. One reason people have felt that the future was fixed was because of divine foreknowledge: If God knows everything that will happen in the future, every event or action is

---

[17] On what follows see also Meynen (2016) and Meynen (2020a).

determined by his knowledge (Kane, 2005). Can people be truly free when their actions are determined in this way? Another form of determinism concerns the laws of physics. If everything that happens is governed by the current state of events combined with the laws of physics, then, it appears, the future is fixed. Even if we cannot predict the future, because of the complexity of the current state of the world and its laws, on a deeper level, it unfolds in a predetermined cause-and-effect manner.

More recently, neurobiological experiments have fueled the debate on free will, particularly the Libet experiment (Libet et al., 1983). In brief, Libet and his colleagues reported that about half a second before a person becomes aware of the urge or intention to perform a motor action (e.g., flexing one's wrist), a characteristic electrophysiological signal can be detected, the "readiness potential" (Libet, 1999). The corollary was that the brain was first, and that consciousness was only following the preceding brain activity; at least that is how some interpreted the findings (Spence, 1996; Wegner, 2002). The debate on the experiment, and how it should be interpreted, also in light of free will, continues (Radder & Meynen, 2013; Mele, 2014).

In his 2007 paper, "The Non-Problem of Free Will in Forensic Psychiatry and Psychology," Stephen Morse has taken a strong position against the relevance of free will for criminal responsibility and insanity in particular (Morse, 2007). He writes: "Solving the free will problem would have profound implications for responsibility doctrines and practices, but, at present, the problem plays no proper role in forensic practice or theory because this ability or its lack is not a criterion of any civil or criminal law doctrine." Yet, not everybody would agree: many have argued for the relevance of free will to criminal responsibility in general, and legal insanity in particular; see for example, Wright (2014).

Still, in none of the standards discussed above are freedom or "free will" mentioned. Knowledge, control, and psychosis are part of the standards discussed, but not free will. Does that imply that it is irrelevant? Free will has to do with decisions about courses of action, not with your knowledge. So, for M'Naghten, free will doesn't seem to be relevant. However, for the control prong, things are different. Let us have a look at the *Stanford Encyclopedia of Philosophy* on free will, where O'Connor writes (O'Connor, 2018; substantive revision, first published 2002):

> The term "free will" has emerged over the past two millennia as the canonical designator for a significant kind of *control* over one's actions.

This quote shows that control and free will are interconnected. So, a control prong in an insanity defense can at least be considered as *related* to free will. Still, we should realize that this quote also states that free will is a *specific kind* of control. This means that the problems surrounding free will need not transpire to all kinds of control. In fact, the concept of control is much less metaphysically contested than the notion of free will. That is not the same as stating that control is unproblematic, which it isn't, but it is definitely less a topic of philosophical controversy than free will.

15.5 BURDEN OF PROOF

We already addressed the issue of the burden of proof, in fact the threshold of proof: the higher the threshold, the more difficult to prove insanity. We now consider in some more detail the burden of proof and related matters: what should be the threshold, who should bear the burden, and who should establish the disorder?

What should be the *threshold* of proof? "Beyond reasonable doubt" is most probably too high for legal insanity. Should it be a preponderance of the evidence, or, a bit higher, clear and convincing evidence? The latter two seem to provide the best options given the nature of the assessment and the nature of the defense. Bijlsma and Meynen recently argued that, in any case, it is important to be clear about the threshold. In the Netherlands, no distinction is made between "clear and convincing evidence" and "preponderance of the evidence." The general term "plausible" (*aannemelijk*) is used, but it is not clear what level of proof that term refers to exactly. So, it is not only important to determine a threshold, but also important to be clear about what the threshold entails. Obviously, determining the threshold, it is important to balance several issues, which I mention briefly. First, the interest of the defendant, who should not be held accountable for crimes committed as a result of a mental disorder. On the other hand, there are victims, who should be able to accept the outcome when a person is considered legally insane and therefore won't be sent to prison. Thirdly, there is society, and the verdict should be acceptable to society as well.[18]

Another topic regards the question of who *bears* the burden of proof. In many Anglo-American jurisdictions, insanity is an affirmative defense. The defendant has to provide the required evidence of insanity. An argument against this is that the chances of a successful defense may be determined to a considerable extent by the defendant's financial resources: is he able to have a good defense lawyer who has the means to build a strong case? In other jurisdictions, the burden is, or has been, on the prosecution (Simon & Ahn-Redding, 2006). Meanwhile, in other systems, the evaluation may be court ordered, and the psychiatrist may immediately report to the judges.

A related issue regarding proof is the following: Who should *establish* the presence of a disorder? Legal insanity predates psychiatry and psychology as academic disciplines. So, long before psychiatrists existed and could inform the court, judgments about legal insanity were made. A legal criterion that was used in the remote past in England was

---

[18] Regarding the threshold, there may be significant differences resulting from the structure of the legal system. In particular, one could argue, the topic is crucial for the common law with their jury system, since the standards must be explicitly stated when an unprofessional jury makes the decision.

the wild beast test. In *Rex* v. *Arnold* (1724), Justice Tracy defined insanity as follows: a defendant "must be a man that is totally deprived of his understanding and memory, and doth not know what he is doing, no more than an infant, than a brute, or a wild beast; such a one is never the object of punishment" (Robinson, 1996, p. 134). Remarkably, no reference is made to illness or diseases of the mind. The standard refers to a lack of understanding and memory, but not to what could be considered its "source": mental pathology. Rather, it refers to nonmedical categories such as infants, brutes, and wild beasts. Nowadays, legal insanity standards generally refer to illness. If such a reference is made, then it is only natural that doctors and/or psychologists assist the court in reaching a decision. In fact, it is common practice that behavioral experts, particularly psychiatrists, inform or advise the court about the presence of mental conditions and, depending on the jurisdiction, about their nature and influence on a person's behavior. In case the experts disagree, which is not uncommon, the jury or the court will have to choose whom to follow. Yet, the decision is based on the expert's testimony. Still, Morse (2011b, p. 894, references omitted) has stated:

> The criminal law can, but need not, turn to scientific or clinical definitions of mental abnormality as legal criteria when promulgating mental health laws. The Supreme Court has reiterated on numerous occasions that there is substantial dispute within the mental health professions about diagnoses, that psychiatry is not an exact science, and that the law is not bound by extra-legal professional criteria. The law often uses technical terms, such as "mental disorder," or semi-technical qualifiers, such as "severe," but non-technical terms, such as "mental abnormality," have also been approved. Legal criteria are adopted to answer legal questions. As long as they plausibly do so, they will be approved even if they are not psychiatric or psychological criteria.

Yet, we have to remind ourselves that Morse is writing about the United States. In principle, the division of tasks that I favor is that behavioral experts establish the presence and influence of a disorder based on their medical/psychological expertise, while the court or jury decides whether the (further) criteria for legal insanity have been met (see also Kooijmans & Meynen, 2017).

15.6 THE ETHICS OF THE EXPERT

Some have taken strong, critical positions on the ethics of giving forensic psychiatric testimony in the courtroom. Well known is Harvard law professor Alan A. Stone's criticism regarding such testimony, first published in 1984, based on a lecture delivered at the Thirteenth Annual Meeting of the American Academy of Psychiatry and the Law, 1982, and later published in 2008. He writes:

> I am not a forensic psychiatrist. What has kept me out of the courtroom is my concern about the ethical boundaries of forensic psychiatry. Let me state what I think the ethical boundary problems are.

First, there is the basic boundary question. Does psychiatry have anything true to say that the courts should listen to?

Second, there is the risk that one will go too far and twist the rules of justice and fairness to help the patient.

Third, there is the opposite risk that one will deceive the patient in order to serve justice and fairness.

Fourth, there is the danger that one will prostitute the profession, as one is alternately seduced by the power of the adversarial system and assaulted by it.

Finally, as one struggles with these four issues – Does one have something true to say? Is one twisting justice? Is one deceiving the patient? Is one prostituting the profession? – there is the additional problem: forensic psychiatrists are without any clear guidelines as to what is proper and ethical, at least as far as I can see.

These are harsh words, but it is good to take them into account, even though they were (first) uttered more than three decades ago – and many things have changed (guidelines, of course, have been developed) since then. Still, basic points of concern remain. First, the question of to what extent psychiatry is relevant for the law. In my view, it is important that forensic psychiatrists continuously reflect on the relevance, value, and appropriateness of their statements – and on how they are, or can be, interpreted and used in the legal realm. For instance, what exactly do forensic psychiatrists know about the relationship between specific mental disorders and crime or risk of recidivism? How should they interpret scientific group level information to the individual defendant? How do they deal with the fact that the defendant's statements may not be truthful and trustworthy? Meanwhile, ultimately, it is the criminal justice system that determines the relevance of psychiatry for the law. Judges, prosecutors, and attorneys will *ask* for psychiatric assistance at those points where they believe forensic testimony can add something. But that does not mean psychiatrists have to answer all of their questions without further reflection. Crucially, behavioral experts have to think carefully about the kinds of answers they provide: do they fall in their area of expertise?

The next two questions posed by Stone are always important to keep in mind: is one serving the defendant (too much) or is one going too far to obtain the kind of information that will please the lawyer, judge or prosecution? It is essential to realize that the relationship with the defendant is not equivalent to a therapeutic (doctor–patient) relationship. This means that one cannot "serve" the interests of a defendant as one would perhaps try to benefit a patient. It is more like an "examiner–examinee" relationship (Gutheil, 2005, p. 346). The unusual nature of the relationship is also addressed in Eastman et al. (2012, p. 248):

> In medico-legal work, forensic psychiatrists need to be thoughtful about the type of relationship they have with individuals they evaluate for legal proceedings. Some professionals argue that these are non-therapeutic relationships which are necessary

for the proper administration of justice; others argue that doctors cannot have non-therapeutic relationships when they are in professional roles ...

The latter, to me, seems to go too far, but clearly, at least in some cases, psychiatrists may experience a tension between the two roles.

In Stone's quote, the risk of "prostituting the profession" is linked to the adversarial system. And that may seem justified: the "battle of experts" is usually linked to the adversarial context.[19] Yet, pressure to cross professional boundaries may also exist in inquisitorial systems.

The ethicist and psychiatrist Paul Appelbaum, partly in response to Stone's criticism of the ethics of forensic psychiatric evaluations, has defined the basic tenets of the ethics of forensic psychiatric testimony (Appelbaum, 1997). To begin with, he acknowledges and stresses that, from a medical ethics point of view, forensic psychiatric experts were in a peculiar situation:

> The bedrock principles of beneficence and nonmaleficence, to which medicine had looked historically, were inapplicable outside the clinical realm. Without these compass points to steer by, forensic psychiatry was condemned to wander in an ethical wasteland, permanently bereft of moral legitimacy.

In other words, forensic psychiatric testimony cannot derive its orientation from the standard bioethical framework, since it is not a doctor–patient relationship in which the four principles of medical ethics apply. These are respect for autonomy, beneficence, nonmaleficence, and justice (Beauchamp & Childress, 2013). The expert's role has also immediate implications for confidentiality, a basic norm in healthcare (Roberts, 2016). In fact, a psychiatrist should inform the examinee that the findings are not confidential and may be shared with judges and jury (Gutheil, 2005). In the courtroom, the media may be present, and information may end up in daily newspapers or television shows. So, in this respect, the context is really different from the standard doctor–patient ethics.

Appelbaum provides guidance through the "ethical wasteland," identifying two overarching principles: truth telling and respect for persons. Both are not alien to the normal medical profession – truth telling is paramount to respecting autonomy and informed consent (Gillon, 1994), while respect is a basic attitude – but here, in the context of forensic testimony, they become, basically, *the* guiding principles, in Appelbaum's view. This makes it clear that the forensic psychiatrist's task when evaluating a defendant's legal insanity is a special one. Not only because of the required expertise, the setting, but also because of the ethical landscape.

---

[19] According to Van der Wolf and Van Marle, "in an adversarial system, expert witnesses – including in forensic psychiatry – are usually appointed by the parties, which could lead to a battle of the experts, while in an inquisitorial system, they are generally appointed by the court. For example, in England, as one of the mentioned solutions for the battle of the experts, a Law Commission advised to have a third expert appointed by the court" (Van der Wolf & Van Marle, 2018, p. 36).

According to Appelbaum, truth telling also implies that the psychiatrist is up to date with the literature, and does not overstate certain results. In addition, it entails respecting the boundaries of one's expertise, which, according to Appelbaum, has a practical implication for expressing one's opinion in insanity cases. He writes (Appelbaum, 2008, p. 197):

> Part of the problem here relates to the proclivity of forensic psychiatrists and other experts to offer "ultimate issue" testimony – that is, to attempt to answer legal/moral questions like whether a defendant is criminally responsible, as opposed merely to presenting descriptive information about a defendant's mental state. With no special expertise in addressing legal or moral questions, psychiatrists who make such judgments are treading on morally perilous terrain. Indeed, I have long believed that psychiatrists should avoid ultimate issue testimony, focusing their attention on descriptions of mental and functional states that they are much better qualified to address. This is not always a simple matter, since some courts will insist on such testimony as a criterion of admissibility, and many attorneys seek experts who will address the ultimate issue.

I believe that this is helpful advice. Ideally, as I already argued in the previous section, the psychiatrist establishes the presence of a disorder (and its impact) while the court or jury determines its implications for criminal responsibility and insanity.

15.7 NEUROSCIENCE AND THE FUTURE OF INSANITY ASSESSMENTS

As discussed in Section 15.2, neuroimaging is sometimes used to inform the court regarding a defendant's insanity. However, there is a debate about its validity, added value, and legal relevance (see Morse, 2006; Catley, 2016; Moratti & Patterson, 2016; Meynen, 2018b).

Neuroimaging may provide reliable information about the presence of a tumor (Burns & Swerdlow, 2003), brain trauma, some neurodevelopmental conditions, and neurodegenerative disease, such as dementia. Meanwhile, in clinical practice, psychiatric disorders such as psychotic illnesses, depression, bipolar disorder, autism, and post-traumatic stress disorder (PTSD), cannot be established using brain imaging. In other words, even after decades of neuroscientific research, there are still no neurobiological assessment tools for clinical psychiatric practice for these disorders. Therefore, in legal practice, in many cases, neuroimaging won't able to add relevant information regarding the presence of a mental disorder within the context of an insanity defense. And, generally, we should not be overenthusiastic or naïve about the value of neuroimaging for insanity assessments (Scarpazza et al., 2018). Still, in certain cases, such as the extortion case described in Section 15.2, where the defendant turned out to suffer from fronto-temporal dementia, neuroimaging is valuable and relevant to establishing a diagnosis and, ultimately, to the question of criminal responsibility. But neuroimaging alone, without further information, will often provide very little information; it has to be judged given other findings and data.

As far as brain function is concerned, neuropsychological assessment can make a valuable contribution as it can help to provide *functional* context to the *structural* findings on a brain scan.[20] For instance, neuropsychological evaluation may show that a defendant's executive functions have deteriorated, which could be due to pathological changes in the frontal lobe. If the brain scan shows a frontal pathology that matches these neuropsychological findings, this corroborates the conclusion that brain pathology is not only present but may have consequences for the defendant's behavior. As a rule of thumb, I suggest that neuroimaging should be combined with neuropsychological assessment to get a clearer picture of how brain changes relate to actual functioning (Meynen, 2018b).

In the remainder of this section, I will briefly focus on new neurotechniques that "read" minds. We will consider their potential value for insanity assessments.[21]

The term "mind reading" may require some clarification. First of all, "mind reading" is an everyday phenomenon: humans constantly try to read each other's minds, using different kinds of information such as facial expressions, gestures, and a person's words (Greely, 2013; Meynen, 2018a). Such "reading" of other people's minds enables us "to predict, explain, mold, and manipulate each other's behaviour."[22] I will understand neuroscientific mind reading as referring to "mind-reading"[23] procedures that rely to a nontrivial extent on brain-derived data.[24] So, the procedure has to involve neurotechniques (e.g., fMRI or EEG) but it may be combined with other technologies as well, such as machine learning algorithms (artificial intelligence). Theoretically, neurotechnological mind reading does not imply committing oneself to a particular position on the mind–brain relationship (such as reductionism). Neurotechnological mind reading, as I conceive of it, is

[20] A structural brain scan shows the structure of the individual brain: examples include CT scans or MRIs of the brain. They may reveal, for example, cerebral infarction or hemorrhage. Functional scans detect functional parameters: they may detect blood flow or electrical activity in order to measure brain activity, and an example is the functional MRI (Roskies, 2013).

[21] On this topic of "mind reading" in relation to (forensic) psychiatry, see also Meynen (2018a, 2019, where the term "neurotechnological thought apprehension" is used, and 2020b).

[22] Heyes and Frith (2014): "Our ability to ascribe mental states to ourselves and others is known as 'theory of mind,' 'mentalizing,' 'folk psychology,' or 'mind reading.' ... Mind reading allows us to predict, explain, mold, and manipulate each other's behavior in ways that go well beyond the capabilities of other animals." As this quote makes clear, other terms are sometimes used to refer to the human capacity of mind reading.

[23] See also Ienca and Andorno (2017) on the notion of "reading" and the state of neurotechnological techniques: "It is true that functional brain imaging cannot really 'read' thoughts, but can only highlight differences between brain activations during different cognitive tasks, and to infer from such differences certain conclusions about an individual's thoughts. However, the fact remains that, even if in an indirect manner, these new tools are increasingly able to determine with a high degree of accuracy certain brain data that belong to the private sphere and deserve to be protected from public scrutiny."

[24] This, and what follows about the concept of mind reading, is in accordance with Meynen (2018a, 2019, and 2020b).

pragmatic: as long as neuroimaging yields useful information about a subject's mental state (broadly conceived), it can be considered neurotechnological mind reading. The broad conception of mental state implies that it includes the ascription of thoughts, emotions, intentions, inclinations, biases, desires, and mental capacities.[25]

At this moment, neurotechnological mind reading is certainly not ready for clinical and forensic psychiatric practice. Yet, to some limited extent, it is possible in laboratory conditions. Some years ago, Gallant and his colleagues were able to reconstruct the movies people viewed using fMRI technology measuring brain activity: the reconstructed movies show a remarkable resemblance to the movies people had been watching (Nishimoto et al., 2011). In the discussion of their results, they write: "This is a critical step toward the creation of brain reading devices that can reconstruct dynamic perceptual experiences" (p. 1644). More recently, Marcel Just's group reported that they were able to identify the physics concepts that subjects were thinking about in an fMRI scanner. The subjects, with some background in physics, thought about concepts like energy, acceleration, and temperature (Mason & Just, 2016). With the help of machine learning, the researchers were able to identify the concepts that the subjects were thinking about. Studies like these merely provide a "proof of principle": they only show that using the combination of neuroimaging and machine learning (artificial intelligence), to some extent, thoughts – mental states – can be identified or "read." Yet, Just et al. used a multiple-choice design, in which the subjects (and the computer) could only choose from a limited set of physics concepts. Furthermore, reading physics concepts is far from psychiatric utility, of course. More recently, however, Just and his colleagues, again using fMRI combined with machine learning, were able to distinguish suicidal youths from nonsuicidal youths.[26] This clearly is the kind of information psychiatrists are interested in.

What could be the value of such developments for insanity assessments? As we have seen, reliance on first-person accounts constitutes a vulnerability, as there is a real risk of faking and malingering (Section 15.2). Perhaps, in some years' time, it might be technically possible to detect and thus obtain psychiatrically relevant information about a person's condition using such brain-based mind reading. For instance, it might be possible to detect hallucinations or delusional thoughts (Meynen, 2018b). Such findings could support the conclusion that the defendant suffers from schizophrenia and increase the likelihood that the defendant was psychotic at the time of the crime. This information may be valuable regarding

---

[25] In principle, this means that also current diagnostic procedures (e.g., those used to detect a brain tumor) could count as mind reading insofar as they yield some information regarding a person's mental capacities. Yet, in this chapter I will focus on types of mind reading that are not (yet) available in clinical practice. On "brain/mind-reading," see also Haynes (2012).

[26] Just et al. (2017). The accuracy is not 100 percent, yet clearly better than chance. On this, and on what follows on "mind reading" and legal insanity, see Meynen (2020b).

the question of his legal insanity. Yet, even if this were technically feasible, it is not self-evident whether – and if so how – it could be used in forensic practice. There may be both legal and ethical issues (Meynen, 2019). To mention just a few: shouldn't defendants be protected against psychiatrists who seek to retrieve information directly from their brains? How about mental privacy? Could defendants be forced to undergo such a neuroimaging evaluation – and would psychiatrists be willing to cooperate with such an involuntary procedure? In my view, given the weaknesses of insanity evaluations, we should not immediately reject possible avenues to strengthen their reliability. On the other hand, given the privacy-invasiveness of such techniques, we should consider legal and ethical qualms very carefully before making use of them. In addition, we should not be overly reliant on these techniques. Suppose that symptoms of schizophrenia are "detected" in a defendant during some mind-reading procedure: does that mean that the defendant heard voices at the time of the crime? Not necessarily. As Scott and Resnick warn, "Persons who have true schizophrenia may also malinger auditory hallucinations to escape criminal responsibility. These are the most difficult cases to accurately assess" (Scott & Resnick, 2016).

15.8 CONCLUSION

Legal insanity is a multidimensional phenomenon in which law, psychiatry, and ethics come together – and it has given rise to much debate. We have considered several central issues. First, we addressed the question of whether the insanity defense should be part of our legal system. Different concerns have been raised, often connected to the reliability of the assessments. Even though responses to these concerns can be provided, these qualms should be taken seriously as they tend to expose vulnerabilities of the defense that deserve attention. Next, we considered the question of what the criterion for legal insanity should look like. Relying on a common – Aristotelean – account of responsibility, I offer that both an epistemic and control component must be included.

Free will is frequently deemed theoretically crucial to justify the defense. However, based on our analysis, I concluded that free will is not related to the epistemic factor which is present in many standards. Notably, the most influential insanity criterion in the Western world, the M'Naghten Rule, merely contains a knowledge component. Free will, therefore, is not relevant to justify that standard. Still, there is a direct link between free will and the control prong, which also regularly features in insanity standards worldwide. As far as the insanity defense includes such a control element, free will could provide a justification.

The burden of proof – in particular the threshold of proof – deserves careful consideration, also in debates about the reliability of psychiatric assessments. It is important to realize that evidence for insanity often requires no more than proof "by a preponderance of the evidence."

By entering the courtroom to provide expert opinion, the psychiatrist leaves the realm of *standard* medical ethics. Meanwhile, it is vital to recognize that there are clearly ethical obligations, in particular truth telling and respect for persons, which apply. Truth telling implies respecting the boundaries of one's expertise. Not providing an opinion on the ultimate issue of the defendant's insanity can well be the expression of such respect.

Nowadays, many feel that neuroscience could help to (better) assess a defendant's criminal responsibility, yet we should be aware of its limitations. These not only regard technical matters of validity and reliability, but they also concern the extent to which neuroscience is relevant to the legal question at hand. Looking to the future, neurotechnological "mind reading" may start to offer new possibilities. But these techniques will have to be carefully assessed, not least from an ethical perspective, before they can be used in a forensic context.

Amidst all the controversy about the insanity defense, there is one thing that seems uncontroversial: the defense is likely to continue to not only cause heated discussions, but also to contribute to the fairness of the criminal justice system.

REFERENCES

American Psychiatric Association. (2013). *Diagnostic and Statistical Manual of Mental Disorders: DSM-5*, 5th ed. Arlington, VA: American Psychiatric Association.

Appelbaum, P. S. (1997). A Theory of Ethics for Forensic Psychiatry. *Journal of the American Academy of Psychiatry and the Law* 25(3), 233–247.

Appelbaum, P. S. (2008). Ethics and Forensic Psychiatry: Translating Principles into Practice. *Journal of the American Academy of Psychiatry and the Law* 36(2), 195–200.

Beauchamp, T. L., & Childress, J. F. (2013). *Principles of Biomedical Ethics*, 7th ed. New York: Oxford University Press.

Bijlsma, J. (2016). *Stoornis en strafuitsluiting. Op zoek naar een toetsingskader voor ontoerekenbaarheid*. Oisterwijk: Wolf Legal Publishers.

Bijlsma, J. (2018). A New Interpretation of the Modern Two-Pronged Tests for Insanity: Why Legal Insanity Should Not Be a Status Defense. *Netherlands Journal of Legal Philosophy* 47, 29–48.

Bijlsma, J., & Meynen, G. (2018). Wat is "aannemelijk"? Over het belang van een helder sanctierechtelijk bewijscriterium. *Nederlands Juristenblad* 34, 2514–2519.

Burns, J. M., & Swerdlow, R. H. (2003). Right Orbitofrontal Tumor With Pedophilia Symptom and Constructional Apraxia Sign. *Archives of Neurology* 60(3), 437–440.

Catley, P. (2016). The Future of Neurolaw. *European Journal of Current Legal Issues* 22(2). http://webjcli.org/index.php/webjcli/article/view/487/651

Eastman, N., Adshead, G., Fox, S., Latman, R., & Whyte, S. (2012). *Forensic Psychiatry*. Oxford: Oxford University Press.

Ferracuti, S., & Roma, P. (2008). Models of Care for Mentally Disordered Prisoners in Italy. *International Journal of Mental Health* 37(4), 71–87.

Gillon, R. (1994). Medical Ethics: Four Principles Plus Attention to Scope. *British Medical Journal* 309(6948), 184–188.

Greely, H. T. (2013). Mind Reading, Neuroscience, and the Law. In S. J. Morse & A. L. Roskies (eds.), *A Primer on Criminal Law and Neuroscience: A Contribution to the*

Law and Neuroscience Project, Supported By the MacArthur Foundation. New York: Oxford University Press.
Gröning, L., Haukvik,U., Meynen, G., & Radovic, S. (2020) Constructing Criminal Insanity: The Roles of Legislators, Judges and Experts in Norway, Sweden and the Netherlands. *New Journal of European Criminal Law* 11(3), 390–410.
Gutheil, T. G. (2005). Ethics and Forensic Psychiatry. In S. Bloch, P. Chodoff, & S. A. Green (eds.), *Psychiatric Ethics, Third Edition*. New York: Oxford University Press, pp. 345–361.
Haynes, J. D. (2012). Brain Reading. In S. Richmond, G. Rees, & S. Edwards (eds.), *I Know What You're Thinking: Brain imaging and mental privacy*. Oxford: Oxford University Press, pp. 29–40.
Heyes, C. M., & Frith, C D. (2014). The Cultural Evolution of Mind Reading. *Science* 344 (6190), 1243091. DOI: https://doi.org/10.1126/science.1243091
Ienca, M., & Andorno, R. (2017). Towards New Human Rights in the Age of Neuroscience and Neurotechnology. *Life Sciences, Society and Policy* 13(5). https://lsspjournal.biomedcentral.com/articles/10.1186/s40504-017-0050-1
Just, M. A., Pan, L., Cherkassky, V. L., et al. (2017). Machine Learning of Neural Representations of Suicide and Emotion Concepts Identifies Suicidal Youth. *Nature Human Behavior* 1, 911–919. DOI: https://doi.org/10.1038/s41562-017-0234-y
Kane, R. (1998). *The Significance of Free Will*. New York: Oxford University Press.
Kane, R. (2005). *A Contemporary Introduction to Free Will*. New York: Oxford University Press.
Kooijmans, T., & Meynen, G. (2017). Who Establishes the Presence of a Mental Disorder in Defendants? Medicolegal Considerations on a European Court of Human Rights Case. *Front Psychiatry* 8, 199. DOI: https://doi.org/10.3389/fpsyt.2017.00199
Libet, B. (1999). Do We Have Free Will? *Journal of Consciousness Studies* 6(8–9), 47–57.
Libet, B., Gleason, C. A., Wright, E. W., & Pearl, D. K. (1983). Time of Conscious Intention to Act in Relation to Onset of Cerebral Activity (Readiness-Potential): The Unconscious Initiation of a Freely Voluntary Act. *Brain* 106 (Pt 3), 623–642.
Ligthart, S. L. T. J., Kooijmans, T., & Meynen, G. (2018). Een juridisch criterium voor de ontoerekeningsvatbaarheid: een uitspraak van het gerechtshof Den Haag geanalyseerd. *Delikt en Delinkwent* 1(9), 101–110.
Linden, D. (2012). Overcoming Self-Report: Possibilities and Limitations of Brain Imaging in Psychiatry. In S. Richmond, G. Rees, & S. Edwards (eds.), *I Know What You're Thinking: Brain Imaging and Mental Privacy*. Oxford: Oxford University Press, pp. 123–135.
Mason, R. A., & Just, M. A. (2016). Neural Representations of Physics Concepts. *Psychological Science* 27(6), 904–913. DOI: https://doi.org/10.1177/0956797616641941
Mele, A. R. (2014). *Free: Why Science Hasn't Disproved Free Will*. New York: Oxford University Press.
Melle, I. (2013). The Breivik Case and What Psychiatrists Can Learn From It. *World Psychiatry* 12(1), 16–21. DOI: https://doi.org/10.1002/wps.20002
Meynen, G. (2016). *Legal Insanity: Explorations in Psychiatry, Law, and Ethics*: Cham: Springer.
Meynen, G. (2018a). Author's Response to Peer Commentaries: Brain-Based Mind Reading: Conceptual Clarifications and Legal Applications. *Journal of Law and the Biosciences*, Advance article.
Meynen, G. (2018b). Forensic Psychiatry and Neurolaw: Description, Developments, and Debates. *International Journal of Law and Psychiatry*. DOI: https://doi.org/10.1016/j.ijlp.2018.04.005

Meynen, G. (2019). Ethical Issues to Consider Before Introducing Neurotechnological Thought Apprehension in Psychiatry. *AJOB Neuroscience* 10(1), 5–14. DOI: https://doi.org/10.1080/21507740.2019.1595772

Meynen, G. (2020a). The Relevance of Free Will, Rationality, and Aristotle for Legal Insanity. In A. Waltermann, D. Roef, J. Hage, & M. Jelicic (eds.), *Law, Science and Rationality (edited volume)*. The Hague: Eleven International Publishing.

Meynen, G. (2020b). Neuroscience-Based Psychiatric Assessments of Criminal Responsibility: Beyond Self-Report? *Cambridge Quarterly of Healthcare Ethics* 29, 446–458.

Moratti, S., & Patterson, D. M. (eds.). (2016). *Legal Insanity and the Brain: Science, Law and European Courts; With a Foreword by Justice Andrâas Sajâo, Vice-President of the European Court of Human Rights*. Oxford: Hart.

Morse, S. J. (1985). Excusing the Crazy: The Insanity Defense Reconsidered. *Southern California Law Review* 58, 777–836.

Morse, S. J. (2006). Brain Overclaim Syndrome and Criminal Responsibility: A Diagnostic Note. *Ohio State Journal of Criminal Law* 3, 397–312.

Morse, S. J. (2007). The Non-Problem of Free Will in Forensic Psychiatry and Psychology. *Behavioral Sciences and the Law* 25(2), 203–220. DOI: https://doi.org/10.1002/bsl.744

Morse, S. J. (2016). Legal Insanity in the Age of Neuroscience. In S. Moratti & D. Patterson (eds.), *Legal Insanity and the Brain: Science, Law, and European Courts*. Oxford: Hart.

Morse, S. J., & Bonnie, R. J. (2013). Abolition of the Insanity Defense Violates Due Process. *Journal of the American Academy of Psychiatry and the Law* 41(4), 488–495.

Nishimoto, S., Vu, A. T., Naselaris, T., et al. (2011). Reconstructing Visual Experiences From Brain Activity Evoked By Natural Movies. *Current Biology* 21(19), 1641–1646. DOI: https://doi.org/10.1016/j.cub.2011.08.031

O'Connor, T. (2018). Free Will (substantive revision, first published 2002). *Stanford Encyclopedia of Philosophy*. https://plato.stanford.edu/entries/freewill/

Parmigiani, G., Mandarelli, G., Meynen, G., et al. (2017). Free Will, Neuroscience, and Choice: Towards a Decisional Capacity Model for Insanity Defense Evaluations. *Rivista di Psichiatria* 52(1), 9–15. DOI: https://doi.org/10.1708/2631.27049

Radder, J. A., & Meynen, G. (2013). Does the Brain "Initiate" Freely Willed Processes? A Philosophy of Science Critique of Libet-Type Experiments and Their Interpretation. *Theory and Psychology* 23(1), 3–21.

Resnick, P. J., & Knoll, J. (2005). Faking It: How to Detect Malingered Psychosis. *Current Psychiatry* 4(11), 13–25.

Roberts, L. W. (2016). *A Clinical Guide to Psychiatric Ethics*. Arlington, VA: American Psychiatric Association.

Robinson, D. N. (1996). *Wild Beasts and Idle Humours: The Insanity Defense from Antiquity to the Present*. Cambridge, MA: Harvard University Press.

Roskies, A. L. (2013). Brain Imaging Techniques. In S. J. Morse & A. L. Roskies (eds.), *A Primer on Criminal Law and Neuroscience: A Contribution of the Law and Neuroscience Project, Supported by the MacArthur Foundation*. Oxford: Oxford University Press.

Salize, H. J. & Dressing, H. (eds.). (2005). *Placement and Treatment of Mentally Disordered Offenders. Legislation and Practice in the European Union*. Lengerich: Papst.

Scarpazza, C., Ferracuti, S., Miolla, A., & Sartori, G. (2018). The Charm of Structural Neuroimaging in Insanity Evaluations: Guidelines to Avoid Misinterpretation of the Findings. *Translational Psychiatry* 8(1), 227. DOI: https://doi.org/10.1038/s41398-018-0274-8; www.nature.com/articles/s41398-018-0274-8

Scott, C. L., & Resnick, P. J. (2016). Forensic Psychiatry. In S. H. Fatemi & P. J. Clayton (eds.), *The Medical Basis of Psychiatry*. New York: Springer, pp. 799–808.

Simon, R. J., & Ahn-Redding, H. (2006). *The Insanity Defense, the World Over*. Lanham, MD: Lexington Books.

Slobogin, C. (2017). Neuroscience Nuance: Dissecting the Relevance of Neuroscience in Adjudicating Criminal Culpability. *Journal of Law and the Biosciences* 4(3), 577–593. DOI: https://doi.org/10.1093/jlb/lsx033

Slobogin, C. (2018). Introduction to this Special Issue: The Characteristics of Insanity and the Insanity Evaluation Process. *Behavioral Sciences and the Law* 36(3), 271–275. DOI: https://doi.org/10.1002/bsl.2342

Spence, S. (1996). Free Will in the Light of Neuropsychiatry. *Philosophy, Psychiatry, & Psychology* 3(2), 75–90.

Stone, A. A. (1984). The Ethical Boundaries of Forensic Psychiatry: A View from the Ivory Tower. *Journal of the American Academy of Psychiatry and the Law* 12, 209–219.

Van der Wolf, M., & Van Marle, H. (2018). Legal Approaches to Criminal Responsibility of Mentally Disordered Offenders in Europe. In K. Goethals (ed.), *Forensic Psychiatry and Psychology in Europe*. Cham: Springer.

Van Impelen, A., Merckelbach, H., Jelicic, M. & Merten, T. (2014). The Structured Inventory of Malingered Symptomatology (SIMS): A Systematic Review and Meta-Analysis. *The Clinical Neuropsychologist* 28(8), 1336–1365. DOI: https://doi.org/10.1080/13854046.2014.984763

Wegner, D. M. (2002). *The Illusion of Conscious Will*. Cambridge, MA: MIT Press.

Welie, J. V., & Welie, S. P. (2001). Patient Decision Making Competence: Outlines of a Conceptual Analysis. *Medicine, Health Care and Philosophy* 4(2), 127–138.

Wright, R. G. (2014). Pulling on the Thread of the Insanity Defense. *Villanova Law Review* 59 221, 221–242.

Zhao, L,. & Ferguson, G. (2013). Understanding China's Mental Illness Defense. *The Journal of Forensic Psychiatry & Psychology* 24(5), 634–657.

16

Thoughts on the Insanity Defence

Lisa Claydon[*] and Paul Catley[†]

16.1 INTRODUCTION

At the start of his chapter Meynen poses three questions. Should the insanity defence be part of our legal system? What should the criterion be for legal insanity?[1] Can neuroscience help to assess a defendant's sanity?

In examining these questions Meynen covers interesting territory that is academically contested, and where approaches differ from jurisdiction to jurisdiction. He also considers the role played by free will in legal insanity judgements. This response will not comment in detail on the assessments he makes as a practitioner, or the professional difficulties involved in the making of an insanity judgement. It will instead concentrate on the attributions the law makes concerning responsibility and consider the basis of insanity in Anglo-American jurisprudence.

The manner and reasons why attributions of criminal responsibility are made are not fixed. Over time definitions of legal insanity have developed to reflect changes in medical understanding and societal attitudes to mental health (see for example: Mackay, 1995; Moratti & Patterson, 2016; White, 2017).

A good starting point is the legal definition of insanity and in Anglo-American understandings of law the foundation is M'Naghten's Case (1843). The M'Naghten Rules are not set out in case law, but arose through the questioning of the puisne judges by Parliament. The judges were asked to justify their decision to find M'Naghten insane. These circumstances highlight that from the beginning the insanity defence was politically charged. Thus the rules are, in a sense, a defensive response to the question posed by the legislature as to why Daniel M'Naghten deserved to be excused criminal liability.

Having considered the structure of the insanity defence and its development and review post M'Naghten, we will then look at the question of the burden and

---

[*] Dr Lisa Claydon, Senior Lecturer, Open University Law School.
[†] Paul Catley, Professor of Neurolaw and Head of the Open University Law School
[1] Throughout the paper, the terms 'insanity' and 'legal insanity' should be read to mean the insanity defence.

threshold of proof, before concluding by addressing two relevant questions. Firstly, why would anyone think that neuroscience would provide a total answer to questions of criminal responsibility in cases of legal insanity? Secondly, why would anyone think that neuroscience would not be relevant to deliberations concerning criminal insanity?

16.2 WHY EXCUSE THE MENTALLY ILL FOR LOWER ABILITY TO CONTROL THEIR ACTS?

Insanity, as Meynen has established, is an excusing condition in many jurisdictions. The operation of the defence and the way that it develops through legislation or codes means that the development of legal insanity is a political as well as a legal undertaking. Amongst commentators, judges, and politicians, very often scepticism is expressed. A typical example of that scepticism is in regard to the question of the relevance of ability to control behaviour to attributions of criminal responsibility.

An expression of this critique appears in an article by Gardner and Macklem (2001), where they consider a claim of provocation and the ruling of the House of Lords that interpreted the defence of diminished responsibility[2] to recognise that a person suffering from mental illness might have less self-control than a person who was well (R. v. Smith, 2000). The authors took particular issue with Lord Clyde's statement that:

> Society should require that he exercise a reasonable control over himself, but the limits within which control is reasonably to be demanded must take account of characteristics peculiar to him which *reduce* the extent to which he is capable of controlling himself. (R. v. Smith, 2000, 678, emphasis in original)

Somewhat quixotically, Gardner and Macklem argue that this should cut both ways and that if this argument is accepted then those with more self-control should be held to a higher standard of control in assessing whether they transgress (2001, p. 625). But this ignores the role of normative standards in criminal law in setting a base for behaviour rather than punishing those who, though they meet the norm, could do better.

The pertinent question in the case of measuring whether lower self-control should excuse is underpinned by two questions that are of importance to society. One is: what is the risk of excusing a defendant who cannot meet the criminal norm and transgresses? The second is whether common morality would be outraged by the excusing of someone who has committed a terrible criminal act. Both questions have political import. Social cognitive neuroscience could undoubtedly assist in these broader discussions by helping to educate society as to the nature of risk. It could also aid societal understanding of the experience of compulsion to commit

---

[2] In the law of England and Wales this is a partial defence to a charge of murder.

criminal acts in the form discussed by Meynen. In expanding this knowledge, it would be drawing on neuropsychology and neuropsychiatry. This commentary takes the view that neuroscience is not just about brain scans but rather about our modern understandings of brains and how they work.

16.3 M'NAGHTEN AS A PRECEDENT

The record of the debate in the House of Lords following the finding that Daniel M'Naghten was insane is informative. It has all the hallmarks of political outrage. M'Naghten's delusion was as to the necessity for M'Naghten to kill the Prime Minister Robert Peel (a member of the Tory Party) in order to protect his own life. He killed the Prime Minister's secretary Edward Drummond, apparently mistaking him for Peel.

M'Naghten's in his statement on arrest said:

> The Tories in my native city have compelled me to do this. They follow and persecute me wherever I go, and have entirely destroyed my peace of mind. ... They have accused me of crimes of which I am not guilty; in fact they wish to murder me, it can be proved by evidence. That is all I have to say. (Walker, 1968, p. 91)

Here seems to be a relatively clear case, legally speaking, of a claim of delusional belief in the need to act for self-preservation.

As has already been stated, M'Naghten was found insane at his trial. However, the subsequent gloss that the rules acquired in their adoption and interpretation by courts around the world gives them different forms.[3] In England and Wales it is debatable whether M'Naghten now could be held to be insane. He may have been suffering from a disease of the mind, but whether he would fit within one of the two limbs of M'Naghten insanity is doubtful. Under the first limb of the rules he seems to know the nature and quality of his act. In terms of the second limb – if he knew it was wrong – this limb has a more modern interpretation. This second limb was refined in the case of R v. Windle (1952). In Windle it was decided that the rules should be interpreted (in England and Wales)[4] to mean that someone could be insane, under the rules, when they could prove that they did not know that their act was legally wrong. Thinking that the act was morally right was deemed, following Windle, to have no relevance to criminal insanity.

As Mackay's research (Mackay, Mitchell & Howe, 2006) has shown, in England and Wales the use of the insanity defence over the years has been low, initially because the sentence for a not guilty by reason of insanity (NGRI) verdict meant confinement to a mental institution without limit of time. The law changed in 1991

---

[3] For fuller discussion of the rules in Anglo-American criminal law see Meynen, Chapter 15 in this volume, Section 15.3.
[4] Hereinafter, referred to as England or English law.

and provided for disposals that were subject to review and the possibility of treatment in the community. However, the number of successful insanity pleas has remained very low – in 2013 the Law Commission estimated that typically there are less than thirty per year (Law Commission for England and Wales, 2013). In other jurisdictions more use is made of the defence (see for example Kogel & Westgeest, 2015).

16.4 THE IMPORTANCE OF CONTROL

Meynen correctly, in our view, argues for a capacity to control element in the definition of legal insanity. As he notes, such an element is present in for example the American Model Penal Code, the Italian Penal Code and the Chinese criminal law – but is missing from the M'Naghten Rules. Lack of control may arise in a number of ways: for example fronto-temporal dementia, as in the Dutch extortion case that Meynen considers, or during an epileptic seizure, a sleepwalking episode or as a result of conditions such as Tourette's syndrome. The extent to which a defendant must lack capacity varies from jurisdiction to jurisdiction. The Model Penal Code refers to a situation where the defendant 'lacks *substantial* capacity ... to conform his conduct to the requirements of the law'; whereas Article 88 of the Italian Penal Code with its reference to a defendant being 'incapable of ... control[ling] his conduct', and the Chinese criminal law with its reference to a defendant being 'unable to control his own conduct', appear to set the threshold higher, requiring on the face of it no capacity to control. A proposed English law reform would adopt a similar approach. The Law Commission recommended that the existing insanity defence should be replaced by a new defence of not criminally responsible by reason of a recognised medical condition.

> The party seeking to raise the new defence must adduce expert evidence that at the time of the alleged offence
> the defendant wholly lacked the capacity:
> (i) rationally to form a judgment about the relevant conduct or circumstances;
> (ii) to understand the wrongfulness of what he or she is charged with having done; or
> (iii) to control his or her physical acts in relation to the relevant conduct or circumstances
>
> as a result of a qualifying recognised medical condition. (Law Commission for England and Wales, 2013, Proposal 3, Paragraph 10.8)

This would afford a capacity-based defence, thereby filling the gap within the M'Naghten Rules. However, it is pitched at a very high threshold: the defendant must 'wholly' lack capacity. This is clearly a higher threshold than the American Penal Code's focus on lacking 'substantial capacity'. It also raises questions akin to those raised by Morse (1985, p. 817) about the difficulty of determining 'whether an impulse was irresistible or simply not resisted'. Will courts be able to determine whether a defendant 'wholly lacked the capacity... to control his or her physical acts in relation to the relevant conduct or circumstances'? Will expert witnesses be able to provide useful advice to the court on this question? Is it simply too high a threshold for an insanity defence? Surely by creating a defence one is anticipating that some defendants will be able to avail themselves of it. One of the advantages of a NGRI verdict is that it enables the court to achieve an appropriate sentence and thereby protect society from the risk of further serious crimes.

16.5 BURDENS OF PROOF AND THRESHOLDS OF PROOF

Meynen in his fifth section explores the burden and threshold of proof. He notes how in many jurisdictions that follow an Anglo-American adversarial approach, the defence is an affirmative defence. He also identifies the problems this may cause where defendants lack the financial resources to gather evidence and employ expert witnesses. In theory, inquisitorial systems avoid these difficulties – court-appointed experts should owe their primary duty to the court and so be neutral as between prosecution and defence.[5] However, Meynen makes the point that this may still leave the expert witness facing ethical and professional dilemmas.

Meynen accepts the idea that the burden of proof should fall on the party asserting the plea of insanity. He favours the threshold of proof being 'a preponderance of probabilities' or 'clear and convincing evidence' rather than 'proof beyond reasonable doubt'. This means that where a court was not satisfied on the balance of probabilities that the defendant was not guilty by reason of insanity it should convict assuming the other elements of the offence were made out, even if the court still had reasonable doubts as to the defendant's sanity. This is the approach currently operating in many jurisdictions including England and Wales. The M'Naghten Rules refer to the presumption of sanity:

> The jurors ought to be told in all cases that every man is to be presumed to be sane, and to possess a sufficient degree of reason to be responsible for his crimes, until the contrary be proved to their satisfaction. (M'Naghten's Case, 1843)

However, the Supreme Court in Canada has taken a different approach. In *Whyte* Chief Justice Dickson observed:

> The real concern is not whether the accused must disprove an element or prove an excuse, but that an accused may be convicted while a reasonable doubt exists. When that possibility exists, there is a breach of the presumption of innocence. (Whyte, 1988, pp. 481, 493)

---

[5] In theory, this is also true in many adversarial systems – see for example Rule 19.2 of The Criminal Procedure Rules 2015 retrieved from: www.legislation.gov.uk/uksi/2015/1490/part/19/made

This, we would argue, is a better approach.[6] That is not to say that in every case the prosecution should have to prove that the defendant was sane, but rather to propose that it should apply where the defence of insanity is raised by the defendant and where the defence is able to provide evidence supporting the defence. Placing an evidential burden on the defendant who wishes to raise the insanity defence achieves an appropriate balance. The defendant has the burden of providing evidence to raise insanity as an issue. The prosecution must then establish to the jury's satisfaction that the defendant was sane, just as it must prove the other elements of the offence.

Such an approach is adopted by the Law Commission for England and Wales' proposed new defence. The party seeking to rely on the defence would have to adduce expert evidence to support the defence, but the burden of proof would then lie with the prosecution to disprove the defence.[7]

16.6 CONCLUSION ON THE ROLE OF NEUROSCIENCE

At the start of this commentary we posed two questions: firstly, why would anyone think that neuroscience would provide a total answer to questions of criminal responsibility in cases of legal insanity? Secondly, why would anyone think that neuroscience would not be relevant to deliberations concerning criminal insanity?

In answering the first question it should be pointed out that it would be unusual for a criminal case to rest entirely on one form of evidence for its success or failure. It may happen that a fingerprint or DNA evidence places the defendant at the scene of the crime. It may also be that a brain scan is highly suggestive that the defendant was suffering from a particular medical condition at the time of the crime that could account for their behaviour. Such evidence could provide useful pointers for either prosecution or defence to explore but would almost certainly not be determinative on its own.

In answering the second question and explaining how neuroscience might be relevant to deliberations about insanity, it will be useful to look at a case from a related area of English law – fitness to plead. In *R v. Sharif* (2010), Sharif was charged with being part of a conspiracy to defraud. His defence team argued that he was unfit to plead as he would be unable to follow the trial proceedings or to give instructions to his lawyers.

In relation to a claim that Sharif had severe brain damage and knew nothing about the fraudulent claims, the prosecution's expert witness, Professor Deakin, concluded

---

[6] In *H v. United Kingdom* App No 15023/89 (Commission decision) (unreported) the European Commission found that placing the burden of proving insanity on the defendant was not unreasonable or arbitrary and found that it related to the presumption of sanity rather than the presumption of innocence. The reasoning behind this decision, even though it upheld the approach of the English courts, was subsequently described as 'unsound' by the Law Commission: Law Commission for England and Wales (2013), Criminal Liability: Insanity and Automatism – a discussion paper paragraph 8.20.

[7] An approach already adopted with the English defence of non-insane automatism.

that it was 'a clear case of malingering' (R. v. Sharif, 2010, 6) – in Meynen's terms, a case of 'faking bad'. Sharif was found fit to plead and a trial date set. While awaiting trial, an EEG scan was conducted. This showed 'enlargement of the extra cerebral spaces in the brain' (R. v. Sharif, 2010, 10). Two further experts commented: one concluding that it indicated 'mild generalised atrophy of the brain' (R. v. Sharif, 2010, 10), the other that Sharif was suffering from a 'longstanding functional psychosis in addition to an organic brain syndrome' (R. v. Sharif, 2010, 10). This evidence was not determinative. Sharif was convicted in 1999 without giving evidence and served a three-year sentence.

It became obvious over the period of his incarceration that it was very unlikely that he had been malingering. A body of neuroscientific evidence was reviewed by a Criminal Cases Review Commission investigation into the fairness of Sharif's conviction. This included neuroscientific and genetic evidence from twelve expert witnesses demonstrating that Sharif was suffering from progressive organic brain damage at the time of his conviction. The weight of this evidence led Professor Deakin to change his mind and state that in his opinion Sharif had not been malingering in 1999. In 2010 the Court of Appeal quashed Sharif's conviction. The case illustrates that neuroscientific evidence can be of value in achieving justice, albeit justice that was delayed by more than a decade in this case.

REFERENCES

Criminal Procedure Rules 2015 UK SI (2015) No 1490 (L.18).
Gardner, J., & Macklem, T. (2001). Compassion without Respect? Nine Fallacies in R. v. Smith. *Criminal Law Review* 623, 623–35.
Kogel, de, K., & Westgeest, E. (2015). Neuroscientific and Behavioural Genetic Information in Criminal Cases in the Netherlands. *Journal of Law and the Biosciences* 2(3), 580–605.
Law Commission for England and Wales. (2013). *Criminal Liability: Insanity and Automatism – a Discussion Paper*. Retrieved from: www.lawcom.gov.uk/project/insanity-and-automatism/.
Mackay, R. D. (1995). *Mental Condition Defences in the Criminal Law*. Oxford: Clarendon Press.
Mackay, R. D., Mitchell, B. J., & Howe, L. (2006). Yet More Facts About the Insanity Defence. *Criminal Law Review* (May), 399–411.
Moratti, S., & Patterson, D. (eds.) (2016). *Legal Insanity and the Brain: Science, Law and European Courts*. Oxford: Hart.
Morse, S. J. (1985). Excusing the Crazy: The Insanity Defense Reconsidered. *Southern California Law Review* 58(3), 777–838.
Walker, N. (1968). *Crime and Insanity in England*. Edinburgh: Edinburgh University Press.
White, M. D. (ed.) (2017). *The Insanity Defense: Multidisciplinary Views on Its History, Trends and Controversies*. Santa Barbara, CA: Praeger.

CASES

H. v. United Kingdom App No 15023/89.
M'Naghten's Case (1843) 10 Clark and Finnelly 200, (1843) 8 ER 718, [1843–60] All ER Rep 229.
R. v. Sharif [2010] EWCA Crim 1709.
R. v. Smith [2000] 3 WLR 654 (HL).
R. v. Windle [1952] 2 QB 826.
Whyte (1988) 2 SCR 3 (1988) 51 DLR (4th) 481.

IV

Evidence

17

Implications of Neurotechnology: Brain Recording and Intervention

Pim Haselager

17.1 INTRODUCTION

It is possible to connect brains and computers directly, bypassing sensorimotor systems, in what is called Brain–Computer Interfacing (Van Gerven et al., 2009). One can do so from brain to computer, for instance by measuring brain activity with electroencephalography (EEG), or functional magnetic resonance imaging (fMRI), and then transmitting the obtained brain signals to a computational system. One can also send signals generated by computational systems into the brain, non-invasively (Polanía et al., 2018; for example, transcranial Direct Current Stimulation: tDCS. Jog, Wang & Narr, 2019; see the Brain Stimulator Net for a brief informal overview), or invasively, via electrodes that are implanted on or within the brain (e.g. Deep Brain Stimulation: DBS; Ramasubbu, Lang & Kiss, 2018). In addition, it is becoming possible to 'close the loop', by connecting brain measurements with brain stimulation, for example to stop epileptic seizures from occurring (Kassiri et al., 2017; Kokkinos et al., 2019). Finally, there are indications that, by using brain recording and brain stimulation, direct communication between brains is becoming possible (Grau et al., 2014; Pais-Vieira et al., 2015). Although these technologies can be aimed at measuring or stimulating brains per se, more often they are applied in order to estimate, use or influence cognitive states and processes. Obviously, there is a great variety in types of cognitive states and processes, as one can distinguish between, for example, personality traits and dispositions (e.g. relatively stable inclinations such as sexual preference, personal taste and habits); qualitative states (e.g. perceptions, emotions, feelings); propositional states (e.g. knowledge, beliefs); or intentions and goals, plans, memories and so on. It is important to realize that successful demonstrations of brain measurement or stimulation in one cognitive domain need not generalize to others.

Especially over the last two decades, there has been growing interest in discussing the ethical, legal and societal implications (ELSI) of technologies developed by neuroscience and artificial intelligence. However, these technologies are in varying states of research and development, often, though not always, still in their early experimental phases, without serious practical applications, with limited and varying task performance, and with different speeds of (expected) progress. For this reason, there can be a – what I would like to call an – *'ELSI gap'* between what currently is possible given the state of science and technology, and the kind of ethical, legal or societal implications that could be considered as relevant to discuss before the technology 'gets there'. The main motivation for starting ELSI discussions before the technology is ready is rather simple: ethical, legal and societal debates about what we would like to have and what we would like to avoid take time too, just like the development of technology. And, as we have learned from the consequences of, for example, internet tracking cookies for privacy, the risk of being too late, and the price one pays for this, is considerable. Technology tends to contribute to the creation of habits and practices that are hard to change once they are established, even if there is agreement about their undesirability. Hence, in what follows, the cases and analyses are to be taken as future-oriented, with all the uncertainties and risks involved in such an enterprise.

Neurotechnologies can raise challenges that are complex in the sense that they require a consideration of a variety of aspects, for example of a philosophical, psychological, ethical and legal nature. Philosophically, there are issues surrounding, for instance, *psychological continuity* or personal identity (Klaming & Haselager, 2013). Psychologically, one can investigate the extent to which neurotechnology may affect a person's *experience of agency* (Haselager, 2013), that is, the extent to which users consider themselves to be the initiators or owners or authors of their actions, affecting their experience of pride or shame, for example. Because of such effects, neurotechnology may have implications for the moral and legal evaluation of actions and/or their outcomes, affecting *responsibility attributions*, individually through, for example, experienced pride or shame, or societally, via communicated praise or blame. Hence, the legal implications of the use of neurotechnology for issues related to liability need to be addressed.

In this chapter, I aim to present a general introduction to the emerging applications of neurotechnology, give some examples and discuss some of their potential implications.

17.2 BRAIN MEASUREMENTS

There are (increasingly) many ways to measure brain structures, states and processes. Some of the most widely used include functional fMRI, Positron Emission Tomography (PET), EEG, magnetoencephalography (MEG), Near Infrared Spectroscopy (NIRS), electrocorticography (ECoG) and other advanced brain monitoring modalities. It would be going too far to discuss all these methods here. Suffice it to say that they vary in their temporal (from milliseconds to several seconds) and spatial (micrometres to centimetres) scales, and differ regarding the brain areas that can be measured (surface cortex to deeper internal brain structures) and have various other relative strengths and weaknesses (e.g., ease of use in naturally occurring contexts vs. sensitivity for movements).

The aims of brain measurement can vary. Brain measurements have been used for *fundamental* research, by supporting theory formation and hypothesis testing regarding the implementation of cognitive functions in brain areas and circuits. More important, for example for legal purposes, is the use of brain measurements for inferring *pathologies*. For instance, brain measurements can be used to establish the presence of brain lesions, or structural deviations from average brain features that are considered to be 'healthy' (e.g., diminished grey or white matter compared to that found on average). Similarly, brain measurements could indicate *functional deficiencies*, such as reduced activity in specific brain areas that could correlate with cognitive deficits resulting in suboptimal task performance. A fourth use of brain measurements is to derive brain signals that could be used to *drive applications*, as happens in Brain–Computer Interfacing. Here, for instance, brain processes involved in imagined movements could be measured and used as a signal to drive an application (e.g., a mouse on a computer screen, or a wheelchair). Finally, one could aim to decode and interpret brain measurements, for example, by trying to derive mental content or behavioural dispositions from brain activity (*brain reading*).

Although measuring brain activity is sometimes called 'brain imaging', and its results are often rendered in the form of pictures, it is important to realize that words such as 'imaging' may be easily misunderstood. Although the results of fMRI are often presented as pictures of a brain with coloured regions indicating different activation levels, such 'pictures' are not to be understood as directly capturing or reflecting brains in action. There is a substantial number of intermediate steps that have to be taken in order to produce such an 'image'. Instead of being a direct capture of the brain measurements, the 'inferential distance' (Haselager, Leoné & van Toor, 2013; Leoné, Van Toor & Haselager, 2016) from brain measurement to interpretation or use is quite substantial. Measurements are indirect. For instance, fMRI does not directly capture brain activity, but rather the flow of deoxygenated blood, averaged over many measurements (normally also over many different subjects). The results are presented as contrasts in blood flow between a target and a control condition, which makes them highly dependent on the specific choices of tasks. Often, repeated measurements are required to obtain a result that presents an 'on-average' indication of the brain in action. Finally, it is standard practice to speak of cognitive neuroscience as establishing the neural correlates of cognitive phenomena, which in general falls short of identifying causal relations between brain activity and cognition. In all, even when a clear brain measurement has been obtained, its cognitive significance is not necessarily equally clear. There are many steps that need to be taken to go from the actual data gathering (the brain measurement) to its final interpretation or use. This means there is significant room for imprecision or error. Hence, the use of brain measurements is better thought of as indicative in relation to cognitive phenomena rather than as direct or absolute 'hard' evidence. Brain measurements can generally best be seen as supportive, rather than 100 per cent reliable providers of information. They enable investigators to make more or less reliable inferences (or 'educated guesses') about the, usually cognitive, targets of investigation.

17.3 BRAIN–COMPUTER INTERFACING AND THE SENSE OF AGENCY

The sense of agency involves an experience that you are the one doing something, in contrast with the experience of something happening to you. It has been described by Gallagher as: 'The sense that I am the one who is causing or generating an action' (Gallagher, 2000, p. 15). For instance, the experience of making a movement is different from the experience of being pushed. The experience does not have to be explicit in the sense of reaching full awareness or being verbally reported. As Gallagher writes (2007, p. 347): 'If someone or something causes something to happen, that person or thing is not an agent (even if they might be a cause) if they do not know in some way that they have caused it to happen. ... The kind of conscious knowledge involved in agency does not have to be of a very high order; it could be simply a matter of a very thin phenomenal awareness, and in most cases it is just that.' Wegner (2003a) indicates that one of the main functions of the experience of conscious will is to indicate an ownership of action. It helps us to appreciate and remember what we are doing, and as an embodied quality it gives the feeling of will a more profound quality than a mere thought. One can think of the sense of agency as an experience of willed action, as a somatic marker of personal authorship or an authorship emotion: an embodied feeling of doing something.

The processes involved in producing a sense of agency turn out to be quite complex. A relevant review of the two main modes involved in creating a sense of agency is Synofzik's multifactorial 'two-step' account (Synofzik, Vosgerau & Newen 2008; Synofzik, Vosgerau & Voss, 2013). Two main aspects of a sense of agency (SA) may be distinguished. A *Feeling of Agency* (FoA) consists of the pre-reflective, non-conceptual aspects of SA. No explicit conscious awareness or identifiable or verbalizable experience of agency is required beyond a mere sense of 'doing'. A neurally implemented comparator (Frith, 1987, 2012; Gallagher, 2000) underlies the FoA. The motor system produces motor commands that would lead to a goal, and this generates predictions of sensory feedback that, when matching with actually obtained feedback, results in a feeling of agency. A *Judgement of Agency* (JoA) refers to the reflective, conceptual aspects of SA, where the acting is more explicitly experienced and can be described. Wegner & Wheatley (1999; Wegner, 2003b) portray it as based on an inferential process that involves three conditions: a thought is perceived as willed action when the thought precedes the action at a proper interval (called the *priority principle*), when the thought is compatible with the reaction (*consistency principle*) and when the thought is the only apparent cause of the action (*exclusivity principle*).

Normally, of course, we judge ourselves to be agents in cases when we actually do engage in actions, and we don't experience it when we don't act. However, in some cases we may feel we are acting when we actually are not. Wegner (2003a, p. 9) has classified this as a case of illusion of control. He describes an occasion where he thought he was playing a computer game, but found out after a while that he was merely watching a demo, using a joystick in vain. Another example is opening a door while someone else on the other side is actually doing that for you. On the other hand, someone might think they are not doing something, while in fact they are. Wegner classifies this as a case of automatism: 'the case of no feeling of will when there is in fact action' (Wegner, 2003a, p. 9). It has been suggested that in some cases people with schizophrenia report hearing voices, while actually producing the sounds themselves (Frith, 2012; Humpston & Broome, 2016). This decoupling of the act with the experience to act can contribute to the attribution of uttered sounds to other, for example alien, agents instead of themselves.

All in all, the sense of agency is the result of various processes that interact in a context-dependent way. It is worthwhile therefore to examine how neurotechnology may affect our agency experiences. In order to do so, I will examine Brain–Computer interfacing (BCI). In BCI, the data acquired via brain measurements are used to drive an application. Often, the user is asked to engage in imaginary movement as a mental task, so that the underlying brain signals can be categorized as a basic signal to drive an application (Van Gerven et al., 2009). For instance, BCI users are asked to imagine (but not to perform) a movement of their left or right hand (e.g. waving the hand up and down). These imagined movements lead to relatively easy-to-detect oscillatory neuronal patterns in right and left motor areas, resulting in two identifiable patterns (left motor cortex activity, right motor cortex activity), that can be distinguished from no clearly identifiable motor cortex activity. This can be used to steer the movement of a cursor on a screen, for example. An important reason why such BCI-mediated actions can lead to confusions in a user's JoA is that user have no way of knowing that they produced reliably identifiable brain states during their imaginary movement task. They may know they genuinely tried imagining a movement of their left hand, and they may experience some of the introspectively accessible phenomenology involved in imagining something (which can vary considerably over persons, or even within persons over time). But they can't possibly know that they produced the right kind of brain states that could be picked up by the BCI, for the simple reason that there is no such thing as brain proprioception. We don't 'feel' our brain activity. This implies that BCI users may know that they tried in virtue of the experienced imaginative act, but they can't be sure they actually succeeded in producing the right brain states. In addition, BCIs still have relatively low information transfer rates and can still be prone to produce mistakes, mainly due to the noise in EEG recordings and occasional classification errors of the algorithms that interpret the data. Information transfer rates can vary greatly (from close to 0 up till 100 bits per minute, and are still well below standard communication channels such as speech (±40–60 bits per *second*). Performance success rates, that is, the BCI successfully performing the action as intended by the user, of 60–80 per cent are quite normal, but even in cases of 90–95 per cent success there still remains room for error (Wierzgała et al., 2018; Abiri et al., 2019). Hence, users have substantial room for uncertainty about whether a performance error was due to their mistake or the BCI's. Suppose, for instance, that a BCI user attempts to go backwards in a BCI-driven wheelchair by imagining a left-hand movement, and finds the wheelchair actually moving forwards and bumping into someone. Would this user have a JoA sufficient to feel responsible for the accident? And would such a feeling of being responsible be correct? A simple pilot experiment we performed (Haselager, 2013; Vlek et al., 2014; see also Lynn et al., 2010) suggests that it may be possible that in BCI contexts users can feel responsible for actions they did not actually perform. The number of subjects was too small to report significance levels, but it may serve here to illustrate the possibility of illusions of agency to mention one observation. Participants were asked to engage in left/right-hand imagined movements, while their brain activity was measured through EEG. On screen, a robot hand was displayed that would respond with a thumbs-up or an OK sign (by touching the thumb with the middle finger creating the shape of an 'o'). Although the EEG signals were measured, we did not use that information to drive the robot hand. Hence, participants thought they were activating the robot hand via their brain activity while performing the imagined hand movements, but saw pre-recorded movie clips. These movie clips included some errors (e.g. where the robot hand made an OK sign when the user had been instructed to produce the thumbs-up sign). We computed the participant's JoA using the following questions, taken from Wegner, Sparrow, & Winerman (2004): 'How much control did you feel that you had over the hands movement?' and 'To what degree did you feel you were consciously willing the hand to move?' We observed JoA ratings above the 50 per cent point of the 1–7 Likert scale. This at least suggests that one had better not rule out the possibility that illusions of agency may occur in BCI-mediated action. In other words, when using a BCI someone may judge themselves to be the author of the act, and thereby have a sense of agency, while causally speaking the actions are not theirs, in the sense that their brain states were not part of the actual causal chain leading to the outcome. Given the transition of EEG-based BCI to the 'direct-to-consumer markets' (Ienca, Haselager & Emanuel, 2018) it is to be expected that such uncertainties may occur outside of the lab as well. It will be important to study the effects of BCI use on JoAs during task performance under naturally occurring circumstances.

17.4 BRAIN STIMULATION, IDENTITY AND PSYCHOLOGICAL CONTINUITY

Like brain measurements, brain stimulation techniques come in an increasing number of varieties. They range from invasive, meaning that the scalp (and often also underlying protective layers, the meninges) is penetrated, to non-invasive, where the contact is made outside or on the skin (for an overview see Luigjes et al., 2019). The class of non-invasive neurotechnology is diverse and rapidly growing. Just to mention a few: transcranial electric stimulation (TES) (Kekic et al., 2016; Woods, Antal & Bikson, 2016); transcranial magnetic stimulation (TMS, Taylor Galvez & Loo, 2018); Transcranial ultrasound stimulation (TUS, Legon et al., 2014); and magnetothermal deep brain stimulation (Chen et al., 2015).

Amongst these techniques, Deep Brain Stimulation (DBS, e.g. Amon & Alesch, 2017) is one that is widely used, and in a growing variety of cases. Initially intended to improve the quality of life of patients with movement disorders, such as Parkinson's disease (PD, e.g. Limousin & Foltynie, 2019), by suppressing tremors, DBS is also applied for patients with depression (Ramasubbu et al., 2019) and obsessive-compulsive disorders (Borders et al., 2018). DBS is invasive in that an electrode is implanted deep in the brain, for example in the *subthalamic nucleus*, or in the *globus pallidus internus* or the *ventral intermediate thalamus*, which could lead to physical complications such as haemorrhage and infections. For my purposes here, the cognitive effects, either the aimed for or the adverse effects, will be the most relevant. In an earlier paper (Klaming & Haselager, 2013), we investigated the potential consequences of DBS for the psychological continuity of an individual. Personal identity, considered as persistence of a person (as being and remaining that particular person) over time, has been suggested, at least since John Locke (Parfit, 1971), to be dependent to a considerable extent on psychological continuity. Basically, the overlapping strands of psychological connections, such as memories, intentions, beliefs, goals, desires, behavioural dispositions, and character style, are thought to make and keep a person that same individual. Perhaps a useful metaphor is that of a rope consisting of various individual strands. Some of the strands may start at different points, or end at others (as e.g., habits may be acquired and lost), but as long as there is substantial overlapping continuity in a substantial number of the strands, the rope continues to be that rope. Some changes, however, may affect this continuity to such an extent that for the persons involved, or for others, the impression of a rupture or radical change in psychological continuity may be unavoidable.

There have been reports of cases that suggest that DBS may lead to changes in cognition and/or behaviour that at least raise the question of whether a change in psychological continuity is observable. For instance, Leentjens et al. (2004) report the case of a sixty-two-year-old Parkinson's patient who developed what appeared to be a manic disorder after DBS. The stimulation caused serious personality changes including chaotic behaviour, megalomania, and mental incompetence leading to financial debts. In this state, the patient did not suffer from motor impairments, but due to his impaired psychiatric functioning he was considered unable to live on his own. When DBS was turned off, his insight and capacity to judge returned. Hence a dilemma resulted: either the DBS could be disabled and the patient would be admitted to a nursing home because of his severe motor impairment, or the DBS would be continued, which meant that the patient would have to be admitted to a psychiatric institution because of severe mental impairment. Several complications followed, such as in which state the patient should be asked whether or not to continue the treatment. The patient's decision with DBS off, hence in a cognitively unimpaired, mentally competent state, preferred to continue the treatment. This led to a further complication, namely whether this decision could be implemented, given that at the time of the case, according to Dutch Health Law (2009, article 2), judicial authorization of treatment in a psychiatric hospital is possible only if the harm cannot be averted by interference of a person or institution. Additionally, a treatment plan focusing on removing the harm that is responsible for the patient's hospitalization is required (Dutch Health Law, 2009, article 38). In this case, of course, it would be easy to comply with the law, i.e. by turning the DBS off, thereby violating the expressed wish of the patient.

Although such examples merely provide single-case illustrations of the type of questions that DBS can raise – and the number of such cases is limited (e.g. Gilbert, Viaña & Ineichen, 2018) – the questions themselves, namely, the impact brain stimulation can have on identity and responsibility, are important to investigate further. For instance, one may ask how much change in an individual's psychological continuity is required before one considers the issue of a potential change in identity that might be morally or legally problematic. After all, we all change continuously over time (see the rope metaphor mentioned above) and it will be hard to identify concrete 'cut-off points'. Hence, how are we to address and classify various forms and levels of change in psychological continuity? Moreover, such questions can and will be understood and evaluated differently by different parties, such as the technology users themselves, their significant others, the involved scientific and clinical teams, moral and legal experts and society at large (e.g. regulators and policy makers, and public opinion). It is not to be expected that all four parties will agree on similar answers to all questions, even regarding the same case. Lewis et al. (2015) asked twenty-seven Parkinson's disease patients whether a 'personality change' had occurred post-operatively; six (22.2 per cent) patients affirmed this, whereas twenty-one did not (77.8 per cent). In comparison, ten of the twenty-three interviewed caregivers (43.5 per cent) perceived a post-operative 'personality change' in the patients. Of these ten patients, three had also rated themselves as changed. Mood changes were noted by twenty-one patients in the interviews, of which twelve (57.1 per cent) described a positive change in mood, whereas nine (42.9 per cent) rated it as negatively changed. One interview is worth quoting here (I = interviewer, P = patient, C = caregiver), because it illustrates the contrast that can exist between the perspectives of people involved, as well as the complexity, for example context dependency, of the assessments:

I: Have you noticed a change of mood since the operation?
P: It has become more fun for me.

I:	What does that mean?
P:	I can afford not to go by the rules, which my wife does not like. I have to admit that. And I can take part in the social aspects of life a lot more....
I:	In your opinion, has your personality changed since the operation?
P:	Yes. The awareness of living and being connected to life has changed. So the most difficult things in life don't always seem the most difficult.
I:	Would you say that your husband has changed his personality through the stimulation?
Caregiver (C):	Yes, absolutely! He is so very positive, but overestimates himself. Getting him to behave in a way I can cope with is very difficult.
I:	OK, so he overestimates himself. Which other personality traits have emerged that perhaps weren't so distinctive before the operation?
C:	He is now so very obsessive with certain things. When we are sitting down, reading or watching TV, he suddenly wants to do this or that. But he then has to do it at that exact moment. And during discussions, he cannot concentrate that well anymore or his thoughts just drift.... I am reminded of my pupils who were always looking for excuses. But maybe I am too sensitive...

Although both the patient and the caregiver notice a change in aspects of personality, in relation to mood, attitude towards life, self-overestimation, obsessiveness and concentration, the seriousness of the implications seem to be assessed differently. Whereas the patient perceives the consequences as 'more fun', the caregiver indicates a loss of self-control, making his behaviour comparable to that of a schoolchild. Hence, it could be interesting to consider questions regarding responsibility for action, perhaps also from a legal perspective, along the lines of assessing the influence of DBS on an individuals' psychological continuity in relation to their capacity for self-control.

17.5 COMBINING BRAIN MEASUREMENT AND BRAIN STIMULATION WITHIN OR BETWEEN BRAINS

Combinations of brain measurement and brain stimulation have been investigated, both within and between brains. Closed-loop neurotechnology enables recorded brain activity to initiate or modulate neurostimulation within the same brain. An example is presented by Kassiri et al. (2017). The Neuropace Responsive Neurostimulator (n.d.), a commercially available closed-loop device for epilepsy treatment, can be implanted in the brain and delivers pulses in a DBS fashion, upon detection of neurophysiological indicators of an upcoming epilepsy seizure. As in the case of traditional DBS, successful applications in one clinical case, like epilepsy, can lead to applications in other domains. A recent patent, for instance, was filed in relation to pain management.[1] Lo and Widge (2017) review closed-loop neuromodulation systems as 'next-generation treatments for psychiatric illness' such as Tourette's syndrome and obsessive-compulsive disorders. The cognitive effects of such closed loops are currently not well known. But in line with earlier analyses of the effects of brain recording and brain stimulation on various aspects of sense of agency and psychological continuity, it will be important to be alert to such effects.[2]

In brain-to-brain interfacing (BTB), data acquired from one brain can be used to stimulate another brain. In one demonstration, brain measurements of one rat brain were fed into another rat brain (Pais-Vieira et al., 2013). The 'encoder' rat performed a task, for example pressing a right- or left-hand lever in response to a right- or left-hand light switching on, receiving food when the location of the pressed lever matched the light location. Information from its sensorimotor cortex was transmitted into the sensorimotor cortex of the receiving 'decoder' rat, enabling it to learn to press the correct lever without perceiving any light stimulus. As Pais-Vieira et al. write, this suggests that BTB technology 'can enable dyads or networks of animal's brains to exchange, process, and store information and, hence, serve as the basis for studies of novel types of social interaction and for biological computing devices' (2013, p. 1). Although concepts such as 'mind melds' have been used, it currently seems more adequate to consider such cases in terms of information transfer, rather than the actual 'joining of minds'. Other studies indicate that the combination of brain reading and brain stimulation can enable two, three or even four brains to collaborate on a task (Pais-Vieira et al., 2015; Ramakrishnan et al., 2015), such as driving a virtual arm. In this way 'Brainets' are created, single computational systems composed of several brains:

> With long-term training we observed increased coordination of behavior, increased correlations in neuronal activity between different brains, and modifications to neuronal representation of the motor plan. Overall, performance of the Brainet improved owing to collective monkey behaviour. These results suggest that primate brains can be integrated into a Brainet, which self-adapts to achieve a common motor goal. (Ramakrishnan et al., 2015, p. 1)

Over the last decade, various investigations of interspecies BTB has been reported. For instance, EEG recording of human brain activity, combined with rat motor cortex stimulation, enabled human mind control of a rat's tail movement (Yoo et al., 2013). Zhang et al. (2019) used EEG recordings of human motor imagery to 'realize human mind control of the rat's continuous locomotion'. Yu et al. (2016) report an

---

[1] 'Systems and Methods for Close-Looped Pain Management', (n.d.) https://patents.google.com/patent/US20180085584A1/en.
[2] See for starting points of this discussion; Bouthour et al., 2019; Klein et al., 2015.

AI-to-brain connection, where input from a computer was used to stimulate the medial forebrain bundle (dopamine increase) and somatosensory cortices (whisker stimulation) of a rat, which improved its maze navigation, reducing the time required to escape from a maze. It is currently entirely unclear what the effects of such (interspecies) BTB or AI-to-brain combinations will be for sense of agency or identity. But it seems reasonable to take seriously the possibility that there will be effects that can give rise to questions about the applicability and legitimacy of traditional responsibility attributions. To be sure, the research reported above should be taken as 'proof-of-principle' studies rather than as exemplifying currently functional applications in real-life circumstances. Thus, this seems a good moment to start investigating and discussing the moral and legal frameworks that are in existence or to be developed, in order to stimulate societally responsible research and design in this area.

Just as a suggestion in this regard, it seems to me that the traditional interpretation of agency and identity will need to be clarified in more detail in order to distinguish and assess the various forms of 'extended minds' (e.g., Clark & Chalmers, 1998; Clark, 2008), that is, the various ways in which human cognition can be supported, augmented or enhanced via technology. For this clarification to be useful, it will be important to shun exaggerated science-fiction labels, while remaining open to the potential novelty of the involved cognitive and experiential effects. Concepts like 'cyborgs', 'person+', 'brainets' and 'mind melds' have been used, but are highly imprecise (except, perhaps, cyborg, which by now is reasonably well defined, e.g. Clark, 2008), and are often vague about the precise effects of the technology, or suggest more than what the effects actually amount to. The kind of changes that neurotechnology might bring about will in general not be of a 'Dr Jekyll and Mr Hyde' type of abrupt and complete personality change (Stevenson, 1886), but will be far more subtle, and likely to be perspective- and context-dependent (see the quote from Lewis et al., 2015, above). There are no 'hard' criteria to establish when someone has changed sufficiently to unequivocally determine that the person in question is no longer him/herself. For this reason, it might be useful to refrain from the exciting labels and develop a more technical terminology to examine the effects of neurotechnology. For example, although far from being new, speaking of 'psychological continuity' instead of 'identity' has the advantage that it is less 'philosophical', less value-laden and presents perhaps a more flexible framework for accommodating a person's partial changeability. It could be useful, for instance, to consider the possibility that emotions could be affected significantly by DBS, but that characteristic patterns of reasoning might not be, or much less so (or vice versa). In relation to law, crucial questions include, for example, whether or not (and if so, to what extent) the capacity to understand the wrongfulness of an act was affected via technology, or the capacity to conform one's behaviour to the law accordingly. Another issue might be whether the use, or in some future cases perhaps also non-use, of technology could be considered as a form of recklessness.

It could also be relevant to consider within-brain closed-loop systems as a kind of 'cognitive bypass'. The loop can provide an external layer for the regulation of cognition of which the user need not be aware, or even in control of. How would this affect a person's capacity for self-control and self-regulation? Depending on type of application and context, the assessments might range from extending, via stabilizing to undermining. Under what conditions, for instance, could someone with a within-brain closed-loop system be allowed to drive?

Regarding BTB, a relevant question concerns the extent to which individuals can be (made) aware of the relative contributions of themselves and other intelligent agents (human, animal or artificial) to cognition and behaviour, in order to develop an adequate sense of (co-)agency. Central here is the question regarding authorship that has been raised by Trimper, Wolpe and Rommelfanger (2014; see also Grau et al., 2014; Hildt, 2015): who owns the thoughts that are collectively generated in BTB? Another issue concerns whether participants in BTB teams at some point in the future could be subjected to investigations regarding (legal) complicity. What kinds of sharing and using brain information could amount to a type of participation in illegal acts that would qualify one as being an accomplice? Will analogues of cockpits and black boxes be required in brainet types of collective action, if only to be able, after the fact, to establish who did precisely what and when? This might be part of a to-be-devised regulatory framework.

17.6 DISCUSSION

The three forms of neurotechnology discussed here (brain decoding, brain stimulation, closed-loop systems within and between brains) present us with several questions regarding agency, identity and responsibility attribution. Obviously, most of the applications of these technologies are still far removed from being applied in everyday contexts. The technology is in a very early phase, often not further than some proof-of-principle demonstrations with animals. Hence questions regarding their implications should be considered as exploratory, or even speculative. Given the development of new techniques for brain measurement and stimulation (e.g. portable or wearable BCIs, thermo- and ultrasound stimulation), and the increasing capacities of machine-learning techniques for analysing the data obtained, it seems safe to say that the field of neurotechnology not only is developing rapidly, but will continue to do so for at least the next couple of decades.

In light of these expected developments, it seems plausible to me that some of our standard concepts may not be applicable in any straightforward way to assess the implications of actions performed by natural agents in neurotechnology-mediated ways. In fact, even this way of phrasing it already assumes a clarity that may not hold in some such actions, or even in many of them. The suggestion that the natural agent (human, animal) performs the action, whereas the technology merely 'mediates', may underestimate the effects of neurotechnology. In other words, the technology for brain measurement and brain stimulation, and the various combinations thereof, could start to transcend our standard framework for determining and attributing responsibility. Hence, we need to be prepared for a future-oriented exploration of some key concepts, central to the human self-image as well as a variety of societal practices. How could or should we characterize the consequences of neurotechnology for the cognitive and behavioural characteristics of individuals, including their own experience of these, as well as their evaluations by others? Such a future-oriented exploration of developing neurotechnology will have to consider and connect a variety of domains, including at least human experience, behavioural interpretation (by various parties), moral assessments, psycho-medical assessments, legal assessments and regulatory policies. Obviously, a lot can be learned here from clinical psychiatry, although the difference between technological and naturally occurring pathologies may turn out be significant. Hence, it would be a worthwhile effort to develop a taxonomy of the different effects of neurotechnologies on cognition and behaviour. Such a taxonomy would be useful to identify effects (either already recognized by clinical psychiatry, or potentially new) that require specific legal attention. It would also be useful to develop a systematized methodology (e.g. extending one already used by clinical psychiatry) for establishing whether such effects actually occur in contexts of neurotechnology usage (and under which circumstances).

Overall, exploratory and speculative questions can be useful to

a) identify in an early stage potential societal concerns and expectations that could be taken into account while developing the technology,
b) analyse, reconsider and perhaps revise our current terminology (both ethical, psychological and legal) in order to accommodate the future impact of technology,
c) propose and discuss ways to regulate the introduction of technology in various fields of application.

It would be nice, for a change, to think about appropriate regulatory frameworks for technology before, instead of only after its introduction into society.

REFERENCES

Abiri, R., Borhani, S., Sellers, E.W., Jiang, Y., & Zhao, X. (2019). A Comprehensive Review of EEG-Based Brain-Computer Interface Paradigms. *Journal of Neural Engineering* 16(1). DOI: https://doi.org/10.1088/1741-2552/aaf12e

Amon, A., & Alesch, F. (2017). Systems for Deep Brain Stimulation: Review of Technical Features. *Journal of Neural Transmission* 124(9), 1083–91. DOI: https://doi.org/10.1007/s00702-017-1751-6

Borders, C., Hsu, F., Sweidan, A. J., Matei, E. S., & Bota, R. G. (2018). Deep Brain Stimulation for Obsessive Compulsive Disorder: A Review of Results by Anatomical Target. *Mental Illness* 10(2), 40–4. DOI: https://doi.org/10.1108/mi.2018.7900

Bouthour, W., Mégevand, P., Donoghue, J., Lüscher, C., Birbaumer, N., & Krack, P. (2019). Biomarkers for Closed-Loop Deep Brain Stimulation in Parkinson's Disease and Beyond. *Nature Reviews Neurology*. DOI: https://doi.org/10.1038/s41582-019-0166-4

Clark, A. (2008). *Supersizing the Mind: Embodiment, Action, and Cognitive Extension*. Oxford and New York: Oxford University Press.

Clark, A., & Chalmers, D. J. (1998). The Extended Mind. *Analysis* 58, 7–19.

Chen, R., Romero, G., Christiansen, M. G. Mohr, A., & Anikeeva, P. (2015). Wireless Magnetothermal Deep Brain Stimulation. *Science* 347(6229), 1477–80. DOI: https://doi.org/10.1126/science.1261821

Dutch Health Law. (2009). Wet Bijzondere Opname in Psychiatrische Ziekenhuizen (Law on Special Admission to Psychiatric Hospitals). http://wetten.overheid.nl/BWBR0005700/geldigheidsdatum_18–11-2009.

Frith, C. D. (1987). The Positive and Negative Symptoms of schizophrenia Reflect Impairments in the Perception and Initiation of Action. *Psychological Medicine* 17(3), 631–48.

Frith, C. D. (2012). Explaining Delusions of Control: The Comparator Model 20 Years On. *Consciousness and Cognition* 21, 52–4. DOI: https://doi.org/10.1016/j.concog.2011.06.010

Gallagher, S. (2000). Philosophical Conceptions of the Self: Implications For Cognitive Science. *Trends in Cognitive Sciences* 4(1), 14–21.

Gallagher, S. (2007). The Natural Philosophy of Agency. *Philosophy Compass* 2(2), 347–57.

Gallagher, S. (2012). Multiple Aspects in the Sense of Agency. *New Ideas in Psychology* 30(1), 15–31. DOI: https://doi.org/10.1016/j.newideapsych.2010.03.003

Gilbert, F., Viaña, J. N. M., & Ineichen, C. (2018). Deflating the 'DBS Causes Personality Changes' Bubble. *Neuroethics*, 1–17.https://doi.org/10.1038/s41582-019-0166-4

Grau, C., Ginhoux, R., Riera, A., et al. (2014). Conscious Brain-to-Brain Communication in Humans Using Non-Invasive Technologies. *PLoS ONE* 9(8). https://doi.org/10.1371/journal.pone.0105225

Haselager, W. F. G. (2013). Did I Do That? Brain–Computer Interfacing and the Sense of Agency. *Minds and Machines*. DOI: https://doi.org/10.1007/s11023-012-9298-7

Haselager, W. F. G., Leoné, F., & van Toor, D. (2013). Data en interpretaties in de cognitieve neurowetenschap (Data and interpretations in cognitive neuroscience. Text in Dutch). *Justitiële Verkenningen* 39(1), 78–89.

Hildt, E. (2015). What Will This Do to Me and My Brain? Ethical Issues in Brain-to-brain Interfacing. *Frontiers in Systems Neuroscience* 9(17), 1–4. https://doi.org/10.3389/fnsys.2015.00017

Humpston, C. S., & Broome, M. R. (2016). The Spectra of Soundless Voices and Audible Thoughts: Towards an Integrative Model of Auditory Verbal Hallucinations and Thought Insertion. *Review of Philosophy and Psychology* 7(3), 611–29. https://doi.org/10.1007/s13164-015-0232-9

Ienca, M., Haselager, W. F. G., & Emanuel, E. (2018). Brain Leaks and Consumer Neurotechnology. *Nature: Biotechnology* 36(9), 805–10. https://doi.org/10.1038/nbt.4240

Jog, M. V., Wang, D. J. J., & Narr, K. L. (2019). A Review of Transcranial Direct Current Stimulation (tDCS) for the Individualized Treatment of Depressive Symptoms. *Personalized Medicine in Psychiatry* 1. https://doi.org/10.1016/j.pmip.2019.03.001

Kassiri, H., Tonekaboni, S., Salam, M. T., et al. (2017). Closed-Loop Neurostimulators: A Survey and a Seizure-Predicting Design Example for Intractable Epilepsy Treatment. *IEEE Transactions on Biomedical Circuits and Systems* 11(5), 1026–40. https://doi.org/10.1109/TBCAS.2017.2694638

Kekic, M., Boysen, E., Campbell, I. C., & Schmidt, U. (2016). A Systematic Review of the Clinical Efficacy of Transcranial Direct Current Stimulation (tDCS) in Psychiatric Disorders. *Journal of Psychiatric Research* 74, 70–86. https://doi.org/10.1016/j.jpsychires.2015.12.018

Klaming, L., & Haselager, W. F. G. (2013). Did My Brain Implant Make Me Do It? Questions Raised by DBS Regarding Psychological Continuity, Responsibility for Action and Mental Competence. *Neuroethics* 6(3), 527–39. https://doi.org/10.1007/s12152-010-9093-1

Klein, E., Brown, T., Sample, M., Truitt, A. R., & Goering, S. (2015). Engineering the Brain: Ethical Issues and the Introduction of Neural Devices. *Hastings Center Report*, 45(6), 26–35.

Kokkinos V., Sisterson, N. D., Wozny, T. A., & Richardson, R. M. (2019). Association of Closed-Loop Brain Stimulation Neurophysiological Features with Seizure Control among Patients with Focal Epilepsy. *JAMA Neurology* 76(7), 800–8. https://doi.org/10.1001/jamaneurol.2019.0658

Leentjens, A. F. G., Visser-Vandewalle, V., Temel, Y., & Verhey, F. R. J. (2004). Manipuleerbare wilsbekwaamheid: een ethisch probleem bij elektrostimulatie van de nucleaus subthalamicus voor ernstige ziekte van Parkinson. *Nederlands Tijdschrift voor Geneeskunde* 148, 1394–7.

Legon, W., Sato, T. F., Opitz, A., et al. (2014). Transcranial Focused Ultrasound Modulates the Activity of Primary Somatosensory Cortex in Humans. *Nature: Neuroscience* 17, 322–9, https://doi.org/10.1038/nn.3620

Leoné, F., Van Toor, D., & Haselager, W. F. G. (2016). *Neurowetenschap en recht* [Neuroscience and law. Text in Dutch]. In M. Boone, C. Brants, & R. Kool (eds.), *Criminologie en Strafrecht*, 2nd ed. Amsterdam: Boom, pp. 163–85.

Lewis, C. J., Maier, F., Horstkötter, N., et al. (2015). Subjectively Perceived Personality and Mood Changes Associated with Subthalamic Stimulation in Patients with Parkinson's Disease. *Psychological Medicine* 45(1), 73–85. https://doi.org/10.1017/S0033291714001081

Limousin, P., & Foltynie, T. (2019). Long-Term Outcomes of Deep Brain Stimulation in Parkinson's Disease. *Nature Reviews Neurology* 15(4), 234–42. https://doi.org/10.1038/s41582-019-0145-9

Lo, M. C., & Widge, A. S. (2017). Closed-Loop Neuromodulation Systems: Next-Generation Treatments for Psychiatric Illness. *International Review of Psychiatry* 29(2), 191–204. https://doi.org/10.1080/09540261.2017.1282438

Luigjes, J., Segrave, R., de Joode, N., Figee, M., & Denys, D. (2019). Efficacy of Invasive and Non-Invasive Brain Modulation Interventions for Addiction. *Neuropsychology Review* 29(1), 116–38. https://doi.org/10.1007/s11065-018-9393-5

Lynn, M. T., Berger, C. C., Riddle, T. A., & Morsella, E. (2010). Mind Control? Creating Illusory Intentions Through a Phony Brain-Computer Interface. *Consciousness and Cognition* 19, 1007–12. https://doi.org/10.1016/j.concog.2010.05.007.

Neuropace Responsive Neurostimulator. (n.d.). www.neuropace.com/

Pais-Vieira, M., Chiuffa, G., Lebedev, M., Yadav, A., & Nicolelis, M. (2015). Building an Organic Computing Device with Multiple Interconnected Brains. *Scientific Reports* 5, 1–15. https://doi.org/10.1038/srep11869

Pais-Vieira, M., Lebedev, M., Kunicki, C., Wang, J., & Nicolelis, M. (2013). A Brain-to-Brain Interface for Real-Time Sharing of Sensorimotor Information. *Scientific Reports* 3, 1319, 1–10. https://doi.org/10.1038/srep01319

Parfit, D. (1971). Personal Identity. *Philosophical Review* 80, 3–27.

Polanía, R., Nitsche, M. A., & Ruff, C. C. (2018). Studying and Modifying Brain Function with Non-Invasive Brain Stimulation. *Nature Neuroscience* 21(2), 174–87. https://dx.doi.org/10.1136/jnnp-2020-323870

Ramakrishnan, A., Ifft, P.J., Pais-Vieira, M., et al. (2015). Computing Arm Movements with a Monkey Brainet. *Scientific Reports* 5, 1–15. https://doi.org/10.1038/srep10767

Ramasubbu, R., Lang, S., & Kiss, Z. H. T. (2018). Dosing of Electrical Parameters in Deep Brain Stimulation for Intractable Depression: A Review of Clinical Studies. *Frontiers in Psychiatry* 9. https://doi.org/10.3389/fpsyt.2018.00302

Stevenson, R. L. (1886). *Strange Case of Dr. Jekyll and Mr. Hyde*. London: Longmans, Green & Co. www.gutenberg.org/ebooks/42

Synofzik, M., Vosgerau, G., & Newen, A. (2008). Beyond the Comparator Model: A Multifactorial Two-Step Account of Agency. *Consciousness and Cognition* 17(1), 219–39. DOI: https://doi.org/10.1016/j.concog.2007.03.010

Synofzik, M., Vosgerau, G., & Voss, M. (2013). The Experience of Agency: An Interplay Between Prediction and Postdiction. *Frontiers in Psychology* 4, 1–8. https://doi.org/10.3389/fpsyg.2013.00127

Systems and Methods for Closed-Loop Pain Management. (n.d.) Patent US20180085584A1. https://patents.google.com/patent/US20180085584A1/en

Taylor, R., Galvez, V., & Loo, C. (2018). Transcranial Magnetic Stimulation Safety: A Practical Guide for psychiatrists. *Australasian Psychiatry* 26(2), 189–92. https://doi.org/10.1177/1039856217748249

Trimper, J. B., Wolpe, P. R., & Rommelfanger, K. S. (2014). When 'I' Becomes 'We': Ethical Implications of Emerging Brain-to-Brain Interfacing Technologies. *Frontiers in Neuroengineering* 7, 4. https://doi.org/10.3389/fneng.2014.00004

Van Gerven, M., Farquhar, J., Schaefer, R., et al. (2009). The Brain-Computer Interface Cycle. *Journal of Neural Engineering* 6(4), 041001. DOI: https://doi.org/10.1088/1741-2560/6/4/041001

Vlek, R., van Acken, J., Beurskens, E., Roijendijk, L., & Haselager, W. F. G. (2014). BCI and a User's Judgment of Agency. In G. Mueller & E. Hildt (eds.), *Brain-Computer Interfaces in Their Ethical, Social and Cultural Contexts*. Dordrecht: Springer, 193–202. https://link.springer.com/chapter/10.1007/978-94-017-8996-7_16

Wegner, D. M. (2003a). *The Illusion of Conscious Will*. Cambridge, MA: MIT Press.

Wegner, D. M. (2003b). The Mind's Best Trick: How We Experience Conscious Will. *Trends in Cognitive Sciences* 7, 65–9. DOI: https://doi.org/10.1016/s1364-6613(03)00002-0

Wegner, D. M., & Wheatley, T. (1999). Apparent Mental Causation. *American Psychologist* 54 (7), 480–92.

Wegner, D. M., Fuller, V. A., & Sparrow, B. (2003). Clever Hands: Uncontrolled Intelligence in Facilitated Communication. *Journal of Personality and Social Psychology* 85, 5–19. DOI: https://doi.org/10.1037/0022-3514.85.1.5

Wegner, D. M., Sparrow, B., & Winerman, L. (2004). Vicarious Agency: Experiencing Control Over the Movements of Others. *Journal of Personality and Social Psychology* 86, 838–48. DOI: https://doi.org/10.1037/0022-3514.86.6.838

Wierzgała, P., Zapała, D., Wojcik, G. M., & Masiak, J. (2018). Most Popular Signal Processing Methods in Motor-Imagery BCI: A Review and Meta-Analysis. *Frontiers in Neuroinformatics* 12, 1–10. DOI: https://doi.org/10.3389/fninf.2018.00078

Woods, A. J., Antal, A., & Bikson, M. (2016). A Technical Guide to tDCS, and Related Non-Invasive Brain Stimulation Tools. *Clinical Neurophysiology* 127(2), 1031–48. DOI: https://doi.org/10.1016/j.clinph.2015.11.012

Yoo, S. S., Kim, H., Filandrianos, E., Taghados, S. J., & Park, S. (2013). Non-Invasive Brain-to-Brain Interface (BBI): Establishing Functional Links between Two Brains. *PLoS ONE* 8 (4), 2–9. DOI: https://doi.org/10.1371/journal.pone.0060410

Yu, Y., Pan, G., Gong, Y., et al. (2016). Intelligence-Augmented Rat Cyborgs in Maze Solving. *PLoS ONE* 11(2), 1–18. DOI: https://doi.org/10.1371/journal.pone.0147754

Zhang, S., Yuan, S., Huang, L., et al. (2019). Human Mind Control of Rat Cyborg's Continuous Locomotion with Wireless Brain-to-Brain Interface. *Scientific Reports* 9(1), 1–12. DOI: https://doi.org/10.1038/s41598-018-36885-0

18

Neuroimaging Evidence in US Courts

Jane Campbell Moriarty

18.1 OVERVIEW OF NEUROIMAGING TECHNOLOGY

Neuroscientific evidence in the US courts includes expert testimony about various types of neuroimages or data from neuroimages, collectively termed here "neuroimaging evidence." The most typical forms of neuroimaging include X-rays, computed tomography scans ("CT scans"), magnetic resonance imaging ("MRI"), positron emission tomography ("PET scan"), single photon emission computed tomography ("SPECT"), electroencephalograph ("EEG"), quantitative EEG ("QEEG"),[1] and functional MRI ("fMRI"). There are two categories of neuroimaging evidence that have the potential to be courtroom evidence, structural imaging and functional imaging, each of which will be explained. This chapter does not address the neuropsychological assessments based upon interviews and so-called "pen and paper tests," commonly used to assess individuals.

Structural imaging depicts the anatomy of the brain and skull, and can be performed using X-ray, CT scans, and MRI. In the trauma setting, X-ray (formally, "radiography") is essentially used for diagnosing skull fractures. CT scans are performed using a machine composed of an array of an X-ray emitter and detectors that rotate around a body part to produce two-dimensional slices. The slices can be postprocessed to create images in different planes or as a three-dimensional rendering. CT is commonly preferred as the imaging device of first choice for traumatic injuries, stroke, intracranial hemorrhages, and other emergency conditions.[2]

MRI employs strong magnetic fields and nonionizing electromagnetic radiation in producing high-resolution images (Langleben et al., 2012). The development of MRI has had an "unparalleled importance" both for diagnostic medicine and for research (Logothetis, 2008). MR imaging has a much greater ability than CT in detecting abnormalities, especially early findings in a disease state. For example,

---

[1] While most would not consider EEG and QEEG as "imaging," they are amongst the forms of neuroscience evidence relevant in courtrooms so are included in the description of "neuroimaging evidence" but they are not described further herein.

[2] For a detailed discussion, see Bigler, Allen, & Stimac (2012).

MR imaging can more easily identify cerebral infarction within a few minutes after onset compared to CT scans, which can identify them only after three or four hours. In addition, MRI can provide anatomic depiction in multiple imaging planes, which helps in lesion detection.

However, as CT is faster, more widely available, and more tolerant of patient motion, it is typically the initial imaging performed for emergency conditions such as stroke and trauma. MR imaging is more commonly used as a problem-solving tool for questions that are unanswered by CT scans. It is also used for serial assessment of long-standing conditions such as brain tumors, multiple sclerosis, and epilepsy.

Structural neuroimaging evidence has many accepted uses in the courtroom. For more than a century, US courts have admitted radiographs as evidence to prove injury or illness in line with their accepted role in clinical medicine (Logothetis, 2008).[3] Over the last several decades, courts have permitted expert witnesses to testify about CT scans and MRIs to provide evidence of injuries (e.g., skull fractures or serious head trauma), medical conditions (e.g., hemorrhages, traumatic brain injury, strokes, and damage from toxins), and certain disease processes (e.g., tumors, Alzheimer's).[4] Historically, structural imaging evidence has been admitted as part of an expert's testimony and was closely related to its accepted clinical use in medicine (Logothetis, 2008). While MRI has multiple appropriate uses in the courtroom as evidence of medical disorders and injuries, its use for other purposes such as explaining cognition or behavior are more controversial, although many courts have admitted such evidence for those purposes.[5]

Functional imaging techniques purport to show activation in the brain – rather than simply structure – and include PET, SPECT, and fMRI (Le Bihan, 2014).[6] Functional MR imaging (fMRI) was developed in the early 1990s and has had a phenomenal impact on basic cognitive research (Logothetis, 2008).[7] It attempts to measure regions of brain activation while the subject is either at rest ("resting state fMRI") or in response to a task ("brain activation fMRI"). The primary technique used in fMRI research is termed blood-oxygen-level-dependent contrast (BOLD), and measures changes in oxygenated blood in the brain (Logothetis, 2008).[8] While researchers have used fMRI to generate thousands of studies, its clinical utility has been far more modest. To date, the primary accepted clinical use of fMRI in medicine has been in presurgical brain mapping, generally for resection of tumors

---

[3] An early reported case in 1918 admitted X-ray evidence as proof of a skull fracture. See *United Laundries Co. v. Bradford* (1918). X-rays were first introduced by Conrad Röntgen in 1895.
[4] For example, physicians routinely use structural imaging, generally CT and sometimes MRI, to diagnose individuals with suspected traumatic brain injury (TBIs). See Granacher (2012) at 43, 46.
[5] See Section 18.3.3, discussing the use of MRI in criminal cases as explanation or excuse for aberrant behavior.
[6] Recently, scientists have begun using diffusion MRI (DMRI), which measures the rate of water diffusion as modulated by brain activity, to investigate neuronal activation.
[7] For discussion of the early use of MRI, see Ogawa et al. (1990); and Kwong et al. (1992).
[8] For a helpful explanation of BOLD fMRI, see Aguirre (2014).

and in epilepsy surgery.[9] Research using fMRI has potential clinically relevant uses for psychiatry, for example, but progress has been slower than anticipated and hoped.[10]

While fMRI research has clearly "ushered in the modern revolution of neuroimaging," there are technical and theoretical limitations that have impaired a seamless transition into either clinical or forensic use (Aguirre, 2014). Substantive critiques about the true value of neuroimaging studies include their low statistical power (due to small sample sizes) (Button et al., 2013),[11] the lack of reproducibility, and other shortcomings (Gilmore et al., 2017).[12] Moreover, populations examined in research studies may not reflect the complexity of actual patient populations. Although the critiques are well grounded, there is much optimism that greater size and reproducibility of neuroscience studies are possible (Gilmore et al., 2017). As Geoffrey Aguirre (2014) explains, "progress is being made in overcoming many practical limitations" in neuroscience research, although theoretical problems persist (Aguirre, 2014).[13]

One form of functional neuroimaging, Diffusion Tensor Imaging (DTI) is used to image white matter in the brain.[14] Researchers have begun to use DTI in research and some investigative clinical practices to visualize the white matter mapping of the brain by measuring the displacement of water molecules using diffusion anisotropy (Assaf & Pasternak, 2007).[15] DTI creates stunning, three-dimensional pictures purporting to show the organization of axonal fiber bundles in the brain (Le Bihan, 2014). To date, DTI is still being studied and further research is required for its clinical use (Granacher, 2012, pp. 53–56). While some researchers believe it may be particularly useful for imaging axonal damage following mild traumatic brain injury (which CT and MRI generally do not detect),[16] DTI is still in the investigatory phase. As such, it has appropriately had a far more limited role in the courtroom than has basic structural MRI or CT scans. However, despite serious concerns being raised establishing that DTI is still in the pre-clinical-use phase, some courts have admitted the evidence in civil cases involving traumatic brain injury (*Ruppel v. Kucanin*, 2011; *Ward v. Carnival Corporation*, 2019),[17] although other courts

---

[9] See, e.g., Silva et al., (2018). "Currently, fMRI is the most commonly used non-invasive neuroimaging modality for surgical planning …".

[10] See Mayberg (2014) noting that that clinical applications of functional neuroimaging are arriving quite slowly, particularly in psychiatry.

[11] The article further explains at length how low sample sizes and/or small effects "negatively affect the likelihood that a nominally statistically significant finding actually reflects a true effect".

[12] The article further discusses problems of reproducibility, transparency, low statistical powers, undetected software errors, and the lack of large-scale studies.

[13] These theoretical concerns include the relationship of brain activity to behavior.

[14] For a detailed explanation of DTI, see O'Donnell & Westin (2011).

[15] For an interesting article about the origins of mapping water diffusion in the brain, see Le Bihan (2014).

[16] For more research on the use of DTI for mTBI, see Niogi & Mukherjee (2010).

[17] See, e.g., *Ruppel v. Kucanin* WL 2470621 (D.C. N.D. Ind. 2011)(unreported); *Ward v. Carnival Corporation*, 2019 WL 1228063 (D.C. S.D. Fl. 2019) These are a few of the cases that have admitted

have excluded the evidence subsequent to a Daubert reliability hearing (*Brouard v. Convery*, 2018).[18] Data from fMRI appear to have been influential with the US Supreme Court in cases involving juveniles *as a group*, as discussed later in this chapter, in Section 18.3.6.[19] To date, fMRI has not figured as prominently in cases involving *individual* plaintiffs or defendants. However, litigants have attempted to introduce fMRI in three cases involving neuroscience lie detection, although attempts to date have not been successful.[20]

PET and SPECT are functional neuroimaging modalities within nuclear medicine that have well-recognized clinical uses and measure brain function based on the uptake of biological molecules, such as glucose, that have a chemical link to isotopes. The presence or absence of these isotopes in the brain can then be imaged and are used for detecting the histological grade of brain tumors, diagnosing Parkinson's disease, and locating seizures' foci (Rushing, Pryma, & Langleben, 2012; Moriarty, Langleben, & Provenzale, 2013). Despite the many clinical indications for PET and SPECT, their use as evidence of traumatic brain injury ("TBI"; particularly mild TBI, "mTBI"), mental illness, or damage due to toxic exposure damage is not well established (Moriarty et al., 2013). The American College of Radiology specifically states that PET has a low degree of utility for imaging brain trauma (Shetty et al., 2016) and is not generally considered useful in clinical psychiatry.[21] Despite these concerns, courts have admitted PET and SPECT to prove or support claims of brain injury or damage in civil and criminal cases (see cases collected in Moriarty, 2008; Rushing, Pryma, & Langleben, 2012; Denno, 2015; Farahany, 2015).

Some researchers use PET and SPECT in an attempt to determine whether violent individuals have abnormal neurological function that would explain their violent behavior (see, e.g., Raine, Buchsbaum, & Lacasse, 1997; Raine et al., 1998), and some have been active in serving as consultants and expert witnesses in cases involving violent behavior.[22] As noted by scholars collecting and analyzing empirical data, PET and other forms of functional neuroimaging have been and continue to be admitted in both the guilt and penalty phase (sentencing) of criminal trials (see

---

evidence of DTI as proof of TBI. Many of the courts cite other courts' findings of reliability as grounds for admission.

[18] See, e.g., *Brouard v. Convery*, 70 N.Y.S.3d. 820, 822–23 (N.Y. Sup. Ct. 2018). This case explains that "based on the issue of general acceptability in a given field, the Court finds that DTI does not (at the time of this writing) have a general acceptance to be used as the standard in clinical/medical treatment of individual patients who are being treated for TBI's."

[19] See e.g., Brief for the American Psychological Association et al., filed in *Miller v. Alabama*, 2012 WL 174239 (2012).

[20] See Section 18.4.

[21] See Mayberg (2014) at S34, noting there is neither "medical [n]or scientific support" for the use of structural or functional neuroimaging to diagnose or treat psychiatric disorders.

[22] See e.g., Gur et al. (2016) for a discussion of Ruben Gur's role as a consultant and expert in death penalty cases.

generally Denno, 2015; Farahany, 2015, discussing neurobiological evidence; Gaudet & Marchant, 2016).

Some in the scientific and medical communities have reservations about the use of PET to diagnose many forms of brain trauma. There are also concerns about the use of such technology to explain behavior, as this involves layering "inference (e.g., PET can reliably diagnose brain trauma) upon inference (e.g., brain trauma is the cause of legally relevant behaviors)" (Moriarty et al., 2013, p. 710). Many of the current forensic uses raise difficult medicolegal questions, "including what constitutes an abnormal scan, whether an allegedly abnormal scan is caused by the trauma, and whether an abnormal scan is meaningfully correlated with brain trauma and/or behavior" (Moriarty et al., 2013).

Litigants and experts, however, continue to push the evidentiary envelope with respect to structural and functional neuroimaging evidence in various types of cases, including both civil and criminal cases. As the science develops and the clinical applications of neuroimaging increase, it is equally likely that neuroimaging will continue to be at issue in the courtroom. Many courts, however, appear not to appreciate the substantial concerns that those in the medical field express about the appropriate use of both structural and functional utility in clinical neurology and psychiatry.

18.2 ADMISSIBILITY STANDARDS

There is both a federal and state system of courts in the United States, with overlapping but independent jurisdiction (*Puerto Rico v. Sanchez Valle*, 2016).[23] As the federal and state government are separate sovereigns (*Abbate v. United States*, 1959), each court system has its own rules for governing the admissibility of evidence. The United States Constitution, federal statutes, regulations, federal case law, and the various federal rules, including the Federal Rules of Evidence ("FRE"), govern the admission of evidence in the federal courts.[24] While state courts have their own evidence rules and cases governing the admission of evidence, many states' rules track the FREs, and state court opinions are often deferential to the US Supreme Court's decisions, particularly in the area of scientific and other forms of expert evidence.[25]

---

[23] This case discusses the fact that states are separate sovereigns from the Federal Government and from one another. Moreover, Native American tribes are also separate sovereigns, but "domestic dependent nations," subject to plenary control by Congress. Id. at 1872.
[24] See generally, Federal Rules of Evidence, 28 U.S.C.A.
[25] For example, the so-called *Daubert* trilogy of cases has been enormously influential not only in the federal courts but in the states as well. See Giannelli et al., (2020) discussing the influence of *Daubert*'s reliability standard on state courts.

Courtroom testimony comes largely from two sets of witnesses: lay witnesses, who provide testimony based upon their personal, perception-based knowledge of the factual events in a case (FRE 602),[26] and expert witnesses, who provide skill or knowledge-based testimony. Expert witnesses often have no first-hand knowledge of the case, but premise their testimony upon evidence primarily supplied by a party or admitted in the case.[27] Witnesses to a crime or accident, parties to the litigation, and any person who saw or heard something relevant to the case all qualify as percipient witnesses to provide factual testimony. Fact witnesses (also called percipient or lay witnesses) are permitted to give opinions, but only about events they witnessed (FRE 701).[28] Thus, a fact witness could describe an accident or provide an opinion about whether the accident victim seemed to be awake, in pain, or possibly even coherent. She could not, however, opine on whether the accident victim had closed-head injury or pupils that were equally reactive to light, subjects only an expert could address under FRE 702 as they are based upon "scientific, technical, or other specialized" knowledge.[29]

Some witnesses provide both lay and expert testimony, such as a treating physician who testifies about factual observations and a medical diagnosis of a plaintiff, for example. Typically, however, expert witnesses have no first-hand knowledge of the case and are generally hired after the case has begun to evaluate the matter and to provide an expert opinion.

---

[26] A witness may testify to a matter only if evidence is introduced sufficient to support a finding that the witness has personal knowledge of the matter. Evidence to prove personal knowledge may consist of the witness's own testimony. As noted in Mueller and Kirkpatrick, Federal Evidence (2018),

> The term "personal knowledge" refers to a combination of perception and memory. "Personal" means that the witness must have *personally* experienced what she is to describe, and that means ordinarily that she must have had direct sensory input that she experienced firsthand, usually in the form of sights and sounds. In other words, personal knowledge means seeing directly the acts, events, or conditions in question, or sometimes hearing them or both. Less often sensory input involves the other senses of touch, smell, or taste, where again personal knowledge means that knowledge produced by the direct involvement of the senses – actually touching or experiencing the taste or smell of something. Id., at §6:6.

[27] See generally, FRE 702 and 703.

[28] If a witness is not testifying as an expert, testimony in the form of an opinion is limited to one that is:

   a) rationally based on the witness's perception;
   b) helpful to clearly understanding the witness's testimony or to determining a fact in issue; and
   c) not based on scientific, technical, *or other specialized knowledge within the scope of Rule 702* (emphasis supplied).

[29] A witness who is qualified as an expert by knowledge, skill, experience, training, or education may testify in the form of an opinion or otherwise if:

   a) the expert's scientific, technical, or other specialized knowledge will help the trier of fact to understand the evidence or to determine a fact in issue;
   b) the testimony is based on sufficient facts or data;
   c) the testimony is the product of reliable principles and methods; and
   d) the expert has reliably applied the principles and methods to the facts of the case.

18.2.1 *Federal Rule of Evidence 702: Testimony by Expert Witnesses*

FRE 702 is the primary rule governing the admission of expert testimony and permits testimony from a sufficiently qualified witness. The testimony must rest on "specialized knowledge" and must be helpful to understanding or resolving the issues in the case. Additionally, the rule has three essential elements that relate to reliability: the testimony must be based upon sufficient facts or data; be the product of reliable methods; and be reliably applied. In sum, the rule provides a number of hurdles that must be overcome before testimony is admissible.[30] Virtually all neuroimaging evidence is presented in court through expert witnesses and is subject to this federal rule or a parallel state rule.

While Rule 702 of the FREs require proof of reliability, some state courts follow a more relaxed approach to the admissibility of expert evidence, employing a "helpfulness" standard or using a hybrid of reliability and other factors (See *Goeb v. Tharaldson*, 2000; *People v. Schreck*, 2001; *Anderson v. Akzo Nobel Coatings, Inc.*, 2011).

18.2.2 *The* Frye *General Acceptance Test*

Amongst states that do not require proof of reliability for expert testimony, many still adhere to the so-called "*Frye* standard" of general acceptance, which requires novel scientific evidence to be generally accepted by the field to which it belongs (see *Frye v. United States*, 1923). In the states that still follow the general acceptance test alone (and there are only a handful that currently do), the test has limited utility, as it often applies only to *novel* scientific evidence.[31] Thus, *Frye* does not apply to many forms of expert testimony, which are often governed by rather amorphous standards such as "helpfulness." For example, the Supreme Court of Kansas has held that the Frye test does not apply to "pure opinion" testimony, which it describes as "expert opinion developed from inductive reasoning based on the expert's own experience,

---

[30] See text of Rule 702. Additionally, the evidence must be relevant to a fact in issue. FRE 401 provides that "Evidence is relevant if:

a) it has any tendency to make a fact more or less probable than it would be without the evidence; and
b) the fact is of consequence in determining the action." The Supreme Court in *Daubert v. Merrell Dow Pharmaceuticals, Inc.*, 509 U.S. 579, 589 (1993) noted that "under the Rules the trial judge must ensure that any and all scientific testimony or evidence admitted is not only relevant, but reliable."

[31] See *Anderson v. Akzo Nobel Coatings, Inc.* (2011), which notes that Frye does not apply to methodology that is already accepted in the scientific community; and *Betz v. Pneumo Abex, LLC.* (2012): "Challenges generally are vetted through the *Frye* litmus, which winnows the field of the attacks by application of the threshold requirement of novelty," but noting that a "reasonably broad meaning should be ascribed to the term 'novel'". But see *People v. Daveggio* and Michaud (2018), which notes the Kelly/Frye test applies only to novel technique in the relevant scientific community *and* potentially to new evidence reflecting a change in the attitude of the scientific community.

observation, or research" (*Kuhn v. Sandoz Pharmaceuticals Corp.*, 2000). The validity of "pure opinion" is only tested by cross-examination, whereas the *Frye* tests controls "when an expert reaches a conclusion by deduction from applying a new or novel scientific principal, formula, or procedure developed by others" (*Kuhn v. Sandoz Pharmaceuticals Corp.*, 2000).

18.2.3 The Daubert Trilogy

While the Federal Rules of Evidence are the primary governing standard for the admissibility of evidence, they must be understood in the context of federal case law, particularly cases from the United States Supreme Court. In the area of expert evidence, three cases are exceptionally influential: *Daubert v. Merrell Dow Pharmaceuticals, Inc.* ("*Daubert*"); *General Electric Co. v. Joiner* ("*Joiner*"); and *Kumho Tire Ltd. v. Carmichael* ("Kumho Tire"). These cases, collectively termed "the *Daubert* trilogy," have been significant in decisions about the admissibility of expert testimony in civil cases, although they have had a more modest effect on decisions in criminal cases.[32]

In *Daubert*, the Supreme Court held that to be admissible, scientific evidence must be both relevant and reliable and explained that scientific reliability was "grounded in the methods and procedures of science." While eschewing a definitive test, the Court listed a number of "observations" that could be helpful to assess the reliability of the evidence: (1) whether the theory can be or has been tested; (2) whether the theory or technique had been subject to peer review and publications; (3) the known or potential rate of error; (4) the existence and maintenance of standards and controls; and (5) whether the technique or theory had been generally accepted in the scientific community (*Daubert v. Merrell Dow Pharmaceuticals Inc.*, 1993).[33]

The *Daubert* factors, so called, are neither mandatory nor exclusive, but have been critical in decisions about whether to admit evidence. These factors are generally seen as a helpful way to evaluate traditional scientific evidence, such as questions of medical causation (see e.g. *McClain v. Metabolife*, 2005) or matters involving air or water pollution issues.[34] They have been an awkward fit for other subjects, such as clinical medicine, psychology, and psychiatry, where the opinions

---

[32] See Giannelli et al. (2020) explaining that Daubert is an "exacting" standard in civil cases but is applied less stringently in criminal cases. For more, see National Research Council (2009). "The vast majority of the *reported* opinions in criminal cases indicate that trial judges rarely exclude or restrict expert testimony offered by prosecutors: most *reported* opinions also indicate that the appellate courts routinely deny appeals contesting trial court decisions admitting forensic evidence against criminal defendants."

[33] For additional explanation, see the Advisory Committee Notes to the Federal Rules of Evidence, Rule 702, 2000 Amendment.

[34] See e.g., *Fisher v. Ciba Specialty Chemicals Corp.* (2007) for admitted expert testimony about DDT contamination on property.

rely heavily upon patient history, clinical observation, and confirmatory testing.[35] In those areas, courts have been more lenient in their analysis of what constitutes reliability, often admitting opinions that do not meet the *Daubert* factors.[36]

Daubert stated that the focus of the trial court's gatekeeping "must be solely on principles and methodology, not on the conclusions they generate" (*Daubert v. Merrell Dow Pharmaceuticals, Inc.*, 1993). In the years after *Daubert*, courts struggled with the distinction between methodology and conclusion. The Supreme Court softened the distinction in the 1997 *Joiner* decision, noting the integral relationship between methodology and conclusions:

> But conclusions and methodology are not entirely distinct from one another. Trained experts commonly extrapolate from existing data. But nothing in either *Daubert* or the Federal Rules of Evidence requires a district court to admit opinion evidence that is connected to existing data only by the *ipse dixit* of the expert. A court may conclude that there is simply too great an analytical gap between the data and the opinion proffered. (*General Electric Co. v. Joiner*, 1997)[37]

The concern about the potential inferential leap from data to opinion – the so-called *ipse dixit* problem – is critical in the evaluation of whether expert evidence is admissible. Many courts have noted that the chasm between the data and the expert's presumptive conclusions is too wide, resulting in exclusion of the expert testimony.[38]

In *Kumho Tire*, which followed *Joiner*, the Supreme Court held that the court's gatekeeping obligation applied to all expert evidence under FRE 702, not solely to scientific evidence, resolving a dispute that had been brewing in the lower courts for several years:

> We conclude that *Daubert*'s general principles apply to the expert matters described in Rule 702. The Rule, in respect to all such matters, "establishes a standard of evidentiary reliability." [and] "requires a valid ... connection to the pertinent inquiry as a precondition to admissibility." [W]here such testimony's factual basis, data, principles, methods, or their application are called sufficiently into question, ... the trial judge must determine whether the testimony has "a reliable basis in the knowledge and experience of [the relevant] discipline." (*Kumho Tire Co., Ltd. v. Carmichael*, 1999)

---

[35] See generally Slobogin (2000), explaining how psychiatry does not fare well using a reliability analysis.
[36] See, e.g. *Westberry v. Gislaved Gummi AB* (1999); and *Chisholm v. Champion* Ent. Inc. (2003) (unreported), noting that most federal circuits have held that a reliable differential diagnosis satisfies *Daubert*.
[37] For a deeper explanation of the relationship between methodology and conclusions, see Faigman, Slobogin, and Monahan (2016).
[38] See, e.g., *Jarvis v. Secretary of the Dept. of Health and Human Services* (2011), finding the proffered theory of vaccine-related neurological injury to be a "bare assertion" connected to the data only by the *ipse dixit* of the expert; *C. W. and E. W., ex rel. Wood v. Textron, Inc.* (2015), stating that the experts' "failure to connect the dots" from the studies to the illness was a "*Joiner* problem ...."

In so holding, however, the court noted that while the judge "may" consider the *Daubert* factors in making that determination, the court is not required to do so in all cases: "*Daubert* makes clear that the factors it mentions do *not* constitute a 'definitive checklist or test' and the factors 'may or may not be pertinent in assessing reliability'" (*Kumho Tire Co., Ltd. v. Carmichael*, 1999). This flexibility, however, is not without limits. While the trial judge is granted "considerable leeway" in determining reliability, "a trial court should consider the specific factors identified in *Daubert* where they are reasonable measures of the reliability of expert testimony" (*Kumho Tire Co., Ltd. v. Carmichael*, 1999).

18.2.4 *The Reliability of Neuroimaging Evidence*

The question of reliability with respect to neuroimaging presents multiple interrelated concerns: whether the method of neuroimaging produces valid and reliable data (reliability generally); whether the neuroimaging was reliably used in the specific case (reliability as applied, including sufficient facts and data); and whether the error rate is known and properly calculated. Relatedly, the court must determine whether the expert or experts are appropriately and sufficiently qualified to present and testify about such neuroimaging evidence and, in some cases must consider whether the testimony arises naturally from the expert's research or is litigation-driven science.[39]

The primary concern is whether the neuroimaging produces valid and reliable data that can be used properly in the courtroom. While there is much agreement that neuroscience research has made substantial progress to illuminate the relationship between brain and mind, there are serious questions about experimental design, reproducibility, statistical interpretation, and whether researchers can agree on the meaning of data patterns (Gilmore et al., 2017).[40] As Geoffrey Aguirre recognizes, the easy access to clinical MRI machines has resulted in a "rapid proliferation of neuroimaging research" in various disciplines (Aguirre, 2014, S17), much of which lacks the sufficient methodological rigor present in more established areas (Aguirre, 2014, S8). Courts are often unaware of many of these concerns.

On the other hand, there is little quibbling over the appropriateness of neuroimaging when it is used in the courtroom for medically accepted purposes, such as CT used to diagnose an emergent head injury or MRI results to prove a brain tumor. However, problems can arise between general reliability and reliability as applied: for example, neuroimaging can be sufficiently reliable for one purpose (CT to

---

[39] The Advisory Committee Notes to the 2000 Amendment to FRE 702 ask courts to consider "[w]hether experts are 'proposing to testify about matters growing naturally and directly out of research they have conducted independent of the litigation, or whether they have developed their opinions expressly for purposes of testifying,'" citing *Daubert v. Merrell Dow Pharmaceuticals, Inc.*, 43 F.3d 1311, 1317 (9th Cir. 1995) (on remand from the Supreme Court).

[40] See also Moriarty & Langleben (2018) at 787, discussing problems of replication.

diagnose skull fracture), but not for another (CT to diagnose Alzheimer's). The problem of using neuroimaging technology for a non-medically-approved purpose is one courts often do not fully appreciate[41] and relates to *Daubert*'s focus on judging reliability not globally, but for the "task at hand" (*Daubert v. Merrill Dow Pharmaceuticals, Inc.*, 1993, p. 597).

Some cases present imaging that either is *contraindicated* for the claimed purpose or has not yet developed into a clinical purpose. For example, although PET is contraindicated as an imaging modality for TBI and other forms of imaging possible brain trauma, it has been introduced in court to support these types of injury (Moriarty et al., 2013).[42] DTI provides another example of potentially unwarranted neuroimaging evidence. Researchers are conducting trials using DTI to determine whether axonal damage follows from mild TBI (see Sections 18.1.1 and 18.5.1). Physicians have not yet accepted DTI for that clinical purpose, yet courts are often unaware of that concern and find the testimony reliable based on a group of small studies.[43] Thus, when faced with two competing experts, courts may not appreciate the distinction between research/clinical investigation and accepted clinical use.

The second concern about the reliability of neuroimaging relates to the implications of the neuroimaging findings. Many cases involve alleged brain damage. Even if the damage is provable by neuroimaging, it is often unclear what behaviors and cognitive deficits are specifically related to such brain damage. As noted by many researchers and commentators, the translation from neuroimaging to cognition and/or behavior is far from certain and "remains deeply controversial" (Greely & Farahany, 2019, at p. 459).

The third concern about reliability relates to the known error rates generated in basic research and translated into courtroom evidence. Perhaps the best example of this concern is presented with neuroscience lie detection, discussed at length later in this paper. While some small studies may provide compelling data, that data is not yet sufficiently reliable for the courtroom. As many have noted, including the researchers themselves, the studies are untested by large-scale trials (Langleben & Moriarty, 2013). While there is a "known error rate" generated in small, controlled lie detection studies, these error rates are not validated by real-world inquiries (Farah et al., 2014). Additionally, until the positive and negative predictive values are calculated, the accuracy of these preliminary conclusions remains unknown

[41] For example, in *United States v. Montgomery*, 635 F.3d 1074 (8th Cir. 2011), the defendant wanted to introduce testimony from a psychologist that PET scans showing alleged abnormalities in the limbic and somatomotor region of the brain were consistent with a diagnosis of pseudocyesis. The court disallowed the evidence but did not recognize that this use of PET (to relate these brain abnormalities to pseudocyesis) was not a medically approved use of PET scan. Moreover, the Court did not appear to appreciate that only a physician is licensed to interpret a PET scan and did not comment on whether it was appropriate for a psychologist to interpret such data.
[42] This article explains how PET is not recommended by the American College of Radiology for most head-trauma imaging, and collects cases where it has been admitted for that purpose.
[43] See *Ward v. Carnival Corporation*, 2019, collecting cases that have admitted DTI evidence to prove TBI.

(Langleben & Moriarty, 2013). Recognizing false positives and negatives is critical for the "real world" use of such data.[44]

The fourth concern relates to the qualifications of the expert witness. As noted in one article, "[t]he growth of neuroimaging as both an area of basic research and as a branch of clinical diagnostic radiology has blurred the lines between the practice of medicine and other areas of expertise" (Moriarty & Langleben, 2018). As the authors note, although only physicians are permitted to order and interpret the results of neuroimaging studies in clinical practice, "non-physician experts are asked to testify about the interpretation of CT, MRI, and PET scans in the courtroom" (Moriarty & Langleben, 2018, p. 786).[45]

18.3 NEUROIMAGING EVIDENCE IN CRIMINAL CASES

Defendants in criminal cases were amongst the first to urge the admission of neuroimaging evidence in trials, primarily as brain-based proof of impaired cognitive function, sanity, or impulse control. One of the early, well-known uses of neuroimaging evidence was during the 1980s, where John Hinckley was charged with multiple crimes for his attempted assassination of President Reagan.[46] Amongst a great deal of other evidence, Hinckley's lawyers also introduced CT images in support of an insanity defense. The defense successfully argued that the atrophy and ventricular enlargement supported Hinckley's claim of schizophrenia and legal nonresponsibility.[47]

Since that time, evidence has been proffered in pretrial matters involving competency hearings, as evidence of a lack of *mens rea* and/or legal insanity during trial, and during sentencing to mitigate the degree of crime.[48] Some have even urged that courts consider a defendant's diagnosis of psychopathy in penalty phase hearings.[49] The trend of using neuroimaging evidence in criminal cases has continued unabated, with an ever-increasing number of defendants seeking to admit such evidence or seeking new trials for failure to use such evidence.[50] Moreover, as

---

[44] For a detailed discussion of the complex problems of getting from the scanner to the courtroom see Greely and Wagner (2011).
[45] To date, little fMRI evidence has been introduced into court, but it too may present complicated issues of expertise.
[46] For the facts of the case in which Hinckley was charged with multiple counts for the attempted assassination of President Reagan, see *United States v. Hinckley* (1982).
[47] For more on this case, see Bigler et al. (2015).
[48] See Snead (2007), noting that in addition to using neuroimaging evidence in the sentencing phase of capital cases, defendants have proffered such evidence "in connection with claims of mental incompetence ... [to] show diminished capacity (or an inability to formulate requisite mens rea) at the guilt phase of criminal trials or as an adjunct to their insanity defenses."
[49] For a fuller explanation of the use of such testimony, see Phillips (2013) and Section 18.3.4.
[50] Empirical studies demonstrate that neuroimaging is often admitted as mitigating evidence during trials and in sentencing and competency hearings (see Denno, 2015, p. 504; Farahany, 2015, addressing neurobiological evidence; Gaudet & Marchant, 2016).

discussed in the empirical studies of neuroimaging evidence, the rate at which courts are addressing neuroscience evidence is also increasing.[51] Given the skepticism with which judges and juries often evaluate mental health evidence in criminal cases, it is unsurprising that defendants attempt to introduce neuroimaging evidence, which is perceived as more scientifically grounded.[52]

Several reasons support the turn toward neuroimaging evidence in the courtroom, particularly to supplement psychological and psychiatric expert testimony. There are well-known shortcomings of using the standard combination of interview and behavioral tests to conduct competency and other forensic psychological evaluations. Primarily, these evaluations measure voluntary responses, which manipulation and malingering can affect.[53] Additionally, such evaluations can be overly subjective (Vincent, 2013) and subject to cognitive bias problems (Scarpazza et al., 2018). Finally, there is often diagnostic disagreement between and amongst clinicians (Vincent, 2013, p. 480).

Moreover, as some persuasively argue, factfinders may find brain-based expert testimony a more compelling form of proof than psychological or psychiatric testimony (see Bigler et al., 2015, p. 312).[54] Many researchers and commentators, however, argue that neuroimaging is neither able to identify mental illness nor sufficiently establish a causal link between most brain images and impaired cognition or impulse control (Mayberg, 2014; see also, Morse, 2007; Brown & Murphy, 2010). However, given that neuroimaging evidence has become more prevalent in criminal and civil cases, there is a pressing need for experts in the field to address its responsible use.[55]

18.3.1 *Competency Determinations*

In the pretrial stage, defendants have sought to introduce neuroimaging evidence as support for claims of incompetency (see generally, Meixner, 2017–2018).[56] The Constitution of the United States prohibits the trial of an individual who lacks mental competency (see *Indiana v. Edwards*, 2008; *Dusky v. United States*, 1960;

---

[51] See, e.g., Farahany, 2015, p. 492, noting the number of judicial opinions addressing neurobiological evidence has jumped from approximately 100 in 2005 to approximately 250–300 in 2012.
[52] For more on the skepticism of fact-finders toward mental health evidence, see generally Perlin (1994); Slobogin (2007); Moriarty (2016).
[53] See Meixner (2017–2018, p. 1002), citing other studies (see also Bigler et al., 2015, pp. 313–314 and Vincent, 2013, p. 480).
[54] Note that "neuroimaging has a level of concrete representation and reproducibility that cannot be achieved by vague techniques such as rummaging in a person's thoughts to uncover motivations and personality structure." See also Moriarty (2016) at 613, recognizing a "need for neurological or laboratory-based expert testimony that might be more persuasive [to fact-finders who are] . . . affected by the skepticism that plagues behavioral-science testimony."
[55] Farahany (2015, p. 488), arguing that neuroscientists need to educate the public and the court about the responsible use of such evidence, as "neuroscience is already entrenched in the US legal system."
[56] Competency may also be relevant at other periods, such as waiving a trial and at sentencing.

Drope v. *Missouri*, 1975). The task for the trial court is to determine whether a defendant "has sufficient present ability to consult with his lawyer with a reasonable degree of rational understanding – and whether he has a rational as well as factual understanding of the proceedings against him" (*Dusky* v. *United States*, 1960). While there is a presumption of competency, once a defendant has raised the issue of incompetency and the court has reason to doubt the defendant's competency, a court must hold a hearing on the matter (see also *Drope* v. *Missouri*, 1975).[57]

Neuroimaging evidence has been used as an adjuvant to support (or dispute) claims of incompetency, provided it can provide fairly concrete evidence of impairment, such as showing severe brain damage or disease.[58] According to Professor Farahany's large set of data (~1500) analyzing US cases involving neuroscience and behavioral genetics evidence, 15 percent were competency matters, with three quarters of those involving competency to stand trial (see Farahany, 2015, pp. 495–496).[59]

In an analysis of the competency issues, another author notes that neuroscience evidence is used largely to "provide imaging and/or other neurological support for a diagnosis (or nondiagnosis) of brain injury or disorder" relevant to mental capacity (Meixner, 2017). John Meixner (2017) conducted a recent one-year search of competency cases involving neuroscience. Many cases were reviews of prior competency hearings that were challenged on appeal or in the context of habeas corpus (postconviction) proceedings. However, in those cases involving neuroscience at the competency hearing, he found it was used generally to indicate the presence of brain injury, and often for the purpose of supporting behavioral evidence about competency (Meixner, 2017).

It is likely that neuroscience evidence will become more common in competency proceedings, as it potentially provides current evidence of the defendant's brain structure and function at the time of the court's evaluation of the defendant's competency. By comparison, the use of neuroscience during trial and in sentencing

---

[57] The federal statute, Determination of Mental Competency to Stand Trial to Undergo Postrelease Proceedings, 18 U.S.C §4241 (2006), provides the procedures for determining competency:

> At any time after the commencement of a prosecution . . ., the defendant or the attorney for the Government may file a motion for a hearing to determine the mental competency of the defendant. The court shall grant the motion, or shall order such a hearing on its own motion, if there is reasonable cause to believe that the defendant may presently be suffering from a mental disease or defect rendering him mentally incompetent to the extent that he is unable to understand the nature and consequences of the proceedings against him or to assist properly in his defense.

> Many states have similar procedural processes.

[58] See Scarpazza et al. (2018), providing a roadmap to use structural imaging to support behavioral observations and conclusions.

[59] A small percentage of the competency issues included waiver of rights, pleading guilty, or confessing.

is typically retrospective, where imaging is used to explain a defendant's prior actions.

18.3.2 *Legal Responsibility*: Mens Rea *and Legal Insanity*

Perhaps the most significant philosophical question about the role of neuroscience in the legal system is whether some degree of abnormal neurobiology should affect our conception of legal responsibility. There is a range of opinions about the current and future role of neuroscience with respect to mental health and legal responsibility (see e.g., Morse, 1996; Greene & Cohen, 2004; Morse & Hoffman, 2007; Vincent, 2009; Pardo & Patterson, 2013; Maoz & Yaffe, 2016; Slobogin, 2017), although the legal system, other than academicians, has been relatively indifferent to the more philosophical debates (see Greely & Wagner, 2011, p. 799). Will neuroscience leave our understanding of legal responsibility unchanged, provide support for or undermine existing psychological and psychiatric concepts, or create an entirely new paradigm for evaluating human responsibility? Aside from the theoretical discussions, the courts are already grappling with the admission of neuroimaging evidence to illuminate defendants' responsibility for criminal acts.

With the exception of strict liability crimes, courts generally interpret criminal statutes to "require that a defendant possess a *mens rea*, or guilty mind, as to every element of an offense" (*Torres* v. *Lynch*, 2016; see also Denno, 2017, discussing these issues).[60] The Model Penal Code and the Supreme Court recognize that wrongdoing must be conscious in order for it to be criminal (American Law Institute, 1985; *Morissette* v. *United States*, 1952) and the concept of *mens rea* generally is what separates wrongful from otherwise innocent conduct (*Elonis* v. *United States*, 2015; Greely & Wagner, 2011, p. 799). Prosecutors are required to prove the defendant's *mens rea* – generally it is not a difficult part of their case.[61]

In most cases, defendants seek to introduce neuroimaging evidence relevant to *mens rea* to reduce the degree of crime to a lesser degree, and not as a complete defense.[62] As noted by empirical research, increasingly defendants use neuroscience evidence to bolster their claims of decreased responsibility for criminal conduct (Farahany, 2015; Greely & Farahany, 2019).

Defendants who claim they should be found not guilty by reason of insanity must raise it as an affirmative defense. There are different constructions for the insanity

---

[60] The other requirement is that the defendant was intentional in his commission of the act, the so-called *actus rea*.
[61] See generally, David L. Faigman et al., Modern Scientific Evidence, §8.2 Mens rea and mental disorder – "Diminished Capacity" (2018–2019).
[62] For a cogent explanation of how neurological impairment might work in a variety of defenses and partial defenses, see Slobogin (2017, pp. 580–582).

defense amongst various states and the federal system in the United States. The most common form of legal insanity employs a cognitive test that considers whether the defendant understands or appreciates the wrongfulness of his conduct. Some states, and the Model Penal Code, recognize a two-pronged test for insanity: both a cognitive test and a volitional test (American Law Institute, 1985).[63] The federal courts and a substantial majority of state courts use some variant of the cognitive test for insanity. This cognitive prong, often termed the M'Naghten test, is based upon an English common-law case from the mid-1800s.[64] A minority of states also employ an insanity defense that has a volitional impairment test similar or identical to the one recognized in the Model Penal Code – frequently termed the "irresistible impulse" test. The volitional test focuses on whether the defendant was able to "conform his conduct to the requirements of law" (American Law Institute, 1985). Although the volitional prong of the test is disallowed in most states and in the federal system, it may become more viable as neuroscience develops more robust data to connect behavior to brain damage.[65]

Under the federal statute, termed the "Insanity Defense Reform Act, or IDRA," the test considers "whether the defendant, as a result of a severe mental disease or defect, was unable to appreciate the nature and quality or the wrongfulness of his acts."[66] Insanity in the federal system is an affirmative defense, which requires that the defendant bears the burden of proving his insanity. Moreover, under the federal statute, he must prove it by clear and convincing evidence, a higher standard than the typical standard, which requires only proof by a preponderance of the evidence.[67]

---

[63] Model Penal Code §4.01. Mental Disease or Defect Excluding Responsibility.

  1) A person is not responsible for criminal conduct if at the time of such conduct as a result of mental disease or defect he lacks substantial capacity either to appreciate the criminality [wrongfulness] of his conduct or to conform his conduct to the requirements of law.
  2) As used in this Article, the terms "mental disease or defect" do not include an abnormality manifested only by repeated criminal or otherwise antisocial conduct.

[64] The so-called "M'Naghten standard" originates with the trial of Daniel M'Naghten in 1843, who was tried for murder and for attempted murder of the prime minister. M'Naghten's Case (1843) 8 Eng. Rep. 718, in which the court considered whether the defendant "was labouring under such a defect of reason, from disease of the mind, as not to know the nature and quality of the act he was doing; or, if he did know it, that he did not know he was doing what was wrong." Id. at 722. For more on this case, see generally, Moran (1981).

[65] See generally, Moriarty (2016) for a discussion of the potential utility of neuroscience for purposes of proving impaired control of volition.

[66] 18 U.S. C. §17, Insanity Defense, provides:

a) Affirmative defense.– It is an affirmative defense to a prosecution under any Federal statute that, at the time of the commission of the acts constituting the offense, the defendant, as a result of a severe mental disease or defect, was unable to appreciate the nature and quality or the wrongfulness of his acts. Mental disease or defect does not otherwise constitute a defense.

[67] 18 U.S. C. §17 (b) (b) Burden of proof. – The defendant has the burden of proving the defense of insanity by clear and convincing evidence. For more on this burden of proof, see generally, Mueller & Kirkpatrick, 1 Federal Evidence, §3:18 (4th ed.), Affirmative Defenses [in Criminal Cases].

Following the enactment of IDRA, a majority of states have followed its lead to a more restrictive interpretation of legal insanity.[68] Some states enacted tests more restrictive than IDRA,[69] and a handful of states eliminated the affirmative insanity defense altogether.[70] The enactment of "guilty but mentally ill (GBMI)" statutes have also further encroached upon the insanity defense (*Clark* v. *Arizona*, 2006).[71] Although the GBMI statutes appear to be a helpful alternative for juries, in reality they simply mean the defendant goes to prison, where he is likely to receive little mental health treatment.[72]

To date, neuroimaging has played a limited role in insanity defense cases as the insanity defense is infrequently raised. Additionally, except in extreme cases, it would be difficult to use neuroimaging to prove the defendant did not understand or appreciate the wrongfulness of his conduct. Moreover, even in those jurisdictions where the volitional prong of the insanity defense is permitted, it is currently difficult to prove that a brain disease or disorder is responsible for the defendant's inability to control his behavior.[73] While there may be a correlation between frontal lobe damage, for example, and a tendency toward impulsive action, there is still little proof to support a claim linking brain damage to criminal behavior. As Professor Slobogin explains, "[t]he fact that a person's brain structure or functioning is abnormal does not mean that the abnormality contributed significantly or at all to a specific act such as a criminal offense" (Slobogin, 2017, p. 585).

When neuroimaging evidence has been admitted in criminal cases to reduce the degree of a crime, the success of such evidence has been less impressive. As Professor Farahany notes in her study, "[p]resented with circumstantial evidence consistent with planning and premeditation and with conflicting neurobiological evidence, judges and juries tend to credit the circumstantial evidence over the neurobiological" (Farahany, 2015, p. 503). While there are many possible reasons juries reject such evidence, it may be that public opinion is simply unreceptive to mental health defenses – even partial ones – whether presented as neuroscience-based or premised upon behavioral science.

There are, however, research data suggesting that neuroscience explanations, when packaged with other expert testimony, may be a helpful addition to psychological or psychiatric testimony relevant to mental states in criminal trials

---

[68] See *Clark* v. *Arizona* (2006), listing state statutes.
[69] See, e.g., TEX. PENAL CODE ANN. §8.01(a) (West, 2015) which states that "[i]t is an affirmative defense to prosecution that, at the time of the conduct charged, the actor, as a result of severe mental disease or defect, did not know that his conduct was wrong."
[70] See *Clark* v. *Arizona* at 752 n.20 which lists the statutes from Idaho, Kansas, Montana, and Utah. For further explanation of the current national standards governing the insanity defense, see Morse (2011).
[71] This section focuses on state statutes concerning GBMI. For a thorough analysis of GBMI, see Slobogin (1985).
[72] See Woodmansee (1996). "In reality, however, GBMI offenders seldom receive mental health treatment during the course of their prison sentences" (Melville & Naimark, 2002).
[73] See, e.g., Farahany (2015, p. 501), noting that neurobiological evidence in criminal cases has not been very helpful for determining responsibility in the guilt phase of trials.

(Scarpazza et al., 2018).[74] Given the legal and public disdain for such behavior-based expert testimony, neuroscience may well be helpful to defendants seeking to overcome fact-finder's skepticism about behavioral testimony. A meta-analysis suggests that while neuroimaging testimony is often unpersuasive with juries determining guilt, a neurological explanation for defendants' mental states is more influential than a clinical psychological explanation (Schweitzer et al., 2011). Although this study is compelling, there is more to be done in the area, a point well explained by the authors (see Schweitzer et al., 2011; for more, see Schweitzer & Saks, 2011; Gurley & Marcus, 2008).

18.3.3 *Psychopathy*

Both the public and academicians are interested in the relationship between criminal law and psychopathy, and the advent of neuroimaging has sharpened that interest (see, e.g., Litton, 2007; Morse, 2008; Kiehl & Hoffman, 2011; Phillips, 2013; Fox, Kvaran, & Fontaine, 2013; Godman & Jefferson, 2014). Dr. Robert Hare, a pioneering expert on the subject of psychopathy, has defined the disorder as a "constellation of affective, interpersonal, and behavioral characteristics, including egocentricity; impulsivity; irresponsibility; shallow emotions; lack of empathy, guilt, or remorse; pathological lying; manipulativeness; and the persistent violation of social norms and expectations" (Hare, 1998; see also Cole Korponay et al., 2017).[75]

Psychopathy is generally estimated at roughly 1 percent of the male population (Hare, 1998; Kiehl & Hoffman, 2011, p. 356). While those with the disorder are disproportionately represented in the criminal justice system,[76] there is growing recognition that not all psychopaths are criminals.[77] Nonetheless, psychopaths often are overrepresented in the criminal justice system: 16 percent of the 6.7M adult males in prison, jail, and on parole or probation are psychopaths, and between 90 and 95 percent of adult male psychopaths in the United States are involved with the prison system (Kiehl & Hoffman, 2011), p. 356, collecting data). Amongst incarcerated inmates, psychopaths comprise between 15 and 25 percent of all male inmates, with nearly 80 percent imprisoned for violent crimes (see Kiehl & Hoffman, 2011, p. 377). Counterintuitively, psychopathy is much more common than most serious mental disorders, such as schizophrenia, bipolar disorder, and paranoia (Kiehl & Hoffman, 2011, p. 356). As many have noted, psychopathy has been largely resistant

---

[74] "Our opinion is that [structural neuroimaging] should support behavioural findings to reduce controversies in court."
[75] "Psychopathy is a mental health disorder characterized by shallow affect, callous disregard for others, and impulsive antisocial behavior."
[76] Apparently, psychopathy is more prevalent in men than in women; Kiehl and Hoffman (2011, p. 356, n.1), citing Nicholls et al. (2005). But see Phillips (2013, p. 14, n.85), which highlights the dearth of research on female psychopaths, although explaining that existing data suggest a slightly lower rate of psychopathy for women.
[77] See, e.g., Babiak (2007), discussing psychopathy in the workforce.

to treatment modalities.[78] And given the disproportionate number of psychopaths who commit murder and other serious violent crimes, neuroscience research about psychopaths is both relevant and important.[79]

For nearly two decades, Dr. Kent Kiehl has imaged the brains of diagnosed psychopaths and others in prison, accumulating a vast database. He claims there is a growing body of research to indicate that psychopathy is "highly correlated to aberrant neuronal activity in specific regions of the brain" (Kiehl & Hoffman, 2011, p. 362). Dr. Kiehl's and others' studies suggest that psychopaths have notably reduced neuronal activity in their paralimbic system compared to other people (see studies cited in Kiehl & Hoffman, 2011, p. 389, n.149; Espinoza et al., 2018). He argues that psychopaths' brain activity is "markedly deficient" in neural areas critical for moral judgment (Kiehl & Hoffman, 2011, pp. 389–390). At the same time, their brains show increased activity in the prefrontal cortex; leading some to conclude that psychopaths are "completely rational yet morally insane" (Kiehl & Hoffman, 2011, p. 390).[80]

Given that psychopathy may develop from abnormal neuronal activity that impairs individuals' conscience and their ability to empathize, should it be considered an excusing mental health disorder to crime under the category of legal insanity? Prominent scholars argue that psychopaths afflicted with a severe form of the disorder have serious deficits of rationality, which could be relevant to both questions of blame and punishment.[81] Such a view, of course, does not mean a psychopath behaving criminally should not be committed – they are dangerous and likely to reoffend (Litton, 2007, pp. 388–389).

Currently, the law does not recognize the view that a psychopath's utter lack of moral concern excuses criminal behavior. The Model Code provides that "mental disease or defect" does not include "an abnormality manifested only by repeated criminal or otherwise antisocial conduct"; a position followed fairly uniformly around the country (American Law Institute, 1985).[82] Moreover, many would argue that psychopaths *do* understand right and wrong, even if their appreciation of that distinction differs from the average person. Psychopathy as a defense would

---

[78] See Phillips (2013, pp. 19–20), collecting studies, but noting that there are some who believe certain types of treatment may be successful.

[79] For research studies, see, e.g. Kiehl et al. (2001) and other studies cited in Kiehl & Hoffman (2011, p. 389, n. 149).

[80] See also Korponay et al. (2017) discussing the association between psychopathy severity and size of prefrontal subregion volume.

[81] See Morse (2008, p. 208) and Litton (2007), who argue that psychopaths' incapacity for moral reasoning indicates a diminished capacity for rationality.

[82] See Model Penal Code §4.01

> 1) A person is not responsible for criminal conduct if at the time of such conduct as a result of mental disease or defect he lacks substantial capacity either to appreciate the criminality [wrongfulness] of his conduct or to conform his conduct to the requirements of law.
>
> 2) As used in this Article, the terms "mental disease or defect" do not include an abnormality manifested only by repeated criminal or otherwise antisocial conduct.

also fail under the volitional prong of insanity, as psychopaths are capable of resisting impulses that are not in their own self-interest.[83] Yet the ample neuroimaging done to date on psychopaths suggests that their neuronal activity is substantively different than most people. Additionally, there is a compelling argument that their rationality is truly impaired by the disorder; while believing they are acting in their own best interest, they often perversely act against it.

While the research on psychopathy is fascinating and presents important areas for continued study, its role in the courtroom is quite limited although there is potential for its use at sentencing. The government might want to use neuroimaging evidence to argue that the defendant poses a continuing danger, whereas the defense might wish to use it to argue he is biologically incapable of remorse. However, there have been efforts to establish that a psychopath may be *less* blameworthy, due to his impaired comprehension of moral blame. During the sentencing phase of convicted murderer Brian Dugan, Dr. Kiehl testified about the defendant's abnormal activity in the paralimbic system using diagrams to help explain Dugan's apparent inability to empathize with his victims.[84] The defense hoped that a neuroscience-based explanation of Dugan's impaired sense of right and wrong might sway the jury; they imposed the death penalty nonetheless.[85]

18.3.4 Sentencing

Neuroimaging evidence has become increasingly common during the sentencing of serious felony cases following convictions, particularly in murder cases and cases where the death penalty is a possible sentence.[86] While judges generally are responsible for sentencing following felony convictions, juries are tasked with deciding between death, or life in prison in capital cases. There is a federal death penalty statute,[87] which is invoked infrequently, and many states have a death penalty as well. During felony sentencing, courts consider much information that would not be admitted during the trial of a case, including hearsay and character evidence, as

---

[83] See Kiehl and Hoffman (2011, p. 371), commenting that psychopaths "can resist sticking their hands in a bee's nest to get honey, they just cannot resist reaching into another person's pocket to take money."
[84] See Hughes (2010) which discusses the case; and Phillips (2013, pp. 40–42) which reviews the neuroscience issues in the case.
[85] How the jury reached the verdict they did appears to be an intriguing story. Dugan's death sentence and those of the others on death row in Illinois were commuted by the Governor. For more on these two issues, see Hughes (2010).
[86] See, e.g., Denno (2015, p. 545, Chart 1), indicating that 553 of the total cases in her 800-case database involved neuroscience evidence at sentencing. Of those, 366 cases were during death penalty cases and 80 of them were non-death-penalty murder cases; Farahany (2015, p. 504), stating "neurobiological evidence seems clearly entrenched in sentencing decisions"; and Gaudet and Marchant (2016) finding that neuroimaging evidence in the penalty phase of capital cases was most commonly admitted as mitigating evidence. For more on neuroscience in capital punishment cases, see Snead (2007); Blume and Paavola (2011); Perlin and Lynch (2016).
[87] See The Federal Death Penalty Act, 18 U.S.C. §3591 (2012).

the formal rules of evidence do not apply at that phase in federal court[88] and in many state courts.[89]

The standard of proof in federal sentencing hearings "is the lowest in the criminal justice system: a fair preponderance of the evidence" (Gertner, 2016). The Federal Sentencing Guidelines provide only that evidence possess a "sufficient indicia of reliability to support its probable accuracy" (FSG §6A1.3).[90] Likewise, many state courts (where the vast majority of death penalty cases are litigated) admit far more evidence at sentencing than would be permissible at trial,[91] although a federal judge has written that the rules governing the reliability of expert testimony are usually applied in sentencing.[92] Despite variation amongst state rules governing states' sentencing procedures, most sentencing hearings admit evidence liberally and the trend has been to admit neuroscience evidence at sentencing, particularly in state court felonies. As noted by Deborah Denno in her large-scale empirical study, "[n]euroscience evidence is primarily used for mitigation" in sentencing, both in felony and death penalty cases (Denno, 2017, p. 504).[93]

In the federal system, the United States Sentencing Guidelines ("the Guidelines") were enacted in 1987 as a rigid and mechanistic system intended to limit judges' role in crafting sentencing, using a grid system of points and mandatory minimum sentences (see Gertner, 2010).[94] Although the Guidelines were held unconstitutional in 2005[95] and reduced to a status of "effectively advisory," they still appear to be exceptionally influential with the judiciary.[96]

The Guidelines permit a judge to evaluate the mental state of the defendant in sentencing, but only in very limited ways. The trial judge may consider whether the

[88] See, e.g., Federal Rule of Evidence 1101 (d) Exceptions. "These rules ... do not apply to the following: (3) miscellaneous proceedings such as: ... sentencing ...."

[89] See McCord and Bennett (2014), citing various state statutes. See also Slobogin (2017) noting that "in most jurisdictions, the usual rules of evidence do not apply."

[90] See also US Sentencing Guidelines Manual §6A1.3(a) (n.d.).

[91] Commentators note there is a lack of uniformity in sentencing rules, particularly those involving death-penalty cases. See McCord and Bennett (2014), which notes the "bewildering variety of approaches about which rules of evidence, if any, apply" during capital penalty phase hearings. For more on the vagaries of capital sentencing, see also Turlington (2008).

[92] See Donald and Bakies (2016), stating that the evidence rules governing expert testimony usually apply during sentencing. For more, see McCord and Bennett (2014, p. 429, n. 49) collecting cases indicating the rules governing expert testimony apply during the sentencing phase.

[93] For an early discussion of the admission of neuroimaging in sentencing (and in trials generally), see Moriarty (2008).

[94] Accord, Stith and Cabranes (1997): "The Guidelines require judges to address many quantitative and definitional issues in excruciating detail, while staying away from larger questions relating to culpability and the purposes of criminal punishment."

[95] The Sentencing Guidelines, which were promulgated in 1987, provided an express and rigid system of punishment, deterrence, incapacitation, and rehabilitation, but were held unconstitutional in 2005 and became "effectively advisory." See *United States* v. *Booker* (2005). For a summary of the history of sentencing pre and post Guidelines, see Donald and Bakies (2016) at pp. 489–492. For a more detailed and critical evaluation of the history of federal sentencing, see Gertner (2010).

[96] Gertner (2018) notes that "the Guidelines ... continue to 'anchor' American sentencing, regardless of whether they are obligatory."

"defendant committed the offense while suffering from a significantly reduced mental capacity ... that contributed substantially to the commission of the offense ..." (FSG §2.13).[97] They also provide that "[m]ental and emotional conditions may be relevant in determining whether a departure is warranted, if such conditions, individually or in combination with other offender characteristics, are present to an unusual degree and distinguish the case from the typical cases covered by the guidelines" (USSGM §5H1.3, 2018).

However, as noted by scholars, the mental capacity sections of the guidelines have not had a substantial effect. In a recent review of cases interpreting this section of the guidelines, the authors note that the role mental capacity plays in federal sentencing is far from dispositive (Perlin & Lynch, 2016).[98] Often, mental health issues play no role in federal non-capital-case sentencing, particularly where the defendant's criminal history suggests the defendant will pose a continuing danger (FSG §5K2.13).[99] Professor Slobogin notes that while some states are more open to mitigating evidence in noncapital case sentencing, other states follow the federal government's limited view (Slobogin, 2017, p. 583).

In death penalty litigation, juries generally consider both the prosecution's aggravating evidence and the defendant's mitigating evidence in deciding whether to apply the death penalty (see Denno, 2015, p. 502, citing Blume & Paavola, 2011). Critically, the US Supreme Court consistently affirms that defendants have a constitutional right to introduce mitigating evidence in penalty hearings (*Kansas v. Marsh*, 2006).[100] "[S]tates cannot limit the sentencer's consideration of any relevant circumstances that could cause it to decline to impose the [death] penalty" (*McCleskey v. Kemp*, 1987). Moreover, the Supreme Court has repeatedly affirmed that "a defendant has wide latitude to raise as a mitigating factor 'any aspect of [his or her] character or record and any of the circumstances of the offense that the defendant proffers as a basis for a sentence less than death'" (*Roper v. Simmons*, 2005).

---

[97] See United States Sentencing Guidelines, 18 U.S.C.A.,§5K2.13 Diminished Capacity (Policy Statement, n.d.). The section does not apply where the mental incapacity was caused by the voluntary ingestion of intoxications or where the defendant poses a danger to the public, amongst other reasons. "Significantly reduced mental capacity" tracks, in large part, the ALI language defining legal insanity: "'Significantly reduced mental capacity' means the defendant, although convicted, has a significantly impaired ability to (A) understand the wrongfulness of the behavior comprising the offense or to exercise the power of reason; or (B) control behavior that the defendant knows is wrongful." Id.

[98] The authors note that "[t]he cases that do take it into account appear to be idiosyncratic, unmoored by any overarching theory or by any uniform reliance on the sorts of external factors about which science potentially may offer some insights, other than the acknowledgement that there may be some biological basis for the behavior at issue."

[99] See Sentencing Guidelines at §5K2.13 (Diminished Capacity). As these guidelines are now advisory, there may be more willingness to depart downward, but as noted, the guidelines are still very influential; see Gertner (2018, p. 53).

[100] "[A] jury must have the opportunity to consider all evidence relevant to mitigation...."

According to Professor Denno's data, neuroscience evidence admitted in sentencing (in both felony and capital cases) includes evidence of serious mental illness (including schizophrenia and other delusional disorders), behavior disorders related to psychoactive substance abuse, and organic mental disorders (Denno, 2015, p. 504).[101] Notably, one half of the cases presented expert testimony that the defendant suffered brain damage, possibly from accidents, childhood beatings, or severe alcoholism (Denno, 2015, p. 504; see also Chart 3, p. 547). In nearly two thirds of these cases, at least one form of brain-imaging test was discussed in the testimony; most prevalent were CT, MRI, and EEG, but testifying experts also relied on PET, SPECT, and QEEG (Denno, 2015, p. 506; see also Chart 4, p. 548).

In sentencing, neuroimaging evidence is often used to confirm or explain traditional forms of mental health diagnoses; it is not used as the primarily diagnostic tool.[102] In many cases, the neuroimaging evidence is helpful in explaining head injury, toxic exposure, blast exposure, disease, or injury. The more questionable use of this evidence, however, is to provide an explanation for behavior, given the concerns about extrapolating from brain injury to behavior. This inferential leap from image to behavior is common in the courtroom, yet many with brain damage do not commit crimes and many without brain damage do (see Mayberg, 2014, p. 39). However, while it is clear from collected data that neuroimaging has been introduced in sentencing and may be particularly helpful in establishing mitigation in some felony and capital cases, sentencing bodies have not always been swayed by such evidence (see Denno, 2015).

18.3.5 Ineffective Assistance of Counsel

Defense counsel are charged with a legal and ethical obligation to provide competent representation to a defendant at "critical stages of a criminal proceeding" (*Lafler v. Cooper*, 2012). These "critical stages" include the decision to enter a guilty plea, during trial, or on appeal (*Lee v. United States*, 2017). Under the so-called "*Strickland*" standard, a defendant must show both that counsel's representation "fell below an objective standard of reasonableness" and that such performance resulted in actual prejudice to the defendant (*Lee v. United States*, 2017; *Strickland v. Washington*, 1984). To demonstrate prejudice, a defendant must show "a reasonable probability that, but for counsel's unprofessional errors, the result of the proceeding would have been different" (*Roe v. Flores-Ortega*, 2000). The Supreme Court described the standard as follows:

---

[101] For her breakdown of specific mental health issues, see Chart 2 at 546; Chart 3 at 547.
[102] See Denno (2015) discussing neuroscience evidence being used to support the confirmed diagnosis. Accord, Blume & Paavola (2011), which argues that "neuroimaging is ... a tool used to confirm the presence of brain dysfunction, not to investigate whether the client in fact has brain damage."

First, the defendant must show that counsel's performance was deficient. This requires showing that counsel made errors so serious that counsel was not functioning as the "counsel" guaranteed the defendant by the Sixth Amendment. Second, the defendant must show that the deficient performance prejudiced the defense. This requires showing that counsel's errors were so serious as to deprive the defendant of a fair trial, a trial whose result is reliable. (*Strickland v. Washington*, 1984)

The ineffective assistance standard is very high and rarely met in most posttrial proceedings (*Strickland v. Washington*, 1984; see also, Smith, 2010), given the "strong presumption that counsel's conduct falls within the wide range of reasonable professional assistance" (*Strickland v. Washington*, 1984). However, claims of ineffective assistance have provided the basis for either a new trial and/or a new sentencing in many capital cases, which constitute a small percentage of all convictions (Marcus, 2016). During the last decade, many defendants have alleged that counsel was ineffective in capital murder cases for failing to employ or properly use neuroscience evidence.[103] These ineffective assistance of counsel claims have proved to be fertile grounds for defense counsel seeking to reverse convictions.

The Supreme Court has repeatedly focused on the role of the attorney in mitigation, particularly as involves the defendants' "cognitive and intellectual deficiencies" (Denno, 2015, p. 506). As noted by Professor Denno, "nearly all of the successful claims [of ineffective assistance] were based on an attorney's failure to appropriately investigate, gather, or understand neuroscience evidence" (Denno, 2015, p. 507). Professor Farahany came to a similar conclusion, based upon her empirical study. Finding that the failure to investigate a brain abnormality frequently constitutes ineffective assistance of counsel, she concludes that neurobiological evidence is "in a rarified position of must-investigate evidence" (Farahany, 2015, p. 505).

Nonetheless, while arguing that trial counsel's failure to investigate and/or present neuroscience evidence about brain damage or serious mental impairment may be a successful strategy for an ineffectiveness claim, that does not always translate into a different outcome on retrial (or resentencing).[104] It is clear, however, that judges are recognizing the importance of neuroscience evidence and over time, it may become more persuasive to juries.

18.3.6 *Juveniles in the Criminal System*

Neuroscience data appear to have been influential in the US Supreme Court on decisions about the death penalty and felony sentencing for juveniles in three key

---

[103] Farahany (2015, p. 504), which notes that 44 percent of the neurobiological claims raised in mitigation were claims made by defendants of ineffective assistance, split between capital cases and other felonies.

[104] See, e.g., Slobogin (2017), which notes that the utility of neuroscience, even at capital sentencing, "may be a mixed bag."

decisions issued by the Supreme Court: *Roper* v. *Simmons* (see *Roper* v. *Simmons*, 2005); *Graham* v. *Florida* (see *Graham* v. *Florida*, 2010); and *Miller* v. *Alabama* (see *Miller* v. *Alabama*, 2012). Unlike the majority of criminal cases in which neuroscience evidence is used on behalf of an individual at trial or sentencing, the evidence in these cases concerned a category of individuals – adolescents. Briefs filed by amicus curiae in the Supreme Court provided a wealth of neuroscience to support the position that adolescents are substantively different from adults in how they think, evaluate risk, and make decisions.[105] The brief of the American Medical Association et al. (2004), for example, relied extensively on neuroimaging studies to support its argument that adolescents' immaturity "mirrors the anatomical immaturity of their brains." The brief of the American Psychological Association (2004) likewise cited neuroscience to provide biological support for its argument about adolescent immaturity.

In *Roper* v. *Simmons* (2005), the Supreme Court of the United States held that the execution of individuals who were under eighteen years of age violated the Eighth Amendment to the US Constitution.[106] The Court noted three differences between juveniles and adults. First, given the lack of maturity and undeveloped sense of responsibility in the young, their actions "often result in impetuous and ill-considered actions and decisions" (*Roper* v. *Simmons*, 2004). Secondly, juveniles "are more vulnerable or susceptible to negative influences and outside pressures, including peer pressure" (*Roper* v. *Simmons*, 2004). And third, the "character of a juvenile is not as well formed as that of an adult" as their personality traits "are more transitory, less fixed" (*Roper* v. *Simmons*, 2004). As a result of these three differences, the court concluded that from a moral standpoint, it would be "misguided to equate the failings of a minor with those of any adult" (*Roper* v. *Simmons*, 2004), given a greater possibility that a minor's character, as compared to an adult's, could be reformed.

In both their written brief and in oral argument, counsel for Simmons emphasized the neuroscience support for his argument that adolescent brains were not the same as adult brains in matters of impulsivity, decision making, and moral judgments,[107] although the Court did not explicitly cite neuroscience studies in its opinion, choosing to mention only behavioral and social science in addition to other forms of legal authority (*Roper* v. *Simmons*, 2004). Professor Laurence Steinberg, a globally recognized expert on adolescents whose work was cited repeatedly in *Roper*, noted that discussions about neurobiological science occupied a "fair amount of discussion" during oral argument (Steinberg, 2017).

---

[105] Amicus curiae, or "friend of the court," is a process by which a person who is not a party to the lawsuit petitions the court to file a brief in the action because of a strong interest in the subject of the case.

[106] "[A] majority of States have rejected the imposition of the death penalty on juvenile offenders under 18, and we now hold this is required by the Eighth Amendment." The Eighth Amendment to the US Constitution provides that "Excessive bail shall not be required, nor excessive fines imposed, nor cruel and unusual punishments inflicted."

[107] See Maroney (2009), citing the oral argument in *Roper* and brief for respondent.

Five years later in *Graham v. Florida*, the Supreme Court again addressed the difference between juveniles and adults in a sentencing context. In *Graham*, the issue before the court was whether a juvenile could be sentenced to life in prison without parole for a nonhomicide crime (*Graham v. Florida*, 2010). The court explicitly stated that "developments in psychology and brain science continue to show fundamental differences between juvenile and adult minds" and that juveniles are "more capable of change than adults" (*Graham v. Florida*, 2010). In holding that the Eighth Amendment forbids the sentence of life without parole for juvenile nonhomicide offenders (*Graham v. Florida*, 2010), the Court referenced neurobiological evidence as support for its recognition of the difference between adults and juveniles.

The issue presented in *Miller v. Alabama* in 2012 was whether an individual sentenced to mandatory life imprisonment without parole for a homicide committed when the individual was under the age of eighteen violated the Eighth Amendment. Justice Kagan, writing for the Supreme Court, concluded that such a law was unconstitutional. "We ... hold that mandatory life without parole for those under the age of 18 at the time of their crimes violates the Eighth Amendment's prohibition on 'cruel and unusual punishments'" (*Miller v. Alabama*, 2012). One of the defendants was only fourteen years old at the time of the homicide.[108] Here, the Court cited its own language in *Graham* that "'developments in psychology and brain science continue to show fundamental differences between juvenile and adult minds' – for example, in 'parts of the brain involved in behavior control'" (*Miller v. Alabama*, 2012). Citing amicus briefs submitted in the case, the Court also mentioned that both developmental psychology and neuroscience confirm and strengthen the court's earlier conclusions in *Roper* and *Graham* (*Miller v. Alabama*, 2012).[109] *Miller* requires that prior to "sentencing a juvenile to life without parole, the sentencing judge take into account 'how children are different, and how those differences counsel against irrevocably sentencing them to a lifetime in prison'" (*Montgomery v. Louisiana*, 2016).[110] The mandate from the Supreme Court was that sentencing juveniles to this "harshest possible penalty" will be an uncommon event (*Miller v. Alabama*, 2012).

While scientists may recognize that neuroscience data do not make the behavioral differences between adults and juveniles "any more real" (Steinberg, 2017, p. 415) the

[108] In *Miller*, Jackson was convicted of homicide and sentenced to mandatory life in prison without parole for his role in a homicide, where he was outside a store when his companions attempted to rob the clerk. When Jackson walked into the store, one of his companions shot the clerk after she threatened to call police. Jackson was convicted under the so-called "felony murder rule," attributing "death caused in the course of a felony to all participants who intended to commit the felony, regardless of whether they killed or intended to kill." *Miller*, 567 US at 491, Breyer, J., concurring, but writing separately to argue that this type of "transferred intent" is insufficient to subject a juvenile to a sentence of life without parole.

[109] In 2016, The Court held that *Miller* announced a new substantive rule and thus, the rule was entitled to be retroactively applied to juveniles whose convictions were final when *Miller* was decided.

[110] See *Montgomery v. Louisiana* (2016), quoting *Miller* and *Graham*.

structural and functional differences between these groups' brains may have been influential to the court in establishing the immutability of these distinctions (Steinberg, 2017, p. 415). Given that brain maturation follows a "specific and predictable pattern" consistent with behavioral changes, neuroscience certainly supports claims (and generally accepted knowledge) that juveniles are less mature than adults.

In the decade and a half since the Court decided *Roper*, neuroscientific progress has "revealed a more nuanced understanding of the physiological markers of youth, how those markers affect behavior, and ways in which young people's brains continue to develop into their mid-20s" (Blume et al., 2020).[111] While the Supreme Court majority's jurisprudential focus on the neurobiological difference between adolescent and adult brains remained strong over that decade in which the cases were written, there were strong dissenting positions in *Miller*, *Graham*, and *Roper*.

Also, many scholars are worried that the consideration of juveniles as a category is problematic, given that not all adolescents are the same and that trials are generally focused on one adolescent, not adolescents as a group. On the other hand, many believe that these cases represent a well-grounded use of neuroscience to explain agreed-upon findings from multiple studies.[112]

18.4 NEUROSCIENCE LIE DETECTION

Perhaps no other area of neuroimaging evidence has engendered more critical commentary than lie detection. To date, there are dozens of published studies about neuroscience lie detection,[113] along with extensive commentary on the subject by science, legal, and ethics scholars (for a sample, see, e.g., Zeki et al., 2004; Pardo, 2005; Wolpe, Foster, & Langleben, 2005; Greely & Illes, 2007; Moriarty, 2009; Brown & Murphy, 2010; Schauer, 2010; Shen & Jones, 2011; Meixner, 2012; Langleben & Moriarty, 2013; Farah et al., 2014). While there are various forms of neuroscience lie detection,[114] this section focuses solely on fMRI lie detection studies.

Neuroscience lie detection studies assume that lying increases cognitive load when compared with truth telling. Studies find that various areas of the brain are engaged during lying and that those areas react in measurable ways during lying but not during truth telling. While there are good reasons to believe that many of these assumptions are well grounded, it is uncertain whether the pattern of activation in lie detection is actually specific to lying or other forms of cognitive thought (see Farah

---

[111] The authors argue that the "bright line" the court chose to use in *Roper* – eighteen years old – is too low, given the developments in understanding of neuroscience. *Id.* at pp. 10–17.

[112] For a helpful explanation of the implications of using neuroscience data with respect to juvenile justice, see Shen (2013).

[113] See summary collected in Langleben et al. (2016); Abe (2011); and Moriarty (2009).

[114] J. Peter Rosenfeld and colleagues have engaged in well-known and extensive work on lie detection using electroencephalograph (EEG) (see, e.g., Rosenfeld, 1999; Rosenfeld et al., 2004).

et al., 2014, p. 125; Moriarty, 2009). For example, while data suggest that there is a "functional contribution of the prefrontal cortex [PFC] to deception" (Abe, 2011, p. 567), it is likewise clear that the activity in the PFC is related to many forms of higher-order thinking (Moriarty, 2009, p. 749; Farah et al., 2014, p. 125). Additionally, many of the studies have found different regions in the PFC activated during deception tasks (Abe, 2011, discussing studies p. 565).

There are multiple concerns about the validity of neuroscience lie detection research. A primary shortcoming is the relatively artificial nature of the testing paradigm and its lack of ecological validity. First, participants are often instructed to lie about matters as part of the test. Additionally, there is little at stake for those involved in the testing; the tests do not approximate real-life concerns; the lies are about unimportant matters; and third, countermeasures may be effective.[115] In addition, many researchers and commentators have noted that there are different types of lies, and memory flaws may be confounding in distinguishing between truth and lies (Langleben & Moriarty, 2013, collecting studies). A number of researchers have noted the lack of replication studies and the relatively small size of all the studies to date (Langleben & Moriarty, 2013, collecting studies). Significantly, much of the original research was based upon group data, although some of the more recent studies have individual data (Langleben et al., 2016).

While these concerns are legitimate and highlight the hurdles for neuroscience lie detection as legal evidence,[116] some data suggest it may be possible eventually to distinguish between truth and lies. "Under certain, controlled laboratory conditions, endorsed lie and truth were distinguished in individual subjects with 76–90% accuracy" (Langleben & Moriarty, 2013, p. 228, collecting studies). In a recent study, researchers conducted a blind, prospective, and controlled within-subjects study to compare the accuracy of fMRI and polygraph in the detection of concealed information (Langleben et al., 2016). That study concluded that the accuracy rates amongst fMRI were very high and that the interrater reliability was much higher with fMRI testing than with polygraph (Langleben et al., 2016). Nonetheless, countermeasures are likely effective for fMRI lie detection (see, e.g., Ganis et al., 2011) and understanding true error rate will require determining the positive and negative predictive powers of lie detection (Langleben & Moriarty, 2013). There are many issues that must be resolved before one can say whether fMRI lie detection will work in the real world. "[The] diverse [research] scenarios, fMRI designs, and data analysis approaches do not allow a direct comparison or an estimate of the overall error rates of the technology. Moreover, they raise the question whether overall error rates are a meaningful variable or whether error rates for each testing scenario need to be evaluated separately" (Langleben & Moriarty, 2013, p. 229).[117]

---

[115] On countermeasures, see Ganis et al. (2011).
[116] The Court of Appeals for the Sixth Circuit upheld the trial court's decision to exclude defendant's fMRI lie detection expert testimony in *United States v. Semrau*, (2012). This case provides an in-depth analysis of the shortcomings of such evidence.
[117] For additional concerns, see Farah et al. (2014).

Litigants in both civil and criminal cases have attempted, unsuccessfully, to introduce fMRI evidence into court to support claims that they were telling the truth.[118] One civil case, *Wilson v. Corestaff*, was in a *Frye* state court jurisdiction, while a criminal case, *United States v. Semrau*, was in a federal *Daubert* jurisdiction. Both cases excluded the evidence. In *Wilson*, the court determined that the testimony did not meet the Frye standard of admissibility:

> Even a cursory review of the scientific literature demonstrates that the plaintiff is unable to establish that the use of the fMRI test to determine truthfulness or deceit is accepted as reliable in the relevant scientific community. The scientific literature raises serious issues about the lack of acceptance of the fMRI test in the scientific community to show a person's past mental state or to gauge credibility. (*Wilson v. Corestaff*, 2010, p. 642)

The court in *Wilson* also held that the testimony impinged upon the province of the jury on the issue of credibility and thus should be treated with a great deal of skepticism – consistent with the way most courts treat polygraph evidence.

In *United States v. Semrau*, Magistrate Judge Tu Pham conducted a thorough two-day hearing to determine whether the proposed evidence met the *Daubert* standard of reliability. The district court adopted the Magistrate's lengthy report and recommendation in its entirety,[119] and the rulings and rationale were affirmed by the Court of Appeals for the Sixth Circuit. The courts all agreed that while the evidence had been tested in a laboratory setting and subjected to some peer review and publication, it was uncertain what the rate of error was, particularly outside of the laboratory. "[T]here are no known error rates for fMRI-based lie detection outside the laboratory setting, *i.e.*, in the 'real-world' or 'real-life' setting" (*United States v. Semrau*, 2012).[120] This concern about ecological validity – real-world application of neuroscience lie detection – is central to the *Semrau* case and reflects a primary concern with those researchers who are engaged in studying the subject:

> There was simply no formal research presented at the *Daubert* hearing demonstrating how the brain might respond to fMRI lie detection testing examining potential deception about real world, long-term conduct occurring several years before testing in which the subject faces extremely dire consequences (such as a prison sentence) if his answers are not believed. (*United States v. Semrau*, 2012, p. 522)

Thus, not only was the error rate essentially unknowable but it affected the other *Daubert* factors as well. "Because the use of fMRI-based lie detection is still in its

---

[118] See *United States v. Semrau* (2012); *Wilson v. Corestaff* (2010). In an unreported trial court decision, *State v. Smith* (2011), a court in Maryland likewise excluded fMRI lie detection evidence. See The MacArthur Foundation Research Network on Law and Neuroscience (2016).

[119] The Magistrate's report can be found at *United States v. Semrau*, 2010 WL 6845092 (W.D. Tenn. June 1, 2010).

[120] *United States v. Semrau*, 2012 (2012), quoting the Magistrate Judge's report and recommendation.

early stages of development, standards controlling the real-life application have not yet been established" (*United States* v. *Semrau*, 2012, p. 522).[121]

In addition to the apparent lack of real-world reliability that fMRI lie detection currently possesses, both the *Semrau* and *Wilson* courts expressed concern that the proposed evidence did not meet the general acceptance test – also known as the *Frye* standard.[122] In *Daubert*, the court included *Frye* as a possible factor in deciding whether evidence should be admissible: "A known technique which has been able to attract only minimal support within the community may properly be viewed with skepticism." In *Semrau*, this attention to the lack of support seemed to be apt, where the magistrate judge and the court of appeals cited ample criticisms by various researchers about the inadequacies of neuroscience lie detection research.[123]

In addition to the problem of reliability, the *Semrau* court (like the court in *Wilson*), excluded the testimony under a rule of evidence that permits courts to exclude evidence if its probative value is substantially outweighed by the danger of confusing the issues or misleading the jury, a process generally termed a "403 weighing."[124] Although there were multiple reasons to exclude the testimony pursuant to this weighing, one issue had implications for lie detection generally. As the Court of Appeals for the Sixth Circuit and many other state and federal courts have held in polygraph cases, using lie detection solely to bolster witnesses' credibility is "highly prejudicial," especially when credibility issues are central to the verdict (see generally, *United States* v. *Sherlin*, 1995; see also *United States* v. *Scheffer*, 1998).[125] Many good reasons support judicial disfavor of polygraph evidence: it has limited reliability; it potentially usurps the jury's role as fact-finder; and is not particularly helpful to the jury, in that it simply vouches for the credibility of a witness (*United States* v. *Charley*, 1999; for more, see Langleben & Moriarty, 2013).

After *Semrau*, interest in using fMRI lie detection seemed to wane amongst litigants. The studies have yet still to be replicated, countermeasures may well be effective, and it is wholly uncertain whether the data will be reproducible in large populations or whether there will be interest in funding such studies. Despite the

---

[121] Semrau also presented numerous other problems about how the tests were administered and interpreted, but most of these issues were unique to the situation and not relevant to the more pressing question of whether fMRI lie detection is a generally reliable scientific method.

[122] While the *Frye* standard was only retained in New York state courts, it has also remained a part of the federal courts' *Daubert* analysis, as explained earlier.

[123] See 2010 WL 6845092 at *13; 693 F.3d at 521–523.

[124] FRE 403, entitled "Excluding Relevant Evidence for Prejudice, Confusion, Waste of Time, or Other Reasons" provides:

> The court may exclude relevant evidence if its probative value is substantially outweighed by a danger of one or more of the following: unfair prejudice, confusing the issues, misleading the jury, undue delay, wasting time, or needlessly presenting cumulative evidence.

Most state courts have a similar rule.

[125] "[J]urisdictions may legitimately determine that the aura of infallibility attending polygraph evidence can lead jurors to abandon their duty to assess credibility and guilt."

chorus of commentary condemning the use of neuroscience lie detection in court, one prominent academic noted that juries' subjective assessments of credibility are markedly unreliable and neuroscience lie detection may already be an improvement (Schauer, 2010, pp. 1191–1220).

Yet, there is much about lie detection that causes most of us distress. The discomfort may rest on our reverence for the privacy of own thoughts, our distaste for giving evidence against ourselves, or our entrenched belief that it is the government's job to prove guilt. As many scholars have written, government-compelled neuroscience lie detection implicates constitutional concerns related to privacy and self-incrimination under the Fourth and Fifth Amendments (see Pardo, 2005; Shen, 2014). But given the current state of the science, the strong rejection of fMRI lie detection by courts, and the distaste for lie detection evidence, it seems unlikely that neuroscience lie detection will become a tool for the courtroom in the near future.

18.5 CIVIL CASES: NEUROSCIENCE AND TRAUMA

For the last few decades, many courts have evaluated scientific and expert evidence using a reliability standard, although some still use the general acceptance test or an even more relaxed standard of mere helpfulness (Giannelli et al., 2020). In their analysis of such evidence, the courts have reviewed prosecutorial expert evidence much more leniently than one would expect, given the shortcomings of much forensic science evidence (Moriarty, 2018).[126] As Professor Erin Murphy notes, that "when it comes to proffers of scientific evidence, civil and criminal proceedings are not in fact created equal" (Murphy, 2016; see also Seaman, 2013). However, in civil cases, many courts have also been willing to permit neuroimaging evidence for various reasons.

Civil cases involving neuroimaging include litigation about brain trauma related to accidents, motor vehicle collisions, products liability, and medical malpractice (Moriarty, 2018).[127] Other cases involve brain injury due to sports concussion (Telis, 2014; Grey, Marchant, & Tyszka, 2015;).[128] Litigants have raised issues of competency related to Alzheimer's disease and other forms of neurodegenerative diseases,[129] and there have been lawsuits about the possible effects of violent video games on

[126] This article discusses how courts have skirted the reliability problem of much forensic science evidence. For more on the shortcoming of such evidence, see both National Research Council (2009), and President's Council of Advisors on Sci. & Tech., Exec. Office of the President, Forensic Science In Criminal Courts: Ensuring Scientific Validity of Feature-Comparison Methods 46 (2016).

[127] See Shen (2016) which discusses the emergence of forensic neuropsychology in the area of civil litigation in the 1980s and 1990s; Taylor (2015) which discusses the history of "neurolaw" in cases of traumatic brain injury; and Liu (2015) which catalogues many types of civil cases involving neuroimaging evidence.

[128] Telis (2014) discusses the individual suits that NFL players have filed against the NFL for concussion-related injuries they sustained playing football.

[129] See cases cited in Jones, Schall, and Shen (2014); and Moriarty (2008). For a helpful discussion of the potential role of neuroscience with respect to these issues, see Grey (2018).

children's developing brains (see *Entertainment Software Association v. Blagojevich*, 2006). Research and extensive legal scholarship addresses the use of neuroimaging to evaluate pain (see e.g., Davis et al., 2017; Pustilnik, 2012; Kolber, 2007), a subject with important implications for litigation. This chapter will focus primarily on civil litigation involving brain trauma and will examine both the difficulties posed by the science and by the proof of such injuries.

18.5.1 *Trauma*

Traumatic brain injury (TBI) is a worldwide public health concern and the leading cause of death in adolescents and children (Aggarwal & Ford, 2013) and contributes to roughly 30 percent of all injury deaths in the United States (Taylor et al., 2017). Approximately 3 million people in the United States seek medical attention annually for TBI (Levin & Diaz-Arrastia, 2015)[130] and over 5 million Americans live with a disability caused by TBI (Aggarwal & Ford, 2013). According to collected US data, most TBIs are caused by falls, road traffic accidents, blunt trauma, and assaults (see Taylor et al., 2017). Military personnel have a substantially elevated risk of sustaining TBI (Levin & Diaz-Arrastia, 2015, p. 506). Military in both the Iraq and Afghanistan conflicts have suffered from a greater percentage of TBIs than those involved in any other major conflict (Eskridge et al., 2012) and between 12 and 20 percent of those returning veterans are diagnosed with TBI as a result of blast exposure (see Moriarty et al., 2013). The aging population likewise suffers from TBI, often due to falls (Roozenbeek, Maas, & Menon, 2013).

TBI can cause a variety of problems related to physical, cognitive, and psychological disorders and is often linked with serious functional impairment (see generally, Stocchetti & Zanier, 2016). Those with TBI often have problems with impulsivity, impaired attention and decision making, and poor executive function (see Aggarwal & Ford, 2013, p. 791; Roozenbeek et al., 2013, p. 231). Many TBI patients subsequently develop depression as well (see Roozenbeek et al., 2013, p. 231).[131] Thus, it is hardly surprising that many cases, both civil and criminal, involve claims of TBI.

TBI is a complicated diagnosis and there are serious questions about how to define, diagnose, and treat the disorder. One international group has proposed a broad definition of TBI to include "an alteration in brain function, or other evidence of brain pathology, caused by an external force," while other groups have different definitional standards (Roozenbeek et al., 2013, p. 232).[132] Nonetheless, as noted by experts in the field, the term TBI "continues to be plagued by ambiguity,

---

[130] For more data, see Faul et al. (2010).
[131] Noting that "30–70% of TBI survivors develop depression."
[132] Citing the Working Group on Demographics and Clinical Assessment of the International Interagency Initiative toward Common Data Elements for Research in TBI and Psychological Health, Menon et al. (2010).

especially at the mild end of the severity spectrum of TBI" (Roozenbeek et al., 2013; see also Granacher, 2008). The confusion about defining mild TBI (mTBI), where it fits on the spectrum of severity, and whether it causes long-term complications are concerns not only for medicine and psychology, but for the legal system. While patient history is used as the "gold standard" approach to diagnosing TBI, there is a recognized need for testing to help strengthen physicians' abilities to better identify TBI in patients – particularly for mTBI and where the report of the injury occurs much later in time (see Roozenbeek et al., 2013, p. 232).

Physicians classify TBI as mild, moderate, or severe, based upon initial Glasgow coma scale (GCS) scores from the ER, coupled with the duration of both loss of consciousness and post-traumatic amnesia (see Levin & Diaz-Arrastia, 2015, p. 506). The American Congress of Rehabilitation Medicine (ACRM) diagnosis of mTBI requires evidence that the head was struck or the brain underwent acceleration/deacceleration movement (coup/contrecoup injury) and one of the following: a GCS score of 13–15 within 30 minutes of presentation; loss of consciousness of up to 30 minutes; post-traumatic amnesia of less than 24 hours; a period of confusion or disorientation, or transient neurological abnormalities not requiring surgery (see Levin & Diaz-Arrastia, 2015, p. 507). Mild TBI and concussion are considered interchangeable terms and sports concussion is a subtype of mTBI (see Levin & Diaz-Arrastia, 2015, p. 506). While mTBIs are a common problem of sports-related injuries and those who suffer falls, they also affect thousands of active duty servicepeople and veterans exposed to head trauma from combat and martial training, activities in dangerous areas, and blast/explosion exposure (see Johnson, Partridge, & Gilbert, 2015; Levin & Diaz-Arrastia, 2015, p. 506). Also complicating the diagnosis of mTBI is its overlap with various disorders, including post-traumatic stress disorder (PTSD), depression, and such physical symptoms as "dizziness, headache, nausea, problems with attention, memory problems, impulsivity, and poor judgment" (Shenton et al., 2018).

Mild TBI, which forms the basis for many contentious legal claims, presents an area of controversy in terms of both imaging and the course of recovery. As is well recognized, individuals with mTBI often have normal structural neuroimaging findings as imaged by either CT or MRI (see studies collected in Belanger et al., 2007; Shenton et al., 2018, p. 56). Thus, in many legal cases involving mTBI, plaintiffs may introduce expert testimony about various aspects of injury, behavior, and cognition, but may not have structural neuroimaging proof to support their claims.

Researchers have begun working with DTI to attempt to image injuries caused by mTBI in the white matter of the brain. Diffuse axonal injury is believed to be the "predominant pathologic mechanism underlying mTBI" (Levin & Diaz-Arrastia, 2015, p. 508). This radiological evidence is the most sensitive tool currently available for imaging diffuse axonal injuries believed to be caused by mTBI (see Shenton et al., 2018, p. 52). While current studies suggest that DTI is may provide superior imaging for identifying white matter injuries in the brain that are not visible on MRI or CT, there is still much to be learned. Critics note that the studies of DTI are relatively new (since 2011); compare groups of people, not individuals (mTBI patients compared to controls); and have not yet been sufficiently standardized for use in individual patients in clinical or forensic use (see Shenton et al., 2018, p. 59). One group of researchers note that although DTI shows great promise, "[there are] inconsistencies across studies in the direction of altered diffusion; between centres [there are] various imaging protocols, quality assurance, and analysis techniques; and the scarcity of normative data applicable across centers [has] to be resolved before clinical application is an option" (see Levin & Diaz-Arrastia, 2015, p. 508). Others, however, are more bullish in their beliefs that DTI is ready for the courtroom and have testified to that effect, sometimes successfully.

Many TBI cases may also include a PET scan, despite serious concerns that PET scans are not clinically appropriate for diagnosing TBI. The American College of Radiology does not recommend PET for imaging brain trauma (Shetty, et al, 2016). In many cases, experts have testified that individuals with mTBI have abnormal PET scans, claiming that such individuals have abnormal functioning in their prefrontal cortex. In these cases, experts will often attempt to correlate the alleged abnormality with behavioral and cognitive deficits (Moriarty et al., 2013). Thus, the courts are often faced with neuroimaging that is either a poor fit (PET) or is or without recognized medical use (DTI) to prove brain trauma. As is clear, however, from the many experts testifying on both of these subjects, many courts are admitting this evidence.

18.6 CONCLUSION

Neuroimaging evidence in the United States has developed at a rapid pace and has become a fixture in many courts around the country. It has been admitted in criminal cases and civil cases and has appeared in US Supreme Court decisions. The use of this evidence is, in most cases, not the primary element of proof. Rather, it is used in ways that support other forms of more traditional expert testimony. Without question, neuroimaging evidence has been helpful in providing brain-based proof for courts dealing with serious questions of law, such as the responsibility of minors for criminal actions. Neuroimaging may also be helpful for those cases in which there is very serious brain trauma or illness – the neurological explanation for severe cognitive deficits may be influential with both juries and judges.

Nonetheless, the problems with neuroimaging evidence are troubling and raise questions about its proper role in the courtroom. Given the concerns outlined in this chapter about the foundational shortcomings of basic neuroscience research and the concerns over reliability, neuroimaging evidence poses formidable challenges for judges attempting to regulate its proper use. More co-created standards between scientists/physicians and the legal profession would likely improve the quality of the scientific evidence, and there are helpful publications emerging that outline areas of consensus (Meltzer et al., 2014). More work in this direction would guide both courts and experts about the use of neuroimaging in the courtroom.

REFERENCES

Abe, N. (2011). How the Brain Shapes Deception. *The Neuroscientist* 17(5), 560–574.
Abbate v. United States, 359 U.S. 187, 195 (1959).
Advisory Committee Notes to the Federal Rules of Evidence, Rule 702, 2000 Amendment.
Aggarwal, N. K., & Ford, E. (2013). The Neuroethics and Neurolaw of Brain Injury. *Behavioral Sciences & the Law* 31(6), 789–802.
Aguirre, G. K. (2014). Functional Neuroimaging: Technical, Logical, and Social Perspectives. *Hastings Center Report* 45, S8–18.
American Law Institute. (1985). Model Penal Code.
Anderson v. Akzo Nobel Coatings, Inc., 260 P.3d 857 (Wash. en banc., 2011).
Assaf, Y., & Pasternak, O. (2007). Diffusion Tensor Imaging (DTI)-based White Matter Mapping in Brain Research: A Review. *Journal of Molecular Neuroscience* 34(1), 51–61.
Babiak, P. (2007). From Darkness Into the Light: Psychopathy in Industrial and Organizational Psychology. In H. Hervé & J. C. Yuille (eds.), *The Psychopath: Theory, Research, and Practice* (pp. 411–428). Mahwah, NJ: Lawrence Erlbaum Associates Publishers.
Belanger, H. G., Vanderploeg, R. D., Curtiss, G., & Warden, D. L. (2007). Recent Neuroimaging Techniques in Mild Traumatic Brain Injury. *The Journal of Neuropsychiatry and Clinical Neurosciences* 19(1), 5–20.
Betz v. Pneumo Abex, LLC, 44 A.3d 27, 53 (PA 2012).
Bigler, E. D., Allen, M., & Stimac, G. K. (2012). MRI and Functional MRI. In J. R. Simpson (ed.), *Neuroimaging in Forensic Psychiatry: From the Clinic to the Courtroom*. Chichester: Wiley-Blackwell, pp. 27–40.
Bigler, E. D., Jantz, P. B., Freedman, D., & Woods, G. W. (2015). Structural Neuroimaging in Forensic Settings. *University of Missouri-Kansas City Law Review* 84, 311–313.
Blume, J. H., Freedman, H., Vann, L., & Hritz, A. C. (2020). Death by Numbers: Why Evolving Standards Compel Extending Roper's Categorical Ban Against Executing Juveniles From 18 to 21. *Texas Law Review* 98, 921–951.
Blume, J. H., & Paavola, E.C. (2011). Life, Death, and Neuroimaging: The Advantages and Disadvantages of the Defense's Use of Neuroimages in Capital Cases – Lessons from the Front. *Mercer Law Review* 62, 909–931.
Brouard v. Convery, 70 N.Y.S.3d 820 (N.Y. Sup. Ct. 2018).
Brown, T., & Murphy, E. (2010). Through a Scanner Darkly: Functional Neuroimaging as Evidence of a Criminal Defendant's Past Mental States. *Stanford Law Review* 62, 1119–1208.
Button, K. S., Ioannidis, J. P., Mokrysz, C. et al. (2013). Power Failure: Why Small Sample Size Undermines the Reliability of Neuroscience. *Nature Reviews Neuroscience* 14(5), 365–376.
Chisholm v. Champion Ent. Inc., 2003 WL 25685508, *4 (D.C. Wyo. 2003).
Clark v. Arizona, 548 U. S. 735 (2006).
C.W. and E.W., ex rel. Wood v. Textron, Inc., 807 F.3d 827, 832 (7th Cir. 2015).

Daubert v. Merrell Dow Pharmaceuticals, Inc., 509 U.S. 579, 113 S. Ct. 2786, 125 L. Ed. 2d 469 (1993).
Davis, K. D., Flor, H., Greely, H.T., et al. (2017). Brain Imaging Tests for Chronic Pain: Medical, Legal and Ethical Issues and Recommendations. *Nature Reviews Neurology* 13 (10), 624–638.
Denno, D. W. (2015). The Myth of the Double-Edged Sword: An Empirical Study of Neuroscience Evidence in Criminal Cases. *Boston College Law Review* 56, 493–551.
Denno, D. W. (2017). Concocting Criminal Intent. *Georgetown Law Journal* 105, 323–378.
Drope v. Missouri, 420 U.S. 162 (1975).
Donald, B. B., & Bakies, E. (2016). A Glimpse Inside the Brain's Black Box: Understanding the Role of Neuroscience in Criminal Sentencing. *Fordham Law Review* 85, 481–502.
Dusky v. United States, 362 U.S. 402, 402 (1960).
Elonis v. United States, 135 S. Ct. 2001, 2010 (2015).
Entertainment Software Association v. Blagojevich, 404 F. Supp. 2d 1051 (N.D. Ill. 2005), aff'd, 469 F.3d 641 (7th Cir. 2006).
Eskridge, S. L., Macera, C. A., Galarneau, M. R. et al. (2012). Injuries From Combat Explosions in Iraq: Injury Type, Location, and Severity. *Injury* 43(10), 1678–1682.
Espinoza, F. A., Vergara, V. M., Reyes, D., et al. (2018). Aberrant Functional Network Connectivity in Psychopathy from a Large (N = 985) Forensic Sample. *Human Brain Mapping* 39(6), 2624–2634.
Faigman, D. L., Cheng, E. K., Mnookin, J., et al. (2018–2019). Modern Scientific Evidence, §8.2 Mens rea and mental disorder – "Diminished Capacity." Thomson West.
Faigman, D. L., Slobogin, C., and Monahan, J. (2016). Gatekeeping Science: Using the Structure of Scientific Research to Distinguish Between Admissibility and Weight in Expert Testimony. *Northwestern Law Review* 110, 859–904.
Farah, M. J., Hutchinson, J., Phelps, E. A., & Wagner, A. D. (2014). Functional MRI-Based Lie Detection: Scientific and Societal Challenges. *Nature Reviews Neuroscience* 15(4), 123–131.
Farahany, N. A. (2015). Neuroscience and Behavioral Genetics in US Criminal Law: An Empirical Analysis. *Journal of Law and the Biosciences* 2, 485–509.
Faul, M., Wald, M. M., Wu, L., & Coronado, V. G. (2010). Traumatic Brain Injury in the United States: Emergency Department Visits, Hospitalizations, and Deaths, 2002–2006. Atlanta, GA: CDC. www.cdc.gov/traumaticbraininjury/pdf/blue_book.pdf
The Federal Death Penalty Act, 18 U.S.C. §3591 (2012).
Federal Rule of Evidence 401
Federal Rule of Evidence 403
Federal Rule of Evidence 602
Federal Rule of Evidence 701
Federal Rule of Evidence 702
Federal Rule of Evidence 703
Federal Rule of Evidence 1101
Fisher v. Ciba Specialty Chemicals Corp., 2007 WL 2302470 (S.D. Ala. 2007).
Fox, A. R., Kvaran, T. H., & Fontaine, R. G. (2013). Psychopathy and Culpability: How Responsible Is the Psychopath for Criminal Wrongdoing? *Law & Social Inquiry* 38 (01), 1–26.
Frye v. United States, 293 F.101346 (D.C. App. 1923).
Ganis, G., Rosenfeld, J. P., Meixner, J., Kievit, R. A., & Schendan, H. E. (2011). Lying in the Scanner: Covert Countermeasures Disrupt Deception Detection by Functional Magnetic Resonance Imaging. *NeuroImage* 55(1), 312–319.

Gaudet, L. M., & Marchant, G. E. (2016). Under the Radar: Neuroimaging Evidence in the Criminal Courtroom. *Drake Law Review* 64, 577–661.
General Electric Co. v. Joiner, 522 U.S. 136, 118 S. Ct. 512, 139 L. Ed. 2d 508 (1997).
Gertner, N. (2010). A Short History of American Sentencing: Too Little Law, Too Much Law, or Just Right. *Journal of Criminal Law & Criminology* 100, 691–707.
Gertner, N. (2016). Neuroscience and Sentencing. *Fordham Law Review* 85, 533–546.
Gertner, N. (2018). Against These Guidelines. *University of Missouri-Kansas City Law Review* 87 49–59.
Giannelli, P., Imwinkelried, E. J., Roth, A., Moriarty, J. C., & Beety, V. E. (2020). *Scientific Evidence*, 6th ed. New York: LexisNexis.
Gilmore, R. O., Diaz, M., Wyble, B., & Yarkoni, T. (2017). Progress Toward Openness, Transparency, and Reproducibility in Cognitive Neuroscience. *Annals of the New York Academy of Sciences* 1396, 5–18.
Godman, M., & Jefferson, A. (2014). On Blaming and Punishing Psychopaths. *Criminal Law and Philosophy* 11(1), 127–142.
Goeb v. Tharaldson, 615 N.W.2d 800 (Minn. 2000).
Graham v. Florida, 560 U.S. 48 (2010).
Granacher, R. P. (2008). Commentary: Applications of Functional Neuroimaging to Civil Litigation of Mild Traumatic Brain Injury. *Journal of the American Academy of Psychiatry and the Law* 36, 323–328, 326.
Granacher, R. P. (2012). Traumatic Brain Injury. In J. R. Simpson (ed.), *Neuroimaging in Forensic Psychiatry: From the Clinic to the Courtroom*. Chichester: Wiley-Blackwell, pp. 43–65.
Greely, H. T., & Farahany, N. A. (2019). Neuroscience and the Criminal Justice System. *Annual Review of Criminology*, 2, 451–471. http://doi.org/10.1146/annurev-criminol-011518-024433
Greely, H. T., & Illes, J. (2007). Neuroscience-Based Lie Detection: The Urgent Need for Regulation. *American Journal of Law & Medicine* 33(2–3), 377.
Greely, H. T., & Wagner, A. D. (2011). Reference Guide on Neuroscience. In National Research Council, *Reference Manual on Scientific Evidence: Third Edition* Washington, DC: The National Academies Press.
Greene, J., & Cohen, J. (2004). For the Law, Neuroscience Changes Nothing and Everything. *Philosophical Transactions of the Royal Society B: Biological Sciences* 359, 1775.
Grey, B., Marchant, G., & Tyszka, C. (2015). Biomarkers for Concussion Susceptibility and Effects. *SciTech Lawyer* 11(2), 12–16.
Grey, B. J. (2018). Aging in the 21st Century: Using Neuroscience to Assess Competency in Guardianships. *Wisconsin Law Review*, 735–780.
Gur, R. C., Gur, O. M., Gur, A. E., & Gur, A. G. (2016). A Perspective on the Potential Role of Neuroscience in the Court. *Fordham Law Review* 85, 547–572.
Gurley, J. R., & Marcus, D. K. (2008). The Effects of Neuroimaging and Brain Injury on Insanity Defenses. *Behavioral Sciences & the Law* 26(1), 85–97.
Hare, R. D. (1998). Psychopaths and Their Nature: Implications for the Mental Health and Criminal Justice Systems. In T. Millon, E. Simonsen, M. Birket-Smith, & R. D. Davis (eds.), *Psychopathy: Antisocial, Criminal, and Violent Behavior*. New York: The Guilford Press, pp. 188–212.
Hughes, V. (2010). Science in Court: Head Case. *Nature* 464(7287), 340–342. DOI: http://doi.org/10.1038/464340a
Indiana v. Edwards, 128 S.Ct. 2379, 2383 (2008).
Insanity Defense Reform Act, 18 U.S.C. §17 (1984).

Jarvis v. Secretary of the Dept. of Health and Human Services, 99 Fed. Cl. 47, 57 (2011).
Johnson, L. S. M., Partridge, B., & Gilbert, F. (2015). Framing the Debate: Concussion and Mild Traumatic Brain Injury. *Neuroethics* 8(1), 1–4.
Jones, O. D., Schall, J. D., & Shen, F. X. (2014). *Law and Neuroscience*. New York: Wolter Kluwer Law & Business.
Kansas v. Marsh, 548 U.S. 163, 171 (2006).
Kiehl, K. A., & Hoffman, M. B. (2011). The Criminal Psychopath: History, Neuroscience, Treatment, and Economics. *Jurimetrics Journal* 51(4), 355–397.
Kiehl, K. A., Smith, A. M., Hare, R. D. et al. (2001). Limbic Abnormalities in Affective Processing by Criminal Psychopaths as Revealed by Functional Magnetic Resonance Imaging. *Biological Psychiatry* 50(9), 677–684.
Kolber, A. J. (2007). Pain Detection and the Privacy of Subjective Experience. *American Journal of Law & Medicine* 33(2–3), 433–456.
Korponay, C., Pujara, M., Deming, P., et al. (2017). Impulsive-Antisocial Psychopathic Traits Linked to Increased Volume and Functional Connectivity Within Prefrontal Cortex. *Social Cognitive and Affective Neuroscience* 12(7), 1169–1178.
Kuhn v. Sandoz Pharmaceuticals Corp., 14 P.3d 1170, 1179 (Kan. 2000).
Kumho Tire Co., Ltd. v. Carmichael, 526 U.S. 137, 119 S. Ct. 1167, 143 L. Ed. 2d 238 (1999).
Kwong, K. K., Belliveau, J. W., Chesler, D. A., et al. (1992). Dynamic Magnetic Resonance Imaging of Human Brain Activity During Primary Sensory Stimulation. *Proceedings of the National Academy of Sciences* 89(12), 5675–5679.
Lafler v. Cooper, 566 U.S. 156, 165 (2012).
Langleben, D. D., Hakun, J. G., Seelig, D., et al. (2016). Polygraphy and Functional Magnetic Resonance Imaging in Lie Detection: A Controlled Blind Comparison Using the Concealed Information Test. *The Journal of Clinical Psychiatry* 77(10), 1372–1380. https://doi.org/10.4088/JCP.15m09785
Langleben, D. D., & Moriarty, J. C. (2013). Using Brain Imaging for Lie Detection: Where Science, Law, and Policy Collide. *Psychology, Public Policy, and Law* 19(2), 222–234. https://psycnet.apa.org/doi/10.1037/a0028841
Langleben, D. D., Willard, D. F. X., & Moriarty, J. C. (2012). MRI and Functional MRI. In J. R. Simpson (ed.), *Neuroimaging in Forensic Psychiatry: From the Clinic to the Courtroom*. Chichester: Wiley-Blackwell, pp. 217–236.
Le Bihan, D. (2014). Diffusion MRI: what water tells us about the brain. *EBMO Molecular Medicine* 4, 1–5.
Lee v. United States, 137 S.Ct. 1958, 1964 (2017).
Levin, H. S., & Diaz-Arrastia, R. R. (2015). Diagnosis, Prognosis, and Clinical Management of Mild Traumatic Brain Injury. *The Lancet Neurology* 14(5), 506–517.
Litton, P. (2007). Responsibility Status of the Psychopath: On Moral Reasoning and Rational Self-Governance. *Rutgers Law Review* 39, 349–392.
Liu, C. A. (2015). Scanning the Evidence: The Evidentiary Admissibility of Expert Witness Testimony on MRI Brain Scans in Civil Cases in the Post-Daubert Era. *New York University Annual Survey of American Law* 70, 479–535.
Logothetis, N. K. (2008). What We Can Do and What We Cannot Do With fMRI. *Nature* 453, 869–878.
The MacArthur Foundation Research Network on Law and Neuroscience (2016). www.lawneuro.org/
Maoz, U., & Yaffe, G. (2016). What Does Recent Neuroscience Tell Us About Criminal Responsibility? *Journal of Law and the Biosciences* 3(1), 120–139. https://doi.org/10.1093/jlb/lsv051

Marcus, P. (2016). The United States Supreme Court (Mostly) Gives up Its Review Role with Ineffective Assistance of Counsel Cases. *Minnesota Law Review* 100, 1745–1768.

Maroney, T. A. (2009). The False Promise of Adolescent Brain Science in Juvenile Justice. *Notre Dame Law Review* 85 89–176.

Mayberg, H. S. (2014). Neuroimaging and Psychiatry: The Long Road from Bench to Bedside. *Hastings Center Report* 44, n.2, s31–s36.

McClain v. Metabolife Int'l, Inc. 401 F.3d 1233 (11th Cir. 2005).

McCleskey v. Kemp, 481 U. S. 279, 753 F.2d 877 (1987).

McCord, D., & Bennett, M. W. (2014). The Proposed Capital Penalty Phase Rules of Evidence. *Cardozo Law Review* 36 417, 420–421.

Meixner, J. B. (2012). Liar, Liar, Jury's the Trier? The Future of Neuroscience-Based Credibility Assessment in the Court. *Northwestern University Law Review* 106, 1451–1488.

Meixner, J. B. (2017). Neuroscience and Mental Competency: Current Uses and Future Potential. *Albany Law Review* 81, 995–1026.

Melville, J. D., & Naimark, D. (2002). Punishing the Insane: The Verdict of Guilty but Mentally Ill. *Journal of the American Academy of Psychiatry and the Law* 30, 553–555.

Menon, D. K., Schwab, K., Wright, D. W., & Maas A. (2010). Working Group on Demographics and Clinical Assessment of the International Interagency Initiative toward Common Data Elements for Research in TBI and Psychological Health. Position Statement: Definition of Traumatic Brain Injury. *Archives of Physical Medicine and Rehabilitation* 91(11), 1637–1640.

Meltzer, C. C., Sze, G., Rommelfanger, K. S., Kinlaw, K., Banja, J. D., & Wolpe, P. R. (2014). Guidelines for the Ethical Use of Neuroimages in Medical Testimony: Report of a Multidisciplinary Consensus Conference. *American Journal of Neuroradiology* 35(4), 632–637.

Miller v. Alabama (2012).

Montgomery v. Louisiana, 136 S.Ct. 718, 733 (2016).

Moran, R. (1981). *Knowing Right From Wrong: The Insanity Defense of Daniel McNaughtan.* New York: Free Press.

Moriarty, J. C. (2008). Flickering Admissibility: Neuroimaging Evidence in the US Courts. *Behavioral Sciences & the Law* 26(1), 29–49.

Moriarty, J. C. (2009). Visions of Deception: Neuroimages and the Search for Truth. *Akron Law Review* 42, 739–761.

Moriarty, J. C. (2016). Seeing Voices: Potential Neuroscience Contributions to a Reconstruction of Legal Insanity. *Fordham Law Review* 86, 599–618.

Moriarty, J. C. (2018). Deceptively Simple: Framing, Intuition and Judicial Gatekeeping of Forensic Feature-Comparison Methods Evidence. *Fordham Law Review* 86, 1687–1708.

Moriarty, J. C., & Langleben, D. D. (2018). Who Speaks for Neuroscience? Neuroimaging Evidence and Courtroom Expertise, *Case Western Reserve Law Review* 68, 783–804.

Moriarty, J. C., Langleben, D. D., & Provenzale, J. M. (2013). Brain Trauma, PET Scans and Forensic Complexity. *Behavioral Sciences & the Law* 31(6), 702–720.

Morissette v. United States, 342 U.S. 246, 252 (1952).

Morse, S. J. (1996). Brain and Blame. *Georgetown Law Review* 84, 527–549.

Morse, S. J. (2007). Criminal Responsibility and the Disappearing Person. *Cardozo Law Review* 28, 2545–2575.

Morse, S. J. (2008). Psychopathy and Criminal Responsibility. *Neuroethics* 1(3), 205–212.

Morse, S. J. (2011). Mental Disorder and Criminal Law. *Journal of Criminal Law & Criminology* 101, 885–968.

Morse, S. J., & Hoffman, M. B. (2007). The Uneasy Entente Between Insanity and Mens Rea: Beyond Clark v. Arizona. *Journal of Criminal Law & Criminology* 97, 1071–1149.

Mueller, C. B., & Kirkpatrick, L. C. (2018). *Federal Evidence*, 4th ed. Egan, MN: Thomson Reuters.

Murphy, E. (2016). Neuroscience and the Civil Criminal Divide. *Fordham Law Review* 85, 619–639.

National Research Council. (2009). Strengthening Forensic Science in the United States. 11.

Nicholls, T. L., Ogloff, J. R. P., Brink, J., & Spidel, A. (2005). Psychopathy in Women: a Review of Its Clinical Usefulness For Assessing Risk For Aggression and Criminality. *Behavioral Sciences & the Law* 23(6), 779–802.

Niogi, S. N., & Mukherjee, P. (2010). Diffusion Tensor Imaging of Mild Traumatic Brain Injury. *Journal of Head Trauma Rehabilitation* 25(4), 241–255.

Ogawa, S., Lee, T. M., Kay, A. R., & Tank, D. W. (1990). Brain Magnetic Resonance Imaging With Contrast Dependent on Blood Oxygenation. *Proceedings of the National Academy of Sciences of the Unites States of America* 87(24), 9868–9872.

Opinion Testimony by Lay Witnesses, FRE 701 section year.

O'Donnell, L. J., & Westin, C.-F. (2011). An Introduction to Diffusion Tensor Image Analysis. *Neurosurgery Clinics of North America* 22(2), 185–196. http://doi.org/10.1016/j.nec.2010.12.004

Pardo, M. S. (2005). Neuroscience Evidence, Legal Culture, and Criminal Procedure. *American Journal of Criminal Law* 33(301), 321–336.

Pardo, M. S., & Patterson, D.M. (2013). *Minds, Brains, and Law: the Conceptual Foundations of Law and Neuroscience*. Oxford; New York: Oxford University Press.

People v. Daveggio and Michaud, 415 P.3d 717, 749 (Cal. 2018).

People v. Schreck, 22 P.3d 68 (Colo. en banc, 2001).

Perlin, M. L. (1994). *The Jurisprudence of the Insanity Defense*. Durham, NC: Carolina Academic Press.

Perlin, M. L., & Lynch, A. (2016). In the Wasteland of Your Mind: Criminology, Scientific Discoveries and the Criminal Process. *Virginia Journal of Criminal Law* 4 (2), 304–360.

Phillips, K. D. (2013). Empathy for Psychopaths: Using fMRI Brain Scans to Plead for Leniency in Death Penalty. *Law & Psychology Review* 37, 1.

President's Council of Advisors on Sci. & Tech., Exec.Office of the President. (2016). Forensic Science in Criminal Courts: Ensuring Scientific Validity of Feature-Comparison Methods 46.

Puerto Rico v. Sanchez Valle, 136 S.Ct. 1863, 1871 (2016).

Pustilnik, A. C. (2012). Pain as Fact and Heuristic: How Pain Neuroimaging Illuminates Moral Dimensions of Law. *Cornell Law Review* 97, 801–847.

Raine, A., Buchsbaum, M., & Lacasse, L. (1997). Brain Abnormalities in Murderers Indicated by Positron Emission Tomography. *Biological Psychiatry* 42(6), 495–508.

Raine, A., Meloy, J. R., Bihrle, S., et al. (1998). Reduced Prefrontal and Increased Subcortical Brain Functioning Assessed Using Positron Emission Tomography in Predatory and Affective Murderers. *Behavioral Sciences & the Law* 16(3), 319–332.

Roe v. Flores-Ortega, 528 U.S. 470, 482 (2000).

Roozenbeek, B., Maas, A. I. R., & Menon, D. K. (2013). Changing Patterns in the Epidemiology of Traumatic Brain Injury. *Nature Reviews Neurology* 9(4), 231–236.

Roper v. Simmons, 543 U.S. 551, 568 (2005).

Rosenfeld, J. (1999). P300 Scalp Amplitude Distribution as an Index of Deception in a Simulated Cognitive Deficit Model. *International Journal of Psychophysiology* 33(1), 3–19.

Rosenfeld, J. P., Soskins, M., Bosh, G., & Ryan, A. (2004). Simple, Effective Countermeasures to P300-Based Tests of Detection of Concealed Information. *Psychophysiology* 41(2), 205–219.

Ruppel v. Kucanin. (2011) WL 2470621 (D.C. N.D. Ind. 2011) (unreported).

Rushing, S. E., Pryma, D. A., & Langleben, D. D. (2012). PET and SPECT. In J. R. Simpson (ed.), *Neuroimaging in Forensic Psychiatry: From the Clinic to the Courtroom.* Chichester: Wiley-Blackwell.

Scarpazza, C., Ferracuti, S., Miolla, A., & Sartori, G. (2018). The Charm of Structural Neuroimaging in Insanity Evaluations: Guidelines to Avoid Misinterpretation of the Findings. *Translational Psychiatry* 8(1), 227–228.

Schauer, F. (2010). Lie-Detection, Neuroscience, and the Law of Evidence. *Cornell Law Review* 95, 1191–1219.

Schweitzer, N. J., & Saks, M. J. (2011). Neuroimage Evidence and the Insanity Defense. *Behavioral Sciences & the Law* 29(4), 592–607.

Schweitzer, N. J., Saks, M. J., Murphy, E. R., et al. (2011). Neuroimages as Evidence in a Mens Rea Defense: No Impact. *Psychology, Public Policy, and Law* 17(3), 357–393.

Seaman, J. A. (2013). A Tale of Two Dauberts. *Georgia Law Review* 47, 889–922.

Shen, F. X. (2013). Legislating Neuroscience: The Case of Juvenile Justice. *Loyola of Los Angeles Law Review* 46, 985, 994–995.

Shen, F. X. (2014). Neuroscience, Mental Privacy, and the Law. *Harvard Journal of Law & Public Policy* 36, 653, 692–707.

Shen, F. X. (2016). The Overlooked History of Neurolaw. *Fordham Law Review* 85, 667, 685–687.

Shen, F. X., & Jones, O. D. (2011). Brain Scans as Evidence: Truths, Proofs, Lies, and Lessons. *Mercer Law Review* 62, 861–883.

Shenton, M. E., Price, B. H., Levin, L. & Edersheim, J. G. (2018). Mild Traumatic Brain Injury: Is DTI Ready for the Courtroom? *International Journal of Law and Psychiatry* 61, 50–63.

Shetty, V. S., Reis, M. N., Aulino, J. M., et al. (2016). ACR Appropriateness Criteria Head Trauma. *Journal of the American College of Radiology* 13(6), 668–679. https://doi.org/10.1016/j.jacr.2016.02.023

Silva, M. A., See, A. P., Essayed, W. I., Golby, A. J., & Tie, Y. (2018). Challenges and Techniques for Presurgical Brain Mapping with Functional MRI. *NeuroImage: Clinical* 17, 794–803.

Slobogin, C. (1985). The Guilty but Mentally Ill Verdict: An Idea Whose Time Should Not Have Come. *George Washington Law Review* 53, 494–527.

Slobogin, C. (2000). Doubts about Daubert: Psychiatric Anecdata as a Case Study. *Washington and Lee Law Review* 57, 919–948.

Slobogin, C. (2007). *Proving the Unprovable: the Role of Law, Science, and Speculation in Adjudicating Culpability and Dangerousness.* New York: Oxford University Press.

Slobogin, C. (2017). Neuroscience Nuance: Dissecting the Relevance of Neuroscience in Adjudicating Criminal Culpability. *Journal of Law and the Biosciences* 4(3), 577–593.

Smith, S. F. (2010). Taking Strickland Claims Seriously. *Marquette Law Review* 93, 515–544.

Snead, O. C. (2007). Neuroimaging and the Complexity of Capital Punishment. *New York University Law Review* 82(1265), 1292–1293.

State v. Smith, 32 A.3d 59 (Md. 2011).

Steinberg, L. (2017). Adolescent Brain Science and Juvenile Justice Policymaking. *Psychology, Public Policy, and Law* 23(4), 410–420.

Stith, K., & Cabranes, J. A. (1997). Judging Under the Federal Sentencing Guidelines. *Northwestern University Law Review* 91, 1247–1283.
Stocchetti, N., & Zanier, E. R. (2016). Chronic Impact Of Traumatic Brain Injury On Outcome And Quality Of Life: A Narrative Review. *Critical Care* 20(1). DOI: http:/doi .org/10.1186/s13054-016-1318-1
Strickland v. Washington, 466 U.S. 668, 688 (1984).
Taylor, J. S. (2015). Neurolaw and Traumatic Injury: Principles for Trial Lawyers. *University of Missouri-Kansas City Law Review* 84, 397–409.
Taylor, C. A., Bell, J. M., Breiding, M. J., & Xu, L. (2017). Traumatic Brain Injury–Related Emergency Department Visits, Hospitalizations, and Deaths – United States, 2007 and 2013. *MMWR. Surveillance Summaries* 66(9), 1–16.
Telis, M. (2014). Playing Through the Haze: The NFL Concussion Litigation and section 301 Preemption. *Georgetown Law Journal* 102, 1841–1868.
Texas Penal Code Annotated §8.01(a) (West, 2015).
Torres v. Lynch, 136 S. Ct. 1619, 1630 (2016).
Turlington, S. (2008). Completely Unguided Discretion: Admitting Non-Statutory Aggravating and Non-Statutory Mitigating Evidence in Capital Sentencing Trial. *Pierce Law Review* 6, 469–483.
United Laundries Co. v. Bradford, 105 A. 303 (Md. 1918).
United States Sentencing Guidelines Manual, §5H1.3. Mental and Emotional Conditions (Policy Statement) (2018).
United States v. Booker, 543 U.S. 220, 237 (2005).
United States v. Charley, 189 F. 3d 1251, 1267 (10th Cir. 1999).
United States v. Hinckley, 672 F.2d 115 (D.C. Cir. 1982).
United States v. Montgomery, 635 F.3d 1074 (8th Cir. 2011).
United States v. Scheffer, 523 U.S. 303, 313–14 (1998).
United States v. Semrau, 693 F.3d 510 (6th Cir. 2012)
United States v. Sherlin, 67 F.3d 1208 (6th Cir. 1995).
Vincent, N. A. (2009). On the Relevance of Neuroscience to Criminal Responsibility. *Criminal Law and Philosophy* 4(1), 77–98.
Vincent, N. A. (2013). A Compatibilist Theory of Legal Responsibility. *Criminal Law and Philosophy* 9(3), 477–498.
Ward v. Carnival Corporation, volume source page (D.C. S.D. Fl. 2019).
Westberry v. Gislaved Gummi AB, 178 F.3d 257, 262–63 (4th Cir. 1999).
Wilson v. Corestaff, 900 N.Y.S.2d 639, 28 Misc.3d 425 (2010).
Wolpe, P. R., Foster, K. R., & Langleben, D. D. (2005). Emerging Neurotechnologies for Lie-Detection: Promises and Perils. *The American Journal of Bioethics* 5(2), 39–49.
Woodmansee, M. A. (1996). The Guilty but Mentally Ill Verdict: Political Expediency at the Expense of Moral Principle. *Notre Dame Journal of Law, Ethics, & Public Policy* 10(341), 341–387.
Zeki, S., Goodenough, O. R., Spence, S. A., et al. (2004). A Cognitive Neurobiological Account of Deception: Evidence From Functional Neuroimaging. *Philosophical Transactions of the Royal Society of London. Series B: Biological Sciences* 359(1451), 1755–1762. DOI: http://doi.org/10.1098/rstb.2004.1555

19

Neuroscientific Evidence in Context

Deborah W. Denno*

19.1 INTRODUCTION

The burgeoning use of neuroscientific evidence in the criminal justice system has introduced controversies regarding the nature and quality of its impact. The criminal law has prioritized the human mind and mental states since the seventeenth century, yet the field of neuroscience is relatively young. Broadly defined as "the branch of the life sciences that studies the brain and the nervous system" (Garland, 2004, p. 206), the term "neuroscience" did not even exist until 1963 (Denno, 2015, p. 496). In turn, many brain-imaging tests that are widely introduced into courtrooms around the country today were not created until the 1970s nor employed clinically until even later (Aono, Yaffe, & Kober, 2019; Moriarty, Chapter 18 in the present volume).

Professor Jane Moriarty has expertly produced an ambitious chapter that examines US courts' use of neuroimaging – among the newest neuroscientific techniques – primarily in criminal law and, on a smaller scale, civil law. In so doing, Professor Moriarty covers a broad scope of topics and admirably weaves together important themes that shed light on this field's future. Professor Moriarty's chapter is limited to imaging tests, an understandable focus given their relative novelty and intricacy.

However, this focus aside, neuroscientific evidence generally and neuroimaging specifically need to be put into some context, legally and scientifically. Criminal (and civil) cases are enormously complex, and legal actors – judges, attorneys, jurors – can be cognitively overwhelmed by the amount of evidence that is introduced into a courtroom. Neuroimaging is just one small piece of a much larger puzzle. In addition, as Professor Moriarty explains, neuroscientific information can be viewed through the lens of many different kinds of evidentiary standards, depending on how such information is being used. The evidentiary standard for mitigation in the penalty phase of a death-penalty case, for example, will be substantially more relaxed than the standard applied for assessing a defendant's level of intentionality in

---

* I am most grateful to Kathleen Ellis and Marianna Gebhardt for their insightful comments.

the guilt phase of a homicide case. This expanse and variability make clear that when it comes to assessing the relevance and applicability of such evidence, there is no "one-size-fits-all" takeaway. At the same time, neuroimaging can at least provide some kind of measured documentation of the brain's condition – no matter how flawed or open to interpretation; this advantage surpasses pre-1960s psychiatry, a profession whose experts relied heavily on mere opinion.

The purpose of this commentary is to consider these and other issues to add context to Professor Moriarty's discussion. The commentary briefly examines the scientific environment in which neuroscientific evidence took hold. It also analyzes the complexities that can arise when deciphering the influence of such evidence in the broader framework of a criminal case involving hundreds of factors, with neuroimaging tests simply being one component.

19.2 NEUROSCIENCE AND MENTAL STATES

Neuroscientific evidence can reveal a vast amount of information about how the brain functions when it is healthy or unhealthy (damaged), as well as simply undeveloped, as in the case of juveniles. Such insights are particularly important in criminal law, an area that relies most heavily on a defendant's state of mind and level of intentionality. That said, there is no scientific measure of a defendant's state of mind (at least not yet). Instead, attorneys must use either direct or indirect (circumstantial) evidence to try to make these assessments. Such an endeavor is not easy.

In most cases, for example, a prosecutor must prove two elements to establish whether a defendant committed a crime: (1) the *mens rea* ("guilty mind"), which pertains to the defendant's mental state at the time the crime was committed; and (2) the *actus reus*, which pertains to the defendant's voluntary act that led to the social harm (such as a victim's injury). Both elements are necessary to determine a defendant's level of culpability and to establish that a defendant's punishment is commensurate with their blameworthiness. While the nature and breadth of *mens rea* have changed across twelve centuries, by the twentieth century *mens rea* had become a core condition for establishing criminality (Denno, 2017).

Yet, *mens rea* and intent are incredibly amorphous concepts and they are established by both direct and circumstantial evidence. In general, direct evidence is often testimonial: a witness testifies that they saw the defendant shoot the victim. If there was no such witness, however (or video, etc.), there would be only circumstantial evidence: for example, the police find a victim died from a gunshot wound and the defendant was the only person in the home at the time. Most cases have a mixture of both types of evidence, but such evidence can be flawed or inadequate, leaving attorneys to try to fill in the gaps to establish a defendant's culpability.

Neuroscientific evidence can be useful in filling these gaps by providing more insight into how the human mind works, or whether there may be defenses or mitigating evidence that would bear on whether the defendant *intended* to shoot the victim, even if intent is clearly implied by the defendant's actions. For example, did the defendant suffer from extensive frontal lobe damage that would suggest those actions were not truly voluntary? Could the defendant not appreciate the nature and quality of those actions? Is the defendant not competent to stand trial? Could that same evidence illuminate the quality of an expert's testimony or extend our understanding of the harm that the victim experienced?

Such questions can go on. Yet, as the scope of Professor Moriarty's chapter indicates, neuroscientific evidence (whether or not it is specifically neuroimaging) can be applied in an immense number of ways and permutations.[1] Indeed, a recent review of the use of such evidence rightly emphasizes that "the purpose of neuroscientific evidence ... is the same as any other kind of evidence that may be introduced into a courtroom" (Aono, Yaffe, & Kober, 2019, p. 3), a pronouncement that would be less significant were it not so frequently overlooked. In essence, neuroscientific evidence is not any more "special" than any other kind of evidence that may be used in a criminal case. Yet both neuroimaging evidence and nonimaging evidence are viewed as more influential than other types of evidence, despite an overall lack of empirical support for that belief (Aono, Yaffe, & Kober, 2019).

In general, there are two major types of neuroscientific evidence – imaging tests, created by computer images of a human brain (such as MRI, PET, and CT scans), and nonimaging tests, which do not rely on computer images but are still diagnostic of brain disorders and injuries (such as the WAIS, WISC, etc.). Professor Moriarty provides a wonderfully detailed overview of the imaging tests, and, within this context, it is perhaps helpful to add that nonimaging tests are a major contribution to the neuroscientific evidence in criminal cases as well, either with or without accompanying imaging tests. It is not unusual for a criminal case to include a number of each type of test in addition to whatever information may be introduced into court, either direct or circumstantial (Denno, 2015).

Indeed, criminal (and civil) cases can involve an extraordinary amount of direct and circumstantial evidence, especially if the stakes are high, such as in death-penalty cases. Without interviews with jurors, sophisticated mock experiments, or large amounts of empirical data, it is difficult if not impossible to decipher what evidentiary pieces ultimately sway a decision maker. This issue becomes all the more important when considering the impact of neuroimaging, because it is only one bit of evidence that decision makers will consider. Indeed, my own research has found that nonimaging tests are still used far more widely in criminal cases and commonly accompany imaging tests. Therefore, legal actors are hardly basing their decisions on imaging tests – or even neuroscientific evidence – alone (Denno, 2015). This influx

---

[1] See, for example, Jones (2013), who offers a framework showing seven different ways in which neuroscience can be applied to law, and Moriarty (2016), who focuses on the insanity defense.

of information and evidence may help explain the conclusion in one recent survey that the impact of neuroscientific evidence is, at most, mitigating in some types of legal cases (primarily death-penalty cases) but that brain-imaging evidence does not appear to be more influential on decision making than nonimaging evidence (Aono, Yaffe, & Kober, 2019).

Such conclusions are also important to keep in mind when we consider past significant cases. For example, Professor Moriarty notes that one of the most prominent and early uses of neuroimaging was in the trial of John Hinckley, Jr. in 1982. Hinckley's lawyers submitted CT images of Hinckley's brain indicating "atrophy and ventricular enlargement" in support of a successful insanity defense. As Professor Moriarty (present volume) rightly notes, "a great deal of other evidence" was also admitted. Given that the Hinckley case ranks among one of legal history's most famous and controversial decisions and attorneys from both sides introduced volumes of information about Hinckley's life, family, and psychiatric condition – not to mention the court's application of a more flexible insanity standard (Bonnie, Jeffries, & Low, 2008) – it is difficult to assess whether Hinckley's CT images were even a blip on the radar of what the jury was processing. As one set of researchers noted, "neuroscience is already being used in criminal cases without regard to how well understood its effects are" and further investigation into its role and application can better illuminate its actual impact (Aono, Yaffe, & Kober, 2019).

With this foundation in mind, it is useful to consider why the influx of neuroimaging evidence is important, how it can be helpful, and finally why it deserves some skepticism in light of Professor Moriarty's concerns about the potential weight of its impact. The next sections put neuroimaging into context, starting with a brief modern history of how the mind started to influence law.

19.3 HISTORICAL OVERVIEW

By the mid-seventeenth century, lawmakers in this country had broadly accepted that an individual's criminal liability necessitated not only that an individual commit an illegal act but also that the act be accompanied by an evil motive. While the concept of an evil motive began as a generalized notion of an intentional mental state, it gradually evolved into a requirement that an individual's liability hinge on a specific state of mind for specific kinds of crimes. These levels of mental-state refinements eventually prompted the law's modern notion of particularized forms of *mens rea* (the defendant's mental state at the time of the crime).

In criminal law, however, no tool yet exists to read an individual's thoughts generally, much less to decipher their mental state at the moment they committed a crime. Rather, the legal system relies on culture, science, and the psychology of the times to attempt to establish for judges and juries each and every defendant's mental state. Freudian psychoanalytic theory, for example, one of the most pronounced cultural phenomena of the twentieth century, had a strong impact on this country's development and interpretation of how the criminal law should formulate key concepts of culpability. While seemingly progressive when introduced, these concepts are a product of the era in which they were created – the early 1950s and 1960s, when Freudian doctrine predominated (Denno, 2005, 2017).

Whether Freudian psychoanalytic theory was ever a suitable foundation for the mental-state requirement of a criminal code is a matter to debate another day. By the 1970s, American psychiatry had experienced a paradigm shift from psychoanalysis to clinical research, which started to stress biological psychiatry. Accompanying this shift was the development and use of many of the kinds of neuroimaging techniques that Professor Moriarty discusses in her chapter. While biological psychiatry embraced some of the language and conceptualization of Freudian analysis, in many ways analysis was ultimately displaced by a cultural and psychological sea change in how the psychiatric profession viewed the mind (Denno, 2005).

This history is important if we are to understand why the legal system embraced neuroimaging in the first place, and why the use of imaging in the courtroom would come to be expected. The legal system's concept of mental state has for centuries reflected the current culture and beliefs. As Professor Moriarty recognizes, older and vaguer psychiatric concepts have created problems in the legal system's interpretation of mental state, especially given that the system's concept of "mind" and intentionality are basically fictions. The capacity of imaging to provide a scientific assessment – however imperfect – of the brain's condition is a much-needed improvement over previous reliance upon a profession whose experts espoused primarily their own opinions.

Because neuroimaging is so intimate, it also enables a more personalized approach in interpreting criminal law concepts, thereby incorporating to a greater degree an individual's particular traits, characteristics, and circumstances. When the criminal justice system embraced Freudian psychoanalysis over a half-century ago, it promoted a more subjective and individualized approach to criminal law, thereby acknowledging the capacity for the psychological sciences to reveal insights on how defendants think and reason. Such an approach encourages an increasingly granular concept of a defendant's level of culpability and, as a result, presumably more effective methods of punishing or rehabilitating (Denno, 2019a).

Again, however, neuroscientific evidence is just one part of the overall picture of determining a defendant's cognitive place in the criminal justice system. The next section discusses how neuroscientific evidence fits within the legal framework in which it is most widely and acceptably applied. Notably, the greatest controversy over the legal system's purported reliance on neuroscience exists in circumstances when the evidence is least likely to be used (for example, lie detection), thus clouding its value in the instances when it is most likely to be used, such as death-penalty cases.

19.4 A RANGE IN EVIDENTIARY STANDARDS

A disproportionate number of criminal cases that rely on neuroimaging evidence are eligible for the death penalty, as Professor Moriarty notes. The evidentiary standard for death-penalty cases, however, is extraordinarily flexible; therefore, any unease over introducing neuroimaging data should be considerably less pronounced than it would be under another evidentiary standard.

In a death-penalty case, neuroimaging evidence can be used in two different ways: (1) at the guilt-or-innocence phase, during which the prosecution must prove that the defendant committed the crime as well as failed the standards for any defenses that the defense may want to introduce (such as insanity, lack of intent, etc.) and/or (2) at the penalty phase, after which a jury has rendered the defendant guilty of a capital offense. Also at the penalty phase the jury must determine whether the evidence of aggravation introduced by the prosecution outweighs the evidence of mitigation introduced by the defense, and, if so, the defendant can be sentenced to death (Denno, 2015).

Evidence is used very differently in these two phases. While the guilt-or-innocence phase involves a factual determination of whether a defendant has committed the crime and also has any defenses, the penalty phase stresses the moral and societal considerations of whether a defendant should be executed. The prosecution's aggravating evidence can comprise those circumstances surrounding a crime (such as the use of a weapon or extraordinary cruelty) and a defendant's prior criminal record. The defense's mitigating evidence usually consists of information about a capital defendant's background and life prior to the crime, which would include the kinds of brain damage and injuries that would make neuroimaging relevant (Denno, 2015).

Overwhelmingly, it is the defense's choice to introduce neuroscientific evidence, including neuroimaging, on behalf of the defendant rather than the prosecution's choice to use such evidence against the defendant (unless the evidence pertains to the victim's injuries) (Denno, 2015, 2017, 2019b). The defense's primary goal is to tell a mitigation "story" on the defendant's behalf in order to counter the impact of the aggravating circumstances as well as to humanize the defendant. Statutory mitigating factors can include the defendant's age (either young or old) and their ability to comprehend the wrongfulness of their conduct (Denno, 2015). As the Supreme Court has pronounced, the defense can introduce mitigating evidence relevant to "any aspect of [the] defendant's character or record and any of the circumstances of the offense that the defendant proffers as a basis for a sentence less than death" (*Kansas v. Marsh*, 548 U.S. 163, 174 [2006], quoting *Lockett v. Ohio*, 438 U.S. 586, 604 [1978]).

This mitigating-evidence standard is highly elastic, subjective, and flexible, enabling the open-ended introduction of a full range of factors that can compel jurors to empathize and connect with a defendant who may have committed an unthinkable crime, including whether a defendant's family continued to provide love and support. Neuroimaging evidence in particular could contribute to mitigation evidence because it can validate existing diagnoses that a defendant is suffering from brain damage and therefore experiencing distorted thought processes or impulsivity, including during the time directly preceding the defendant's criminal acts. Mitigating factors based on neuroscientific evidence can also shed light to jurors on the defendant's worldview, including whether the defendant was under a high degree of stress or fear (Denno, 2015). In the case of John McCluskey, for example, a jury rejected the death penalty, deciding instead to sentence McCluskey to life in prison without the possibility of parole, because of brain scans indicating pervasive damage to his frontal lobe and his attorneys' explanation that this condition was a mitigating factor that hindered his ability to plan or intend his crime (Denno, 2015).

In addition to this mitigation standard, the Supreme Court has firmly held – in a series of opinions – that defense attorneys are constitutionally required in capital cases to thoroughly investigate "all reasonably available mitigating evidence" relevant to a defendant's background and circumstances (*Wiggins* v. *Smith*, 539 U.S. 510, 524 [2003] (emphasis omitted)). My research has shown that defense attorneys' failures to investigate relevant neuroscientific evidence in particular heightens the likelihood that they will be rendered ineffective. The presumption is that, had attorneys included neuroscientific evidence, their clients' case outcomes would have been different (that is, they may not have received the death penalty) (Denno, 2015).[2]

With such constitutional encouragement for the admissibility of neuroscientific evidence, including neuroimaging, what are some of the drawbacks? Professor Moriarty articulates them well, questioning in particular whether neuroimaging data is sufficiently valid and reliable to be used in court cases, specifically whether – or to what extent – the data measure certain types of brain damage or are in any way connected to an individual's behavior. There is no doubt that, in theory, there can be "inferential leap[s] from image to behavior" as Professor Moriarty notes. Because experts are nearly always the interpreters of neuroimaging results, Professor Moriarty also rightly questions whether most are qualified and appropriate for the cases in which they testify. The criminal justice system's overreliance on neuroscience can be seriously misleading, potentially encouraging unjustified presumptions regarding a defendant's injuries or actions.

That said, Professor Moriarty's important points bring the spotlight back to case complexities and the need for "triangulation" in all cases, in other words, multiple measures of the injuries and behaviors at issue. My own research has shown, for example, that several different neuroimaging tests are typically used in criminal

---

[2] These outcomes were in accord with the standard of ineffective assistance of counsel laid out by the Supreme Court in *Strickland* v. *Washington*, 466 U.S. 668, 688 (1984).

cases to assess the same brain injuries and behaviors; in addition, neuroimaging techniques are nearly always accompanied by nonimaging tests as well as other indicators of brain trauma across time. A well-researched death-penalty case, for example, would incorporate volumes of evidence over an individual's lifetime, including hospital and school records, interviews with family and friends, and, increasingly, indicators of mental illness or disabilities going back generations (Denno, 2015, 2019b). As in the Hinckley case, a defendant's neuroimaging testimony would be simply one of hundreds of factors explaining a defendant's mitigation story – either confirming, conflicting with, or contradicting whatever damage or disorder a defendant is trying to explain.

Admittedly, such evidence has created plenty of debacles. Professor Moriarty's concerns are well grounded. But the solution could be to provide more – not less – by way of neuroscientific evidence in the courtroom to ensure proper validation or disregard for the arguments being offered.

19.5 CONCLUSION

Neuroscientific evidence has become an increasingly influential component of a broad range of criminal and civil cases involving various evidentiary standards and purposes. That said, when viewed in context, the evidence is just one small part of a much larger puzzle of information that legal actors must decipher in order to assess in the courtroom the intricacies of a defendant's brain and behavior. In essence, there is no "one-size-fits-all" approach to determining the relevance and utility of neuroscientific evidence. Incorporating an array of neuroscientific measures in the courtroom – both imagining and nonimaging techniques – would enhance efforts to support or refute arguments raised by either the prosecution or the defense.

REFERENCES

Aono, D., Yaffe, G., & Kober, H. (2019). Neuroscientific Evidence in the Courtroom: A Review. *Cognitive Research: Principles and Implications* 4. DOI: https://doi.org/10.1186/s41235-019-0179-y

Bonnie, R. J., Jeffries, J. C., Jr. & Low, P. W. (2008). *A Case Study of the Insanity Defense: The Trial of John W. Hinckley, Jr.*, 3rd ed. St. Paul, MN: Foundation Press.

Denno, D. W. (2005). Criminal Law in a Post-Freudian World. *University of Illinois Law Review* 3, 601–774.

Denno, D. W. (2015). The Myth of the Double-Edged Sword: An Empirical Study of Neuroscience Evidence in Criminal Cases. *Boston College Law Review* 56, 493–551.

Denno, D. W. (2017). Concocting Criminal Intent. *Georgetown Law Journal* 105, 323–378.

Denno, D. W. (2019a). Neuroscience and the Personalization of Criminal Law. *University of Chicago Law Review* 86, 359–401.

Denno, D. W. (2019b). How Courts in Criminal Cases Respond to Childhood Trauma. *Marquette Law Review* 103, 302–363.

Garland, B. (2004). *Neuroscience and the Law: Brain, Mind, and the Scales of Justice.* New York: Dana Press.

Jones, O. D. (2013). Seven Ways Neuroscience Aids Law. In A. M. Battro, S. Dehaene, M. S. Sorondo, & W. J. Singer (eds.), *Neurosciences and the Human Person: New Perspectives on Human Activities.* Vatican City: The Pontifical Academy of Sciences, pp. 181–194.

Kansas v. Marsh, 548 U.S. 163, 174 (2006) (quoting LOCKETT V. OHIO, 438 U.S. 586, 604 [1978]).

Moriarty, J. C. (2016). Seeing Voices: Potential Neuroscience Contributions to a Reconstruction of Legal Insanity. *Fordham Law Review* 85, 599–618.

Strickland v. Washington, 466 U.S. 668, 688 (1984).

Wiggins v. Smith, 539 U.S. 510, 524 (2003).

20

Some Issues in Interpreting Neuroscientific Evidence

Bartłomiej Kucharzyk[*]

Neuroscience is not the holy grail of legal fact-finding. One can, of course, imagine, even if it strongly contradicts the contemporary view on human memory (Loftus, 2005; 2018), that one day eyewitnesses will not be questioned but, instead, connected to some kind of projector. However, even then one would simply have a lot of evidence similar to CCTV recordings. Regardless, for now the possibilities offered by neuroscience to fact-finders are much more modest and the pitfalls one faces exploring them are numerous. This paper concerns several of those pitfalls. Some are mentioned in Jane Moriarty's chapter (Chapter 18), yet it seems reasonable to consider them once more. The other issues addressed below may be less conspicuous but therefore arguably also more dangerous.

20.1 KINDS OF NEUROSCIENTIFIC EVIDENCE

First of all, it is crucial to bear in mind that neuroscientific data are not homogeneous. Neuroscientists utilize neuroimaging as well as, among other things, psychological tasks and tests, neurological instruments, chemical and biological research methods (such as those from the field of cellular biology), and the classical techniques of psychophysiological response (such as blood-pressure or electrodermal-activity changes) measurement (Andreassi, 2006). Moreover, neuroimaging methods and data, which are central to modern neuroscience, may be roughly divided into the structural – concerning the static architecture of the brain, and the functional – showing how the brain works. Both structural and functional data, which are basically huge sets of numbers, are processed with the use of dedicated software that provides aggregate information which is more comprehensible. It includes:

- images (visualizations) of the brain structure from CT and MRI,
- brainwave patterns – and their changes caused, for example, by stimulus exposure – from EEG and MEG,

---

[*] The author obtained financial resources within the doctoral scholarship No. 2017/24/T/HS5/00417 from the Polish National Science Center.

- locations (areas) and magnitudes of changes in brain activity in response to stimuli or during the task performance from PET, fMRI, and NIRS.

Also functional data are often visualized, hence the colored brain images illustrating the results of fMRI experiments (Goldstone, Pestilli, & Börner, 2015).

From the legal perspective, yet one more distinction within neuroscientific, and in particular neuroimaging, data seems important: individual (single case) versus group (mostly experimental) data. The former concern the structure or functioning of a particular person's brain and come from clinical research or medical practice (or they may be acquired by an expert for use in a legal trial). The latter are the results of research conducted on a sample (group of subjects) from a predetermined population, for instance a population of healthy adults or people with a specific neurological condition. This research is often experimental, so, simplifying slightly, it explores possible statistical differences in the structure or functioning of the brain between two or more groups of people (e.g. healthy vs. patients) or between the functioning of the subjects' brains in different situations (e.g. stress vs. relaxation). Individual data, for example a CT scan of the defendant's brain, would seem to have more use in courts, but the issue is not that simple. The interpretation of individual data is usually based on conclusions resulting from group data (inductive reasoning). For example, to establish that a particular person's brain is structurally damaged, one must compare its scan with a brain image statistically typical for the population of healthy people. Subsequently, to claim that some damage has affected the brain areas related to, for instance, self-control, one needs to refer to the results of research which has identified such areas in groups of healthy people and to remember that modern neuroscience tends to recognize functional neural networks rather than dedicated brain areas (Knight, 2007). On the other hand, to show that the brain processes of self-control do not work properly, one needs to find research – based on functional neuroimaging – illustrating the (statistically) normal functioning of these processes. Moreover, images of the structure or activity of the brain should also be collated with, among other sources, information on the subject's behavior, for example the results of psychological tasks and tests (Parsons, 2001).

Due to these complex interpretive tasks, a neuroscience expert's opinion on a particular subject inevitably includes, directly or indirectly, both kinds of data. Group data may be considered as statistical evidence, arguments, background knowledge, and so on, but it is clear that without considering them, one cannot use neuroscientific evidence at all.

20.2 ASSUMPTIONS AND INFERENCES

Even these introductory remarks suggest that the interpretation of neuroscientific evidence may be very problematic. The general issue may be well illustrated by the classic *United States* v. *Hinckley* case. In 1981 John Hinckley, Jr. attempted to assassinate US President Ronald Reagan. Hinckley's bullets wounded Reagan, police officer Thomas Delahanty, Secret Service agent Tim McCarthy, and Press Secretary James Brady (Clarke, 1990). However, in the 1982 trial he was found not guilty by reason of insanity (NGRI). The defense evidence included a CT scan showing, according to their expert witnesses, that Hinckley suffered from an organic brain disease. Thus, one of the defense arguments may be reconstructed as follows:

1. The CT scan shows that Hinckley's brain structure is abnormal.
2. The abnormal structure of the brain disrupts brain functioning.
3. This disrupted brain functioning leads to aberrant behaviors and mental disorders (in Hinckley's case, possibly schizophrenia).
4. Those behaviors and disorders constitute "legal" insanity (see below) and therefore are grounds for not finding Hinckley responsible for his actions.

Such multilevel arguments are quite typical in interpreting neuroscientific evidence (Moriarty, Langleben, & Provenzale, 2013). Those "cascades of inferences" (Schum & Martin, 1982) may be even more intricate when functional data are overtly involved. For example, in 1992 Herbert Weinstein was accused of strangling his wife and attempting to disguise it as a suicide (Rushing, 2014). His insanity defense was based on:

- an MRI scan revealing a large cyst in the arachnoid mater, pressing the left frontal, temporal, and insular regions of Weinstein's brain (individual structural data),
- a PET scan showing that the areas of brain tissue pressed by the cyst were not metabolizing glucose at the expected rate (individual functional data),
- theories and research linking acts of aggression to dysfunction within the prefrontal cortex and impaired connections between the frontal lobe and associated limbic brain regions (group functional data).

One can thus reconstruct the following argument:

1. The MRI scan shows a large cyst pressing upon a part of Weinstein's brain.
2. The PET scan demonstrates that this part of Weinstein's brain does not function properly.
3. Neuroscience suggests that it is a part of the human brain crucial to controlling aggression (or at least that its dysfunctions may cause acts of aggression).
4. Weinstein's act of aggression should thus be attributed to his brain condition ("insanity").
5. Weinstein could not control his actions, so he is not criminally responsible.

In general, the problem with cascades of inferences may be described in terms of the multitude of assumptions. "Piling inference upon inference" – as Jane Moriarty put it – leads to the proliferation of presuppositions, doubts and questions: "what constitutes an abnormal scan, whether an allegedly abnormal scan is caused by the trauma, ... whether an abnormal scan is meaningfully correlated with brain trauma and/or behavior" (Moriarty et al., 2013, p. 710) etc. Those should be seen as fracture points – each assumption may be false and the more assumptions one makes, the more error-prone the argument is.

Because of this variety of inferences and assumptions, some more specific pitfalls with the interpretation of neuroscientific evidence may be pointed out, all of which contribute to the cascade-of-inferences problem.

20.3 SPECIFIC PITFALLS

Pitfalls related to early-level inferences are quite obvious and have been widely discussed in the literature. Most crucial here are the issues of reliability and the theoretical validity of neuroscientific tools, methods, and experiments. In the domain of basic research, they involve reservations in relation to, inter alia:

- the quality of hardware, software, and statistical analysis (Plant & Quinlan, 2013; Eklund, Nichols, & Knutsson, 2016),
- the sample sizes and statistical power (Button et al., 2013; Turner et al., 2018),
- publication bias, reproducibility, lack of replications, and failed replications (Chambers et al., 2014; Gilmore et al., 2017; Poldrack et al., 2017).

"Bad science" (Smaldino & McElreath, 2016) simply cannot form the basis for valuable evidence (see Buckholtz & Faigman's 2014 critique of Schauer, 2010).

In the field of applied neuroscience, the most important early-level questions concern the scope of a given method accepted in clinical use (e.g. can PET reliably diagnose brain trauma?) or other practical applications (Schleim & Roiser, 2009) and qualifications of the potential trial experts (Moriarty & Langleben, 2017). It is worth noting that those basic and applied early-level issues are in the focus of the *Daubert* standard and, therefore, of most papers on the admissibility of (neuro) scientific evidence (Feigenson, 2006; Moriarty, 2008; Brindley & Giordano, 2014; Rushing, 2014; Murphy, 2016).

The mostly technical problems above are followed – at the mid-level – by a series of strictly inferential issues stemming from interpretation of individual data and results of experimental research. A good example of an inferential problem is the reverse inference practice. While the classic reasoning in experimental neuroscience takes the form of "if cognitive process X is engaged, then brain area Z is active," many researchers use – suspiciously often to explain the unexpected activations *ex post* – a more problematic kind of inference:

1. In the present study, when task comparison A was presented, brain area Z was active.
2. In other studies, when cognitive process X was putatively engaged, then brain area Z was active.

3. Thus, the activity of area Z in the present study demonstrates engagement of cognitive process X by task comparison A.

(Poldrack, 2006, p. 59)

Such an inference goes "backward" – from the brain activation to the cognitive process – and hence may be called a reverse inference. It is of course not deductively valid: using it one commits the fallacy of affirming the consequent. The brain area Z may be, and most probably is, active not only when the cognitive process X is engaged, but also when processes Y, V, Q, and so on are engaged. Moreover, correlation is not causation – the activation of the area Z "in other studies" could just have coincided with the engagement of the process X (for example, due to a third variable, related both to the activation and the process X). Therefore, the activation of the brain area Z "in the present study" does not guarantee the engagement of the cognitive process X and may even not be its substantial premise. Hence, the usefulness of reverse inference depends strongly on the selectivity of activation of the brain area in question (Poldrack, 2006).

The above remarks alone allow one to have doubts about some possible forms of neuroscientific evidence, especially fMRI lie detection (is brain area L active "because" the person is lying or due to other mental processes? see Farah et al., 2014), but the reverse inference issue is particularly significant in combination with the group-to-individual (G2i) inferential problem (Faigman, Monahan, & Slobogin, 2014): "science's generalized, population-level knowledge of a phenomenon does not necessarily provide an appropriate empirical foundation for making inferences about the instantiation of that phenomenon in any given individual" (Buckholtz & Faigman, 2014, p. 864).

The G2i problem is intimately connected to the (inter-)individual differences in brain functioning and structure. In the hypothetical fMRI lie detection experiment described by Buckholtz and Faigman (2014), the dorsolateral prefrontal cortex (DLPFC) was *on average*, across thirty subjects, statistically significantly more active while lying compared to truth telling. However, in the case of some subjects there was no difference or even higher DLPFC activity during truth telling in comparison with lying. If a court used DLPFC activity as an individual-level biomarker for lying, measurements for some witnesses and defendants would be misleading. Lies by "no difference" subjects would not be detected (false negatives) and subjects showing increased DLPFC activity during truth telling would be incorrectly recognized as liars (false positives).

The G2i pitfall lurks whenever group data are applied to inferences concerning an individual. Looking back to the Weinstein case: do the premises that some part of his brain does not function properly and that – given the group data – this part is important in controlling aggression, guarantee that Weinstein had no neural capability for inhibiting criminal impulses? They do not, and for several different reasons. First, what does it mean that a part of Weinstein's brain did not function properly? It means that the PET scan "demonstrated that the areas of brain tissue that were compressed by the cyst were not metabolizing glucose at the expected [i.e. *average* in a group of control subjects – B.K.] rate" (Rushing, 2014, p. 62). Hence, it actually means that this area in Weinstein's brain did not metabolize *typically* – we cannot be sure whether this impaired Weinstein's capacity for self-control (besides, we cannot even be sure that this area is in fact so important, and, specifically, that it plays a causal role in controlling aggression). The level of metabolism could have been unusually low before the cyst appeared and, even if it was not, it might still be sufficient to exert control. Secondly, neural variability (individual differences) may not only concern the patterns of activation but also the structure of the brain and the locations of its functions (Brett, Johnsrude, & Owen, 2002). We cannot know for sure where exactly the "aggression center" was to be found in Weinstein's brain – if such a thing even exists (see De Boer et al., 2015). Last, but not least, the human brain is quite flexible – it changes structure and function due to experience (Kolb & Whishaw, 1998) and it can also change itself in order to compensate for damage (Ward, 2005). This could well have been the case with Weinstein's brain in relation to self-control. Considering all the above possibilities, the insanity defense argument in *The People of the State of New York* v. *Herbert Weinstein* seems rather weak.

But the pitfalls within cascades of inferences do not end here. High-level inferences are related less to the evidence and more to the legal rules, so they entail questions of a philosophical, normative, and dogmatic – rather than scientific – nature. Arguably, the most urgent high-level challenge in interpreting neuroscientific evidence is the lingua franca problem:

> [M]ost legal rules that reference the mind are underspecified to a degree that confounds appropriate operationalization by scientists. To a cognitive neuroscientist, legal standards like "volitional capacity" and "irresistible impulse" are inherently meaningless. They do not map on to specific mental processes or discrete brain circuits. ... Conversely, cognitive science constructs such as "action cancellation" or "delayed reward discounting" represent valid and distinct species of cognition that can be measured reliably and precisely, yet are foreign to legal decision-makers. There is no coherent framework for linking legal standards referencing mental function to specific, quantifiable cognitive processes. (Buckholtz & Faigman, 2014, p. 864)

Both Weinstein's and Hinckley's insanity defense arguments, and many similar trial inferences based on neuroscientific evidence, suffer from the lingua franca problem.

In the Hinckley trial, the in-force legal standard for insanity was the American Law Institute Test from the Model Penal Code (Slovenko, 1982):

> A person is not responsible for criminal conduct if at the time of such conduct as a result of mental disease or defect he lacks substantial capacity either to appreciate

the criminality [wrongfulness] of his conduct or to conform his conduct to the requirements of law. (Model Penal Code, §4.01(1))

But even today, neuroscientists do not have valid and reliable tools to measure an individual's capacity – either past or present – to understand the difference between right and wrong or to behave in accordance with the law. And, even if such measures existed, setting the norm for "substantial" would not be a task for scientists.

Hence, the evidentiary value of neuroscientific data in the Hinckley trial was at best very limited. However, since the insanity issue had been more or less adequately raised, the burden of proving sanity beyond reasonable doubt was placed upon the prosecution. The NGRI verdict caused public outrage (Hans & Slater, 1983) which led, inter alia, to the passing of the Insanity Defense Reform Act of 1984 (Caplan, 1984). The burden of proof was shifted to the defense, a requirement of the severity of a given mental disease/defect introduced and the volitional alternative (incapacity to conform) eliminated. The federal legislators even tacitly acknowledged the lingua franca problem:

> No expert witness testifying with respect to the mental state or condition of a defendant in a criminal case may state an opinion or inference as to whether the defendant did or did not have the mental state or condition constituting an element of the crime charged or a defense thereto. Such ultimate issues are for the trier of fact alone. (Federal Rules of Evidence, Rule 704(b), later amended)

However, acknowledging a problem is just a first step toward solving it. From the perspective of neuroscience, the insanity defense and other legal constructs pertaining to mental states remain something of a puzzle (Buckholtz, Reyna, & Slobogin, 2016).

20.4 SOME FURTHER ISSUES

Numerous significant issues in interpreting neuroscientific evidence have been sidelined in this chapter due to its nature as a commentary. However, a few at least deserve to be mentioned, albeit in passing.

First, one should consider the problems of external and incremental validity (Buckholtz & Faigman, 2014): Can the conclusions from a particular experiment be generalized and applied outside the laboratory, particularly in courts, and to what extent? Does neuroscientific evidence add value to traditional psychiatric and psychological expertise, or is it virtually redundant?

Second – the pitfalls of scientific authority bias: Do lawyers and people in general expect too much from neuroscience (Buckholtz & Faigman, 2014)? Are jurors excessively impressed by brain images (McCabe & Castel, 2008; McCabe, Castel, & Rhodes, 2011)? Is neuroscientific evidence potentially highly prejudicial (Brown & Murphy, 2009)? Do expert's credentials guarantee the credibility of their opinion?

How can a layperson assess the former and the latter? Do judges and jurors have the requisite intellectual tools to comprehend neuroscientific testimony and discern bad science and unfounded conclusions (Schacter & Loftus, 2013)?

Finally, there is the futility of explaining individual behavior. Neuroscience-oriented defense arguments could be summarized by means of the formula "his brain made him do it" (Gazzaniga, 2011), which sounds like a variation on the good old fundamental attribution error (Ross, 1977). Correlation shall not prove causation (Pearl & Mackenzie, 2018) even if we had access to a live stream from the defendant's brain at the time of the misdeed.

REFERENCES

Andreassi, J. L. (2006). *Psychophysiology: Human Behavior & Physiological Response*, 5th ed. New York: Psychology Press.

Brett, M., Johnsrude, I. S., & Owen, A. M. (2002). The Problem of Functional Localization in the Human Brain. *Nature Reviews Neuroscience* 3, 243–249.

Brindley, T., & Giordano, J. (2014). Neuroimaging: Correlation, Validity, Value, and Admissibility: *Daubert* – and Reliability – Revisited. *AJOB Neuroscience* 5(2), 48–50.

Brown, T., & Murphy, E. (2009). Through a Scanner Darkly: Functional Neuroimaging as Evidence of a Criminal Defendant's Past Mental States. *Stanford Law Review* 62, 1119–1208.

Buckholtz, J. W., & Faigman, D. L. (2014). Promises, Promises for Neuroscience and Law. *Current Biology* 24(18), 861–867.

Buckholtz, J., Reyna, V. F., & Slobogin, C. (2016). A Neuro-Legal Lingua Franca: Bridging Law and Neuroscience on the Issue of Self-Control. *Mental Health Law & Policy Journal* 5, 1–30 (Vanderbilt Public Law Research Paper No. 16–32).

Button, K. S., Ioannidis, J. P., Mokrysz, C., et al.(2013). Power Failure: Why Small Sample Size Undermines the Reliability of Neuroscience. *Nature Reviews Neuroscience* 14(5), 365–376.

Caplan, L. (1984). *The Insanity Defense and the Trial of John W. Hinckley, Jr*. Boston, MA: David R. Godine.

Chambers, C. D., Feredoes, E., Muthukumaraswamy, S. D., & Etchells, P. (2014). Instead of "Playing the Game" It Is Time to Change the Rules: Registered Reports at AIMS Neuroscience and Beyond. *AIMS Neuroscience* 1(1), 4–17.

Clarke, J. W. (1990). *On Being Mad or Merely Angry: John W. Hinckley Jr. and Other Dangerous People*. Princeton, NJ: Princeton University Press.

De Boer, S. F., Olivier, B., Veening, J., & Koolhaas, J. M. (2015). The Neurobiology of Offensive Aggression: Revealing a Modular View. *Physiology & Behavior* 146, 111–127.

Eklund, A., Nichols, T. E., & Knutsson, H. (2016). Cluster Failure: Why fMRI Inferences for Spatial Extent Have Inflated False-Positive Rates. *Proceedings of the National Academy of Sciences* 113(28), 7900–7905.

Faigman, D. L., Monahan, J., & Slobogin, C. (2014). Group to Individual (G2i) Inference in Scientific Expert Testimony. *The University of Chicago Law Review* 81(2), 417–480.

Farah, M. J., Hutchinson, J. B., Phelps, E. A., & Wagner, A. D. (2014). Functional MRI-Based Lie Detection: Scientific and Societal Challenges. *Nature Reviews Neuroscience* 15(2), 123–131.

Feigenson, N. (2006). Brain Imaging and Courtroom Evidence: On the Admissibility and Persuasiveness of fMRI. *International Journal of Law in Context* 2(3), 233–255.

Gazzaniga, M. S. (2011). Neuroscience in the Courtroom. *Scientific American* 304(4), 54–59.
Gilmore, R. O., Diaz, M. T., Wyble, B. A., & Yarkoni, T. (2017). Progress Toward Openness, Transparency, and Reproducibility in Cognitive Neuroscience. *Annals of the New York Academy of Sciences* 1396(1), 5–18.
Goldstone, R. L., Pestilli, F., & Börner, K. (2015). Self-Portraits of the Brain: Cognitive Science, Data Visualization, and Communicating Brain Structure and Function. *Trends in Cognitive Sciences* 19(8), 462–474.
Hans, V. P., & Slater, D. (1983). John Hinckley, Jr. and the insanity defense: The public's verdict. *Public Opinion Quarterly* 47(2), 202–212.
Knight, R. T. (2007). Neural Networks Debunk Phrenology. *Science* 316(5831), 1578–1579.
Kolb, B., & Whishaw, I. Q. (1998). Brain Plasticity and Behavior. *Annual Review of Psychology* 49(1), 43–64.
Loftus, E. F. (2005). Planting Misinformation in the Human Mind: A 30-Year Investigation of the Malleability of Memory. *Learning & Memory* 12(4), 361–366.
Loftus, E. F. (2018). Eyewitness Science and the Legal System. *Annual Review of Law and Social Science* 14, 1–10.
McCabe, D. P., & Castel, A. D. (2008). Seeing Is Believing: The Effect of Brain Images on Judgments of Scientific Reasoning. *Cognition* 107(1), 343–352.
McCabe, D. P., Castel, A. D., & Rhodes, M. G. (2011). The Influence of fMRI Lie Detection Evidence on Juror Decision-Making. *Behavioral Sciences & the Law* 29(4), 566–577.
Moriarty, J. C. (2008). Flickering Admissibility: Neuroimaging Evidence in the US Courts. *Behavioral Sciences & the Law* 26(1), 26–49.
Moriarty, J. C., & Langleben, D. D. (2017). Who Speaks for Neuroscience? Neuroimaging Evidence and Courtroom Expertise. *Case Western Reserve Law Review* 68(3), 783–804.
Moriarty, J. C., Langleben, D. D., & Provenzale, J. M. (2013). Brain Trauma, PET Scans and Forensic Complexity. *Behavioral Sciences & the Law* 31(6), 702–720.
Murphy, E. (2016). Neuroscience and the Civil/Criminal *Daubert* Divide. *Fordham Law Review* 85, 619–639.
Parsons, L. M. (2001). Integrating Cognitive Psychology, Neurology and Neuroimaging. *Acta Psychologica* 107(1–3), 155–181.
Pearl, J., & Mackenzie, D. (2018). *The Book of Why: The New Science of Cause and Effect*. New York: Basic Books.
Plant, R. R., & Quinlan, P. T. (2013). Could Millisecond Timing Errors in Commonly Used Equipment Be a Cause of Replication Failure in Some Neuroscience Studies? *Cognitive, Affective, & Behavioral Neuroscience* 13(3), 598–614.
Poldrack, R. A. (2006). Can Cognitive Processes Be Inferred from Neuroimaging Data? *Trends in Cognitive Sciences* 10(2), 59–63.
Poldrack, R. A., Baker, C. I., Durnez, J., et al.(2017). Scanning the Horizon: Towards Transparent and Reproducible Neuroimaging Research. *Nature Reviews Neuroscience* 18 (2), 115–126.
Ross, L. (1977). The Intuitive Psychologist and His Shortcomings: Distortions in the Attribution Process. In L. Berkowitz (ed.), *Advances in Experimental Social Psychology*, Vol. 10. New York: Academic Press. pp. 173–220.
Rushing, S. E. (2014). The Admissibility of Brain Scans in Criminal Trials: The Case of Positron Emission Tomography. *Court Review* 50, 62–69.
Schacter, D. L., & Loftus, E. F. (2013). Memory and Law: What Can Cognitive Neuroscience Contribute? *Nature Neuroscience* 16(2), 119–123.
Schauer, F. (2010). Can Bad Science Be Good Evidence? Neuroscience, Lie Detection, and Beyond. *Cornell Law Review* 95(6), 1191–1220.

Schleim, S., & Roiser, J. P. (2009). fMRI in Translation: The Challenges Facing Real-World Applications. *Frontiers in Human Neuroscience* 3, 63. DOI: https://doi.org/10.3389/neuro.09.063.2009

Schum, D. A., & Martin, A. W. (1982). Formal and Empirical Research on Cascaded Inference in Jurisprudence. *Law & Society Review* 17(1), 105–152.

Slovenko, R. (1982). The Insanity Defense in the Wake of the Hinckley Trial. *Rutgers Law Journal* 14, 373.

Smaldino, P. E., & McElreath, R. (2016). The Natural Selection of Bad Science. *Royal Society Open Science* 3(9), 160384. DOI: https://doi.org/10.1098/rsos.160384

Turner, B. O., Paul, E. J., Miller, M. B., & Barbey, A. K. (2018). Small Sample Sizes Reduce the Replicability of Task-Based fMRI Studies. *Communications Biology* 1(1), 1–10.

Ward, N. S. (2005). Neural Plasticity and Recovery of Function. *Progress in Brain Research* 150, 527–535.

21

Explanation-Based Approaches to Reasoning about Evidence and Proof in Criminal Trials

Anne Ruth Mackor, Hylke Jellema and Peter J. van Koppen[*]

21.1 INTRODUCTION

In this chapter we discuss explanation-based theories on reasoning about evidence and proof in criminal trials that view such reasoning in terms of evaluating competing explanations. The theories are all grounded in the cognitive psychology of decision making (notably Cohen, 1977; Kahneman, Slovic & Tversky, 1982; Pennington & Hastie, 1993; Gigerenzer & Engel, 2006; Gigerenzer, 2007; Bennett & Feldman, 2014). They aim to describe how people actually reason when they have to make sense of a great deal of evidence in, for example, criminal trials. According to these theories, people in such contexts typically construct one or more causal explanations for the evidence.

The explanation-based approaches that we discuss in this chapter extend these empirical findings by developing theories that are, in varying degrees, normative. That is, they are concerned with the question of how people should reason about legal evidence if they want to do so in a rational manner. These theories investigate to what extent people actually reason in a rational manner but also to what extent they should change their manner of doing so. In particular, we discuss three theories, namely Allen and Pardo's relative plausibility theory, Amaya's theory of inference to the most coherent explanation and Van Koppen's theory of anchored narratives or, as it has also been called, the scenario theory. These three theories have the following in common: (i) that causal explanation, more specifically inference to the best explanation (IBE), is at their heart; (ii) that coherence is a core criterion to assess the quality of explanations; and (iii) that as normative theories, they try to stay close to how people actually reason, both in everyday life and in criminal trials. We have chosen to discuss these three theories in some depth instead of giving an overview of all explanation-based theories or trying to give a general characterization of explanation-based approaches.

---

[*] The authors thank Christian Dahlman, Jaap Hage, Ronald Meester and Henry Prakken for their comments on an earlier version of this chapter.

In the literature about evidence and proof in criminal law, explanation-based approaches are generally contrasted with probabilistic, more specifically Bayesian, approaches (Tillers & Green, 1988; Schum, 1994; Fenton, Neil, & Berger, 2016). In Section 21.3 we discuss Bayesian critiques of explanation-based approaches and in Section 21.4 we discuss explanation-based critiques of Bayesian approaches.[1] Here we briefly mention the most salient differences. The approaches differ in particular with respect to the three core characteristics just mentioned.

One important difference between normative explanation-based and probabilistic approaches is that the latter do not aim to stay, or focus on staying as close as possible to how human beings actually reason. Next to that, although the notion of probability plays a role in explanation-based approaches, it is not the core notion used to assess the quality of the explanations. Instead, coherence plays a central role. In the last few years a debate has been going on about the question of whether explanatory coherence can be explicated in probabilistic terms (Shogenji, 1999; Fitelson, 2003; Olsson, 2005 and 2019; Siebel, 2011; Schippers, 2016). Finally, causality and explanation mark the perhaps most important differences between explanation-based and probabilistic approaches. There is no room here to provide an extensive analysis of causality and explanation. However, in a nutshell, to state that A is a cause of B is not merely to claim that B happened after A, or that there is a correlation between the occurrence of A's and B's, or that the occurrence of A makes the occurrence of B more probable, but that A is efficacious in bringing about B. Accordingly, on an explanation-based approach, first and foremost there is and should be a causal explanation of evidence, and only then should factfinders assess the probability that certain events happened. An explanation is an answer to a why-question, and a causal explanation is an answer to a why-question in which the cause is said to explain why the evidence has occurred. Thus, a causal explanation does not merely predict or retrodict the probability that the evidence occurs, but it aims to answer the question of why the evidence has occurred. Moreover, it allows for counterfactual reasoning (for answering questions as to when and why evidence would have occurred) by offering information about causes and mechanisms. It is said that in this manner, causal explanations aim to offer more than probabilities; namely, knowledge or understanding.

In Section 21.5 we discuss the question of whether a productive partnership between explanation-based and probabilistic approaches is possible. First, however, we describe the three explanation-based theories in some detail.

---

[1] We do not compare the explanation-based approach to a third, argumentative, approach in which logical inference is a core notion (Bex et al., 2003; Anderson, Schum & Twining, 2005; Walton, Reed & Macagno, 2008; Bex et al., 2010). Unlike explanation-based theories and some Bayesian approaches, the argumentative approach is generally seen as useful only to reason about details of a case but not to reason about and to model a complete criminal case (Prakken, 2020). For this reason, the argumentative approach is not dealt with in this chapter.

21.2 THREE EXPLANATION-BASED APPROACHES

21.2.1 *The Story Model of Pennington and Hastie*

The starting point of the scenario theory of Van Koppen (Section 21.2.4) and, to a lesser extent, of the relative plausibility theory of Allen and Pardo (Section 21.2.2) is psychological research into the way people actually reason when they have to deal with a great amount of evidence. Both Van Koppen and Allen and Pardo refer specifically to the story model of Pennington and Hastie (1993). Therefore, this section starts with an exposition of the model.[2]

The story model is a descriptive psychological theory about cognitive strategies that factfinders use to process trial information in order to make decisions about evidence and proof. Pennington and Hastie claim that factfinders typically use one central strategy, namely active story construction. In doing so, factfinders impose a narrative story organization on the trial information (Pennington & Hastie, 1993, p. 194; Bennett & Feldman, 2014;). Their model offers an analysis, both of the structure of these stories and of the dynamics of the way in which people construct and reason about stories.

21.2.1.1 The Structure of Stories

Stories consist of elements, which are called *episodes*. Episodes consist of specific elements, such as an initiating event, a psychological response, sometimes a goal, an action and a consequence. Episodes have a specific structure: the elements are chronologically connected through physical and mental causal relationships. Stories can be thought of as a hierarchy of episodes (Pennington & Hastie, 1993, p. 197). Take for example the following episode that is also a simple story: a husband has an argument with his wife (initiating event), which makes him angry (psychological response). Because he intends to hurt her (goal), he beats his wife (action), which causes her death (consequence).

21.2.1.2 The Dynamics of Stories

Factfinders construct stories by reasoning from *three kinds of knowledge*. They use:

a) case-specific knowledge, i.e. evidence;
b) knowledge about similar events to infer facts and causal relationships;
c) knowledge about what makes a story complete: knowledge about the typical elements of stories, episodes and their elements, and about the connections in and between episodes. (Pennington & Hastie, 1993, p. 194)

---

[2] This section is an adaptation of section 2.1 of Dahlman and Mackor (2019).

Factfinders use (b) and (c) to 'fill out' a story. Thus, on the story model, a story consists of evidence, inferred facts and the causal relations between them. Unlike the normative scenario approach, Pennington and Hastie do not always sharply distinguish between the elements, that is the hypotheses in the story, and the evidence for the story.

Pennington and Hastie (1993, p. 195) mention in particular *three types of reasoning procedures* that factfinders use to establish intermediate and final conclusions:

- deductive reasoning from world knowledge;
- reasoning from analogy to other – experienced and hypothetical – episodes;
- reasoning by evaluating alternate conclusions that contradict the initial conclusion.

Finally, Pennington and Hastie (1993, pp. 198–9) mention three *certainty principles* that factfinders use to assess stories, namely coverage, coherence and uniqueness. These principles help a fact trier to determine how acceptable a story is for him and how confident he is about the truth of the story:

1. COVERAGE. Coverage deals with the question of to what extent the story explains the occurrence of the evidence. The greater the coverage, the more acceptable the story and the more confident the factfinder will be.

2. UNIQUENESS. A story is unique if it is the only coherent story that can account for the evidence. If there is more than one coherent story, all stories are in principle acceptable, but confidence in each of them will diminish.

3. COHERENCE. Coherence has three components: consistency, plausibility and completeness.

   3a) consistency is about two questions, namely (1) whether the story is consistent with evidence believed to be true and (2) whether all of its elements are consistent with other parts of the story.
   3b) plausibility deals with the question of whether the story fits into the factfinders' background or world knowledge.
   3c) completeness is about the question of whether the structure of the story has all its parts, such as episodes, elements of episodes and causal relationships in and between episodes. missing information (story gaps) and lack of plausible inferences make a story incomplete and decrease confidence in the story.

Pennington and Hastie state that consistency, plausibility and completeness can be fulfilled to a greater or lesser degree and that the values of the three components combine to yield the overall coherence of the story (Pennington & Hastie, 1993, p. 199). They do not offer a further specification of the components of coherence, nor of the way the individual weight of the components is assessed and the way in which these weights are combined. Moreover, given the fact that a consistent set of statements need not be coherent, their analysis of coherence, which is only in terms of consistency and completeness, may not be fully adequate.

21.2.2 *Allen and Pardo's Relative Plausibility Theory*

In recent decades Allen and Pardo's *relative plausibility theory* has arguably been one of the major contributing factors in a shift in thinking about legal evidence – from probabilistic to explanatory thinking (Allen & Pardo, 2019b, p. 1). We now turn to an explanation of their theory, drawing mainly on a recent special issue of the *International Journal of Evidence and Proof*, which was dedicated to a renewed defence of their theory and to the responses of fourteen critics (Allen & Pardo, 2019a, 2019b).

Allen and Pardo state that their goal is to explain the different facets of juridical proof of the American legal system, thereby making that system understandable. They propose a theory which they believe is not just descriptively appropriate in light of that system, but also normatively (Allen & Pardo, 2019b, p. 2). They focus on proof standards and how to interpret these in terms of explanations (more on that in Section 21.2.2.1). However, they seek to explain many other aspects of legal proof as well, including (i) jury decision making; (ii) how evidence is presented by the parties and used in argumentation; (iii) how evidence is processed by humans; (iv) how rules of evidence create the trial structure; and (v) the structure of litigation before and after the trial (Allen & Pardo, 2019b, pp. 3–4). So, while their goal of explaining reasoning and decision making is related to that of Pennington and Hastie's story model, Allen and Pardo's goal is broader. As they themselves put it, whereas the story model is an empirical description of juror reasoning, relative plausibility theory is an explanation of the 'standards of proof and other features of the proof process' (Allen & Pardo, 2019b, p. 17, n. 86).

The core of the relative plausibility theory is that juridical proof involves determining the comparative plausibility of competing explanations (Allen & Leiter, 2001, pp. 1527–8). In their words: 'The primary message of relative plausibility is that from beginning to end the legal system pushes the parties to provide competing explanations, and these explanations structure the decision that is subsequently made' (Allen & Pardo, 2019b, p. 4). For instance, parties in dispute try to show weaknesses in the cases of their opponents and try to show that their own version of reality is true. Factfinders then have to determine which of these competing explanations best explains the available evidence and to decide accordingly (Pardo & Allen, 2008, p. 228).[3] We now turn to three central aspects of the relative

---

[3] Pardo and Allen (2008) have also called their account 'inference to the best explanation'. However, Laudan (2007) and Nance (Nance, 2001) call inference to the best explanation a misnomer. They point

plausibility theory: explanations, plausibility and their account of the proof standards.

21.2.2.1 Explanations

As with Pennington and Hastie's story model, the relative plausibility theory proceeds from the premise that humans process evidence 'holistically'. According to Allen and Pardo, holistic processing means that people structure evidence and evaluate it by tying it to (causal) explanations when making inferences (Allen & Pardo, 2019b, p. 10).[4] In that respect, the two approaches are very similar. Allen and Pardo use the empirical research underlying the story model – which is evidence that people reason holistically – to support their own theory (Allen & Pardo, 2019b, pp. 16–17). However, their notion of an 'explanation' is not exactly the same as that of a 'story'.

Allen and Pardo's definition of an 'explanation' is somewhat general: it is 'an answer to the question "what happened" in the particular context of the dispute in question' (Allen & Pardo, 2019a, p. 7). In other words, it is an answer to the question of what caused the evidence in this particular case. For example, suppose there is a rape case in which DNA evidence was found, where we have a witness statement of the (alleged) victim that the defendant sexually assaulted her and we have another witness who states that he has seen the defendant running away from the crime scene. One explanation of such evidence is that the defendant did indeed assault the victim. A competing explanation is that the evidence was fabricated by the victim. Both are answers to the question: what happened that caused this evidence (the DNA evidence, the report and the witness)?

Allen and Pardo see stories as a specific type of (causal) explanation that have the form of a chronological narrative (Allen & Pardo, 2019b, p. 34). Such a story is therefore a specific series of chronologically and causally connected events. However, they claim that not all (causal) explanations take such a chronological form. So, while stories are explanations, not all explanations are stories. In contrast with stories, explanations can also be 'disjunctive' and 'general' (Allen & Pardo, 2019b, p. 13, n. 86). Disjunctive explanations are made up of mutually exclusive events – so 'this happened or that', while

---

out that in criminal cases, Allen and Pardo's theory implies that the factfinder does not always choose the best theory. That happens, for example, when the best explanation is not good enough or when the disjunction of multiple explanations in favour of innocence are jointly more plausible than the best explanation implying guilt.

[4] Allen and Pardo contrast holistic reasoning with the sequential updating presumed by probabilistic models in which, or so they claim, evidence is processed item by item. A more in-depth critique of probabilistic approaches is given in Section 21.4. The probabilistic approach to evidence and the probabilistic critique of explanation-based approaches is discussed in Section 21.3.2.

general explanations can be of the form 'something (else) happened' (Pardo, 2013, pp. 598–599).[5]

Furthermore, while they do not say that explicitly, another possible difference is that not all good explanations have to contain the elements that good stories do, such as a motive and an action. Allen and Pardo note that in areas like no-fault divorce, anti-trust litigation and contract litigation, explanations often do not take the form of stories. However, they also point out that in criminal trials and tort cases, explanations are usually stories (Allen & Pardo, 2019b, p. 27).

21.2.2.2 Plausibility

According to the relative plausibility theory, explanations should be judged and compared in terms of their plausibility. Allen and Pardo contrast the notion of plausibility with that of probability, which is the key concept in probabilistic approaches to legal evidence. While they do not offer a very precise distinction between the two concepts, we can roughly interpret it as follows. According to them probability is a quantitative concept, leading to statements such as 'I believe that the probability that the defendant is guilty is 0.92' (Allen & Pardo, 2019a, p. 4 n.15). Yet, as Pardo and Allen point out, such probabilistic conclusions either require objective numbers or rely on subjective degrees of belief. Yet, objective numbers are usually difficult to obtain or estimate in legal contexts (Allen & Pardo, 2019b, pp. 9–10). Furthermore, probability theory sets hardly any constraints on subjective degrees of belief. The Kolmogorov axioms of probability, which are discussed in Section 21.4, set only very weak limits on what kinds of probabilities are acceptable, such as that the probability of events should be between 0 and 1. However, such constraints do not rule out many kinds of reasoning that we would ordinarily call irrational and that conflict with the legal system's goal of obtaining accurate outcomes (Allen & Pardo, 2019b, pp. 9–10). For instance, if a factfinder believes that the probability that a defendant is guilty is 100 per cent, on a probabilistic account no amount of evidence can result in any other conclusion. However, we would not call a factfinder who convicts all defendants, even when there is overwhelming evidence for their innocence, rational. Yet nothing in probability theory rules out such a dogmatic and irrational stance.

Plausibility, on the other hand, is a non-numerical notion and its assessment depends on the evidence and our background beliefs. More specifically, an explanation is more plausible when 'it is consistent, simpler, explains more and different types of facts (consilience), better accords with background beliefs (coherence), is less ad hoc, and so on; and is worse to extent [sic] it betrays these criteria' (Pardo &

---

[5] For instance, Allen and Pardo (2019b, p. 24) mention that plaintiffs in *res ipsa loquitur* cases may win by proving that 'the defendant did something negligently and thereby caused my injuries' without being able to identify a specific cause.

Allen, 2008, p. 230).⁶ However, Allen and Pardo say little else about how these criteria should be interpreted and applied.

While plausibility differs from probability, the goal of assessing the plausibility of competing explanations is to reach probabilistic conclusions. Allen and Pardo write that '[e]xplanatory criteria guide inferences and judgments about likelihood' (Allen & Pardo, 2019b, p. 17) and that 'the better the explanation, the more likely true' (Pardo & Allen, 2008, p. 9, n.45). Nevertheless, we should not conclude that 'the best explanation' therefore simply means 'the most likely explanation' or that inferences about plausibility are identical to probabilistic judgements (Allen & Pardo, 2019b, p. 20). Instead, inference to the best explanation is a method of arriving at probabilistic conclusions. That fits with how other authors, such as Lipton (2004) and Poston (2014) have described the role of IBE. We discuss the relation between explanation-based and probabilistic approaches in more detail in Sections 21.4 and 21.5.⁷

21.2.2.3 Proof Standards

While Allen and Pardo aim to explain various aspects mainly of the American proof process, they focus in particular on proof standards. Proof standards determine when certain key propositions, such as whether the defendant is guilty, count as legally proven. Allen and Pardo interpret such proof standards in terms of a comparison of the plausibility of different explanations. Whether an explanation satisfies the proof standard depends on the strength of the possible explanations supporting each side (Allen & Pardo, 2019b, p. 13). For instance, under the 'preponderance of the evidence' standard, which is used in civil cases, the party with the most plausible explanation wins (Allen & Pardo, 2019b, p. 14). Under the more stringent 'clear and convincing evidence' standard, which is also used in civil cases, a party wins if their explanation is clearly more plausible than that of the other party (Allen & Pardo, 2019b, p. 15). However, in this chapter we are primarily concerned with criminal law and therefore we restrict ourselves to a discussion of the beyond-a-reasonable-doubt standard.

On the relative plausibility theory, guilt is proven beyond a reasonable doubt only if there is a sufficiently plausible explanation that implies guilt and there is no plausible explanation which is consistent with innocence (Pardo & Allen, 2008, p. 238). Allen and Pardo contrast their interpretation of that proof standard with a probabilistic interpretation, according to which the standard should be interpreted as a probability threshold. Guilt is then proven if the probability that the defendant committed the criminal act of which he is accused exceeds a certain threshold (e.g. 95 per cent).

---

⁶ Pardo and Allen (2008) seem to derive these criteria from Thagard (1978). Amaya also builds upon Thagard's theory, but – as we will see in Section 21.2.3 – her theory is more precise and detailed.
⁷ Allen and Pardo (2019b, p. 12, n.74) explicitly refer to Lipton's approach.

In conclusion, Allen and Pardo offer an alternative to probabilistic accounts of legal evidence.[8] In doing so they have put the discussion about explanation-based versus probabilistic approaches on the agenda. However, their account remains underspecified on several points. In particular, they say little about the nature of explanatory reasoning and about what makes explanations plausible. While they state that explanatory reasoning is holistic and distinguish criteria such as coherence, they do not elaborate upon these terms. In the next section we turn to Amaya's theory, which offers a detailed analysis both of the concept of coherence and of the process of coherence maximization.

21.2.3 *Amaya's Theory of Inference to the Most Coherent Explanation*

Amaya's theory of inference to the most coherent explanation (Amaya, 2009, 2013, 2015) is built on Thagard's theory of explanatory coherence (Thagard, 2000).[9] Amaya offers a detailed analysis of coherence and the role it should play in inferences in evidential judgements in law. Thus, Amaya's theory is an analysis of both of the *concept* of coherence and the *process* of coherence maximization. Coherence is claimed to play a role in the generation and the pursuit as well as in the justification of evidential judgements in criminal law.

The purpose of Amaya's theory is not to describe or explain legal practice, in America or elsewhere. Thus, it is much less focused on legal practice than Allen and Pardo's theory. Also, although Thagard developed his theory as competitor to a probabilistic model, Amaya's goal is not, unlike those of Thagard and Allen and Pardo, to criticize probabilism. Finally, although Amaya's theory focuses on coherence, it does not make use of the story model and the role coherence plays in this model. In particular, she claims that her notion of coherence as constraint satisfaction differs from the notion of narrative coherence as it is used in the descriptive story model (Amaya, 2015, p. 109).

The two most important ingredients of Amaya's theory are coherence and inference to the best explanation. On Amaya's view, the best explanation of a (criminal) fact is the one that does best on a test of coherence (Amaya, 2009, p. 137). A third and fourth component of Amaya's theory are a responsibilist epistemology (Amaya, 2013, p. 24) and the demand that standards of justification should be contextualized (Amaya, 2013, p. 27). In a responsibilist epistemology, justification is not analysed exclusively in terms of evidential support, but also in terms of what a factfinder has done or failed to do, more particularly in terms of how *thorough* or *robust* the investigations have been (Amaya, 2009, p. 154). The fourth component, the demand of contextualization, implies that the theory of inference to the most coherent

---

[8] We discuss their critique of probabilistic interpretation of the proof standard in Section 21.4.
[9] This section is an adaptation of Dahlman and Mackor (2019), section 2.2.

explanation should *fit the specific context* in which it is applied. In this section, the focus is on criminal law, more specifically on its rules and principles.

21.2.3.1 Coherence

Amaya relies on Thagard's analysis of coherence, in particular on his analysis of explanatory coherence. Thagard (2000, pp. 15 ff.) defines coherence as the satisfaction of a set of positive and negative constraints – coherence and incoherence relations – among a set of elements. The set of elements E is divided into two disjoint subsets A (accepted) and R (rejected).[10]

The main elements in the assessment of evidentiary judgements in a criminal case are hypotheses (H) and evidence (E). The main, but not the only, type of coherence involved in these judgements is explanatory coherence.[11]

Thagard (2000, p. 43) distinguishes seven principles of explanatory coherence. Amaya states that when applying Thagard's theory to a particular problem, it must be further specified and contextualized. In her application of Thagard's theory in the context of criminal law, she adds two coherence principles, namely to E4 and to E7 (see later on in this section) and she stresses that next to explanatory coherence, deliberative coherence should play a role too. She does not, however, offer a further specification of the elements (H and E) in the set. More specifically, Amaya does not distinguish between kinds of hypotheses and between types of evidence. In particular she does not incorporate the distinction between episodes and the different kinds of elements that the story model distinguishes.

We list Thagard's seven principles of explanatory coherence and also the two subprinciples Amaya adds to them:

E1: symmetry
Explanatory coherence is a symmetrical relation, unlike explanatory relations and relations of conditional probability.[12]

E2: explanation
  a) a hypothesis (h) coheres with what it explains, evidence (e) or another hypothesis (h);

---

[10] A problem with the idea of constraint satisfaction is that the constraints are not equally important and must therefore be weighted. Thagard's theory does not answer the question of according to which criteria weights should be assigned.

[11] Thagard (2000) distinguishes between explanatory, analogical, deductive, visual, conceptual and deliberative coherence.

[12] For instance: whereas two propositions H and E cohere with each other equally, explanation is asymmetrical in that H causally explains E, but E does not causally explain H. E is part of an evidential explanation of H, i.e. E is a reason to believe H. The asymmetry of conditional probability is even more obvious in that the probability that H is true given E, i.e. $p(H|E)$, is not the same as the probability that E is true given H, i.e. $p(E|H)$. Those who do not distinguish between these two probabilities commit the so-called prosecutor's fallacy.

b) hypotheses that together explain another proposition (h or e) cohere;
c) the more hypotheses are needed to explain something, the lower the degree of coherence.[13]

E3: analogy
Similar hypotheses that explain similar pieces of evidence cohere.[14]

E4: data priority
Propositions that describe the results of observations and evidence have a degree of acceptability on their own.

For the context of criminal law, Amaya (2013, p. 13) adds the principle that factual hypotheses that are compatible with innocence have a degree of acceptability on their own. She adds this principle to satisfy the demand of the presumption of innocence.

E5: contradiction
Contradictory propositions are incoherent with each other.

E6: competition
Hypotheses that explain a proposition but that are not explanatorily connected are incoherent (i.e., they are incoherent even if they do not contradict each other).

E7: acceptance
The acceptability of a proposition in a system depends on its coherence with other propositions.

For the context of criminal law Amaya (2013, p. 13) adds the principle that the guilt hypothesis may be accepted only if it is justified to a degree sufficient to satisfy the reasonable-doubt standard.

21.2.3.2 Inference to the Most Coherent Explanation

Amaya (2009, 2013, 2015) not only offers an analysis of the concept of coherence but also of the process of coherence maximization. She argues that that process is an explanatory inference, that fits the model of inference to the best explanation.[15] Amaya uses Lycan's (1988, 2002) definition of IBE:

---

[13] That principle expresses the epistemic virtue of simplicity. Note that simplicity is an ambiguous term. It can refer to the number of hypotheses but it can also refer to the number of hypotheses in relation to the number of pieces of evidence they explain. Thagard (1978) also discusses other epistemic virtues, such as consilience and analogy. Allen and Pardo (2019b) also refer to epistemic virtues, among which simplicity and consilience, as criteria to assess the quality of explanations.

[14] Thus, analogical coherence plays a role in the assessment of explanatory coherence. Pennington and Hastie (1993, p. 195) too claim that people reason by analogy to experienced or hypothetical episodes and that in their doing so, analogies play an important role in 'filling out' the story in parts where evidence is missing.

[15] Note that just as a distinction is made between the descriptive story model and the normative scenario approach, a distinction is made between descriptive and normative theories about IBE. Lipton (2004), for instance, offers an analysis that is primarily descriptive, giving an account of how people actually

F1 ... Fn are facts in need of explanation
Hypothesis H explains F1 ... Fn
No available competing hypothesis explains Fi as well as H does

---

Therefore, H is probably true

As was explicated above, Amaya's criterion of best explanation is best on a coherence test. She states that an inference to the most coherent explanation consists of the following explanatory inference steps (Amaya, 2013, p. 16):

1) the specification of a base of coherence, i.e. the set of factual hypotheses and evidence over which the coherence calculus proceeds;
2) the construction of a contrast set that contains a number of alternative theories from which the most coherent is to be selected;
3) refining and revising the alternative theories by means of coherence-making mechanisms, in particular addition, subtraction and, the combination of the two, reinterpretation. That can result in a revision of the contrast set (2), but it can also lead to revision of the base set (1);
4) the evaluation of the coherence of the alternative theories by means of the principles of explanatory coherence E_1–E_7;
5) the selection as justified of the most coherent theory, provided that its degree of justification satisfies the applicable legal standard of proof, which is the beyond-a-reasonable-doubt standard in the context of criminal law.

21.2.3.3 Coherence versus Intuition

Amaya explicitly considers the possibility that the theory that best satisfies the criteria of coherence nevertheless seems intuitively unjustified (Amaya, 2013, p. 18). She points out that errors may have been made in step 1, the selection of the elements of the base set of hypotheses and evidence. In particular, it is possible that relevant evidence has been ignored. In step 2, the construction of the contrast set, factfinders can also fail and as a consequence of that they will at best end up with an inference to the best of a bad lot (Van Fraassen, 1989). That critique is discussed in Section 21.3.2.

Problems can also arise in the inference to the most coherent explanation (step 4). Amaya points out that people suffer from coherence bias, since they may inflate some alternatives and deflate others in order to maximize coherence. By ignoring or misrepresenting evidence or alternative hypotheses, they distort the set of evidence and hypotheses that threatens their beliefs.

How can factfinders prevent these errors? Amaya explicitly mentions the duty to actively search for alternative hypotheses (Amaya, 2013, p. 26); she also mentions the

reason. He also offers a tentative normative approach, giving an account of how people should reason if they want to be rational.

duty to gather additional evidence about propositions that are less certain and instructs factfinders to believe all and only propositions that are supported by available evidence (Amaya, 2013, pp. 25–6). These duties are part of her responsibilist epistemology, which entails the demand to perform robust investigations.

In conclusion, Amaya offers a detailed analysis, both of the concept of coherence and of the process of coherence maximization. Amaya does not, however, make use of the story model. We now turn to an approach that explicitly takes the descriptive story model as its starting point for a normative theory.

21.2.4 *Van Koppen's Scenario Theory*

The theory of anchored narratives, or the scenario approach as we call it here, has its roots in the story model of Pennington and Hastie.[16] Wagenaar, Van Koppen and Crombag (1993) developed the story model into both a descriptive and a normative theory. In this chapter we only discuss the normative version of the scenario approach. The normative theory only deals with criminal trials and explicates how people should reason if they want to make rational decisions about evidence and proof. Since 1993, the approach has been developed further, especially by Van Koppen (2011, 2013) and more recently by Van Koppen and Mackor (2020).

Like the theories of Allen and Pardo and Amaya, the scenario approach conceives of reasoning about evidence in criminal trials in terms of explanations, more specifically causal explanations. An important difference between the scenario approach and the theories of Amaya and of Allen and Pardo is the central role that stories or scenarios play. Amaya does not make use of the story model, and we have seen that Allen and Pardo refer to Pennington and Hastie's theory, but claim that parties offer explanations which can but need not be stories (Allen & Pardo, 2019b, p. 3 n. 7 and p. 13 n. 86).

Another difference between the relative plausibility theory and the scenario theory is that the former is primarily an explanatory account of the American system of legal proof, whereas the latter is primarily a normative theory. A possible reason for that difference may be that the American legal system has already developed a complex set of rules of evidence. One of Allen and Pardo's aims is to show that these rules are rational. Such a set of rules is lacking in the Netherlands and in many other countries. Accordingly, in the Netherlands and elsewhere, there was and still is a need for a normative theory that offers legal practitioners a set of criteria that can guide them through reasoning with evidence in criminal law.

A final difference between the relative plausibility theory and the scenario approach is that the former emphasizes that probabilism is incorrect and incompatible with trials (Allen & Pardo, 2019b, abstract, p. 1), whereas the latter does not make such a bold claim. On the contrary, in its more recent version (Van Koppen &

---

[16] This section is based on Van Koppen and Mackor (2020, section 1).

Mackor, 2020), the value of triangulation – that is, of comparing the analyses of different approaches to reasoning about and with evidence – is emphasized and it is argued that explanation-based and probabilistic approaches are not only compatible but also complementary.[17]

The scenario theory is underpinned by insights from three different disciplines: psychology, epistemology and philosophy of science. From psychology it takes the notion of stories or scenarios (Pennington & Hastie, 1993). From psychology and epistemology, it takes the idea that in everyday life people both use and should use IBE (Harman, 1965; Lipton, 2004) to create, evaluate and select scenarios. From epistemology the scenario theory takes a coherentist view of knowledge (Amaya, 2009, 2013, 2015; Thagard, 2000) as opposed to foundationalist theories. Finally, insights from the philosophy of science are applied in scenario theory, in particular Popper's falsificationist theory (Popper, 1963), drawing on the analogy between the assessment of scientific theories and the assessment of scenarios.

The scenario approach is based on the following core notions: scenario; coherence; background knowledge; IBE, alternative scenarios and discriminating facts; falsification; and prediction. These notions are spelled out below.

21.2.4.1 Scenarios

The core notion of the scenario approach is 'story', 'narrative' or 'scenario'. Following Pennington and Hastie (1993), the scenario theory entails that a scenario is a hypothesis about an action (or event), offering a chronological and causal description of that action. A scenario consists of at least a central action and a scene that makes the central action understandable. A scenario can have more elements, which can be categorized under one of these headings: scene, motive, action, actor, consequences. In a complete scenario all these components are described. The scenario approach emphasizes that the scenario of the prosecution should be compared to at least one alternative scenario.

21.2.4.2 Coherence

The central question in the scenario approach is: why should we believe that the indictment is true? The scenario approach endorses a coherentist view of knowledge to answer that question. Coherentist views should be distinguished from foundationalist, in particular empiricist, views. Scenarios are not anchored, as foundationalist empiricists see it, in facts about the case under investigation or in our sensory experiences of these facts, but in a coherent web of statements about the world. In that web, some statements, in particular statements about observations that are

---

[17] Van Koppen's (2011) more critical view of probabilistic approaches to evidence and proof is discussed in Section 21.4.

accepted as true, have more weight than others, but none of the statements are foundational or anchored in 'the world' or in our observations of 'the world'.[18]

According to the scenario approach, for a scenario to be coherent it should minimally fulfil the following three criteria:

a) it must be internally coherent,
b) it must be coherent with background knowledge,
c) it must be coherent with all the evidence about the case.

These criteria are derived from, but differ slightly from, those of Pennington and Hastie (1993).

First (a), a scenario must be internally coherent. For a scenario to be internally coherent, it must be internally consistent (i), complete (ii) and detailed (iii).

i) The criterion of internal consistency demands that statements within one scenario do not contradict each other.
ii) A scenario can be more or less complete. That means that it can have more or fewer of the elements mentioned earlier, as for instance scene, motive, action, actor, consequences.
iii) Detailedness concerns the level of detail of the content of each of the elements.

The more details there are, the fewer story gaps the scenario contains. We distinguish between *story gaps* and *evidence gaps*. A story gap is a gap in the story being told. For instance, the simple story 'I was in Amsterdam this morning and am in London now', has a gap, namely how I got from Amsterdam to London. An evidence gap is a gap in the anchoring of a part of the scenario via sub-scenarios in background knowledge. So, if there is no evidence that I was in Amsterdam this morning, the story has an evidence gap on that point. If there is a story gap, there cannot – for lack of a story – be an evidence gap. Conversely, the more details in the story, the more options to predict and confirm facts, but also the larger the risk of falsifications and evidence gaps (Popper, 1935).

Second (b), a scenario must be coherent with our general background knowledge. In fact, world knowledge is paramount in every aspect of the scenario theory. It determines our judgement about whether a piece of evidence is relevant to what needs to be proven. It also determines how strong evidence is considered as proof of something. It also determines how we interpret scenarios and evidence. And it determines what additional probing must be done before a proposition is considered proven. At the same time, our general – and usually shared – background knowledge of the world changes all the time. In this sense background knowledge may be as dynamic as scenarios can be.

---

[18] Compare Thagard's principle E4 about data priority. See Section 21.2.3.

The central claim the scenario approach makes is that each and every word and sentence in each scenario carries a lot of general world knowledge that we take for granted. It is usually left implicit, but that world knowledge guides us through the scenarios and sub-scenarios. Part of that background knowledge is contained in scripts and the concept of a scenario is related to that of a script (Taylor & Crocker, 1981; DiMaggio, 1997; Kleider et al., 2008). Scripts contain general background knowledge about the world and the object of the script.

For example, if a scenario entails that a husband killed his wife, we can derive the fact that the suspect and victim knew each other, had a heterosexual relationship, perhaps have children, and much more. That information is based on what we call our shared knowledge of the world. It is often taken for granted, but it may become important any time in a case and can lead to a discussion about evidence.

The distinction between the internal coherence of a scenario and coherence of the scenario with background knowledge can be explicated as follows. A fairy tale, for example, can be internally coherent, but not coherent with background knowledge. The same holds for a story that is internally consistent, but empirically impossible or extremely implausible, such as the scenario in which the defendant has travelled by car at an average speed of 300 km/h.

Third and finally (c.), a scenario must be coherent with specific knowledge about the case under consideration.

The scenario approach is also called the theory of anchored narratives because we can rephrase criteria 2 and 3 as the demand that the scenario must be 'anchored', not in 'the world', but in narratives about the world that are accepted as true. The answer to the question 'Why should we believe . . . ?' is the evidence that will always take the form of another scenario or multiple scenarios. These scenarios are called sub-scenarios. These sub-scenarios, when accepted, form the evidence in the case that, in the end, is anchored in generally accepted knowledge about the world. In practice the – in principle endless – regression into next levels of sub-scenarios ends.

An important question, however, is why we should be justified in accepting scenarios that are internally coherent, coherent with the evidence at hand and with our general background knowledge. Stated differently, how can we argue that the story model is not just a good descriptive theory of how people reason, but also a good normative model of how people should reason? Another important question is whether the normative model differs from the descriptive model and, if so, in which respects.

21.2.4.3 Inference to the Best Explanation (IBE), Alternative Scenarios (AS) and Discriminating Facts

According to the scenario approach, factfinders are instructed to construct at least two scenarios and to assess and compare them. Like the other two theories discussed in this chapter, that assessment and comparison are interpreted in terms of inference to the best explanation (IBE), which consists in accepting a scenario on the grounds that it provides a better explanation of the evidence than any alternative scenario that has been proposed.

According to the scenario approach, a fact that 'makes the difference' in the comparison of one set of scenarios, a discriminating fact, need not make a relevant difference in the comparison of a different set of scenarios or of one of the scenarios against another scenario. So, for example, seemingly incriminating evidence that there is blood of the victim on the defendant does not discriminate between the 'guilty' scenario, and the alternative scenario in which the defendant told the police that he was walking close to the victim when they were attacked by an unknown perpetrator (Van Koppen, 2011, 2013; this example is discussed in Van Koppen & Mackor, 2020). Again, it is pointed out that our general knowledge plays an ineliminable role in assessments of relevance and weight of evidence, in choice of scenarios, in choice of evidence and in assessing the relation between evidence.

21.2.4.4 Falsification

In the scenario approach, insights from Popper's philosophy of science are applied, emphasizing the importance of falsification. Popper's theory entails that one should not only look for evidence that a scenario can explain, but first and foremost for evidence that can be used to falsify the scenario (Popper, 1963). On that point, the normative scenario approach is different from actual practice since people are inclined to confirm, not to falsify (Lewicka, 1998; Meissner & Kassin, 2004; Oswald & Grosjean, 2004; Ask & Granhag, 2005).

The process of falsification tests whether a scenario is inconsistent with evidence. In the scenario theory, evidence does not consist of 'facts out there' but sub-scenarios that are accepted as true. The only good manner of doing so is by searching for reasonable alternatives for each scenario and sub-scenario and then trying to find evidence that best discriminates between the scenario and its alternatives. The importance of assessing and comparing alternative scenarios is also stressed by Allen and Pardo (2019b) and by Amaya (2009, 2013, 2015). However, neither Allen and Pardo nor Amaya mention an important manner of testing a scenario, namely that of deriving sufficiently precise and risky predictions from the scenario and investigating whether they can be falsified or confirmed.

21.2.4.5 Creation, Accommodation, Prediction

Imagine a scenario that was created only after all the evidence was known. In that situation, the scenario is likely to offer neat explanations for all the facts. That, for instance, often holds for the prosecution's scenario which is usually formed after the police have carried out an extensive investigation. Then the scenario is made to accommodate all the evidence uncovered by the police. The same often holds for the defendant who, until trial, invokes their right of silence and only then comes up with an explanation to accommodate all the evidence presented by the prosecution. However, sometimes these explanations are in some way ad hoc. For example, sometimes implausible auxiliary hypotheses are added which play no other role than to make the scenario fit the facts (see Mackor, 2017, for the analysis of such a Dutch case).

Therefore, it is relevant to assess whether a scenario was solely created on the basis of the evidence or whether the scenario in part *predicted* the evidence. More specifically, we need to distinguish three different relations between a scenario and facts, namely creation, accommodation and prediction (Mackor, 2017). One of the strengths of explanation-based approaches is that a hypothesis, or more specifically a scenario, enables factfinders to predict facts. Testing of predictions is an important way to assess the quality of explanations, both in science and in criminal trials.

The first step in a criminal case is the creation of a scenario. It is created, typically by the police during the investigation, on the basis of one or a few or many known facts. The scenario is created on the basis of certain facts, but it is also created in order to explain those very same facts. After the scenario has been created, police investigations will continue. Three situations can be distinguished. First, if a novel piece of evidence does not cohere with the scenario, the conclusion may be that the scenario should be rejected. However, secondly, one may also conclude that the scenario need not be rejected, but that it must be accommodated. If the core of a scenario, for example, the defendant is the culprit, is falsified by evidence, the scenario will be rejected. If only a minor aspect of a scenario is falsified, the scenario can be accommodated. By means of adding or deleting elements, the scenario can be improved in order to explain facts that were not yet known when creating the scenario (Popper, 1963). Third, the police may discover evidence that was actually predicted on the basis of the scenario. A scenario gains strength especially if a detailed and risky prediction is confirmed (Lipton, 2007). However, it is also possible that no confirmation or falsification is found. In that case the scenario has an evidence gap. A scenario with evidence gaps is less strongly supported than a scenario without, depending on the number and size of the evidence gaps (see Mackor, 2017 for an analysis of a case with evidence gaps).

In conclusion, in the scenario approach it is stressed that the weight of the evidence is not only determined by the question of whether it discriminates between a scenario and an alternative scenario and by the question of how well established or reliable the evidence is, but also by the question of whether the evidence was used to create or accommodate the scenario, or whether it was unknown and predicted by the scenario.

21.3 PSYCHOLOGICAL AND PROBABILISTIC CRITIQUES OF EXPLANATION-BASED APPROACHES

Explanation-based theories have been criticized on several grounds. The most familiar critique is that they are underdeveloped since core notions such as coherence, inference to the best (causal) explanation and plausibility are insufficiently defined. In this section we discuss more specific points of critique that have been launched by empirical scientists, more in particular psychologists, and by Bayesian probabilists.

21.3.1 *Psychological Critique of Explanation-Based Approaches*

Explanation-based and story-model approaches to legal decision making in criminal cases can be criticized on psychological grounds, namely that they justify rather than counteract weaknesses and fallacies in human reasoning. First, decision makers typically tend to overvalue evidence that supports their favourite decision and undervalue evidence against the favourite decision. They simply do not evaluate competing scenarios. That tendency, commonly denoted as confirmation bias (Nickerson, 1998), is seen as a general human cognitive process. It is part of what is called the human tendency to keep our vision of the world without too much dissonance (Festinger, 1957). It is also referred to as a holistic evaluation of evidence (Schweizer, 2014). And, indeed, the story as presented by, for instance, the prosecution can be appealing to such an extent that evidence pointing in the other direction is ignored (Schweizer, 2014; Wagenaar et al., 1993), sometimes leading to miscarriages of justice (Gross, 1998, 2008; Gross et al., 2005; Huff & Killias, 2008).

Second, decision makers usually rely on simple – fast and frugal – heuristics rather than careful consideration of alternatives (Gigerenzer & Engel, 2006; Gigerenzer, 2007). A normative model that directs decision makers to evaluate competing scenarios does not come naturally to humans.

Nevertheless, the story model (Pennington & Hastie, 1993) and, following that, the scenario approach (Wagenaar et al., 1993; Van Koppen, 2011, 2013) and the theory of Allen and Pardo (Allen & Pardo, 2019b), have been built on how people actually reason in decision making in criminal cases. There is, for instance, a host of research on how jury members decide on cases (see for an overview Vidmar & Hans, 2007; Hans, 2008; Van Koppen, 2009; Vidmar, 2009, 2011). All of this research demonstrates that people think and decide about the world in the form of stories, of scenarios. However, were the story model to be a descriptive model of actual decision making in criminal cases, it should allow for the confirmation bias (Oswald & Grosjean, 2004; O'Brien, 2007; Kassin, Dror & Kukučka, 2013),[19] and the coherence bias, according to which factfinders maximize coherence by discounting

---

[19] Also see B. M. O'Brien, 'Confirmation Bias in Criminal Investigations: An Examination of the Factors that Aggravate and Counteract Bias' (Unpublished diss., University of Michigan, 2007).

contradicting evidence, inflating supporting evidence and by interpreting ambivalent evidence in a way that is coherent with the emerging decision (Simon, 2004, p. 522; Schweizer, 2014, p. 66). People have the tendency to look for verification of their hypotheses and do not seek to falsify their hypotheses.

Another point of critique is that much of what happens in criminal cases cannot be grasped in the form of a scenario or story. For instance, Simon (2019, p. 3) argues that in many instances, in criminal cases, there is not much of a story to tell. Simon gives the example of a neighbour who hears a dreadful shout in the night. However, Simon's critique misses the mark. Although a shout in the night may not be a full-blown story in the sense of 'human action sequences connected by relationships of physical causality and intentional causality between events' (Pennington & Hastie, 1993, p. 196), it is a story all the same. Through our general world knowledge, a shout in the night points to a crime taking place, with everything that brings such an occurrence to mind, based on our knowledge of the world. It may cause somebody to have a look outside or phone the police.

A third point of critique is that, on any explanation-based approach, a hypothesis or a scenario is offered that can causally explain the evidence at hand. Thus, the argument runs from the hypothesis to the evidence and not the other way around. In everyday life, however, people reason in both directions.[20] That happens, for instance, in a police investigation, especially in the first stages, right after the crime is discovered. Based on what the police uncover, in other words the evidence, they try to build scenarios of what may have happened (De Poot et al., 2004). In a later stage, often the very same evidence is used to assess the veracity of the scenarios built. From the point of view of confirmation bias that may seem an unsound practice. In actual criminal cases it is unavoidable.

The points just mentioned may be a valid critique of how people are actually inclined to reason in criminal cases. However, they miss the mark with respect to normative theories. Take for instance Van Koppen's scenario theory. On this approach factfinders should formulate scenarios that are resistant to additional 'why-should-I-believe-you' questions. Therefore, according to scenario theory, decision makers are forced to consider formulating strong scenarios and cannot get away with sloppy work on that part. Second, since scenarios must always and explicitly be compared to other competing scenarios, this instruction functions as a hallmark prevention of confirmation bias. In particular, the instruction to try to falsify the favourite scenario is an excellent practice in preventing confirmation bias. Finally, the obligation to formulate a scenario as precisely and in as detailed a manner as possible makes it feasible to formulate precise and possibly risky predictions, the outcomes of which might confirm or falsify the scenario.

---

[20] Bex (2011) has developed a hybrid theory according to which factfinders reason causally within the scenario, but argue evidentially, from evidence to story, when they connect the scenario and the evidence for it.

21.3.2 Probabilistic Critiques of Explanation-Based Approaches

The approaches we have discussed so far all rely on inference to the best explanation. As we have seen, IBE is an inference from an explanation being the best out of the available ones to the conclusion that the explanation is probably true. One important strand of criticism aimed at IBE, and thus at explanation-based approaches in criminal law, comes from Bayesian probabilism, a normative model for evidential reasoning which we discuss in more detail in Section 21.4.

Many Bayesian probabilists defend the view that factfinders who draw conclusions based on the evidence in a case should do so in accordance with probability theory. That does not necessarily mean that factfinders should engage in actual probabilistic calculations in their decision process.[21] Rather, it means that factfinders' conclusions should be consistent with those they would have reached if they had (correctly) applied probabilistic calculations (Friedman, 1997, p. 289). However, some theorists have argued that explanation-based approaches are, at least potentially, in conflict with Bayesian probability theory. We examine five objections from adherents of Bayesian probability theory and the responses of adherents of explanation-based approaches. The first four objections target the idea that there is a necessary link between an explanation being the best explanation and that explanation being probably true. The last objection asks why a good story would also be a probable story.

21.3.2.1 A. The Bad Lot Problem

The bad lot problem is possibly the best-known argument against IBE in philosophy of science (Van Fraassen, 1989). It has also been raised against IBE in legal contexts. For instance, Amaya calls it 'the most serious problem that a model of IBE for law has to face' (Amaya, 2009, p. 152, n.13). The problem is that in IBE we should choose the best[22] explanation out of the available ones. However, an explanation can be the best without being good. If all available explanations are bad ones, even the best explanation will be poor. In that case IBE would tell us to accept a bad explanation as true. In criminal law that would imply that a defendant could be convicted on a weak case.

One response to that objection has been to amend the definition of IBE by adding the demand that the best explanation should also be sufficiently good on its own

---

[21] Although it has been suggested that it may be useful to do so when it comes to evidence that has a statistical basis, such as DNA evidence (Stein, 1996, p. 35; Allen, 1997, p. 258). Probabilistic methods are also proposed for reconstructing and analysing cases by experts (cf. Kadane & Schum, 2011; Fenton et al., 2016). See, however, the discussion below.

[22] Given a specific definition of explanatory goodness. See Ylikoski and Kuorikoski (2010) for an overview of how philosophers have interpreted this term. Furthermore, see the above accounts that define how well an explanation does in terms of criteria such as, for example, simplicity (Allen and Pardo), coherence (Amaya and van Koppen), or the absence of story gaps (van Koppen).

(Lipton, 2004, pp. 63, 154). However, even if the best explanation is good on its own, it may still not be enough to guarantee its probable truth, if we have failed to consider even better explanations. That worry is not unique to IBE. However, it does mean that factfinders have to ensure that they are reasonably sure that they have considered all relevant explanations. For instance, Amaya (2009, pp. 154–5) states that 'we need to have some reason to believe that the set of hypotheses from which we have inferred to the best is "good enough"'. Similarly, Van Koppen (2011, p. 52) emphasizes that the scenario-based approach requires that factfinders consider all 'reasonable' scenarios.

21.3.2.2 B. Dutch Book Argument

Another critique of IBE has been formulated by Van Fraassen (1989). That critique starts with the well-known Dutch Book argument. According to that argument, whenever an agent's degrees of belief in certain propositions (such as the proposition that the defendant is guilty) violate the maxims of probability theory, that agent risks having the Dutch Book argument made against them (Vineberg, 2016).

> A Dutch Book is a series of bets that guarantee that the agent will lose money. That argument presupposes a hypothetical betting scenario where the agent has to bet on the truth of some propositions. The betting scenario is used as an analogy for decision making in real life. The Dutch Book argument is too complicated to fully explain here. What is important, however, is that Bayesians often use the Dutch Book argument to support the idea that any agent who reasons in a way that deviates from the precepts of (Bayesian) probability theory is irrational.

Van Fraassen applies that argument to IBE. According to him there are only two options: either IBE is in accordance with Bayes' rule, namely when it implies that we have to update our beliefs in accordance with Bayes' rule, or IBE instructs us to update our beliefs in a different manner, in particular by giving a bonus to the explanation that best explains the evidence. Van Fraassen has argued that IBE is superfluous in the former case while, in the latter, it deviates from the precepts of Bayesian probability theory and is therefore irrational.

Most adherents of IBE adhere to the first view but claim that even though IBE is consistent with Bayes' rule, nevertheless it is not superfluous. Lipton (2004), among others, has claimed that IBE is a heuristic for a Bayesian calculus which is both fruitful and feasible. We briefly discuss possible relations between Bayesian probabilistic and explanation-based approaches in Section 21.5.

21.3.2.3 C. Disjunctive Explanations

Another reason why choosing the best explanation may not lead us to the most probable conclusion is the problem of disjunctive explanations. That objection has been raised in particular against the theory of Allen and Pardo (e.g., Clermont, 2017; Nance, 2019), but if valid, it would also seem to hold against Amaya's and Van Koppen's theory. In essence, the argument is that while one explanation may be much better than any competitor, it might still be less probable than the disjunction of all competitors. For instance, suppose that there is a criminal case in which 'the defendant murdered his wife' is the best explanation. However, suppose further that the disjunction 'either the victim committed suicide or it was an accident or someone else than the husband killed her' is jointly more probable. In such cases the one-to-one comparison that explanatory accounts seem to promote could lead us in the wrong direction.

As a response to that problem, Allen and Pardo (2019b, pp. 23–8) state that nothing in their theory prohibits factfinders from considering such 'disjunctive' explanations.

21.3.2.4 D. Are Criminal Trials about Comparing Explanations?

At its core, IBE is a comparative notion: it presupposes that we compare the quality of different explanations. However, it has been argued that criminal trials need not be about comparing explanations. Rather, the onus is on the prosecution to prove the defendant's guilt. While the defendant may offer his or her own version of the facts, he or she does not have a duty to do so (Clermont, 2015, p. 359). Apart from the fact that the defendant has the right to remain silent, he can also attack the prosecution's case by offering counterarguments against the scenario and the evidence for it, without offering an alternative scenario or explanation. So, it seems that IBE is doing little work. On a probabilistic view, what is going on in criminal trials is that the prosecution needs to prove that it is probable beyond a reasonable doubt that the defendant committed the act of which he or she is accused. That account seems to fit better with the structure of criminal trials.

One response is to claim that proving beyond a reasonable doubt in fact means that the prosecution's scenario must be demonstrated to be better than any alternative reasonable scenario (Wagenaar et al., 1993; Van Koppen, 2011), even if the defence does not come up with an alternative of its own. In that sense every criminal trial is comparative, although it must be noted that in practice the comparison is typically left implicit.

Another response has been that we should not take the name 'inference to the best explanation' too literally. Instead, IBE is often used to describe explanatory reasoning in general. Such explanatory reasoning does not have to be comparative. For example, according to Allen and Pardo's theory, a defendant's guilt can only be proven beyond a reasonable doubt if there is a plausible explanation implying his or her guilt and no plausible explanation implying his or her innocence. That means that factfinders do not necessarily have to look at how well explanations perform compared to one another (Pardo & Allen, 2008). However, the approach would still be explanatory since factfinders would still be involved in causal explanatory reasoning.

21.3.2.5 E. Good versus Probable Explanations

Explanation-based accounts use qualitative criteria to evaluate explanations. For instance, both in the descriptive story model and in the normative scenario approach, how good an explanation is depends, among other things, on the number of evidence gaps and story gaps (Pennington & Hastie, 1993, pp. 190–9; Bex, 2011, pp. 91–2; Van Koppen & Mackor, 2020). Similarly, Allen and Pardo mention criteria such as simplicity, accordance with background beliefs and lack of ad hoc-ness as marks of a good explanation (Pardo & Allen, 2008, p. 230). However, they have not argued why these criteria are truth-conducive. In other words, the question is what reason we have to believe that the better a story is, the more likely it is to be true.[23] In the absence of an argument, it is unclear why such criteria should have a normative status, and showing a reliable connection between these criteria and the probability of explanations has proven to be difficult. Take the notion of coherence as an example. Epistemologists have given 'impossibility results' for coherence, that is, mathematical proofs that suggest that more coherent theories are not necessarily more probable than less coherent theories (e.g., Bovens & Hartmann, 2003; Olsson, 2005, 2019). However, others have criticized these results.[24]

In response to that critique, defenders of explanation-based approaches have referred to epistemologists and philosophers of science who have done work on epistemic virtues such as simplicity, robustness and coherence, showing how these virtues can be truth-conducive (Thagard, 1978; McMullin, 1996; Douglas, 2009; Cabrera, 2017). These insights can also be applied in the context of criminal law (Mackor, 2017, Dahlman & Mackor, 2019). We will briefly return to this topic in Section 21.5.

In conclusion, the link between inference to the best explanation and the probable truth of the best explanation is problematic for various reasons. Advocates of explanation-based approaches have partially responded by amending their theories to ensure a better fit with probabilism (e.g. by allowing for the possibility of disjunctive explanations and elaborating on epistemic virtues). However, that does not mean that explanation-based approaches are just Bayesian approaches in disguise. It does show, however, how probabilistic considerations can be an incentive to improve explanation-based approaches. Moreover, the opposite might also be true, namely that Bayesian approaches can be improved by adding insights from explanation-based ones. We elaborate on the latter claim in the next section.

---

[23] In fact, research on lying defendants shows that a false story may sometimes be more believable than a true one (Granhag & Strömwall, 2004).

[24] See Schippers (2016) for a recent contribution that summarizes the debate.

21.4 COMPARING BAYESIAN PROBABILISTIC AND EXPLANATION-BASED APPROACHES

In the previous section we discussed probabilistic critiques of explanation-based approaches. In this section we first briefly explicate the Bayesian probabilistic approach and then discuss several well-known points of critique of Bayesianism, in particular those endorsed by Allen and Pardo (2019b), Amaya (2015, pp. 79 ff.) and Van Koppen (2011, chapter 9).

21.4.1 Bayesian Probabilistic Approach and Its Critiques

Bayesians claim that a factfinder's evaluations of any hypothesis are degrees of belief, which express how confident the thinker is in the truth of the hypothesis (Kaye, 1979). Furthermore, they state that these degrees of belief, if rational, should obey the axioms of probability theory.

These axioms are most popularly expressed in the form of the Kolmogorov axioms which, stated informally, are:

i) The probability of any event is equal to or greater than 0.
ii) The probability that at least one of all the possible outcomes of a process will occur is 1.
iii) If A and B are mutually exclusive outcomes, then the probability of either of them happening is the sum of the probability of A happening and the probability of B happening.

In this chapter we take Bayesian probabilists to be theorists who claim that when a thinker receives new evidence, he or she should update his or her degrees of belief in line with Bayes' theorem. The theorem states that the probability of a hypothesis given the new evidence (its posterior probability), $P(H|E)$, is a function of the likelihood of the evidence given the hypothesis, $P(E|H)$, the prior probability of the hypothesis, $P(H)$, and the marginal probability of the evidence, $P(E)$:

$$P(H|E) = \frac{P(E|H)*P(H)}{P(E)}$$

In its 'odds' form, in which one hypothesis (H_1) is compared to another hypothesis (H_2), it reads as follows:

$$\frac{P(H_1|E)}{P(H_2|E)} = \frac{P(E|H_1)*P(H_1)}{P(E|H_2)*P(H_2)}$$

Like IBE, Bayesian probabilism has been applied in legal contexts (Fenton et al., 2016). However, its status as a normative epistemic theory, in particular for the evaluation and the assessment of legal evidence and legal proof, is disputed.

The main point of critique concerns the values that Bayesians have to assign to the prior probability and to the likelihoods. The crucial question is where probabilists find these values. Roughly, two options are available. The first, and most generally chosen, option is to accept that those values are subjective, and thus are to be chosen by the individual. The other option is to search for objective values. These values might either derive from logic (for example, the probability that a fair coin will land heads or tails is 0.5) or from statistics (an example would be the probability that a woman who has been killed, has been killed by her partner or ex-partner, which is said to be 0.52 (Nieuwbeerta & Leistra, 2007)). We now turn to several influential critiques of probabilism that revolve around the problem of assigning the required values.

21.4.2 *The Problem of the Prior*

Bayes' rule gives a way of updating one's prior probability. However, it says nothing about how to assign the initial probability, one's degree of belief in the truth of a hypothesis before evidence (Van Koppen, 2011, p. 214; Amaya, 2015, p. 82; Allen & Pardo, 2019b). For instance, it, as said, does not forbid incorporating prejudices for or against the defendant and neither does it prohibit a factfinder setting their prior degree of belief in the defendant's guilt to 0.9999, or even to 1. Such a factfinder could easily end up convicting the defendant, regardless of the evidence. That seems an unreasonable choice, but it would not be irrational from a probabilistic point of view which in itself allows for purely subjective degrees of belief, even though there are some rules one needs to adhere to, to make sure these beliefs follow the axioms.

Another worry about the prior degree of belief concerns the presumption of innocence. After all, if we set the prior probability of guilt at 0, we can never prove the guilt of the defendant. However, if we set the prior higher than 0, that seems to conflict with the presumption that the defendant is innocent until proven otherwise (Van Koppen, 2011, p. 216; Amaya, 2015, p. 85). There have also been discussions as to whether the prior probability for guilt should be set at a normatively fixed standard. However, there is no agreement as to what that fixed standard should be either. All suggestions made so far seem highly problematic (Fenton et al., 2017; Dahlman, 2018).

One response of Bayesians has been to claim that setting the prior probability is not very important. They state that, after a sufficient number of updates, priors eventually 'wash out'. In other words, the assignment of priors will converge on the 'right' posterior probability (Edwards, Lindman & Savage, 1963). However, the problem is that such washing out requires a great deal of evidence, which we sometimes have in a mundane criminal case, but which we seldom have in a criminal case where the evaluation of evidence is not clear-cut (Godfrey-Smith, 2009; Van Koppen, 2011, pp. 214 ff.; Amaya, 2015, p. 83; Dahlman, 2018).

21.4.3 *Absence of Data*

We have seen that probabilities can be set either subjectively or objectively. Most Bayesians adhere to the view that the values of priors are set subjectively. The same seems to hold for the values that are assigned to the likelihoods. In a scientific context at least some objective information will be available, but in legal cases we usually lack the required objective data to assign meaningful probabilities to either priors or likelihoods (Van Koppen, 2011, pp. 220–2, 226; Amaya, 2015, pp. 83, 85; Allen & Pardo, 2019b).

For example, when Bayesian probability theory is applied in statistical contexts, the prior is typically set using base-rate information – information about how often the event that we are interested in (e.g., whether or not someone has a certain disease) occurs in the relevant population (e.g., people over sixty-five years old). This information might be available in medical research, for example, but in criminal law we almost never have such base-rate information. For instance, we do not know how often defendants are falsely accused or how often witnesses lie. In the absence of such base-rate information, it is unclear how the relevant probabilities can be meaningfully estimated. The same holds for the assessment of the evidence. In science we often have objective and reliable information, but in criminal cases there is rarely objective, precise, let alone quantifiable information either about the probability that evidence occurs $P(E)$ or about the probability that the evidence occurs if the hypothesis is true $P(E|H)$ (Van Koppen, 2011, p. 213). Take, for instance, the numbers attached to DNA evidence, which are usually presented in rather precise terms. These numbers are based on a theoretical calculation in which important elements are left out. For instance, rates of laboratory errors and crime-scene errors are not incorporated (Gill, 2016; Thompson, 2009, 2011). Furthermore, they hide severe problems with interpreting DNA mixtures (Butler, Kline & Coble, 2018).

We have seen that one approach to tackling this problem is to say that the relevant probabilities are subjective degrees of probability, rather than frequencies. However, this solution comes with its own problems. Although these degrees of belief are constrained by the Kolmogorov axioms, these axioms hardly put any limits on the acceptable degrees of belief. This in turn means that 'in the subjective-Bayesian model someone can, without being contradicted and unpunished, entertain the most outrageous prejudices' (Hofstee, 1980, p. 81, our translation). Earlier we mentioned the example of a factfinder who believes that the probability that a defendant is guilty is 100 per cent. On a probabilistic account this implies that no amount of evidence can result in another conclusion. However, we would not call a factfinder who convicts all defendants, even when there is overwhelming evidence for their innocence, rational. Yet nothing in probability theory rules out such a dogmatic and irrational stance.

Another response of Bayesians to the problem of lack of data has been to admit that Bayesian probabilism needs something else to assign reasonable values to the prior probability and to the likelihood. In doing so they distinguish between Bayes' theorem and a Bayesian approach to evidence which allows for more principles than Bayes' theorem. Fenton and colleagues for example (Fenton et al., 2017; Lagnado, Fenton & Neil, 2013) propose to use specific legal idioms and causal structures. This seems to be a fruitful approach. However, one could argue that what they then do is to use an explanation-based, more specifically, a scenario approach, to solve the problem.

21.4.4 Problems of Feasibility and Complexity

Some versions of probabilism require calculations which are, in the practice of criminal cases, almost never feasible to make. The first problem is that humans are typically not very good at making calculations with probabilities (Saks & Thompson, 2003, pp. 338–9). For example, it turns out that it is hard to avoid committing the notorious prosecutor's or defence attorney's fallacy. Another problem, already addressed in Section 21.4.3, is that there is no knowledge or belief in criminal law about evidence that allows for a precise numerical assessment. Even though on a Bayesian approach we do not model the 'facts' or evidence about the facts, but rather our beliefs about them, the problem is that we often have no idea what probability we should attach to a certain belief about a piece of evidence.

Take for instance the number accompanying DNA evidence. Even if we were to accept that DNA evidence is an example of evidence that allows for the most precise calculations, DNA is no more than a first step in a chain of evidence. If we have a solid match between the DNA of a suspect and the DNA in a specimen from the crime scene, it just moves the discussion. It moves it to the question of what the meaning of the specimen at the crime scene is. Can it be accepted as coming from the perpetrator? And with what probability (Thompson, 2009, 2011; Van Koppen, 2011; Gill, 2016)? These are the problems of feasibility.

Second, the more evidence there is in a case, the more calculations are required to calculate the posterior probability of whatever hypothesis we are interested in. In fact, the number of calculations needed increases with the amount of evidence. So, computing the relevant probabilities quickly becomes unmanageable, even for experts. That is the problem of complexity (Amaya, 2015, pp. 83, 86; Allen & Pardo, 2019b, pp. 38 ff.).

One response to these worries has been the introduction of Bayesian network approaches, which express the dependencies between hypotheses and evidence graphically (Fenton et al., 2016; De Zoete et al., 2019) and in which computers do the calculations. These Bayesian networks (BNs) may be more insightful for laymen. However, the question remains of whether these networks are insightful enough for non-experts to meaningfully engage with. Thus, they do not seem helpful as a means for a factfinder to make decisions. For example, Fenton et al. (2020, p. 20) admit that a BN model is not as easily accessible as scenario-based approaches. They also admit that they use causal structures to place constraints on the feasible range of probabilities (Fenton et al., 2020, p. 19). Building such a network still requires a great deal of effort and expertise. So, the Bayesian network approach only solves the problem of feasibility to the extent that the time and resources are available to construct these networks, and they do not seem to solve the problem of complexity to such an extent that they may be helpful in decision making.

21.4.5 Paradoxes of Proof

Another strand of criticism against probabilistic approaches to criminal evidence is that they lead to so-called paradoxes of proof. We will restrict ourselves to discussing the two most commonly mentioned paradoxes, both of which have been used as an argument in favour of explanation-based approaches. These paradoxes relate to Bayesian interpretation of the criminal standard of proof, according to which guilt has to be proven beyond a reasonable doubt. That standard is sometimes interpreted as the demand that guilt has to be proven with a probability of 0.95 or more (Dane, 1985; Connolly, 1987; Dhami, 2008).[25] The two paradoxes we discuss are the conjunction paradox and the paradox of naked statistical evidence.

21.4.5.1 The Conjunction Paradox

The conjunction paradox was formulated by Cohen (1977, pp. 58–67) and it is one of the central arguments of Allen and Pardo (2019b) against Bayesian models of legal proof.

The paradox begins with the observation that the beyond-a-reasonable-doubt standard requires that all elements of a crime have to be individually proven. For instance, proving a murder might mean proving both 'killing' and 'intent'. Allen and Pardo claim that the probabilistic approach therefore implies that the factfinder has to prove that the probability of each individual element exceeds the threshold (Allen & Pardo, 2019b, p. 13). However, suppose that the threshold for proof beyond a reasonable doubt is 0.95 and that both elements are proven with 0.96 probability. Assuming independence (which is, by the way, questionable as regards the relation between an intention and the subsequent act) the probability of the conjunction of these two claims would then only be 0.92 – below the threshold of 0.95. So, although all elements are proven beyond a reasonable doubt, the probability of the crime as a whole does not sanction convicting the defendant. Pardo and Allen see that as

---

[25] What the threshold should be has been a subject of debate for some centuries (Volokh, 1997), of which the most well-known participant is probably William Blackstone with his proposition: 'all presumptive evidence of felony should be admitted cautiously: for the law holds, that it is better that ten guilty persons escape, than that one innocent suffer' (Blackstone, 1765–1769, book 4, chapter 27). The threshold varies, depending on the seriousness of the crime the defendant is charged with (De Keijser & Van Koppen, 2007; Van Koppen, 2011), the attitude of factfinders (De Keijser, De Lange & Van Wilsem, 2014), how the rule is explained to a jury (Stoffelmayr & Diamond, 2000) and what legal politics dictate (Dershowitz, 1996).

a serious problem for probabilistic interpretations of the proof standard because it violates one of two basic premises of the legal system.

First, a fundamental goal of the proof standard is to distribute errors in a way that leads to very few false convictions (at the expense of more false acquittals). For example, if we have a threshold of 0.95 for proof beyond a reasonable doubt, we would have a maximum of 1 in 20 cases that would end in a false conviction. However, suppose that we allow conviction based on the above conjunction. That would mean that the number of false convictions could be higher, since a case where the probability of guilt is 0.92 could also be proven beyond a reasonable doubt. Second, suppose that the probabilist claims that proof beyond a reasonable doubt instead means that the probability of the conjunction of elements has to be at least 0.95. That would allow situations where the weak proof of one element is compensated by very strong proof for the other elements (as long as the probability of the conjunction is high enough). That would violate the requirement that all elements of a crime have to be proven beyond a reasonable doubt. In other words, the probabilistic interpretation of the beyond-a-reasonable-doubt standard either violates the legal system's requirement of a just error distribution or the requirement that all elements of the crime have to be proven beyond a reasonable doubt.

However, many probabilists deny that the conjunction problem is as problematic for them as Pardo and Allen make it out to be, for instance by offering probabilistic interpretations of the proof standards that do not face the problem (e.g., Spottswood, 2016; Schwartz & Sober, 2017; Wittlin, 2019).

21.4.5.2 The Paradox of Naked Statistical Evidence

The second paradox also relates to the probabilistic explication of the proof standards (Nunn, 2015). Take the following example (adapted from the so-called Prison Riot Hypothetical of Nesson, 1979, pp. 1192–3): there were 100 prisoners in a prison yard and we know (from camera footage) that 99 of them participated in the killing of a prison guard and that only one of them did not. However, the camera footage is too grainy to make out the identity of the killers and of the single bystander. Proper investigations have been carried out, but no further incriminating or exculpating evidence has been found. The paradox that Bayesians are faced with is this: given a probability of 0.99, it seems permissible to convict one and even all of the prisoners. However, many people have objected to that conclusion because it conflicts with their intuitions.

Now suppose that we have a witness instead of the camera footage, one whom we know to be 99 per cent reliable, and he claims that he saw prisoner X kill the guard. Can we now convict prisoner X? Many believe that these two cases differ: that we can convict based on the witness evidence, but not on the camera evidence. The question is why.

Probabilists can reply in several ways to the problem of statistical evidence. They can reject common intuitions about statistical evidence as irrational. Second, they might agree with the intuition, but argue that the difference between statistical and non-statistical evidence can be accounted for within the probabilist framework. For one thing, they might point out that the cases differ as regards their likelihood ratio. Interestingly, there also seems to be a relevant difference between the two cases from an explanation-based perspective, namely that in the latter case, the hypothesis that the prisoner participated in the killing seems to offer a much better causal explanation of the fact that the witness stated he saw prisoner X kill the guard, than the hypothesis that the witness was mistaken or intended to frame the prisoner. In the former case, on the other hand, it seems that the hypothesis that the prisoner is innocent can explain the camera images, and thus the fact that there is a 0.99 probability that the defendant participated in the killing, roughly equally well (Di Bello, 2019). So, explanation-based approaches seem to fit with common intuitions about when to convict or not based only on statistical evidence (Mackor, in press).

21.4.6 Conclusion

So far, we have not discussed arguments against using the Bayesian probability theory in general.[26] Instead, we have discussed arguments specifically directed against using the Bayesian model for evidence in criminal cases. The problem with Bayesianism in criminal cases seems to be threefold. First, in itself it lacks a way of meaningfully assigning or even delineating priors and likelihoods. It needs something else, such as causal structures and idioms, to set constraints (Lagnado et al., 2013; Fenton et al., 2020). Second, it may not be a psychologically feasible way of reasoning and in any case, it is less feasible than explanation-based approaches. That seems especially pressing when Bayes' rule is used to model all of the evidence in a criminal case, rather than to analyse a part of the evidence (Prakken & Meester, 2017). Third, it may lead to paradoxes of proof, although recent work on Bayesian approaches that overcome these paradoxes looks promising (De Zoete et al., 2019).

In conclusion, it seems that both explanation-based approaches (see Section 21.3.2) and Bayesian probabilistic approaches (this section) are confronted with several problems, and the question has been raised of whether the approaches can be combined to overcome some or all of the problems on both sides. We briefly discuss the relation between Bayesian and explanation-based approaches in the next and final section.

---

[26] Furthermore, we have not discussed alternative probabilistic approaches. In particular we did not discuss the Dempster–Shafer theory, which has also called the theory of belief functions. See Shafer (1976) and for an application to criminal law Meester and Kerkvliet (2016).

21.5 EVALUATION AND CONCLUSION

In this chapter we have discussed three different explanation-based approaches to reasoning about evidence and proof in criminal trials: Allen and Pardo's relative plausibility theory, Amaya's theory of inference to the most coherent explanation and Van Koppen's scenario theory. Whereas Allen and Pardo aim to explain the American legal system, in particular the different standards of proof, Amaya and Van Koppen offer explicitly normative theories, aimed at improving legal reasoning.

We have shown that causal explanation, more specifically inference to the best explanation (IBE), is at the heart of these theories and that coherence is a core criterion to assess the quality of explanations. We have also pointed out that all three theories stay close to how people actually reason, both in everyday life and in criminal trials. Since Allen and Pardo's theory is explanatory, it obviously stays close to actual reasoning, but the same holds for Amaya's and Van Koppen's normative theories. In respect to these three issues in particular, explanation-based approaches differ from Bayesian approaches. Bayesian approaches do not aim to stay close to how people actually reason, and probability, rather than causal explanation and coherence, is their core notion.

In this final section we briefly address the question of how Bayesian and explanation-based approaches to reasoning about evidence and proof in criminal trials might relate to each other. First it should be noted that on an abstract level the structure of analysis of Bayesian and explanation-based approaches seems to be the same. They both instruct factfinders to assess two things. A factfinder both has to assess the quality (the prior probability or the plausibility) of the hypothesis or the scenario in itself, and to assess how probable or how well explained the evidence is in the light of the hypothesis or the scenario. However, they use different concepts (causal explanation versus probability), and explanation-based approaches propose a holistic and qualitative approach, whereas Bayesians propose an atomistic approach, which is necessary to allow for a quantitative analysis.

Lipton (2004) has offered a well-known view about the relation between Bayesian and explanation-based or IBE approaches. Even though Lipton primarily focuses on the comparison of Bayes and IBE as descriptive theories, his classification is also useful for the comparison of the normative theories. In this section we confine ourselves to brief discussion of the relation between Bayesianism and explanationism as normative theories.

Lipton has distinguished three possible views of the relation between explanation-based and probabilistic approaches, namely that the Bayesian, or the explanation-based approach, or both, are incorrect as normative theories; that they are correct and compatible; or that they are correct and complementary.

In Section 21.3.2 we discussed Van Fraassen's argument according to which the explanation-based approach is either incompatible with Bayesianism and therefore irrational, or compatible but accordingly superfluous (Van Fraassen, 1989). However, several defenders of explanation-based approaches have argued that there is a middle way between irrationality and redundancy. They defend the view that Bayesianism and explanation-based approaches are not just compatible, in that they can exist next to each other, but rather that they are complementary and can be an aid to each other (Okasha, 2000; Lipton, 2004; Hitchcock, 2007; Psillos, 2007; Poston, 2014).

On most of these complementary views, explanation-based approaches should conform to Bayes' rule. At the same time, these views hold, firstly, that epistemic virtues such as simplicity, robustness and coherence can be truth-conducive and thus that an assessment of a scenario and the relation between scenario and evidence in terms of virtues, which is deemed to be cognitively more feasible than a Bayesian analysis, can be a heuristic to a Bayesian assessment of a scenario. Next to that, these complementary views hold that explanation-based considerations can or even should be used to help to determine (1) which hypotheses are to be tested and (2) which evidence is relevant, and to help to assign weights to (3) the priors and (4) the likelihoods. The general idea is that the weight of the prior can be assessed by determining how well background knowledge would explain the hypothesis, and similarly that the likelihood can be assessed precisely by determining how well the hypothesis would explain the evidence.

On a weak complementary view, Bayesianism would allow for explanation-based considerations to fulfil this role. On a strong complementary view, these explanation-based considerations are indispensable and thus mandatory in order to turn subjective beliefs into something more objective.

This strong complementary view is closely allied to a yet stronger view, namely that explanation-based approaches are correct and Bayesian approaches are not applicable to criminal cases. In Section 21.4 we have discussed several points of critique of applying Bayes' rule in criminal cases. One of these was that Bayes' rule does not say anything about the choice of the hypotheses and the evidence nor about the weight that can or should be assigned to them. Summarizing this view quite bluntly, it has been claimed that in itself Bayes' rule allows for 'garbage in, garbage out'. For that reason, even subjective Bayesians might want to defend the view that Bayes' rule should only be used if the priors and likelihoods can be determined with some precision and objectivity or if they can be expected to 'wash out' (Douven, 2017). In most criminal cases, however, priors and likelihoods can neither be determined with sufficient precision and objectivity, nor 'wash out'. That is an important difference between applying Bayes' rule in a legal and a scientific context. Accordingly, this critique of Bayesianism is not so much that it fails in general as a normative approach, but rather that it should not be used in criminal cases.

Another argument for this critical view of Bayesianism is that complex cases can only be analysed with the help of Bayesian networks to do the complex calculations.

Although the fact that a network can do the calculations for us can be regarded as a strength of Bayesianism, it can also be seen as a drawback since these calculations are likely to be opaque to legal factfinders. In particular in a legal context, that is a serious drawback since legal decisions should not only and not even primarily result in reaching (probable) truth, but first of all in a decision that is justified in a manner which is understandable to the court, to the parties involved and preferably also to society at large. Even though it might be acceptable that some part of a judicial decision is technical and difficult to understand, even for judges and parties of a case, this seems questionable when almost all of the decision becomes opaque to them. However, that might happen if a complete case is modelled in Bayesian terms.

Finally, on a slightly less critical view, Bayes' rule should not be applied with respect to criminal cases as a whole. However, this view acknowledges that it can be used and indeed be useful with respect to those parts of the scenario and the evidence about which the priors and likelihoods can be established with sufficient precision and objectivity (in some cases DNA evidence might be an example; Prakken & Meester 2017). Moreover, on this view, a Bayesian approach can also be useful to protect factfinders against several fallacies, such as base-rate neglect, causal fallacies and the prosecutor and the defence attorney fallacy. Finally, on such a view, a comparison of an explanation-based analysis and a Bayesian network analysis of the same case might be useful to analyse differences and agreements in the analysis. In this manner, a Bayesian analysis might work as a kind of triangulation of the explanation-based analysis.

In conclusion: explanation-based approaches stay close to how people reason in everyday life and in criminal cases and they offer tools with which to reason in a structured way about evidence and proof in criminal cases, and therewith avoid certain fallacies and biases such as confirmation bias. As regards the possible relation between Bayesian and explanation-based approaches, there does not seem to be agreement at the moment. As far as our own view is concerned, we do not reject a Bayesian approach in general. However, we agree with the critical view that Bayes' rule can be used to analyse parts of the scenario and to prevent factfinders from committing certain fallacies, but that – at least for now – it should not be used to analyse legal cases as a whole.

REFERENCES

Allen, R. J. (1997). Rationality, Algorithms and Juridical Proof: A Preliminary Inquiry. *International Journal of Evidence and Proof* 1, 254–275.

Allen, R. J. & Leiter, B. (2001). Naturalized Epistemology and the Law of Evidence. *Virginia Law Review* 87, 1491–1550.

Allen, R. J. & Pardo, M. S. (2019a). Clarifying Relative Plausibility: A Rejoinder. *International Journal of Evidence and Proof*. Advanced online publication. DOI: https://doi.org/10.1177/1365712718816760

Allen, R. J. & Pardo, M. S. (2019b). Relative Plausibility and Its Critics. *International Journal of Evidence and Proof.* Advance online publication.
Amaya, A. (2009). Inference to the Best Legal Explanation. In H. Kaptein, H. Prakken & B. Verheij (eds.), *Legal Evidence and Proof: Statistics, Stories, Logic.* Farnham: Ashgate, pp. 135–160.
Amaya, A. (2013). Coherence, Evidence and Proof. *Legal Theory* 19, 1–43.
Amaya, A. (2015). *The Tapestry of Reason: An Inquiry Into the Nature of Coherence and Its Role in Legal Argument.* Oxford: Hart.
Anderson, T. J., Schum, D. A. & Twining, W. L. (2005). *Analysis of Evidence*, 2nd ed. Cambridge: Cambridge University Press.
Ask, K. & Granhag, P. A. (2005). Motivational Sources of Confirmation Bias in Criminal Investigations: The Need for Cognitive Closure. *Journal of Investigative Psychology and Offender Profiling* 2, 43–63.
Bennett, W. L. & Feldman, M. S. (2014). *Reconstructing Reality in the Courtroom: Justice and Judgement in American Culture*, 2nd ed. New Orleans: Quid Pro.
Bex, F. J. (2011). *Arguments, Stories and Criminal Evidence: A Formal Hybrid Theory.* Dordrecht: Springer.
Bex, F. J., Van Koppen, P. J., Prakken, H. & Verheij, B. (2010). A Hybrid Formal Theory of Arguments, Stories and Criminal Evidence. *Artificial Intelligence and Law* 18, 123–152.
Bex, F. J., Prakken, H., Reed, C. & Walton, D. (2003). Towards a Formal Account of Reasoning about Evidence: Argumentation Schemes and Generalisations. *Artificial Intelligence and Law* 11, 125–165.
Blackstone, W. (1765–1769). *Commentaries on the Laws of England.* Oxford: Clarendon.
Bovens, L. & Hartmann, S. (2003). *Bayesian Epistemology.* Oxford: Oxford University Press.
Butler, J. M., Kline, M. C. & Coble, M. D. (2018). NIST Interlaboratory Studies Involving DNA Mixtures (MIX05 and MIX13): Variation Observed and Lessons Learned. *Forensic Science International: Genetics* 37, 81–94.
Cabrera, F. (2017). Can There Be a Bayesian Explanationism? On the Prospects of a Productive Partnership. *Synthese* 194, 1245–1272.
Clermont, K. M. (2015). Trial by Traditional Probability, Relative Plausibility, or Belief Function? *Case Western Reserve Law Review* 66, 353–391.
Clermont, K. M. (2017). Common Sense on Standards of Proof. *Seton Hall Law Review* 48, 1057–1080.
Cohen, L. J. (1977). *The Probable and the Provable.* Oxford: Clarendon.
Connolly, T. (1987). Decision Theory, Reasonable Doubt, and the Utility of Erroneous Acquittals. *Law and Human Behavior* 11, 101–112.
Dahlman, C. (2018). Determining the Base Rate for Guilt. *Law, Probability and Risk* 17, 15–28.
Dahlman, C. & Mackor, A. R. (2019). Coherence and Probability in Legal Evidence. *Law, Probability and Risk* 18, 275–94. DOI: https://doi.org/10.1093/lpr/mgz016
Dane, F. C. (1985). In Search of Reasonable Doubt: A Systematic Examination of Selected Quantification Approaches. *Law and Human Behavior* 9, 141–158.
De Keijser, J. W., De Lange, E. G. M. & Van Wilsem, J. A. (2014). Wrongful Convictions and the Blackstone Ratio: An Empirical Analysis of Public Attitudes. *Punishment and Society* 16, 32–49.
De Keijser, J. W. & Van Koppen, P. J. (2007). Paradoxes of Proof and Punishment: Psychological Pitfalls in Judicial Decision Making. *Legal and Criminological Psychology* 12, 189–205.
De Poot, C. J., Bokhorst, R. J., Van Koppen, P. J. & Muller, E. R. (2004). *Rechercheportret: Over dilemma's in de opsporing* [Detectives' portrait: On dilemma's in police investigations]. Alphen aan den Rijn: Kluwer.

De Zoete, J., Fenton, N., Noguchi, T. & Lagnado, D. (2019). Resolving the So-Called 'Probabilistic Paradoxes in Legal Reasoning' with Bayesian Networks. *Science and Justice* 59, 367–379.
Dershowitz, A. M. (1996). *Reasonable Doubt: The Criminal Justice System and the O. J. Simpson Case*. New York: Simon and Schuster.
Dhami, M. K. (2008). On Measuring Quantitative Interpretations of Reasonable Doubt. *Journal of Experimental Psychology: Applied* 14, 353–363.
Di Bello, M. (2019). Plausibility and Probability in Juridical Proof. *International Journal of Evidence and Proof*. Advance online publication. DOI: https://doi.org/10.1177%2F1365712718815355
DiMaggio, P. (1997). Culture and Cognition. *Annual Review of Sociology* 23, 263–287.
Douglas, H. (2009). *Science, Policy, and the Value-Free Ideal*. Pittsburgh: University of Pittsburgh Press.
Douven, I. (2017). Abduction. In E. N. Zalta (ed.), *Stanford Encyclopedia of Philosophy*. https://plato.stanford.edu/entries/abduction/.
Edwards, W., Lindman, H. & Savage, L. J. (1963). Bayesian Statistical Inference for Psychological Research. *Psychological Review* 70, 193–242.
Fenton, N. E., Lagnado, D. A., Dahlman, C. & Neil, M. (2017). The Opportunity Prior: A Simple and Practical Solution to the Prior Probability Problem for Legal Cases. *Proceedings of the 16th edition of the International Conference on Artificial Intelligence and Law*. ACM Online Library, pp. 69–76.
Fenton, N. E., Neil, M. & Berger, D. (2016). Bayes and the Law. *Annual Review of Statistics and Its Application* 3, 51–77.
Fenton, N.E., Neil, M., Yet, B. & Lagnado, D. A. (2020). Analyzing the Simonshaven Case Using Bayesian Networks. *Topics in Cognitive Science* 12(4), 1092–1114. DOI: https://doi.org/10.1111/tops.12417
Festinger, L. (1957). *A Theory of Cognitive Dissonance*. Evanston, IL: Row, Peterson.
Fitelson, B. (2003). A Probabilistic Theory of Coherence. *Analysis* 63, 194–199.
Friedman, R. D. (1997). Answering the Bayesioskeptical Challenge. *International Journal of Evidence and Proof* 1, 276–291.
Gigerenzer, G. (2007). *Gut Feelings: Short Cuts to Better Decision Making*. London: Penguin.
Gigerenzer, G. & Engel, C. (eds.). (2006). *Heuristics and the Law*. Cambridge, MA: MIT Press.
Gill, P. (2016). *Misleading DNA Evidence: Reasons for Miscarriages of Justice*. Amsterdam: Academic Press.
Godfrey-Smith, P. (2009). *Theory and Reality: An Introduction to the Philosophy of Science*. Chicago: University of Chicago Press.
Granhag, P. A. & Strömwall, L. A. (eds.). (2004). *The Detection of Deception in Forensic Contexts*. Cambridge: Cambridge University Press.
Gross, S. R. (1998). Lost Lives: Miscarriages of Justice in Capital Cases. *Law and Contemporary Problems* 61, 125–149.
Gross, S. R. (2008). Convicting the Innocent. *Annual Review of Law and Social Sciences* 4, 173–192.
Gross, S. R., Jacoby, K., Matheson, D. J., Montgomery, N. & Patel, S. (2005). Exonerations in the United States: 1989 Through 2003. *Journal of Criminal Law and Criminology* 95, 523–560.
Hans, V. P. (2008). Jury Systems Around the World. *Annual Review of Law and Social Science* 4, 275–297.
Harman, G. H. (1965). The Inference to the Best Explanation. *Philosophical Review* 74, 88–95.

Hitchcock, C. (2007). The Lovely and the Probable. *Philosophy and Phenomenological Research* 74, 433–440.
Hofstee, W. K. B. (1980). *De empirische discussie: Theorie van het sociaal-wetenschappelijk onderzoek* [The empirical discussion: Theory of social science research]. Amsterdam: Boom.
Huff, R. & Killias, M. (eds.) (2008). *Wrongful Conviction: International Perspectives on Miscarriages of Justice*. Philadelphia: Temple University Press.
Kadane, J. B. & Schum, D. A. (2011). *A Probabilistic Analysis of the Sacco and Vanzetti Evidence*. New York: Wiley.
Kahneman, D., Slovic, P. & Tversky, A. (eds.) (1982). *Judgment Under Uncertainty: Heuristics and Biases*. Cambridge: Cambridge University Press.
Kassin, S. M., Dror, I. E. & Kukučka, J. (2013). The Forensic Confirmation Bias: Problems, Perspectives, and Proposed Solutions. *Journal of Applied Research in Memory and Cognition* 2, 42–52.
Kaye, D. H. (1979). The Paradox of the Gatecrasher and Other Stories. *Arizona State Law Journal*, 101–109.
Kleider, H. M., Pezdek, K., Goldinger, S. D. & Kirk, A. (2008). Schema-Driven Source Misattribution Errors: Remembering the Expected from a Witnessed Event. *Applied Cognitive Psychology* 22, 1–20.
Lagnado, D. A., Fenton, N. E., & Neil, M. (2013). Legal Idioms: A Framework for Evidential Reasoning. *Argument and Computation* 4, 46–63.
Laudan, L. (2007). Strange Bedfellows: Inference to the Best Explanation and the Criminal Standard of Proof. *International Journal of Evidence and Proof* 11, 292–306.
Lewicka, M. (1998). Confirmation Bias: Cognitive Error or Adaptive Strategy of Action Control? In M. Kofta, G. Weary & G. Sedek (eds.), *Personal Control in Action: Cognitive and Motivational Mechanisms*. New York: Plenum, pp. 233–258.
Lipton, P. (2004). *Inference to the Best Explanation*, 2nd ed. London: Routledge.
Lipton, P. (2007). Alien Abduction: Inference to the Best Explanation and the Management of Testimony. *Episteme* 4, 238–251.
Lycan, W. G. (1988). *Judgment and Justification*. Cambridge: Cambridge University Press.
Lycan, W. G. (2002). Explanation and Epistemology. In P. K. Moser (ed.), *The Oxford Handbook of Epistemology*. Oxford: Oxford University Press, pp. 408–433.
Mackor, A. R. (2017). Novel Facts: The Relevance of Predictions in Criminal Law. *Strafblad* 15, 145–156.
Mackor, A. R. (in press). Different Ways of Being Naked: A Scenario Approach to the Naked Statistical Evidence Problem. *IFCOLOG*.
McMullin, E. (1996). Epistemic Virtue and Theory-Appraisal. In I. Douven & L. Horsten (eds.), *Realism in the Sciences*. Leuven: University of Leuven Press, pp. 1–34.
Meester, R. & Kerkvliet, T. (2016). Assessing Forensic Evidence by Computing Belief Functions. *Law, Probability and Risk* 15, 127–153.
Meissner, C. A., & Kassin, S. M. (2004). 'You're Guilty, So Just Confess!' Cognitive and Behavioral Confirmation Biases in the Interrogation Room. In G. D. Lassiter (ed.), *Interrogations, Confessions, and Entrapment*. New York: Kluwer Academic, pp. 85–106.
Nance, D. A. (2001). Naturalized Epistemology and the Critique of Evidence Theory. *Virginia Law Review* 87, 1551–1618.
Nance, D. A. (2019). Belief Functions and Burdens of Proof. *Law, Probability and Risk* 18, 53–76.
Nesson, C. R. (1979). Reasonable Doubt and Permissive Inferences: The Value of Complexity. *Harvard Law Review* 92, 1187–1225.
Nickerson, R. S. (1998). Confirmation Bias: An Ubiquitous Phenomenon in Many Guises. *Review of General Psychology* 2, 175–220.

Nieuwbeerta, P. & Leistra, G. (2007). *Dodelijk geweld: Moord en doodslag in Nederland.* Amsterdam: Balans.
Nunn, G. A. (2015). The Incompatibility of Due Process and Naked Statistical Evidence. *Vanderbilt Law Review* 68, 1407–1433.
Okasha, S. (2000). Van Fraassen's Critique of Inference to the Best Explanation. *Studies in History and Philosophy of Science, Part A* 31, 691–710.
Olsson, E. J. (2005). *Against Coherence: Truth, Probability, and Justification.* Oxford: Oxford University Press.
Olsson, E. J. (2019). Dahlman and Mackor on Coherence and Probability in Legal Evidence: A Commentary. *Law, Probability and Risk* 18, 295–303. DOI: https://doi.org/10.1093/lpr/mgz017
Oswald, M. E., & Grosjean, S. (2004). Confirmation Bias. In R. F. Pohl (ed.), *Cognitive Illusions: A Handbook on Fallacies and Biases in Thinking, Judgment and Memory.* Hove: Psychology Press, pp. 79–96.
Pardo, M. S. (2013). The Nature and Purpose of Evidence Theory. *Vanderbilt Law Review* 66, 547–613.
Pardo, M. S. & Allen, R. J. (2008). Juridical Proof and the Best Explanation. *Law and Philosophy* 27, 223–268.
Pennington, N. & Hastie, R. (1993). The Story Model for Juror Decision Making. In R. Hastie (ed.), *Inside the Jury: The Psychology of Juror Decision Making*, 2nd ed. Cambridge: Cambridge University Press, pp. 192–221.
Popper, K. R. (1935). *Logik der Forschung: Zur Erkenntnistheorie der modernen Naturwissenschaft.* Vienna: Springer.
Popper, K. R. (1963). *Conjectures and Refutations: The Growth of Scientific Knowledge.* London: Routledge & Kegan Paul.
Poston, T. L. (2014). *Reason and Explanation: A Defense of Explanatory Coherentism.* New York: Palgrave Macmillan.
Prakken, H. (2020). An Argumentation-Based Analysis of the Simonshaven Case. *Topics in Cognitive Science* 12(4), 1068–1091. DOI: https://doi.org/10.1111/tops.12418
Prakken, H. & Meester, R. (2017). Bayesiaanse analyses van complexe strafzaken door deskundigen. Betrouwbaar en zo ja: nuttig? [Bayesian Analyses of Complex Criminal Cases by Experts. Reliable and If So: Useful?] *Expertise en Recht* 5, 185–197.
Psillos, S. (2007). The Fine Structure of Inference to the Best Explanation. *Philosophy and Phenomenological Research* 74, 441–448.
Saks, M. J. & Thompson, W. C. (2003). Assessing Evidence: Proving Facts. In D. Carson & R. H. C. Bull (eds.), *Handbook of Psychology in Legal Contexts*, 2nd ed. Chichester: Wiley, pp. 329–45.
Shafer, G. (1976). *A Mathematical Theory of Evidence.* Princeton: Princeton University Press.
Schippers, M. (2016). The Problem of Coherence and Truth Redux. *Erkenntnis* 81, 817–851.
Schum, D. A. (1994). *The Evidential Foundations of Probabilistic Reasoning.* New York: Wiley.
Schwartz, D. S. & Sober, E. (2017). The Conjunction Problem and the Logic of Jury Findings. *William and Mary Law Review* 59, 619–692.
Schweizer, M. (2014). Comparing Holistic and Atomistic Evaluation of Evidence. *Law, Probability and Risk* 13, 65–89.
Shogenji, T. (1999). Is Coherence Truth Conducive. *Analysis* 59, 338–345.
Siebel, M. (2011). Why Explanation and Thus Coherence Cannot Be Reduced to Probability. *Analysis* 71, 264–266.
Simon, D. (2004). A Third View of the Black Box: Cognitive Coherence in Legal Decision Making. *University of Chicago Law Review* 71, 511–586.

Simon, D. (2019). Thin Empirics. *International Journal of Evidence and Proof.* Advanced internet publication. DOI: https://doi.org/10.1177/1365712718815350

Spottswood, M. (2016). Unraveling the Conjunction Paradox. *Law, Probability and Risk* 15, 259–296.

Stein, A. (1996). Judicial Fact-Finding and the Bayesian Method: The Case for Deeper Scepticism About Their Combination. *International Journal of Evidence and Proof* 1, 25–47. DOI: https://doi.org/10.1177%2F136571279600100103

Stoffelmayr, E., & Diamond, S. S. (2000). The Conflict Between Precision and Flexibility in Explaining Beyond a Reasonable Doubt. *Psychology, Public Policy, and Law* 6, 769–787.

Taylor, S. E., & Crocker, J. (1981). Schematic Bases of Social Information Processing. In E. T. Higgins, C. A. Herman & M. P. Zanna (eds.), *Social Cognition: The Ontario Symposium on Personality and Social Psychology.* Hillsdale, NJ: Erlbaum, pp. 89–134.

Thagard, P. R. (1978). The Best Explanation: Criteria for Theory Choice. *The Journal of Philosophy* 75, 76–92.

Thagard, P. R. (2000). *Coherence in Thought and Action.* Cambridge, MA: MIT Press.

Thompson, W. C. (2009). Painting the Target Around the Matching Profile: The Texas Sharpshooter Fallacy in Forensic DNA Interpretation. *Law, Probability and Risk* 8, 257–276.

Thompson, W. C. (2011). What Role Should Investigative Facts Play in the Evaluation of Scientific Evidence? *Australian Journal of Forensic Sciences* 43, 123–134.

Tillers, P. & Green, E. D. (eds.). (1988). *Probability and Inference in the Law of Evidence: The Uses and Limits of Bayesianism.* Dordrecht: Kluwer Academic.

Van Fraassen, B. C. (1989). *Laws and Symmetry.* Oxford: Oxford University Press.

Van Koppen, P. J. (2009). Jury Trials: Opposed. *E-Journal USA* 14 (7), 18, 23–24.

Van Koppen, P. J. (2011). *Overtuigend bewijs: Indammen van rechterlijke dwalingen* (Convincing evidence: Reducing the number of miscarriages of justice). Amsterdam: Nieuw Amsterdam.

Van Koppen, P. J. (2013). *Gerede twijfel: Over bewijs in strafzaken* (Reasonable doubt: On evidence in criminal cases). Amsterdam: De Kring.

Van Koppen, P. J., & Mackor, A. R. (2020). A Scenario Approach to the Simonshaven Case. *Topics in Cognitive Science* 12(4), 1132–1151. DOI: https://doi.org/10.1111/tops.12429

Vidmar, N. J. (2009). Jury Trials: In Favor. *E-Journal USA* 14(7), 18–22.

Vidmar, N. J. (2011). The Psychology of Trial Judging. *Current Directions in Psychological Science* 20, 58–62.

Vidmar, N. J., & Hans, V. P. (2007). *American Juries: The Verdict.* Amherst, NY: Prometheus.

Vineberg, S. (2016). Dutch Book Arguments. In E. N. Zalta (ed.), *The Stanford Encyclopedia of Philosophy* (Spring 2016). Metaphysics Research Lab, Stanford University. https://plato.stanford.edu/archives/spr2016/entries/dutch-book/.

Volokh, A. (1997). n Guilty Men. *University of Pennsylvania Law Review* 146, 173–211.

Wagenaar, W. A., Van Koppen, P. J. & Crombag, H. F. M. (1993). *Anchored Narratives: The Psychology of Criminal Evidence.* London: Harvester Wheatsheaf.

Walton, D. N., Reed, C. A. & Macagno, F. (2008). *Argumentation Schemes.* Cambridge: Cambridge University Press.

Wittlin, M. (2019). Common Problems of Plausibility and Probabilism. *International Journal of Evidence and Proof.* Online advanced publication. DOI: https://doi.org/10.1177%2F1365712718815349

Ylikoski, P. & Kuorikoski, J. (2010). Dissecting Explanatory Power. *Philosophical Studies* 148, 201–219.

Dissenting Opinions

22

A Non-Naturalist Account of Law's Place in Reality

George Pavlakos*

22.1 LEGAL NATURALISM AS A METAPHYSICAL THESIS

For the present purposes, I shall proceed on the basis of the understanding that legal facts are facts about the content of the law in a given legal system at a given time. For example, 'it is the law in Greece that the police cannot enter university grounds unless a special permission has been granted by the Senate'; or 'According to UK law, killing is forbidden'.[1] While it is uncontroversial that legal facts obtain in the actual world, given that law is a derivative feature of reality, we may ask what it is in virtue of which such facts obtain. The question involves two further sub-questions: (a) What is the relevant relation of dependency between law and its determinants? (b) Which determinants does the relation pick out? As to the first sub-question, I have argued elsewhere (Chilovi & Pavlakos, 2019) that the relation between legal facts and their determinants is better understood as one of *metaphysical grounding*, a view that seems to be widely shared in the recent literature (Greenberg, 2004; Rosen, 2010; Plunkett, 2012). Although answers to the second sub-question about the determinants of legal facts abound, a theoretically interesting dividing line, which

---

* I am grateful to the editors for inviting my contribution to such a timely volume. Jaap Hage has provided rigorous and detailed feedback on an earlier draft, which led to considerable improvement of the text. Carsten Heidemann has prompted me to think hard about the success of a ground-theoretic reconstruction of Kelsen's theory of law. If I continue to stand by the fruitfulness of the project, it is because his challenging criticisms have strengthened my intuition that Kelsen was involved in the same enterprise that today goes by the name of metaphysical explanation. Samuele Chilovi has been an intellectual companion over the last three years and our collaboration, apart from being pure fun, has opened fresh pathways for my own thinking; several of this chapter's ideas would not have been possible without his input to our collaborative venture. Further, I wish to thank the editors of *Revus* for allowing me to use portions of Pavlakos (2019) in the second part of the chapter; and last but not least, Susan Hoehn and Oliver Brandenberger for their congenial hospitality in Lenzerheide, where the final draft was written.

[1] For the purposes of the present discussion I adopt the following working definition of a legal fact (LF): 'for every proposition p, system s, if p is law (valid) in s, we can state truly that it is a fact that p is law in s, or that s validates p, and call this a "legal fact"'. The formulation goes back to work I have developed together with Sam Chilovi in Chilovi & Pavlakos (2019, pp. 71–4).

coincides with traditional debates, involves the question of whether the determinants of law are entirely descriptive or partly moral in kind.[2]

Embracing a unifying standpoint, I suggest understanding naturalism about the law as comprising accounts of legal facts in terms of more fundamental, descriptive facts of both a social and physical nature: facts about social practices and collective actions, mental states and attitudes; but also physical facts about the brain and other physiological states of the relevant agents.[3] Although such an inclusive notion of legal naturalism might evoke disbelief, there exist reasons to suggest its fruitfulness. Adopting a convention for the limited purposes of this chapter, I shall understand legal naturalism as encompassing any broadly naturalist strategy in legal theory.

Accordingly, the naturalist project, as understood for the present purposes, contains two aspects: on the one hand legal naturalism is a metaphysical thesis about the determinants of legal facts; on the other it aims at an explanation of legal facts. In what sense is legal naturalism a metaphysical thesis? It is so in the sense that it advances a claim about how more fundamental, non-legal facts determine or constitute facts about the content of the law. Given that legal facts are not fundamental parts of the social and physical environment, a question arises about which (simpler) facts make them what they are. This question concerns the *grounding relation* that obtains between different levels of reality: the less fundamental level of legal facts (the grounded facts) and the more fundamental level of their constituents (the grounds):

> law is clearly not a fundamental feature of reality. If, say, it is the law in the United States that one ought to drive on the right-hand side of the road, or that one may freely walk on hills at night, this must be so in virtue of other, more fundamental things. Law being derivative, it owes its existence to more basic entities; it depends on them. Correlatively, when someone wants to find out what the law is, an adequate way of doing so would involve precisely appealing to those things that the law is determined by. (Chilovi & Pavlakos, 2019, p. 54)

The grounding relation is a *metaphysical* one because it tracks the dependency of some non-fundamental fact from a collection of more fundamental facts; this dependency is commonly expressed by saying that the grounded fact obtains 'in virtue of' its grounds. Accordingly, and adopting a somewhat sketchy classification, any legal theory that takes descriptive facts of a social or physical

---

[2] For the distinction between descriptive and non-descriptive facts see also fn. 16, this chapter.
[3] This inclusive definition purports to capture not only positivist accounts of legal facts but also any conceivable strongest, 'physicalist' account of legal facts. Typically, in the case of law, a physicalist thesis would be one about the physicalist nature of the mental states, dispositions and attitudes which play the role of determinants of legal facts. The case of such strong physicalism about the law would probably require the truth of some version of legal positivism, which argues that the determinants of law include such facts as are amenable to reductive, physicalist explanations.

nature to be the immediate grounds[4] of legal facts will be classified as naturalist.[5]

Additionally, the 'in virtue of' relation has an *explanatory* ambition: just as causal explanation aims to explain something *because of* something else, stating the obtaining of some fact *in virtue of* its determinants involves an explanatory operation. The explanatory ambition of grounding is a common theme both in general metaphysics and recent legal theory. Metaphysicians employ the ground-theoretic apparatus in order to move beyond relations which merely depict patters of correlation amongst facts of different levels of fundamentality (Kim, 1993, p. 167). Leading authors such as Fine, Schaffer and many others who are involved in the debates about consciousness agree that relations of metaphysical dependency are able to play an explanatory role (Fine, 2001; Audi, 2012; Schaffer, 2016; Dasgupta, 2017; Litland, 2017; Wilson, 2018; Chilovi & Pavlakos, 2019). Similarly, in the philosophy of law, Greenberg has emphasized the link between metaphysical determination and explanation by formulating the condition that anything that counts as a ground of a legal fact must also explain it.[6]

Notably, a key effect of the explanatory dimension of grounding is that it imposes demands on any substantive view which is advanced as a correct metaphysical account of the facts in a domain. To that extent, the demands of explanation are of a general value and can be used to appraise a wide range of metaphysical accounts. For our present concerns, it is of particular significance that a violation of the explanatory demands of grounding would undermine the truth of legal naturalism, as a view that aims to account for deep explanations of legal phenomena. Let me next turn to an explication of the explanatory demands of grounding and a discussion of their demandingness.

22.2 THE DEMANDS OF EXPLANATION

The demands stemming from the explanatory dimension of grounding presuppose a link between grounding and explanation, which can be formulated as the requirement that if a collection of facts D fully determines some fact F, then D must also explain how F obtains.[7] Given this requirement, each of the facts in D must contribute to an explanation of F, while the full ground D must provide a complete explanation of F. Further, the requirement posited by the link helps to elucidate the general structure of a valid argument against the success of naturalist

---

[4] For the notion of an immediate ground, see (Correia & Schnieder, 2012, pp. 25–8).
[5] Jaap Hage in Chapter 2 of the present volume adopts an equally inclusive understanding of naturalist legal theories.
[6] M. Greenberg (unpublished MS, on file with author). 'Legal Interpretation: How Does Law's Epistemology Relate to Its Metaphysics?'
[7] This section draws on common work which I have developed with Samuele Chilovi in Chilovi and Pavlakos (2019) and S. Chilovi and G. Pavlakos, 'Grounding, Explanation, and Legal Positivism' (in preparation).

claims. A brief survey of the relevant philosophical literature will be of help at this juncture.

Notably, explanatory gap arguments have been deployed in the philosophy of mind to argue against physicalism as the (metaphysical) claim that mental facts are determined by, and are nothing over and above, physical facts. Arguments that belong to this family include Chalmers' conceivability argument (Chalmers, 1996) and Jackson's knowledge argument (Jackson, 1986). These arguments have a common structure: (i) they start by establishing an epistemic gap between physical and mental (phenomenal) truths, by establishing the failure of a kind of epistemic entailment (specifically, of a priori entailment) from the physical to the mental; (ii) then they argue that the epistemic gap implies a corresponding metaphysical gap; finally, (iii) they conclude that there is a metaphysical gap between the physical and the mental, and hence that physicalism is false. The shape of the argument is then the following (Chalmers, 2010, p. 110):

1) There is an epistemic gap between physical and phenomenal truths
2) If there is an epistemic gap between physical and phenomenal truths, then there is a metaphysical gap and physicalism is false

---

3) Physicalism is false

Chalmers' and Jackson's arguments can be viewed as specifying different sorts of epistemic gaps, and different arguments in favour of the existence of such gaps. Let me visit them in turn.

Chalmers (1996) argues from a premise about conceivability and a premise that links conceivability with metaphysical possibility, to the negation of physicalism. Schematically, where P is the conjunction of all microphysical truths about the actual world, and Q an arbitrary phenomenal truth about the world:

1) It is conceivable that P&¬Q.
2) If it is conceivable that P&¬Q, it is metaphysically possible that P&¬Q.
3) If it is metaphysically possible that P&¬Q, then physicalism is false.

---

4) Physicalism is false.

This argument says that if it is conceivable that there be a world that is physically indiscernible to ours but that lacks some actual phenomenal truth, and if this suffices for there to be a metaphysically possible world with those features, then physicalism should be false. A world that duplicates all the physical features of actuality while lacking some actual phenomenal features is a 'zombie world'.

The epistemic gap at work in the argument consists in the fact that one can rationally conceive of P without Q, as per premise (1). So one is not required to conceive Q upon reflectively conceiving P: the epistemic entailment fails. The thesis that a zombie world is conceivable thus involves the idea that such a world is coherent under rational reflection, that it does not result in any contradiction: an ideal reasoner with complete physical knowledge of the actual world would not be bound to conclude that there are no zombies. In other words, P is conceivable if it cannot be known a priori to be false, or be ruled out. So, the relevant notion of conceivability is a broadly epistemic one.

Relatedly, Jackson's knowledge argument (Jackson, 1986) constitutes a further way of arguing from epistemological premises to metaphysical conclusions. His argument starts with the claim that the violation of an epistemic constraint has a certain metaphysical impact (it leads to the falsity of physicalism), and then claims that the constraint is indeed violated. The relevant epistemic constraint here is one of deducibility: phenomenal truths are not (a priori) *deducible* from physical truths, even by a perfect reasoner. In the case Jackson famously invites us to imagine, Mary is a scientist with unrestricted deductive powers and who has complete knowledge about the physics of colour and colour vision, but who has lived all her life in a black-and-white room. Despite all her physical knowledge and inferential abilities, it seems that there is something Mary doesn't know: what it's like to see red. Thus, for all her physical knowledge, she lacks phenomenal knowledge since she cannot deduce the latter from the former.

The form of the argument is the following:

1) If there are phenomenal truths that are not deducible from physical truths, then physicalism is false.
2) There are phenomenal truths that are not deducible from physical truths.

---

3) Physicalism is false.

Finally, returning to the legal domain, we encounter a parallel strategy in the argument Greenberg (Greenberg, 2004, 2006a, 2006b) deploys against the view that legal facts are grounded in descriptive social facts.[8] The argument involves an epistemic constraint on law determination, together with the contention that descriptive social facts on their own fail to satisfy this constraint because of an explanatory gap between the legal and whatever counts as the domain of non-legal explanantia. A putative formulation of his argument, adjusted to the context of naturalism, might take the following shape:

1) If a collection of facts D fully grounds a legal fact L, then D must generate a complete explanation of L.
2) There is an explanatory gap between legal facts and social and physical facts.

---

3) Legal naturalism is false.

[8] The type of determination that is implicit in Greenberg's discussion is constitutive (rather than causal or merely modal) in character. Given current developments in metaphysics that cash out constitutive determination in a grounding-based terms, the epistemic argument against positivism can thus be re-interpreted as involving the contention that the *grounding* of legal facts is subject to an epistemic constraint. For a ground-theoretic reconstruction of Greenberg's law determination see Chilovi and Pavlakos (2019).

22.3 THE EPISTEMIC DIMENSION OF EXPLANATORY GAPS

A key element of the strategies explored earlier was the formulation of the explanatory gap argument, both in the domain of mind and law, in *strong epistemic terms*. The epistemic gloss of explanation represents the gap as resulting from the inability to transition between two epistemic states (i.e. states of knowledge or belief). Thus, in the case of consciousness, the gap results from the inability to derive knowledge of a conscious state from knowledge of a collection of physical facts. Similarly, in the legal domain, the gap is located in the inability to derive knowledge of a legal fact from a collection of descriptive facts.

This inability points to a key requirement of successful explanation: the transparency between the epistemic state that plays the role of the *explanans* and the one that plays the role of the *explanandum*. Accordingly, the *epistemic constraint* of metaphysical explanation can be formulated as follows:[9]

> EC: If a collection of facts D fully grounds a legal fact L, one can in principle deduce (knowledge of) L from (knowledge of) D.

Given EC, there emerges a particularly helpful way of understanding the explanatory gap; that is, to represent it as an instance of an inferential failure to derive the target concept of the explanation from the concepts depicting the *explanantia*. This meets with support from the phenomenology of legal interpretation: in everyday legal practice lawyers employ legal reasoning with an eye to 'working out' the content of the law from the more fundamental concepts that depict its grounds (Greenberg, 2004).

The epistemic dimension helps clarify the gap in an instructive way, by relating the failure to derive knowledge of the facts in a domain to the inability to determine which amongst several possible interpretations of the target concept is the correct one. We know from Kripke's discussion (Kripke, 1982) of Wittgenstein's rule-following considerations – for brevity *Kripkenstein* – that the said inability can be modelled as the discrepancy between normatively determinate applications of a concept and the putative descriptive determinants of such applications. This rendering carries special force within the legal domain, in particular with respect to naturalist accounts of the content of the law. Kripkenstein, operating in a cognate context of philosophical enquiry,[10] suggests that the epistemic gap between the

---

[9] I limit the scope of the formulation to the legal case. See our discussion in Chilovi and Pavlakos, 'Grounding, Explanation, and Legal Positivism' (in preparation) and Greenberg (unpublished MS).
[10] Namely the context of discussing the determinants of semantic facts (facts about the meaning of words/concepts) in the later work of Ludwig Wittgenstein.

correct application of a concept and its determinants gives rise to a paradox: The example concerns a person who had added correctly two natural numbers, 57 and 68, which exceed the range of numbers previously added by the same person. The sceptic's challenge is to explain what makes it the case that the person meant addition (and, hence, applied the function correctly) as opposed to meaning quaddition, where quaddition is a function exactly similar to addition up to the point where one of the arguments reaches 57, from which point onwards the function's value becomes 5. Disturbingly, any attempt to answer the sceptic, through reference to the past history of applying addition, collapses because any such reference can be made consistent with the meaning of quaddition.

The paradox arises, *pace* Kripkenstein, because a key condition for any account of the meaning of a concept is that concepts be understood as normative in a strong sense;[11] that is, that they be understood as rules or standards which guide rational thought and language. Yet, there is nothing in the collection of descriptive facts that constitute the past practice of applying a concept[12] which could determine the unique course of action[13] recommended by the relevant target concept. Thus, the source of the epistemic gap lies in the *epistemic possibility of having multiple mappings from the same set of descriptive facts of past practice to different meanings* for any single collection of such facts is logically compatible with different interpretations of the target concept that is at stake. Whether a course of action is prescribed by the relevant concept cannot be determined merely by reference to facts of past practice (Wittgenstein, 1953, §201). Kripkenstein, in raising the sceptical paradox, points to a key feature of explanations that involve facts of different levels of fundamentality, as is the case with legal facts and their determinants. In such contexts, it is opaque as to why the obtaining of the source is linked to the obtaining of the result given that it is logically possible that the source obtains without the result obtaining.[14] Opacity accounts for the explanatory gaps which undermine

---

[11] Arguably, understanding concepts as strongly normative grounds the epistemic dimension of explanation. Only under the assumption that concepts are normative in a strong sense is it possible to understand the grounds of a target domain as 'reasons' for the obtaining of the facts in the domain; see Hattiangadi (2007, pp. 3–4; Ginsborg, 2018). In this spirit, Chilovi and Pavlakos 'Grounding, Explanation, and Legal Positivism' (in preparation), offer a detailed discussion of epistemic rationality and the requirement that the grounds of legal facts be epistemic reasons. Cf. with (Brożek, 2013) who argues for a weak normativity of concepts and uses it to develop a naturalistic solution to the rule-following paradox.

[12] For reasons of simplicity, I include in the facts of practice any of the facts deemed inert by Kripkenstein in determining the meaning of a concept: that is, all the physical and psychological facts involved in past instances of the relevant practice.

[13] The 'course of action' referred to here is, in the first instance, action with respect to the inferential moves guided by the concept. To this extent, the Wittgensteinian view I am discussing assumes that all concepts are 'practical' or 'action-guiding' in that minimal sense. Obviously, any evaluative concept will also have additional practical impact.

[14] I am paraphrasing a definition offered by Schaffer (2017, p. 4). In doing so, I restrict the scope of opacity to logical possibility, leaving out cases of a priori entailment and conceivability, which are also discussed by Schaffer.

complete explanations of the target domain (in our case, legal facts). Here is a useful definition:

> *Explanatory Gap*: There is an explanatory gap between source and result if and only if it is opaque why the obtaining of this particular source is linked to the obtaining of that particular result (as opposed to some other result, or no result at all). (Schaffer, 2017, p. 3)

This, then, is the argument against legal naturalism, stated in full: One cannot deduce knowledge of facts of legal content (L) from knowledge of descriptive facts about social practices (D) because it is *epistemically possible to have multiple mappings from the same collection of descriptive facts to legal content*. Therefore, there is an explanatory gap, D does not fully ground L, and legal naturalism is false.

22.4 NON-NATURALIST STRATEGIES IN LAW

Notably, the epistemic gap argument in law draws a different conclusion to the cognate arguments in the domain of mind. In a nutshell, failure to deduce knowledge of legal facts from descriptive non-legal facts has been understood as suggesting a shortcoming at the level of the putative explanantia (i.e. the relevant descriptive non-legal determinants) rather than requiring a revision of the way we conceive the explananda (i.e. the legal facts).

Accordingly, proponents of such arguments in the philosophy of mind take the epistemic gap to imply an ontological gap and thus argue that the grounded facts are not amenable to explanation, hence they are ontologically fundamental.[15] In contrast, the moral Greenberg draws for the legal domain (Greenberg, 2004) is that the grounding facts need to be supplemented by adding additional facts *of a different kind* to the inventory of descriptive social facts, which positivism takes to compose the grounding base of explanation.[16] Doing so will, in turn, resolve the indeterminacy of the possible deviant mappings and allow us to perform correct derivations from the base facts to the legal facts they ground. Further, Greenberg proceeds to argue that the additional facts that are required are value facts, ultimately helping himself to a non-naturalist position.

I turn next to discuss the consequences of the epistemic constraint on the explanation of legal facts for non-naturalist strategies in legal theory. Broadly

---

[15] With regard to mental facts see Chalmers (1996); Jackson (1986); and Levine (1983). It should be added that the result is yet different with respect to the domain of meaning, where epistemic gap arguments are taken to support some version of eliminativism about the grounded facts: that is, the claim that semantic facts do not really exist. See the sceptical reading of Kripke (1982) and the very perceptive analysis of Kripke's account in (Hattiangadi, 2007).

[16] Without going into a justification of the different route taken in law, an obvious explanation is the implausibility of deeming legal facts to be either fundamental components of reality, in the way Chalmers and Jackson take phenomenal facts to be, or non-existent, in the strong sense Kripke holds semantic facts to be non-existent.

speaking, we can distinguish between two non-naturalist strategies in the literature: the *additional grounds* strategy and the *bridging the gap* strategy. I shall discuss a paradigmatic instance of each strategy without passing a conclusive judgement about which strategy wins.

First, the *additional grounds* non-naturalism. This strategy takes the lesson of the epistemic constraint as recommending the broadening of the grounding base of the explanation of legal facts. In other words, the strategy runs, if one cannot derive knowledge of the target domain (law) from the knowledge of any amount of descriptive facts, then no collection of descriptive facts can fully ground the legal facts. *E contrario* one must arrive at the full grounding base by adding to the relevant descriptive facts a collection of non-descriptive facts[17] which can meet the demands of the epistemic constraint. Prominent in respect of this strategy is Mark Greenberg's account of law determination.[18]

Although it cannot be discussed here in full, an evident objection to this strategy would challenge the capacity of the expanded grounding base to meet the epistemic constraint. In other words, it would remain uncertain how the addition of, say, moral facts to a collection of descriptive facts D would enable the resulting collection of facts D* to epistemically necessitate the inference from the knowledge of D* to the knowledge of some target legal fact. To recall Kripkenstein's argument from earlier, given the possibility of multiple mappings from a collection of facts to legal content, it is not clear how adding further facts of any kind to the grounding base would close the gap of the explanation.

22.5 KELSENIAN NON-NATURALISM

Bridging the gap non-naturalism is the second strategy. Roughly put, this strategy looks for an intermediary or a *bridge* in virtue of which the epistemic gap between legal facts and their grounds can be joined. In exploring this option, I shall turn to a long-standing account of law from the first half of the twentieth century, Hans Kelsen's Pure Theory of Law. While Kelsen's non-naturalism has long been recognized and discussed in the literature, no one to my knowledge has discussed it in ground-theoretic terms.[19]

---

[17] As an aide-memoire: descriptive facts will typically include physical and social facts whereas non-descriptive will comprise deontic, moral and other evaluative facts broadly conceived.

[18] In his wide-ranging paper 'Are the Cognitive Sciences Relevant for Law?' Jaap Hage advances a constructivist account which involves non-legal normative facts in the explanation of legal facts (Hage, Chapter 2, present volume). Although he claims that such constructivist facts are ultimately grounded on social facts of acceptance it is not clear that his account does not help itself to 'acceptance-independent' value-facts, such as moral or prudential reasons for action. Thus, Hage's view seems to me to be better characterized as a version of *additional grounds* non-naturalism. Either that, or it fails to generate the requisite explanation of legal facts.

[19] The only exception is an earlier attempt I made in Pavlakos (2019), which is, however, incomplete. For a discussion of Kelsenian non-naturalism that sets it into the context of the history of ideas see Paulson (2018).

The extent to which Kelsen's account of law is cast in language that is compatible with the contemporary ground-theoretic debates in legal theory is astonishing. To begin with, Kelsen identified legal norms as the object of cognition of the Pure Theory of Law, his rendering of legal science, and sought to preserve the independence[20] of the realm of legal objects (norms) from both non-normative, brute facts and value facts. But the independence of the realm of legal norms from both fact and value is accompanied by two explanatory challenges: first, to explain[21] how knowledge of a set of non-normative psychological and physical facts can generate knowledge of legal norms. Second, to explain *that* knowledge without making reference to any robust value facts.

The first challenge relates to the non-fundamental nature of legal facts and arises because:

> at least part of the essence of the law ... appears to occupy the realm of nature, to have a thoroughly natural existence. If one analyses a parliamentary enactment, say, or an administrative act ... one can distinguish two elements. There is an act perceptible to the senses, taking place in time and space, an external event ... And there is a specific meaning, a sense that is, so to speak, immanent in or attached to the act or event. (Kelsen, 1992, p. 8)

Accordingly, Kelsen shares the contemporary view that legal norms are not fundamental but depend on more basic facts,[22] which are available to the senses. 'How do more fundamental, non-normative facts contribute to/determine legal norms?' This is the key explanatory task for legal science in general, and more specifically to the Pure Theory of Law.

Kelsen's understanding of a legal norm fits quite closely with the working definition of a legal fact that was suggested earlier.[23] Kelsen explains the contribution of more fundamental facts in terms of meaning or content: the same set of facts can be interpreted in an objective or in a subjective way, out of which only the former corresponds to the content of a legal norm. The norm-creating acts of the Captain of

---

[20] The independence referred to in this context is primarily epistemic, not metaphysical, for Kelsen recognizes that law is not independent of the realm of naturalistic facts (Kelsen, 1992, p. 8). However, given the priority of epistemology over metaphysics, which occupies a central position within Neo-Kantian philosophy, questions concerning the existence-conditions of things are treated as addressing conditions for making valid judgements about those things. For the main tenets of Neo-Kantianism see the excellent discussion in Heidemann (2013).

[21] Kelsen contrasts the explanation he is interested in with causal explanation. While there is insufficient textual evidence that he was engaged in strict constitutive explanation, it is plausible to attribute the key tasks involved in this type of explanation to him. I aim to develop this point in more detail in future work but will assume its truth for the present purposes.

[22] Kelsen is not very precise in his use of the term 'fact', which seems to include both the naturalistic facts that arise in the context of intentional action, such as acts of will and their expressions, but also facts of social practice, such as the doings and sayings of legal officials. Since nothing much turns out for my account on introducing more fine-grained distinctions, I will understand 'fact' to include all of the above.

[23] Note 1, this chapter.

Köpenick, Kelsen's proverbial figure of the impostor, possess only a *subjective* meaning; in contrast, an identical act issued by a government official acting within their powers possesses the *objective* meaning of a (legal) norm. It is this objective meaning, attached to the relevant set of non-normative facts, which explains how these contribute to or determine the content of legal norms. To that extent, the explanatory task obtains – also for Kelsen – between facts about the content of the law and their (more fundamental) determinants. And relatedly, facts about 'the objective meaning of the law' can be readily understood as facts 'about the content of the law'.

Instructively, Kelsen took subjective meaning to consist in any meaning attached to facts by their authors, including the meanings conferred on them by such normative orders as morality, ethics and religion. In contrast, objective or legal meaning requires a specifically legal cognition:

> External circumstances are always a part of nature, for they are events perceptible to the senses, taking place in time and space; and, as part of nature, they are governed by causal laws ... what makes such an event a legal (or an illegal) act is not its facticity, not its being natural but ... its meaning, the objective sense that attaches to the act. The specifically legal sense ... comes by way of a norm whose content refers to the event and confers legal meaning on it ... The norm functions as a scheme of interpretation. (Kelsen, 1992, p. 10)

Thus, the object of legal cognition (objective meanings or norms) presupposes the activity of legal science, while legal cognition cannot have as its object anything but legal norms:

> To comprehend something legally can only be to comprehend it as law ... To characterize acts occurring in nature as legal is simply to claim the validity of norms whose content corresponds in a certain way to that of actual events. (Kelsen, 1992, p. 12)

In this way, validity becomes the special mode of the existence of legal norms, in a manner that draws a strict separation between the realm of fact and the normative sphere of legal norms:

> To speak ... of the validity of a norm is to express ... the specific existence of the norm, the particular way in which the norm is given, in contradistinction to natural reality, existing in time and space. The norm as such, not to be confused with the act by means of which the norm is issued, does not exist in space and time, for it is not a fact of nature. (Kelsen, 1992, p. 12)

22.5.1 *Facts About the Content of the Law*

Notably, Kelsen's discussion provides an important insight to the contemporary debate: his detailed discussion of the objective meaning of a legal norm makes a contribution to a more fine-grained understanding of facts about the content of the law, which adds considerable richness in the context of the ground-theoretic discussion of law determination: Kelsen introduces an abstract account of the structure of facts about the content of the law under the notion of *imputation* (*Zurechnung*). On Kelsen's view, imputation describes the linking relation that is expressed by the legal Ought, whose content is stated in the hypothetical sentence of the legal norm (*Rechtssatz*): 'If A is, then B ought to be'. In the first edition of the Pure Theory of Law, we read:

> The Pure Theory ... [understands] the legal norm as a **hypothetical judgment** that expresses the specific linking of a conditioning material fact with a conditioned consequence. ... Just as laws of nature link a certain material fact as cause with another as effect, so positive laws ... link legal condition with legal consequence .... If the mode of linking material facts is causality in the one case, it is **imputation** in the other. (Kelsen, 1992, p. 23)

And a little later:

> Expressing this connection, termed 'imputation', and thereby expressing the **specific existence, the validity**, of the law – and nothing else – is the 'ought' in which the Pure Theory of Law represents the positive law. That is, 'ought' expresses the unique sense in which the material facts belonging to the system of the law are posited in their reciprocal relation. In the same way, 'must' expresses the law of causality. (Kelsen, 1992, p. 24)

A key advantage of rendering legal facts along the lines of imputation is additional clarity about the explanatory task that is involved in law determination. In particular, what would need to be explained – the target legal facts – are no longer characterized in some vague terms, but are given a more concrete structure, that of the hypothetical formulation that is proposed by imputation. This carries over to the explanatory/epistemic demands of law determination. In other words, when looking for the determinants of law, we are looking for such facts that can direct/guide a thinker to deduce knowledge of the putative legal facts from knowledge of their determinants. Ultimately, the rendering of the structure of the legal explananda in terms of imputation offers significant theoretical guidance when attempting to bridge the gap between legal facts and their grounds.[24]

22.5.2 *A Sceptical Challenge*

In line with the now familiar epistemic demands of law determination, as discussed above, Kelsen directly addresses the question about which of the two meanings is in play, the objective or the subjective. The question gains momentum because the more fundamental determinants, which partly constitute the content of the law, *are*

---

[24] See Section 22.5.3.

by themselves incapable of discriminating between subjective and objective meaning. In Kelsen's words:

> The *possible* content of the norm, however, is the same as the *possible* content of an actual event, for the norm refers in its content to this actual event, above all, to human behavior. (Kelsen, 1992, p. 12)

And elsewhere:

> the subjective meaning may ... coincide with the objective meaning attributed to the act in ... the legal system. (Kelsen, 1992, p. 9)

Kelsen can be helpfully reinterpreted as suggesting that it is (epistemically) possible that there exist multiple mappings from the same set of facts to different subjective meanings, alongside the objective meaning of legal cognition. This is so, because the same set of facts is epistemically compatible with multiple interpretations and there is nothing in the facts themselves capable of determining any mapping as being the correct one. This raises a paradox very similar to the one diagnosed by Kripkenstein earlier.[25] According to the paradox there exist no grounds for opting for the objective meaning of a collection of facts (i.e. the legal content) as opposed to any of the available subjective meanings (i.e. other deviant contents), which epistemically are equally possible as interpretations of the relevant collection of descriptive determinants.

22.5.3 Kelsen's Bridge

The lack of anything supporting the objective over the subjective interpretation of the relevant facts makes it epistemically possible that the putative determinants obtain without the relevant legal facts obtaining. This, as we saw, leads to opacity which ultimately opens up the gap of explanation. I shall now propose understanding Kelsen's way out of the paradox in line with a state-of-the art strategy for bridging explanatory gaps of this kind.

As an antidote to explanatory gaps, the literature has proposed linking principles (call these *bridging principles or bridges*), which aim to restore the transparency of the linking relation between the grounding facts (sources) and the grounded facts (result). Bridging principles purport to provide substantive information for all the concrete transitions from more fundamental sources to less fundamental results in order to make transparent how a less fundamental target is linked to more fundamental sources (Schaffer, 2017, pp. 10 n).[26]

---

[25] Section 22.3.
[26] Bridging principles, in the context of inter-level explanations, perform the function of linking a source to a result in a transparent manner, that is, by eliminating opacity in the sense explained earlier. Whether in the case of law transparency requires a bridging principle that engages moral facts amongst the explanantia of legal facts is controversial. Kelsen obviously thought transparency may be generated, without making reference to moral facts. A more detailed enquiry into the requirements

Skipping a taxonomy of possible types of explanatory gaps and respective bridges, I will suggest understanding Kelsen's idea of the *basic norm* (*Grundnorm*) as a genuine contribution to the overcoming of the explanatory gap in the domain of law. My proposal is that the *Grundnorm* represents Kelsen's version of a bridging principle which aims to make epistemically transparent how lower-level facts are (explanatorily) linked to legal norms. Accordingly, the *Grundnorm* can be thought of as a bridging principle for epistemic transparency, which does not require more demanding forms of dependence (e.g. logical entailment).[27] Let me adumbrate the role of the *Grundnorm* as a bridging principle.

As submitted earlier, the context of explanation of legal norms is opaque, because it is epistemically possible that we can know all the relevant descriptive facts without knowing that the target legal fact obtains. The ensuing explanatory gap is modelled by Kelsen as an Is-Ought gap, whereby it is not possible to derive an Ought-fact (legal norm) from any given set of Is-facts (lower-level facts).[28] Although Kelsen does not use ground-theoretical vocabulary, the strategy he employs for bridging the gap can be recast in ground-theoretic terms. I shall suggest that Kelsen can be usefully understood as arriving at a bridging principle whose role is to create transparency in the context of an inter-level explanation by providing substantive information about the linking relation at work.

For simplicity, Kelsen's bridging strategy can be understood as aiming to develop a model that maps the determinants of law (descriptive facts) onto legal content, that is, facts with the structure of imputation, as submitted earlier. The model can direct/ guide a thinker to deduce knowledge of some concrete legal fact from knowledge of a concrete collection of descriptive facts, by making it intelligible how the latter determine the former and, consequently, restoring transparency between the two levels of explanation. Now, the complex task of constructing the model can, for the sake of simplicity, be represented as follows.

To begin with, Kelsen's vocabulary supports an interpretation of the Is-Ought gap as one about the demands of inter-level explanation, i.e. the link in virtue of which some collection of descriptive facts (e.g. acts of will and their subjective meaning) contributes to the determination of some fact of objective meaning (a norm):

> of inter-level explanations, which involve a transition from non-normative to normative facts, might conclude that something like the prohibition of inferring an Ought from an Is makes additional demands on the structure and content of bringing principles. However, this enquiry must be deferred to a future occasion.

[27] Logical entailment aside, a further version of transparency depends on knowledge of essences, as when we can derive knowledge of 'water' from our knowledge of molecules of hydrogen and oxygen plus our knowledge of the essence of water (i.e. 'water is H_2O'). This version is equally not required for Kelsenian epistemic transparency.

[28] This requires more unpacking: the opacity that generates the explanatory gap between Ought-facts (legal norms) and Is-facts (non-normative facts) is due to the fact that there exist logically possible mappings from the same source (set of facts) to multiple subjective meanings, which *are not* legal norms.

That an assembly of people is a parliament, and that the result of their activity is a statute (in other words, that these events have this 'meaning'), says simply that the material facts as a whole correspond to certain provisions of the constitution. That is, the content of an actual event corresponds to the content of a given norm. (Kelsen, 1992, p. 9)

And he explicitly searches for a model capable of constraining possible mappings from descriptive determinants to deviant meanings, with an eye to establishing the required link between those determinants and legal content. In a first step he suggests that 'the norm function ... as *a scheme of interpretation*' (Kelsen, 1992, p. 10; my emphasis – GP). On one level, the idea of the 'norm as a scheme of interpretation' may serve the function of the requisite model just by relying on the hierarchical structure of a concrete legal order. Recall that Kelsen has – via the notion of 'imputation' – already built the requirement of validity into legal content: that is, imputation tells us that legal content requires the authorization of some official by a higher norm of the legal order. But, eventually, the idea of validity can only serve as the requisite model up to a point, on pain of an infinite regress. For, sooner or later, the hierarchical series of norms of any legal order will run out.

Ultimately, the idea of the 'norm as a scheme of interpretation' needs to overcome the limitations of any concrete hierarchical series of norms. To deliver the requisite model for constraining deviant mappings and bridging the epistemic gap, Kelsen *must* come up with a conception of the norm that does not itself depend on some pre-existing concrete norm. And that's exactly what he does: he suggests that the norm that can function as the model (or scheme) of interpretation be understood as the abstract formulation of 'objective meaning' that 'authorizes' the transition from more fundamental sources (non-normative facts) to less fundamental results (objective 'meaning-facts' or norms).

Not to put too fine a point on it, Kelsen's bridging strategy consists in bringing together his idea of imputation as the abstract formulation of objective meaning (i.e. the norm), and the requirement of the 'norm as a scheme of interpretation', with an eye to delivering the model that can bridge the pertinent epistemic gap. As one would expect, cut off from the context of any concrete legal order, the norm becomes a free-floating, pure instance of imputation which can no longer itself rely on any actual authorization to ground its own 'objectivity'. Its 'objectivity' must be 'postulated' or 'presupposed'. Indeed, Kelsen calls the norm whose objective meaning does not require an earlier authorization, but is logically[29] presupposed, the *Grundnorm* (basic norm):

A positivistic science of law can only state that this norm is presupposed as a basic norm in the foundation of the objective validity of the legal norms, and therefore

---

[29] Kelsen talks about logical presupposition, but it should be clear by now that the *Grundnorm* is more akin to an a priori synthetic proposition, in the sense of a transcendental presupposition of legal cognition.

presupposed in the interpretation of an effective coercive order as a system of objectively valid legal norms. (Kelsen, 1967, p. 204)

In incorporating objective meaning in an 'ungrounded', 'pure' form, the *Grundnorm* basically postulates the application of imputation with respect to any actual, functioning legal order. Along these lines, the *Grundnorm* generates the model that can rule out deviant mappings from any given collection of descriptive facts and provides a bridge that links those facts to legal content (the objective meaning of a legal norm).[30]

Accordingly, imputation is a bridging principle *for epistemic transparency*. Consistent with the programme of Neo-Kantianism, which arguably informs Kelsen's account, imputation is not a principle of the ontological constitution of the objects of the legal discipline (legal norms), but instead a necessary presupposition for the intelligibility of antecedently constituted lower-level materials qua legal norms. 'Necessary presupposition' in this context should be understood as a (synthetic) a priori principle that makes intelligible how the knowledge of legal facts obtains.[31]

22.6 SUMMING UP

I began by suggesting that naturalistic accounts of legal phenomena are best understood as metaphysical explanations of how a legal fact obtains in virtue of its more fundamental determinants, consisting of a collection of non-legal, physical or social facts. I then discussed the explanatory constraints implicit in the relation of metaphysical determination and demonstrated how those can generate an argument that undermines naturalism in a number of domains, including law. Usefully, the same constraints that condemned naturalism were employed to craft a non-naturalist account capable of meeting the demands that metaphysical explanation poses in the legal domain. Kelsen's idea of the *Grundnorm* proved to be a perfect candidate for this task, both in terms of anticipating the concerns of the ground-theoretic analysis and of delivering a philosophically capacious solution that can live up to the standards of contemporary debates in metaphysics.

REFERENCES

Audi, P. (2012). Grounding: Toward a Theory of the In-Virtue-of Relation. *The Journal of Philosophy* 112, 685–93.
Brożek, B. (2013). *Rule-Following*. Kraków: Copernicus Press.

---

[30] It is in this sense that Kelsen's controversial claim about legal science *constituting* its object should be interpreted best: that is, the cognition of legal norms depends on the conditions that make their knowledge intelligible. See Kelsen (1928, p. 62) and Heidemann (2013).
[31] In Neo-Kantian parlance Kelsen submits that imputation serves the purpose of a necessary presupposition that justifies the possibility of the factum of legal science.

Chalmers, D. J. (1996). *The Conscious Mind: In Search of a Fundamental Theory*. Oxford: Oxford University Press.
Chalmers, D. J. (2010). *The Character of Consciousness*. Oxford: Oxford University Press.
Chilovi, S., & Pavlakos, G. (2019). Law-Determination as Grounding: A Common Grounding Framework for Jurisprudence. *Legal Theory* 25, 53–76.
Correia, F., & Schnieder, B. (eds.) (2012). *Metaphysical Grounding: Understanding the Structure of Reality*. Cambridge: Cambridge University Press.
Dasgupta, S. (2017). Constitutive Explanation. *Philosophical Studies* 27, 74–97.
Fine, K. (2001). The Question of Realism. *Philosophers' Imprint* 1, 1–30.
Ginsborg, H. (2018). Normativity and Concepts. In D. Star (ed.),*The Oxford Handbook of Reasons and Normativity*. Oxford: Oxford University Press, pp. 989–1014.
Greenberg, M. (2004). How Facts Make Law. *Legal Theory* 10, 157–98.
Greenberg, M. (2006a). Hartian Positivism and Normative Facts: How Facts Make Law II. In Hershovitz, 2006, pp. 267–90.
Greenberg, M. (2006b). On Practices and the Law. *Legal Theory* 12, 113–36.
Hattiangadi, A. (2007). *Oughts and Thoughts: Rule-Following and the Normativity of Content*. Oxford: Clarendon Press.
Heidemann, C. (2013). Facets of 'Ought' in Kelsen's Pure Theory of Law. *Jurisprudence* 4, 246–62.
Hershovitz, S. (ed.) (2006). *Exploring Law's Empire: The Jurisprudence of Ronald Dworkin*. Oxford: Oxford University Press.
Jackson, Frank. (1986). What Mary Didn't Know. *Journal of Philosophy* 83, 291–5.
Kelsen, H. (1928). *Die Philosophischen Grundlagen der Naturrechtslehre und des Rechtspositivismus*. Berlin: Pan Verlag.
Kelsen, H. (1967). *Pure Theory of Law*. 2nd German ed., translated by Max Knight. Berkeley: University of California Press.
Kelsen, H. (1992). *Introduction to the Problems of Legal Theory*. 1st German ed., translated by B. Paulson and S. Paulson. Oxford: Clarendon Press.
Kim, J. (1993). *Supervenience and Mind: Selected Philosophical Essays*. Cambridge: Cambridge University Press.
Kripke, S. (1982). *Wittgenstein on Rules and Private Language*. Cambridge, MA: Harvard University Press.
Levine, J. (1983). Materialism and Qualia: The Explanatory Gap. *Pacific Philosophical Quarterly* 64, 354–61.
Litland, J. E. (2017). Grounding Ground. *Oxford Studies in Metaphysics* 10, 279–315.
Paulson, S. (2018). The Purity Thesis. *Ratio Juris* 31, 276–306.
Pavlakos, G. (2019). Kelsenian Imputation and the Explanation of Legal Norms. *Revus* 37, 47–56.
Plunkett, D. (2012). A Positivist Route for Explaining How Facts Make Law. *Legal Theory* 18, 139–207.
Rosen, G. (2010). Metaphysical Dependence: Grounding and Reduction. In B. Hale & A. Hoffmann (eds.), *Modality: Metaphysics, Logic and Epistemology*. Oxford: Oxford University Press, pp. 109–36.
Schaffer, J. (2016). Grounding in the Image of Causation. *Philosophical Studies* 173, 49–100.
Schaffer, J. (2017). The Ground between the Gaps. *Philosophers' Imprint* 17, 1–26.
Wilson, A. (2018). Metaphysical Causation. *Noûs* 52, 723–51.
Wittgenstein, L. (1953). *Philosophical Investigations*, ed G. E. M. Anscombe & R. Rhees. Oxford: Blackwell.

23

The Law and Cognitive Sciences Enterprise: A Few Analytic Notes

*Pierluigi Chiassoni**

23.1 THE LAW AND COGNITIVE SCIENCES ENTERPRISE

The present collection of essays purports to contribute to the Law and Cognitive Sciences Enterprise (L&CSE) as a further and relatively recent line of interdisciplinary inquiry inside of contemporary legal culture.

Like its 'Law & ...' sisters, the L&CSE aims at satisfying the call, which appears to be deeply felt amongst jurists and jurisprudents, to enrich law and legal scholarship with the secure benefits flowing from foreign disciplines in the social or natural sciences.

In the case of the L&CSE, as the authors of these collected essays make clear, the purpose consists in bringing to the fore the many ways in which the outputs of the several branches of learning devoted to exploring the functioning of the human mind – either as an 'object' in itself, or considered in its relations to the structure and functioning of the human brain[1] – can be put to work in carrying out a renovation of law and legal thinking. They conceive of the cognitive sciences'-induced renovation of the legal world as a sweeping phenomenon: ranging from the more abstract level of the general theory of law, legal reasoning and legal interpretation (see Hage, Chapter 2; Brożek, Chapter 7), to more specific corners of the legal maze like the elucidation of the notions of human agent and human mind arguably embodied in, or presupposed by, existing laws in the criminal or civil sectors (see Kurek, Chapter 4; Palka, Chapter 11); the elaboration of models of evidentiary reasoning (see Mackor, Jellema, & van Koppen, Chapter 21), the psychology of trial judges (see Hoffman, Chapter 8), the use of neuroimaging evidence in courts (see Moriarty, Chapter 18); and the theory of insanity defence in criminal law (see Meynen, Chapter 15).

Interdisciplinary enterprises are difficult undertakings. The scholars willing to enrol – I am thinking, in particular, of those who are trained as jurists or legal

---

* University of Genoa (pierluigi.chiassoni@unige.it).
[1] Namely: psychology, cognitive neuroscience, biology, sociology, economics, philosophy, artificial intelligence, and so on (see Hage, Chapter 2, §2.1).

philosophers – must be conscious that they are threading, if not through a veritable minefield, surely an insalubrious neighbourhood. Let me mention just a few of the dangers which interdisciplinary (legal) scholars are likely to face. It may happen that they end up acting amateurishly – to be sure, out of a sincere passion for the 'new frontier' they are discovering and mapping to general benefit. It may also occur, however, that they unreasonably expect the foreign fields of learning to do jobs such fields are structurally unable to do; that they tend to exaggerate the payoffs that law and legal scholarship may get from them; that they come to confuse the levels and functions of the several kinds of discourse at stake; that they pay an uncritical deference to experts from foreign fields; or even, last but not least, that they become possessed by an innovation frenzy, which may go from urging the throwing out of old but tried-and-trusted and valuable furniture of the legal world, to the extreme of promoting an imperialist takeover by non-legal disciplines, in force of which traditional legal tasks (like, e.g., the identification of the legal standards to be enacted by legislators or applied by judges) are no longer to be carried out by lawyers but, rather, by (the competent variety of) non-legal experts, leaving lawyers with the subsidiary task of putting externally produced content into the proper legal forms.

The several contributions to the present collection are safe from the flaws I have just recalled. There is no room, accordingly, for wholesale knockdown critiques, but only for queries upon issues of (relative) detail. In the following, assuming the external standpoint of an analytic jurisprudent, I will consider four issues in turn, corresponding to as many claims made and argued for in support of the L&CSE. These are:

1) The relevance issue (are the cognitive sciences really relevant for the law?);
2) The metaphysics of law issue (do we need cognitive sciences in view of a renewed 'metaphysics of law'?);
3) The Hume's law or Hume's guillotine issue (are the cognitive sciences really undermining the so-called Hume's law?);
4) The psychological theory of legal interpretation and legal reasoning issue (are the cognitive sciences useful in working out an adequate model of legal interpretation and legal reasoning?).

While dealing with the issues above, I will only take a few of the essays in this collection into account.[2] This is by no means to be understood as an implicit censure to the ones I will not consider. My jurisprudential cast of mind and programme of research are to be regarded as solely responsible for that.

An avowal is in order before proceeding. While I think any serious scientific enterprise can be of help to the legal profession in carrying out its multifarious daily activities, I also think, contrary to any form of scientific imperialism, that (cognitive)

---

[2] As we shall see in a moment, these are the essays by Jaap Hage, Corrado Roversi, Jane Campbell Moriarty, Anne Ruth Mackor, Hylke Jellema, Peter J. van Koppen and Bartosz Brożek.

sciences can replace *neither* the *normative ethics commitment* each responsible lawyer (in the broadest sense of the term) has necessarily to undertake in relation to the positive legal system(s) s/he happens to serve, *nor* the (legal) *norm-expertise* and (legal) *norm-engineering*, from drafting to interpretation and systematization, which represent the matter and purpose of legal studies (of 'law as an autonomous discipline').

23.2 ARE THE COGNITIVE SCIENCES REALLY RELEVANT FOR THE LAW?

Philosophy is the art of pretending to ignore what everybody knows or assumes to know. Acquaintance fatally breeds an appearance of knowledge, the shortcomings of which are liable to be disclosed by careful philosophical investigation, often to people's utmost discomfort.

Here and now, everybody – every reasonable person – seems to take it for granted that cognitive sciences *are* relevant for law. Taking stock of that common view in a true philosophical spirit, Jaap Hage devotes his contribution to the task of carefully inquiring on precisely *which* grounds the relevance of cognitive sciences to law can be safely affirmed (Hage, Chapter 2, §2.1). As an outcome of this, he comes to envision a three-pronged relevance.

First, cognitive sciences are relevant to law, Hage claims, since they are able to provide law with useful pieces of information. These are likely to be particularly worthwhile in determining both the facts to which existing legal rules ought to be applied (relevance in evidentiary reasoning), and the facts that must be taken into account by lawmakers, if they wish to make good (i.e., working and effective) laws (Hage, Chapter 2, §2.4).

Second, cognitive sciences are relevant to law, Hage claims, since they are able to 'determine' or 'establish' the 'content of the law' (Hage, Chapter 2, §§2.3, 2.5, 2.6). Normativist legal theorists like Kelsen entertain the idea of there being two separated realms of 'is' (*Sein*) and 'ought' (*Sollen*), and regard the realm of 'ought' as unfit for scientific investigation.[3] However, they are wrong. There 'is no hard difference between IS and OUGHT', because 'ought-facts', the stuff of which the law is made, are 'facts', being, more precisely, 'constructive facts that depend in the last instance ... on acceptance by the members of some group' (Hage, Chapter 2, §2.7).[4]

Third, but by no means least important, cognitive sciences are relevant to law, Hage claims, because they are likely to undermine ('disrupt') the traditional image of mankind that underlies the law of the present age. Present law assumes human beings to be rational, reasons-responsive agents. The cognitive sciences, however,

---

[3] 'If law is approached from the traditional perspective, it is seen as normative – belonging to the realm of OUGHT. If it is also assumed that descriptive sciences belong to the realm of IS, and that there is a logical gap between IS and OUGHT, then the cognitive sciences cannot inform us about the content of the law' (Hage, Chapter 2, §§2.2.3, 2.5.3).

[4] 'As the expression "ought-facts" suggests, an ought is a fact' (§2.5.6).

bring to the fore that human beings 'often do not know what motivates them', 'that it is not obvious what agents and actions are', and suggest momentous reforms should take place to accommodate existing law (private, constitutional, and, above all, criminal law) to such a fact (Hage, Chapter 2, §2.7).[5]

Leaving aside the first count of relevance which Hage considers, which is uncontroversial, the second and third ones deserve a few comments.

Let us start with Hage's second claim. This claim – it must be noted – would be (mostly) uncontroversial, were it not for its critical dimension. As we have seen, in the making of it Hage strikes a blow against normativist legal theorists, and particularly their foremost representative, Hans Kelsen, for considering the law to be outside of the realm of scientific inquiries, since, being made of norms, it would belong to the realm of the 'ought'. Whereas – so Hage's argument goes – contrary to Kelsen's view, it must be acknowledged that cognitive sciences *are* able to *determine* or *establish the content of the law*, because the law is a social phenomenon made of deontic facts ('ought-facts').

Ought-facts – we are told – are a variety of 'constructive' or 'constructivist' *social facts*. Namely, they are social facts that exist if, and only if:

1) they exist as *brute social facts*, i.e., because a relevant number of the component of a social group knowingly *accepts their existence* as social, not natural, facts; *and*,
2) they consist in the fact (case, state of affairs) *either* that something *ought to exist*, or that something *ought not to exist*.[6] In the former situation, as Hage makes clear, the ought-fact can be 'expressed' by the symbolic logic formula '$O(p)$', while in the latter situation it can be 'expressed' by the symbolic logic formula '$O(\neg p)$'.[7]

In light of the preceding clarifications, we must pause to ask what it means to claim that the cognitive sciences are able to *determine* or *establish the content of the law*.

If we leave aside any natural-law reading of that claim as preposterous, the claim can only mean that cognitive sciences are *capable of knowing*, and *informing people about*, the *legal* ought-facts that obtain (are the case) *in a given society*.

Such a claim by Hage, however, seems to be simultaneously troublesome and trivial. More precisely, as we shall see in moment, it looks *troublesome* from the

---

[5] 'Perhaps criminal law is the field where the impact of a modified image of mankind will be most strongly felt ... a lack of reason-responsiveness takes away criminal responsibility and ... makes retributive criminal law impossible. ... If a role for criminal law is to remain, it must be confined to measures that promote a better future. In other words, criminal law must become completely consequentialist' (§2.6.8).

[6] I hope this reconstruction of mine to be faithful to what Hage is saying in a key passage of his essay (see Hage, Chapter 2, §2.5.4).

[7] Contrariwise, according to Hage, the fact that *it is not the case that* a fact (p) ought to exist is expressed by the formula $\neg O(p)$ (see Hage, Chapter 2, §2.5, and Brożek, Chapter 7, §7.3).

standpoint of cognitive sciences' assumed capacities, and *trivial* from the standpoint of the normativist conception of scientific knowledge of law as endorsed, for example, by Hans Kelsen.

In order to show why this is so, it is necessary to cast a closer glance at Hage's notion of a (legal) ought-fact.

We are told, as we have seen, that, say, the ought-fact according to which a certain fact (p) ought *not* to exist can be 'expressed' by the formula: 'O(¬p)'.

Now, from the standpoint of deontic logic, such a formula is ambiguous. It is in fact liable to two quite different readings. On the one hand, 'O(¬p)' can be understood as expressing a *norm*: namely, the *categorical norm* according to which 'It is obligatory not-p (¬p)', or, what is the same, 'It is forbidden p'. On the other hand, 'O(¬p)' can be understood, alternatively, as an elliptical expression for a *normative proposition*: namely, as an elliptical formulation for the (true-or-false) proposition to the effect that 'According to the legal system LS_i, it is forbidden p', or, in a perhaps clearer way, 'The norm "It is forbidden p" exists in/belongs to/is valid in/ is binding in the legal system LS_i'.

The principle of charitable interpretation suggests ruling out the first of the two possible readings. Indeed, according to it, Hage's *ought-facts* would be tantamount to *norms*. They would be no facts at all. As a consequence, only the second reading appears to be viable. This reading, however, suggests that legal ought-facts, whatever they are, are the *matter* of *normative propositions*, that is, *what* normative propositions *are about*. It suggests, more precisely, that legal ought-facts are facts *having* (somehow) *to do* with the existence (membership, validity, bindingness) of legal norms in a legal system.

Once we accept the second reading, the ability of the cognitive sciences 'to determine or establish the content of the law' can be given a clear meaning. It is tantamount to the ability of cognitive sciences (a) to ascertain which norms are valid (existing, belonging to, binding) in a legal system at a certain time, and (b) to describe the results of their inquiries by means of normative propositions (possibly formulated by means of unambiguous logical forms).

If the conclusion I have just set forth is correct, it should be apparent by now why Hage's claim is at the same time both troublesome and trivial.

To begin with, it is a troublesome claim, perhaps due in part to some degree of rhetorical exaggeration, since the existence of legal norms is not, and cannot be, a matter of *purely* mental phenomena. External – mostly linguistic – behaviours by individuals acting as normative-authorities or lawmaking bodies, and their empirical outputs (constitutions, statutes, customary practices, etc.), are also needed for legal norms 'to exist' in a legal order, and these behaviours cannot be ascertained by a bunch of sciences dealing with the functioning of the human mind *only*. The knowledge of ought-facts cannot be obtained just by means of the cognitive sciences.

Secondly, as soon as we get a clear idea of what ought-facts are (i.e., the *matter* of normative propositions), and as soon as we reformulate it to meet the objection

I have just considered, Hage's claim appears also to be a trivial uncontroversial claim from the very standpoint of normativist legal theorists like Kelsen. Hage, as we have seen, claims the existence of legal norms to be a suitable matter for genuinely scientific investigations on the basis of his theory of ought-facts. However, contrary to what Hage suggests, Kelsen makes a similar claim too. From his 1940s writings onwards, Kelsen was in fact amongst the first legal theorists to propose drawing a sharp distinction between *legal norms (Rechtsnormen)*, which are the outputs of acts performed by *norm-authorities*, and *legal propositions (Rechtssätze)*, which purport to *describe* valid legal norms (the *content* of valid legal norms), and are formulated by legal science. Furthermore, and in that very connection, Kelsen claimed legal norms to be fit for scientific investigations, distinguishing two different but mutually synergic kinds of scientific enquiry: namely, the empirical, but not causal-explanatory, enquiries of normative legal science ('normative (particular) jurisprudence'), on the one hand, and the empirical, and causal-explanatory, enquiries of legal sociology ('sociological jurisprudence'), on the other (see e.g. Kelsen, 1945, pp. 162–80).

Let us move to Hage's third and final claim. As you may recall, it states that cognitive sciences are relevant to law, because they are likely to undermine ('disrupt') the image of human beings as rational, reasons-responsive agents, which underlies the law of the present age, suggesting the need for sweeping law reforms.

It is worthwhile rehearsing, albeit briefly, Hage's argument. On the one hand, the actual machinery of law is built upon an image of human beings as rational, reasons-responsive agents. Think of such legal institutions as contractual and other acts-in-law, the principle of autonomy in private law, the right to vote 'about the course of government' and 'about future legislation' in constitutional law, or criminal responsibility. On the other hand, however, cognitive sciences bring to the fore the many ways in which human beings act out of irrational motives, casting light on the 'dictates' of competing, pulling apart, 'selves' within one and the same body (and brain), and emphasize the sweeping scope of self-delusion, automatic reactions to environmental stimuli, ignorance about one's (true) interests, and, not least, the opportunist manipulations of advertisers, politicians, spin doctors, and other like rogue fellows. Accordingly, cognitive sciences are to be resorted to, if we want the law ('our law') to be in tune with the real psychological nature of human beings.

Hage's argument is powerful. Nonetheless, two caveats seem to be in order, if only for the sake of putting a check to a too-hasty surrender of traditional, individualistic (moral and) legal thinking to the rule of (some) scientific paradigms – a surrender that, it must be noticed, is likely to be dangerous for the legal protection of individual human beings.

First, as Hage acknowledges, the law ('our law') is already endowed with a vast array of tools for coping with irrational, self-deluding, or manipulated agents. Think, for instance, of the institutions of duress, fraud, and mistake in private law, or the several forms and limits of personal liability in criminal law.

Second, Hage's argument seems to suffer from the informal fallacy of generalization. From the fact that – to be sure, in many situations – human beings do act as irrational, self-deluding, or manipulated agents, it does not seem to follow that they never act as rational, reasons-responsive agents. So that, for instance, insofar as the criminal law is considered, we should throw out of the window any idea of personal responsibility and retributive justice, in favour of a society-geared, utilitarian approach.

Summarizing, one may argue that the law ('our law') already takes into account *both* images of human agents: the rational *and* the irrational one. As a consequence, Copernican law reforms, or even more moderate frontier-shifting ones based on suggestions coming from the cognitive sciences, should be the matter of careful reflexion about their practical (legal and moral) effects.

23.3 DO WE NEED A COGNITIVE-SCIENCES-BASED 'RESEARCH ON THE METAPHYSICS OF THE LAW'?

In the last two centuries we have become accustomed to the fact that the disciplines professionally dealing with 'the law' ('law in general', law 'as a social, rule-governed, phenomenon', or, more suspiciously, 'the nature of law') are known by unpretentious denominations like '(general) jurisprudence', 'general theory of law', or, simply, 'legal theory', and make up an intellectual enterprise characterized by a combination of empirical investigation and conceptual analysis, broadly conceived to include conceptual detection, conceptual reconstruction, and conceptual therapy.[8]

Corrado Roversi, in the essay he contributes to the present volume, 'Cognitive Science and the Nature of Law' (Chapter 6), seems to be well aware of that (Roversi, Chapter 6, §6.1). Nonetheless, he prefers to conceive the enterprise he purports to cultivate as 'research in the metaphysics of [the] law', where the phrase 'metaphysics of (the) law' stands for the research's peculiar object of inquiry (Roversi, Chapter 6, §6.1).

To be sure, one may regard Roversi's move as being ultimately harmless – Should we care for *labels*? – and legitimate – Has not any author a (quasi) absolute *privilege* in relation to his or her work? I can see the point. Nonetheless, as soon as I recall the history of legal thought from Bentham onwards, Roversi's move seems to me a misleading and potentially obnoxious rehabilitation of an obscure bygone expression. In the following, I will try to provide some reasons why I think this is the case.

---

[8] Conceptual detection concerns how concept-bearing words are used in fact in a certain community – it accounts for ongoing conceptual and terminological apparatuses (frameworks, 'structures'); conceptual reconstruction sets forth proposals concerning the reformulation of existing conceptual and terminological apparatuses; conceptual therapy warns against certain uses of words and forms of expressing thoughts by means of words. I have briefly considered these operations in Pierluigi Chiassoni (2019, pp. 10–15).

Roversi sets himself to the task of accounting, albeit in a tentative way, for 'the nature of law from a psychological point of view' (Roversi, Chapter 6, §6.4). More precisely, he purports to show how cognitive psychology can cast precious light on two theses 'about legal metaphysics' (Roversi, Chapter 6, §6.4).

The first thesis, having to do with 'the root of law', claims that 'legal facts are a subset of social facts' (§6.1), and social facts 'depend necessarily, and at least partly, on mental states' (Roversi, Chapter 6, §6.1).

The second thesis, having to do instead with 'the structure of law', claims that 'law is a normative organization of sanctions and authorities' (Roversi, Chapter 6, §6.3.1).[9]

In regard to the first thesis, cognitive psychology brings to the fore that the existence of legal facts – like, for example, marrying, setting up a joint venture, enacting legal rules, or conferring legal statuses by means of legal rules – *also* depends on the *same kind* of mental states on which *joint activities* (like, e.g.: hunting in teams for a buffalo), *introducing social norms* ('Spare the best ribs of the buffalo for the whole tribe'), *attributing a social status* ('Red Eagle will be the leader of the hunting team until the next Moon'), or *attributing social statutes by means of social norms* ('Whoever kills a buffalo with just one arrow-shot will be the leader of the hunting team') depend:

> law is *ultimately rooted* in four distinct and progressively more complex layers of sociality, moving from joint action [to the introduction of social norms, to attributing social statutes] to symbolic status attribution by way of social norms. (Roversi, Chapter 6, §6.2.1)

In regard to the second thesis, cognitive science requires us to carry out inquiries on the psychology of authority, the psychology of punishment and sanctions, and the psychology 'behind the concept of validity' (Roversi, Chapter 6, §6.3.2). Such inquiries will lead, for instance, to discovering that resort to legal sanctions depends on mental states typically entertained by humans, such as rage, moral disgust, and expectations for a fair reaction to the violation of legal rules (Roversi, Chapter 6, §6.3.2).

From the standpoint of an analytic jurisprudent, there is nothing objectionable in Roversi's intriguing project; yet a few remarks are warranted.

First, it seems advisable to abandon the phrase 'metaphysics of (the) law' in favour of some less obscure, less misleading, and plainer expression, like, for example 'law' or 'legal reality'. 'Metaphysics of (the) law' fatally evokes the premodern idea of a set of 'principles' or 'essential features' calling for a philosophical enquiry capable of grasping the very 'nature' (the very 'ontology') of legal phenomena by delving into their depths in ways that are not available to different forms of investigation.

---

[9] See also § 6.1: 'legal institutions are peculiar social institutions that put in place a framework consisting of sanctions, along with the authority to define, apply, and enforce shared rules of conduct in a formal way, namely, in terms of legal validity'.

However, from an analytic point on view, and, if I am correct, also from Roversi's own, there is no form of knowledge of legal phenomena besides the knowledge that can be gathered from empirical inquiries and conceptual analysis. That being the case, *why* should a scholar indulge in using such a suspicious expression, even though it may happen to be in tune with some fashionable lines of inquiry (to wit, those belonging to 'social ontology')?

Second, if the goal of 'research in the metaphysics of (the) law' is the *scientific knowledge* of the social phenomenon of law, as it can be pursued by means of a combination of empirical and conceptual investigations, it would be worthwhile outlining a map of the several disciplines that should cooperate towards the realization of that goal. However, as soon as we set to that task, 'research in the metaphysics of (the) law' looks, again, like an inappropriate obscure cumbersome denomination. Why not talk directly of 'scientific knowledge of law' instead, and bring to the fore that such a knowledge is likely to result from the interaction of no fewer than three disciplines, namely, legal theory (as an analytic enterprise), legal sociology (as an empirical and explanatory enterprise concerning legal phenomena as social phenomena), and cognitive psychology (as an empirical and explanatory enterprise concerning the mental faculties, states, and activities typically related to legal phenomena)?

Third, and finally, leaving aside any (misleading) longing for 'the metaphysics of (the) law' will perhaps contribute to avoiding any resort to metaphorical language in the formulation of theoretical theses about the law in general. Metaphors are brilliant ways of providing defective accounts of the things at stake. Is not the image of 'the root(s) of law' desperately imprecise, and, one may even say, utterly unscientific?

23.4 HUME'S LAW AND THE PRACTICAL LIMITS OF COGNITIVE SCIENCES' DISCOVERIES

In his essay for the present book, as we have seen (*supra*, §23.2), Jaap Hage claims that:

> There are good reasons not to make the distinction between IS and OUGHT too strictly ... there is no fundamental difference between the OUGHT and the IS. As the expression 'ought-facts' suggests, an ought is a fact. This means that sciences, including the cognitive sciences, which give us information about the facts, can also give us information about what ought to be done. (Haage, present volume, §§2.1, 2.5)

I have already argued that such a claim cannot be used against normativist theories of law, and Kelsen's theory in particular, for Kelsen is to be numbered amongst the strongest supporters of the view according to which legal norms are also amongst the entities that are fit for truly scientific enquiries.

The issue I wish to touch upon in this section is different. Hage's claim takes into account just one of the possible different ways of understanding 'the is–ought distinction'. He considers the is–ought distinction as an *ontological divide*: namely, one running between two areas, spheres, or realms of entities. On the one hand, there is the realm of causally related natural or social *facts*; on the other hand, there is the realm of norms as prescriptions (in the broad sense of the term) concerning somebody's behaviour (if you like, as the 'meanings of acts of will directed to somebody else's behaviour', to recall Kelsen's well-known definition) (see e.g. Kelsen, 2017 [1960], §4), and considered, to scientific purpose, as entities outside of the flux of causal relations. However, at least one other way of conceiving the is–ought distinction is available, which is worthwhile recalling because it must be recognized as endowed with foundational value for any reflection upon interdisciplinary investigations about the law. This is the conception that reads the is–ought distinction as a *discursive divide*: that is, as a distinction concerning *two kinds of discourse*; descriptive discourse, made of empirically true or false sentences, on the one side, and prescriptive discourse, made of sentences expressing prescriptions, recommendations, advices, norms of behaviour, and so on, which, contrariwise, are neither true nor false, on the other side.

We are used to thinking of the distinction between descriptive and prescriptive discourse as having not only a pragmatic, semantic, and syntactic dimension (where the pragmatic one is ultimately paramount), but also as presenting a logical dimension. The logical dimension concerns the inferential relationships between descriptive sentences and prescriptive sentences. The logical dimension is captured by a sentence that goes under the name of 'Hume's law' or 'Hume's guillotine': no prescriptive sentence (no norm, recommendation, advice, rule, principle, etc.) can be logically derived as a conclusion from a set of purely descriptive (and non-contradictory or practically pointless) premises, and vice versa.[10] In Bentham's terminology, Hume's law is the basis for carefully distinguishing between two sorts of jurisprudence (and jurisprudents): on the one side, expository jurisprudence deals with what, and how, the law *is* in fact; on the other side, censorial jurisprudence deals with what, and how, the law *ought to be* (see Bentham, 1988 [1776], 1996 [1789], 2010).

If we adopt the standpoint of the discursive conception of the is–ought distinction, if we set ourselves to use Hume's law as a tool for assessing the discourses making up

---

[10] On Hume's law, see, e.g., Prior (1960, pp. 199–206); Celano (1994); Gonzáles Lagier (2017, ch. IV). A few words are needed to explain the 'non-contradictory or practically pointless' caveat I put in the text. First, *ex falso quodlibet*. Second, suppose you are a theist, and you want to derive the norm that 'Men ought not to kill' from the fact that God has commanded them not to kill. From the assumption 'God has commanded men not to kill', you may derive 'God has commanded men not to kill *or* men ought not to kill'. From this conclusion, however, there is only a way to derive the norm that 'Men ought not to kill'; and it consists in *negating* your starting assumption: i.e., you must assume that it is *not* the case that God has commanded men not to kill ('God has not commanded men not to kill'). But, in such a way, the logical derivation of the no-killing norm you cherish requires the affirmation of the moral indifference, and irrelevance, of God as to that norm.

the outputs of the L&CSE, both in themselves and as regards their pragmatic function, it is apparent that there is no way in which the discoveries of the cognitive sciences could ever affect, least of all disrupt, the distinction between descriptive and prescriptive discourse and Hume's law.

Consider one of the discoveries Hage mentions: namely, that adult human beings are not the fully fledged rational agents they are supposed to be in traditional legal and economic thinking (Hage, Chapter 2, present volume, §§2.1, 2.6). Suppose that statement to be true. Clearly, no normative consequence follows *from it alone*: no normative conclusion, in morality or law, can be derived solely by it, about which moral or legal principles ought to inform, say, 'our' criminal, or contract, or family law.[11]

The view according to which cognitive sciences' discoveries belong to the realm of scientific description and explanation, and should not be considered as immediately affecting the realm of ethical evaluation and social norms appears – I would say, fortunately – to be well rooted in many contributions to the present volume.

The first noteworthy instance of adherence to the discursive is–ought divide is provided by Jane Campbell Moriarty's 'Neuroimaging Evidence in the US Courts' (Moriarty, Chapter 18). The essay contains a section devoted to 'Psychopathy' (Moriarty, Chapter 18, §18.3.3).[12] We are used to label as 'psychopaths' people

---

[11] Another discovery, worthwhile mentioning here, is the well-known 'Libet Experiment'. It is often quoted to question the very possibility of 'free will' and the idea of thoroughly conscious voluntary actions, which belong to the psychological bedrock of the is–ought distinction. But in fact this is done pointlessly – and paradoxically, according to John R. Searle (2001, ch. 9). Indeed, after recording that there are situations in which a brain impulse towards the performance of a certain act *can* precede 'any (at least recallable) subjective awareness' and conscious decision to perform that act, the authors conclude as follows:

> These considerations would appear to introduce certain constraints on the potential of the individual for exerting conscious initiation and control over his voluntary acts. However, accepting our conclusion that spontaneous voluntary acts can be initiated unconsciously, there would remain at least two types of conditions in which conscious control could be operative. (1) There could be a conscious 'veto' that aborts the performance even of the type of 'spontaneous' self-initiated act under study here. This remains possible because reportable conscious intention, even though it appeared distinctly later than onset of RP, did appear a substantial time (about 150 to 200 ms) before the beginning of the movement as signalled by the EMG. Even in our present experiments, subjects have reported that some recallable conscious urges to act were 'aborted' or inhibited before any actual movement occurred; in such cases the subject simply waited for another urge to appear which, when consummated, constituted the actual event whose RP was recorded ... (2) In those voluntary actions that are not 'spontaneous' and quickly performed, that is, in those in which conscious deliberation (of whether to act or of what alternative choice of action to take) precedes the act, the possibilities for conscious initiation and control would not be excluded by the present evidence. (See Libet et al., 1983, p. 641)

See also the dispute between Joshua Green and Selim Berker on the relevance of neuroscience discoveries to normative ethics (Green et al., 2001, pp. 2105–8; Berker, 2009, pp. 293–329); on the issue, see also, for example, Michael S. Pardo and Dennis Patterson (2016, ch. 10). A recent, well-argued defence of Hume's law against the criticism of neuroethics scholars can be read in Daniel Gonzáles Lagier (2017, ch. IV).

showing shallow emotions, callousness to other people's interests and sufferings, and a propensity to break social norms and expectations – people, we may say, showing the adoption of a 'reversed morality', like the many characters of the novels of the Marquis de Sade. We know that people we are used to labelling as 'psychopaths' are characterized by a 'neuronal activity that is substantively and markedly different than most people' (Moriarty, Chapter 18). We know, furthermore, that these people have an impaired instrumental rationality, that they are liable to believe they are acting in their own 'best self-interest', though they are 'often' acting, in fact, in ways that are 'perversely' against their best self-interest (Moriarty, Chapter 18). We also know, however, that such knowledge is disputable. On the one hand, there are plenty of people we would not regard as 'psychopaths', who, nonetheless, entertain false beliefs about the courses of action that are in their own best self-interest. On the other hand, there is evidence that 'psychopaths' *are* endowed with relevant doses of instrumental rationality. It has been observed that they can 'resist sticking their hands in a bee's nest to get honey', while they 'just cannot resist reaching into another person's pocket to take money' (Moriarty, Chapter 18, n. 83).

These are the data we have. Now, as our good old friend Hume suggests, empirical data are not self-qualifying entities. They do not tell us: 'Look, I am a case of serious mental disease deserving neither moral blame, nor legal punishment'. They – fortunately – do not, and cannot, do any job to save us from our inescapable responsibilities as moral agents and lawmakers. Accordingly, a few questions deserve to be recalled, which the technical account by Jane Campbell Moriarty elicits.

1) Which is the relationship between the (so-to-speak) moral hardware and moral software of 'psychopaths'? Is it the case that they wish to act, and act, as they do, because their brains work differently than those of most people, or is it rather the case that their brains work differently than those of other people, because they wish to act, and act, as they do?
2) It is a fact, apparently, that not every psychopath turns into a lawbreaker: not every psychopath commits murder, rape, or other (heinous) crimes. Is not such a fact something that cast a dim light upon any deterministic, excusing disease view, about the psychopathic mind (and actions)?
3) Provided we know that there are people with psychopathic minds, what should be the *moral* relevance of such a fact? Should we consider psychopaths as responsible, accountable, and blameable moral agents, namely, as a minority of morally full-bloodied, but 'anti-social' fellows, or, rather, should we consider them as a bunch of irresponsible, unaccountable, un-blameable moral agents, namely, as a minority of mentally disturbed, often socially dangerous fellows?
4) Provided we know that there are people with psychopathic minds, what should be the *legal* relevance of such a fact? Should we consider psychopaths as responsible, accountable, and punishable legal agents, or should we rather consider them as irresponsible, unaccountable, unpunishable legal agents,

who, being dangerous, should nonetheless be put under careful legal observation and control?

Clearly, perhaps with the exception of the first puzzle, no neuroimaging technique, no neuroimaging data, can provide by themselves any answer to the moral or legal puzzles recalled at points 2, 3, and 4.

Another clear instance of adopting the discursive is–ought divide (the distinction between descriptive and prescriptive discourse and Hume's law) as a paramount tool in assessing theories and critiques is provided by A.R. Mackor, H. Jellema, and P. J. van Koppen in 'Explanation-Based Approaches to Reasoning About Evidence and Proof in Criminal Trials' (Chapter 21). After having provided an account of four explanation-based approaches to evidentiary reasoning (i.e., the 'story model' approach, the relative plausibility approach, the inference to the most coherent explanation approach, and the scenario approach), the authors consider the critiques that those approaches have undergone from scholars appealing to human psychology (Mackor, Jellema, & van Koppen, Chapter 21, §21.3.1). All the critiques argue that those approaches are not true to the facts, for the following reasons: (i) decision makers usually do not proceed by comparing alternative explanatory hypotheses of the same set of facts, but they tend, rather, 'to overvalue evidence that supports their favourite decision and undervalue evidence against the favourite decision'; (ii) criminal cases may be so simple that there is 'not much of a story to tell' about them; and (iii) the direction of fit between story (explanatory hypotheses) and evidence doesn't usually go from the former to the latter, but 'in both directions', namely, from evidence to hypotheses and from hypotheses to evidence. According to Mackor, Jellema, and van Koppen, however, the psychological critiques above are utterly unsubstantiated. Indeed, explanation-based approaches – they emphasize – are not meant to provide true descriptions of what is going on in people's minds, of how people do in fact reason when they decide about evidentiary propositions. They do not belong, in other words, to the realm of 'is', to wit, to *descriptive* discourse. They are, rather, *prescriptive* theories, setting forth how people should (ought to) reason, in order to make decisions concerning the proof of legally relevant facts. Being prescriptive discourses, they are not truth-apt discourses. The direction of fit goes from the world to (prescriptive) discourse, so that the world become how it ought to be; and not the other way round.'[13]

---

[13] The same Humean spirit also pervades Gerben Meynen's contribution, Chapter 15, 'The Insanity Defense'. The whole essay is built upon the need to preserve the difference between the scientific, descriptive account of how the brain of a certain agent is, and works, in fact, on the one hand, and the resolution of the moral and legal ('ultimate') issues concerning the moral and criminal responsibility of that very agent, on the other.

23.5 PSYCHOLOGICAL THEORIES OF LEGAL REASONING AND LEGAL INTERPRETATION

In his contribution to the volume, Chapter 7, 'The Architecture of the Legal Mind', Bartosz Brożek purports to put 'the findings of cognitive science' to work in view of casting light on the 'mental mechanisms that are utilized in legal thinking' (Brożek, Chapter 7, §7.1).

The essay contains a critical side (*pars destruens*) and a constructive side (*pars construens*). In the critical side, Brożek considers in turn four 'theories of legal reasoning', namely: 'deductivism', 'dialecticism', 'coherentism', and 'intuitivism'. He claims that they should be rejected since, at most, each offers just an incomplete, unilateral, account of legal reasoning: one that only focuses *either* on logical inferences and structures (deductivism); *or* on the comparison of alternative ways of rationally arguing about the right answer to a legal problem (dialecticism); *or* on the need to arrive at the right answer by considering which one fits 'the broader context of legal knowledge' (coherentism); *or*, finally, on the role of intuitions ('hunches') in solving legal problems (intuitivism) (Brożek, Chapter 7, §7.1). In fact, as Brożek emphasizes, cognitive science makes it clear that lawyers, 'in their cognitive efforts', 'cannot limit themselves to only some of these mechanisms'; that they typically resort to three connected mental capacities ('mechanisms'): that is, intuition, imagination, and thinking in language. On this footing, the constructive part of the chapter is devoted to clarifying the three 'mechanisms' and bringing to the fore how they work when legal issues are at stake.

Intuition is an unconscious, fast, automatic, problem-solving capacity based on past experience and training; it is typically afoot whenever lawyers face an 'easy case', be it concerning the finding of facts or the solution to a legal problem (Brożek, Chapter 7, §7.2).

Imagination (or *mental simulation*), so far as legal reasoning is considered, can concern, again, either the reconstruction of the facts of a case at hand ('heuristic' or factual imagination), or the interpretation of a legal provision at stake (interpretive or 'hermeneutic' imagination). Interpretive imagination, in particular, encompasses three typical mental activities: first, the activity consisting in identifying the classes of things to which a certain legal term refers ('exemplification'); second, the activity consisting in translating a whole legal provision into another sentence that is presented, and used, as an exact synonym of the former ('paraphrase'); third, the activity of checking the interpretations of a legal provision in the light of its context ('embedding', or, as we may also say, systematic reading) (Brożek, Chapter 7, §73). The three activities – Brożek remarks – would fit into Allan Paivio's 'dual coding theory', according to which, when we 'process language expressions' in 'our minds', we typically put to work both an 'analogical code' – that is, we resort to mental images of the things to which the expressions refer – and a 'symbolic code', that is, we look for conceptual associations between the expression at stake and other expressions in the same or in other languages (Brożek, Chapter 7, §7.3).

Thinking in language, finally, has to do with such operations as 'abstraction', 'theorizing', and 'dialogicalization'. For instance, it promotes the passing from a casuistic penal code phrased in terms of stealing 'oxen', 'goats', 'boats', and so on, like Hammurabi's code, to modern penal codes phrased in terms of 'movable property' (abstraction); it works out the general parts of criminal codes, distinguishing, for example, between different kinds of criminal offences, different kinds of intentionality, and different kinds of sanctions (theorizing); it promotes, finally, the elaboration of ways of arranging the discipline of a certain matter that are alternatives to the extant ones (dialogicalization) (Brożek, Chapter 7, §7.4).

Brożek's essay provides powerful evidence of the explanatory capacity of the cognitive sciences in relation to traditional jurisprudential issues like legal reasoning and legal interpretation.

From the vantage point of analytic jurisprudence, a few comments are, nonetheless, in order.

1) 'Legal reasoning' and 'legal interpretation' are ambiguous expressions. Both of them can be used to refer, in particular, *either to* a *mental activity* or a *mental process*, that is, the activity of legal reasoning, the activity of interpreting a legal provision, as they develop 'in the mind' of a lawyer, a jurist, or a judge; *or*, rather, *to* the *external output* of such a mental activity (legal reasoning–output, legal interpretation–output). Legal reasoning–output and legal interpretation–output are *discursive entities*, made of strings of pronounced or written sentences in a natural language.

A theory of legal reasoning or legal interpretation as a mental process cannot be but a psychological theory, one to be worked out with the aid of the cognitive sciences.

In contrast, a theory of legal reasoning or legal interpretation as discursive entities cannot be but a theory consisting in discourse analysis: that is, one concerned with ways of reasoning or interpreting; with the tools – the forms of argument – that are, can be, or ought to be put to work to argue for a certain legal conclusion (interpretive or otherwise); with the data or resources that are, can be, or ought to be employed in building up those forms of arguments; and so on.

As soon as we pause to reflect on the ambiguity of 'legal reasoning' and 'legal interpretation', therefore, the four theories of legal reasoning Brożek considers appear to be heterogeneous. On the one hand, intuitivism is an instance of a psychological theory of legal reasoning: it purports to tell us by what sort of mental process judges come to decide what they do decide. On the other hand, deductivism, dialecticism, and coherentism look like as many instances of discursive theories of legal reasoning (and interpretation). They can be, in turn, of a descriptive or of a normative variety, as Brożek correctly remarks. But, in any case, they do not deal with processes going on in the mind of a lawyer, a jurist, or a judge, but, rather, with different sorts of tools and resources that they in fact employ or ought to employ.

2) The distinction between psychological and discursive theories of legal reasoning and legal interpretation should perhaps be put at the center of any fruitful approach and used to provide the basic terminological and conceptual framework for any reflection upon those paramount topics in legal theory. This distinction can be put to a double use. On the one hand, it can work as a classificatory tool, by which 'theories of legal reasoning' and 'theories of legal interpretation' can be identified from the standpoint of their object and purpose. On the other hand, it can work as a tool for critically assessing the 'theories of legal reasoning' and the 'theories of legal interpretation' set out in the province of jurisprudence. Every 'theory' should make it clear which object it is about: in particular, whether it is mental or discursive; furthermore, it should use tools that are adequate to its proposed object. A theory dealing with legal interpretation as a mental process, for instance, should avoid employing tools that are fit for discourse analysis, and vice versa, and this in order to avoid the flaw of methodological syncretism.

3) Descriptive psychological and descriptive discursive theories of legal reasoning and legal interpretation are obviously distinct but complementary enterprises. They should be developed in a synergetic, mutually reinforcing way. The point is trivial, but nonetheless it is worthwhile making. Consider Brożek's psychological model of legal interpretation, as an imagination activity typically encompassing operations such as exemplification, paraphrase, and embedding (Brożek, Chapter 7, §7.3). First, the same outcome could have been reached by way of a discursive analysis of interpretive reasonings as discursive entities. Accordingly, discursive theory can be used as a (confirmatory or disproving) check to psychological theory. Second, discursive theory is likely to add relevant details to the skeleton outlined by psychological theory. It can cast light, for instance, on the interpretive directives and interpretive resources that, in a certain legal culture or sector thereof, at a certain time, are typically put to work while arguing for the exemplifications, paraphrases, and embeddings (systematic interpretations) actually carried out by lawyers, jurists, and judges.

REFERENCES

Bentham, J. (1988 [1776]). *A Fragment on Government*. Cambridge: Cambridge University Press.
Bentham, J. (1996[1789]). *Introduction to the Principles of Morals and Legislation*, eds. J. H. Burns & H. L. A. Hart with an Introduction by F. Rosen. Oxford: Clarendon Press.
Bentham, J. (2010). *Of the Limits of the Penal Branch of Jurisprudence*, ed. P. Schofield. Oxford: Clarendon Press.

Berker, S. (2009). The Normative Insignificance of Neuroscience. *Philosophy & Public Affairs* 37(4), 293–329.

Celano, B. (1994). *Dialettica della giustificazione pratica. Saggio sulla legge di Hume*, Torino: Giappichelli.

Chiassoni, P. (2019). *Interpretation without Truth: A Realistic Enquiry*, Cham: Springer.

Gonzáles Lagier, D. (2017). *A la sombra de Hume. Un balance crítico del intento de la neuroética de fundamentar la moral*. Madrid, Barcelona and Buenos Aires: Marcial Pons.

Green J., Sommerville, R. B., Nystrom, L. E., Darley, J. M., & Cohen, J. D. (2001). An fMRI Investigation of Emotional Engagement in Moral Judgement. *Science* 293(14), 2105–2108.

Kelsen, H. (1945). *General Theory of Law and State*. Cambridge, MA: Harvard University Press.

Kelsen, H. (2017[1960]). *Reine Rechtslehre* (2nd ed.). Tübingen: Mohr Siebeck,

Libet, B. Gleason, C. A., Wright, E. W., & Pearl, D. K. (1983). Time of Conscious Intention to Act in Relation to Onset of Cerebral Activity (Readiness Potential): The Unconscious Initiation of a Freely Voluntary Act. *Brain* 106, 623–42.

Moriarty, J. C. (2016). Seeing Voices: Potential Neuroscience Contributions to a Reconstruction of Legal Insanity. *Fordham Law Review* 85, 599–618.

Pardo, M. S., & Patterson, D. (2016). The Promise of Neuroscience for Law: 'Overclaiming' in Jurisprudence, Morality, and Economics. In M. S. Pardo & D. Patterson (eds.), *Philosophical Foundations of Law and Neuroscience*. Oxford: Oxford University Press.

Prior, A. N. (1960). The Autonomy of Ethics. *The Australasian Journal of Philosophy* 38, 199–206.

Searle, J. R. (2001). *Rationality in Action*. Cambridge, MA, and London: The MIT Press.

24

The Cognitive Approach in Legal Science and Practice: A History of Four Revolutions

Jerzy Stelmach

24.1 LAW AND COGNITION

For someone who has devoted much of his attention to the methodological aspects of jurisprudence (cf. Stelmach, 1994; Stelmach & Brożek, 2006; Brożek, Brożek, & Stelmach, 2013), often tackling and analysing various 'cognitive approaches' in both legal science and practice, writing about the influence of cognitive science on contemporary legal theory should pose no great challenge. However, it would seem that the contemporary debate on the subject has undergone something of a sea change. It transpires that the problem is still the same, namely that of applying the findings of the natural sciences to legal research and practice, which themselves do not necessarily make reference to transparent, intersubjective criteria for the verification or falsification of their own claims. However, both the context of their discoveries, that is the context which serves as the framework for the formulation of the claims which are key for the standpoint of cognitive science, as well as the context of their justification, have changed dramatically.

As a result, one cannot talk about there having been a single, uniform 'cognitive revolution' but rather a number of them. The greatest difficulty concerns the last of these, the 'fourth revolution'. On the one hand, contemporary applications of the cognitive science to the law are certainly 'mediated' by those previous positions which have featured in the ongoing debate about the (criteria) of humanities and social sciences over the last 150 years, including, of course, legal science and practice. On the other hand, however, this approach has distanced itself from the earlier positions, putting forward not only its own conception of cognition but also its own vision for the reconstruction of the humanities and social sciences.[1] Yet another problem is to be discerned when defining the limits to this debate, as there seems to be no unanimity in this respect. I have encountered at least two different kinds of contemporary 'cognitive turn' in the humanities and the social sciences. According to the first, narrower, more specialized and technical understanding, 'the cognitive approach' is above all a 'repair

---

[1] While I distinguish between the humanities and the social sciences here, I have no desire to enter into the discussion as to how they may be defined.

programme', devoted to the attempt to apply the tools and theories developed in psychology, or at least some of its fields, together with neuroscience to the humanities and social sciences. In the case of the second, the understanding is much broader – it is the choice of a philosophical position, one which has preferences not only in terms of cognition but also ontological, anthropological and even ethical ones.

What, therefore, are the cognitive revolutions? Do they take the form of a recurring 'fashion for science' which stems from the need to improve at least some aspects of the humanities and social sciences, amounting to a 'collection of new words' which define problems which have long been known by general epistemology, or perhaps they are something more? After all, 'a fashion for science' has been a recurring theme in the philosophical debates. It has always been present in philosophy, on the one hand, as an expression of opposition to all kinds of irrationalism and anti-empiricism and, on the other, of the call to improve (re-educate) the humanities and social sciences. At the same time, each subsequent cognitive revolution has introduced its own lexicon, redefining at least some of the key concepts of general epistemology in the process. Opponents of this way of thinking will claim that these are only 'new words', which merely describe previously defined things, phenomena and relationships. Their advocates, however, claim that they constitute a new approach to at least some concepts in the field of the theory of cognition in the humanities and the social sciences. In my opinion, these 'cognitive revolutions' are ultimately 'something more' than just the manifestation of certain fashions or collections of new words, primarily because they lead to paradigms that may redetermine the limits of potential discourse on the cognitive status of the humanities and social sciences.

24.2 FOUR REVOLUTIONS

I decided to describe as many as four 'cognitive revolutions', despite having doubts as to whether distinguishing between the first two makes any sense. Ultimately, however, I decided upon a more developed distinction, seeing it as allowing me to present the history of the attempts to apply a naturalistic approach to cognition in the humanities and the social sciences in the fullest possible manner.

Paradoxically, the impulse behind the first cognitive revolution was the anti-naturalistic conception, formed by nineteenth-century philosophy, which underscored the opposition between the humanities and the natural sciences. The anti-naturalists sought to safeguard the autonomy of the humanities, the goal of which was 'understanding', in contrast to the objective of the natural sciences which sought to 'explain' phenomena. The idea of the 'science of understanding' (*Verstehenswissenschaft*) was a prominent one in nineteenth- and twentieth-century humanities, as well as in the philosophy of law in the twentieth century.[2] This trend in hermeneutics, termed the

---

[2] In terms of the hermeneutics of the humanities, I would put Friedrich D. E. Schleiermacher and Wilhelm Dilthey in first place, while in terms of the methodological strand of legal hermeneutics, I would place in it Emilio Betti, Helmut Coing, Karl Engisch, Karl Larenz and Josef Esser.

methodological, was based on suppositions which, in my opinion, were counterfactual. This contradiction can be discerned in the work of Wilhelm Dilthey, regarded as the creator of the most well-known version of the methodological conception of hermeneutics (see Stelmach, 1991, pp. 27f.). Dilthey advocates 'cognitive objectivism', the epistemological universalism of Immanuel Kant, while at the same time accepting that 'understanding' is of a strongly subjective and psychological nature. Is 'understanding' thus to be understood as an objective, historical, connected with 'life' understood as a universal process, cognitive disposition, or rather as a particular phenomenon in the sphere of psychology, the capability to access the mental dispositions of other people and which Dilthey terms *Hineinversetzen*? (see Stelmach & Brożek, 2006, p. 178). Whichever is true, we are confronted here with a certain ambiguity and the juxtaposition of 'understanding' and 'explanation' does not correspond to the differences in how the humanities and the natural sciences are actually practised. Finally, regardless of how we define 'understanding' and 'explanation', it is unquestionable that the humanities do not simply 'understand' and the natural sciences 'explain'.

The response to this anti-naturalistic project was an extreme naturalism, primarily expressed in the postulate of physicalism, and which appeared in the second stage of positivism, known as empirio-criticism, before being more precisely defined and developed in the third stage of positivism, referred to variously as neo-positivism, logical empiricism or the philosophy of the Vienna Circle. This postulate has also featured in later philosophy (see Ayer, 1982, pp. 170f.). These attempts to make the humanities and social sciences more scientific, by means of models developed in the natural sciences, particularly physics, were usually enacted in general philosophy and ethics. In the first case, it was a project to construct a so-called scientific philosophy, while the latter sought an empirical ethics that would utilize the explanatory models developed in physics. The debate initiated by the Vienna Circle on the philosophy of science and the naturalistic concept of ethics was one which lasted until the 1970s (see Reichenbach, 1992; Schlick, 2011). However, in legal science and practice, the 'postulate of physicalism' did not play such an important role, even though of course certain 'naturalistic elements' can also be 'traced' there. They were already to be found in nineteenth-century Continental legal positivism, where amongst others the naturalistic concept of 'sovereign will' appeared, and somewhat later, in the work of the representatives of the neo-positivist school of Scandinavian legal realism, especially that of Karl Olivecrona (1939). The school of American legal realism also had a rather naturalistic character, although it is no longer possible to easily show its direct links with philosophical positivism.

In my opinion, the anti-naturalistic conception of juxtaposing the humanities with the natural sciences, as well as the naturalistic idea of making the humanities and social sciences more 'scientific' by means of the application of models developed in physics, were faulty and did not lead to the 'cognitive breakthrough' which these approaches had earlier claimed. Due to their extreme positions and considerable simplifications, they ultimately proved to be of little use to either legal science or practice.

The second revolution was related to another conception of naturalism, one which was somewhat more refined. Naturalism in this form cannot be reduced to one single postulate. Instead, it was a multi-element branch of philosophy, one which tackled issues in ontology as well as epistemology. The former can be termed 'ontological naturalism' while the latter would be 'methodological naturalism'. Both played a significant role, especially in meta-ethical and philosophical discussions concerning fundamental problems related to the question of the existence of moral norms and legal rules, the nature of normativity, the interpretation of concepts such as necessity, obligation and entitlement, and, finally, normative meaning. One cannot hope to understand contemporary ethics and meta-ethics, as well as the legal philosophy and theory, without a familiarization with this concept, which arose on the basis of 'second stage naturalism'.[3]

Against this 'second naturalism', two charges are most frequently formulated. The first is that it is also not free from the errors present in the former version of naturalism, especially those related to the adoption of the 'reductionist thesis', which leaves it open to the 'open-question argument', namely the charge of having fallen into the 'naturalistic fallacy'.[4] The other is that, because of the presence of numerous views, the boundaries blur in this concept, essentially becoming akin to 'moderate naturalism', and at least to some of the 'soft' anti-naturalistic positions. The debate on the weaknesses of naturalism was, in my opinion, one of the contributing factors for the turn towards analytical research by proponents of the naturalistic approach, both advocates of the 'hard' (logical-mathematical) type of *horseshoe analysis*, and the 'softer' versions (limited to the analysis of natural language) – known as *soft-shoe analysis*.[5] As a result, numerous analytical conceptions arose in meta-ethics and the philosophy and theory of law, the starting point of

---

[3] Scores of the most talented philosophers, ethicists and legal philosophers and theorists of the era took part in this debate and it suffices to mention only Ludwig Wittgenstein, Bertrand Russell, Charles L. Stevenson, Hans Albert, Chaim Perelman, Alf Ross, Maria Ossowska, Jerzy Wróblewski and Kazimierz Opałek.

[4] The 'open-question argument' or 'naturalistic fallacy' was described for the first time by George E. Moore. This fallacy seems to accompany all ethical and legal concepts that permit the possibility of deriving propositions about obligations from those about facts. The 'open-question' argument leads us to the conclusion that every naturalistic analysis of ethical predicates (broadly normative) must be incorrect in some way. The essence of Moore's reasoning amounts to the fact that, regardless of what empirical proposition we propose as a criterion for recognizing (accepting) a certain moral value, it will always be possible that something that possesses this property will be devoid of moral value, and in turn something which has a moral value will be devoid of this empirical property. To conclude that a particular ethical trait is empirical on the basis of the premise that if something possesses one property then it also has a second one, is to commit a 'naturalistic fallacy' (see Moore, 1993, pp. 89f.; also Stelmach, 2012, p. 137 and others).

[5] This distinction was introduced by Józef M. Bocheński (1993, pp. 36f.).

which was essentially the adoption of a naturalistic conception of being and cognition.[6]

The next 'cognitive breakthrough' in the humanities and social sciences, termed here as the 'third revolution', no longer appealed directly to naturalism but rather to the 'the idea of interdisciplinarity'. The task of making at least some of the humanities and social sciences more scientific was meant to be carried out by making them open to other disciplines that met scientific criteria, particularly psychology, sociology and economics. This 'opening up' of the humanities and social sciences to psychology and sociology could also be discerned in the first two revolutions, as well as in legal science. A new perspective, however, was that of economics. Research undertaken in the 1960s by proponents of the so-called Chicago School, Ronald Harry Coase, Armen Albert Alchian and Guido Calabresi, bore fruit in the creation of a new trend termed *Law & Economics*. At this point it is worth noting that Oliver Wendell Holmes, the renowned lawyer, Supreme Court judge and precursor of American legal realism, had written already in 1897 in his famous essay, *The Path of the Law*, that in a rational science of law, the conscientious interpreter of rules might be a man of the present, but the man of the future would be a statistician and master of economics (Holmes, 1897, p. 469). The conception of the economic analysis of law was finally adapted to the field of law by Richard Posner, who published his book *Economic Analysis of Law* in 1973, in which he attempted in detail to justify the thesis of the economic effectiveness of the traditional system of common law.

Even though no 'interdisciplinary research programme' appeals directly to a particular form of naturalism, these naturalistic elements are still strongly discernible within them. With the aid of the empirically guided sociology and psychology, efforts were made to naturalize certain key concepts in the humanities and social sciences, particularly those connected with ethics (meta-ethics) and jurisprudence. However, the question of the limits of economic naturalization remains open (cf. Załuski, 2013, p. 289ff.).

This somewhat exaggerated declaration of 'neutrality' towards naturalism claimed by proponents of the 'interdisciplinary approach' allowed them to avoid the problems I wrote about in connection with the first two revolutions, but it also meant that the whole programme suffers from a certain ambivalence, a result of the heterogeneity and eclecticism stemming from the lack of a coherent ontological and epistemological basis to the project discussed here.

Thus, finally, we can turn to the fourth revolution which we are currently experiencing, one which has the ambition of opening up the humanities and social sciences to 'reality', free from previous errors and limitations, on the basis of cognitive science, psychology, or at least for some of its varieties, and neuroscience.

---

[6] I will limit myself here to supplying two examples. I interpret Herbert L. A. Hart's *rule of recognition* as a certain factual principle which has its source in empirical experience (see Hart, 1961, pp. 100f.). A similarly naturalistic pedigree also seems to be possessed by the 'non-linguistic concept of norms' formulated by Kazimierz Opałek and Jan Woleński (see Opałek, 1985; also Opałek & Woleński, 1988).

This time, it is concerned with directly introducing elements of knowledge, tools, theories and models developed in these sciences into the humanities and social sciences. In my opinion, the reception of scientific methods and theories which we saw in the previous revolutions did not meet the requirements of 'being real', or, in other words, of being 'implemented' or 'applied' and 'mediating', because they did not lead to permanent changes, that is, they did not shape the humanities and social sciences into sciences in the more precise sense of the term. Could the fourth revolution have such an impact? Are we able to move beyond the mode of declarations expressed in imperfect, conditional terms? I will try to answer these questions in Section 24.4 of this chapter, discussing the consequences of this last cognitive revolution for legal science and practice. Unfortunately, I am not sure if I will be able to avoid using the above-mentioned conditional terms. Furthermore, in contemporary philosophy and legal theory, there are (so far?) not many examples which confirm the supposition that we are truly experiencing a genuine 'cognitive' breakthrough.

When we examine the course of subsequent revolutions, we can observe a process that I could term 'modification', 'expansion' and, in the case of the last of them, a 'deepening of paradigms'. In this regard, it is worth focusing on two myths about cognitive revolutions. The first is expressed in the belief that we are dealing with the same naturalistic paradigm, that is, the revolution is still essentially the same. The other, on the contrary, proclaims that they are paradigms which are fully independent of one another, and each of the revolutions is autonomous with regard to the others. And the truth, as is usually the case, probably lies somewhere in the middle. In any case, at least one finding seems to be certain, namely that all of the cognitive revolutions discussed here, irrespective of the declarations they made, have strongly naturalistic features.

24.3 THE CURSE OF KIRCHMANN

In 1848, the Berlin prosecutor Julius Hermann von Kirchmann gave perhaps his most famous prosecuting statement. In his *Die Werthlosigkeit der Jurisprudenz als Wissenschaft*, he not only criticized the current state of the development of legal science but also claimed that the knowledge possessed by lawyers was completely without value, perhaps even parasitic. Jurists in this conception were spiders living off a dying tree. Turning from what was healthy, they made their nests and wove their webs from what was sick. As a result, legal science which was only rooted in the past had become the handmaid of chance, error, passions and misunderstandings (see Kirchmann, 1848; also Stelmach, 2013b, p. 21).

There is much to suggest that the truth and relevance of the charges formulated by Kirchmann remain valid. Regardless of any ultimate assessment of 'the charges of Kirchmann', it is worth noting that it was the first time that a critical opinion had been voiced, one which rejected jurisprudence, and thus also the legal method, denying it any scientific value and which, moreover, provoked the fury of the legal world of the time. What is interesting is that Kirchmann has not found many continuators. In contemporary legal science, this 'critical element' is not particularly visible. Of course, the most important legal paradigms often find themselves in opposition to one another, but the debate between them never seems to touch directly upon the problem of their scientific basis. This is especially discernible in the methodological debate which was conducted in German legal science in the second half of the twentieth century. Even within this school, which was deliberately termed *Methodenlehre* since it directly concerned legal methods, it was relatively rare to find deeper reflections on the scientific basis of jurisprudence (see Engisch, 1963; Savigny, 1976).[7]

I perhaps belong to the decided minority who, like Kirchmann, think that jurisprudence is not a science. It is not after all a research method, and the interpretation strategies used by legal science and practice simply do not meet the basic requirements of science.

There are two arguments that are usually formulated against such a position. The naturalistic argument permits the reduction of the normative sphere (the world of ought) to empirical facts, that is to objects that can be tested using standard scientific methods, especially those developed by empirical and analytical (logical) sciences, enabling the conversion of normative statements (rules/norms) into factual sentences, i.e. statements that can be directly assigned a truth value. On the other hand, there is the second, anti-naturalistic argument. It highlights the special ontological and epistemological status of the normative sciences, that is the sciences dealing with the study of the world of obligations, and posits that they are subject to different requirements from the natural sciences. The naturalistic argument can be questioned by highlighting the consequences of the adoption of a reductionist thesis, including the 'naturalistic fallacy', or showing that propositions about obligations are cognitively not the same as those which express obligations (rules/norms) (see Stelmach, 2012, p. 139ff.). It is even easier to question the anti-naturalistic conviction that there are criteria for the acceptability of certain statements in the normative sciences which have nothing in common with the scientific criteria adopted in science written with the capital S. Because, after all, why should these criteria be acceptable?

This is why, in my opinion, none of the arguments raised above may establish the question of the scientific basis of jurisprudence in a satisfactory manner, which might in turn suggest that 'Kirchmann's curse' is still very much alive and well, and will probably continue to be so, as long as legal science and practice distance themselves from the exact and natural sciences, especially mathematics, logic, economics, psychology and, finally, neuroscience.

---

[7] Rarely does not mean, however, never.

At the same time, I would like to emphasize that the charge raised here primarily concerns the doctrinal study of law and legal practice. Certainly, the philosophy and theory of law have not remained indifferent to the natural sciences. On the contrary, many philosophical and theoretical fields of law have undertaken attempts to incorporate the methodological concepts developed in the above-mentioned sciences and, after all, they have taken part in the successive cognitive revolutions.

In a manner different to the philosophy and theory of law, legal doctrine and legal practice have remained in their 'own world'. Unfortunately, while constructing their 'scientific identity' and autonomy, they did not take into account the subsequent 'cognitive revolutions'.[8] The distancing of the legal doctrine and practice from the ongoing debates on the cognitive status of the humanities and social sciences stemmed in the past, and also today, from at least several related reasons. The first of these I would term the 'science complex of lawyers'. This is mainly a result of the lack of philosophical education on the part of the vast majority of lawyers, especially in terms of methodology and logic. Courses in logic which are part of legal curricula (if they are there at all!) focus on classical propositional calculus or only elements of it, which cannot be directly applied in legal interpretation, or else teach the so-called legal logic, which is not a logic in the pure sense, because all the arguments (reasoning) to which this logic refers are disputable. The second reason, which is in fact a consequence of the first one, is the distancing of legal doctrine and legal practice from the philosophy and theory of law, that is, from those legal disciplines which have already dealt with the 'cognitive opening up'. Admittedly, we meet, we discuss, but somehow nothing comes from this. At best, the representatives of legal doctrine and practice treat us, that is philosophers and theoreticians of the law, indulgently, as harmless madmen, or at worst, less leniently, as already dangerous madmen who are trying to violate the methodologies of a status quo which has been developed for centuries. The third reason is the anti-naturalistic vision of law, commonly adopted by representatives of both legal doctrine and practice, which is expressed in the conviction that the law is subject to a special ontological and epistemological status, and consequently that lawyers can independently determine the criteria for the recognition of statements made by themselves and their interpretative decisions. The fourth reason is in turn 'legal opportunism' which expresses itself above all in the maintenance of a tradition, as a result of which there is considerable reluctance to conduct any kind of radical (revolutionary) change. An example of this opportunism, or perhaps more kindly, legal conservatism, is the widespread acceptance of lawyers and legal practitioners of the 'principle of inertia' (*Prinzip der Trägheit*), which states that unless there are justified, detailed circumstances and reasons, there is no need to change the convictions, practices and customs

---

[8] The assessment formulated here stems primarily from my negative experiences associated with Continental legal science and practice. In contrast, examples of a positive 'reception' can be found in American jurisprudence, if only in the case of the economic analysis of law.

which were assumed earlier.[9] Finally, the fifth reason may simply be laziness, manifested in a lack of a desire on the part of lawyers to engage in any of the additional intellectual efforts which are necessarily connected with learning any new method, procedure or interpretative standard from any other science.

24.4 LAW AND COGNITIVE SCIENCE

In the final part of the chapter, I would like to attempt to answer the following question: what can contemporary cognitive science offer legal science and practice? In other words, in this final section I would like to consider the potential consequences which the fourth cognitive revolution has for legal science and practice (Stelmach, 2018).[10]

The first of these consequences would be the potential introduction into legal discourse of elements of knowledge (methods and models) stemming directly from psychology and neuroscience. They would facilitate new conceptions and, in the opinion of advocates of the cognitive approach, the proper (correct) definition and interpretation of a series of concepts which are of crucial importance for every possible legal epistemological conception (e.g., legal reasoning, intuition, imagination, understanding, argumentation etc.). In this context, we must ask ourselves whether legal cognition is a 'model' case, or whether it is 'special' in relation to the other types of cognition that we encounter in the humanities and social sciences. In my opinion, the former approach to legal epistemology is faulty. Legal cognition and, in the case of Gadamer, understanding, interpretation and application, cannot be regarded as a 'model case'. Gadamer, after all, supplied no sensible arguments in favour of this position (see Stelmach, 2011b). I also treat positions which maintain that legal cognition is a 'special case' in comparison to what we have in the humanities and social sciences in a similar manner. The so-called *Sonderfallthese* of Alexy, despite being better justified than that of Gadamer, is also unacceptable for similar reasons (see Alexy, 1991, p. 263 and others). It is impossible to show that legal cognition and its constituents such as intuition, imagination, understanding or argumentation, which Alexy discussed, are essentially any different or more remarkable than any other model or method used in any other field of knowledge.[11] The rejection of both positions, and the resulting rejection of the anti-naturalistic vision of law, permit legal science and practice to adopt the 'cognitive perspective', namely one which allows it to directly exploit the tools (methods) and theories (models) which have been developed in psychology and neuroscience.

[9] Amongst others, Chaim Perelman has written about the principle of inertia. In his opinion, the principle can be interpreted in at least two ways: negatively, as a manifestation of conservatism and even legal opportunism, or positively as an expression of the need to maintain the durability and continuity of a certain tradition, and in the case of the relationship between law and other academic disciplines to continue the interpretive tradition in law (see Perelman, 1963, p. 86).
[10] Also of crucial significance for my considerations here was the text by B. Brożek (2018a, pp. 73f.).
[11] Bartosz Brożek adopts a similar position in this respect (see Brożek, 2018b, p. 13).

The second consequence would be the possibility of defining the scientific criteria for legal science and practice, that is, the ability to construct canonical models for both the theoretical and practical propositions formulated therein. Accepting the distinction made here – between the practical and the theoretical discourse – we should make an effort to build two different canonical models of the statements formulated in these discourses. In the first case, it would be a model enabling the verification or falsification of theoretical (descriptive) theses, based on intersubjectively verifiable and communicable criteria, and consequently on assigning unequivocal logical values to these assertions, that is, truth or falsehood. In the second case, in turn, it would be a model that allows the recognition of practical propositions, that is, normative judgements, which include, amongst others, hypotheses and interpretative decisions. With regard to normative judgements, we speak less often about their verification or falsification, but more about the need to use 'softer criteria' than the truth for the assessment of such claims, for example equity, justice, rationality, validity, reliability, effectiveness and, finally, an economic understanding of efficiency. I am convinced that the vast majority of misunderstandings related to the discussion about the cognitive (scientific) status of legal science and practice, and the propositions and judgements formulated therein, stem precisely from the lack of a distinction between the two discourses (see Stelmach, 2006, p. 893 and others).

As a result of these consequences, three questions arise. The first is whether we really have the opportunity to construct an adequate scientific model for both of these legal discourses? The second is, if so, will they once again be naturalistic models? The third is whether these models will be free from the errors which scarred the earlier forms of naturalism? As an optimist, I would answer the first question in the affirmative. The very distinction between two legal discourses, the theoretical and the practical, which shows the unique nature of the debate on the subject of the scientific and cognitive status of legal science and practice, is a good starting point in the debate on the scientific models that can be effectively applied in legal discourse. As for the second question, from the whole of the line of reasoning undertaken in this chapter, an affirmative answer also follows. Each of the possible models of science with which we had to deal in all the previous 'cognitive revolutions' had some factual dimension, and thus were in some sense naturalistic models. It seems that the most difficult thing is to give a definite positive answer to the last question asked here. However, in this case I am also ready to answer in the affirmative.

The source of all these disputes is the acceptance, whether openly or tacitly, of the assumption of a dualism of between Is and Ought. A consequence of this assumption was the reductionistic thesis, whose acceptance was in turn synonymous with the charge of the 'naturalistic fallacy'. It is only by rejecting the dualism of Is and Ought, and thus acknowledging obligation as only a form of being in existence, that we can free naturalistic thinking from the aforementioned mistakes and inconsistencies.[12]

---

[12] I discuss this problem in more detail in the articles (Stelmach (2011a; 2013a, p. 45 and others, pp. 205f.).

Finally, I would like to emphasize that the models of legal science alluded to above, both for theoretical and practical legal discourse, should have, in connection with the assumptions made here, a clearly factual character.

A third consequence would be the use of the language of psychology and neuroscience to redefine at least some legal and juridical concepts. Perhaps this would be the most important and the most interesting use of knowledge in the field of psychology and neuroscience for legal science and practice. Using the language of psychology and neuroscience, one could attempt to revise theories of normativity, philosophy and theory of law, the understandings of necessity, obligation, and entitlement and, ultimately, the cognitive status of legal rules. The standard language used by legal science and practice does not provide the opportunity to change existing concepts. Lawyers have become prisoners of their own linguistic habits, their once adopted terminological conventions and definitions. Without opening these up to other fields of knowledge and the languages which accompany them, we will continue to 'stew in our own juices', endlessly debating what is essentially always the same. Is it possible to say something new about normativity, necessity or the cognitive status of legal rules using the language we currently have at our disposal? In my opinion: no. If we want to propose a solution which will not merely be an imitation of those which already exist, which after all we don't really accept, we must begin with language. First, we have to find it and then utilize it in the correct manner. Why not, therefore, use the language of psychology and neuroscience?

Utilizing this kind of language would open up the way to redefining some of the untouched legal and juridical notions from different fields and branches of law, especially criminal and private. I have in mind here notions such as guilt, responsibility, will, intent, error, consciousness or liability. What unites these notions and many other similar ones? It is that it is impossible to define and correctly interpret them without making reference to knowledge from psychology or, more broadly, cognitive science. It should be recalled that at least in Continental (European) legal science, these notions were defined at the turn of the nineteenth century or at the beginning of the twentieth (in terms of their codification in Germany) by making use of the psychological theories which were known and accepted at the time, theories which have largely been rejected since. Meanwhile, contemporary legal science and practice, above all in the Continental tradition, has consistently tried to ignore this fact. The attachment to tradition, to the previously described 'principle of inertia', turns out to be stronger than the need to open up legal doctrine and practice to new areas of scientific research. Therefore, speaking today about the use of neuroscience and other related fields, especially psychology, neuropsychology and psychiatry, this seems to be not only 'wishful thinking' or a 'cognitivist postulate', but simply 'a common-sense demand', resulting directly from changes taking place in both the near and far environment of law.

The last of these considerations, namely the fourth consequence, would be the ability to alter the current interpretive paradigms in the law, both the naturalistic and anti-naturalistic ones, and thus change perceptions of the acceptable boundaries to the interpretation of law. It could be argued whether this would constitute a genuine, deep shift in the current interpretive theories, or whether it would only be a certain modification stemming from the new 'cognitive perspective'. Regardless, without opening up to other fields of knowledge, in this case psychology and neuroscience, it would be difficult to imagine there being more fundamental changes, but also any more significant modifications of these theories, something which I have already indicated when discussing the first and third consequences in particular.

However, the second part of the postulate, concerning the potential to change perspectives on the limits to the interpretation of law, should arouse no controversy. By utilizing elements of knowledge from other sciences, in this case from psychology and neuroscience, we also change the limits of what is permissible, that is, we change the possible interpretation of law.

I am obviously aware that these consequences are closely related. I believe, however, that they are worth delineating between in order to show the benefits of adopting the 'cognitive perspective' to the fullest extent possible.

For balance, however, it is worth devoting a moment to the consideration of the eventual 'losses' or rather 'risks' that the unthinking adoption of the 'cognitive approach' in legal science and practice might entail. The first would be the potential risk of the relativization of a legal field which had previously been regarded as unified. In this case, it would not only be the 'strength of tradition' or the 'principle of inertia' which I have already mentioned but rather the entire 'legal experience' that is connected with the functioning of lawyers in the normative space, one in which the rules governing the empirically understood reality were never respected. The second risk accompanies the adoption of a naturalistic perspective. Wanting to stave off the basic objections that were formulated against naturalism, I accepted that the strict dualism of Is and Ought simply does not exist. As a legal theoretician, I could afford such a philosophical extravagance. But can a lawyer afford it? Certainly not, because they cannot defend their position anyway, and even if they could, they would not want to involve meta-theoretical disputes over the coherence of the naturalistic model. The third risk is of lawyers giving up 'their own field' to cognitive scientists, that is, to representatives of the sciences who usually have little knowledge of the law. Lawyers, in turn, do not know much about psychology and related fields of science. Therefore, they must simply accept elements from these sciences 'on faith', which may lead to the introduction of theories and models to legal discourse that are useless, or at best ineffective. Making legal science and practice more scientific at such a cost simply makes no sense. The fourth, and final risk, is the risk of the wholesale elimination of the so-called 'anti-naturalistic perspective' from legal science and practice. Without wishing to overplay the role of legal anti-naturalism, it should be highlighted that it allows the maintenance of a certain minimum balance, necessary for lawyers, between the legal world, which according to their deepest convictions is governed by specific normative principles, and the empirical world.

In light of this, where might we expect the further development of legal science and practice to take place? Will its essence be the above-mentioned pursuit of balance between a non-cognitive (anti-naturalistic) approach and a cognitive (naturalistic) one? Or perhaps it will lead to a 'cognitive breakthrough', leading to further revolutions? Unfortunately, at this point we do not have the requisite knowledge which would allow us to formulate these predictions in a convincing fashion.

REFERENCES

Alexy, R. (1991). *Theorie der juristischen Argumentation. Die Theorie des rationalen Diskurses als Theorie der juristischen Begründung*, 2nd ed. Frankfurt am Main: Suhrkamp Verlag.
Ayer, A. J. (1982). *Philosophy in the Twentieth Century*. New York: Vintage.
Bocheński, J. M. (1993). *Logika i filozofia* (Logic and Philosophy). Warsaw: Wydawnictwo Naukowe PWN.
Brożek, A., Brożek, B., & Stelmach, J. (2013). *Fenomen normatywności* (The Phenomenon of Normativity). Kraków: Copernicus Center Press.
Brożek, B. (2018a). Epistemologia prawnicza z perspektywy nauk kognitywnych (Legal Epistemology from the Perspective of Cognitive Science). In B. Brożek, Ł. Kurek & J. Stelmach (eds.), *Prawo i nauki kognitywne* (Law and Cognitive Science). Warsaw: Wolters Kluwer, pp. 73–99.
Brożek, B. (2018b). *Umysł prawniczy* (The Legal Mind). Kraków: Copernicus Center Press.
Engisch, K. (1963). *Wahrheit und Richtigkeit im juristischen Denken*. Munich: Hueber.
Hart, H. L. A. (1961). *The Concept of Law*. Oxford: Oxford University Press.
Holmes, O. W. (1897). The Path of the Law. *Harvard Law Review* 10, 457–78.
Kirchmann, J. H. v. (1848). *Die Werthlosigkeit der Jurisprudenz als Wissenschaft*. Berlin: Verlag Julius Springer.
Moore, G. E. (1993). *Principia Ethica*. Cambridge: Cambridge University Press.
Olivecrona, K. (1939). *Law as Fact*. London: Stevens & Sons.
Opałek, K. (1985). Argumenty za nielingwistyczną koncepcją normy: Uwagi dyskusyjne (Arguments in Favour of a Nonlinguistic Conception of Norms: A Discussion). *Studia Prawnicze* 3–4, 203ff.
Opałek, K., & Woleński, J. (1988). Logika i interpretacja powinności (Logic and the Interpretation of Obligation). *Krakowskie Studia Prawnicze* XXI, 13–30.
Perelman, Ch. (1963). *The Idea of Justice and the Problem Argument*. London: Routledge and Kegan Paul.
Reichenbach, H. (1992). *The Rise of Scientific Philosophy*. Berkeley: University of California Press.
Savigny, E. v. (1976). *Juristische Dogmatik und Wissenschaftstheorie*. Munich: C. H. Beck.
Schlick, M. (2011). *Problems of Ethics*. Charleston, SC: Nabu Press.
Stelmach, J. (1991). *Die hermeneutische Auffassung der Rechtsphilosophie*. Ebelsbach: Verlag Rolf Gremer.
Stelmach, J. (1994). *Współczesna filozofia interpretacji prawniczej* (Contemporary Philosophy of Legal Interpretation). Monographs of the Faculty of Law and Administration of Jagiellonian University. Kraków: Jagiellonian University Press.

Stelmach, J. (2006). Die Grenzen der juristischen Erkenntnis. In B. Dauner-Lieb, P. Hommelhoff, M. Jacobs, D. Kaiser & Ch. Weber (eds.), *Festschrift für Horst Konzen zum siebzigsten Geburtstag*. Tübingen: Mohr Siebeck.

Stelmach, J. (2011a). And If There Is No Ought? In J. Stelmach & B. Brożek (eds.), *Studies in the Philosophy of Law: The Normativity of Law*. Kraków: Copernicus Center Press, pp. 15–20.

Stelmach, J. (2011b). Interpretacja bez granic (Limitless Interpretation). *Forum Prawnicze* 2 (4), 13–18.

Stelmach, J. (2012). The Naturalistic and Antinaturalistic Fallacy in Normative Discourse. In J. Stelmach, B. Brożek, & M. Hohol (eds.), *The Many Faces of Normativity*. Kraków: Copernicus Center Press, pp. 137–44.

Stelmach, J. (2013a). O problemie prawdziwości norm inaczej (The Problem of the Truthfulness of Norms in Another Way). In A. Brożek, B. Brożek & J. Stelmach (eds.), *Fenomen normatywności* (*The Phenomenon of Normativity*). Kraków: Copernicus Center Press, pp. 45–54.

Stelmach, J. (2013b). Positivistische Mythen der juristischen Methode. *Augsburger Rechtsstudien* 75, 21.

Stelmach, J. (2018). Co może zaoferować neuroscience nauce prawa i praktyce prawniczej? (What Can Neuroscience Offer Legal Science and Practice?). In B. Brożek, Ł. Kurek & J. Stelmach (eds.), *Prawo i nauki kognitywne* (Law and Cognitive Science). Warsaw: Wolters Kluwer, pp. 160–6.

Stelmach, J., & Brożek, B. (2006). *Methods of Legal Reasoning*. Cham: Springer.

Załuski, W. (2013). *Game Theory in Jurisprudence*. Kraków: Copernicus Center Press.

For EU product safety concerns, contact us at Calle de José Abascal, 56–1°,
28003 Madrid, Spain or eugpsr@cambridge.org.